I0822170

Redmond:
The Parnellite

Redmond:
The Parnellite

Dermot Meleady

First published in 2008 by
Cork University Press
Youngline Industrial Estate
Pouladuff Road, Togher
Cork, Ireland

British Library Cataloguing in Publication Data
A CIP catalogue record for this book is available from the British Library

ISBN–13: 978–1–85918–423–3

Typeset by Tower Books, Ballincollig, Co. Cork
Printed by ColourBooks Ltd, Baldoyle, Co. Dublin

www.corkuniversitypress.com

For my mother,
and in memory of my father

Contents

List of Figures

Acknowledgements

I am deeply grateful to Professor Tom Dunne, formerly of Cork University Press, for his receptiveness to the idea of this book, and for his support and suggestions regarding the manuscript; and to the editors, readers and all associated with Cork University Press in the production of the book. For reading part or all of the manuscript and offering suggestions and encouragement, I am indebted to Dr Carla King, St Patrick's College, Drumcondra and Professor Michael Laffan, University College Dublin.

I wish to acknowledge the help of Jarlath Glynn, Wexford County Librarian, Fr Matt Glynn, PP, Tagoat, County Wexford, Michael and Sylvia O'Connor, Wexford, and Jamie and Mary Ryan, Ballytrent House, County Wexford for helping me to explore the Wexford background of the Redmond family. My thanks are also due to the directors, librarians, keepers and staffs of the National Library, the National Archives, the manuscript library of Trinity College, Dublin and the library of St Patrick's College, Drumcondra for unfailing patience and courtesy.

To my family, I am grateful for their support and their patience with my frequent absences while engaged in research and writing. I also wish to thank William O'Brien of the Woodenbridge Hotel, County Wicklow, and Murt O'Sullivan for various forms of help and encouragement, and William Sexton for his advice, based on exhaustive knowledge of the source material, and for many stimulating discussions of the constitutional nationalists of the Redmond era. Finally, I am grateful to Kevin Myers who, unknowingly, made me aware, through an Irishman's Diary column in the *Irish Times* of 23 April 1996 ('A great reconciler is traduced again') of the long period of 'calumnious neglect' since the last appearance of a full-length biography of Redmond; and to my friend Evan Salholm, Librarian of St Patrick's College, Drumcondra, for suggesting that I try to fill the gap.

Abbreviations

NLI	National Library of Ireland
NAI	National Archives of Ireland
CBS	Crime Branch Special
F.J.	*Freeman's Journal*
I.D.I.	*Irish Daily Independent*
I.R.B.	Irish Republican Brotherhood
I.N.A.	Irish National Alliance
I.I.L.	Irish Independent League
U.I.L.	United Irish League

Introduction

John Edward Redmond (1856–1918) has managed the difficult feat, over the almost ninety years since his death, of becoming at once a neglected and a controversial figure. His role as leader of the Irish Parliamentary Party in the United Kingdom Parliament in winning major reforms under the British administration, culminating in the attainment of Home Rule legislation for his country, was long ago swept out of the popular consciousness with the eclipse of the Irish Party in the aftermath of the events of 1916. His achievements now form part of the prehistory of the Irish state, of interest mainly to scholars, whose excavations have been very slow to change the public perception of the period. Predictably, that perception has been dominated by the view of those who founded the Irish state, which saw 1916 as a 'year zero' and ignored the decades of peaceful constitutional struggle which had gone before. The fascination of modern readerships with the doings of colourful and extreme figures from the 1916–1923 period, even those of relatively minor historical significance, has encouraged authors to concentrate on representatives of the 'physical force' tradition. The bloodstained sacrifices of the latter have been extolled at the expense of men such as Redmond and John Dillon, whose mode of self-sacrifice took the more humdrum form of wearying decades of service on the benches of Parliament.

Also forgotten is the very prominent position, incidental to his role as Irish Party leader, which Redmond once occupied in the Edwardian House of Commons. There he was regarded as one of its two or three best orators, and was spoken of, during the years of post-Gladstonian Liberal disarray, as the real leader of the Opposition, and even as a potential Prime Minister had he decided to abandon the cause of his nation's legislative independence. His status as the hero of British democrats during the fight to curb the veto power of the House of Lords in 1910-11 has, like the Liberal party of that era, long disappeared from the popular memory.

The controversy attaching to Redmond's memory arises from two crucial decisions made by him. The first, in the wake of the signing into law of the third Home Rule Bill in September 1914, was to encourage nationalist Irishmen to enlist in the British forces fighting in the Great War. The second, following negotiations with the leaders of Ulster Unionism in the summer of 1916, was to accept a limited and, as he understood it, temporary partition of Ireland in order to bring Home

Rule into immediate operation. Both decisions, notwithstanding the widespread popularity of the first at the time it was made, were cast in retrospect by the inheritors of the Sinn Fein tradition as the inevitable results of a 'de-nationalisation' attendant on too many years spent in the British parliament. His relative isolation, in his later years, from developments in Ireland, the result of his preoccupation with work at Westminster for at least six months every year, contributed to the lasting image of a remote figure more at home in the House of Commons than in his own country. (The third element in the Sinn Fein indictment of Redmond, that based on his supposed acceptance of conscription, was never founded on truth.)

By his detractors on the republican wing of nationalism, Redmond is presented as either a fool or a knave, willing to squander Irish lives by the tens of thousands in the interests of an imperial power, without winning anything worthwhile in return. For a minority, long unjustly labelled 'West British', on the other hand, Redmond's name is symbolic of a more inclusive concept of the nation than that which prevailed in nationalist Ireland throughout most of the twentieth century. It represents the possibility of the reconciliation of the British and Irish components of the Irish psyche, and perhaps the one-time only hope, however slim, of forging a common allegiance for Ulster unionists and Irish nationalists and of thus avoiding partition.

Five biographies of John Redmond have been published, four of them full-length works. The first, produced during his lifetime by his nephew, Louis G. Redmond-Howard, did not have his approval, but contained valuable material on Redmond's family background, youth and schooling. The first study of Redmond's whole life appeared in 1919, the year after his death, and was the work of a British journalist, Warre B. Wells. Basing itself for the early life on Redmond-Howard's work, it gave a lucid survey of Redmond's important role in the political events of the previous decade. However, Wells did not have access to Redmond's papers, and the book revealed little that was new of his character and motivations. Stephen Gwynn's 'John Redmond's Last Years', published in the same year, was a reminiscence based on intimate acquaintance and personal involvement by one who was a M.P. and a staunch defender of the Irish Parliamentary Party from 1906 onwards. A Protestant and the grandson of the Young Irelander, William Smith O'Brien, Gwynn had begun as a protégé of Dillon but soon found himself closer to Redmond in temperament and political character. The book, more than half of which was concentrated on Redmond's actions and tribulations during the years of the Great War, gave a detailed first-hand account of his final attempt to salvage a Home Rule settlement in the Irish Convention of 1917; it was infused with admiration and affection for his personal qualities, modulated by tender criticism of his limitations.

The son of Stephen, Denis Gwynn, a U.C.D. professor and prolific writer on Irish national subjects, published the last full treatment of

Redmond's life in 1932. Its great strength was its use of Redmond's papers, recently made available to the author by Redmond's son, Captain William Archer Redmond, in documenting his dealings with British leaders during the years of the passage of the third Home Rule Bill and afterwards. Like its predecessors, however, it provided only the most cursory treatment of Redmond's early career as a young lieutenant of Parnell and as the leader of the embattled Parnellite minority faction of the Irish Party during the 1890s. With the wound of partition still raw in 1932, the biography offered no critique of Redmond's failure, or of that of nationalism generally, to understand Ulster unionism. Instead it sought to rehabilitate him in nationalist eyes by pointing out Redmond's distrust of and capacity to criticise the perceived vacillations of the Liberal leaders on the Ulster issue. Finally, a short biographical study by Paul Bew, suggesting fruitful new approaches to Redmond's life and work, was published in 1996. Bew focused in particular on Redmond's part in the 'conciliation' initiatives of the later 1890s and early 1900s when he made common cause with Irish unionists to win ameliorative measures for Ireland by taking advantage of the Tory Government's constructive unionist policies.

Clearly a new biography of Redmond is long overdue. Firstly, simple justice demands that his efforts on behalf of his country be given due recognition, and that an unprejudiced attempt be made to understand the motives and significance of his beliefs and actions. The great national excommunication that wrote out of history the nationalist Irishmen who voluntarily served with the British armies in the Great War has been lifted in the past decade. On 11 November 1998, President McAleese stood alongside Queen Elizabeth at Messines, Belgium, to dedicate the Peace Tower at the site where the 36th (Ulster) Division and the 16th (Irish) Division fought together, and where Major William ('Willie') Redmond, the brother of John Redmond, was killed at the age of 56. It is only proper that the amnesia surrounding the memory of the man who did more than any other to recruit those nationalists be similarly lifted.

Secondly, recent political events have opened up the possibility of new perspectives on Redmond's career. The cessation of violence by the I.R.A. in the 1990s, and the acceptance by it of the power-sharing arrangements first proposed in 1973, amounted to an effective acceptance that the 25-year armed campaign to drive Northern Ireland out of the United Kingdom had ended in failure. Violent republicanism was thus seen to be no more successful in undoing partition than Redmond had been in averting it. As its part in the Belfast (Good Friday) Agreement of 1998, the electorate of the Republic of Ireland abandoned the long-sacrosanct clauses of the Irish constitution which laid claim to the territory of the whole island, thus nullifying the nationalist repudiation of Redmond on that issue in 1918. Although Redmond did not recognise a 'principle of consent' in his own day, he was prepared in practice to go to almost any lengths to avoid conflict between the two Irish communities. In this sense, the characterisation by Seamus Mallon of the Belfast Agreement as 'Sunningdale for slow learners' can be adapted for the whole period of eighty years to become 'Redmondism for slow learners'. More controversially, there is also a growing receptiveness to the view that, if the Treaty of 1921 is validated by its being 'the freedom to achieve freedom', the Home Rule settlement of 1914 can be seen in a similar light as having had the potential to evolve towards more complete forms of independence. (A former Taoiseach, John Bruton, spoke along these lines in 2004, generating a letters controversy in the *Irish Times*.)

It has been said that, to the young men and women in the turbulent atmosphere of Ireland in 1913-14, Redmond and his classically honed oratory seemed as antiquated as Victorian aspidistras. Yet to us he is more 'modern' than that: he belongs in many ways to the eighteenth century rather than to the nineteenth. He sought legislative independence for his people as the most rational way of organising its political life. The dark hatreds of religious and ethnic atavisms were foreign to him. Although both a devout Catholic and an admirer of the Gaelic revival who had his children taught the Irish language, he made no mystical identifications between the soul of the nation and its religion or language. There were limits to his interest in cultural nationalism; his youthful grounding in Shakespeare and the English classics gave him too much respect for the best of the British heritage for him to retreat into cultural exclusivism. His rhetoric at its best, in its self-control, its calm and sanguine appeal to reason, its gift for presenting a complex case with both clarity and passion, yet without demagoguery, places him alongside Grattan and O'Connell as a transmitter of Enlightenment values in Ireland. It is difficult to imagine him, like DeValera, looking into his own heart to find what the Irish people wanted. And although he took, with a grave sense of responsibility, the decision to urge his followers to enlist for service in a war which soon turned into mass slaughter, and extolled the bravery of troops of 'a fighting race', he could never have exulted, as Pearse did, that 'the old heart of the earth needed to be warmed with the red wine of the battlefields'.

Redmond has also a contemporary relevance on an issue that is far from settled: Ireland's appropriate role in international affairs. Though he was a strong advocate of the essential 'Sinn Féin' idea – of self-sufficiency as an antidote to the paralysis of the colonial cast of mind – it is clear from his frequently expressed support for federalism that he could not envisage a future Ireland that did not cede some of its sovereignty to a larger entity. The active involvement of thousands of Irish people in the expansion, administration and defence of the British Empire of his day, and in the education of its subjects, made isolationism for him an undesirable goal. In his speech at the Cambridge Union in 1895, he unveiled his ideal of 'that great Imperial Senate which, in future, he believed, would govern this Empire', to which a self-governing

Ireland would send its representatives to join those of 'those mighty dominions throughout the world which had been won by Irishmen just as much as by Britons'. The British Commonwealth as it evolved from the 1920s onwards, of which the Irish Free State remained a member for 27 years, fell considerably short of this vision, being based on free association rather than federal rule. Less than two decades after leaving it, however, the Irish Republic was applying to cede sovereignty to a different supra-national body, the European Economic Community. Would Redmond have approved? Would he have criticised the tendency of the Republic to stay aloof from the military alliances of the Anglophone world, although it has relied on those allies for its practical defence? John Bowman has noted, in his study of DeValera and the Ulster question, that the latter Irish leader worried about being cast in the 1914 role of Redmond when, in 1939, he found himself faced with a demand for Irish participation on the Allied side in the war, with the question of partition still unresolved. From this dilemma flows Ireland's so-called 'traditional' (actually expedient) policy of military neutrality and the modern debate about whether Ireland is, or should be, closer to 'Boston' or to 'Berlin'.

Redmond and his fellow-Parnellites experienced the heady sensation of near-success, in the 1886 Home Rule Bill, while still very young men. The motivation derived from that experience sustained them through the long decades of tedium and disappointing reverses to come as they agitated for Irish self-government. However, participation in the Westminster Parliament as the 'ambassadors of the Irish nation' was much more than a matter of waiting patiently for the right conjunction of forces to win Home Rule legislation. A close study of Irish politics in the Parnell and Redmond periods cannot fail to reveal the extent to which constitutional nationalism improved the lives of the Irish people. In the thirty-five years between 1881 and 1916, legislative reforms were enacted which revolutionised the franchise and local government, and initiated a revolution in land ownership. Some reforms, such as the old age pension provisions and the National Insurance Act, would have come in any case as part of membership of the United Kingdom. But there was nothing inevitable about the final form taken by much of the legislation for land reform, labourers' housing and other improvements. Parliamentary time had to be fought for, amendments to be sought and won, and negative amendments to be fended off. The Irish nationalist people, in joining the organisations set up to support and maintain their parliamentary representatives in this vital work, which involved discipline, self-sacrifice, knowledge of parliamentary procedure and political skill, continued that schooling in democracy which had begun in the era of Daniel O'Connell a century earlier. Redmond and his colleagues thus left a rich legacy which would underpin the stability of the future independent Ireland as one of the few uninterruptedly democratic states in Europe in the twentieth century.

1 The Tradition

> My heart is with the town of Wexford. Nothing can extinguish that love but the cold sod of the grave, and when that day comes I hope you will pay me the compliment I deserve of saying that I always loved you.[1]
>
> Last testament of the first John Edward Redmond

I

The first John Edward Redmond, during his six years as a member of the British Parliament, spoke only three times in the House of Commons. Two of his interventions advocated minor amendments to the Fisheries (Ireland) Bill, which was being debated in the summer of 1863.[2] The third, later that session, concerned the appointment of the superintendents of county jails in Ireland.[3]

The few hundred electors of Wexford borough may have been dissatisfied with the parliamentary productivity of the man whom they had sent unopposed to Westminster in 1859. At the general election of 1865 they unseated him by 153 votes to 107, giving the seat to a member of the Devereux family, arch-rivals of the Redmonds in Wexford's political and commercial life.[4] However, Redmond's activities in other areas of the life of his home town and county more than compensated for his deficiencies as a representative. His death, at the age of fifty-nine, followed closely on his election defeat, and two years later his contemporaries erected the memorial that still stands in Redmond Square near the centre of Wexford, which carries the inscription addressed to the people of the town quoted at the head of this chapter. The eulogy delivered by the mayor of Wexford at the laying of the foundation stone in March 1867 gives an idea of the character of this Redmond, and of the status his family had attained in his native county:

> We have assembled here today in order to discharge a heartfelt and gratifying duty – that of placing on record a monument of a people's love and gratitude for a distinguished citizen and fellow-townsman – a man characterised by many of those attributes which in their combination have, in every age of the world, advanced the cause of civilisation and national prosperity, and acted as beacon lights to mankind . . . John Edward Redmond was no ordinary man. Born to a large and ample fortune, gifted with an intellect of superior order, and trained in the best schools, he used all those advantages and gifts, not for his own proper gain, but to extend employment – to

Figure 1. John Edward Redmond (1806–1865), M.P. for Wexford Borough (1859–1865), grand-uncle of the subject. *Courtesy of the National Library of Ireland.*

> develop the resources of the country – and, above all, to turn the natural, but theretofore neglected capabilities of his native town and county to the best account.[5]

The mayor went on to detail the many-sided contribution made by Redmond. He had presided over the large and prosperous banking establishment founded by his father and uncle, opened up a new artery of communication from the south-eastern baronies of Forth and Bargy into the town, extended the line of quayage, enlarged the area for building and the facilities for commercial traffic, and built a small shipyard for construction and repair of local shipping. Not content, he had worked tirelessly until he gave Wexford a new bridge, and though beset by 'an ungenerous and heartless opposition', had spent a fortune in bringing the railway to the county. But his crowning achievement had been

> that magnificent undertaking which his giant intellect and untiring energies carried into execution before he was called away to receive the reward of his virtues . . . the reclamation of our submerged mudlands, and the turning of a waste of waters into broad and smiling pastures – thereby adding, for all time to come, to the productive territory of our island.[6]

John Edward Redmond could trace his ancestry, through twenty-four generations in the paternal line, to Sir Alexander Redmond, or

Raymond, who, according to the pedigree kept by the family, was 'of the same stock' as Raymond Fitzwilliam de Carew, known as Le Gros. The latter was one of the leaders of the small Anglo-Norman invasion force that landed in south-eastern Ireland in 1171, an event which for all nineteenth-century Irish nationalists marked the beginning of the long history of English interference in Ireland. The nineteenth in the line of descent, Oliver Redmond, migrated from the south of County Wexford to Ballynacurry in the north and 'lost his patrimony in the troubles of 1641', actually forfeiting his lands in 1653 after Oliver Cromwell's outright defeat of the rebellion of the Gaelic and Norman-Irish nobles.[7]

Oliver Redmond's cousin, Alexander Redmond, of the family's most prominent branch, successfully defended his castle, known as The Hall (Redmond Hall, near Fethard in south County Wexford), from the royalist Sir Thomas Aston in 1642, but was twice more besieged in 1649, the second time by Cromwell in person. Over seventy years of age by then, he capitulated 'upon honourable terms' to Cromwell. Following his death soon afterwards, his son Robert joined the royalist army as the English Civil War was drawing to a close. Notwithstanding this display of loyalty, the Restoration did not reverse the confiscation of the Redmond estate, and in 1666 most of Robert's lands were transferred under the Act of Settlement to the Protestant Sir Nicholas Loftus (Lord Ely), and Redmond Hall was replaced by Loftus Hall. Such dispossession was a fate suffered by most of the Catholic gentry, of both Gaelic and Anglo-Norman descent, at that time, or later following the Williamite settlement of the 1690s.[8]

Meanwhile, the son of Oliver, Gabriel Redmond, according to the pedigree, married Mary Redmond of Kilmichael in the north of the county, the daughter of an unrelated family of Redmonds of Gaelic ancestry.[9] Later, he 'purchased considerable property and by a decree of peace in 1684 obtained letters patent on his estate'. Confiscation must have occurred again in the 1690s, but the family evidently managed to stay on the property, as Gabriel's son John is known to have been farming on at least part of it, at Killagowan near Oulart, probably as head tenant, before 1750.[10]

The connection of this John Redmond of Killagowan with the political Redmonds of the nineteenth century is the subject of some uncertainty. The family pedigree states that one of his five sons, who became a merchant, was Edward Redmond, the grandfather of the first John Edward. On the other hand, Hilary Murphy cites a controversy in the Wexford *People* in 1908 in which it was claimed that John Edward's forebears, dispossessed descendants of The Hall Redmonds, were ordinary farmers at Harveystown, Taghmon, in the eighteenth century. This assertion was repeated in a 1990 essay by Kevin Whelan. The aim of the 1908 writer seemed to be to dissociate the family of the leader of the Irish Parliamentary Party from the Ascendancy alliances made through marriage by some of the Killagowan Redmonds, and to portray them as content to endure social eclipse as the price of preserving the 'faith of their fathers' during the period of Penal Laws. His opponent in the controversy held, on the contrary, that the parliamentarians were probably descended from a younger son of one of the Killagowan family, an assumption that is compatible with the claim made in the pedigree.[11] Significantly, all of these lineage models agree in pointing to an Anglo-Norman ancestry, although the pedigree did not claim this to be undiluted, in view of the intermarriage with the Gaelic Redmonds. The latter fact certainly casts as fanciful the claim of Denis Gwynn to see in the parliamentarians 'the heavy, thick-set build which has persisted through every generation' of the descendants of Raymond Le Gros.[12]

The later rise to prominence of the Redmond family in Wexford forms part of the story of the resurgence of the Catholic former gentry in Ireland from the early eighteenth century onwards. This revival of fortunes reversed some of the effects of the dispossessions and the penal legislation that followed them. It took place earliest, and was at its most pronounced, in those south-eastern parts of the country most influenced by Anglo-Norman settlement. Many of the old landed families were able to obtain long leases or freeholds on farms that had formerly been part of their estates. A thriving class of Catholic merchants had continued to exist in Wexford through the harshest times of the seventeenth century. As the town became a thriving port with strong trading links with Liverpool, Bristol, and other British as well as continental centres, this class was now augmented by sons of farmers whose prosperity enabled them to partake in the commercial life of the town and county.[13]

Edward Redmond prospered in the commercial life of Wexford, and his eldest son, Walter, born in 1768, became one of the leading malt factors in the town (all twenty of whom were Catholic in 1796).[14] Walter founded the Wexford bank mentioned in the eulogy of his nephew, and ran it in partnership with his brother John (the father of John Edward), who later became its sole proprietor. This bank was the only one in the south to survive the provincial banking crisis of 1820, being able to pay its liabilities in full, probably because of the Redmonds' substantial capital reserves.[15] It continued to prosper until it went into voluntary liquidation in 1834 and was taken over by the Bank of Ireland.

Walter's wealth not only enabled him to buy Bettyville, a large house in the suburbs of Wexford town, it also placed him in a position of advantage when the legislation against ownership of land by Catholics was repealed in 1793. Described in the memorial of the agreement as 'Walter Redmond of the city of Dublin merchant' (he had a property at 106 Townsend Street), he purchased in 1799 Ballytrent House and estate, at the south-eastern tip of County Wexford, from a Protestant family implicated in the insurrection of the previous year, for £7,750. He was able to offer this house, together with £15,000, as a dowry for his daughter Anna Eliza, his only child. By the time of his death in 1822, he had acquired land in the county amounting to some 5,000 acres, as well as properties in Dublin. His status as one of the few Catholic resident landlords in Wexford was a mark of how far his family had travelled to regain its former position of social prominence among the gentry of the county.[16]

Walter Redmond, like other wealthy Catholics of his place and time, played a leading role in endowing and building the new institutions that would later raise his Church to a dominant position in Ireland. He provided the land on which St Peter's College was built in 1818, and left a bequest to have an orphanage established in the town (later run by the Sisters of Mercy). His sons, and son-in-law, John Hyacinth Talbot, were contributors to St Peter's and to the building of its chapel in 1838; the latter engaged the services of the famous architect Augustus Pugin for the task.[17] He took a leading part in the campaign to remove the market tithes, a form of taxation in support of the Established Church, which the Catholic merchants of Wexford found particularly oppressive.[18] Yet, with the continued denial to Catholics, until 1829, of the right to take seats in Parliament and hold judicial appointments and other government posts, he did not live long enough to see the increasing self-confidence of his class reflected in political power.

The brothers Walter and John died within four months of each other in 1822, both in their early fifties (a third brother, Patrick, had died in early manhood). All Walter's wealth, along with Ballytrent House, passed to Anne Eliza. Her death only four years later left everything in the hands of Talbot, her husband, who rented out Ballytrent to members of the Redmond and Talbot families over the subsequent decades.[19]

The government of Wexford town, a typical 'rotten borough', was for many decades under the joint control of two Protestant families, those of Loftus (marquis of Ely), the original dispossessors of the Redmond ancestors, and Nevill, who took turns to represent it in Parliament. This cosy arrangement lasted until 1829, the year of the Catholic Emancipation Act, when a dispute between the families led to a parliamentary election. The Nevill interest favoured reform of the borough by admitting prominent Catholics to the franchise; the Ely side was totally opposed. The methods used by the second marquis of Ely to gain victory for his candidate gave rise to a petition by the Nevill candidate, which in turn led to a House of Commons Select Committee to scrutinize the ways of Wexford politics over the previous half-century. Letters written by Ely were revealed, which showed his determination to hold back the Catholic tide: he would order in non-resident freemen from his country estate to vote to keep out 'those damned papists, with Redmond at their head' and vowed that he 'would dispute every inch with them'. The petition was successful and the Ely candidate was unseated.[20] It was thus that in 1830, ten years before the Municipal Corporations Act expanded the franchise for local elections throughout Ireland, the Catholics of

Wexford were able to secure a great increase in the number of freemen admitted to the franchise, and by 1833 they had sufficient power in the corporation to elect one of its grain merchants as the borough's, and indeed Ireland's, first Catholic mayor.[21]

The year 1835 marked another important step in the realization of the potential opened up by emancipation. The general election in January put the Liberal administration of Lord Melbourne into power. The new Irish executive was exceptional in the entire century, until William Ewart Gladstone's first Home Rule Bill, for its friendliness to Catholic and nationalist interests, particularly in its appointment as under-secretary of Thomas Drummond, termed by Daniel O'Connell's biographer, Oliver MacDonagh, 'the greatest Irish public servant of the nineteenth century'. An even-handed approach characterized the new appointments to judicial and other offices of national management; roughly one-third of these were of Catholics, and within half a decade a similar proportion of such posts would be in Catholic or liberal Protestant hands.[22] In 1841 the political representation of the Wexford borough finally passed into Catholic possession with the election of Sir Thomas Esmonde, member of another Wexford gentry family of Anglo-Norman descent, in the Liberal interest. After 1847 it passed to the Catholic Devereux family, which held it unopposed until 1859.

The two sons of John Redmond, orphaned in their teens in 1822, were still young men when emancipation was passed and were among the first to exploit the new possibilities for their class. Both inherited the banking interests of their father, acting as agents in Wexford for the Bank of Ireland in the 1830s,[23] but both had aspirations beyond business. Patrick Walter (the Redmond referred to in Ely's letter), born in 1803, stood for Parliament as, interestingly, a Conservative candidate for his native county in 1835, but came last of four in the list.[24] His political affiliation seems to have incurred the hostility of some of the Catholic clergy, notwithstanding the family's active role in the religious life of Wexford. He soon became involved in the civil administration of the county, becoming a justice of the peace in the year of his election defeat.[25] In the same year, while living at Somerton, not far from Ballytrent, he became one of the deputy lieutenants of the county,[26] joining his cousin-in-law Talbot, appointed to the same post three years earlier, in the upper tier of the county establishment.[27] He was high sheriff (a post that rotated among the deputy lieutenants) in 1844 and 1845, and remained a deputy lieutenant, as well as a magistrate, until his death in 1869.[28] For the last twenty years of his life, he maintained a residence in Dublin, in the new township of Pembroke to the south-east of the city. There, among the tall houses being built for the legal, commercial and other élites who were deserting the Georgian streets of the city centre, he owned Pembroke House, the most valuable dwelling on Pembroke Road.[29]

The other son, the John Edward already mentioned, combined his many business activities with the role of magistrate from the mid-1830s onwards.[30] It was many more years before he could spare the time to enter national politics, standing in the Liberal interest as, according to a descendant, 'an advocate of the removal of all civil and religious disabilities'.[31] His election, coming late in his life, when he lived at Newtown Lodge, an opulent Italianate villa at The Deeps, a scenic spot on the River Slaney near Wexford, may have been as much a testimonial in honour of his life's work for the borough as a mandate of representation.

The brothers Redmond seem to have stood at opposite poles within the circumscribed and gentlemanly world of Wexford politics as it reflected the issues in contention between the two great parties of the United Kingdom. A clue to their affiliations may be found in the respective London clubs to which they belonged in their later years. Patrick Walter evidently held on to the Conservative convictions of his youth, giving the Union Club as one of his addresses in the 1860s, while John Edward favoured the Reform Club.[32] They shared, however, the exceptional status of being among a minority of Catholics within a still predominantly Protestant county government hierarchy. As late as the mid-1880s, Protestant justices of the peace in all of Ireland outnumbered Catholics in a ratio of 4:1, while the ratio of populations was exactly the reverse.[33]

II

John Edward Redmond and his wife, Margaret Archer, had no children. His brother Patrick Walter, on the other hand, married twice and had five children. Two of those by his first wife, Esther Kearney of Rocklands, were to play an important role in the public fortunes of the family. One carried on the military, the other the political, strand in the family tradition.

Pursuit of a military career with continental armies was a common career choice for many of the Catholic élite. Such service was, among other things, a means of retaining social status, since entry to the higher levels required proof of noble descent.[34] Two of the uncles of Edward Redmond had been officers in the Spanish army, while his brother Michael was in the French service, and later, according to the family pedigree, 'in 1763 aide-de-camp to the Emperor of Germany'.[35] Patrick Walter's eldest son, John Patrick Sutton Redmond (born in 1824), followed in the military tradition, but in the less usual manner of joining the British army. He entered the army as an ensign at the age of eighteen, and served with the 61st Regiment of Foot throughout the Punjab campaign of 1848–49. He was awarded a Commander of the Bath for his part in the siege of Delhi. Having been a colonel in the Gloucestershire Regiment, he retired in 1881 with the rank of lieutenant general.[36]

The military tradition in the Redmond family also took a more local form. Members were active on both sides in the great insurrection of

1798. Walter Redmond was enrolled in the Shelmalier cavalry, a branch of the loyalist yeomanry, a force which in Wexford included a strong Catholic component, although distant cousins of his were involved in the local leadership of the rebellion.[37] William Kearney, an ancestor of Patrick Walter's wife, was also active on the rebel side. Some fanciful embellishments to the tradition were added later during the political career of the second John Edward Redmond: there is no evidence that the 'beautiful and accomplished Miss Redmond' leading the rebels on horseback, depicted in an old print to be found in certain Wexford houses, was any more than a distant relative.[38]

Patrick Walter's second son, William Archer Redmond, born in 1825, took the political path. Given the best education available at Stoneyhurst (the Jesuit college in Lancashire at which his uncle had been educated) and Bonn, he took a Bachelor of Arts degree in Trinity College, Dublin.[39] In 1848 he married Mary Louisa Hoey, the daughter of Major Michael Hoey, of Hoeyfield in County Wicklow, a Protestant officer in the Wicklow Rifles. He is recorded as living at various addresses in Dublin between then and 1858. Later he took up residence at Ballytrent House, which remained the property of Talbot. His interdenominational marriage was typical of many such in the Wexford area, reflecting the relatively good relations between members of the two faiths among the middle and upper classes in an age when tensions between Catholic self-assertion and Protestant evangelicalism were manifesting themselves in the 'battle for souls'. Not only were there many examples of intermarriage in Wexford, but members of the two communities were willing to support each other's educational charities and even more specifically religious causes. A local historian has commented on the prevalence in the religious attitudes of the local Catholic élite of certain features, such as sabbatarianism, which were not typical of Catholic Ireland as a whole. These may have been the result partly of the greater degree of contact of the south-east with Britain, and partly of respectful rivalry with native Protestants.[40]

When, in 1872, Richard Devereux, Wexford's leading Catholic layman, who had replaced the first John Edward Redmond as M.P. for the borough, resigned the seat, William stood in the by-election and won it back for the Redmonds.[41] (He had already replaced his father as a magistrate in 1870, and remained one for the rest of his life.) Changes were under way in Ireland. The abortive Fenian insurrection of the mid-sixties, followed by Gladstone's attempt to 'pacify Ireland' with the disestablishment of the Church of Ireland in 1868 and the Land Act of 1870, had ended the two decades of political torpor that followed the Great Famine. The Protestant and former Tory barrister Isaac Butt had recently founded the first Home Rule movement. The first public meeting of the Home Government Association had been held in September 1870. William Redmond's election address of 1872 set out his stance on the issue:

> In reference to the question of legislative independence which now occupies the attention of the country under the name of Home Rule, I will at once declare my conviction that Ireland possesses the indefeasible right to be governed by an Irish Parliament . . . I hold that the restoration of Home Rule is absolutely essential to the good government of the country, to the development of its resources, to the removal of the wasting curse of absenteeism and to the final establishment in peace and liberty of the Irish race upon Irish soil.

He was equally clear as to the limits he envisaged on both the means and the end: 'I am convinced that ample means exist to achieve this result within the limits of the Constitution, and without infringing upon our loyalty to the throne . . .'[42]

The election of Ireland's first batch of Home Rule M.P.s (six were elected in eight by-elections in 1871–72), of whom Redmond was one, opened a new chapter in the history of constitutional nationalism.[43] The four-day Home Rule Conference in the Rotunda, Dublin, in November 1873, called into being 'by public requisition of 24,000 Irishmen of every shade of patriotic opinion and every occupation and profession',[44] was attended by over a thousand delegates. It laid the foundations for the election of fifty-nine Home Rule M.P.s in the general election of the following year, to be led in Parliament by Isaac Butt. The restoration of an Irish parliament in Dublin, governing the domestic affairs of the country, was now the central political aspiration of the vast majority of the Catholic community, the four-fifths of the population of the island which had been politically quiescent until the end of the eighteenth century and which had been excluded from participation in the semi-autonomous Anglican-dominated parliament won under the leadership of Henry Grattan in 1782 and abolished by the Act of Union of 1800.

The newly elected members were soon regarded by Irish opinion as relatively ineffective in getting Westminster to listen to their demand. This early Home Rule party has been well characterized as 'a fairly prosperous body of Irish gentlemen' whose aim was 'to persuade an assembly of English gentlemen that the cares of Irish government could safely be devolved upon them'.[45] It was not long before a rift developed between the majority, including Butt, committed to a policy of winning over English public opinion by force of reason, and a small group of obstructionists who had decided that a more fruitful approach was to 'annoy' Parliament into granting Irish self-government by keeping the Irish question to the fore and making the normal working of the House of Commons impossible. The principal obstructionists were the Belfast merchant and ex-Fenian Joseph Biggar (who initiated the policy), Frank Hugh O'Donnell and Charles Stewart Parnell. These men won fame at home in the late seventies by their tireless energy in speaking in the House on any and all subjects, and by their demonstration of indifference to English opinion and institutions. By 1879, Parnell, in particular, had achieved huge prestige in Ireland as one who knew how to 'stand up to' the English.

William Redmond was re-elected in 1874 for Wexford borough, as he would be at the following election in the very different conditions of April 1880. At the 1873 conference Redmond had been partly responsible for ensuring that Butt's party would be loose-knit and undisciplined: he had proposed the resolution, adopted by the conference, that rejected the notion of binding all members to a pledge to act and vote as a single body with a common policy.[46] As a close associate of Butt's, he had, on the face of it, nothing in common with the obstructionists. Yet neither is he easily classified with their opponents, the sham Home Rulers of the party, contemptuously dubbed 'Whigs' by other nationalists. Together with such colleagues as Alexander Martin (A. M.) Sullivan, M.P. for Louth and a close Butt lieutenant,[47] he belonged to a 'centre' group within the party, committed rhetorically but sincerely to a vague 'active policy', yet equally committed to the principle of freedom of action of each M.P., sharing what David Thornley has called Butt's 'reverence for the institutions of Parliament' and unwilling to jettison the 'moral influence' of the party in the House of Commons.[48]

The author of his son John's first posthumous biography claims that Redmond was opposed to 'the Bolshevist methods of Biggar and the Land League';[49] another biographer says simply that he was not a supporter of Parnell's methods, and spoke less and less after Parnell took over the party.[50] A third, however, writes that he was 'one of Parnell's early supporters when a revolt developed against the conservative leadership of Isaac Butt'.[51] It is true that Redmond did not speak at all in the 1879 session, and only once in that of 1880, after Parnell became chairman. But these were years in which he was suffering serious ill-health from heart disease,[52] and, in any case, he had never been a prominent contributor to debates, speaking only five or six times in each session. He was absent from the Dublin City Hall meeting on 17 May 1880, which elected Parnell to the chair, but sent a message in agreement with the Parnellite policy of opposition.[53]

His brief but incisive speeches on the national issue showed a tone of increasing impatience as the decade went on. In the March 1874 debate on the Queen's Speech, he said that the prodigious majorities by which Home Rule members had been returned showed the strength of Irish feeling on the management of the country's affairs, and that 'either they must give serious and earnest consideration to the causes of the dissatisfaction which existed, or they must go on governing the country by force, terror and coercion'.[54]

Later that year he objected to the renewal of coercion legislation in the defensive terms that would become a familiar part of nationalist speeches in the following decade. The people of Wexford had told him they were at a loss to understand why these Acts were being continued:

Figure 2. William Archer Redmond (1825–1880), M.P. for Wexford Borough (1872–1880), father of the subject. *Courtesy of the National Library of Ireland.*

'To retain such powers caused great discontent in Ireland, and their renewal was no bulwark to the order and peace of Ireland; on the contrary, it was a most dangerous policy.'[55] Four years later, his language had become even sterner:

> [Ireland's] demands were listened to, but thought no more about . . . Last Session they asked them to grant an amnesty to the remaining Irish political prisoners. This request, made with moderation, was refused with insult . . . A vast number of the Irish people, let him tell the House, said the Home Rulers asked for too little. And they said the Home Rulers did not ask it in the right way . . . He himself was

> opposed to desperate courses; but he could assure the House, however they might think the demands he had alluded to were exaggerated, that the day would never come when the people of Ireland would retire from them.[56]

These were words that could have come from any of the active section. Redmond's activity in the Irish Amnesty Association in London in the 1870s, and his willingness to appear on amnesty platforms to demand the release of those still imprisoned in the aftermath of the Fenian rebellion, also marked him out as different from his colleagues on the right of the party. One of his first public speeches, at an amnesty meeting in Enniscorthy in 1869, was remembered by his son John on a similar platform in the same town twenty-three years later; at William Redmond's death it was recalled that he had taken part in nearly every such meeting in the county.[57] Butt himself was an active campaigner for amnesty, and chaired one of the first great amnesty public meetings at Cabra, Dublin, in October 1868, attended by an estimated 200,000 people.[58]

The uneasy relationship between constitutional nationalists and physical force extremists, the outcome of disagreement as to methods and only limited congruence of aims, was expressed in a letter from Patrick Ford, editor of the New York *Irish World*, to Butt in 1875:

> for all my admiration for your ability, honesty of purpose, and self-sacrificing devotion, I feel assured that Ireland could never rise to the true dignity of her nationhood by means of the proposed federal arrangement, and that the Irish people – however much disposed to cheer Home Rule now – would ultimately be dissatisfied with that arrangement.[59]

The nadir of the relationship, and the limits of criticism beyond which it was not prudent for constitutionalists to go, were marked by the assassination by Irish republicans, in Ottawa in April 1868, of the Wexford-born Thomas D'Arcy McGee, the ex-Young Irelander who had gone on to become a founding father of the Canadian federation. McGee had returned to his native town in May 1865 and made a speech in which he 'denounced the revolutionaries himself included as honest fools, with the emphasis on foolishness: the rising of 1848, in his view was the product of immaturity, of the triumph of wishful thinking over objective reality.'[60]

The amnesty cause was the one forum in which constitutionalists and extremists could work together, in a symbiotic relationship. The respectability of the first could provide powerful leverage for the early release of political prisoners, while the popular following of the second gave the constitutionalists a reserve of manpower at times of elections, as exemplified by the support enjoyed by Butt in his own Limerick constituency from the 'advanced' nationalist John Daly and others during the 1874 election campaign.[61]

William Redmond's attitude to the Land League was ambiguous. The embrace of the league and the 'New Departure' policy [62] in 1879 by the increasingly powerful group centred on Parnell widened the divide in the party, alienating most of those members drawn from the landlord class. Although Redmond, who had asserted at the 1873 conference that Home Rule represented no threat to property,[63] stayed aloof from the new movement, whether from illness or disapproval, he did address a huge crowd in Hyde Park, London, in late November 1879 to protest at the arrest of Michael Davitt and two other league leaders for seditious language.[64]

Redmond's speeches in the House of Commons also reflect his interest in the agitation for university education for Irish Catholics, in the reform of the borough franchise and in the temperance movement. In 1873 he criticized a Liberal Bill to open the governing body of Trinity College to all religious denominations:

> [The Bill] was designated to uphold that secular system which the people of Ireland would never accept . . . They did not wish to see Trinity College drawn down to the level of the 'godless' Colleges, for Trinity College had been regarded with more good feeling than had been attached to other Government institutions in that country. The Roman Catholics took a pride in its renown.[65]

Dealing in 1876 with the pressing need for Irish electoral reform, he expressed the hope that

> the House would not, by rejecting this motion, strengthen the impression which existed to a considerable extent in Ireland, that it was futile to come to the House of Commons, or appeal to the Government, for the redress of any grievance, no matter how plainly it might be demonstrated.[66]

Redmond's stance on temperance legislation also marked him as different in a party closely linked with the drink trade. (A. M. Sullivan shared his views on this, as on other matters.) In London he was a regular attender at meetings of the League of the Cross, a total abstinence association founded by Cardinal Henry Edward Manning.[67] Speaking in May 1876 to second a resolution to close public houses in Ireland on Sundays, he assured the House that his motive was

> to increase and secure those home comforts at present too often endangered by the absence of the father of the family, squandering his money which he should keep for those comforts in the public-house . . . On Sunday after morning worship [the Irish peasants] had little or nothing else to do; and after loitering about, what was more natural than that they should go to the public-house? And then, unfortunately, they drank away their wages and their wits.[68]

Rejecting arguments that the measure would not have the desired effect, he pointed to the experience of Scotland, where Sunday closing had been in force for over twenty years. But his most telling example came from his own town. They had had voluntary Sunday closing in Wexford for twenty years, introduced by the late bishop, who had

> appealed to the publicans to abstain from selling liquors for that one day. He was supported not only by Catholics, but by Protestants of all classes in the diocese, and the public-houses were closed, and with the best results, for, in 1872 . . . the venerable prelate said that in all cases of drunkenness and disorder there had been a marked diminution.[69]

Significantly, the member who spoke immediately after Redmond to oppose the measure, Philip Callan, M.P. for North Louth, alleged that 'concealed Sabbatarianism was at the bottom of the whole of this agitation'.[70]

On Redmond's death shortly after the general election of 1880, the *Tablet*, the English Catholic review to which he had been a regular contributor, called him a 'man of large and cultivated intellect, refined and sensitive nature, and his fearless assertion of principle was ever combined with a heart ever sensible of warm and generous emotions'.[71] Other assessments reflect the difficulty of categorizing him politically. The conservative *Wexford Independent* wrote:

> Although many have considered his political bias of too extreme a character – his scholarly acquirements, great natural ability, oratorical power, and, above all, his gentlemanly and Christian bearing, won him troops of friends; whilst his eloquent advocacy of the temperance movement has made an impression on the hearts of those, who have been struggling for years to rescue our people from the degrading vice and bondage of drunkenness, that can never be obliterated.[72]

The *Nation*, itself a supporter of the 'active' policy, claimed in its death notice that Redmond had been 're-elected at the last general election as a supporter of the active policy'; in a short front-page obituary, recalling that he had been for a long time in failing health, it stated: 'Mr. Redmond was not a very active politician, but he was an honest one.'[73]

2 Beginnings and Bereavements

I was taught there by precept and example the lessons of truth, of chivalry and manliness . . . to accept success without arrogance and defeat without repining.

John Redmond in 1914 remembering
his schooldays at Clongowes[1]

'The Green above the Red!' Aye, friend,
O'er Ireland's sacred shore
The Green above, and, God defend,
We'll win our own once more!

John Redmond, May 1880[2]

I

Two girls, Esther and Dorothea, were born to William and Mary Redmond, and then, on 1 September, 1856, a boy, christened John Edward after his great-uncle.[3] The birth took place at William and Mary's Dublin home, 35 Upper Rutland Street, on the fringe of the city's Georgian north side.[4] At some point during John's first decade the family moved from Dublin and settled at Ballytrent House. The lonely coastal mansion near the south-eastern tip of County Wexford, looking out to the Tuskar lighthouse and St George's Channel, was his home for the rest of his childhood. The children were joined in 1861 by the fourth and last child, William Hoey Kearney, who was to be his older brother's loyal follower and confidant in a 34-year partnership that would end only with his death in uniform in Flanders in 1917. While John was still a boy, Esther became a nun of the Order of Marie Reparatrice in London, a community devoted to missionary work in India.[5]

Little is known of his early years, but his nephew, L. G. Redmond-Howard, wrote that he showed signs from the first of exceptional ability, and that he enjoyed literature as well as sports and hunting. He was sent at the age of twelve to the Irish Jesuit college at Clongowes, in County Kildare,[6] the secondary boarding school that educated many of the sons of the Catholic upper middle class and included Cardinal Paul Cullen and the Fenian John O'Leary among its graduates. John's admission took place about a decade before the Intermediate Education Act of 1878 began a modest state support for Catholic secondary schools, instituting the system of centralized external examinations and payment by results. The curriculum was 'liberal' in the old sense, with the accent heavily on the classics, aimed at conferring the 'veneer of gentility'[7] on the children of those who had been successful in business or farming and preparing them for entry to the higher professions. It was not a nationalist one: the boys were being groomed, not as the ruling class of a future self-governing Ireland, but as administrators of the expanding British Empire, or as members of the religious orders engaged in missionary work in the geographically coterminous entity sometimes called 'Ireland's spiritual empire'. When the Clongowes Union held its inaugural dinner in November 1897, Lord Chief Baron Christopher Palles and Lord Chief Justice Peter O'Brien, along with Redmond, were among the illustrious past pupils present.[8]

Much of the information we have about Redmond's time at Clongowes has come down to us from his nephew, who interviewed his old master, Father Robert Kane, and received written testimonies from another mentor and from a schoolmate. The material was gathered for use in the first biography of Redmond, published in 1910 when he was at the height of his influence and occupied a commanding position in the House of Commons. The testimonies may thus be coloured by a concern to make the best possible impression on British opinion. Father Kane's closing remarks read like a character reference: 'I can only say this – that while they are in the hands of John Redmond, the destinies of Ireland are safe, as far as ability of mind and nobility of character are concerned. I have known him from a boy . . .'[9] The picture that emerges is of a talented, serious, rather high-minded student whose slight priggishness did not adversely affect his popularity. The chief characteristic

Figure 3. Ballytrent House, County Wexford, where John Redmond was raised.

Figure 4. John Redmond as Hamlet at Clongowes, 1874.
Courtesy of the National Library of Ireland.

noted by Father Kane was his 'maturity': '"Jack" always had a grand old-fashioned respect for his father, and thus he acquired part of his father's refinement and polish, and the close intimacy between them gave him a maturity of mind which at once placed him in a different category to that of his companions.'[10] He evidently had a capacity to identify with authority. He had once approached the priest after a classroom confrontation with a particularly rowdy classmate, asking 'Why didn't you knock him down, sir?'[11]

With a reputation of being one of the most religious boys in the school, he was well liked because of the 'very kind and easy way he had about him', as the schoolmate recalled. He was good at games – 'a first-rate bowler and a smart batsman' – but distinguished himself most through his aptitude for English literature. It was 'excellence in the speaking and writing of English' that ensured 'there was no more prominent boy' all through his time at the school.[12] He impressed Father Kane with his ability to recite by heart passages from Byron, Shelley, and especially, Shakespeare, and his essays were 'always well ahead of those of the other scholars'. It was not so much the display of knowledge in itself, as 'the elevated and dignified way he had of looking at any given subject', which struck the master.[13] Clongowes, with its drama and debating societies, provided good opportunities for the public display of ability in spoken English. Excelling in elocution classes (he was the favourite pupil of Bell,[14] the great elocutionist), he always took the leading roles in the school plays, and was remembered as 'the greatest actor that was ever seen at Clongowes'. He played Macbeth in 1873, and Hamlet the following year, at the age of seventeen.[15] He would carry his love of the classics of English literature with him into his political career, when he frequently embellished his speeches and lectures with quotations from Shakespeare, Shelley and other poets.

His other arena was the school's debating society, at which he was regularly awarded the medal for best speaker. He seems to have been instrumental in bringing about a change in the content of the debates, turning them away from strictly classical themes to questions of Irish history and current politics. The minutes book of the society, which would have provided an interesting insight into the genesis of his political thinking, was unfortunately destroyed in the fire that burned down the study hall in 1886. There were public days, such as Academy Day, when parents and other guests would come, and 'then John Redmond really shone. In addition to the public debate I would induce him to recite a Latin ode or declaim one of Cicero's speeches,' said Father Kane.[16]

However, in spite of his talents, or perhaps because of them, he was not the most industrious of students, in his master's assessment. He could be overtaken by other students who worked harder: 'One might describe Jack as being "almost lazy" – not idle but dreamy, "literary" and dilettante. Towards the exams, however, he would make up for lost time, and by sheer ability account for his apparent lack of industry during previous terms.'[17] This has the ring of truth: a certain indolence would characterize phases of his political career, especially in its first decade, and may have been among the reasons for his failure to advance to the front rank of his party under Parnell. In later life he regretted that the relaxed style of education he had experienced had been superseded by the 'cramming' system following the introduction of the Intermediate Examination. But he had no doubts as to the role played by his old school in his formation. At one of the Clongowes Union dinners, at which he was guest of honour, he declared: 'All I am I owe to the Jesuit fathers. I was taught there by precept and example the lessons of truth, of chivalry and manliness . . . to accept success without arrogance and defeat without repining.'[18]

His formal education at Clongowes came to an end in 1873, but he seems to have spent a further year there as a member of a small philosophy class formed by the rector, enjoying an arrangement, inconceivable nowadays, under which, according to Redmond-Howard, certain privileged students could live in private rooms and 'were allowed to keep their dogs, and occasionally were permitted to shoot'.[19] Hunting with gun and dog would all his life be a favourite leisure pursuit.

Redmond went to Dublin to matriculate at Trinity College in October 1874, following in his father's footsteps. He enrolled for a degree in classics, but his earlier promise as a student was not fulfilled. In the list of thirteen junior freshmen taking the Hilary term examinations for honours in February 1875, four are listed in the 'first rank', while Redmond appears second last of those in the 'second rank'. His name does not appear on any other examination lists for that or the following year. Stephen Gwynn comments that 'after two years his father took his name off the College books for good'. That was in July 1876.[20]

We can only speculate as to the reasons for his poor performance at Trinity. It may have been the result of the tendency to laziness already noted, or he may have found the content of the courses less exciting than the issues of the day, given a personal relevance as they were by his father's involvement in them. His schoolmate John Gannon, who met him again during his year at the college, later remembered 'the interest he took in John Mitchel's election for Tipperary [in February 1875] and how he deprecated the policy of not going to Parliament which Mitchel announced'.[21] Distraction by family matters may be another reason. His father's role as a M.P. necessitated his spending long periods in London, leaving his mother in sole charge of young William (known as Willie). Willie was at this time in his early teens, and from what we know of his impulsive and rebellious, though good-natured, character as an adult, it is possible that his mother found him too much to handle, and that John's presence was required at times to keep him under control. More certainly, there is the fact that his parents were actually estranged by the early 1870s. Father Kane told Redmond-Howard that he 'had been matured by his home life and his devotion to both his parents and sisters'. In his 1918 obituary of John

Redmond, he amplified, with masterly delicacy, his explanation for this early maturing:

> One cause of this was only known, I think, outside the boy's own home, to Father Carbery and myself. The characters of his father and mother were very dissimilar. Their son was the confidant of each and the comforter of both. It has always seemed to me that this circumstance made John a man in mind and character while still a boy in age and humour.[22]

The rift erupted in early 1873 into correspondence between both parents and, of all people, Isaac Butt. Mary had, for reasons unknown to us, been compelled to leave the family home at Ballytrent and wrote to Butt seeking advice on the taking of a legal case against her husband in line with her 'determination to be reinstated in his affections and my position'.[23] Butt's reply was impartial as to the cause of the dispute – 'I cannot and I do not say who is in fault and possibly as is generally the case there are faults on both sides' – but begged her to reconsider an action that would wreck William's budding political career:

> think very seriously before you take a step which may draw all the secrets of your home before a mocking public and may end in irretrievable mischief to your husband – and in destroying all hope of that reconciliation which you must feel no decision of a legal tribunal could ever really effect.[24]

There were other dimensions to the quarrel, as evidenced by a later letter from Mary which told Butt that she had been informed that it was her daughter Dorothea who was the main obstacle to her being restored to her home, as she refused to live there with her, and that William was arranging to have Dorothea live with him in London.[25] It seems that legal proceedings were avoided when Mary accepted the advice of two clerical acquaintances, including an archbishop, whom Butt had advised her to see.

It is tempting to find in this experience of family disharmony the origins of some of John Redmond's best-known personality traits. In acting as a go-between for his parents he must have honed those conciliatory skills which, in the years after 1900, were conceded by all sides to have played such a crucial part in consolidating the fragile reunion of the Irish party, and which would again be displayed in the abortive attempts to avert partition in the 1914 negotiations with Edward Carson and in the 1917 Irish Convention. In his concern at the risk to his father of exposure of the family quarrel can be seen the roots of his later secretiveness and reserve regarding his private life. It is even possible that his one-time fear of the revelation of his father's marital difficulties may have given him a reflexive sympathy with Parnell, augmenting 'the double ties of private friendship and political allegiance',[26] when the latter's affair with Katharine O'Shea became public property in 1890.

The premature end to Redmond's Trinity career coincided with his father's wish to have his son with him in London, both as an assistant and as a political apprentice who could be groomed to take his place. In London he began to study for the bar, and apart from this the only certain information about him for the next three years is that he sometimes attended Parliament as a visitor and watched debates, and accompanied his father in political activities. He was present in the House of Commons during the session of 1876, and was greatly impressed by a Home Rule speech of Butt's, who quoted lines from *Macbeth*, as he recalled years later during the debate on the second Home Rule Bill in 1893, when he used the same quotation.[27] In January 1877 he was taken, along with William, to meet ex-political prisoners, including Michael Davitt, the thirty-year-old former Fenian just released on ticket of leave from Dartmoor having served seven years of a fifteen-year sentence on a conspiracy conviction.[28]

The nineteen-year-old Redmond could see for himself, as he sat in the Strangers' Gallery in June 1876, the disunity and indiscipline of the party under Butt's weak leadership, as members subverted their own leader's moderate motion, which called for a select committee inquiry into the demand for Irish self-government. The following year he would have seen the systematic blocking, by obstructionist tactics, of a large raft of British legislation by Biggar and Parnell, the new M.P. for Meath, in what Thornley has observed 'might better be known as the policy of retaliation', and the open repudiation of that policy in the House by Butt.[29] It was obvious in 1877, when Parnell displaced Butt as chairman of the Home Rule Confederation of Great Britain, the Irish nationalist organization in England, that the latter's policy of conciliation and persuasion was now seen as ineffectual by nationalists, and that support for the 'active policy' better expressed the mood in the Home Rule electorate. And in 1878 Redmond could witness the collapse of Butt's remaining authority as his instinctive loyalty to the British Empire put him on collision course with colleagues who saw opportunities to turn British difficulties in the East – arising from Russian expansionism and war in Afghanistan – to Irish advantage. The fate of Butt must have been in his mind when, nearly four decades later, he found himself in an analogous predicament.

II

As Butt's party disintegrated, developments in agriculture exacerbated the political crisis. In the late seventies a long period of relative prosperity for Irish agriculture came to an end. The partial failure of the potato crop in 1877 brought the threat of starvation to the poorest sections of the rural population. The importation of cheap corn from the newly cultivated areas of the American West brought about a fall in prices in the following year which badly affected the ability of the tenants to pay their rents. The two old spectres of eviction and famine came back to haunt the nation. In 1878 evictions rose to their highest level in over a decade; by 1880 they had doubled again. Scenes of rural distress were particularly bad in the west of Ireland; it was there that Michael Davitt founded the Land League of Mayo with the aim of achieving the transfer of ownership of the soil from the landlords to the tenants.

In the autumn of 1878 the New Departure came into being. This arose from a proposal put by Davitt and John Devoy, the US-based Fenian leader, aimed at attracting 'extreme men', previously supporters of secret revolutionary societies, into support of an open movement that would include a Parliamentary Party with a vigorous, independent policy. The chief planks of such a movement, as outlined by Davitt at a series of meetings in American cities, would be the achievement of national self-government and agitation for the settlement of the land question. In Davitt's words:

> What was wanted was to link the land or social question to that of Home Rule, by making the ownership of the soil the basis of the fight for self-government. Tactically it would mean an attack upon the weakest point in the English hold on Ireland, in the form of a national crusade against landlordism.[30]

Shortly after Butt's death, Parnell in June 1879 publicly associated himself with the Land League of Mayo and spoke, alongside Davitt, at a meeting in Westport at which he exhorted the peasantry under threat of eviction: 'You must show the landlords that you intend to hold a firm grip on your homesteads and lands. You must not allow yourselves to be dispossessed as you were dispossessed in 1847.'[31]

Parnell's election as the first president of the Irish National Land League, on its formation in Dublin in October 1879, set the seal on the New Departure. Those Fenians willing to abandon their disapproval of all parliamentary activity *per se,* and their aloofness from social issues, could now ally themselves, under a charismatic leader, with agrarian radicals, parliamentarians committed to an aggressive nationalist policy, and the militant American-Irish organization, Clan na Gael, led by John Devoy.

In the first quarter of 1880, Parnell and John Dillon, a prominent young Home Ruler and son of the noted Young Irelander of the 1840s, John Blake Dillon, were in the United States on a speaking tour, addressing huge gatherings on behalf of the Land League. Attention in Wexford, as elsewhere in nationalist Ireland, was turning to the selection of candidates for the election everyone knew was imminent. Political activists of Parnellite sympathy were busy launching campaigns against sitting M.P.s seen by them as sham or nominal Home Rulers. At a meeting of the Wexford Independent Club held at Gorey on 17 December 1879, a letter was read from Canon Thomas Doyle, parish priest of Ramsgrange, one of the growing number of politically active clergymen in the nationalist movement, urging the selection of two candidates to replace the sitting Wexford county M.P.s Sir George Bowyer and the Chevalier Keyes O'Clery.[32] According to Canon Doyle, O'Clery had 'violated his pledged word to those who conferred on him the highest honour in their gift'.[33]

Redmond came from London in March 1880 to help in his father's campaign in Wexford borough.[34] Remarkably, in the light of his inactivity in Parliament and his poor attendance at important meetings, the latter was able to escape the kind of criticism visited on many of his fellow-members. It was not as if the *Nation*, now the watchdog of the Parnellites, would be fobbed off easily by verbal expressions of support for the active policy. On 20 March it ran a review of the constituencies and an assessment of election addresses, the good, the bad and the ambiguous. It was well able to distinguish between obvious Whigs such as Bowyer ('the hateful old humbug') and 'Whigs in disguise' such as Villiers Stuart, whose election address was called 'indefinite, vague, misleading'. Others were assailed for inactivity: 'these gentlemen and some others whose addresses have not yet appeared belonged to the stay-away and do-nothing classes, and without a distinct and clear promise to adopt the active policy for the future they should not be sent back to Parliament'.[35] William Redmond's address included a promise that, if elected, he would 'engage to be among the most earnest, active and determined upholders of the national demand'.[36] This was indefinite and vague enough, yet he escaped without censure. Sympathy for his illness, his past services to the amnesty cause, or the prestige of the Redmond name in Wexford may have helped him. It is also possible that he had privately intimated his intention to resign some time soon in the new Parliament and hand over to his son.

With William's campaign going smoothly in the borough, John had time to observe the more exciting county campaign. The contest in the county was one of seven in Ireland in which there was open antagonism between Whigs and Parnellites,[37] and one violent incident there attracted more attention than any other in the entire campaign. This was the so-called 'Enniscorthy outrage' at which Parnell was attacked and prevented from speaking. A public meeting to select the two county candidates was scheduled for the early afternoon of Easter Sunday, 28 March in the town centre. The platform was already occupied by Keyes O'Clery and a group of priests, both supporters and opponents, when Parnell arrived accompanied by John Barry and Garret Byrne, his two nominees for the county seats, along with members of the Wexford Independent Club, a band and green banners. Since Bowyer had announced that he would not stand again as a Home Rule candidate, it seemed that Parnell would have no difficulty in getting one, at any rate, of his nominees accepted; this was to be Barry, a Wexfordman. But resentment had been aroused by the attempt, in the eyes of local people, to impose the outsider Byrne, from the neighbouring county of Wicklow, on the constituency at the expense of O'Clery.[38]

Figure 5. Charles Stewart Parnell in 1880.
Courtesy of the National Library of Ireland.

The crowd of several thousand, determined to show its opposition to his attempt to 'dictate' their choice of candidate, was predominantly hostile to Parnell, who had great difficulty in pushing his way to the platform, and even greater difficulty in being heard when he tried to speak. Fighting broke out around the platform, mud and stones and an egg were thrown, shouts of 'No dictation', 'Down with Byrne' and 'Cheers for O'Clery' filled the air, and members of the Independent Club were bundled off the platform. Father Joseph Murphy appealed to local tradition against the intruding Parnellites: 'Here in the shadow of Vinegar Hill is it to be told that the priests and the bishop and the people of Wexford cannot select their own candidate?'[39]

One of those on the platform from the beginning was a 'Mr. Redmond', presumably Redmond senior, but it is not clear whom he was there to support. Redmond junior was certainly present, by his own account, 'to share in the welcome which I thought the men of my native county would gladly accord to Mr. Parnell on his return from America' but not to take any active part against the Chevalier.[40] He described the experience to Parnell's biographer, R. Barry O'Brien, nearly two decades later:

> I met Parnell in 1880 after his return from America. I was at Enniscorthy with him. It was an awful scene. There were about 4,000 to 5,000 people there. They all seemed to be against him. I remember one man shouting, though what he meant I could not tell: 'We will show Parnell that the blood of Vinegar Hill is still green'. The priests were against Parnell. Parnell stood on the platform calm and self-possessed. There was no use in trying to talk. He faced the crowd, looking sad and sorrowful, but not at all angry; it was an awful picture of patience. A rotten egg was flung at him. It struck him on the beard and trickled down. He took no notice of it, never wiped it off, and was not apparently conscious of it; he faced the crowd steadfastly, and held his ground. One man rushed at him, seized him by the leg, and tore his trouser right up from bottom to top. There was no chance of a hearing, and we got away from the platform and went to the hotel to lunch. Parnell ate a hearty lunch while a waiter was busy stitching his trousers all the time. It was a comical sight.

On that day Redmond had his first experience of political violence:

> Afterwards we went for a walk. We were met by a hostile mob, and I was knocked down and cut in the face. I got up as quickly as I could and made my way to the railway station. When Parnell saw me he said: 'Why, you are bleeding. What is the matter?' I told him what had happened, and he said, smiling: 'Well, you have shed your blood for me at all events.'[41]

The Enniscorthy meeting ended by adopting Barry and O'Clery. The following evening O'Clery was burned in effigy at the Redmond monument in Wexford town by a Parnellite crowd, to the accompaniment of music provided by the St John's Independent Band. The Parnellites ultimately had their way: Keyes was defeated in the election, thanks to a vigorous campaign led by Canon Doyle and some other priests, and Barry and Byrne became the new M.P.s. The Council of the Home Rule League passed a resolution holding all who took part in the attack on Parnell 'in lasting reprobation', while the *Nation* called it, with characteristic hyperbole, 'the most disgraceful incident recorded in recent Irish history', which had sent 'a shock of indignation and horror' through the country.[42]

The general election brought the Liberals back to power, returned sixty-one Home Rulers and strengthened the Parnellite component of the Irish Party. Forty-five members assembled at Dublin's City Hall on 17 May and elected Parnell sessional chairman to replace William Shaw, who had held the post since the death of Butt, by 23 votes to 18. When the new Parliament met on 29 April 1880, the Irish Party, reflecting the hopes of the public for remedial measures from the Liberal Government, suspended obstruction and behaved with moderation. Although the Queen's Speech contained no relief provisions, the Parnellites used the tactic of bringing in a Bill providing for the compensation of tenants evicted for non-payment of rent, and this forced the Government to introduce its own Compensation for Disturbance Bill on 18 June. This passed through the Commons on 26 July, receiving united support from Whigs and Parnellites. Its success seemed a vindication of moderate methods. However, when the House of Lords, on 3 August, threw out the Bill by a large majority, moderation was at an end. Agitation and unrest broke out in Ireland: there were riots at evictions, assaults were made on tenants taking the place of evicted occupiers, and a party of Fenians carried out a robbery of forty cases of firearms from a ship in Cork harbour.

Relations between the Parnellites and the new Government now began to worsen by the week. Dillon, newly elected and just back from the heady atmosphere of Irish-America, shocked the Commons by warning of 'bloodshed and massacre' to come. Back in Ireland on 16 August, he kept up the inflammatory talk, advising the Land League to send 'two active young men' to visit each farmer who had not yet joined the organization and 'persuade' him to do so; he also forecast a general strike against rent.[43] Few were ready to defend Dillon, but the chief secretary, William Forster, brought even moderate nationalists, and the *Freeman's Journal*, to the former's side by declaring that the wickedness of the speech could be equalled only by its cowardice. The activists went back to obstructive tactics, with nineteen members holding up the discussion on the estimates for the Royal Irish Constabulary (RIC) and forcing an all-night sitting of the House on 24–25 August. Yet Parnell held himself open to conciliation, denying that obstruction was a settled policy.

III

Information about Redmond during 1880 is sketchy. After the election, he returned to London, where he seems to have continued his law studies in a desultory manner. He lived on a modest income derived from the rentals of several properties in the Wexford area, the leasehold interest of which he had purchased from his father the previous year.[44] Such an independent income was an indispensable, but perhaps not sufficient, condition of a career in politics in the era before the payment of salaries to M.P.s. He apparently felt the need to supplement it. In May he obtained a job as a clerk in the Votes Office of the House of Commons, at a yearly salary of £300 (valued at £20,000 in 2005). T. M. Healy wrote many years later that 'straitened means alone forced him to accept a post in the Bill Office'.[45] He also began to write the Parliamentary Letter for the *Weekly Register*. The surprise caused in some circles at his taking money for part-time journalism illustrates the expectations gentlemen parliamentarians held of each other. The Liberal attorney-general, Sir Charles Russell, heard about the job from the editor, Wilfred Meynell, who told the story to Redmond-Howard:

> And when, as Attorney-General, he learned of the humble weekly sovereign that used to be John Redmond's modest reward, he exclaimed: 'My God! You don't mean to say the fellow *took* it?' 'Better men have taken less', was the reply of the veteran journalist, 'and worse have taken more!'[46]

Redmond's attendance with Parnell at Enniscorthy suggests that he was preparing himself to become a candidate for the active section; if so, these jobs were a means of gaining an intimate knowledge of parliamentary procedure. Yet he did not put himself forward in March, when, with his inside track to Parnell – we can only presume he had first met him through his father – he would have had little difficulty in getting a nomination. We are led to the conclusion that the constituency he desired was the borough of Wexford, and that he expected to step into his father's shoes at a near date. William Redmond's condition is consistent with this. Suffering from chronic ill health, ambivalent, to say the least, about the direction the party was taking, unable to give the commitment of energy and time required for party work, and with a son in whose formation and education for political life he had invested much, he had every reason to resign soon and allow the seat to be inherited by John.

John Redmond was thus a politician-in-waiting. We know that he had time on his hands during 1879 and 1880, because he had time to write verse. A few of the two dozen or so pieces that have survived offer insights into his personal and family life, and there are attempts at nature sonnets and love poetry, but otherwise there is little in the nature of personal revelation. Much of the material is political verse, written in the romantic style popularized by the Young Ireland versifiers of the 1840s and, though old-fashioned, still flourishing in the 1880s in the columns of the *Nation*. Given his political ambitions, it would have been understandable if he had tried to have it published, but he seems to have kept it to himself. However, these pieces do give a valuable insight into the early development of his politics.[47] In 'Vinegar Hill', dated 27 September 1879, he tells of standing 'on the spot where my forefathers died' and thinking 'how each sod marks a hero's grave', when his musings make the past live again:

> Bold rebels stood round me and claimed me aloud
> A brother to join in the fray.

Having sworn to conquer or die with the rebels, he awakes from the dream to find '. . . o'er the hill's frowning crest the ensign of slavery flies', a sight from which the dead are happily spared. At last a voice from the river bids him: 'Honour the martyrs for Liberty's sake!'

Another poem on the 1798 theme marks the death of a last survivor of the insurrection; is it dedicated 'In Memoriam William Christopher Penrose who fought at Vinegar Hill, Oulart, Hacketstown and Ross; *obiit Jan.* 25th 1880, *aetat*: 98':

> The last link broken in the living chain
> That binds us to a past of memories deep
> No more – the last is freed from earthly pain
> And calmly lies with comrades long asleep!

His example will inspire the rising generation:

> Thy memory yet shall live in younger hearts
> Around our country's flag we too will stand
> Till every trace of tyranny departs.

Although Redmond does not claim to have known the old rebel personally, these pieces are consistent with what he told his nephew much later about the influence of Wexford's '98 tradition on his youthful mind:

> For myself, the rising of Wexford county in '98 is one which from my very earliest youth has exercised a powerful fascination upon my mind. This is but natural. I had been reared and nurtured in the midst of the hills and valleys that witnessed the struggles of '98; I had been taught to regard every scene as a monument of the heroism of our forefathers, and to remember that well nigh every sod beneath my feet marked a hero's sepulchre. My boyish ears had listened to the tales of '98 from the lips of old men who had themselves witnessed the struggles, and I scarcely know a family who cannot tell of a father or grandfather or some near relative who died fighting at Wexford, at Oulart, or Ross . . . one of my proudest recollections has ever been, as it is today, that in that dark hour of trial, there were not wanting men of my race and name who attested by their lives to their devotion to Ireland.[48]

Another piece, 'Famine and Freedom', dated 27 January 1880, adopts the outlook of a Young Irelander in the grim conditions of the 1840s:

O'er all the land a shadow lies
For British-nurtured Famine rears its head,
With breaking heart and maddened cries
Fair Erin mourns the dying and the dead!
O'er all the land a gloom is cast,
A brooding sorrow darkens to despair;
The nation's life is ebbing fast
And curses mingle with her dying prayer
. . . .
Cursed be the Rule that Famine breeds
Cursed the Law built up on Irish slain! . . .

Looking around, he sees 'verdant soil, made rich by Nature's every choicest gift', yet those who toil on it 'starve in spite of industry and thrift'. Must this always be Ireland's fate? His answer has the character of a political manifesto:

No! by the memory of the dead
The martyr'd dead who fell for Freedom's cause
By every drop of blood they shed
We swear to battle against British laws!
The land is ours! Ere cowards came
In friendly guise to plunder and to slay,
Our fathers owned the soil – the same
On which their sons must work and starve today!

'And that's the Reason Why', written in May 1880, contains remarkably extreme sentiments for an employee in the House of Commons:

Why do we hate your Royal red?
(Aye, Saxon, *hate*'s the word)
Make answer heaps of Irish dead
And women's prayers unheard.
Your English red meant Irish shame
In days not long gone by.
To us its name still means the same
And that's the reason why.

Other verses deal with family and other relationships. There is a touching piece, ('To Mere St. Lelia, on the completion of her ninth year of reparation'), dated 18 November 1879, addressed to his sister Esther, the Reparatrice nun, who had been sent home from the Indian mission to recuperate from illness, and would die the following year: [49]

. . . .
I loved thee dear nine years ago
Ere convent veil had screened those eyes of blue.

Now love I less? Ah! Sister – No!
Those years were full of proudest thoughts of you.
Reparatrice! From India's sand
Thrice welcome for thy suffering and pain;
God grant that in our own dear land
Our Irish lily yet may bloom again.

'Spes Mea', written for Valentine's Day 1880, links political and amorous aspirations:

To win in Erin's heart a place
Would seem the sweetest hope for man,
But to thy face of winning grace
My hope will turn – Kilkenny Nan!
. . . Thy Valentine fain would I be
Tho' miles divide and waters part ,
Love leaps the sea and rests with thee
Thou art my hope, my other heart!

Redmond's verse may indicate only the smallest of poetic talents, but it points to a strong sensibility hidden behind the reserve that would often be noted among his chief characteristics. This reserve, along with the measured rationality and discipline of his oratory at its best, would be interpreted by some in later years as coldness and used against him in times of political conflict. Yeats's remark about Parnell, that he was reserved despite his sensibility, rather than for want of it, applies equally to Redmond.[50]

The evidence of early immersion in the traditions of 1798 goes a long way to acquit him of the charge of opportunism levelled by some writers in commenting on his participation in the centenary commemorations in 1898.[51] Throughout his career he put himself forward as an authority on the insurrection, lecturing to large audiences in Australia on the subject as early as 1883,[52] and publishing a pamphlet on it in 1886.[53] He was, of course, a politician rather than a historian and made a politician's use of the events of that bloody and traumatic episode, playing down the impact of sectarian atrocities (at least on the rebel side) and emphasizing the noble ideals and heroism of the insurgents. As a campaigner against the Union of 1800, he was concerned to show that British Prime Minister William Pitt and his colleagues had provoked the rebellion in a conspiracy to bring an end to Ireland's semi-autonomous Parliament. As a constitutionalist, he was keen to portray the United Irishmen as frustrated constitutionalists driven reluctantly to violent rebellion. As a Home Ruler more sensitive than many of his colleagues to the concerns of Protestants, he did not embrace the paradigm of the rebellion as a 'faith and fatherland' crusade by an enraged Catholic peasantry, which was becoming dominant in his own lifetime due to the influence of Father Kavanagh's 1870 *Popular History of the Insurrection of 1798*, but emphasized the co-operation of Catholics and Protestants in its leadership. Although there were contradictions within his rhetoric in 1898, there were no aspects of the 'bandwagon' about it. He advanced an interpretation of the rebellion which was, as Malcolm Campbell has pointed out, remarkably consistent throughout his career.[54] It was an interpretation which, in some respects, resembles the modern 'consensus' – equally sanitized and tailored to suit contemporary political purposes – which emerged at the bicentenary commemorations in 1998.[55]

Despite his tendency to romanticize rhetorically the insurrection, his closeness to the '98 tradition may have been the source of the actual nervousness of popular violence that would characterize his career. His attitude is certainly compatible with having grown up in a county still traumatized by the violent deaths of more than 20,000 people in a couple of months, less than sixty years before his birth. While he would always uphold the right – and possible need, if at some future time constitutional methods were deemed to have failed – of the Irish nation to use armed force to win its freedom, his actions betrayed an anxiety to discourage outbreaks of violence, large or small, for fear of the consequences for the people themselves. His constant appeals at public meetings for peaceful behaviour within the law and his condemnation of agrarian outrages reveal none of the mentality of the agitator who seeks to radicalize a population by provoking its exposure to the violence of state forces. More than once, at eviction scenes, he expressed the belief that leaders should not advocate violent resistance unless they were prepared to take part themselves.[56]

IV

With Parliament in recess throughout the autumn of 1880, land agitation in Ireland spread through the west and south of the country. The chief Parnellite M.P.s travelled the country, speaking at huge weekend demonstrations from mid-September to late November. At the first, at Ennis on 19 September, Parnell himself proclaimed the Land League policy towards 'land-grabbers' – those taking farms from which others had been evicted – in terms that gave the doctrine of social ostracism, shortly afterwards to be known as 'boycotting', a powerful new impetus. The left and right wings of the nationalist movement, represented respectively by the ex-Fenians sympathetic to Davitt and by the Catholic clergy (but without the support of the Whig parliamentarians), gradually came together behind this campaign, as shown by the presence of no fewer than eight priests on the platform at Ennis. The *Freeman's Journal*, previously cautious about backing Parnell, gave him its first unequivocal endorsement the day after the meeting. The Government decided to prosecute the Land League leaders on charges of conspiracy to prevent the payment of rent. Prosecutions were brought against five M.P.s – Parnell, Biggar, Dillon, T. D. Sullivan and Thomas Sexton – and against other prominent members of the league.[57]

On Saturday 30 October, William Redmond was staying with his half-sister Theresa in Cork city, having spoken in Dublin the previous week at temperance meetings, when he suffered a heart attack. John was summoned from London by wire, and arrived on Monday. He was with his father when he died early on Tuesday, 2 November, the day on which the trials of Parnell and the others opened in Dublin.[58]

Within a week, it was clear that Redmond would not be taking over his father's seat, since Parnell had other ideas. Tim Healy, an energetic Parnellite journalist in London working for the *Nation* and an aspirant to a parliamentary seat, had been asked by Parnell in September to organize the Land League in Wexford. He had recently been charged with making an intimidatory speech in Bantry, and his election to the seat would strike a blow at the Government. According to Healy's account, the Wexford Independent Club telegraphed Parnell to say they would accept anybody nominated by him; Redmond also telegraphed to say that, although he wanted the seat, he would not stand against a Parnell nominee. Parnell replied to Redmond, stressing the importance of having Healy returned, but intimating that if he (Redmond) surrendered his claim, he would not be forgotten.[59]

On Sunday 7 November, Redmond told a meeting assembled at the Redmond monument:

> His family had for generations served them in Parliament. He had no objection to representing the town, but at the present time he thought it was a duty to Ireland to withdraw in favour of Mr. Healy. If he (Mr. Redmond) was elected it would have no significance outside the town, but by selecting Mr. Healy they were striking a blow in this ancient town which would be felt in the three kingdoms [loud cheers] . . . I am a young man, and at some future time I may ask you for your suffrages . . .[60]

Proposing a vote of thanks to Redmond for standing aside, a member of the club praised him 'for his thoroughly unselfish, disinterested, and noble conduct in waiving his claims to our support'. Healy publicly thanked 'the worthy and brilliant son of a worthy and distinguished father, who is such a loss to Ireland, for his abnegation at such a crisis'.[61] The same day, however, he wrote to his brother, claiming that Redmond's compliance with Parnell's wishes was not all it appeared to be: 'Redmond leaves today. He has acted frankly since the Club gave him his *Dimittis*, but had he got any encouragement from them he would have gone forward in spite of Parnell.'[62]

Healy was elected unopposed for the Wexford seat on 24 November. That Redmond felt the disappointment keenly is shown in the letter he wrote a month later to Father Patrick Furlong, the parish priest of New Ross, a member of the Council of the Home Rule League and one of the priests who had campaigned against the Whigs in March:

> Allow me in the first place to thank you for the high opinion you express as to my qualifications. So far as that opinion relates to the fact of my being heart and soul with the people at the present crisis, it is a truthful one. In reply to your letter, I beg to say my great desire would have been to succeed my father in Wexford, and it was only after a tough struggle with my feelings that I was able to withdraw in favour of Healy. My desire still would be, at the very first opportunity, to ask the electors of Wexford for their votes, and in the event of a dissolution of Parliament, Mr. Healy has been good enough to say he would go elsewhere, if the people still desired me to represent them.[63]

The possibility of another borough seat becoming vacant in the county, that of New Ross, must have been adverted to by Furlong, since Redmond added that he would be 'very proud to stand for Ross if adopted by the popular Party', but nothing had been confirmed by the end of the year.

Before Christmas, Redmond made two attempts (both titled 'The New Year 1881') to put into verse his feelings about the year of double bereavement and disappointment now ending:

> The year is dying! Ah! How few
> Will weep its death! For me
> I watch impatient for the new
> My soul yearns to be free
> From that hard year of Death and pain
> Whose memory aye will live in grief and fear!
> As withering flowers kiss the rain
> My spirit weary greets the coming year,
> Thrice welcome child,
> 'Time sweetens grief', Hope fondly said and smiled.
>
> * * *
>
> . . . Years smiled at first, Death's stealthy hand too fast
> Ere life had fully blossom'd seared my heart.
> Come, Future! Hide this hideous Past away . . .[64]

3 Passion and Pragmatism

> The floor was littered everywhere with papers. All things were in disorder. A dozen dishevelled, weary Irishmen were confronting some 100 or so infuriated Englishmen, some of them in evening dress and in shirts that had been white the evening before last. Of intelligent debate there was absolutely none . . . The galleries were crowded. No one knew what was going to happen . . .
>
> Redmond in New York, 1896, remembering the scene in the House of Commons on his arrival to take his seat on 2 February 1881[1]

> His primary object in that House would ever be to endeavour to overthrow the government, or, rather, misgovernment, of his country by this Parliament.
>
> Redmond in the House of Commons, 11 March 1881[2]

I

Early in January 1881, J. W. Foley, M.P. for the County Wexford borough of New Ross, resigned his seat. Letters from Father Furlong had suggested to Redmond that, if he chose to stand in the by-election, his adoption by the party was highly probable. He replied that he was ready to go to the constituency at a day's notice.[3] After some weeks of uncertainty Redmond was adopted as the candidate of the Home Rule party and elected unopposed for New Ross on Tuesday 1 February.[4]

Although impatient to enter Parliament, he had told Furlong in December that he would not stand unless supported by all sections of the 'popular' party, as defeat would be 'a serious matter for me'. His remarks to the priest also indicated that his funds were limited:

> I presume the expense of a contest would be much the same as in Wexford – if it were likely to be *very much* more, it might cause me some inconvenience unless I had timely notice. In Wexford at the General Election I did everything for my poor father and we dispensed with the services of a solicitor as conducting agent. I suppose we could do the same in Ross . . .[5]

Though modest, he was in no doubt about his own credentials:

> If elected you would have a young and I am afraid, very inexperienced politician as your representative, but you would have one whose whole heart was in the cause, and who, quite irrespective of

Figure 6. John Redmond around the time of his first election, 1881.
Courtesy of the National Library of Ireland.

his own devotion to that cause is too proud of the traditions he has inherited ever to bring disgrace upon his name by betraying his principles.[6]

Entering Parliament, Redmond became the youngest of the group of brilliant young Parnellites, new to the House since the spring of 1880 (in Healy's case, since November), who augmented the original 'active policy' ranks of Biggar, O'Donnell, John O'Connor Power, James Lysaght Finigan and Parnell himself and were now in the thick of both parliamentary activism and land agitation. In that year, Parnell was 34 years of age, T. P. O'Connor 33, Thomas Sexton 33, Dillon 30 and Healy 26. By-elections would add the remaining Parnellite 'lieutenants', William O'Brien and Timothy Harrington, in 1883. Most of these men would dominate constitutional nationalist politics for more than three decades to come.

The characteristics that distinguished this group have been described thus: 'They were, as compared with the whigs, fresh to politics; they had a streak of "fenianism", a streak of more exotic radicalism; and they were committed to a very advanced land programme, which they had not themselves evolved.'[7] Other features that marked them out from the Whigs were their tendency to make their living from paid work in journalism or the law, rather than from landed wealth, and to live in England, mostly in London and Liverpool. Encouraging Irish electors to vote for these 'carpetbaggers', as they were often disparagingly called by the Whigs, meant weaning them away from attachment to the old families which had supplied candidates of local standing, and winning their support for a national programme advanced by a national leader and a party with centrally chosen nominees. Redmond combined features of both groups. His base in London and his occupations, though they were not his sole source of income, gave him much in common with the other new recruits. On the other hand, there was something Whiggish about his having a family tradition in Wexford politics and in his strong desire to carry on that tradition in Parliament, rather than place himself at the disposal of the party and Parnell to deploy him where they might. There is some evidence of family opposition, not to his entry into politics, but to his intended orientation within the party. According to Healy, his brother William, not yet twenty but a lieutenant in the militia, telegraphed him with the message, 'For God's sake don't disgrace the family by joining the Land League and Parnell.'[8] Given the army position of his uncle, his mother's unionist background and his father's centrist position in the party, this story has plausibility.

When Parliament opened on 7 January, the Queen's Speech outlined a dual programme for Ireland: coercion legislation would be brought in to curb the 'extended system of terror' in the country, and a Land Bill would address the main agrarian grievances. Parnell, in his amendment to the Address to the Queen, argued that the Land Bill should be taken first, thus making coercion unnecessary. When this was rejected, the Irish Party launched a filibuster, proposing one amendment after another and prolonging the debate over eleven nights until 20 January. Four days later William Forster, chief secretary for Ireland, brought in the Protection of Person and Property (Ireland) Bill, and the party intensified its obstruction. Extended sittings were forced on the House, that of 25 January lasting for twenty-two hours, while the sitting that began on Monday 31 January lasted until Wednesday morning, a total of forty-one hours, making it the longest on record. That afternoon, one which proved to be climactic in the history of the use of the obstruction tactic, Redmond arrived to take his seat. He found 'one unbroken scene of turbulence and disorder', with Parnell on his feet waiting to be heard amid the roars and howls of English M.P.s.[9] He wrote hurriedly to Furlong:

> On arriving at the House this morning I found the fight had been suddenly stopped by a ruling of the Speaker of which I fancy we are destined to hear a good deal . . . Our 'chaps' are full of fight but, I fear, if the rulings of the Speaker are maintained it will be difficult to make a successful stand.[10]

In later years he told the story, not quite accurately, of how he had taken his seat, made his maiden speech and been ejected from the House all on his first day in Parliament.[11]

The Irish members, taken completely by surprise by the Speaker's ruling of the morning, were unable to prevent the passage of the first reading of the Coercion Bill. However, during the afternoon sitting, one of the party's best debaters, A. M. Sullivan, through clever jousting with the Speaker, succeeded in bringing in an adjournment motion, leading to a fresh series of Irish speeches that further obstructed business for the rest of the afternoon.[12] During that afternoon Redmond was sworn in as a new member and was able to observe his colleagues effectively neutralizing the Speaker's ruling.

The following afternoon the first business was a resolution of Gladstone's to amend the rules of procedure to defeat obstruction. Before this was reached, Home Secretary William Harcourt informed the House that Davitt had been arrested in Dublin for violating the conditions of his parole. When the Speaker then called on Gladstone to put his resolution, John Dillon stood up to demand an explanation for the arrest. Refusing to resume his seat, he was named and suspended by a vote of the House, and withdrew only when the sergeant-at-arms was called. A. M. Sullivan argued with the Speaker, protesting at 'the reign of law being over, and the reign of force having commenced'. At length Gladstone rose again, and then Parnell stood up and moved 'that the right honourable gentleman [Gladstone] be no further heard'.[13] Hansard at this point records: 'From this incident forward, the Business of the House proceeded under indescribable confusion.' To British members' cries of 'Name him! Name him!', Parnell repeatedly clashed with the Speaker until Gladstone moved that he be suspended for the rest of the sitting. This required a vote of the House, but the Parnellites refused to leave their seats for the division lobby. Parnell was suspended and removed by the sergeant-at-arms, but Finigan rose and put Parnell's motion again, and another ejection followed. This time the sergeant-at-arms was able to report the names of those twenty-seven members who, by refusing to quit their places, were flouting the authority of the chair. Gladstone moved their suspension, and one by one they uttered a brief refusal and then withdrew under duress.[14] When the sergeant-at-arms reached him, Redmond's words, his first as a parliamentarian, were: 'As I regard the whole of these proceedings as unmitigated despotism, I beg respectfully to decline to withdraw.'[15] Within his first twenty-four hours in the House, he had indeed taken his seat, made a 'maiden speech' of a kind, and been suspended.

The following morning, the *Freeman* beseeched the Irish people to remain calm, despite events that would 'send a less excitable race into a noble rage', and, giving the names of the suspended, declared 'they shall be written on the memory-tablets of Ireland'. At New Ross, the Land League branch adopted a resolution condemning both the Coercion Bill and those Irish members who had 'deserted the active Parliamentary party and Mr. Parnell at such a momentous crisis',[16] a reference, not only to Shaw and the other eleven Whigs who had formally seceded from the party on 16 January, but to a substantial centre group of about fifteen who remained aloof from Parnell.

It has been suggested that, if there were ever a moment when Parnell might have fulfilled the expectations implicit in the New Departure – and his own apparent commitment made at an emergency meeting of the Land League executive in London on 1 and 2 February – by withdrawing the Irish Party from Parliament and bringing it to Dublin, this was it.[17] Public opinion was aroused by the land crisis, the Davitt arrest, the looming threat of coercion and the fight made against it in Parliament by the active wing. The party would lose little in the short term since its only weapon, obstruction, had been destroyed by the action of the Speaker and the introduction of the new rules. It was a time to choose between the quasi-revolutionary policy of 'concentration' (withdrawal to Dublin) and continuation on the constitutional path. In the event Parnell had no hesitation in choosing the latter course.[18] The view that Parnell reached this decision partly because he was unsure of the degree of party support for a policy of concentration is supported by what Redmond wrote to Furlong after the events of 3 February:

> I quite agree with you in thinking that we made a mistake on Thursday. That is *now* the opinion of four fifths of the Party (Parnell included). We acted, however, on the impulse of the moment and without consultation, and I am not sorry a remarkable protest was made against Davitt's arrest:[19]

Two days before the first Coercion Bill was finally passed by the Commons, Redmond again referred to the effect of the mass suspension in terms that showed already a coolly pragmatic concern with parliamentary tactics over theatrical gestures: 'What is thought of the fight made against the Coercion Bill? I think the great error was allowing ourselves to be suspended while the new rules were passed. Only for that incident it would have taken some time to pass them and they would probably have been modified'.[20] It was evident that many of Parnell's closest supporters not only would have opposed pulling out of Parliament, but actually regretted what had happened there, notwithstanding that Parnell, according to his biographer, had deliberately allowed the Dillon incident to escalate into one affecting the whole party.[21]

Redmond played an active part in the struggle to delay the passage of the Bill, speaking once on the second reading (his real maiden speech) and three times in Committee in support of amendments. The Government and the Speaker were slow to use their new powers,[22] and allowed the debate to spread over a total of fifteen nights. In his maiden speech, Redmond gave signs already that he had inherited his father's sensitivity to the 'tone of the House':

> . . . it was his strange fortune, on the first occasion of taking his seat, to find himself placed in a position of direct antagonism to the feeling and authority of the House. Such a position was painful, and would have been altogether intolerable, had he not been convinced that he was only fulfilling his duty to his constituents and his country, and that it must, sooner or later, inevitably be the fate of every Irishman who entered Parliament to represent the national aspirations of his countrymen, to be placed in direct antagonism to English politicians, whether Liberal or Conservative.

Arguing that coercion legislation was unnecessary, he pointed to the 'calumnies' being hurled against Ireland, Wexford being an example: fifty-six 'outrages' had been recorded for the county for 1880, but almost all of these were merely cases of threatening letters; such dishonest statements were 'blackening the character of a people whom he knew to be the most law-abiding and God-fearing in the United Kingdom'. Rejecting denunciations of 'the unwritten law of the [Land] League', he defended it on the grounds that it had

> prevented thousands of those evictions which the Government had acknowledged to be inhuman and unjust, but which they had failed to arrest; and he thanked God that there was an unwritten law in Ireland, strong enough to cancel the 'sentences of death' which Irish landlords had levelled against their tenants . . .

He denied the right of the 'English Parliament' to govern Ireland; the only hope for her peace and prosperity lay in 'having an Assembly of her own once again – a native Parliament, hallowed by the glories of the past'.[23] Writing to Furlong the following day, he exulted: 'I made my maiden speech last night, and was successful far beyond my expectation, but I am told the *Freeman* wire was broken so my vanity will receive a salutary lesson in the shape of a report of probably three lines.'[24]

Parnell was absent in Paris for most of February, at first for a Land League executive meeting, later in order to meet notable figures of the

French left, such as Victor Hugo and the Communard Henri Rochefort. These well-publicized visits were part of an effort to divert the attention of the 'advanced men' from his abandonment of the withdrawal policy. They were the action of, in Conor Cruise O'Brien's telling phrase, 'a master of constitutional politics, adept at the cape-work of the pseudo-revolutionary gesture'.[25] The visits drew fire from Archbishop Edward McCabe of Dublin, who denounced the seeking of allies from the ranks of 'impious infidels' who were 'sworn to destroy the foundations of all religions'.[26] The Whigs George Errington and Henry Bellingham, as well as A. M. Sullivan, also protested against them. Redmond gave his own sceptical views to Furlong, reflecting the general unease at the leader's long absence:

> Parnell's absence was and is a great injury to effective action by the party and I am most anxious for him to return, the more so as I don't anticipate much practical result from his work in Paris . . . I would employ any means against the English Government but I don't think Rochfort [*sic*] and that lot can do anything for us and I think Parnell is wasting his time.[27]

The Coercion Act, passed on 28 February, empowered the authorities to arrest any person on suspicion of agrarian offences or treasonable actions and to hold them in prison for any period up to 30 September 1882.[28] The next day, the Government introduced the complementary Peace Preservation (Ireland) Bill, also known as the Arms Bill. This took nine nights of debate, and passed the Commons on 11 March. The debate was notable for an altercation on 3 March between Dillon, as usual setting the pace in extremism of language, and the Home Secretary, Harcourt. Dillon wanted the Irish people to supply themselves with arms; if he were a farmer, he would shoot anyone coming to turn him out of his house and land. 'If they wanted to provoke a civil war in Ireland – but it could not be a civil war, for the Irish people had not the means of waging a civil war – he wished they had . . . (*Cries of "Oh!" and "Withdraw!"*).' He then withdrew 'civil war' and substituted 'bloodshed'. A furious Harcourt said that the speech would 'bring horror and disgust' and that 'the language of assassination' used by Dillon showed the real nature of the Land League.[29]

Redmond's response, coming after those of Healy and T. P. O'Connor, and in the presence of Parnell, was remarkably assured. He first dissociated the league from Dillon's language:

> The honourable member for Tipperary had not, as the right honourable gentleman [Harcourt] cleverly asserted, spoken authoritatively on behalf of the Land League. The honourable member spoke in that manner for himself, upon his own responsibility . . . He did not compromise the Land League or any of its members, whose policy in the present crisis was one of passive resistance . . .

But with regard to Dillon's expression of regret that the people had not the means of waging war, 'he (Mr. Redmond) agreed entirely with the honourable member; because he was firmly of opinion that if the only thing wanting – the possibility of a successful rising against this country – existed, it would be an ample justification for the Irish people at the present moment'.[30] These comments drew a 'Hear, hear' from Parnell. This renunciation, on grounds of expediency rather than of principle, of violence for national aims would be a rhetorical constant with Redmond, as with other Parnellites. It differentiated them both from O'Connell, with his categorical aversion to insurrection, and from the Fenians, who would have doubted – probably correctly – whether Parnellites would ever view the time as right for the use of physical force. The moderate *Freeman* the following day responded to Dillon in a similarly ambivalent manner. A leader deeply deplored the speech for both its nature and its effect in England: it was a time for urging self-restraint, not uttering words that could encourage the shedding of blood. But neither did it take exception to Dillon's reference to civil war: that was something on which all nationalists could agree.[31]

Redmond's own speech against the Bill combined an appeal to the traditions of the Liberal Party with a warning to the Government:

> They had seen a great Party pledged to a policy of redress – a Party who were the friends and champions of freedom all over the world, after all their professions, having recourse to the degrading weapon of despotism . . . they had succeeded in establishing a reign of terror in Ireland . . . it exposed the sham of Constitutionalism in Ireland . . . the day might come when the hate with which the Government were filling the breasts of the Irish people might be a source of danger to England in her hour of peril.[32]

With the coercion debates ended, the neophyte M.P. could reflect on the experience of his first six weeks in Parliament. He had made a confident start; his years of familiarity with the House ensured that he had not been overawed either by its British luminaries or by the rhetoric of colleagues such as Dillon. William O'Brien in later years remembered him in those early months: 'His frank and handsome presence, his self-restraint of manner and remarkable faculty of lucid and captivating oratory, gave early promise, which he has not disappointed, of success in a House which has by no means lost the gusto for grace and ornament of speech.'[33] Redmond wrote to Furlong on 26 February:

> I have already tasted something of the anger of the House. The last time I spoke . . . I was fairly howled at, and I must say it is not nearly so unpleasant a sensation as I fancied. I had got up quite without preparation and the only effect the shouts had was to inspire me with plenty to say. Tim Healy, however, bears off the palm – I think if English members could they would flay him alive. He is able to rile them more than Biggar, O'Donnell and Finigan rolled into one.[34]

He had also been speaking outside the House, accompanied by Edmund Leamy, the new M.P. for Waterford: 'Did you see our invasion of Forster's constituency – Bradford? It was rather cheeky for the two youngest members of the Irish party to beard the lion in his den.'[35]

In April he went touring again in the north of England, addressing 'some fine meetings' in Leeds, Darlington and Hartlepool, among other venues.[36] These meetings were another part of Parnell's alternative to secession from Parliament: that of 'widening the area of the agitation' to win the support of the English masses for the Irish cause.

II

The Government now turned its attention to redress. On 7 April Gladstone introduced the Land Law (Ireland) Bill. The Bill conceded to a great extent the Irish demand for judicial fixing of rents – effectively establishing dual ownership of the land – and also provided finance to help tenants to purchase their holdings. However, despite its welcome by the Catholic hierarchy and moderate nationalists generally, its chances of acceptance were vitiated by the rising tension in the countryside. Evictions were again on the increase, and attacks on landlords' agents and process-servers rose accordingly. The left of the party led by Dillon attacked the Bill almost immediately, the latter declaring at a meeting in Dublin that if he were to vote for it, he 'would be only helping to rivet the collar of the master around the tenants'.[37] Parnell tried to steer a course between the opposed approaches by maintaining a non-committal stance. At a Land League convention chaired by him in Dublin on 22 April, he skilfully obtained a resolution that allowed the Parliamentary Party the freedom to accept the Bill if certain amendments were adopted by the Government, while avowing that only the abolition of landlordism would satisfy the Irish people.[38]

Dillon, however, seized the initiative. In the last week of April he made another series of extreme speeches in Ireland, bringing about his arrest, under the Coercion Act, on 2 May.[39] Parnell was compelled to make a gesture of protest. At a party meeting on 5 May, he moved that the party abstain on the second reading of the Bill, and threatened to resign if this were not carried. His motion was passed by 18 votes to 11.[40] The large number of 'active section' members who opposed abstention reflected the unhappiness of much of the nationalist centre. Archbishop Thomas Croke of Cashel, the best-known clerical supporter of the league, and the *Freeman* and the *Nation* all condemned the decision.[41]

Redmond was one of those who supported abstention. He told Furlong on 9 May: 'I never felt so uncertain about any vote but I think my reasons were sound. I was not influenced by Dillon's arrest and in my speech at the meeting I protested against connecting it with our action.'[42] He was in favour of abstention on its own merits on the grounds that it would make the Government more willing to accept amendments in Committee and thus secure support on the crucial third reading, while it did not imperil the passage of the Bill. But he was upset by Parnell's threat to resign and also fearful of a new split:

> a most unfair thing, in my opinion, to announce, but of the two evils, the resolution was accepted by some who were on its own merits opposed to it. I am sincerely sorry at the whole affair. Of course the air is full of rumours but it is really hard to say what the final result will be. It is most important we should have no split.[43]

This letter crossed with a telegram from Furlong to Redmond, which must have expressed concern at the abstention vote. Redmond showed this to Parnell and wrote back that the latter had asked him to give Furlong his reasons for favouring abstention. These made no mention of a gesture of protest but reiterated the practical argument, that abstention now was crucial to any chance of winning amendments later. Redmond added:

> He [Parnell] is most anxious for the country to support our action, more especially as I cannot see how we can change our front even if it seemed wise to do so. The men who came to our meeting and *voted* and then declared themselves unwilling to abide by the resolution seem to me to occupy an anomalous position. They are few, however . . . We are all in a most difficult and painful position, and it will be deplorable if we have a further secession from the party.[44]

It seemed that conciliation measures from the Government tended to divide, as coercion tended to unite, the Irish members. The following day Parnell showed his concern to appease the moderates by addressing an open letter to Croke, which emphasized that the party's tactic would not harm the Bill.[45]

In the parliamentary division on 19 May, thirty-five Home Rulers abstained with Parnell.[46] Fourteen members voted for the Bill (together with the twelve who had seceded), but Redmond's fears were not realized.[47] He told Furlong that his only concern had been for the possible defection of members who had voted for abstention on 5 May, who were in the habit of coming to meetings of the active section; but not many of them were among the fourteen who had defected: 'I am sure you were pleased and relieved to find how loyally most of our men acted. The few who voted for the Bill I think made a great mistake but happily they are too few to make a "split".'[48] Meanwhile he had received a taste of the displeasure of the 'advanced men':

> Did you see how the Fenians treated Dr. Cummins and myself at Blackburn? All through the North of England they are bitterly opposed to the Land League and have formed a gang to break up our meetings. Of course a little organisation on our side will prevent this. It is a great pity. They are decent fellows most of them, but very foolish.[49]

Redmond had not yet spoken on the Land Bill at the time of the abstention vote. He had his chance to indicate his real attitude on 12 May, during the second reading, when he balanced measured criticism with an appreciation of the 'great principles' recognized therein, namely 'that landlordism in Ireland was an evil'. It was the duty of all Irish M.P.s to approach the discussion in a spirit of fairness and liberality; it would ill become them to approach it 'in a spirit of carping criticism'. He welcomed 'with pleasure' the facilities it afforded for the creation of a peasant proprietary, though it appeared to him that some of the provisions for that purpose were inadequate and absurd. His party's criticism focused on four areas. The existing courts would not be able to fix the judicial rents, and a new type of tribunal would be needed to do the job; no provision was made to have fair rents fixed retrospectively, so that huge numbers hopelessly in arrears due to accumulation of rack rent would face eviction; leaseholders were excluded from the Bill; increased facilities were provided to encourage emigration, on the assumption that it was too slow, but two and a half million had emigrated since 1853 – 'What nation on earth could stand such a drain as that?' he asked. He ended by assuring the House that if the Government listened to the suggestions that would come from the Irish representatives, they would, 'in truth, inaugurate an era of conciliation, and there would be some chance that the Land Bill would be formed into a wise, lasting and beneficial measure of reform'.[50]

These remarks were similar in tone to those made by many other members of the party. During the long Committee stage, which now began and continued until 27 July, the party occupied itself with the double task of getting its own amendments accepted and defending the Bill against pro-landlord amendments from the Tories. In this it was led with enormous ability by Healy and Sexton. Redmond's part in these debates was small: he made five contributions, in the main supporting amendments put by others. He told Furlong in June:

> The Land Bill is beginning to make way and I should not be surprised if we found a disposition on the part of Gladstone to make concessions to us where he can do so with safety to the ultimate chances of the Bill passing, but he has a very difficult card to play.[51]

A few weeks later he was less optimistic. At a large Land League demonstration in New Ross on Sunday 3 July, with Furlong in the chair, he told his audience that the people were suspicious of the Bill because they had no confidence in the men who had lied to justify coercion. While it had some 'important principles', it 'lacked finality' and was a scheme for emigration. All the party's efforts to improve it had been fruitless to date, and one concession after another had been made to the Tories. In August the House endured late night sittings to consider certain amendments made by the House of Lords, and he was one of those who entered a vigorous protest against one such change to the provisions on arrears.

Speaking at 3 a.m. on 12 August on T. D. Sullivan's motion to adjourn, he warned that the fate of the Bill would be endangered by such last minute amendments.[52]

Near the end of the 1881 session Redmond clashed with Gladstone in the House when he spoke strongly on a Parnell amendment on Supply for the Irish Executive, which asserted that the Coercion Acts were not being administered impartially. He linked coercion with the fate of the Land Act, which had now passed all stages and was awaiting royal assent. It would not do, he said, to hold out remedial measures while at the same they administered 'a despotism the like of which was unknown even in Russia'. Some two hundred men had been arrested but not tried and had no chance to face their accusers or offer evidence in their own behalf. If justice was to be at all regarded, these men must be released from prison,

> and [they] said that what was called the remedial measure [the Land Act] must fail so long as one of these men was detained in prison . . . [otherwise] so long would the Representatives of Ireland prolong and intensify a state of feeling which would be not only inconvenient and embarrassing to the Government, but also a source of danger.

And he uttered a criticism commonly made by nationalists of British reforms:

> As regarded the Land Act, he would not venture to say whether it was a bad or a good measure; but this he would say – the Irish people did not owe it to the Prime Minister. All the burning words which had been spoken by the Irish members in respect to the conditions of the tenants had been disregarded until the country was brought within a measurable distance of civil war; and then terror, not a feeling of justice towards the Irish people, wrung the measure, such as it was, from the Liberal Government.[53]

Gladstone's reply put Redmond on the defensive. He claimed, plausibly, that his words implied that there would be no fair trial for the Land Act until every coercion prisoner was free. Redmond denied having said this; rather he had argued 'that it would be utterly impossible for the Act to have a fair trial in Ireland unless the Government liberated [the prisoners]'. Gladstone replied, 'But the honourable Member further said that his endeavours would be to move in that direction', and chided him for the harshness of his speech, claiming that reforms such as the 1869 Church Disestablishment or the 1870 Land Act were not responses to Irish agitation. Embarrassed, Redmond again denied saying that the Act would not be given a fair trial, only that 'there could not be any such thing as a pacified Ireland'.[54] The next day, he was adamant that he and his friends had been 'misrepresented, unintentionally': 'He never said . . . that they would do all they could to prevent the Land Bill . . . having a fair trial in Ireland. On the contrary, they felt that whatever good was in that Bill should be extracted from it by the Irish people for their benefit.'[55]

Part of that 'good' was, for Parnell, that it would bankrupt a third of the landlords, which was more than the league could do, and make the rest amenable to being bought out rather than face the legal expense of going to the land courts every fifteen years.[56] Others did not make such a cool appraisal in a revolutionary atmosphere. With the passing of the Land Act, the pressures on Parnell from the left became more acute. Though the bishops welcomed it, the Irish-Americans were for rejection and Dillon was in radical disagreement with the whole policy of the party towards it: he had written to William O'Brien on 12 July from Kilmainham jail that the differences between 'certain members of the L.L. Executive and myself on the one hand, and Parnell and the Parliamentary section of the Executive on the other' were becoming 'daily wider'.[57] At the National Convention of the Land League, which began at the Rotunda on 15 September, Parnell braved a flood of rejectionist oratory and won the agreement of the divided delegates for the middle course of 'testing the Act'. The plan was to encourage the tenants not to rush *en masse* into the land courts but to submit only selected cases. With Parliament in recess in September, it was easy for M.P.s to deploy verbal extremism to cover the essential moderation of the plan. At a succession of rallies in late September Parnell stressed 'the hollowness of the Act'.[58] Dillon and another militant, Father Eugene Sheehy, were released from jail, and the latter took his place on the platform at a huge demonstration in Cork on 2 October at which Parnell made more negative noises.[59]

These developments were misunderstood in London. In William O'Brien's words,

> While . . . it took all Parnell's strength to save the Act from summary rejection by followers of his own, who mistook his policy for pusillanimity, he was assailed by Gladstone, on the other hand, as the cold-blooded politician who was withholding the blessings of the Act from a people thirsting to receive them.[60]

The following Friday, Gladstone, taking the 'test case' policy to mean that the Act was being undermined, replied in his famous speech at Leeds, threatening the league with the 'resources of civilisation'. Two days later, on 9 October in Wexford, Parnell appeared to challenge Gladstone to have him arrested, calling him a 'masquerading knight-errant' and appealing to the Irish insurrectionary tradition.[61] According to Healy, who left Dublin by train for Wexford that morning with Redmond and John Barry, Parnell had not read Gladstone's speech when he got on the train at Rathdrum. Healy read it to him and his reply was composed jointly by himself and Healy (and possibly some of the others) *en route* to the meeting. Parnell, remembered Healy, 'stirred the Wexford folk . . . not easy to move, being largely of Norman or Welsh blood . . . to their entrails'.[62]

Redmond welcomed Parnell to Wexford in a short speech aimed at the farmers of the county: 'Their attitude should be to ignore the existence of this Land Act until they had ascertained its character, until it had been tested.'[63] The following day, at the conferring of the Freedom of the Borough on Parnell, he reflected his leader's new-found militant tone: 'The movement was not started to obtain tenant-right for the people of Ireland. Time was when the people of Ireland would gladly have accepted that, but the landlords would have no compromise. The watchword now was "No surrender"'.[64] It was at the wild scenes on that day that Parnell, in Healy's recollection, turned to him and, in a tense whisper, said 'Healy, we have pushed this movement as far as it can constitutionally go.'[65]

On 12 October, Chief Secretary Forster returned from an urgent Cabinet meeting in London. The following day Parnell was arrested and lodged in comfortable accommodation in Kilmainham jail. Dillon was re-arrested, other leading Land Leaguers were locked up within forty-eight hours, and rioting with baton charges took place on the streets of Dublin for three nights.[66] On 18 October the arrested 'suspects' released their 'No Rent Manifesto', drawn up by O'Brien, which advocated a 'general strike against rent'.[67] Such a strike had been the preferred option of the rejectionists at the National Convention in September; a cable from Patrick Ford, editor of the New York *Irish World*, 'in the name of eight hundred Irish-American branches, adjured the Convention to unfurl the banner of No-Rent'.[68] Coming from the jailed leaders, it was intended, not as a repudiation of rent, but as a tactic to withhold it until constitutional rights of free speech and association were restored.[69] O'Brien later remembered that 'even a man so little inclined to headstrong passion as Mr. J. E. Redmond declared in Wexford: "Yesterday we were willing to test the Act, today it is our duty to trample upon it. Until Parnell is released, I say it is the duty of the people to strike against all rent!"'[70] Two days later, the Land League was proclaimed as an unlawful organization.[71]

In an open letter to the tenants of County Wexford on 25 October, Redmond responded to these developments. Perhaps mindful of the fact that Dillon had been arrested on a charge of incitement to the non-payment of rent, he made no mention of the manifesto. He told them the land movement did not depend on any one man, but on the loyalty of the people to one another. They must for the time being avoid formal meetings, because 'for force we are not prepared', but there was nothing to stop informal consultation and individual action. It was not illegal to refuse an evicted farm, or to refuse contact with one who had taken such a farm. They should remember the 'unlimited support' of their brethren in America: £40,000 had been guaranteed already to sustain evicted families.[72]

III

Within a short time it was evident that the No Rent Manifesto was a failure. The clergy and almost all the nationalist press condemned it. Most tenants paid their rents while many flocked to the land courts to seek fairer ones. All this, it has been suggested, was no more than Parnell expected: he looked to this failure to strengthen his hand in the moderate course he knew would have to be taken later.[73] Redmond, on the other hand, seems to have invested his hopes in the manifesto (ironically, in view of the fact that Dillon was unenthusiastic), and was correspondingly disappointed at the attitude of Father Furlong and of the tenants. He wrote that if the strike against rent were supported, it would be 'the proper way and indeed the only possible way of hitting our enemies'. The fact that it was not getting general support, he wrote to Furlong,

> makes me feel very despondent. I fear the people are not equal to the sacrifice demanded from them. They are doubtful, they fear the risk, they see the Land Act working favourably and they take grave note of the words of Dr. Croke, and of the silence of men like Father Tom [Doyle], yourself and others . . . I confess I feel greatly disheartened.[74]

In November, a by-election in County Derry presented a chance to exact electoral revenge on the Liberal Government. The Liberal candidate was A. M. Porter, the solicitor-general. Redmond and Leamy were sent north to campaign for C. J. Dempsey, the Home Rule candidate. During the three-week campaign, Redmond shed his previous moderation of tone and borrowed from Dillon's rhetoric. Frank Hugh O'Donnell, who was also asked by Parnell to go to Derry, remembered: 'I heard young Redmond and Leamy make some of their very best speeches in this hillside campaign.'[75] At Limavady on 14 November, Redmond commented that Gladstone had come before the people 'as an inspired prophet . . . almost as a sort of demi-god', but when he found a spirit of independence abroad, 'so soon was the veil torn from the political Mokanna', revealing the features, 'distorted with passion', of a tyrant.[76] At Derry City he told his hearers that the Government was trying to steal their votes on the pretence that they had got the Land Act for them, but Gladstone's conduct would 'remain an indelible blot on his reputation as a wise statesman, and, more than that, upon his character as a humane man'.[77] At Maghera he called on those present to 'raise their hands to show they had no gratitude for the Land Act and only revenge for the Coercion Minister and his hirelings'.[78]

On 5 December, Dempsey withdrew from the contest 'in answer to the voice of Kilmainham', and called on his supporters to vote for the Tory candidate.[79] Many, though not quite enough, nationalist voters responded to this early harbinger of the 'Vote Tory Manifesto' of four years later; Porter was returned. Redmond pronounced himself nevertheless happy that the thousand nationalist voters in Derry had obeyed their duty, swallowed old animosities and voted for the Tory.[80] According to O'Donnell, 'the Catholics voted splendidly alongside of their hereditary enemies the Orangemen, in order to beat the coercionist'. He had a pleasant time at the Limavady polling booth, where he shared agency duty with the master of the local Orange Lodge, 'a splendid Irishman, who said that Ulstermen would never be against home rule if we kept the priests out of it'.[81]

Later in the month, Redmond and Leamy visited Parnell in Kilmainham and must have reported to him on the Derry campaign.[82] No doubt Redmond also was able to give a first-hand account of extraordinary events near Parnell's home in Wicklow during the previous week. Lands owned by the leader had been ploughed and manured by supporters who came from all the surrounding counties. Special trains had been laid on from Dublin, while 600 carts and 183 ploughs, decorated with green ribbons and laurels, were employed. Redmond was there with the local M.P.s. He told the crowd: 'It had another and greater significance besides that of an expression of the affection and constancy of a people towards an individual man. It was a demonstration in favour of the principles for which this man and his friends are suffering.'[83]

Throughout the winter of 1881–82 there was mounting disorder in Ireland, with daily accounts of outrages and horrifying murders perpetrated by the agrarian secret societies. The *Freeman* reacted to two such murders in February with the cry that 'no honest Irishman' of whatever party or creed could read of such events without 'a sensation of shame and horror and indignation' and prayed 'that such dark deeds will not draw upon our country the vengeance of Heaven'.[84] Dismayed by these reports, Redmond directed his anger publicly at the Government for removing the only people capable of curbing the violence, the natural leaders of the people now among the 350 'suspects' in prison.[85] His contention seemed justified by information given by Forster to Gladstone in a letter of 7 April that the figures for serious crime in the last quarter of 1881 and in the first quarter of 1882 were each worse than for the combined first three-quarters of 1881 (Forster, of course, did not attribute this to the arrest of the leaders, as did Redmond).[86]

The febrile quasi-revolutionary atmosphere, combined with the absence of Parnell's cool judgement, seemed to throw Redmond off balance in these months. The level-headedness he had displayed the previous year was replaced by an increasing extremism of language and at times self-contradiction. In his contribution to the debate on the Address in February 1882, his tone was uncompromising. His dark mood cannot have been improved by the news that his brother William, not yet twenty-one, had been arrested on 6 February for Land League activities.[87] He told the House:

> He [JER] never took part in the deliberations of the House without feeling how useless, how humiliating it was for Irishmen who had national aspirations to come to the House and to take part in its proceedings at all . . . day by day the English Government were lessening the confidence the Irish people had in Parliamentary government . . . day by day they were destroying the belief in constitutional agitation which, up to the present, the Irish party had endeavoured to keep alive . . . if, instead of giving them conciliation, England gave them hate, they would be prepared to pay back that hate with hatred.

Forster's name, he predicted, would in future be cursed with those of Cromwell and Castlereagh.[88]

The next day, he interrupted Forster's speech on the Address, and afterwards moved to adjourn in order to give the Irish members a chance to see the chief secretary's speech in print. He dealt with the Land Act, the 'maliciously untrue' charges made against those in prison, and the No Rent Manifesto. Parnell had

> never concealed his belief that the bulk of the tenants would never benefit by [the Act], and all the experience they had had since then went to confirm that opinion . . . the Government's so-called 'message of peace' was proving a message of ruin and destruction to thousands of tenants . . . [the land court] was paralysed already . . .[89]

The chief secretary had tried, he said, to justify the arrests and the suppression of the league on the grounds of intimidation. His reply was that pressure, in the form of boycotting, on tenants who took evicted farms was not intimidation but 'exclusive dealing', which Forster admitted was legal. Charges of 'treasonable behaviour' had been made against people on the basis of one or two sentences in speeches, as in the case of his colleague Sexton. As for the No Rent Manifesto, its meaning had been deliberately misrepresented: 'It never was a demand that the people should pay no rent whatever. It was simply a cry to withhold rent till the landlord party and the Government came back to the path of constitutional action.'[90] He said that Parnell and the party had always resisted this tactic, urged on them by many in America and in Ireland, until driven to it by the Government's actions. In a revealing passage, he brought the implications of 'no rent' home to himself:

> it could not be denied that it pressed hardly upon individuals. No one deplored that hardship more than he did. His connections and friends belonged wholly to the landlord class, and it was no personal interest, as had often been asserted against him, but love of his country alone which led him to take the course he did.[91]

Later that month, he again attacked Forster directly, landing a blow on the chief secretary by showing up inconsistencies with his previous attitude to the leaders of the Land League.[92] An accusation of dishonesty had to be withdrawn; he had meant the term in the sense of 'violation of pledges given to the House'. Over the following weeks, working in tandem with Healy, Sexton and others, he concentrated his fire on the conduct of the police and the treatment of the coercion prisoners. A long stream of parliamentary questions culminated in a resolution on 13 March.[93] Two days later the *Freeman* commented:

> The debate on the treatment of the suspects raised by Mr. Redmond on Monday night is already bearing good fruit, and there is reason to believe the Chief Secretary will be compelled by pressure from his own side of the House to mitigate very greatly the conditions to which they are subjected.[94]

On 17 March Forster conceded some changes in the conditions, allowing two extra hours for exercise and lifting the embargo on chess. The next day thirty-seven M.P.s from both sides of the House petitioned the prime minister for mitigation of the hardships, maintaining that 18 hours of solitary confinement in 24 was 'cruel and unnecessary' and 'doing more harm than good' to peace in Ireland.[95]

The same issue of the *Freeman* that had praised Redmond's resolution of 13 March also chided him and others for a different action – their criticism of colleagues. This referred to a party meeting at which the centrifugal tendencies encouraged by Parnell's departure were evident: it had passed a resolution calling the attention of constituents to 'the habitual absence of several of their representatives in the present Session of Parliament'. This and a similar resolution singling out a particular M.P. for reproof were, according to the paper,

> instances of that over-zeal natural to young men, but which sometimes defeats its objects . . . for a meeting of ten members to pass in effect a vote of censure on their colleagues, and threaten to hold them up to the anger and condemnation of their constituents and the country, is a very wrong step . . . The guiding hand of Mr. Parnell has, in fact, been frequently missed since the opening of the Session.[96]

Sexton, one of those at the meeting, wrote a long letter to the paper defending the action. Redmond was unapologetic in a speech to a London Irish audience on 19 March. Forty-six members were pledged to follow Parnell, but, he asked,

> Where were they today? Was it because Mr. Parnell was in prison that, like cowards, they should take advantage of his absence and remain away themselves? They were told that they were young and should moderate their zeal, but on behalf of the young men, he would say that they had no desire to shove themselves to the front or pose as the Irish party; what were they to do, however, when deserted by the senior members?[97]

The issue very soon became critical with the imminent vote on the Government's Cloture (closure) legislation, aimed at putting a final end to obstruction. A meeting of sixteen M.P.s on 27 March resolved that the party should vote against the Government and requested all Irish members to attend and so vote on the following Thursday. It declared the occasion to be 'of supreme importance' to the House of Commons and to Irish interests; any member failing to turn up would be 'guilty of an unpardonable breach of the trust reposed in him'. The object was as much to inflict a defeat on the Government as to avert the closure measures in themselves, and this was too much for some of the semi-Whigs still in the party.[98] On 31 March, the *Freeman* announced that freedom of speech had been 'strangled' at two o'clock that morning. Four Home Rulers were missing from the division, but worst of all was the 'melancholy' fact that some Irish members had voted for the Government, whose slim majority of thirty-nine could have been overturned by a united Irish vote.[99]

The ranks of an angry active section were swollen to twenty-four when the party met next and resolved to call on constituents to 'record their opinion' of the conduct of those M.P.s who had been absent, abstained or voted with the Government.[100] At the London branch of the Land League the following Sunday, 2 April, Redmond said that the cloture division 'had set an indelible mark upon the Irish representatives who deserted the interests of their country, and nothing could ever rehabilitate them into popular favour'.[101] Most of the offending members, in fact, would be banished from Home Rule politics at the general election of 1885. One such was the Buttite Mitchell Henry, M.P. for Galway, who told his constituents in a letter to the *Freeman* that he had always opposed obstruction and favoured conciliation.[102]

That spring, the anarchy in the countryside and the No Rent campaign continued to form the major themes of Redmond's speeches. At the London meeting he reflected the growing concern in the party that the worsening disorder was due to the removal of all restraining influences. He also seemed to have changed his mind about the success of the rent strike, asserting, against the general evidence, that rents were not being paid: three-quarters of the districts he knew were standing by 'what has been erroneously called the No Rent Manifesto'.[103] On tour with Biggar in Edinburgh, he placed the moral responsibility for 'every drop of innocent blood shed' on the heads of Gladstone and Forster: 'He held that the cry that was ringing through the land was pharisaical and hypocritical, and his answer was simply "If you lay blood at my door, show me your hands. Are they clean?" (*cheers*).'[104] As if aspiring to fill the shoes of the absent Dillon, still in Kilmainham, he denounced the Land Act as 'a sham and a falsehood' and flirted with the rhetoric of violence: 'If the Government . . . tried the means which they used in '98 against them, then the duty would remain to the Irish people to meet those means as best they could.'[105]

The day after this speech, Parnell was released on parole and began the negotiations that would lead to his release and the 'Kilmainham treaty'. Redmond, like most others, was unaware of this as he lapsed further into oratorical hyperbole. At Bradford on 11 April, he lashed out at a verbal effigy of the chief secretary:

> the greatest outrage in Ireland today was Forster (*cheers, hisses, cries of "Buckshot", "Brigand"*) . . . Ireland lay prostrate in the dust . . . a gag upon her mouth and manacles in her hands, towered over by a brutal form with the key of a dungeon in one hand and a blood-stained bayonet in the other, a scowl of hate in his eye, the fear of the coward and the bully in his heart . . . a Cromwell in ferocity, but, withal, a Forster in imbecility and weakness (*cheers*) . . . Today, amidst the clash of bayonet and sabre, she heard the sound that was wafted across to her over the fair Atlantic. It was the sound of the united voice of ten millions of Irishmen, who sent a message to Ireland of allegiance to her in the defence of her freedom (*cheers*).[106]

Back in the House on 20 April, Redmond returned to his campaign of questioning the chief secretary and the home secretary on behalf of the victims of coercion.[107] He again called Forster 'dishonest' and this time was named and suspended from the House for the sitting.[108]

IV

By late April, Healy and Sexton, the effective leaders in Parnell's absence, gave indications of being anxious to return to a more moderate policy. At the same time, Parnell was coming to an understanding with Gladstone and Joseph Chamberlain. Two channels of communication – one via Captain William O'Shea, a Home Rule M.P. and the husband of Parnell's secret lover, the other via Justin McCarthy M.P. – allowed negotiations to proceed. The terms agreed were that, in return for the release of the suspects and an undertaking by the Government to amend the Land Act with regard to tenants in arrears, the Home Rule party would do its utmost to pacify the country, agree that the amended Act was 'a practical settlement of the land question' and co-operate with the Liberal Party in its programme of general reform.[109] The party had decided to bring in its own Bill to specify the amendments required. This was drawn up, at the request of Parnell, by Maurice Healy, the brother of Tim, and Redmond was chosen by ballot to present it in Parliament.[110]

On 26 April, Redmond introduced this Bill, eliciting from Gladstone the response that 'that gentleman had said everything he could towards a fair prospect for the working of the system of land laws in Ireland'.[111] Gladstone pledged that the question of arrears would be dealt with promptly. The air was now thick with rumours of an impending change in the Government's Irish policy.[112] On Tuesday 2 May, Parnell, Dillon and J. J. O'Kelly were released from Kilmainham and Gladstone announced the resignations of Chief Secretary Forster and Lord Lieutenant Cowper.[113] Parnell was back in the House two days later, observed by Healy 'striding to his place as if nothing had happened'.[114] On Saturday 6 May, the *Freeman* reported that 'the wild joy of the people . . . manifested everywhere throughout Ireland was nowhere more conspicuous than in Dublin last night'.[115]

That evening, all the expectations raised on both sides of the Irish Sea by the new course were thrown into disarray by the assassination in the Phoenix Park of the new chief secretary, Lord Frederick Cavendish, just arrived in Dublin, and the under-secretary, T. H. Burke, by members of the Invincibles secret society, armed with surgical knives. The shocked reaction of almost all nationalists was expressed in the black-edged columns in which the *Freeman* announced the news on Monday, calling it 'a crime which will fill the world with horror and dismay'.[116] Dublin went into mourning that week, black crepe covering the shuttered shops. The only defiant note came from the Fenian Jeremiah O'Donovan Rossa, who in his New York newspaper refused to join 'the cowardly crowd of politicians and . . . milk-and-water Land Leaguers . . . they [the assassins] shall not have one word of condemnation from us'.[117] This was disowned by another Fenian veteran, John O'Leary, who told the *New York Herald* on 15 May that 'the time when O'Donovan Rossa had any claim to represent any appreciable section of the Fenians is long passed' and recorded his 'utmost horror and loathing' at the murders.[118]

The day after the murders, Redmond was in Manchester to address a meeting in the Free Trade Hall. According to his own subsequent account, he had heard a rumour that Cavendish and Lord Spencer, the incoming viceroy, had been murdered; there was no mention of Burke. Redmond, having asked for enquiries to be made at the detective office but getting no further details, moved a motion denouncing the murder of Cavendish. On behalf of the Irish of Manchester, he expressed 'their consternation and their horror at the news . . . of the assassination of a man who is utterly guiltless so far as Ireland is concerned (*cheers*)'.[119]

Having undoubtedly read the papers of the previous two days, he must have realized immediately the implications for the Kilmainham agreement:

> I am here to say that the men who have shed this innocent blood are enemies of us (*great cheering*) – are enemies of our country and our country's cause . . . A few – maddened, perhaps, but none the less criminal – men have been able to cast upon the name of Ireland . . . the disgrace which will attach to a dastardly and cowardly crime'.[120]

Yet he was not above extracting political capital from the atrocity: the primary responsibility for every drop of innocent blood spilt was to be laid at the door of a system of government alien to the wishes of the people, and until it was brought into harmony with those wishes such acts would continue to disgrace the country.[121] This made his condemnation somewhat less unequivocal than that issued by Parnell, Davitt and Dillon later that day in their manifesto to the Irish people.[122] In Redmond's defence, however, it can be argued that they had more time to reflect and consult on an appropriate response.

The Times of 8 May reported his speech, but added the accusation that he had withheld any mention of Burke's murder. It commented: 'Not more than four days have elapsed since the policy of conciliation was thus set in motion and already we have its hollowness exposed by the tragedy in the Phoenix Park.'[123] Redmond's reply to *The Times* in the House the next day was not published. On 18 May he repeated his explanation there and complained of the refusal of *The Times* to print his reply. The paper, obviously in no mood to have its suspicions regarding the Kilmainham deal assuaged, reported this speech but omitted the part dealing with the affair.[124]

There is, however, a difficulty with Redmond's explanation of his omission. It is credible that he had not heard the news if he had not seen that morning's (Sunday) papers, but it is strange that he should have sent out for information to a police office rather than simply ask for a newspaper to check the rumour, and that none of those arriving at the meeting showed him one. Parnell had read of both murders in the *Observer* early that morning at a small Surrey railway station near Katharine O'Shea's home.[125] O'Brien had read of them on a Paris boulevard the same day.[126]

The Phoenix Park outrage meant that, as in the previous year, a measure of redress (this time the Arrears Bill) would be accompanied by a dose of coercion. The Prevention of Crime (Ireland) Bill was introduced by Harcourt on 11 May, providing for the suspension of trial by jury, authority for the lord lieutenant to suppress public meetings and newspapers, and other punitive measures. The Irish Party had no option but to offer an impassioned resistance to such a measure.[127] The second reading passed quickly, Redmond being among a small group of Irish members taking an effective part in the debate. He would be more than ready to vote for any measure that would put a stop to outrage and crime, he said, but the only effect of this Bill would be 'to increase the exasperating cause of crime in Ireland'. He attacked what he saw as the inconsistency of an approach that simultaneously targeted the secret societies *and* open constitutional agitation:

> the Irish members were either the representatives of the Irish people, and their opinions were worth considering, or they were arrant rebels, who ought to be hanged or sent to penal servitude. But the Government, while adopting their proposals with respect to arrears, called them traitors in the same breath, and introduced a Bill whereby it would be possible for the judges to send them to penal servitude.[128]

In language that may have been intended for the ears of Harcourt, who was known to think that Irish demands would only be satisfied with total separation of Ireland from Britain, his meaning was clear:

> For his own part, while he was desirous of seeing the English connection, so far as the Crown was concerned, maintained in Ireland, he rejoiced in his heart at every fresh evidence, like what they had in this Bill, of the utter incapacity of this Parliament to rule over Ireland. It proved to the world that the English government of Ireland rested upon nothing but brute force.[129]

On 24 May Dillon made a militant defence of boycotting, which Gladstone called 'heartbreaking' to all who desired harmony between the two countries. The next evening Parnell neutralized its effect by making 'one of the most brilliant of his "balancing" speeches', which deeply impressed the House, including even Harcourt.[130] Redmond also replied to Dillon that evening, adopting Parnell's tactic of disowning Dillon by claiming that he had been misrepresented. He then attempted to distinguish between boycotting 'in itself', as practised under the control of the Land League, and boycotting in the absence of such control, which led to 'outrage, crime and intimidation'. These comments evoked an emphatic 'No!' from Gladstone.[131]

Parnell attempted through private channels to persuade the Government to moderate the terms of the Coercion Bill, but to no avail in the teeth of Harcourt's opposition. The party was thus thrown back on the old weapon of obstruction, which, however, could no longer be wielded in the old crude way. A group of about twenty members, led by Biggar and Sexton, managed to prolong the Bill's passage through Committee from 1 June to 4 July, using a process of detailed scrutiny, which avoided the censure of the Speaker. Redmond played an active part in this process, moving and speaking often on amendments to the various clauses.[132] The climax came at the end of a twenty-eight hour sitting, when the interventions of Redmond and Justin McCarthy finally snapped the patience of the chairman, who suspended seventeen members, including Parnell and Dillon, for the rest of the sitting.[133] The *Freeman*, praising 'the patient endurance and dauntless pluck' of the party, proclaimed 'the indignity is the Government's. The honour remains with the expelled.'[134] This incident marked the end of obstruction; the activists took no further part in the debate, and the Bill became law on 12 July.

In the meantime, the Arrears Bill had been introduced, and now proceeded rapidly through Committee. Gladstone fought off attempts by Tory and some Liberal members to 'emasculate' it.[135] Redmond, perhaps exhausted by his efforts in the coercion proceedings, took no part in this new debate. He was, however, one of only six members present at a midnight meeting on 31 July that called on all Irish members to be in their place the following Thursday in order to strengthen the prime minister's hand in resisting House of Lords amendments.[136] The Irish landlords in that House realized that the Bill offered them their only chance of recovering at least some of their arrears, and this ensured the defeat of the more destructive amendments from their colleagues. The Bill received the royal assent on 18 August. It was an immediate success. Out of 135,997 claims submitted under it (by which if the tenant paid one year's arrears and satisfied the Land Commissioners that he could pay no more, the state would pay half the outstanding sum to the landlord and cancel the rest), 129,952 were allowed.[137]

With Parliament about to go into recess, Redmond, Healy and Sexton were among only ten Irish members still present on 5 August in a depleted House to vote against a Government Bill to increase the pay of officers of the RIC.[138]

Many of the Irish Party were in Dublin for the celebrations of 15 August, which in 1882 embraced not only the Catholic religious feast of the Assumption but the centenary commemoration of the inauguration of Grattan's (Protestant) Parliament, the Industrial Exhibition in the Rotunda and the unveiling of the O'Connell monument in the capital. Redmond was one of twenty M.P.s who marched in procession (behind massed ranks of Catholic clergy) from the Mansion House to join the huge crowds at O'Connell Bridge. Parnell, always ill at ease at such public occasions, made a very short speech. At a banquet given by the lord mayor that evening, McCarthy, Dillon, Redmond and Healy spoke in reply to a toast to the M.P.s of the Irish Party. Redmond told the guests that the party was 'destined before it left the House of Commons to work out the emancipation of Ireland'. He then returned to the issue of party discipline that had exercised him earlier in the year: the Irish people had a duty to make sure that M.P.s represented their views; his blood boiled when Englishmen taunted the activists with being only 'a fraction' of the Irish representation. The following day the Freedom of the city was conferred on Parnell and Dillon. Later that week Redmond was one of those elected to the Mansion House Committee to administer a national fund for the relief of evicted tenants.[139]

The events in the Phoenix Park and the renewal of coercion did not ultimately derail the Kilmainham settlement. The Land League was not reinstituted, and the party settled down to a campaign of purely constitutional activity, an effective abandonment of the New Departure that was bound to displease the left wing of the movement. Parnell could do nothing about the opposition of the secret societies or the old-style Fenians, but he did succeed in bringing the remnants of the league organization under his control. During the summer of 1882, he secured repossession of the league funds in Paris and began the winding down of the Ladies' Land League, which had been spending money freely on the care of evicted tenants and was a natural centre of militancy. These actions alienated Dillon and Davitt, who, however, did not openly oppose Parnell. In late September, Dillon announced his retirement from political life 'for the next few years', ostensibly for reasons of health, but undoubtedly also because he could not stomach the new policy. Davitt immersed himself in preaching his new gospel of land nationalization, a campaign that was a fortunate opportunity for Parnell, allowing him to appear in the role of defender of original Land League principles.[140] Two other strokes of luck helped to insulate him from criticism, particularly from America: an attack on him by Forster linking him with the Phoenix Park murders; and, in 1883, the 'Roman Letter' from the Vatican warning the Irish clergy against associating themselves with the Irish National League, which was seen as the result of English intrigue at Rome. His response to these events helped to neutralize all significant opposition from within the movement.[141]

The chief political events in the remainder of the year were, in Ireland, the foundation of the Irish National League to replace the Land League, and, in the House, the fight against the new cloture regulations, now being pushed through in their definitive form. The former was planned at a conference in September at Avondale, Parnell's Wicklow home, in which Healy, Sexton, Dillon and Arthur O'Connor joined the Land League veterans Davitt and Thomas Brennan. Its five major objectives were national self-government, further land law reform, local government reform, extension of the franchise and encouragement of the labour and industrial interests of the country. The national conference to institute the new league met on 17 October, and Redmond supported T. P. O'Connor in speaking against a Davitt amendment aimed at preventing the party from having a dominant voice on the executive. Later, with Leamy, he was among those elected on to the league's organizing committee by the Mansion House Committee.[142]

V

October 1882 has been called the Thermidor of the land war. Parnell told Davitt and O'Brien that he saw no option but to 'duck' for a few years to allow coercion to run its course.[143] It would be part of the new policy to campaign for an amendment of the 'Healy clause' in the Land Act, which was supposed to prevent tenants' improvements from attracting rent increases but which had been neutralized by a series of court decisions. Verbal militancy was still a potent weapon, serving both to maintain a sense of urgency with the Government and to disguise from the agrarian radicals the Parnellites' embrace of purely constitutional methods. Redmond, speaking at a by-election meeting in Ennis on 12 November, was still urging boycotting (in so many words) and telling tenants not to go into the Land Court 'until we obtain the amendment'. A few days later he condemned the Land Act as 'a mockery and a delusion'.[144]

There is no basis for Healy's assertion in his memoirs that 'the opening years of John's career were not enterprising. He was of a retiring disposition, and the House for long knew little of his powers.'[145] On the contrary, Redmond's performance during these first two years of his parliamentary career marked him out as a promising contender for the front rank of the party. That he did not join the front rank was due partly to his youth, partly to the surfeit of talent already there when he took his seat. The party had, in Sexton and Healy, two superb parliamentarians of complementary abilities and tireless energy who were a match for any of the British leaders. O'Brien wrote later:

> Mr. Sexton's breadth of view, his dignity of language and grasp of great principles and, in a special manner, of financial intricacies, completed in a debate the effect of his nimble colleague's airier and more pungent sallies.[146]

These two were reinforced by T. P. O'Connor and Arthur O'Connor, the latter renowned for his grasp of parliamentary procedure.

A rare personal glimpse of Redmond at this time is presented in the reminiscences of Katherine Tynan, then a young poet active in the Ladies' Land League. She remembered him as a frequent visitor to their office, often in company with Edmund Leamy:

> I should not like to say that these visits did not make a purple patch for some of us . . . He was a very attractive young man in those days, and he had the gift of pleasant manners and a charming voice. He was very young, with still much of the charm of the boy about him . . .[147]

In later memoirs, she recalled Redmond with Leamy and James Carew, 'the bucks of the young Irish parliamentary party' strolling about the 1882 Industrial Exhibition 'very much fluttering the hearts of some of the girls'. Redmond was then 'a young man in love, very much in love and unashamed as young men used to be at that time'. As a procession one day went past the League offices in Upper Sackville Street, outside which scaffolding with seats had been erected, she saw him

> sitting by a fair-haired girl whispering in her ear, with an absorption in her which took no account of anyone or anything else . . . He was bonny then, not heavy with responsibilities as I remember him later . . . [His oratory was] rather of the debating society kind than pure unmeditated oratory, sped by passion into passionate words, such as was the gift of his colleague and friend, Edmund Leamy.[148]

It was in the late summer of 1882 that Redmond began his lifelong association with Aughavanagh, the former barracks in the heart of the south Wicklow mountains which Parnell used as a shooting lodge. He later recalled to Barry O'Brien how, while walking up a mountain one day, he and Parnell met an old tenant of the latter, whom Parnell took to task for not keeping the mountain clear of sheep while he was shooting.[149] The same hills would become part of the fabric of his life, providing rest and relief from the crowded corridors of political life.

Whatever Redmond's relationship with the unknown 'fair-haired girl', it was about to be cut short. It must have been at least partly with a view to finding an alternative outlet for his energies that Parnell conceived the idea of asking him to undertake a fundraising mission to Australia, New Zealand and the United States.[150] The need to ensure continuity in the supply of funds from the Irish overseas had become acute at a time when the American organization was split by factionalism. The Australian Irish constituted a fresh, relatively untapped source of financial support and, with an attitude to Irish affairs markedly less extreme than that of most of Irish–America, an insurance in the event of the collapse of support from America for the new policy. John would be accompanied on the tour by William, who had another reason for going. Following his release from prison in May, he had spent the summer in the States with Davitt, but since his return home, had placed himself in danger of renewed arrest. On 27 November, Col. Tottenham asked the chief secretary in the House if his attention had been drawn to remarks of William Redmond reported in a Cork paper that 'he, as a Nationalist, yearned to see Ireland a free nation, untrammelled by any shadow of British law, but . . . it could only be accomplished by the swords and united arms of the Irish people . . . it was the duty of every man . . . to prepare for that revolution.'[151] William wisely left for the south of France shortly after this speech, and was strongly advised by Parnell not to come home when the warrant for his arrest was issued. The warrant charged him with counselling boycotting, but the Government was known to be considering a treason prosecution, which would have meant a sentence with hard labour.[152]

In the first week of December 1882, John Redmond sailed for Australia, carrying with him letters of introduction from the veteran Young Irelander, sometime member for New Ross, later minister of the province of Victoria, Sir Charles Gavan Duffy.[153] He would be absent from Ireland for fifteen months.

4 The Mission

It began with a rant; it has gone on to a riot; it may end in rebellion, and in the vigour necessary to restrain rebellion.
Victorian Banner, Australia, 24 March 1883[1]

. . . all that they contended for was a federal arrangement whereby the will of Ireland should be supreme in Irish affairs, but whereby also Ireland would remain a portion of the general Empire and a much more integral part than she was at present.
Redmond at Bathurst, New South Wales, March 1883[2]

I

Accounts of the ten months spent in Australia and New Zealand by John and William Redmond are scarce. Neither seems to have kept a journal of the visit. Surviving correspondence is limited to a progress report sent by Redmond to the treasurer of the new National League in Dublin, Alfred Webb, and a congratulatory letter from Parnell. Redmond's busy correspondence of 1881 with Father Furlong appears to have been in abeyance, possibly due to the estrangement over the No Rent Manifesto. William published a book about a much later visit to Australia, but made no references to the mission of 1883, except to say that its success was helped by Irish priests, and that he found Australian women 'both decorative and useful'. We are thus left with Redmond's own summary account given in public speeches in the weeks after his return home in the spring of 1884. For a detailed narrative we must turn to the principal Australian newspaper that made a reasonable effort to keep up with events in Ireland, and was in sympathy, moderately, with the Parnellite movement, the weekly *Freeman's Journal* of Sydney.[3]

Australia was, in the early 1880s, a federation of self-governing colonies under the British crown, with a white population of some three million people. About one-third were of Catholic Irish descent or birth, the rest of mainly English and Scottish origin.

The Redmond brothers arrived into the heat of the Australian summer at Adelaide on Monday 5 February 1883. John had broken his journey at Naples to allow William to join him. Responding to an extravagant address of welcome from the secretary of the city's branch of the National League, which referred to him as 'the representative of those who have uprooted the deadly upas-tree of landlordism that so long paralysed the arm of industry', Redmond declared it 'an inspiriting sign of the indestructibility of Irish nationality to find that here, divided from Ireland by the breadth of the entire universe, one should find himself surrounded by Irish hearts, yearning as deeply as any for the emancipation of their motherland'.[4]

According to Redmond's later account of the visit, they were confronted on arrival with 'false cablegrams' claiming that the Land League was implicated by irrefutable evidence in the Phoenix Park murders. This produced 'a state of public opinion which made it extremely difficult to commence work'. Almost all of the colony's press had taken up the suggestion that the Redmonds had come to collect money for future assassinations. The result was a blanket refusal to allow them the use of public halls for their meetings. In addition, many leaders of the Irish community had 'given way before the storm of odium raised' and either passively or actively opposed their mission, although a minority of that class had 'stood by them manfully'.[5]

At his first major meeting in Adelaide on 9 February, with a large attendance of Catholic clergy, M.P.s and other influential citizens, Redmond devoted a large part of his address to a history of the recent land agitation and, in particular, the events of the previous winter in Ireland. Gladstone's Land Act had been regarded by the league as a step in the right direction, and 'hence the League did not reject it, though it was false in its principle, if accepted as a finality'. The league had acted constitutionally in testing the Act, and the test had proved it unsatisfactory. Turning to the No Rent Manifesto, he said it 'was never the manifesto of the Land League, and the cry of "no rent" was a malicious imputation of its enemies'. He then spoke of the 'winter of unutterable horror' that had passed over Ireland, when

> true Irishmen and the enemies of Ireland stood aghast at the daily record of outrage and crime . . . [but] the truth was, that from the commencement the Land League set its face against violence and outrage of every kind up to the moment of the suppression of the League in 1881. Never was there so large a movement which accomplished so great a work in any nation upon earth with less cost of human blood and human suffering. When the League was suppressed, however, and when its leaders were imprisoned, then its responsibility for peace in Ireland ceased, because its restraining influence, felt in every hamlet in the land, was destroyed with the imprisonment of its leading representatives . . . with the final imprisonment of Michael Davitt [the Government] found themselves face to face with a maddened and despairing people.[6]

This account of recent events was, by itself, likely to draw the fire of the local establishment. But it was Redmond's use of language in expressing the Irish national demand embodied in the programme of the new National League that rang alarm bells in the loyal press: 'They did not base their claim upon their grievances alone but on their imperishable right. England could never, in the nature of things, make Ireland part of herself. Ireland must have a separate existence.'[7]

The use of a phrase such as 'separate existence' may have seemed to Redmond perfectly compatible with the concept of autonomy within the Empire, but to Australian ears, unused to such subtleties, it must have sounded very like the separatism they had been warned against. In the city where Redmond was due to speak next, the *Sydney Morning Herald* told its readers that if the Adelaide speech had been reported correctly, 'we fail to find anything in it which commends itself to our moral sense or practical judgment, and after considering the scheme, it appears to us that no loyal Australian can support it'.[8]

The local *Freeman* stepped in to defend Redmond against what it called 'grossly misleading and fallacious statements' by the *Herald* and its sister paper the *Echo* to the effect that his programme entailed total severance from England. On the contrary, every Irishman knew that Home Rule was merely 'a modification, in the federal direction, of the movement carried on by O'Connell, whose loyalty no man questions'. Redmond was not of the 'advanced' party – he was an M.P. and had sworn strict allegiance to the queen. Unless he was a perjurer and a traitor, 'it cannot truly assert that the self-government which they ask for is coincident with the sovereign independence of Ireland'. Criticizing the *Herald* for 'condemning a man unheard', it said that Redmond should be listened to when he denied that it was ever the intention of the signatories that the No Rent Manifesto should be interpreted as an incitement to the tenants to pay no rent at all. They had got it wrong when they said that the manifesto had rendered the Land League unlawful, as it had been effectively outlawed for months previously.[9]

A few days after the meeting, a counter-lecture was delivered by one Edward Riley, 'lately from England', who tried to refute Redmond's arguments. The meeting, which *Freeman* described as 'of the most partisan character, the Orange feeling predominating', carried unanimously a resolution expressing 'want of confidence' in the league and 'refusing countenance to its objects till the League clearly defined the purposes to which the subscriptions were to be put'.[10] The controversy had now aroused much interest, and the newspapers were deluged with letters on the subject.

On 19 February, the Redmonds arrived in Sydney in company with J. W. Walshe, the chief National League organizer in Australia. The news of the confession of James Carey, the member of the Invincibles who testified against his accomplices in the Phoenix Park murders, had just reached the southern hemisphere. Unfortunately, Carey's claimed membership of the Land League lent credibility to efforts to identify the league with the murders. Following the appearance of articles in this vein in the *Herald*, the *Echo* and the *Evening News*, the Freemasons and the lessees of the Gaiety Theatre revoked the contracts allowing the use of their venues by the Irish envoys. The *Freeman* deplored the making of

Figure 7. 'Parnell Party Portraits' (*Weekly Irish Times*, 17 March 1883).
Courtesy of the National Library of Ireland.
The most prominent of Parnell's followers in the Irish Parliamentary Party.

such charges, combined as it was with a refusal to hear the Redmond case. It reminded readers that the Land League had the support of a majority of the hierarchy and clergy at home and abroad; none would dare to maintain that they were therefore complicit in assassination. It pleaded: 'Then why not hear him? . . . Is this the British fair play which we hear so much of on Sydney platforms and in the Press?'[11] Years later,

Redmond told Barry O'Brien that when he arrived in Sydney the Phoenix Park murders were the talk of the colony:

> I received a chilling reception. All the respectable people who had promised support kept away. The priests would not help me, except the Jesuits, who were friendly to me as an old Clongowes boy. The man – a leading citizen – who had promised to take the chair at my first meeting would not come. Sir Harry Parkes, the Prime Minister, proposed that I should be expelled [from] the colony, but the motion was defeated. The Irish working men stood by me, and in fact saved the situation. They kept me going until telegrams arrived exculpating the Parliamentary party. Then all the Irish gradually came around and ultimately flocked to my meetings.[12]

Redmond managed at the last minute to obtain the use of the Academy of Music, 'a room of moderate size behind a small, dingy shop of three narrow windowpanes', where the meeting went ahead on 22 February.[13] The audience of largely plebeian Irish heard him repeat his impassioned account of the previous two years, when 'the Government tore the mask of constitutionalism from its face and an absolute reign of terror commenced', and give an uncompromising defence of the actions of the league and the Irish Party. However, he gave his remarks a 'loyal' tinge, which showed that lessons had been learned from the Adelaide experience:

> If the interpretation which has been placed by a certain section of the colonial press upon the object of my visit to Australia were a correct one, and if I really held the principles the press has attributed to me, I would require a considerable amount of audacity to stand upon the platform this evening (*hear, hear*). The cordiality and warmth of your reception shows me that you are not in favour of the practice of condemning a man unheard (*great applause*).

The means employed in his cause were consistent, he maintained, not only with morality and honour, but with loyalty to the sovereign and to the constitution of the Empire. He justified the policy of testing the Land Act as a sensible means of avoiding the blocking of the land courts and minimizing legal expenses, and gave figures to illustrate the inefficiency of the working of the Act. Cleverly, he pulled parliamentary rank on the 'stupid insolence' of a member of the local legislature 'who presumed to ask the local Government of this country to step in and prevent a member of the Imperial Parliament (*prolonged cheering*) from the exercise of his undoubted right to explain to the public the principles which he holds and advocates (*cheers*)'. He then deployed his ancestry and family connections to useful effect:

> Those who have charged me with such a crime [disloyalty] should at least have inquired who I was and what position I held, and what character I bear in my own country. For three generations my family

> have represented in the House of Commons that part of Ireland of which I am now the Parliamentary representative, and at the present time the head of my family serves Her Majesty as a general of the British army (*applause*).

He told the audience that the No Rent Manifesto was never the policy of the league, but the last weapon in the armoury of the leaders, 'a call upon the people to suspend the payment of what they acknowledged as a debt for a certain definite time', and went on to claim, implausibly, that although the call 'was only partially responded to, it achieved its object, and before six months were over the Government had to acknowledge itself defeated, Mr. Forster was dismissed from office, and the leaders of the people were released'. Drawing a clear demarcation between the mainstream movement and the secret societies, he said that Parnell and his followers in the moderate section had 'been opposed with relentless animosity by the desperate minority' and that Carey and his associates had 'followed the League and its leaders with unrelenting enmity and sought to destroy the national movement'.[14]

As an essay in tailoring rhetoric without jettisoning vital principles, the speech was a triumph. Redmond was given a standing ovation, and the meeting adopted a resolution of sympathy with the aims of the National League, and recorded its satisfaction that none of the murder suspects was ever connected with the Land League.[15] The reviewer for the *Evening News* felt that his five shillings had not been spent in vain. His description of Redmond embraced physical appearance and oratorical style:

> a figure compact and well built, below the middle size; a face of refined and almost delicate expression, if it were not relieved in the latter respect by the firm expression of the mouth, which, together with the somewhat aquiline shape of the nose, gives to the entire countenance an unmistakeable air of self-confidence and decision . . . I recognised in him what I do not often in his compatriots, that is, that his eloquence, while plentifully interspersed with that fanciful imagery so dear to the Celtic heart, was regulated by extreme good taste. As an intellectual treat the lecture was as thorough as any I have enjoyed for many a day. It was spoken apparently *ex tempore*, and certainly, so far as I could judge, there was not a sentence, nor even a word, which could have been improved by the most careful elaboration.[16]

Feelings had been aroused in the Irish community by Parkes's action in the New South Wales legislature, and this led to disorder on the streets. There was some violence outside a meeting held at the Protestant Hall on 6 March to protest against the Redmond mission. The *Freeman* reported that Parkes was hooted by about two thousand Irishmen as he left the meeting; the *Herald* said that a crowd of seven to eight thousand were waiting to attack Parkes.[17] The *Freeman* had earlier accused the

Herald of incitement to disturbance in the city, by predicting, while affecting to dread, a riot if the meeting at the Masonic Hall took place, and then expressing astonishment that no trouble had followed the Academy meeting.[18]

II

Over the following weeks, Redmond addressed a series of meetings and established branches of the league in population centres in New South Wales. At Orange, where they arrived by train from Sydney, the brothers stayed as guests of James Dalton, a member of a locally prominent extended family of Irish immigrants, now a wealthy trader and justice of the peace. The prejudice on display in Sydney had followed them: Redmond was denied the use of the School of Arts and the Oddfellows Hall as venues, and was forced to lecture in an auction mart. Incensed by this, local Irishmen, including Dalton and several other JPs, presented him with an address which welcomed him as one of 'that noble band which has won a world's admiration by its resolute resistance to the oppressive proceedings of a foreign senate' and went on to criticize 'the existence in Ireland of what is practically martial law'. In response, the colony's government demanded the JPs' resignations; when they refused, it withdrew their commissions.[19]

It was at Orange that Redmond met James Dalton's younger half-sister Johanna, one of a large circle of admirers who, according to the *Freeman*, 'were all charmed with his singular personal qualities as they were moved by his astonishing oratorical powers and graces'[20]. Johanna was also a sister of Thomas Dalton of Sydney, a member of the legislative assembly. The couple would be married six months later. It was at this time also that William met Eleanor Dalton, the eldest daughter of James, whom he would marry in London in February 1886.

Redmond's multiplying encounters with colonists of Irish descent, most of them of moderately nationalist sympathies but including a small pro-Fenian minority, forced him further to clarify his attitude to separatism. At a meeting at Bathurst chaired by John Meagher JP, a descendant of County Clare emigrants, he listened to separatist sentiments from a speaker, J. H. Roughan, who supported a resolution of sympathy with the principles of the National League. If he had time, said Roughan, 'he would show them that the real hope of Ireland is separation from England (*A voice: 'That is so.' Mr. Redmond: 'No, no.'*) He did not want to bind their distinguished visitor to that programme, but these were the opinions of the most advanced Irishmen (*'No, no'*).' The chairman followed with the statement that 'the majority of Irishmen in Australia – as well as Irishmen in Ireland – did not want the dismemberment of the British Empire (*hear, hear*). They merely wanted the same freedom, the same government, and the same privileges for Ireland as they enjoyed themselves (*hear, hear*).' In acknowledging the vote of thanks, Redmond endorsed Meagher's remarks. He did not question the good intentions or the patriotism of Roughan, but

> he did question his right to stand upon the platform of the Irish National League and advocate principles which the League did not hold. The League was charged with a desire and intention of dismembering the Empire, and of separating England from Ireland, whereas all that they contended for was a federal arrangement whereby the will of Ireland should be supreme in Irish affairs, but whereby also Ireland would remain a portion of the general Empire and a much more integral part than she was at present.[21]

The largest meeting was a St Patrick's Day demonstration at the huge Sir Joseph Banks Pavilion in Botany. There he referred to the recent violence and asked Irishmen to avoid any interference with freedom of speech, even when it found vent in 'calumnies and falsehoods'. He hoped St Patrick's Day would not be 'desecrated by disorder, or by the sight of a single man in a state of intoxication'. Thanks to the publicity provided him by 'a certain section of the press', he said sardonically, his work had progressed more quickly than he had ever anticipated. He had already had the pleasure of sending home £1,000 and hoped to send another £1,000 the following week. He regretted that opposition to him was emanating from local Orangemen. Somewhat optimistically, he asserted that their brethren at home would repudiate their actions. He had stood on Land League platforms with Orangemen, and the largest meeting he had ever attended was presided over by an Orangeman.

In a scorching attack on the man who had tried to have him expelled, he claimed that Sir Henry Parkes, following the display of 'good sense' by the people of New South Wales, 'reminded him very much of a shark without a tail', and called him 'a man of whom it could be said at the end of his long career that he had been in private life without honesty, and in public life without principle (*enthusiastic cheers*)'. Turning to Home Rule, he cited twenty-five British dependencies that enjoyed it, including the Australian and New Zealand colonies for over forty years, and the Dominion of Canada, which provided 'the most striking illustration of the fact of Home Rule antagonising the law of disintegration in great empires'. Last year both Houses of the Canadian parliament had sent an address to the queen begging her to concede to Ireland the same measure of self-government as Canada had, and he suggested the Australian legislatures might do likewise. 'If granting Home Rule to a dependency meant dismemberment of the Empire, the Empire had been dismembered twenty-five times', he said, to general applause and laughter.[22]

At the St Patrick's Night banquet that evening at Nithsdale, Liverpool Street, there were tense moments before the start of Redmond's speech, when the chairman, the Limerick-born J. P. Garvan, a member of the legislature, prefaced his introduction with a very strong denunciation of the crime which

> had estranged for a time from a land so unfortunate as to produce such monsters the feelings of the fair and liberal-minded men of England and Scotland . . . no privilege, however sacred, was worth obtaining by the sacrifice of one iota of honour, let alone such a diabolical and hideous crime, revolting to our common humanity, and the mere mention of it being perpetrated on Irish ground brought shame to the cheek of us all (*applause*).

Redmond, who had interjected with a vigorous 'hear, hear' at several points during this tirade, clearly sensed an overstatement of the case:

> . . . no greater act of villainy, no act of greater atrocity could have been committed . . . but I refuse to be drawn into any vindication of myself (*loud cheers*) – or of those with whom I have been and am associated – and if I thought that in any allusions which you have made to that matter you were insinuating in the remotest degree that what has been stated in this land many times was true – (*the chairman*: *No*) – that is, that either I or the men with whom I am associated were implicated even in the remotest degree of sympathy with this atrocious crime, I would leave my place at this table (*cheers*).[23]

After that, there were toasts to the queen and the royal family, and the band played 'God Save the Queen'. Redmond, in his response to the toast 'To the day we celebrate', gave eloquent expression to his generous Young Ireland concept of Irish nationality:

> the Irish nation which I love – the Irish nation for which I am struggling (*loud cheers*) – is not a nation of one sect, of one creed, or of one class, or of one party. It is a nation composed of all that is good of every creed, of every party, of every class.

His feelings were of pride at the fact that 'here Irishmen have shown to the world that under a free constitution and with equal chances they can be as industrious, as law-abiding and as loyal – (*loud cheers*) – as either their English or Scotch brothers'. There was no parallel, he claimed, for the chequered history of the Irish race throughout the world, except perhaps in that of the Jews. Irishmen had become good citizens and achieved prosperity in every land, but had yet preserved, just as had the Jewish race, 'the distinct individuality of the national type (*enthusiastic cheering*)'.[24]

At the end of March, the Redmonds and Walshe went to Queensland, and were welcomed in Brisbane by Kevin Izod O'Doherty, a veteran of the Young Ireland movement, transported in 1848 and now a respected medical practitioner. Failing to obtain a suitable hall, the organizers had to arrange for Redmond to lecture at short notice in a Catholic schoolroom. The chairman regretted that this might give a 'sectarian tinge' to the movement; a protest was recorded at the conduct of those 'who had, perhaps by design, caused the meeting to be forced into a denominational schoolroom'. At this and a subsequent meeting at Goodna, Redmond's themes were again the dissociation of the movement from the aim of dismembering the Empire and a concern to emphasize the width of the gulf between the Land League and the Invincibles.[25] At Gympie, a town with a large Irish population, which had grown out of a gold rush two decades earlier, he received a warm welcome from several thousand people who crowded the railway station. Here he had more success in getting a venue, and lectured to an audience of over seven hundred at the Varieties Theatre. Telling them that he cared nothing for the disapproval of those who chose to revile him, he asserted that the movement was in exactly the position of Grattan and the Volunteers of 1782, who had said: 'We know our duty to our sovereign, and we are loyal; we know our duty to ourselves and are determined to be free.' He was applauded strongly when he expressed the belief that in working to achieve self-government, they were doing 'the best thing to consolidate and strengthen the Empire of the Queen'. He had praise for the ladies of Gympie:

> I have found wherever the Irish women take up the cause of their country that that cause is certain to succeed, and the presence here today of the Irish ladies of Gympie is sufficient to tell me that come what may the Irishmen of Gympie will be bound not only by their patriotism, but [by] motives which perhaps touch each of them more closely, to stand up for the cause of their country.[26]

Hostility to the tour from the colony's establishment was less severe than in New South Wales. The premier, Sir Thomas McIlwraith – 'no Irishman, but a broad and liberal Scotchman', commented the *Freeman* – sent Redmond, unsolicited, a free pass for the Queensland railways. At Maryborough, the municipal council at first refused the use of the town hall, but two of its members who met Redmond felt that he had been misrepresented and succeeded in having the decision reversed.[27]

Leaving William in Queensland with Walshe to carry on the work of organization, Redmond returned to New South Wales in mid-April to a string of meetings in the smaller towns. Here the pattern of refusal of the use of public buildings was repeated. At Tenterfield, in the constituency of Sir Henry Parkes, he failed to obtain the exhibition building and was forced to give the lecture in the grounds of a Catholic church. In Maitland and Newcastle the only available venues were again Catholic schoolrooms.[28] Everywhere he found it necessary to explain the situation with regard to the Phoenix Park murders. On 12 May he was back in Sydney in a much improved setting, lecturing at the Opera House for two hours on 'Self-Government'. In language of scrupulous moderation, illuminated with copious quotation from Butt, he set out, as he had not done at Adelaide, the precise extent and limits of the national demand. The mild tones of his indictment of 'English rule' were a far cry from his excoriation of Forster in the House of Commons the previous year:

> At first [Ireland] was ruled brutally, but, I freely admit, Englishmen of today desire to do her justice (*cheers*) – though they neither have time to attend to her wants, nor knowledge to understand them. The Imperial Parliament is already over-burdened with all kinds of work, and day by day the pressure is growing intolerable.

He drew on the cases of the Netherlands, Switzerland and the United States for examples of the successful working of federal arrangements.[29] At Goulborn, an admittedly partisan reporter for the *Freeman* described his delivery: 'For nigh two hours an enraptured audience hung upon his words . . . Never during his brilliant lecture did he pause for a word, never repeat an idea or an expression. With masterly well-ordered ease the brilliant flow was kept up from beginning to end.'[30]

Yet moderation and masterly oratory were not enough to open the doors of public venues. In town after town throughout a six-week campaign, he was thrown back on the use of rooms in Catholic schools, or, in one case, a produce store belonging to an alderman. At Temora he had his best reception since Gympie, and was met in fiercely inclement weather by an 'enormous cavalcade' of buggies. According to the *Freeman*, 'the ladies were evidently pleased, for they joined right heartily in the ringing Irish cheer which woke the echoes of the bush, and heralded the coming of the best abused, and therefore, from an Irish point of view, the best recommended man in Australia'.[31]

The months of June and July were spent in Victoria. On his arrival in Melbourne, Redmond could tell the welcoming members of the Australian National League central committee that more than £6,000 had been collected in three months, but there had also been the moral success of overcoming opposition based on prejudice. He gave a press conference at which he asked that the public judge the Irish demands on their merits and that the press report his speeches in full or not at all. Responding to the plausible assertion that he had moderated his tone since coming to Australia, 'he challenged any man to prove this by quoting from any of his speeches delivered in Australia, in the House of Commons or on the hillsides of Ireland. His tone was moderate because he was a moderate man, and represented a body of men who were moderate politicians.'[32] Despite his pleas for fair play, however, the difficulty in securing venues continued. He complained of the attitude of the press on 9 June in 'St. Michael's schoolroom'. He could go anywhere in England and Scotland, even at the height of the anti-coercion campaign, he said, and be sure not only that he would get a hall, but that the press would report verbatim what he said and give him the right of reply when they misreported him.[33]

In spite of these difficulties, it would be a mistake to conclude that Redmond's activities were confined within the boundaries of the Irish Catholic community. Writing in June to Alfred Webb in Dublin, he was at pains to deny reports, which he had read in some home papers, that his mission had proved a failure. He told of having held 'upwards of seventy meetings, attended by large and enthusiastic audiences of all creeds and political opinions, and presided over by Ministers of the Crown, members of both Houses of Parliament, mayors of cities, and justices of the peace'.[34]

He delivered three lectures in Melbourne, two of them in St Patrick's Hall to large audiences. In the second, entitled 'Home Rule – Its Real Meaning', he stressed the essential moderation of his goal, 'a middle course between separation on the one hand and over-centralisation of government on the other', and asked why Australians should not concede 'that which they themselves acknowledge is the source and the cause of their own prosperity and their own loyalty'.[35] In the third lecture, on 20 June, again defending the Land League against the charge of organizing violence, he demonstrated that the dramatic rise in the murder rate had followed the Coercion Acts and the suppression of the league; the violence had decreased when the Forster policy was abandoned. And he had a new charge to counter, since news had arrived of explosions in Britain, the first fruits of the new 'dynamite policy' launched by O'Donovan Rossa partisans. He told his audience that the arrest and punishment of the Phoenix Park murderers would have a good effect (news of their executions had come through in May): 'I believe that the Irish people are rapidly learning lessons of political moderation and self-restraint as well as a religious toleration and upon these three things I base my hope for a near future of triumph for our cause.'[36]

Another piece of news from home that reached the Redmonds was that of William's election, *in absentia* on 16 July, to the Wexford borough seat, now vacated by Healy who had gone to win a famous victory for the party in Monaghan. The opponent was The O'Conor Don, a Catholic nobleman and ex-Buttite M.P. with a Gaelic clan title and a decidedly Whiggish allegiance to Home Rule. Local Liberals and Tories threw their weight behind him, but he managed only 126 votes against 307 for Redmond. The crowd on polling day again bucked the stereotype of stolid Wexford reserve and engaged in stone-throwing, leading to a police charge with fixed bayonets. In Ireland the result was seen, in conjunction with Healy's victory, as the final nail in the coffin of Whiggery.[37]

Redmond returned to Sydney on 1 August, having addressed at least forty meetings on his tour of Victoria and raised a further £4,000 there.[38] Meanwhile, William went to Tasmania to deliver a personal account of the workings of the Coercion Acts.[39]

III

During August, the planned visit to New Zealand was postponed until October. The change of plan was occasioned by the wedding of John and Johanna, which took place on 4 September in the little church of St

Mary's on North Shore, near Wheatleigh House, the residence of Thomas Dalton. The *Freeman* reported that the 'young Lochinvar' had charmed all with his 'singular personal qualities'; his young bride could not fail to be 'a most loyal and devoted "home ruler"'. William, as best man, spoke with 'a simple tenderness and graceful chivalry that was as touching as it was admirable . . . as a special mark of honour, the toast of "Our Victorian Visitors" was proposed'.[40]

October saw the Redmond brothers in New Zealand, with Redmond beginning his tour in Auckland while William visited the towns of the west coast with Walshe. There was the same mixed reaction as in Australia, the Irish community (its more affluent members excepted) laying on a warm welcome while the population at large gave them a cooler reception. Part of this response arose from concern, also voiced in Australia, lest the introduction of Irish political issues into the local discourse lead to a revival of intercommunal strife.[41] As early as March, the Catholic bishop of Auckland, John Luck, had written of his intention to abstain from any part in the programmes of political agitators 'whoever they may be'. Although he sympathized with the 'faithful, generous and long-suffering Irish nation', he did not see the wisdom of 'mixing oneself up in an adopted country in the feuds and strifes of the land of one's birth, especially when the land of one's adoption is at the very antipodes of the field of action'.[42]

On his arrival in Wellington for the keynote lectures, Redmond was presented with an address of welcome by a number of Irish residents. He expressed the hope that citizens would come and 'show the manliness of their English character, which was not to condemn a man before he was heard'. The two lectures he gave on 15 and 16 October, the first on the 'real meaning' of Home Rule, the second on the Irish land question, were received enthusiastically. The *Evening Post* devoted the leader columns of two issues to favourable comment on the lectures, doubting whether the Irish National League and its cause could have been 'more ably and judiciously represented'. The merits of his cause aside, there could be no two opinions about his style:

> the striking eloquence of his diction, the lucidity of his arguments, and the felicitous persuasiveness of his style all were calculated to prepossess his hearers strongly in his behalf... there is genuine pleasure in listening to so gifted an orator . . . with all the fire of his vivid declamation and all the histrionic embellishment with which an accomplished orator can adorn the subject of his burning eloquence.

And it was clear that initial scepticism regarding the cause had been mollified:

> When the most moderate members of the Irish Home Rule party, of whom Mr. Redmond distinctly declares himself to be one, tell us, as Mr. Redmond did last night, that what they desire for Ireland is only such a power of local self-government as New Zealand and other

> British colonies now possess – indeed, less than this, for they would be content still to leave in the hands of the Imperial Parliament powers now exercised independently by colonial legislatures – our sympathies as colonists are irresistibly attracted by what appears *prima facie* so reasonable a demand.[43]

Press coverage was similarly benign as the brothers reunited and held the final meetings of the tour in Christchurch and Dunedin. Although the prominent Irish, as at Auckland, stayed away, it was evident that Redmond's combination of eloquence and moderation in the presentation of his case had helped to disarm criticism. The Catholic *Tablet* of Dunedin summed up the tour as 'thoroughly successful', opining that a better man than Redmond could not have been found for the mission and praising his 'complete want of assumption or conceit of any kind, and the perfect simplicity of his manners and bearing'.[44] With fundraising results greatly exceeding the original target of £1,000 for all of New Zealand, thanks especially to an enthusiastic response in the Irish centres on the west coast, the Redmonds returned to Melbourne to round off their mission.

It was now time to hold a convention to centralize authority over the three hundred branches of the league that had been established throughout the colonies. On 7 November, about two hundred delegates representing the chief branches in Australia, Tasmania and New Zealand assembled in St Patrick's Hall, Melbourne. In the chair was Kevin O'Doherty, who had welcomed the Redmonds to Brisbane; on the table in front of the Young Ireland veteran, in a kind of posthumous reconciliation, stood a large bust of Daniel O'Connell. There were resolutions deploring the state of Ireland and petitioning for Irish Home Rule, expressing support for the Parnell policy and agreeing to contribute to the Parnell testimonial fund, at that moment nearing the sum of £40,000 at home. The most interesting resolution agreed was a proposal that each colony guarantee financial support for one Irish member in the imperial Parliament. O'Doherty's speech emphasized the extremely moderate consensus among the Antipodean Irish: 'I can confidently aver that, as regards my own countrymen, a year or two of residence under the free Australian sky suffices to make loyal men of those who have been driven here from home with soured and embittered hearts.' He stressed the importance of denouncing the dynamite policy carried on by some of the extreme nationalists in America, whose 'senseless and abominable outrages' aroused bitter feelings. 'Let them understand,' he said, 'that in Australia they are regarded as the bitterest enemies of our country.' Another delegate thought that Australians should assist the Irish to obtain self-government out of gratitude for the fact that 'as Irish-Australians, they enjoyed every privilege which free men could wish for, and lived under a constitution as near perfection as could be found in any country'.[45]

The tone of Parnell's letter to Redmond, dated 5 September, which was read to the convention, was in perfect harmony with this atmosphere. Having praised the 'magnificent' response of Australians to his exertions, it implied that the Irish had nothing to learn from them in moderation:

> we are all glad to learn that the Australian organisation has adopted the same moderate principles as the National League, and that our people are persevering in their present attitude of patient forbearance, no matter what provocations they may receive. You will have seen that the entire absence of crime of any kind from the movement in Ireland is a sufficient indication that our exertions in dissuading the people from illegal courses have been so far successful.[46]

Redmond's address ascribed the success of the mission to four factors: the support of the Catholic bishops and priests, the unselfish but indispensable organizing work of Walshe, the support of the bulk of the working population of the Irish community, and 'the unconscious kindness of the press', whose hostile leading articles had been 'huge gratuitous advertisements'. The convention was, he said,

> the free parliament of the Irish people of Australia speaking out their minds on the demands of the people in Ireland. He thanked them all from the bottom of his heart. He hoped that before his life closed he would have an opportunity to re-visit these shores . . . But whether his life was long or short, one of the proudest recollections of it would be that in his political youth he was able to do a great and useful work for home and his self-respecting countrymen in Australia.[47]

After the convention, he paid a flying visit to Adelaide to speak on Wexford in 1798,[48] then returned to Sydney for a farewell lecture on the same theme on 30 November. According to the *Freeman*, every inch of space was taken up in the Gaiety Theatre for the two-hour lecture. Beside Redmond on the platform was Father Patrick Kavanagh, the Wexford Franciscan whose *Popular History* propagated what was becoming the most influential, 'faith and fatherland', model of the rebellion.[49] Remarkably, although Redmond acknowledged his debt to the priest for 'many details', he diverged significantly from his interpretation and drew explicitly on the earlier work of Dr R. R. Madden, *The United Irishmen: Their Life and Times*, published in the 1840s, with its emphasis on Protestant participation and the non-sectarian aims of the leaders. Presenting the insurrection as the consequence of provocation by English ministers intent on an Act of Union, Redmond was nevertheless unequivocal as to the limits of its relevance for contemporary Ireland:

> I am quite prepared for disapproval at my choice of subject . . . I may be told that I am raking up the wrongs and miseries of the past for no

> good end . . . that I am a rebel today because I sympathise with men who were termed rebels one hundred years ago. Thank heavens times and circumstances have changed since the year 1798, and we in our day are able to struggle for our national rights by legal and constitutional means, which, to our outlawed and penalised forefathers were as impossible as an armed rising would be to the Ireland of today.

Acknowledging the vote of thanks, Redmond told his listeners that from the general public of Sydney he had received 'very determined opposition, but I am bound to say not very much foul play (*laughter*)'. But he would never forget the 'generous confidence' with which nine-tenths of the Irish-descended of New South Wales had received him, and he expressed pride in the fact that he had won over the great majority of Australian Irish to the Home Rule cause.[50]

As his visit drew to a close, he could certainly congratulate himself with, as Campbell states, 'subtly shifting Australian and New Zealand opinion on the Irish question'.[51] Two decades later, the support of colonial legislatures for the Home Rule demand would be an important weapon in the nationalist armoury. The importance of the mission for the constitutionalist organization at home can be seen if its financial yield is compared with the contributions from America. The full sum raised in Australia and New Zealand in ten months was nearly £15,000, which, even when the considerable expenses are deducted, compares very favourably with Irish-American subscriptions, which had sunk to only £2,000 in 1883 and were just over £3,000 in 1884.[52] The *Freeman*'s valedictory was lavish in its praise for the manner in which Redmond had coped with the obstructions placed in his path:

> That Mr. Parnell had picked the right man for the work, was evident immediately hostilities were commenced . . . It was nothing but Mr. Redmond's good judgment, his temper and nerve, his scorn of stupid insolence, his masterly dignified refutation of grave slanders publicly uttered, and above all his wonderful control over his own feelings, and his perfect knowledge of those of his countrymen in the colonies that saved us from those scenes of violence and national animosity which a certain section of the Press had more than once prophetically pictured, and which several 'respectable' papers – to their everlasting disgrace, be it said – had beyond doubt done their very best and worst to originate.[53]

Redmond's experiences in Australasia left a lasting imprint on his political attitudes. The view that Irish autonomy within the Empire, apart from being the only form of self-government attainable in the realm of practical politics, might in itself be a worthwhile goal, was one his family traditions made congenial to him; it was now strengthened by what he had seen and heard in the past year. Federalist ideas would break through the more orthodox elements in his rhetoric at intervals over the coming decades.[54] According to his friend and biographer, Stephen

Gwynn, Redmond came to know more and care more about the Empire than most imperialists, having seen so many of the Irish engaged in building it and feeling that it belonged as much to them as to the English, Scots or Welsh.[55] It was a sentiment that would find expression in his speech on the first Home Rule Bill in May 1886, in which he dealt with the proposal to abolish the Irish representation at Westminster after Home Rule. He opposed the idea that 'Ireland's voice should be excluded from the Councils of an Empire which the genius and valour of her sons had done so much to build up and of which she was to remain a part.'[56]

IV

Leaving Sydney on 6 December on board the *Zealandia*, the Redmond brothers with Johanna sailed for San Francisco, arriving there on 1 January 1884. The contrast between the political atmospheres of Irish-America and Irish-Australasia could not have been greater. The Irish National League of America, launched the previous year to replace the American Land League, and supposedly representing moderate opinion, was heavily influenced by Clan na Gael thinking and infiltrated by its members. Its first elected president was Alexander Sullivan, the dominant figure in the 'Triangle', the triumvirate that ruled one faction of Clan na Gael. Although the Clan avoided public identification with the dynamite policy, Sullivan and other members were implicated in the bombing campaign in Britain, which began in 1883.[57]

Since Parnell's visit to the United States four years previously, Patrick Ford, the editor of the extremist weekly *Irish World*, had built a reputation as the most successful fundraiser for the Irish nationalist cause. He claimed to have collected $350,000 for the Land League, $8,000 for the relatives of the hanged or imprisoned perpetrators (he called them 'victims') of the Phoenix Park murders, and $55,000 for the defence of Patrick O'Donnell, executed for shooting dead James Carey, the Invincible-turned-informer. This represented an average of $14,000 (equivalent to nearly £3,000) a month over thirty months.[58] Ford's paper, while welcoming the Redmonds as 'earnest and patriotic Irishmen who have laboured and are labouring zealously and honestly in the Irish cause', reflected the growing dissatisfaction in Irish-America at the failure of their colleagues at home to advance the expected revolution. Having heard of Sexton's statement that the Irish Party recognized the queen as the constitutional sovereign, it wondered how this was to be reconciled with the declared aim of Parnell to 'make Ireland a nation'; if they accepted such a proposition, then their pursuit was 'not nationhood but municipal reform'.[59] A week before the Redmonds' arrival, Ford had unveiled his latest venture, the 'Emergency Fund'. As they travelled across the continent, holding 'large and enthusiastic' meetings at San Francisco, Denver, Chicago and other centres, they could read of the avowed object of the fund, prominently displayed in the *Irish World* each week:

> to aid the Active Forces on the Other Side in Every Practical Mode of Warfare for the Recovery of Irish National Independence, to Stimulate to Deeds of Heroism, to Punish Informers, to Reward Heroes Whilst Living, and to Honour their Memories When They have Passed from the Scene of Action, and to Look After the Dependants of Men Who May Fall for Ireland, but Who Before They have Fallen shall have Struck SUCCESSFUL BLOWS Against the Common Enemy.[60]

They spent two weeks in Chicago, where Redmond gave a 'course of lectures on Irish affairs'.[61] The climax of their stay was a 'grand reception' on 29 January at the Armoury of the 1st Cavalry on Lake Michigan, where Redmond addressed an audience of six thousand. The brothers were escorted there, in a procession of 3,500 people, by 32 divisions of the Ancient Order of Hibernians, the Clan-na-Gael Guards and 8 companies of the Hibernian Rifles. In this atmosphere, Redmond unsurprisingly jettisoned some of his Antipodean moderation of language and reverted to the heated rhetoric of 1882. Parnell himself had succumbed to similar influences in Cincinnati, where he was reported as saying that he would not be satisfied until they had 'destroyed the last link which keeps Ireland bound to England', a speech that would come back to haunt him at the Special Commission in 1889.[62] Redmond, although wanting it understood that he deplored, detested and denounced Irish crime, mitigated that condemnation in a remarkable passage in which he told the story of a woman who had been wounded by a police bayonet at an eviction mêlée:

> Picture that scene to yourselves, you stern moralists who rail at Irish crime, but know nothing of English provocation. Picture that scene, you fireside philosophers who would reform humanity on a theory, but make no allowance for human nature and human passion . . . I say that Irish crime is due to English misgovernment; that England has sown the wind and is reaping the whirlwind.

His response to the Fenian embrace was most evident in the peroration, when he used phrases which he had studiously avoided in Australia. There was no talk of the impossibility of armed uprisings. Instead he declared: 'I would be very frank in this matter. I believe that all means which brave and honest men would consistently adopt are justifiable for Ireland.'[63] Before sailing from New York at the end of February, Redmond made contact on 12 February with the Devoy wing of the Clan, though it seems he did not meet its leader.[64]

Redmond visited the southern hemisphere only once; he would return to the United States many times. Although it was the Australian trip that had the more profound influence on his politics, he needed to learn its lesson only once. America was a different matter. With its greater accessibility and its much greater, and more radicalized, Irish population, it was potentially a much more prolific source of funds for the movement at home. Over the coming years he would develop his facility for playing to the gallery of Irish-America, seeming to find intoxication in its atmosphere. Genuine enthusiasm was evident in his farewell oration at the Dublin banquet in 1906 to two young nationalist M.P.s, T. M. Kettle and Richard Hazleton, then embarking on their first mission to the US, as he told them they would see the future there: an Irish race already emancipated, thriving and powerful.[65] At home, his rhetoric was under constant guard as he sought to win Britons and moderate unionists to the Home Rule cause. In the unbuttoned ambience of Irish-America, however, immersed in a culture that blamed all of Ireland's woes on the British connection, he appeared at times to enjoy throwing away the restraints.

On a 1902 visit to Boston, a local report headlined 'Mr. Redmond Wishes People Could Learn Use of Arms' quoted him as telling officers and men of the Massachusetts 9th Regiment, who had given a drill exhibition in his honour:

> You come of a grand old fighting race, one of the great fighting races of the world . . . Unfortunately, Ireland, the cradle of your race, is a disarmed country, a land where men are forbidden to learn the use of arms, forbidden to bear arms, and the thought that surged through my heart in witnessing your maneuvers tonight was this, that if only on the old soil of Ireland we had the opportunity, for five or ten years, of teaching our people the use of arms as you do here, we could very soon and very speedily settle the Irish question (*tremendous cheering*).[66]

Two years later in New York, according to a local paper, he made it clear that

> he was just as anxious as any Irishman the world over to see Ireland separated now and for all time from British control. 'If it were in my power tomorrow to absolutely emancipate Ireland I would do it. It is just as possible for Ireland to have absolutely separate existence as a nation as Switzerland, or any other nation of small dimensions.'[67]

Rhetorical eruptions such as these helped to raise the indispensable funds, and could do little practical harm, since he would always insist that only the representatives of the Irish people at home could decide on the means to be employed in the struggle for self-government. Nevertheless, reports of them did cross the Atlantic and damaged the Home Rule movement in unionist eyes by seeming to confirm suspicions that it was a cover for separatism.

The year in Australasia began as a fundraising mission and ended by confirming Redmond in a political creed; the visits to the United States would become for him both a recurring political necessity and a form of personal recreation.

5 At Parnell's Command

> Mr. Redmond . . . seems now to take delight . . . in openly and continuously insulting those with whom a strange stroke of fortune has placed him on a footing of nominal equality.
>
> Sir Henry Lucy, parliamentary diarist[1]

> He trusted the House would accept with readiness the statement of the Representatives of the Irish people that, on the whole, they were satisfied with this [Home Rule] Bill, and that, so far as their judgment went, it provided a final settlement of the question.
>
> Redmond in the House of Commons, 13 May 1886[2]

I

The Ireland to which Redmond returned on 8 March 1884 had calmed considerably in the fifteen months of his absence. While agrarian agitation continued in some areas, the edge had been taken off the campaign by the combination of coercive legislation and the desire of the tenants to avail of the practical benefits of the Land Act. Even before he had left Ireland, agrarian crime as a whole was showing a sharp downward trend, with 59 outrages in September 1882 compared with 225 in the same month of the previous year, and this trend had continued.[3] In the House of Commons, Irish legislation had ceased to dominate parliamentary time, and the attention of the Government was focused on passing the great Third Reform Bill, aimed at enlarging the franchise in the United Kingdom. Parnell's effective abandonment of the New Departure in May 1882 had neutralized the agrarian left wing; the Fenian component detached itself from the movement and resorted to sporadic dynamite attacks in England in 1883 and following years (including bombs left at four London rail stations, one of which exploded, the week before Redmond's return).[4] The twin tasks facing Parnell's capable leadership were now the creation of a united and disciplined party and the maximization of its electoral strength in time for the next general election.

On arrival at Queenstown, Redmond immediately declared his 'unswerving allegiance to Mr. Parnell'. Replying to an effusive address of welcome from Davitt, he asserted that the condition of continued Australian support would be 'that an active, vigorous, uncompromising attitude shall be maintained by the organisation at home; and secondly, the suppression by every means in the power of the National leaders of anything in the shape of outrage or crime'.[5] At Cork the Redmond brothers were fêted with the standard nationalist addresses of welcome, an open-air demonstration of several thousand people by the light of tar-barrels, and a torchlight procession led by six of the city's bands. Similar receptions awaited them a few days later, when they arrived by rail in Dublin, and that weekend in Wexford, where William was greeted as the borough's new M.P.[6] At Cork, Redmond stated that he had come home

> more than ever convinced that if this movement is to obtain the sympathy and respect of other nations throughout the civilised world, in addition to being a patriotic movement, it must be a just and honourable one (*hear, hear*); one conducted on lines consistent with the traditions of an ancient and honourable race (*cheers*).[7]

The lesson of what he had seen was clear: 'Anywhere we went,' he said, 'we found self-governed communities, with free institutions administered by Irishmen, although in our own country we are told that we are unfit to govern ourselves.'[8]

With his domestic audience in mind, however, he placed less emphasis on the 'loyal' aspects of his Australian experience, and was anxious to correct some reports that had filtered back from there. There was a defensive tone in his indignant denial of a claim made by Archibald Forbes, an English war correspondent who appears to have trailed the Redmonds for part of their tour. Forbes, in an article in *Contemporary Review*, alleged that Redmond had begun his visit by speaking in his 'usual seditious manner', but, faced with the wrath of loyal citizens, had changed his tone and, by a 'droll irony', had ended by speaking enthusiastically of the sovereign. Redmond branded as a 'deliberate falsehood' the allegation that he 'had gone so far to propitiate the enemies of my race as to ask meetings of Irishmen to cheer for the Queen (*hisses*)'.[9]

Despite his avowal that his trip had imbued him 'with energy' to proceed in his political career, Redmond was in no hurry to return to intensive political work. He resumed the light duties of a party whip, but it was mid-June before he made a significant contribution in the House, on the Sunday Closing Bill. For the rest of that year, and most of the following, his attendance was constant but he spoke far less often than might have been expected on the basis of his performance in 1881–82. In those first years in the House, the quantity of his interventions, in terms of number of questions asked, contributions in Committee, and set-piece speeches, while it did not approach that of the leading stars of the party, Healy, Sexton, Biggar and O'Donnell, had been respectably in the middle range of activity. By contrast, in 1884–85, his work-rate in the House placed him among the most inactive members of the party. Neither did his name appear often among the M.P.s who attended the many weekend demonstrations throughout Ireland during these years, organizing the National League, preaching the Parnellite gospel and preparing the ground for the general election.

Several factors may account for this seeming indolence. No doubt he felt entitled to a rest from the rigours of extensive travelling and changes of climate. As a newly married man, some of his energies were no doubt absorbed in home life, and the birth of the couple's first child, a daughter named Esther (Essy), in June 1884 can only have intensified this. Katherine Tynan met him at a dinner party in London at the house of Dr John Rae, the Arctic explorer who had brought home the relics of Lord Franklin:

> [He] had brought home an Australian wife, full of life and very unconventional, with whom again he was very much in love . . . He recited after dinner and his unsophisticated choice was Longfellow's 'Wreck of the Hesperus' . . . At the close, one almost expected to see him standing up as the head-boy of the school to receive his prize.[10]

The much quieter political atmosphere of 1884 gave him an opportunity to resume the law studies he had begun when he first went to London, and which had been interrupted by his entry into politics. He told Father Furlong in October 1885, some weeks before the general election: 'The fact is for the last year I have been making up for lost time at my legal work and have been cramming into that twelve months the work of three years. I am now happily at an end.'[11]

He was not the only Irish M.P. taking advantage of the lull to complete law studies: Healy was called to the bar in November 1884 and Leamy in June of the following year.[12] (Healy managed, however, to combine his studies with a prodigious work-rate in Parliament.) As a parliamentary fighter, Redmond in this period fell far short of some of his colleagues, particularly Healy. William O'Brien later wrote of him that although his rare contributions in the House were always done 'with grace',

> His comparative uselessness where the blows were flying was partly due to the fact that the weapons wanted in such a warfare were not orations, but what were prosily called 'a few words', (though hot ones), and may also, I think, be attributed partly to a diffidence which genuinely led him to the belief that his brother Willie was the greater orator of the two.[13]

William, sworn in as a M.P. on 24 March, and still only twenty-three in 1884, spoke more often in the House than his brother, and began a near-manic round of attendance at weekend open-air rallies and other meetings in Ireland, where he came to be much in demand as a 'sensational' speaker.[14] Early on, he developed his reputation for unguarded and intemperate language. Although the two brothers were often mistaken for one another physically, there was no confusing their rhetoric. The word 'hatred', for example, in Redmond's mouth, even at the height of the tumults of 1881–82, was usually applied to abstractions such as 'English rule', but William could speak of the people being 'united in their hatred of England'.[15] At a National League meeting he descended into racial hatred with the assertion that the people were determined 'to use all the means in their power till they drove every man of English blood from every official position in this country . . . this was a struggle between the Celtic race and the Saxon race'.[16] A party colleague, J. J. Clancy, dissented from this remark, saying that what mattered was not the rulers' race but 'the removal of the hand of government in Ireland moved by a London head'.[17] Again, at Bradford William told the audience that the Irish in England 'must not forget that the people among whom they lived were undoubtedly the enemies of their race'.[18] Whereas Redmond at Wexford could euphemistically declare that it was the duty of the people to organize to make land-grabbing impossible, William, in a fiery speech at Kells, taunted the police and incited the crowd by calling the grass-grabber 'more loathsome to me than the ugliest snake ever God created'.[19]

More seriously for the image of responsibility that Parnell was trying to instil in the minds of British voters and statesmen, William became fond of winning easy applause by openly identifying himself with the current enemies of Britain in a manner that would have horrified his Australian audiences. At Dundalk in April 1885, two months after the news of the fall of Khartoum and the death of General Gordon, he praised the 'brave Arabs' who had given the British 'a touch of what his fellow-countrymen gave them in the blessed days of '98'.[20] He went on to place his hopes in Europe's most despotic regime (war with Russia being seen as inevitable in that month): 'he believed that if the cheer they had just given could reach the Russian bear, it would wake up that old animal to set about that clawing which he hoped to God he was soon going to give to the British lion (*loud and prolonged cheering*)'.[21] Above all, in language that had almost brought about a second spell in prison in 1882, he constantly adverted to the need for violent methods if constitutional means failed, an eventuality to which Redmond and others now seldom referred.[22]

Living in the shadow of an acclaimed older brother, William may have felt it necessary to use extreme rhetoric in order to establish a separate identity. His youth, and youthful appearance, made it difficult for him to be taken seriously in Australia and America, as he told the welcoming party in March 1884, and this may have driven him to greater lengths to win respect.[23] Instead, it made his excesses tolerable. Katherine Tynan wrote in 1913 of his 'evergreen boyishness, which makes him so much beloved, and in the House of Commons used to excuse any indiscretion'.[24] William O'Brien's wife, Sophie Raffalovich, found him to be more lovable than his brother, the latter impressing her as the abler, more intellectual of the two.[25] There seems to have been a strong element of impulsiveness in William's temperament. Certainly, only thoughtlessness, or extreme naïvety, can account for his remarks at Belleek, County Fermanagh, in November 1885, when, having told the religiously mixed audience that Parnell fought for oppressed Protestants as well as Catholics, he proceeded to tell them that this was a struggle 'for which their fathers had fought and died in every part of the country . . . a battle they had been waiting for for centuries'.[26]

The death in October 1884 of the 54-year-old M.P. for Meath, A. M. Sullivan, severed a link with the generation of Young Ireland. To Redmond's generation, he embodied the type of an incorruptible constitutional nationalist; he had also been a colleague of his father's, sharing the latter's zeal for temperance reform. Redmond's closeness to him, and the possibility that Sullivan may have played some part in grooming him for political life, is attested to in a letter written to him by Sullivan's widow, Frances, the following year: 'Mr. Sullivan always spoke of you as *his* boy and I feel a deep interest in you . . .'[27]

At the party meeting of 22 October, Redmond seconded Parnell's resolution mourning Sullivan's death.[28] He presided at the first meeting to set up a tribute to raise funds for his widow and children and the following year helped to organize a benefit concert in St James's Hall.[29] The eulogies bestowed on Sullivan, who had denounced Fenianism in pre-New Departure days, were controversial in 'advanced' quarters. A meeting of the Young Ireland Society voted to rescind its resolution of condolence with the Sullivan family; one of the members who so voted was Frederick J. Allan, a member of the Irish Republican Brotherhood (IRB).[30] As it happened, Allan was arrested the following week on a treason-felony charge, but the charges were later allowed to drop. Ironically, Redmond was to find himself in close political association with Allan for much of the 1890s, when the latter was manager of the Parnellite *Independent* newspaper publishing company.

II

Redmond's few major speeches of 1884–85 put across the party message of hostility to the Liberal government and, in line with Parnell's policy of seeking the balance of power at the general election, the need to maintain an independent stance between the two British parties. At the public banquet given for him and William by the nationalists of Wexford at the town hall on 16 April 1884, his theme was the Reform Bill, the great question of the day. This measure proposed to replace the property-based franchise in Irish counties and boroughs with a household franchise, thus expanding the electorate from about 200,000 to over 600,000.[31] The attitude of indifference affected by Redmond to this major extension of democracy to the masses may surprise us, but it reflected the pragmatic stance that has been noted in Parnell at this time.[32] They should make it clear to the people, he said, that the Irish Party were in no way indebted to the Liberal Party for the reform about to be granted, firstly because they knew they could not carry it through the House of Commons for England without Irish support and its consequent extension to Ireland, and secondly, because 'they [the Irish Party] could very well afford to do without it'. Even with the present franchise they could return seventy men at the next election pledged to follow the present leader and policy of the party. The extension of the franchise would confer no more than perhaps ten further seats: 'It mattered little to them whether they had 70 or 80 members in the Imperial Parliament. With 70 members of true mettle they could work wonders.'[33] For Redmond, there were also limits to the value of an extended franchise in the absence of Irish self-government, despite the claim that Ireland's rulers were responsible to those they ruled by being responsible to the House of Commons in which the Irish people were represented: 'That argument was based upon the supposition that Ireland was a part of England as much as Kent or Yorkshire (*cries of 'No'*) . . . but Ireland was . . . a distinct country . . . the Almighty so willed it when He traced the lines of the universe.'[34]

Extending the vote to the labourers and poorer farmers may have seemed to Gladstone and others a good way to lessen Parnell's influence, which so far had been based electorally on tenant-farmers who had done relatively well out of the land war. This prospect alarmed Parnell for a reason not envisaged by the Liberal leaders: such an unpropertied vote would be more open to influences from the left, which he would find hard to control. Redmond's instinctive conservatism was similarly alive to the danger of the national drive for self-government being swamped by a new tide of agitation based on the demands of specific class interests. His priority that day was clear: 'He would not hesitate in casting the vote which would send out of office that Ministry without whom they could maintain their ground – a Ministry who to Ireland had broken every pledge by which they had obtained the vote of the Irishmen in English constituencies.'[35] The following month, the party, though it had voted for the Reform Bill's second reading, got the chance to act on this threat when 32 members voted with the Tories on a censure motion, reducing an expected Government majority of 92 to 28, and imperilling the fate of both Government and franchise measure. There was 'indescribable excitement' in the House at this 'moral defeat' for the Liberals, reported the *Freeman*.[36]

When Tory peers in the House of Lords defeated the Reform Bill in July, a crisis ensued in which the Government faced the options of dissolution or an autumn session in which to try again to pass the Bill. Rallies for the Bill took place all over Great Britain, including an enormous demonstration of 120,000 people at Hyde Park on 21 July. Gladstone opted for the second course, and the Irish Party was finally faced with a decision on how to vote on the Bill. On 24 October, Redmond delivered what the *Freeman* called 'a carefully thought-out and felicitously-worded indictment of the entire policy of the Administration',[37] in which he followed Healy in asserting that the turning out of 'this Government of coercionist Radicals and hypocritical Whigs' was the primary mission of the party at the moment:

> Let no man tell him that it was their duty to tolerate such an Administration because they hoped to receive the boon of a Franchise Bill. The time had arrived when the franchise must be extended in England and Scotland, and Irishmen knew that no statesman dare withhold it from Ireland, and at the same time profess to govern the country constitutionally. They cared not whether they got this boon from a Whig or from a Tory Government.[38]

But the Redmond–Healy view on the Bill was not the only one in the party. Another section, as the *Freeman's* London correspondent wrote, thought that voting against the Franchise Bill might play into the hands of the enemies of Ireland.[39] When the party met on 7 November to decide on its vote, Redmond found himself in the minority. The decision was to support the Government, and the second reading passed by a huge majority. The party had proved, said the *Freeman*, 'their earnest desire, despite all incentives to revenge against the Government, to enfranchise not only an additional half million of their own countrymen, but a million and a half of the democracy of Great Britain'.[40]

Whatever his doubts about the franchise reform, Redmond was not slow in applying the new language of democracy. The day after the Reform Act received the royal assent, he spoke with Biggar at the Manchester Free Trade Hall. His task, as a member of the seven-man executive of the Irish National League of Great Britain, was to ensure the passing of a resolution expressing confidence in the Irish Party. Asking the Irish voters to keep themselves unpledged at the next election, he warned them especially to beware of seduction by the Radicals. The Irish Party was the only Radical section in the House, he said, inviting them to look at what it had done in a few years:

> Young, poor, many of them totally unknown, they had banded together almost as if by the providence of God, and they had wrought a revolution in Ireland as great as the blood of France had brought about before the united enemies of Europe. Talk of democracy. They had raised the democracy of Ireland throughout the country . . . and had taught the people how to use that mighty and stupendous power which was to be found in the will of a free, united and determined people.

At the next election no one would be returned who was not 'an independent democrat in all his feelings', determined to wipe out British misrule in Ireland.[41]

Hostility to British Radicals dictated by parliamentary tactics did not imply a lack of sympathy on Redmond's part with the reforming impetus that swept through the politics of the period. Although social reform was not for him, as a Home Ruler, a first priority, he did show, then and for long afterwards, a desire to improve the lot of the most downtrodden stratum in the Irish countryside, the agricultural labourers. One of the legislative results of Parnell's efforts in the 1883 session was the Labourers (Ireland) Act, which authorized Boards of Guardians to build cottages with plots of land attached for letting to labourers, the rent being used to pay the interest on the money borrowed for the purpose.[42] Though its scope was inadequate to the scale of the problem, Redmond told the Wexford rally in September 1884 that he was glad that greater efforts were being made in the county to give labourers the small benefits of the Act. It was 'little better than a sham and a mockery' and it was the duty of the Irish Party to have it amended, he said. He told farmers that if they did not treat their labourers better, they would lose the sympathy of men like him, who had not gone into politics to benefit a single class.[43]

However, his concern for the welfare of rural workingmen does not seem to have extended to the working and unemployed classes of the cities. At this time the Georgian centre of Dublin, including the street of Redmond's birth, had entered on its long decline into dereliction as the tradesmen and casually employed labourers of the city crowded into the large houses vacated by the professional classes. In autumn 1884, the *Freeman* ran a series of articles on 'The Slums of Dublin', which publicized the full horror of the destitution of the urban poor.[44] The Government set up a Royal Commission chaired by the Radical Charles Dilke[45] to inquire into the problem, and Sexton was nominated by his party to sit on it. The report which it issued led to the Housing of the Working Classes Act, 1890, which provided for the first register of tenement property and the first measure to deal with dangerous buildings.[46] However, although the question was taken up by a local branch of the National League, the problem failed to ignite as a nationalist political issue.[47]

The blind spot of Home Rulers on the slum problem is explained in part by the concentration of their attention on the single issue of legislative independence, seen as the prerequisite for addressing Ireland's social ills, as the Union was seen as their sole cause. 'Labour must wait' was an attitude in vogue among nationalists long before Eamon de Valera uttered the phrase in the 1920s. But a deeper reason for their lack of concern with the problem was the wide diffusion of tenement ownership among the population, nationalist as well as unionist, and the tendency of nationalist politicians of the period to own urban properties in the affected areas. Dillon had inherited three tenement houses near the city centre, which by 1913 were in a very dangerous condition (though beyond his control because sublet on a long lease);[48] William Redmond inherited a row of cottages, together with a church, at North Strand, Dublin, from his mother.[49]

Social reform of a different kind was, however, close to Redmond's heart. The role of alcohol abuse in exacerbating the poverty in the city was notorious, and was highlighted in the *Freeman* articles. Temperance reform was an issue on which his own convictions met those of contemporary British Radicals. A King's Inn acquaintance of this time later wrote that it was the fact that Redmond was almost a total abstainer that first brought them together. The law students customarily dined at tables of six, with a fixed quantity of wine at each table. Since the writer did not drink wine, and Redmond never took more than half a glass, the two of them were in great demand at certain tables. The writer, coming from a Protestant home in which the nationalist movement and the drink trade were seen as closely connected, seems to have been surprised at meeting a Catholic nationalist temperance reformer.[50]

His convictions were displayed when, in June 1884, the Government tried to renew the Sunday closing (of public houses) legislation. The debate showed up divisions within the Irish Party on the temperance issue. William O'Brien disagreed with the Bill on principle ('the lives of the Irish people were sufficiently joyless already'), while others, such as Tim Harrington, felt that it would not achieve the desired effect. Redmond was one of a very small group who spoke in support of the Bill, in spite of the opportunity to embarrass the Government. The strength of his commitment was evident from the fact that, though he could contemplate losing a measure of the magnitude of the franchise reform in the interests of voting out the Government, he would not use this Bill in the same way. In a brief contribution, he said that he was an avowed supporter of the principles of Sunday closing when elected, and 'I have never, since I have been a Member, received any representations on the subject from my constituents, except those of cordial approval of the course I have always taken upon measures of this character.'[51] Healy, for whom the discrediting of the Government took precedence over all else, talked out the limited available time for the Bill in a rambling speech while claiming to support its principle.[52] In his memoirs, he claimed that he induced William Redmond, as one whose father was a temperance advocate, to speak at length in support of it, thus helping to kill the Bill.[53] The Irish Association for the Prevention of Intemperance (IAPI) blamed the Government for the fate of the Bill, claiming that it had made the task of opponents easy by putting it down for days when debate had to finish early.[54]

There was more to Redmond's advocacy of temperance legislation than the legacy of Wexford's sabbatarian movements; it had a political dimension relevant to the nationalist struggle. In his Sydney lecture on the 1798 insurrection, he spoke of how, after a string of victories, the insurgents had lost the town of New Ross through drunkenness: 'How many losses had not Irishmen suffered since that day through the same cause?'[55] Lecturing on the same theme at Glasgow in March 1885, he alleged that Wexford town had been lost when part of the rebel army broke into the spirit stores.[56] At the annual meeting of the IAPI in Dublin in 1886 he declared that 'he regarded no duty as more important than that of supporting the temperance movement', and that, following the extension of the franchise, the placing of the regulation of the liquor traffic in the hands of the people would more effectively repress vice.[57] A remark of the late secretary of the association, the Ulster Liberal M.P. T. W. Russell, to the effect that the Irish Party was dependent on the drink trade as its backbone, caused him to retaliate in kind. As well as violating the non-political nature of the association, Russell was, he said, hypocritical for claiming to be a temperance reformer while standing on an election platform in County Tyrone surrounded by publicans. ('A voice: 'He must have been drunk (*cheers*)').[58]

In furtherance of his 'Ireland sober, Ireland free' stance, Redmond made an attempt to enlist the forces of temperance among the Catholic Irish in Britain in the ranks of the Home Rule agitation. In November 1884 he was part of a deputation that called on Cardinal Henry Manning to see whether some 'common line of action' could be adopted between National League branches and those of the League of the Cross in London.[59] Little seems to have come of the initiative. Contrary to his prediction regarding the forces of reform, the strength of the publican lobby in nationalist politics increased over the years, such that Sunday closing Bills failed every year in the 1880s and early 1890s. Redmond, who had sponsored the Bill every year, found himself unable to vote for the Liberal's Bill in 1893, and voted, for reasons of party unity, against the measure that made Sunday closing permanent in 1906.[60]

III

In the early months of 1885 preparations began for an election that all sides knew could not be long delayed. The Cabinet began a prolonged debate over its Irish strategy in the knowledge that the enlarged franchise would greatly strengthen Parnell's hand. Decisions had to be made with regard to two matters: the renewal of the coercion legislation, and a suitable measure of redress with which to balance it. A faction led by Earl Spencer, the lord lieutenant,[61] wanted a strong Coercion Act, renewable for three years. Meanwhile, secret negotiations took place in these months between Parnell and the leader of the Radical section of the Liberal Party, Joseph Chamberlain, using Captain O'Shea as an intermediary. The subject was a scheme for Irish local government, with a 'central board' having both administrative and limited legislative powers, which might be offered to the Irish as a quid pro quo for an agreement not to obstruct coercion. Parnell, although willing to accept such a scheme, was at pains to make clear that it would not be a substitute for a restored Irish parliament, which would remain the party's demand. In the end, in spite of Gladstone's support for it, the Cabinet decided against the scheme, and a shamefaced prime minister had to announce, on 15 May, that coercion would be renewed without any accompanying remedial measure.[62] The *Freeman* announced on 16 May:

'Lord Spencer has triumphed.' Chamberlain and two other Radicals, Dilke and George Shaw Lefevre, resigned from the Cabinet.[63]

From the opening of Parliament on 19 February, it had been clear that the Government was skating on thin ice. The Tories put down a motion of censure on the mishandling of the Sudan situation following the fall of Khartoum. The division resulted in the Government's majority being reduced to fourteen when forty-two members of the Irish Party voted with the Tories. This led to rumours of a deal between the two; there were signs in the House of a Tory–Nationalist *rapprochement*.[64] Such manoeuvring, along with the contacts with Chamberlain, was part of Parnell's game of encouraging the British parties to bid for the Irish vote. Central to the Tory overtures was Lord Randolph Churchill, now seen as the rising star of Toryism who would bring his party into the new era of mass democracy. Parnell met him in mid-May and received a pledge from him that if he were in Government he would oppose the renewal of coercion. Parnell agreed that in that case he would have the Irish vote.[65] On 20 May, Churchill came out publicly against the renewal.[66]

Redmond's role in the House in these months was unspectacular but vital. As one of the party's whips, he had the job of ensuring that members were in their places for crucial votes in which there was a chance of defeating the Government. After a string of such votes, the end came when thirty-eight Irish members were mustered in the early hours of 9 June to vote against a budgetary measure to raise duty on spirits. The Government was defeated by 12 votes. According to the *Freeman* report, the Irish Party and the Tories were 'utterly carried away with the enthusiasm of victory'.[67] On 13 June, the queen accepted Gladstone's resignation. Lord Salisbury took office as prime minister shortly afterwards. Earl Spencer left Ireland, and it was announced that the earl of Carnarvon, a Tory peer with atypical Home Rule sympathies, would replace him as lord lieutenant. The new chief secretary, replacing Sir George Trevelyan, would be William Hart-Dyke. It was now certain that the general election would be held on the new registers in November.[68] Redmond told the Camden Town branch of the National League of Great Britain on 17 June of the 'sweet revenge' for the party in hurling from power the Government that had imprisoned 1,000 Irishmen without trial and judicially murdered innocent men. But their attitude to the Tories should be one of reserve:

> The Tories had been at any rate consistent in their demands for coercion, and for his part he must say that he preferred open and avowed enemies to false and treacherous friends . . . It was not at all to his mind clear that the Tories would fall back on the evil prejudices of the past.[69]

In fact, the new Tory regime got off to the best possible start. Abandoning coercion, it pushed through three reform measures in its first six weeks. On 14 August, when Parliament was prorogued, the royal assent was given to an expanded Land Purchase Act (the Ashbourne Act), a more generous Labourers' Act and the Educational Endowments Act, a measure that pleased the Catholic hierarchy by allotting funds worth £140,000 to benefit Catholic schools and colleges.[70] At Gorey on 23 August, Redmond praised the Land Purchase Act, which 'he had no hesitation in saying was considerably in advance of the original proposals of the Land League', and the Labourers' Act, which he regarded 'with far greater pride and favour than the Land Purchase Bill'.[71] As Lord Carnarvon and his wife steamed along the west coast of Ireland on holiday, some nationalists allowed themselves to dream that the gift of self-government from a Tory administration would soon follow.

IV

With the election imminent, the question of where he would stand became urgent for Redmond. Under the new Redistribution Act, boroughs such as New Ross and Wexford were to be abolished or 'merged' into their counties. In April, when the legislation was going through the House, Redmond had seen its implications for his own future, and feared a scramble for seats by the 'merged' members.[72] His ambition to carry on the Redmond tradition in the representation of Wexford now entailed winning one of the two county seats. A possible obstacle to this ambition, however, lay in the culture of Parnellism itself, which saw the placing of the choice of candidates in the hands of the leader and a few confidants as the best guarantee of a strong party. If necessary, local preferences would be overridden, as also might the preferences of members to stand for certain constituencies. In January, Parnell had called a second convention in Tipperary when the first mutinied and refused to accept the candidate nominated by him in consultation with Archbishop Croke; Parnell went to Thurles to preside, persuaded the previously selected candidate to withdraw and had his own man accepted. The Whig and Tory papers spoke of Parnell's 'dictatorship', a charge to be repeated many times over the coming years. The links binding a potential candidate to a particular constituency for family, historical or other reasons were no longer sacrosanct. The sole criterion was to be the extent to which, in Parnell's judgement, the attributes of a candidate matched the needs of the party. The high-profile 'lieutenants' were happy to allow Parnell to deploy them in this way in the 'difficult' Ulster constituencies. Healy had already left Wexford for Monaghan and would soon move to South Derry, while O'Brien would shortly leave his Mallow base for South Tyrone, and Sexton, another southerner, would stand for a Belfast division. William Redmond had also agreed to fight an Ulster seat, in North Fermanagh. For John, however, the ties of place and family tradition were in potential conflict with loyalty to Parnell and to the party's needs.

In early May, he told Father Furlong:

> Of course my highest delight would be, to be one of the members for the County, but I will hold myself unreservedly at the disposal of Parnell and go wherever I am sent. If however Small goes North I hope I will be allowed to remain in Wexford if the Club are satisfied with such an arrangement.[73]

J. F. Small, a northerner who was Healy's election agent in the Monaghan by-election in 1883, had been elected in the same year to Garret Byrne's Wexford county seat when the latter resigned. A speech made by Small at a demonstration at Taghmon, County Wexford, on 24 May gave Redmond the impression that he was saying farewell to the constituency.[74] Small's participation during the summer in a by-election campaign in his home county of Down must have strengthened this impression.[75] However, Small was present on the platform with Redmond in the north Wexford town of Gorey on 23 August, when the latter made a coded claim to the constituency seat: 'He could point to others of his blood who had given good service in the same cause (*cheers*). He thought he could now claim to have done his duty with "honesty and steadfastness"'.[76]

At the end of September he was made suddenly aware of opposition, probably the result of his inactivity, to his candidature within Wexford. He wrote urgently to Furlong that he had heard nothing since last speaking to Parnell, who had 'highly approved' of his standing for the Wexford seat, 'until this morning when I received a letter from Willy saying Cardiff and several others in Wexford had written to Parnell expressing dissatisfaction at my standing, and that "the O'Clery Party" were supporting me. Can you tell me the meaning of this?' He was in the dark as to the matter and could not go over to Ireland until his final law examinations had finished in late October. He was ready to 'drop out at a word from Parnell', but did think

> a point might be stretched in my favour in Wexford. It is no hardship on Small who may if he chooses accept a certain seat in his own town of Newry. It is no injury to the Party for there are plenty of strong men ready to fight the doubtful six seats in Ulster (Willy amongst them) . . . I would however sooner never have a seat than allow myself to be made a party to any intriguing or disunion.[77]

The next day he received a letter from Healy to say that Small had complained to him that they had 'made the arrangement behind his back without giving him notice'. Acknowledging the favour he owed Redmond from the last election, Healy added: 'Personally I am in a fix between you both, considering how you retired for me in '80'.[78] On 5 October, Redmond told Furlong that he was far from wishing to force himself on the county, but he presumed that if Small were called elsewhere and Parnell recommended him (Redmond) for the seat, the club and convention would not refuse to adopt him. If he thought they would, he would 'save the Convention the necessary trouble'. He wrote again a few days later to say that he wanted no unpleasantness and had suggested no further action until he, Small and Parnell had a meeting to settle the matter. He insisted, however, on his claim, saying that when he was in Dublin 'a meeting of some 15 of the leading men (informally)' had decided that he should stand for the Wexford seat.[79]

Two weeks later Redmond received some advice from 'a friend and a sincere well-wisher', Frances Sullivan, who had heard from several sources that there was 'great sourness' at his insisting on standing for Wexford instead of putting himself in Parnell's hands to go where he was sent:

> There is a general feeling that you are a good man for fighting a hard place and that you would be thrown away in a safe place and I heard that you are the only man of the active set who has insisted on choosing your seat . . . I know you so well that I feel pained at anyone finding fault with you and I have said you have been obliged to give up politics more or less till your examinations are over, then you would come over and help as much as any other . . . You have done noble work in dark days and I want you to be in the front when the wishes of the people are realised which must be very near.[80]

The County Wexford Independent Club met on 21 October and resolved to recommend the sitting county members Barry and Small to the selection convention for the two seats. This resolution was forwarded to Parnell, who replied that he had brought it before his colleagues, but had been advised that Small had accepted an invitation to stand for South Down. Support for Redmond from an anonymous source appeared in the Wexford *People* of that week. Published as a report of a meeting of a remote branch of the National League, the article extolled his virtues and implored Parnell 'not to deprive us of his labours, his experience, his eloquence and truthfulness in public and polemic matters'. It went on to disparage Small, suggesting that he would attend to his law business first and only afterwards 'to your duties'. The colourfully parochialist scribe went on to give Home Rule a whole new meaning:

> So give us a Wexfordman in the person of John Redmond, and let the Newry coroner go seek the suffrages of his Northern brethren, for he would not do here . . . No stranger, no foreigner, Home Rule, home manufacture, home production, the native born should be preferred before the alien, in politics.[81]

This evoked a hostile reply in the following issue which denounced 'the cowardly intriguers', and deplored seeing 'introduced into honest Irish politics, black designs and Russian and French diplomacy, that makes one blush for the manhood of such politicians'.[82]

Now in Dublin, with the examinations behind him, Redmond wrote to Furlong on 27 October to deny two charges, of intrigue and of threat, which the priest had informed him were being made against him. He had been in no communication, direct or indirect, with anyone in Wexford except Furlong. The charge of threat accused him of saying that he would abandon the party altogether unless Parnell nominated him for Wexford. This he denied ever having said:

> On the contrary I always told him what indeed he well knew, that I would be bound by his wishes, but from the first he was quite favourable to my going to Wexford . . . It is, however, quite true that to some of my colleagues I said something to the effect that if not adopted (Parnell having approved of my going) I would 'drop out'. This was an ill-considered expression but by no means in the nature of a threat. It was preceded and followed by expressions of my willingness to place myself in the hands of the Leader . . . Parnell says he will come to the Convention and Healy yesterday came to me and said if I wished he would also attend to support me.[83]

The matter took another ten days to settle. Healy wrote on 3 November, the day on which Small was finally selected for South Down at the Newry convention.[84] He had, he said, communicated with nobody in Wexford about Small's withdrawal or Redmond's desire to stand for the county, but felt sure that his candidature would be adopted by acclamation:

> I have been deeply pained by the rumours of discussion in the County and by the tone of a letter addressed to me on the subject to which I gave no reply. It would be a very poor reward indeed for your great services to the Irish cause if your name was not greeted with the [most] perfect unanimity by the Convention.[85]

The fulsome tone of this letter, and Healy's previous one of 1 October, contradict the account of the episode given by him in his memoirs. Redmond had joined the ten-man committee of the party, which met daily at Morrison's Hotel in Dublin to select candidates.[86] Healy recalled:

> In our electoral committee . . . I supported the retention of Small in his Wexford seat, and advocated that John Redmond (like William) should attack an Ulster constituency. This angered Redmond, who complained to me of unfriendship. I tried to soothe him by saying I was mindful chiefly of the Ulster situation, but he would not be pacified.[87]

If he did express such views to Redmond in the committee, he could hardly have been 'deeply pained' at their expression by others in Wexford.

A second theme in Healy's account pertains to the possible reasons why Small was induced to give up the Wexford seat, and raises the possibility that the secret of Parnell's affair with Katharine O'Shea may have played a part in the adoption of Redmond as candidate for Wexford. According to Healy, when Small was Healy's election agent during the 1883 Monaghan by-election, he had mistakenly opened a telegram addressed to Parnell, thinking it was a message *from* the latter. It read: 'The Captain is away. Please come. Don't fail – Kate.' Healy was angry with Small, but there was no remedy since the envelope had been torn up. Healy says that, years later, he heard that Small kept the telegram and passed it to Philip Callan, M.P. for Louth. This part of the story has been corroborated;[88] what follows is speculation on Healy's part: 'The Chief must have heard of this, for at the Dissolution in November 1885, he removed Small from Co. Wexford, and gave the seat to John Redmond.' At the next election, eight months later, Small was 'displaced' altogether.[89]

There are strong grounds for giving credence to this story. According to Parnell's biographer, F. S. L. Lyons, the possession by Callan of his secret may have been the reason for Parnell's decision to remove him from his constituency in 1885, first offering him an alternative seat further north, and, when that was refused, imposing his own candidate on Louth and conducting a personal campaign against Callan that ended his political career.[90] If indeed Parnell had heard about the telegram, there would be consistency in his treating Small in a similar manner to Callan. The possibility also offers the only real explanation why Parnell was willing to make an exception, in Redmond's case, to his rule of sending the most able members to the most difficult constituencies. The alternative, that Parnell felt some residual obligation to Redmond for the latter's standing aside for Healy in 1880, does not seem credible in a leader of Parnell's forcefulness, and given the scale of what was at stake in 1885. We are left with the strong likelihood that the fulfilment of Redmond's desire to represent his home county came about because of Parnell's need to neutralize those in possession of his secret. If, as is likely, Redmond knew nothing of the telegram, it is probable that he felt an enormous sense of obligation to Parnell. This in turn may have been a prime motivating factor in Redmond's loyalty to his leader five years later, when the latter's secret was at last exposed and his career faced destruction.

For the moment, however, it was only a question of how to present the *fait accompli* to the public. The unanimity called for by Healy was exactly what came about at the Wexford convention on 5 November. The *Freeman* reported that Redmond had been proposed by Father Furlong and that he and John Barry had been adopted 'without a note of division'. Regarding Small, it said that he had wished to stand again in Wexford, adding with no trace of irony, 'but these are days in which localism has been subordinate to Nationalism, and it is the distinguished characteristic of the Irish party that as Parliamentary representatives their influence and their strength is not limited by the boundaries of the particular seat for which they have been returned.' Parnell engaged in some interesting dissimulation:

> these two gentlemen are almost too good for so good a constituency (*cheers*) for you know in these days it is the best men who are selected for the most difficult – I will not say for the worst – constituencies. We cannot now any longer consider the county of Wexford as a difficult constituency. Mr. Small, the member for the county, has acted with great magnanimity, and has shown a considerable spirit of self-sacrifice.

Redmond ignored the contradictions implicit in this speech, replying simply that he was not ashamed to say that it had been his 'earnest desire and ambition' to represent the people of the county. Recording his deep obligation to Small, he reminded those assembled that five years previously he had 'acted a similar part . . . at the word of command of the same leader'. In a concession to any lingering criticism, and probably by prior agreement with Parnell, he added that he was still ready to go elsewhere to a more difficult constituency (while still representing Wexford) if commanded, and that he expected that he might be called on to do so.[91]

V

Aside from his preoccupation with his own seat, Redmond threw himself into party work from the time of his return to Ireland. The county conventions, which had begun in early October, were each attended by two or more M.P.s carrying written instructions to use any means necessary to ensure the selection of the candidate already chosen by the caucus in Morrison's Hotel.[92] Redmond spoke at the South Tyrone convention on 29 October and at Kildare and Limerick during the first week of November. In between he attended the annual convention of the Irish National League of Great Britain in Glasgow. The management of the votes of the Irish community in Britain, most of whom would be voting for the first time under the new franchise, was a critical part of the Parnellite strategy for the election. It was still too early to give definite voting advice, as both Gladstone and Lord Salisbury, the Tory leader, were making equivocal statements at this time which hinted at the concession of self-government in some form. On 1 November, the league passed a holding resolution, counselling voters 'to hold aloof from all British parties . . . but to await the advice of the executive of the National League and to stand by that advice when given'.[93]

Redmond's speech at Glasgow expressed the nervous optimism of one who found it difficult to believe that so much had changed in such a short time. He saw signs of hope, he said, so great that he sometimes feared that the prospect was too bright to last and that the evil destiny of Ireland might re-assert itself. The leading men of all parties were now discussing, not whether Home Rule should be granted, but what form it should take. For him, Home Rule was 'simply the restoration to Ireland of representative government'. But what if it led to separation? His answer echoed Parnell's speech at Wicklow in October when he said there could be no guarantees, but 'England would be just as powerful the day after such a Parliament was granted'. One thing was sure: Ireland could not be more disloyal than she was today.[94]

He spent the rest of November in Britain, with the exception of a flying visit to campaign in North Wexford, where he denounced the 'so-called "loyal classes"' for forcing a contest on the constituency by putting up a candidate, Viscount Stopford, to oppose him.[95] He spoke at meetings in Stockport, Bury and Bolton, but there was still no definite advice for Irish voters. However, Gladstone's refusal to set out specific Home Rule proposals in advance of the election, together with the fact that the Tory leaders had not closed the door on Irish hopes, finally prompted Parnell to authorize the publication of the famous 'Vote Tory Manifesto', released on 21 November. This urged the Irish in Great Britain to vote, except in a few individual cases where Liberal members were friends of the Irish cause, 'against the men who coerced Ireland, deluged Egypt with blood, menaced religious liberty in the school, freedom of speech in parliament, and promise to the country generally a repetition of the crimes and follies of the last administration'. There were seven signatures on this document, including those of Redmond, Healy, Sexton and T. P. O'Connor, though only the last of these was its author and there seems to have been little or no consultation as to its issue except between O'Connor and Parnell.[96]

In Liverpool on 22 November, Parnell preached the message of the manifesto.[97] The following day, Redmond's promise to stand in a second constituency was fulfilled when Parnell introduced him to the voters of Liverpool's Kirkdale division:

> Mr. Redmond is a gentleman of great ability, he has another seat in Ireland, and he has offered, if he be returned for the Kirkdale division, to leave his constituency in Wexford and to place himself at your service. I believe it is just possible to return Mr. Redmond . . . at all events we are going to have a good hard try.[98]

This announcement came late, less than a week before the Liverpool elections. Redmond must have known that he stood little chance of winning Kirkdale, but his token effort allowed him to redeem his pledge to stand in a 'difficult' constituency. Despite his campaigning on a 'Home Rule is good for the Empire' theme, he came last of three candidates in the election. The other Home Rulers standing in Liverpool fared better, T. P. O'Connor winning the seat in the heavily Irish Scotland division, while Captain O'Shea, standing as a Liberal and despite Parnell's furious efforts on his behalf, was narrowly defeated in the Exchange division.[99]

The ideal outcome of the general election from Parnell's point of view would have been a small Tory majority dependent on Irish Party support in the House of Commons. The 'Vote Tory Manifesto' fell far short of producing that. However, it gave a result nearly as good: a total of 335 seats for the Liberals and 249 for the Conservatives, with Parnell holding the balance with his 86 seats – 85 in Ireland and 1 in Liverpool – which could be used either to double the Liberals' majority or to wipe it out, as the situation might demand. Most gratifying for nationalists was the winning of a (bare) majority in the nine-county province of Ulster. Among the 17 of 33 Ulster seats won by prominent Parnellites were South Derry (Healy), South Tyrone (O'Brien), East Donegal (Arthur O'Connor), and the two in Fermanagh (William Redmond and Henry Campbell). The *Nation* boasted: 'Ulster is Ireland's at last. Nevermore will a West-British faction or a bitter Orange clique be able to rise in the House of Commons and deny that a united Ireland demands the restoration of a native parliament.'[100] In the other three provinces the Parnellites won every seat except the two belonging to Trinity College, Dublin. The *Freeman* exulted at 'the tide of Nationalist triumph sweeping over the country carrying before it Whiggery, Toryism, bogus "loyalty" and all the other rubbish that until now cumbered the field of Irish politics'.[101]

The Ulster seats won by Parnellites all had very substantial Protestant minorities. Although the elections there were not quite the 'sectarian head-counts' they would become in the twentieth century, partly due to the success of the Land League in attracting support from Protestant tenant-farmers, the polarization of Ulster along ethno-religious lines had been a fact of Irish political life for two centuries, and the nationalist victories excited great alarm in the Protestant community. The growing prosperity of north-east Ulster, dependent as it was on robust links with industrial England and Scotland, was a further factor strengthening the support of that community for the Union. The evolution of the pro-union and anti-nationalist identity among the various social strata of Presbyterian and Episcopalian populations in Ulster is a subject beyond the scope of this biography, but one thing can be stated with certainty about the Protestant community as a whole. If its consent to Home Rule was ever to be won, its fears for its position as a minority on the island had to be taken seriously by nationalists. The aftermath of the 1885 general election was a time for avoiding the temptations of triumphalism, forgetting past injustices and giving substance to the inclusive rhetoric that had been the legacy of Thomas Davis to the nationalist movement.

The reactions of the two leading nationalist newspapers quoted above were not encouraging in this regard. Neither were those of some prominent Home Rulers in the days following the election. Harsh things uttered during the campaign were predictable; what is more remarkable is the absence of attempts at binding up wounds in its aftermath. An example is the speech of J. J. Clancy, newly elected member for North County Dublin, at Finglas, in which he castigated his unionist opponents for having the temerity even to stand in the election. The contest, he said, had been forced on them 'wantonly and recklessly' by the 'Orange minority' who had no hope of success. Any candidate who could get only one-eighth of the vote should be 'compelled to pay a heavy fine for causing the excitement, the irritation, the trouble, the inconvenience and the pecuniary expense which his appearance in the field necessarily entails on the particular portion of the public whose favour he vainly seeks'.[102] Such intolerance in the mouth of a junior member might be dismissed were it not that similar sentiments had already been voiced by the most eminent Parnellite cleric in the country, Archbishop Croke, after the election in Tipperary, and even by Redmond in Wexford.[103] The Clancy speech is a particularly fine example of the struggle between atavism and inclusivism in the nationalist mind. In one breath he berates 'the utterly contemptible character of this miserable faction . . . the paltry West Britonism of the "loyal minority" . . . the garrison of Cromwellian landlords and their miserable parasites'. In the next he is 'boding no ill to the interests of the Protestant section of our fellow countrymen'.[104]

Healy, who had just fought and won two seats in Ulster, discounted loyalty as a factor in the voting of Ulster Protestants. They did not 'care a jackstraw' about England, but were told that if nationalists got the upper hand, the Protestant farmers would be expelled and the land given to the Catholics.[105] The *Daily Express* the following month did in fact report rumours of 'auctions' and 'lotteries' of Protestant farms taking place in Catholic chapels in Ulster, anticipating their confiscation under Home Rule. Although the *Freeman* called it 'a preposterous story' and the Presbyterian *Londonderry Standard* termed it 'a wicked joke',[106] it is easy to see how such stories gained currency when William Redmond, who had won a small number of votes from Protestant tenants opposed to an unpopular landlord, blundered in with talk of 'hundreds of years of tyranny, oppression and degradation'.[107] More would be needed to win Protestant votes than the formalism of Healy, as a Catholic representing a mixed northern constituency, in getting a Protestant representing a southern Catholic constituency to second his resolution hailing the recent nationalist victories in Ulster.[108]

The identification of the Irish Party with the political advancement of the Catholic community was of course unavoidable, but this did not in principle conflict with the wider objective of forging a nation from disparate elements. But a closer and more explicit identification with the powerful religious leaders of that community had been under way since 1884 with the party's agreement to sponsor Catholic demands in the field of education, in return for which the hierarchy pledged its support for the Home Rule programme. In October 1884 just before Parliament reassembled, Redmond attended a party meeting at which the alliance was effectively sealed: the party unanimously resolved to 'press the unsatisfied claims of Catholic Ireland in all branches of the Education Question'.[109] Parnell, alive to the power of the bishops to influence the party's electoral fortunes, replied to their letters: 'I need scarcely say how highly my colleagues and I value the mark of confidence in us which the resolutions of the hierarchy convey.'[110]

The gradual conversion of the Catholic hierarchy's attitude of distrust of the Protestant Parnell to one of cautious endorsement was accelerated the following year when Cardinal McCabe died and his place was taken as archbishop of Dublin by the more nationalist William J. Walsh. The nationalist press gave huge publicity to the proceedings surrounding his enthronement in September 1885. Even before he arrived from Rome, no fewer than sixteen M.P.s attended a large gathering of clergy and laity at the pro-cathedral to prepare an address of welcome.[111] The following week Redmond and Davitt were in a group that greeted Walsh on his arrival at Kingstown, while another half-dozen M.P.s waited at Westland Row station.[112] At a reception at Clonliffe College after the solemn enthronement on 7 September, the Redmond brothers were among fifteen members of the party present for the address.[113]

Archbishop Walsh's elevation had come at a crucial moment to help Parnell secure control over the county conventions which selected the candidates for the election. These conventions consisted of four delegates from each National League branch in each county and the M.P.s representing the Dublin caucus, the third element being any Catholic clergymen wishing to attend. Large numbers did so, to the extent that the attendance at the 32 conventions averaged about 150 laymen and 50 priests. The latter were instructed directly by Walsh, and acted as a disciplined block vote to help ensure the selection of those candidates approved by party headquarters.[114]

Despite his participation in the religious ceremonies, Redmond was the only prominent Catholic in the party to voice any awareness that a contradiction might be perceived between the trenchantly expressed demand for Home Rule and the growing identification of Church and party. Speaking at the fortnightly National League meeting in Dublin the day after Walsh's enthronement, he defended the presence of politicians at the recent religious events, and attempted to shift elsewhere the responsibility for investing those events with political significance:

> Of course that [the party] was a political organisation, but it was utterly impossible to divest this event to which he had alluded – the entry of Archbishop Walsh into his diocese – of all political significance; and if political significance attached to it, that fact was due not to them, but rather to their enemies, who tried through the dearest interest which many of them had – their religion – to strike a blow at their Nationality (*applause*).[115]

What Redmond most likely had in mind were the intrigues of British diplomacy at Rome which had succeeded in 1883 in eliciting a papal letter opposing the involvement of clergy, and of Archbishop Croke in particular, in promoting the 'Parnell testimonial', the national subscription fund set up that year when Parnell's perilous personal financial position became known.[116] Redmond's attempt to minimize the political significance of the events, by implying that Catholic nationalists would ideally prefer to keep their religion separate from their politics, was about as far as he could go in the current atmosphere of religious hubris, but it showed at least a degree of sensitivity to what Protestant opinion might be on the matter.

VI

As 1885 came to an end, the *Freeman* was cautiously quoting a report that Gladstone was preparing a scheme to give 'any measure of Home Rule compatible with the maintenance of Imperial interests'. It rejoiced: 'With bewildering suddenness the Home Rule "Never" has vanished for all time from British politics, and we are today in face of a general craving by England, as complete as it is surprising, for a settlement of the Irish National Question in accordance with Irish ideas.'[117] The 'Never' referred to was that uttered by Chamberlain in September at Warrington when he replied to one of Parnell's Home Rule pronouncements.[118] The paper was, however, mistaken: the Radical leader made an uncompromising speech before Christmas accusing the Tories of having purchased office by a 'discreditable surrender of principles'. Parnell's 'personal caprice' could turn them out at any time, but he would first like to see them 'drink to the dregs the cup of humiliation which they filled for themselves'. In an ominous allusion that showed the direction of his thinking, he reminded his Birmingham audience that 'to preserve the Union the Northern States of America poured out their blood and their treasure like water'.[119]

The new Parliament assembled in mid-January 1886. The Irish Party's honeymoon with the Tories melted like Irish winter snow when rumours circulated that the latter were contemplating the suppression of the National League and some form of coercion to deal with boycotting, coupled with a local government scheme.[120] Less than a week after the Queen's Speech, Lord Salisbury's administration was out of office, defeated by 79 votes, 74 of which came from Parnell's Home Rulers.[121] Gladstone returned as prime minister with the pro-Home Rule John Morley as chief secretary. For the next two months, the political world in both islands was gripped by a huge sense of expectancy. The twin topics of speculation were the scope of Gladstone's intentions and the question of how long Chamberlain and other dissidents would stay in the Cabinet when those intentions became known. Parnell had reached the pinnacle of his power and influence, having behind him 'virtually the whole of articulate Irish nationalism at home and abroad'.[122] Archbishop Walsh, in a letter to the prime minister on behalf of the hierarchy, had formally stated that only Home Rule could satisfy 'the legitimate aspirations of the Irish people'.[123] On the left, John Dillon, who had returned from Colorado in time to be elected in November, recognized Parnell as 'the accredited leader and ambassador of the Irish people'.[124]

In early February, there occurred the bizarre episode of the 'Galway mutiny'. If Parnell had been prepared to bend his own informal rule in the case of Redmond's seat, he now engaged in a much more flagrant violation of the party's new formal code, that is, the requirement that each prospective candidate pledge 'to sit, act and vote with the parliamentary party'. When a vacancy arose in Galway, he announced that Captain O'Shea, the narrow loser of the Liverpool seat in November, would be his candidate. His colleagues were dumbfounded; so enraged were Healy and Biggar at the imposition of a Whig who refused to take the party pledge that they went to Galway to campaign for Michael Lynch, the local candidate. The knowledge or suspicion that O'Shea's wife was Parnell's mistress was common currency among the leadership by this time, and this fuelled the bitterness of the affair. An open split was avoided only when Parnell arrived in Galway a few days later and turned the issue into one of his personal leadership, overawing an angry crowd by telling them, 'I have a parliament for Ireland in the hollow of my hand.' Opposition to O'Shea was withdrawn and the crisis passed, but the event was the first harbinger of the tensions in the party that would destroy Parnell five years later.[125]

Redmond, his brother and forty-eight other M.P.s signed a letter calling on the Galway electors to support Parnell.[126] There is evidence that Parnell helped Redmond avoid a potentially embarrassing confrontation with his Wexford constituents. He was due to attend a demonstration there on Sunday 7 February, but just before he crossed to Ireland on the Friday night, the same night O'Shea's candidacy was announced, he was asked urgently by Parnell to travel instead to Monaghan to assist in another by-election.[127] He would have been certain to face tough questioning in Wexford about the imposition of a non-pledge-bound candidate, especially since it was the Wexford Independent Club that had first suggested the pledge.

Back in the House, he was now one of four party whips. Here and at public meetings, his task was to enforce the new Parnellite policy of 'forbearance' while Gladstone wrestled in private with the intricacies of Irish self-government. At Scotstown, County Monaghan, he invited a by-election crowd to admire the spectacle of the aged statesman, who had done more for Ireland than any other Englishman, devoting in his seventy-seventh year the last hours of his life to settling the Irish question. Peace was threatened, he admitted, by the prospect of wholesale evictions arising from inability to pay rent caused by a slump of 40 to 50 per cent in agricultural prices. The Government would have to act to prevent this, but in the meantime he appealed to those menaced by eviction 'to bear and forbear, in the confidence which you must have that the moment is near at hand when you will be rooted as absolute owners of the soil you till today'.[128] At Brentford the same month, his theme was similar:

> no single word should pass from the lips of any member of the Irish party that might embarrass or retard Mr. Gladstone while preparing his plans for settling the Irish Question [or] . . . retard the chance of that great statesman ending a glorious career by a crowning act of justice to Ireland.[129]

The greatly enlarged party, ironically reversing previous tactics, now practised a self-imposed silence in the House, as the parliamentary correspondent of the *Freeman* wrote:

> It will be obvious that the necessity for speech in such a party is very small . . . The time of the House is the most precious possession next to its votes which belongs to the Government of the day, and for the moment it is the interest of Ireland to assist the Government of the day. Every unnecessary speech is a waste of Ministerial time and in that way is opposed to the Irish policy.[130]

But if the feelings of a British majority were in the mind of the nationalist press, no such consideration was afforded to the 'Protestant fellow-countrymen' in Ulster who had used the new democratic franchise to vote in unprecedented numbers for sixteen anti-Home Rule M.P.s. Parnell did appeal to northern nationalists, as the St Patrick's Day celebrations approached, to 'do nothing to excite the irritation of the Orange section of our countrymen',[131] but this did not restrain the writers of the popular press. Petty abuse and mockery seemed to be the order of the day, with words like 'stupid' and 'imbecilic' in frequent use when the *Freeman* referred to loyalists. As the long wait for Gladstone's Bill continued, the paper rejoiced at the unease and discomfiture of the Ulster Protestant M.P.s, and at their unpopularity in the House.[132]

Redmond wrote to Furlong as the party waited:

> I can't describe to you the anxiety of us all here about the situation. Every hour new rumours are floated and no one knows what to believe. One thing seems certain – Gladstone is going to propose a thoroughgoing scheme and will not give way an inch until he is beaten at the polls, if such a disaster should occur.[133]

On 26 March Gladstone finally presented his proposals to the Cabinet, causing the immediate resignations of Chamberlain and Trevelyan. On 8 April, he introduced the Government of Ireland Bill in the Commons. Between these dates, Parnell and Gladstone met in private for the first time, and Parnell immediately reported on that meeting to an inner circle of colleagues, which included Healy, Sexton, O'Brien and Dillon. The Bill provided for an Irish parliament with an Irish executive responsible to it for the government of domestic affairs. Matters over which control would be retained by the Westminster parliament included the crown, war and peace and foreign relations. There was disappointment among the Irish leaders at the Bill's financial provisions. The difficulty was twofold. One aspect concerned customs and excise, over which Parnell had hoped the Home Rule parliament would have control; the other was a disagreement on the size of the 'imperial contribution', the annual amount that Ireland should pay to the British Exchequer. Gladstone wanted this to be set at one-fifteenth of the total, while Parnell argued that it should be one-twentieth or less. According to Healy,

> as Parnell unfolded details, however, we grew disheartened at the niggardliness of Gladstone's offer as regards finance . . . 'Gentlemen,' answered Parnell, 'I share your regrets. I took up my hat today at one point to leave, and break off the negotiations with Gladstone. If any of you wish to resume them, and you think you can do better, take my place.' Towards midnight, chastened, we went out into the fog and frost.[134]

When the full party met immediately after the Bill's first reading, there was general dissatisfaction with the financial clauses, as well as with two other matters. These were the retention of London control over the RIC for a number of years, and the division of the parliament into two 'orders', of which the 'upper' one would be only partly elective and weighted in favour of property, each order having a veto on legislation passed by the other. The party meeting agreed that Parnell should give the Bill a cautious welcome, voicing objections on the above issues but stating that, if those provisions were amended in Committee, the Bill would be accepted by the party and the people.[135] By contrast, the initial press reaction verged on the ecstatic: the *Freeman*'s London correspondent greeted the 'matchless eloquence . . . marvellous power . . . stupendous scheme' of the prime minister.[136] This accorded better with the wave of euphoria that swept the country. The readership of O'Brien's *United Ireland,* which less than a year previously had been excoriating Gladstone's 'coercion' Government, rose from its average of 90,000 weekly to 125,000 in the week it published a colour portrait of the prime minister.[137] The details of the Bill seemed less important than the fact that the principle of Irish self-government had been conceded by a great British party and leader and embodied in legislative form.

Redmond had expressed fears, when he wrote to Furlong in March, about the possible consequences in Ireland of a House of Commons rejection of the Bill: 'The reaction in Ireland must inevitably be so terrible if things go wrong now . . . I am absolutely afraid to contemplate the possibility of failure now.'[138] A month later at a National League meeting in Dublin, following the favourable reception of the measure in every quarter, from extreme Irish-Americans to the Catholic bishops, he was

Figure 8. W.E. Gladstone moving the Second Reading of the Home Rule Bill, House of Commons, 10 May 1886 (Weekly News, 15 May 1886).
Courtesy of the National Library of Ireland.

Parnell is in the second row, right foreground. To his left are Tim Healy, T.P. O'Connor, John Redmond and Joseph Biggar.

more optimistic as he recalled the historical parallels on which those fears were based. He had in mind the events of 1795, when Lord Fitzwilliam, sent to Ireland in that year to reform Parliament and bring a final end to the anti-Catholic Penal Laws, was suddenly recalled, with disastrous consequences, against the advice of the great Irishman, Edmund Burke:

> He would not like to take the responsibility of saying that a reversal of the present policy would lead to bad results . . . he knew that the Irish people had changed since then. They had acquired powers within the constitution which they did not then possess. Education and enlightenment had spread amongst them . . . under no possible provocation could events occur at all similar to the events which marked the recall of Lord Fitzwilliam from Ireland in 1795.[139]

The debate on the second reading of the Bill, which began on 10 May, gave Redmond his chance to establish his reputation with the kind of set-piece oratory at which he excelled. He rose well to the occasion, delivering a powerfully eloquent and closely argued speech that dealt, one by one, with the objections to the Bill from the opponents of Home Rule. He began by accepting, in common with all the party's leading members in the debate, that the Bill provided a final settlement of the Irish question. He went on to make the case for self-government based on the two arguments of right and of expediency, citing 'the miserable record of 85 years of coercion, disaffection and ever-increasing poverty'. Dealing with the objection that the Bill would lead on to separation, he went into the details of the Canadian experience to show that Home Rule there had not damaged the Empire. On this point Lord Arthur Hill, the member for West Down, interrupted him to say that Ireland was now held by force. Redmond thanked him for the word, asking:

> But did the present Bill propose to take away that force, which, he presumed, meant the English Army and Navy and the Police? No; it still left these forces under Imperial control. But in addition to physical force, they would have working on the side of connection and against separation the moral force springing from justice conceded, which the English Government of Ireland had never yet had upon its side.

Turning to the chief objection summed up in the word 'Ulster', he relied on superficial numerical arguments (later singled out by the *Freeman* for special praise) to refute the idea that Ulster was a Protestant province. Alluding to the recent suggestion by Chamberlain, to a Birmingham Liberal audience on 21 April, that he would be willing to support the second reading if a separate assembly were conceded to Ulster, he demonstrated that such a parliament, based on the election results, must inevitably contain a majority of Catholics. He asked:

> Was Ulster anti-National? Out of the nine counties of Ulster, only one – namely Antrim – went solid against Home Rule, and if his hon. Friend the Member for Sligo (Mr. Sexton) had secured 38 more votes [in West Belfast], not even one solitary county in Ulster or in Ireland would have declared against Home Rule . . . In the face of these facts, it was the utmost folly to speak of Ulster as anti-National.[140]

The fragility of some of those nationalist majorities, and the fallibility of arguments that sought to make a distinct community disappear politically by resorting to electoral majorities would soon become apparent. Sexton had employed similar devices in a speech in January, winning acclaim from nationalists but only intransigent responses from Ulster unionists. As to the threats of unionist leaders to fight rather than submit to a Dublin parliament, Redmond dealt with them light-heartedly, apologizing for alluding to such a 'frivolous matter'. Given the imprecise and rather overblown nature of the threats – William Johnston, M.P. for Belfast South, had repeatedly stated that if Home Rule were passed he and his friends would 'line every ditch from Belfast to the Boyne with rifles'[141] – he found it easy to show on the basis of population statistics that loyalists would be swamped if they attempted to take over the province. In the end, he could only offer, in noble and ringing phrases, assurances that the fears of Protestants were groundless:

> He deeply regretted having to speak of Protestants and Catholics in connection with the matter at all. Theirs was not a sectarian but a national movement. If Home Rule were granted, the Protestant minority would have equal rights and liberties with their Catholic fellow-countrymen. The truth was the Catholics of Ireland entertained feelings of deep respect and affection for their Protestant fellow-countrymen. Protestants had led the national movements of Ireland for generations . . . there was not a single one of the Catholic leaders of the people today who would not reject with scorn and derision any settlement of the National Question which did not secure for the Protestants of Ireland full civil and religious liberty.

His party was willing to accept the first Order (upper House) proposed in this Bill, which many saw as contrary to democratic principles,

> because, although they knew the fears of their Protestant fellow-countrymen were unworthy and unfounded fears, at the same time they recognised those fears, and they desired by every means in their power to give guarantees to every section and every creed amongst their countrymen, that their sole object in this movement was to build up a united and a prosperous Irish nation.[142]

This speech, coming as it did relatively early in the debate, and some weeks before the leading Parnellite lieutenants had spoken, made a strong impact in the House. The *Freeman* correspondent wrote: 'Mr.

Redmond was heartily congratulated by all his colleagues on his most brilliant Parliamentary effort, and many English members came to me and spoke with delight of its impressiveness and of its temper.'[143] The only regret of Liberal members who heard it was that it did not have a full House, it being delivered during the dinner hour.[144] The Tory diarist Sir Richard Temple was not moved: of this speech and of Dillon's, also conciliatory, he remarked, 'What can we say of them now, when we remember their former speeches?'[145] The replies of the northern M.P.s pointed to a frosty reception in Ulster for assurances of the kind Redmond had given. Sir James Corry, member for Mid-Armagh,

> preferred to base his judgment upon experience and upon history rather than upon any promises or assurances whatever . . . whatever hon. Members below the gangway [the Home Rulers] might now say, they would not, in a short time, be in a position to keep their promises, even if they wished to do so, because they would be driven out by a force which they could not resist.

Speaking for the only industrialized part of the country, he was convinced that Home Rule would be a great blow to its commercial prosperity:

> He had always been proud to call himself an Irishman, and pleased to have the ships of his firm registered as sailing from the port of Belfast, so that the port might become known all over the world. One reason for his pride in doing this was the connection with Great Britain.

He asked the eighty-five nationalist members

> what any single one of them, or what all of them put together, had ever done to promote the commercial prosperity of Ireland? . . . Over and over again in that House they had been told that they were aliens, and had no right to call themselves Irishmen; and he was afraid that if an Irish Government were set up in Dublin the people of the North would be looked upon as aliens, and would be likely to have a rough time of it.

Corry did not fit the nationalist stereotype of the bigoted Orangeman, yet his words carried a veiled threat. He had never seen his way to join the Orange Order, he said, and his co-religionists, the Presbyterians of Ulster, had zealously supported Gladstone in the past. But 'if the worst came to the worst, they knew pretty well in Ulster how to take care of themselves'.[146]

During May, optimism in nationalist Ireland about the Bill's prospects began to evaporate as the obstacles came into view. On the very day of his great speech, Redmond wrote pessimistically to Furlong about the short-term outlook:

> I fear the Bill is doomed. Chamberlain wants to humiliate Ireland by making the proposed assembly in Dublin simply a vestry and to give Ulster one to itself. Better the Bill to be lost than for Gladstone to concede this. Time is on our side and I don't think we need fear a short delay – as success in the near future is assured.[147]

A later letter, on 24 May, revealed why he was sanguine regarding the longer term.

> I believe we will carry the Second Reading by a few votes . . . I won't believe in defeat until the figures are announced. One thing is certain: the masses of the people here are with Gladstone. On Saturday at Sunderland, I spoke to about 3,000 English working men and never witnessed greater enthusiasm. If the Bill be defeated the Seceders will pay dearly for it when the election comes.[148]

On 27 May, Gladstone announced the Cabinet's decision that if the Bill passed its second reading, they would not proceed with it but rather re-introduce it in the autumn session.[149] This was intended to stop the haemorrhage of Liberal support from the Government, but it angered Parnell and prompted him to consider whether the party should vote against the second reading, thus bringing down the Government.[150] Nationalist hopes were now fluctuating wildly from day to day. The veteran Radical John Bright, in whom Redmond had earlier placed his hopes, came out against the Bill. The effect of his letter on a sizeable group of Liberal waverers whom Chamberlain met on 31 May made it seem that all was lost.[151] The following day, when Sexton, in what the *Freeman* called 'the finest effort of his life', attacked Chamberlain's proposals, the pendulum seemed to have swung back.[152] Finally, on 7 June, despite a masterly last-minute speech by Parnell in which he again emphasized that he regarded the Bill as a final settlement (reversing previous declarations that no guarantees could be given on this matter), the second reading was defeated by 341 votes to 311. Such a majority was, in O'Brien's words, 'not one to intimidate a nation that has outlived Cromwells and King Williams by the score'.[153] A swing of 16 votes would have carried the opposite result. Nationalists consoled themselves with the thought that the principle of Home Rule was still alive. 'The Bill is lost, but Home Rule triumphs,' declared the *Freeman*.[154]

VII

The party certainly acted as if it did not see the defeat as anything more than a momentary pause in an unstoppable advance. Dillon, at the fortnightly National League meeting in Dublin, praised the Irish people for accepting the defeat with 'perfect calmness and dignity'.[155] Gladstone was more popular than ever among the newly enfranchised masses. Unionists (the collective term for Tories and Chamberlainite seceders) complained of 'Gladstoneolatry'.[156] With dissolution of Parliament and a fresh general election imminent, it seemed as if the game was still to play. The only blot was the serious sectarian rioting in Belfast and other Ulster towns, which began just after the Bill's defeat and continued throughout the summer. It was announced that Redmond would be in charge of electioneering in Lancashire, helped by his friend James Carew and the newly elected Patrick O'Brien. On 17 June he spoke at a large Home Rule rally at Birmingham, where he pulled out all the stops to appeal to British sentiment:

> The Irish did not seek to be separated. Their desire and their interest was to be connected with the empire, but they demanded in the name of men whose fathers had just as great a share in building up that empire as yours their rightful place, as partners and not as slaves. She asked the people of England to have confidence in the Irish race . . . in return they promised that in future the Imperial greatness of the country would have no more loyal defenders than the men who were only the enemies of England when England seemed the enemy of Irish freedom.[157]

The dissolution took place on 26 June. All the major political figures returned to electioneering at a frenetic pace. Gladstone himself was one of the first in the field, addressing huge meetings in Edinburgh and Glasgow. Parnell realized that the battle would be decided in the English constituencies, and campaigned accordingly, appearing in front of mainly English audiences for the first time. T. P. O'Connor was reported to be making three speeches nightly in London, using a team of fast horses to get around.[158] For Redmond, who was also very active in the London area after leaving Lancashire, and for his colleagues, the experience of first-hand contact with the 'English democracy' left a lasting impression. It helped to cement their adherence to the 'Union of Hearts', the alliance with the Gladstonian Liberals that would endure for the next four years and become controversial only in the circumstances of the party split. Dillon told a Dublin meeting that no impression had been more forcibly marked on his mind in the campaign than that the English masses were for Home Rule. When Redmond spoke at Enniskillen on 11 July, his words suggested that he had been quite carried away by the emotions of the campaign:

> Mr. Gladstone, by the conception of one bold gracious thought, by the performance of one patriotic act, has entirely changed the character of the struggle, and the hearts of the two peoples have been touched and completely changed . . . As if by magic, by that one act, the scales have fallen from the eyes of the English people, and their hearts have been opened up to the true facts of the case . . . a great wave of sympathy has passed over England (*cheers*) and I assert here that . . . from this day our struggle is not with the people of England, but with a certain class, and that the masses of the English people are on our side (*cheers*) . . . The scales have fallen from the eyes of

> Irishmen too. They see now that . . . the masses of the English people had not the slightest responsibility for all the misgovernment of the past . . . I have just come from England, where for the last fortnight I have been working in support of the Home Rule candidates, and I there witnessed scenes which deeply touched my heart. I witnessed enormous masses of Englishmen cheering for Home Rule and for Ireland as ardently as you cheer for it today (*loud cheers*).[159]

Irish nationalists may have been misled by the size of the audiences at these meetings, or carried away by the novelty of being cheered by English crowds. In the minds of the wider British population, the 'Vote Tory Manifesto' of eight months previously may have left an impression of cynicism. Whatever the cause, when the results of the election came in mid-July, it was obvious that Home Rule had been resoundingly defeated. The Tories had won 318 seats; the secessionist Liberals (now called Liberal Unionists) had 77 seats, while Gladstonian Liberals had only 193. The Irish Party was almost unchanged at 85 seats, giving an overall Unionist majority of 117. Healy and O'Brien had both lost their Ulster seats, and Sexton had won West Belfast, all by narrow margins.[160]

There was little outward sign, in the wake of such a comprehensive defeat, of the deflation that might have been expected among the Home Rulers. Their public utterances maintained a strong emphasis on the positive. Not only had they had time to prepare themselves for the possibility of defeat, given the attitude of the Chamberlainites in the spring, but they seemed genuinely mesmerized by the magnitude of what had been achieved. The ousting from power, within the space of seven months, first of one, then of the other, British party, followed by the conversion of the first to the principle of satisfying Ireland's national demand, seemed almost as much as could be absorbed for the moment. The introduction of a Home Rule Bill by the greatest statesman of the age, and the attendant transformation of British Liberal opinion, were successes that seemed almost to compensate for the fate of the Bill.

If we look for the motivating force that sustained men like Redmond, through the long decades of tedium and disappointment to come, in their commitment to the constitutional nationalist cause, it must be found in the fierce energies liberated during that thirteen-month period, which began with the overthrow of the Liberal Government in June 1885 and ended with the electoral defeat of Gladstone. To Redmond, not yet thirty, the rate of progress in six years must have seemed miraculous. The story of his remaining years is the history of an unceasing effort to return to that 'place' from where the promised land had been glimpsed and everything seemed possible.

6 The Land and the Law

> I assert here today that the government of Ireland by England is an impossibility, and I believe it to be our duty to keep it so.
>
> Redmond at Chicago Convention of Irish National League of America, 19 August 1886[1]

> The fight made there that day was one more effective blow against the accursed system of Irish landlordism (*cheers*). He condemned the act of the resident magistrate ordering a bayonet charge of police upon unarmed men . . . the events there that day had shown to the country how that monstrous engine the battering ram can be defeated.
>
> Redmond at eviction scene at New Ross, 16 August 1888[2]

I

Even as the Home Rule Bill was being considered by the House of Commons, the stage was being set for a different scene. A new crisis on the land was imminent, brought on by the general depression of agricultural prices that had begun in 1885. The slump tended to cancel the effect of the reductions in rent, of up to 20 per cent, which the land courts were awarding to tenants under the 1881 legislation. There were widespread reports of inability to pay rents. Evictions rose from 698 in the first quarter to 1,309 in the second quarter of 1886, and were still rising by the autumn.[3] While the Bill was in Parliament, the lid had been kept firmly on land agitation by National League local branches, instructed from the centre. With its defeat and the prospect of a disturbed winter in the country, the party did not need to look far for an alternative arena of action. However, another matter required Parnell's immediate attention, one that would entail a second trip to America for Redmond. In the wake of the rejection of Home Rule, he was alert to the danger of the National League organization in the US being taken over by open advocates of the dynamite policy. The delegates of Clan na Gael were likely to be the most numerous and most vocal element at the Irish National League of America Convention, due to take place in Chicago on 18–19 August 1886.

The Clan faction ruled by Alexander Sullivan's Triangle (the other faction was that of Devoy) had already promoted terrorist bombings in

England. The monies collected in Patrick Ford's Emergency Fund appeal, during the visit of the Redmond brothers to America in early 1884, were not long in being put to use. In February and March that year, a bomb had exploded at Victoria Station and 'infernal machines' had been discovered at three other stations.[4] At the end of May, three large explosions rocked London, including one at Scotland Yard, causing no injuries.[5] The climax of the campaign came the following January when bombs in Westminster Hall, the Tower of London and the House of Commons caused massive damage, but again miraculously no injuries.[6] At the same time Ford continued to detonate his weekly verbal fireworks against the futility of constitutional methods. With Gladstone's conversion to Home Rule, his stance had moderated somewhat.[7] However, with the election reverse of 1886 being seen by many Irish-Americans as a fresh insult to the Irish race, the *Irish World* wrote of the English people hardening their hearts, and urged the Irish Party to abandon conciliation and return to obstruction. This advice was publicly rejected by Davitt, who, although he retained close ties of friendship with Sullivan, was unpopular with Clan members for his renunciation of violence.[8]

Parnell was anxious lest the capture of the league by the extremists might face him with the choice of breaking altogether with the American organization or seeing critical damage done to the Liberal alliance and the Home Rule cause in Britain. His own appearance at Chicago to counter the threat would raise the stakes too high, ending, as it might, in his own resignation as leader. He asked William O'Brien and Sexton to attend the convention, but the latter declined, and Redmond agreed to take his place. John Deasy M.P. was the third member of the delegation. Davitt was already making his way, independently, to the convention. As bloody rioting raged nightly in the streets of Belfast in the early weeks of August, with loyalist crowds confronting and even firing at the police, the delegates took their leave from Queenstown. 'Mr. Parnell's slightest word is to me an order,' explained O'Brien. Redmond told reporters that they were taking the message to their brethren

> that while we are willing to meet a policy of conciliation and justice with good will and the hand of friendship, we are just as determined . . . to meet repression with resistance (*cheers*) and to take care, come weal or woe, that the Irish cause is not put back from the position to which we have advanced it.[9]

Arriving in New York a week later, they were, as described in O'Brien's characteristic style, 'boarded and captured by the dynamiters, and, it may with substantial truth be said, never quitted their custody until we steamed out of New York harbour a fortnight afterwards'.[10]

Having reached Chicago on the evening before the convention, after an overnight train journey in unbearable heat, they learned that the Triangle had nominated a public advocate of the bombing policy for the presidency of the league. There followed an intensive late-night grapple with the Clan leaders in the hotel, in which the delegates sought to impress on Sullivan and Ford that the judgement as to the methods to be used in the struggle must be left to the representatives of the Irish people at home. To the Americans' argument that constitutionalism had achieved nothing except a blow in the teeth, O'Brien and Redmond countered that the conversion of the Liberal Party to Home Rule, backed by millions of British votes, had transformed the situation utterly, and that they were no longer fighting a single 'England', but the weaker, ultimately, of two Englands, that over which the forces of reform had always prevailed in the past. To throw all this away with a policy of outrage that would alienate their best friends in Britain would be suicidal lunacy. At the same time, they made clear that if the Tories were about to implement coercion, although they had no power to fight England, 'we had a thousand ways of shaming and tormenting her, and at any peril of our own liberties and lives, the government of Ireland by force could and would be made impossible'. That kind of talk seemed to sway Ford, but the domineering Sullivan was more difficult to convince, driven as he was by personal animus against Parnell.[11]

Afterwards Redmond and O'Brien retired to the latter's room to consider how to proceed. It was, for Redmond, his first intimate contact with the underworld of the secret societies. In O'Brien's recollection,

> it would have been for most men a daunting one. He found himself groping darkly amidst intricacies and pitfalls where the clash between at least three transparently honest Irish organisations, open or clandestine, was rendered still more unintelligible by cross-currents of American politics of the least ideal order. All he did quite clearly see was that the existence of the Irish movement was at stake, but that was enough to make him an ally of unflinching fidelity throughout the midnight battle with 'the Triangle', as well as an orator of unfailing charm in the easier hours of the next day's triumph.[12]

It was dawn when Davitt, who had stayed up to continue the caucusing with the Americans, came to their door to tell them that the candidacy of the dynamite advocate had been dropped, and the nominee for president was now the respectable John Fitzgerald, the Nebraska 'Railway King'.

After that, the convention itself was relatively plain sailing. O'Brien was everywhere, indefatigably lobbying, giving interviews and extolling the virtues of Parnell and Gladstone from the platform.[13] The delegates voted confidence in Parnell's policy and gratitude to Gladstone and to 'the English, Scotch, and Welsh democracy' for their support for 'the greatest, noblest living English statesman'. Redmond's speech was a bravura display, firmly rooted in nationalist tradition, yet drawing on his new understanding of the Irish–British relationship. Asking the convention the twin questions, 'Are we worthy of your confidence, and have we a right to claim your continued support?', he dwelt on the assertion that the principle embodied in the Irish movement was that which had been the soul of every such movement for seven centuries: 'the principle of rebellion against the rule of strangers'. But, he continued,

> Let no man desecrate that principle by giving it the ignoble name of hatred of England. Race hatred is at best an unreasoning passion. I, for one, believe in the brotherhood of nations, and bitter as the memory is of past wrongs and present injustice inflicted upon our people by our alien rulers, I assert the principle underlying our movement is not the principle of revenge for the past but of justice for the future.

He referred to the Home Rule settlement, now 'temporarily defeated', as offering 'a future of freedom and amity between the two nations' and 'a blessed oblivion of the past':

> Last April Ireland was ready to forget and forgive. She was ready to sacrifice many things for peace, as long as the one essential principle for which she struggled was conceded. She was willing, on the day when the portals of her ancient senate-house were re-opened, to shake hands with her hereditary foe, and to proclaim peace between the democracies of two nations whom the Almighty placed side by side to be friends, but who had been kept apart by the avarice, the passions, and the injustice of a few.

As to their programme for the immediate future, their duty was clear. Though they could be 'trusty friends' if given liberty, they must show that 'as slaves we can be formidable foes'. In words that would be used against him for years to come, he added, 'I assert here today that the government of Ireland by England is an impossibility, and I believe it to be our duty to keep it so.' The national movement was in the hands of a man 'who can be bold as well as cautious'. The present prime minister had recently prescribed twenty years' coercion as a cure for Irish discontents. He had no doubt that the Government would ultimately resort to stern measures, because 'to the concession of justice and liberty there is no alternative but coercion'. But the Irish-Americans were to be in no doubt that in return for unswerving adherence to principle and to a policy of fight,

> we, and no others, are entitled to decide for ourselves upon Irish soil and upon our own responsibility what our policy for the future is to be. This is the condition upon which you have given your support to us in the past, and it is the condition upon which alone we can accept your support for the future.[14]

The *Freeman* correspondent reported that Redmond's speech was 'universally pronounced one of the most polished and powerful pieces of oratory ever delivered to an Irish-American audience . . . and produced a most excellent impression'.[15]

The confidence with which Redmond could demand autonomy of judgement for the Irish Party, even in the wake of its recent defeat, signified the attainment of a new phase in the evolution of constitutional nationalism. Hitherto, the followers of the parliamentary road had had to adopt a somewhat defensive posture when presenting their case to nationalists. In the light of the failure of O'Connell's mass movement in the 1840s, the treachery of Sadleir and Keogh in the 1850s and the ineffectiveness of Butt, constitutionalists had much to live down.[16] These failures left them with a negative argument only – that violent methods, however nobly conceived, had not worked either. Further, whatever grounds had existed in 1798 for belief in military parity between peasant pikemen and eighteenth-century infantry and cavalry, there were none whatever for holding on to such beliefs when the experience of the 1848 revolutions and the Paris Commune had proved that non-professional forces could not prevail in the open against a modern army. Now, however, constitutionalists had positive arguments on their side. By observing a quasi-military discipline as parliamentarians, by following a code of incorruptibility in refusing to take favours from the political establishment and by maintaining their independence from both British parties, the Parnellites had achieved something that no militarists had ever done: they had brought around one of those great parties, the party of progress, and its prestigious leader to embrace their cause. Henceforth, for men like Redmond, there need be no apologetic looking over the shoulder at the Fenians.

Redmond's attitude to political violence was consistent throughout his career. On the one hand, he would always maintain, inside and outside the House of Commons, that the Irish nation had a sovereign right to use physical force to win and defend its freedom. On the other, any scenario in which such a situation might materialize was to him a construct of fantasy, at least as long as the nationalist population remained unarmed. As already mentioned, there was enough in the folk memory of '98 in his own county to urge extreme caution in contemplating a rebellion by an unarmed people. But though advances in military technology had made a repetition impossible, the insurrections of the past could and should be respected and praised. Redmond looked at these, as did most nationalists, through the prism of the nineteenth-century romantic cult of battlefield honour, courage and self-sacrifice. The other type of violence, that of the dynamiters, or that which went on in the actual Ireland of his day, the violence of the Moonlighters who assassinated landlords on lonely country roads, fired into the houses of tenants who had taken farms of those evicted, or occasionally shot and killed policemen, fell into the category of crime, was the action of 'desperate men', and was to be severely condemned, even if it resulted from great provocation. The possibility that Moonlighter-type acts would one day be harnessed to political objectives, as in the 'guerrilla days' of the 1920s, was probably beyond his powers of imagining.

II

On 14 September, Parnell introduced his Bill to deal with the agricultural crisis. It proposed a three-pronged approach: to enable leaseholders to apply for judicial revision of rents, to have all judicial rents more than one year old revalued on the basis of current prices, and to suspend all ejectments on the payment of three-quarters of the original rent.[17] It failed to pass its second reading, the Liberal Unionists suspecting it was part of a plot to bring Gladstone back to power.[18] Chief Secretary Sir Michael Hicks-Beach ominously hinted at a return to coercion, and Dillon challenged the Government to do its worst.[19]

On Monday 18 October the papers carried reports of a National League demonstration at Woodford, County Galway, near the estate of Lord Clanricarde, at which the speakers were Dillon, O'Brien and three other M.P.s. Clanricarde and his tenants were locked in conflict over arrears as well as the current rents, and evictions had already taken place, with more pending. Dillon proposed a new tactic: the tenants should offer a reduced rent payment, which, if refused by the landlord, should be lodged with a trusted person who would use it to give support to those evicted for non-payment of the full rent. Tenants on every estate should adopt this tactic, acting as a body and refusing to make any payment until the reduction was accepted for all.[20] The following weekend O'Brien published in *United Ireland* an article by Tim Harrington, secretary of the league, entitled 'A Plan of Campaign', setting out the same advice in more detail, with special emphasis on the novel aspect of the common defence fund. The article foresaw the need for boycotting: 'That the farms unjustly evicted will be left severely alone, and everyone who aids the victims shunned, is scarcely necessary to say.'[21] The second phase of the land war had received its blueprint and its title.

To its initiators, it was an emergency response to the alarming reports they were receiving from many parts of the country forecasting a return to bloody agrarian violence, which could only seriously damage the Irish Party's alliance with the Liberals. Organizing the resistance in a quasi-legal framework by effectively putting Parnell's rejected Bill into force seemed to O'Brien the only alternative to disaster.[22] In the eyes of Tories and their landlord supporters, however, the Plan of Campaign seemed like a revival of the No Rent Manifesto at the behest of the Chicago convention.

British readers who followed Irish affairs could read of the Woodford *démarche* in the mass-circulation *Pall Mall Gazette,* whose editor, W. T. Stead, was present at the meeting. Over the next four years, the name of Clanricarde, along with those of a dozen or so other estates, such as Massarene (County Louth), Coolgreaney (County Wexford), Ponsonby and Kingston (County Cork), O'Callaghan/Bodyke and Vandeleur (County Clare), deFreyne (County Roscommon) and Smith-Barry

(County Tipperary), would become household words on both sides of the water. They would be the scenes of mass meetings and their attempted suppression, actual or attempted evictions and tenant resistance, massive police and military deployment and arrests of M.P.s and sympathizers, Irish and British. Weekend public meetings in the last two months of 1886 saw the adoption of the Plan of Campaign throughout the country. Parnell stayed aloof and would make no public comment on it for eighteen months. Its effect on the Liberal alliance worried him greatly, Morley having told him in December that the effect on English opinion was 'wholly bad; it offends almost more even than outrages'.[23] O'Brien later gave an account of a strange meeting he had with Parnell in the freezing mist of a December morning at the back of Greenwich Observatory, when he tried to reassure him about the Plan, and agreed that it should be limited to the eight estates where it was already in operation.[24]

Redmond was one of the first Parnellites to embrace the Plan. Speaking at the central branch of the league on 9 November, he hailed its enthusiastic reception by the people and the fact that it had first emanated from them rather than from the leaders. His speech is interesting for the divergent emphases of his own and Dillon's contributions. His concern at this stage was to calm the fears of English sympathizers by emphasizing the reasonableness and legality of the demands of the tenants. In this spirit he interpreted recent official actions as practical concessions of the demands in Parnell's Bill. General Sir Redvers Buller, who had been sent to Kerry to impose order in a county notorious for agrarian outrage, had refused to allow police assistance at evictions where it was clear that the tenants could not pay the rent; Judge Curran at Kerry County Court granted rent reductions and struck out arrears; another judge refused to grant an eviction unless satisfied the tenant was solvent.[25] To Redmond these actions, combined with the reductions already given by large numbers of landlords, were a practical vindication of the Plan. Dillon, on the other hand, warned the tenants to beware of judges granting rent reductions: they did this in order to divide and conquer, setting the tenants against each other: 'He would advise the tenants when they are processed to keep away from the court, no matter what terms the county court judge offered, because those terms were offered by the enemy. [Their attitude should be] "Fear the Greeks, even when bearing gifts."'[26] The words of the two men marked out the difference of political temperaments that would characterize their relationship throughout the decades to come: the one sanguine (to use one of his favourite self-descriptions), confident that concessions could only strengthen the cause; the other suspicious of concessions, fearful of their sapping effect, unsure that a victory was worth anything until final victory was won.

The difference extended to their respective concepts of what the Plan was about. For both men, it was first of all a tool to win rent reductions and avert mass evictions. Both also saw it as a means of keeping the party close to the people. But Dillon, for whom the agrarian and political struggles were viscerally interlinked, also looked on the Plan as a means of taking the fight to the landlord class in the hope of weakening one of the buttresses of unionism in Ireland. He told a meeting in Kildare in May 1888 in a speech devoted entirely to the agrarian question, 'This struggle is the same struggle which was fought for generations by our forefathers and which has been handed down to us as a sacred heritage.'[27] Redmond's conception of the Plan's political dimension was concerned less with its destructive effects on the landlord class than with the dividends it might yield in forcing English opinion to choose between coercion and the granting of self-government. The campaign he envisaged was one in which the tenants would act up to, but not beyond, the boundaries of the law, and respond to the forces of the state with passive forms of resistance, evoking in turn the sympathy of public opinion across the water. The two concepts of the Plan would be aired publicly, and bitterly, as one of the issues in dispute during the Parnell split in 1891.[28]

With the first of many prosecutions of Dillon begun in late November, the Government's intentions were becoming clear to Redmond. On 5 December at Glenbrian, in his own constituency, he showed an almost indecent impatience for the deployment of coercion, telling the meeting that the slide towards it had already begun (this was four months before the introduction of the Crimes Act by Arthur Balfour). The people's victory, he said, was that, without a single outrage, they had forced the Government to give up reliance on the ordinary law, thus fulfilling Gladstone's prophecy that it must be either Home Rule or coercion for Ireland. If they kept Ireland free from crime next year, the Government would fall and Gladstone's chance would come again. They could settle the land question themselves that winter if they adopted the Plan of Campaign on every estate.[29] Meanwhile, William was implementing the Plan in Ulster, joking at Enniskillen about having become a land agent, since he now took care of the money of local landlords.[30] All over the country tenants were paying their rents to trusted receivers, usually nominees of the league.

On 16 December, Dillon and O'Brien were arrested in the act of receiving rents, and three days later the Government proclaimed the Plan of Campaign as an 'unlawful and criminal conspiracy'.[31] As reports circulated at Westminster in the last days of the year about the Government's readiness to bring in a Crimes Act in the next session, the two leaders, with William Redmond and three other M.P.s, appeared in court in Dublin on charges arising out of the Woodford meeting. Dillon was bound over to be of good behaviour for twelve months and released on bail.[32] Despite this, at Arklow on 2 January 1887 he was as provocative as ever, telling the crowd that if they could not carry on a legal, open policy by the light of day, 'we will do it by moonlight too'.[33]

Redmond and Dillon shared a platform at a demonstration at Enniscorthy on 16 January at which the former declared himself glad that the Plan was being taken up by the Wexford tenants; the whole county was behind Dillon and they were all 'criminal conspirators' if he was. Dillon recalled the scenes of eighty-eight years previously, when the bodies of the dead were piled high and 'the blood of your fathers ran like water down the streets'.[34]

Redmond worked hard to promote the plan in early 1887. In a level-headed speech at Claremorris, County Mayo, on 19 January, he urged the adoption of the Plan on the surrounding estates, contrasting the distressing scenes at the recent evictions at Glenbeigh, County Kerry, an area where the Plan was not adopted, with the victory that their neighbours had just won on the nearby estate of Lord Dillon, where the landlord had been induced to grant a 20 per cent abatement of rent, and where peace now reigned and lives and property were protected.[35] At the central branch meeting on 1 February, he gave his view that, with hardly a day passing without news of a Plan victory, the Plan had been 'the salvation of the people of Ireland'; the absence of crime during the winter had been remarkable, when compared to the 1879–81 period.[36]

Dillon continued to force the pace of events in north Wexford, and Redmond cannot have been too happy at another 'invasion' of his constituency on 20 February by Dillon, who defied an official ban to hold a meeting at Coolgreaney. Significantly, the tenants on the Brooke estate, labouring under rents that were 30 per cent above the valuation and the average on neighbouring estates, had called on Dillon, rather than their own M.P., for assistance. Redmond was on his way north to Louth when he heard of the proclamation, and had to make a sudden turnabout to be with his constituents. He and Dillon evaded police roadblocks to hold a series of smaller meetings in and around nearby Castletown, thus helping the people to 'trample on the Government's proclamation'.[37] Shortly afterwards, the trial of Dillon, O'Brien and the three other M.P.s collapsed when the jury disagreed.

On 3 March, in the House of Commons, Redmond protested that the Government's action in seeking to prevent meetings was illegal; the country was beginning, he said, to realize the inevitable result of 'firm and resolute Unionist government'. Anyone who had read its history could predict

> that the course of action on which the Government are entering can have only one ending – namely, the suppression of free speech, and the imprisonment of Members of this House and other popular leaders . . . Hon. Gentlemen who have never read a line of Irish history may laugh; but so sure as the sun will rise tomorrow, they will laugh very differently this day six months if the policy of the Government is carried out.[38]

The sooner they brought in their Coercion Bill, the sooner would come the crisis, which would open the eyes of the English people to the failure of the Government to rule Ireland. Then room would be made for a government

> which prefers to base its rule upon conciliation, and upon the golden link of affection, instead of depending upon bayonets and bullets ('*Oh, oh!*'). I repeat, upon the golden link of affection. You Gentlemen opposite are having your innings. Try your bayonets and bullets, and we will see what the result shall be.[39]

Two days later Arthur Balfour replaced Hicks-Beach as chief secretary, and the following week the Plan of Campaign saw its first fatality when a boy was shot dead by police during a riot at a meeting in Youghal, County Cork of tenants of the Ponsonby estate.[40] The new chief secretary was immediately christened 'bloody Balfour' by nationalists.[41] The police came under fire from Moonlighters in two ambushes in County Kerry within the next month, and two constables were shot and injured.[42]

Balfour introduced his Criminal Law Amendment (Ireland) Bill – popularly known as the Crimes Bill or Coercion Bill – on 24 March. Redmond was one of the first to speak on its first reading. Addressing himself to those members who did not support coercion on principle, but regarded it as 'a hateful and desperate expedient', he asked them to question whether an exceptional state of agrarian violence existed, and whether the ordinary law had broken down. Using the official returns for the three months ending the previous December, he showed that serious agrarian crime was almost non-existent: there was not a single case of murder, manslaughter, attempted murder or any other serious crime in that period. Nine counties were totally free of even trivial agrarian offences. This line of argument had been anticipated by the Liberal Unionist speaker just before him, Viscount Lymington, who contended that the power of the National League was now such that intimidation was rampant in the country, making outrages no longer necessary. But Redmond was able to quote from the statements of judges at the recent assizes who had congratulated their grand juries on the peaceful condition of their counties. In a fine peroration, Redmond summed up the contradictions in the Unionist policy:

> But yesterday you enfranchised the mass of the Irish people, and today you declare that, so far from being capable citizens, they are not worthy of exercising the common rights and privileges of the Constitution. You call on Irishmen to be loyal to England, and you persist in keeping English law what it has been for centuries in Ireland – an engine of national humiliation and oppression.

Two categories of men would rejoice at the introduction of this Bill: the Ulster Tories, who had opposed every effort made by Parliament to remedy Irish grievances – 'are they safe guides for Englishmen on this Irish Question?' – and the extreme faction in Irish politics, those who hated the idea of reconciliation between the two nations, and whose secret organizations derived new vitality from coercion. It was because he hoped for a settlement of the great question 'upon peaceful and honourable lines, and within the limits of the Constitution' that he deplored the introduction of the Bill.[43] Sir Richard Temple, who had previously listened to Dillon speak 'treason with passionate vehemence' for nearly three hours, commented on Redmond's effort:

> By this time it was past midnight . . . I had never heard him make a set speech before. This one was really well delivered, quite different from the florid, turgid style too common on the Irish benches. It was fluent without being verbose, eloquent without being bombastic, earnest without being over-strained. In delivery it was the best speech – indeed, one of the few really well-delivered speeches – I have heard from the Irish benches.[44]

The Crimes Bill passed the Commons on 8 July after a total of forty-five nights of debate, and only after the Government had forced it through Committee using the closure.[45] The resistance put up by Dillon, Healy, Sexton, T. P. O'Connor and some of the Gladstonians ensured a lengthy passage. It also ensured that the House was frequently kept up late: there were twenty-four sittings until after 2 a.m., and many others that lasted as late as 6 a.m., in the period between April and September.[46] This was not obstruction in the old sense, but simply the process of scrutinizing every clause minutely. It was work that suited the individual genius of Healy in Committee; in O'Brien's words, 'he would swoop down like a Captain of guerrillas from his mountains',[47] and pursue with anger and sarcasm, and terrier-like persistence, the smallest points of the Bill.

Redmond took no part in this cut and thrust; he did, however, speak from one of the twenty-two platforms at a massive rally in Hyde Park in April, at which tens of thousands heard him, Sexton and other Home Rule M.P.s, together with Davitt and many English Radical M.P.s, denounce the Bill.[48] At New Ross on 8 May, where he and Leamy prevented an attack upon the police, he derided it as 'a weak, halting and half-hearted measure, compared with what would be necessary if oppression had a chance of defeating the Irish people'.[49]

III

As evictions went ahead on Plan of Campaign estates in the spring and summer of 1887, each month seemed to put a different locality in the spotlight. In March it was Youghal; in June, Bodyke; in July, Coolgreaney. The novel element that distinguished these evictions from those of Land League days was the publicity that attended them. Responding to the interest in Britain in Irish affairs awakened by the 'Union of Hearts', British newspapers sent reporters to cover the events, while British Radicals and their friends came to see for themselves. The reaction of many was shock at the practical implications of the enforcement of the law in relation to landlords' rights.

The Bodyke and Coolgreaney affairs brought Redmond into conflict with Davitt for the first time. The latter at this time was a kind of roving radical-without-portfolio. An honorary secretary of the National League but not an M.P., soured by his failure to win support for his land nationalization ideas, he was also out of sympathy with the Plan of Campaign, since it seemed to him that the rent reductions demanded set a falsely high standard of what the tenants should pay.[50] The prestige of his name ensured that his criticisms of the movement were indulged by the nationalist press. As the evictions were proceeding at Bodyke, Harrington, speaking at the central branch meeting chaired by Redmond on 7 June, counselled the people to retain their 'noble attitude' of self-control. He recalled Parnell's advice, on the night of the introduction of the Coercion Bill in Parliament, that they should submit to any oppression rather than retaliate, and should remember Gladstone's words that the Liberals had been able to come so far with the Irish Party because the Irish people had stayed within the law. Even where cruel evictions were occurring, there was no comparison with the position of six or ten years previously, since the tenants now made common cause and had an estate fund for support when evicted, with a pledge of further financial support from the league when that was exhausted. Redmond earnestly endorsed this advice; he considered that

> anything in the shape of active resistance at the present moment would be fraught with danger and disaster to the people themselves, and . . . to the path of that cause, which was not the cause of the tenants alone, but the cause of all classes of people in the community.[51]

When Davitt the following day in fiery language called for a vigorous response from the tenants, the *Freeman* excused his 'emotional words', though injudicious, as 'the natural expression of a heart full to overflowing'.[52]

In the week beginning 11 July, Redmond stayed in the Coolgreaney area while evictions on the Brooke estate went ahead in the presence of English and American visitors. Elaborating on his advice of the previous month ('let them not be guilty of the madness and the folly either of tolerating one single act of crime or outrage or the equal folly of throwing themselves unarmed on the bayonets and muskets of their enemies'), he told the people that they should not strike an Emergency man unless struck first, but if they saw one lay a hand on a woman, it was their duty to strike him down. The fire that had burned the roof of one tenant's house could, he said, be seen all over England; he had received a telegram from W. T. Stead, who had published the story in the *Pall Mall Gazette*, telling him that it had caused a sensation.[53]

A few days later, Davitt arrived, unexpected, at the scene and told the people that he would not mince words: they had shown very little courage or determination, and the blame lay with those who advocated passive resistance.[54] That weekend, at a rally in nearby Arklow to support the tenantry, Dillon remonstrated mildly with his old colleague for his criticism of the advice from central office. But the most heated words of reply came from Redmond. Although he deeply respected Davitt's record, he said, he had read his speech with regret:

> Mr. Davitt yesterday said that if he were in the position of one of these tenants he would resist within the house to the death. Well, that is an advice I frankly tell you I am not prepared to give to the tenants (*bravo*) . . . that advice ought only to be followed if the position of the tenants was desperate . . . These men who have been cast out of their homes have other homes that will be provided for them; they have thousands of friends at home and abroad and they will not be allowed to suffer.

To Davitt's call that the tenants should learn from those who had resisted at Bodyke, Redmond replied that the display of courage had been as great as at Bodyke (a reference to one house at which boiling gruel had been thrown at Emergency men armed with crowbars). Did Davitt want an unarmed crowd to attack soldiers and police? 'I would be long sorry to give that advice, and would not dream of giving it if I was not prepared myself to take the lead (*cheers*).'[55] The row was defused when Davitt backed down, saying that he had not meant to suggest that resistance should be to the death. The following week, Redmond, in company with his brother and William Scawen Blunt, an English sympathizer who was also a Catholic and a landlord, was in court for the inevitable trial of the tenants charged with assault at the evictions, while Davitt was back in Dublin.[56]

Meanwhile, the Union of Hearts was bearing fruit in new and unprecedented ways. In a display of solidarity, two Radical M.P.s, C. A. V. Coneybeare and C. E. Schwann, with no fewer than eighty other members of the Liberal Party, arrived in Dublin and enrolled as members of the National League.[57] A spate of by-election victories for Gladstonian Liberals in the summer of 1887 initiated a trend that would endure for the next three years, and encouraged the hope among Home Rulers that the Tory repression was but the dark before the dawn of the final triumph of their cause.[58]

From July onwards, the Government was on a collision course with the Irish Party, and in particular with Dillon and O'Brien, the backbone of the Plan of Campaign. O'Brien was the first prominent nationalist to be prosecuted under the Crimes Act, for speeches delivered at Mitchelstown to tenants of the Kingston estate in August. The scene was now set for a tumultuous autumn and winter. O'Brien and John Mandeville, chairman of the local Board of Guardians and the leader of the tenants, were ordered to stand trial at Mitchelstown on 9 September. They refused to appear, but a crowd gathered in the town when the warrants were issued for their arrest, an impromptu public meeting took place, police batons were drawn against blackthorns and in the ensuing riot, the police panicked, retreated indoors and fired into the crowd, killing three and wounding others.[59] The event was immortalized as the 'Mitchelstown massacre', and Gladstone would taunt the Tories for years to come with the cry 'Remember Mitchelstown!'[60] At the inquests the following month, which received huge publicity, verdicts of wilful murder were returned against the police. A similar verdict was returned the same day following the shooting of an elderly tenant by Emergency men near Coolgreaney.[61]

O'Brien was arrested and sentenced to three months' imprisonment on 24 September.[62] At the Liberal Party Conference at Nottingham in mid-October, Gladstone asked, 'Where now is the middle course?' between conciliation and coercion.[63] That weekend, the police batoned another meeting at Woodford held under the auspices of the English Home Rule Union, and Blunt was arrested, charged under the Crimes Act and later given a two-month sentence.[64]

By 1 November, Mandeville had joined O'Brien in jail on a two-month sentence.[65] The story of O'Brien's battle with the Tullamore prison governor for the right not to wear the prison uniform, and of the farcical smuggling in of a suit of Blarney tweed, has been vividly told by Joseph V. O'Brien.[66] A demonstration of 50,000 in Trafalgar Square demanded his release, while liberal-minded Britons were also disturbed at the news of the jailing of Edward Walsh, editor of the *Wexford People* and friend of Redmond's, for publishing a report of a speech of the latter and a report of a suppressed meeting, offences deemed to be incitement under the coercion legislation. Balfour had pledged that coercion would not impinge on the freedom of the press.[67] The plight of Mandeville was constantly in the news, his state of health causing concern due to his subjection to a bread-and-water diet and his being forcibly stripped and beaten by warders for refusing to wear prison clothes.[68] Although he was released before Christmas, his death from pneumonia six months later, at the age of thirty-nine, was generally held to be a result of his rough treatment, and exacerbated nationalist bitterness.[69]

In the midst of the escalating tension, Redmond embarked on speaking tours in the west of England in late September and in Lincolnshire in early October, in which he aroused the sympathy and indignation of his audiences with his accounts of the summer evictions and the Mitchelstown events. When he returned to his London home, domestic concerns took priority: Johanna gave birth to a girl, who was named after her mother, on 26 October at their Clapham residence. The couple were now the parents of three children, their son William Archer having been born on 16 October the previous year. That Redmond's income had been placed under considerable strain by the expenses of two general elections seems evident from the fact that in July 1886 he sold part of the interest in his inherited Wexford properties for £500 (equivalent to £35,000 in 2005).[70] The inadequacy of his income throughout the 1880s was revealed at the Special Commission, at which he was named as one of only five M.P.s in receipt of subsidies from Parnell, which averaged £100 each annually.[71] On 9 November 1887, his decade-long law studies finally bore fruit when he was called to the bar.[72] This immediately opened up a new field of activity for him: following in the footsteps of Healy, he would act as defence counsel in a string of prosecutions of nationalists over the next three years.[73]

With the *Daily Express* calling for the full suppression of the National League and an end to the 'sham fight' that the repression so far constituted in its eyes, Balfour assured an audience at Birmingham on 4 November that the new legislation would soon make the Plan of Campaign a thing of the past. Gladstone at the same time was registering his 'panic and grief and dismay' at the unfolding events in Ireland.[74] Before the year ended, three more M.P.s were in jail, with further prosecutions pending.[75] Redmond sounded a defiant response to the Government at the central branch meeting on 6 December. It was idle and childish, he claimed, to suppose that coercion would stop the work of the league. Didn't the Government know that the Plan was now at work far more widely in the country than twelve months previously? The people now understood it as they had not at the start. As for prosecutions, he had seen men going into court proud to be given sentences for doing something for the national cause.[76] He returned to this theme again at the central branch meeting on 31 January 1888 and analysed the working of the coercion legislation over six months. Although more than 400 men had been prosecuted, over half of them for illegal assembly or incitement, the total effect on the movement was, he asserted, very small; the people were not intimidated. He added that the newspapers would be doing a great service to the fight against it if they reported in detail the statements of magistrates, which in many cases showed outrageous ignorance of, or contempt for, the law.[77]

Redmond's warning contained more than a little bravado. The Plan was in reality being squeezed by the new laws, which made it difficult for suppressed league branches to meet, and thus reduced the flow of funds to central branch. The financial support of the evicted on those estates, such as Clanricarde, which showed no prospect of an early settlement, therefore became a critical issue. This tended to cancel out the effect of victories such as that at Mitchelstown, where the Kingston tenants won their demand. Lack of tenant solidarity was reflected in the relatively small number of farms remaining derelict following evictions. The number of such farms was recorded as 1,405 on 1 January 1889 and reached a peak of only 2,088 in 1891. Given the much higher number of evictions, it was obvious that the intimidatory powers of the league were not as effective as was often supposed. The bulk of the population seemed, in fact, more intimidated by the stringent measures of Balfour. Troops of Hussars were being used to augment police strength in breaking up public meetings, and acts such as selling *United Ireland*, cheering for William O'Brien or even grimacing at the police were being prosecuted in front of specially appointed 'removable' magistrates. Reported cases of boycotting fell from 4,835 on 31 July 1887 to 2,469 at the end of the year, while serious agrarian crime remained very low outside of Kerry and Clare.[78]

The pressure of coercion on the operation of the Plan also had a political effect: it tended to personalize the struggle as a duel between Balfour on one side and O'Brien and Dillon on the other. The enormous publicity generated by O'Brien's many spells of imprisonment and his colourful exploits in evading arrest or, as in one case, disappearing from a courtroom following conviction, ensured him a warm place in the affections of ordinary nationalists. His release on 20 January 1888 was celebrated at a 'magnificent' demonstration in Dublin.[79] As Redmond remarked at the central branch meeting that greeted T. D. Sullivan on his release from prison, 'the only result of Balfour's attempt to degrade the political prisoners had been to make him [Sullivan] and his colleagues who suffered with him in prison the most popular public men in Ireland'.[80]

A new political leadership, making its decisions independently of the party leader, was clearly in the process of formation. By contrast, Parnell was becoming a remote figure in the popular mind. He made no public appearances at all in Ireland in the four years after 1886, his only communication with the nationalist electorate being through his occasional 'pronouncements' published in the nationalist press. His prestige, however, stood high with that electorate, and it was chiefly the actions of his enemies, and one action in particular, which ensured that it remained so through these years. *The Times* chose the date of the vote on the second reading of the Crimes Act, 18 April 1887, to publish a facsimile of what purported to be a letter from Parnell to an anonymous recipient. The letter, dated 15 May 1882, explained that his denunciation of the Phoenix Park murders was forced on him for policy reasons, and that although Cavendish's death was regrettable, Burke had got no more than his just deserts. Parnell that night denounced the letter in the House as 'a villainous and bare-faced forgery'. Legal action was risky for Parnell, and he sought instead a select committee to investigate the charge. This was refused, and it was the summer of the following year before the Government agreed to set up a commission of inquiry, consisting of a panel of judges. In the meantime, *The Times* had gone on to make further charges against the Irish Party as a whole in a series of articles entitled 'Parnellism and Crime', and other incriminating letters allegedly written by Parnell had come to light; all of these were included in the commission's terms of reference. The Special Commission began its sittings on 17 September 1888, and sat on more than 120 days over the next 15 months. Much of its proceedings were dull in the extreme, as counsel for the *The Times* ploughed unpromising ground in efforts to substantiate its charges of treason and complicity in serious crime against sixty-four members of the party, including Redmond. But regarding the pivotal allegations against Parnell, the outcome was decisive. The sensational events of February 1889, when the impoverished ex-Fenian journalist Richard Pigott broke down under cross-examination by Parnell's counsel, Sir Charles Russell, confessed later to having forged the letters and Parnell's signature, then escaped from London and shot himself in a Madrid hotel, generated a huge wave of sympathy for Parnell on both sides of the water, vindicated his reputation in the eyes of the Liberals and cemented the 'Union of Hearts'.[81]

These events did not change Parnell's status in Ireland, which increasingly was that of a deity to be worshipped from afar. At Westminster, his frequent absences, partly due to the bouts of serious illness which often laid him low, and partly to his sojourns at Eltham with Katharine O'Shea, became a source of demoralization in the party. Absenteeism was contagious, and more than thirty members, including Redmond, were missing from a division in May 1888 in which the Government had a majority of only eight. Important opportunities to humble or even defeat the Government were being lost, as the *Freeman* commented after a similar occurrence in June.[82] These influences would slowly erode the substance of Parnell's hold on the minds of many nationalists, leaving it a brittle carapace that collapsed easily when the split came in late 1890.

As far as the Plan was concerned, the biggest worry for O'Brien and Dillon was Parnell's continuing aloofness from it. Parnell told a *Freeman* interviewer in November 1887 that it would not become him either to criticize or to approve its management, since he had not been consulted about its initiation and he had been unable since then to take any active part in it.[83] His anxiously awaited speech to the Liberal Eighty Club on 8 May 1888 was a shattering disappointment to the two Plan leaders. Although he gave credit to the Plan for having saved thousands from eviction and for having, in fact, pacified the country, he saw in it the political defect that it offered the Tories an excuse for coercion. He hoped to replace it with a new scheme that would 'correspond in every respect with the method of organisation known as Trade Unionism in England'. In the meantime, he urged that the Plan not be expanded, and that the party and the league be kept clear of it. His advice to Irishmen was to rely upon 'the great Liberal party of England'.[84] Clearly, Parnell's mind was on the 'flowing tide' of Home Rule by-election victories, of which there were five more in the first half of 1888, and which seemed to promise the early demise of the Unionist coalition and another chance for Gladstone.[85] Nationalists could now contemplate the ironic spectacle of a Liberal ex-home secretary, Lord Harcourt, who had presided over the pre-1885 coercion, being more supportive of the Plan than was the 'Leader of the Irish race'.[86]

O'Brien's and Dillon's sense of betrayal was so strong that the former immediately penned an editorial for *United Ireland*, surrendering, under protest, to Parnell's judgement. The article was stopped by Dillon and Harrington before it could wreck the movement.[87] Redmond made no public comment on Parnell's speech. We do not know whether he felt about it as his colleagues did, or, if he did, whether he voiced his misgivings privately. Not having invested as much of himself in the Plan, and seeing it as secondary to the political struggle, he is unlikely to have shared their anger.

Redmond did, however, defend the Plan from the second body blow it received in these months. This was the rescript issued by Pope Leo XIII, which condemned the Plan and boycotting and forbade the clergy to take part in either. The document was the outcome of the long tour of Ireland the pope's personal envoy, Monsignor Persico, had made since his arrival the previous July, which was itself the product, partly of diplomatic lobbying in Rome by an English mission led by the duke of Norfolk, and partly of anti-Plan of Campaign complaints sent there by two Irish bishops.[88] The rescript was issued on 20 April 1888, and was met with a calmly disingenuous reception from those Catholic clergymen involved with the Plan. One curate's response, reported in the *Freeman*, was typical of many: 'some little news from Rome . . . don't fret in the slightest . . . don't mind it, remember when their great archbishop would return (*loud and prolonged cheering*) that he would make all their consciences pretty easy . . .[89] Redmond's first reaction was to join with other M.P.s in convening a meeting of the party's Catholic members. Dillon came out in advance of this meeting with the first public criticism of the rescript, saying at Drogheda that Irish Catholics would not accept the bidding of Rome in political matters.[90] Redmond and thirty-nine other M.P.s adopted and signed a series of resolutions on 17 May, one of which stated that while they unreservedly acknowledged the spiritual jurisdiction of the Holy See, they could 'recognise no right in the Holy See' to interfere with the Irish people in the management of their political affairs.[91]

At a mass meeting in the Phoenix Park on 20 May, Redmond made his own position clear. Admitting that 'absolute submission' was required of Catholics in spiritual matters, he contended nonetheless that if the Catholics of Ireland abated their independence of thought and action in political matters they would be 'the veriest slaves and unfit for any measure of freedom'. The central and strongest idea of their movement, he declared, was that Ireland should not be ruled by any power outside Ireland – whether that be a parliament, a king or a number of cardinals, 'or the sovereign Pontiff himself'. Were such interference from Rome to be tolerated, Home Rule would be a 'sham' and an Irish parliament would be 'a mockery, a delusion and a danger': 'If they submitted now to Roman dictates in carrying on their battle for freedom, when they did obtain that freedom the Court of Rome would claim, and rightly claim, an equal right to interfere and to be admitted to the counsels of their Parliament.' They owed it to their Protestant fellow-countrymen to make it clear that Home Rule did not mean Rome Rule. Going a step further, perhaps, than most of his colleagues would have done, he said that if he had to choose between submission to the Parliament of Westminster and submission to 'the decrees of conclaves of cardinals at Rome', he would prefer to be a slave to a Parliament, 'which at any rate deliberates in the light of day' and was in some degree subject to the influence of public opinion, than to a conclave of cardinals 'sitting in secret and utterly ignorant of the simplest facts of the situation in Ireland'.[92]

The debate did not stop there, since not all Catholics found it so easy to draw a clear boundary between the political and spiritual spheres when the morality of actions was in question. One such, the M.P. Sir Joseph McKenna, dissented from his colleagues, saying that it was fallacious to put politics and religion in separate domains, since questions of morality belonged to both; otherwise how could the Phoenix Park murders, for example, be denounced as immoral?[93] One member of the hierarchy, Bishop Edward O'Dwyer of Limerick, declared it to be the duty, under pain of sin, of every Catholic, priest and layman, to obey the rescript. Dillon, in what was the start of a long public controversy between the two men, answered that the bishop spoke only for himself and 'a small minority of the Catholic Church in Ireland, who are on the side of the oppressor against the oppressed, of the rich man against the poor, of the landlord against the tenant'.[94] Redmond sought to address the question of the Plan's morality. At Ashford on 21 May, he outlined the kind of boycotting that was acceptable to him:

> nothing more than the defensive weapon which I believe to be absolutely necessary to save the people of today and of tomorrow . . . such a boycotting as that I believe to be not only an effective weapon whose use is absolutely justified in morals but on the ground of expediency also.[95]

At Wexford the following Sunday, he returned to the papal letter:

> Is condemnation to be reserved only for those who by oppressions of that kind may have been led into excesses, whilst nothing is said of the provocations [of the evictors and exterminators] which have been the real cause of whatever excesses have occurred? . . . No, we believe not unconsciously the Holy See has been misled by the calumny of our enemies in Rome and elsewhere into an act which the whole world today interprets as an interference with our political freedom.[96]

IV

Before the papal rescript and Parnell's Eighty Club speech diverted attention, the situation on the Plan estates and in the neighbouring towns in early 1888 was as turbulent as ever. March saw the dispersal of a meeting at Youghal with such violence that another Mitchelstown was only narrowly averted.[97] At Ennis on 8 April sabres were drawn by the cavalry and pressmen were injured in a police baton charge. At Kilrush the same day, when the police were ordered to disperse the crowd as he was starting to speak, Redmond told the resident magistrate of the 'profound responsibility' he felt to avoid bloodshed, and advised the people to disperse peacefully. During May, both O'Brien and Dillon received jail sentences, of three and six months respectively, but the former succeeded in getting his sentence reviewed and remained free, while the latter was lodged in prison in late June.[98]

In mid-June Parnell hosted a dinner in London for the imprisoned M.P.s, of whom there were now up to a dozen. Redmond may have decided it was time to have his name added to the roll of honour of those who had served time for their part in the struggle. If so, there were many opportunities available to court prosecution. He made a militant speech in Dungloe in County Donegal on 19 July, which came close to incitement, urging the people not to co-operate with a police inquiry but to 'stamp it out with your feet'.[99] Three days later he was in his own constituency, and addressed a meeting convened at Scarawalsh to protest against a recent eviction. He wished them to make it plain 'to every man in the county' that the evicted farm was to remain idle, and that no farmer in the district should have anything to do with working it. If Captain Thomas Walker (the landlord) was determined to fight, he would find out that in doing so he would 'have arrayed against him the united hostility of the whole people amongst whom he lives and amongst whom he hunts'; he would find that 'his injustice to this man will confront him wherever he goes'.[100] This threat of the boycott weapon was enough to have Redmond and Edward Walsh, who also spoke, charged with using intimidation towards Walker. Soon afterwards William was also prosecuted for his part in inciting tenants to resist the sheriff at an exceptionally violent eviction scene on 16 August at Coolroe in south County Wexford. Although the police charged with fixed bayonets, they were repulsed, with several injured, and the battering ram rendered ineffective. The crown alleged that William's words – 'Bravo, Wexfordmen, I am proud of you . . . give it to them' – 'admitted but of one construction'.[101]

William received a three-month sentence at Wexford on 14 September, and twelve days later Redmond was given five weeks, both sentences without hard labour. No appeal was made in either case, Redmond telling the court that he had no desire 'to shirk or to shrink from' the consequences of his words. He would bear his sentence with a cheerful mind and an easy conscience, certain that under the ordinary law no jury in Ireland or Great Britain would have convicted him of intimidation. At the courthouse he was accompanied by Johanna, Father Furlong and other friends and met by a brass band.[102] Inside, he was met by William, who exclaimed on seeing him with his close-cropped hair and convict clothes, 'Good heavens, what a ruffian you look!'[103] A few days into his sentence he was transferred to Tullamore jail, the scene of O'Brien's and Mandeville's stand against the wearing of prison clothes. The authorities there seemed to wish to avoid a repetition of that episode, and when he refused prison clothes he was not asked again to wear them. Having been put on bread and water in Wexford for refusing to exercise with ordinary prisoners, he was treated better in Tullamore, being allowed to exercise alone. He asked for books and was given just one – *The Imitation of Christ* – which, he told a friend, he knew from cover to cover by the end of his sentence. On his release, 'none the worse but lighter by a stone', according to the *Freeman*, he had no complaints, telling the crowd of supporters and fellow-M.P.s who met him on his arrival in Dublin that he had been treated 'with the utmost respect'.[104]

A few weeks of rest followed. He wrote to Furlong on 15 November:

> I have been taking the world very easy since my release – doing little more than eating and sleeping. I am all right again now – my only reminder of Tullamore is a pain in my back which I get every afternoon and which no doubt is the effect of the plank bed. I never had a night in a bed during my five weeks.[105]

His prison term was, in truth, at the lenient end of the range of sentences to which Irish Party members were subjected: 22 of them served terms ranging from 14 days to 6 months between July 1887 and May 1889. Compared with the total of 11 months served by William O'Brien before 1890, the 7 months of the Monaghan M.P. Patrick O'Brien, or the 6 months with hard labour given to the Kerry newspaper editor Edward Harrington for reporting meetings of suppressed league branches – a sentence branded 'savage, vindictive and atrocious' by Morley[106] – Redmond's term was a mere taste of prison life. Nevertheless, it would serve him as a useful piece of political capital in the stormy years ahead, enabling him to hold his own when such exploits became weapons of warfare between pro- and anti-Parnellites after the split.

With regard to his involvement in the Plan of Campaign, his imprisonment was a watershed. Unlike William O'Brien, he courted no further prosecution after his release and did not try to speak at proclaimed meetings or agitate publicly again at sites of evictions. Instead, he continued his work for the Plan in two different but related areas. First, he greatly expanded his legal work, defending dozens of tenants prosecuted for resisting eviction, conspiracy to discourage payment of rents or other offences under the Crimes Act. Occasionally he appeared for the next of kin at inquests at which prison treatment was suspected as a cause of death; in one case, he represented the relatives of a boy shot dead by the police.[107]

From the few pieces of correspondence to survive from those years, an exchange in November 1889 between him and M. J. Horgan, the Cork solicitor who had handled the trial of ninety-seven tenants of the Ponsonby estate, suggests that he charged only modestly for his services, and again points to his tendency to shun the spotlight. Telling Horgan that he would not dream, under the circumstances, of taking anything like the full fees, he returned £116 of his payment, retaining only 30 guineas. Healy had been paid £211 for his part in the same trials and had won praise in the nationalist press for his pledge to donate £100 to the Tenants' Defence Association. Horgan returned Redmond's refund cheque 'in order that you may act similarly if so disposed. I don't see why your generosity should not be known as well as Mr. Healy's.' Redmond did not take up the suggestion; instead he felt 'bound' to return the cheque a second time, saying that he did not consider it an act of generosity and 'my only doubt is whether I am justified in taking even the fees which I have retained'. The episode would not have become public had it not been for the later controversies of the Parnell split. In July 1891, the *Freeman* published a letter from the Parnellite Horgan in which he recounted the story and contrasted the respective attitudes of Healy and Redmond to their fees (which were, of course, paid from Plan of Campaign funds), claiming that Healy's donation was actually the fee paid to him for an earlier case.[108]

Redmond's second area of activity lay in the increasing role he played in the management of the affairs of the Plan estates. This came about through the enforced absences of O'Brien, who spent over half of 1889 in jail, and of Dillon, who left the country on a fundraising tour of Australia and New Zealand in March and did not return for thirteen months. Dillon's departure was a desperate response to the crisis in the funding of the Plan, which was exacerbated by the fall in the number of league branches from 1,031 to 975 between April 1888 and April 1889 as a result of coercion. O'Brien and Dillon reckoned in late 1888 that a minimum of £25,000 would be needed to keep going for another year, but a fresh wave of evictions in January made the situation more acute. Despite Parnell's continuing aloofness, Dillon had no option but to appeal to him for an immediate release of £5,000, and the assurance of a further £5,000 by 1 March from the funds held in Paris, to avert the imminent collapse of the regular maintenance payments to the evicted.[109]

Redmond was helped by Tim Harrington and T. P.Gill, another Parnellite M.P., in keeping the campaign going. Much of the work involved protracted efforts to reach settlements by arbitration.[110] In the summer of 1889, the Plan faced its greatest challenge yet when a landlord syndicate was set up, with the secret encouragement of Balfour, to come to the rescue of a small number of key estates, the first of these being the Ponsonby property in Cork. The syndicate was now run by a committee headed by A. H. Smith-Barry, the landlord of extensive estates in Cork and Tipperary. As Redmond explained to the meeting of the central branch in June, the landlord and tenants had agreed a deal on the Ponsonby estate until Smith-Barry appeared on the scene as an 'interloper and a stranger'; his syndicate of wealthy Englishmen had paid more for the estate than the landlord had been willing to take from the tenants, had rejected all settlement proposals and had now begun eviction proceedings.[111]

By way of retaliation, O'Brien, while briefly out of prison that summer, persuaded Parnell to found the Tenants' Defence Association as a protection against the landlord combination, and to announce this on 10 July as an 'official act of the whole Irish party'.[112] Although publicly Redmond might try to play up the significance of Parnell's move – 'Mr. Parnell when he strikes at all strikes hard and quickly,' he weakly told a meeting of tenants in Killarney – behind the scenes, the leader's commitment to the initiative was half-hearted; long wrangles took place between him and O'Brien, which revived the crisis of May 1888 in their relations. Parnell would neither call off the Plan nor throw himself fully behind it, and promised only to send Sexton as his representative to the convention that would launch the new association.[113] By the time that took place, on 28 October in Thurles, events had been set in train that would take the Plan of Campaign to its final and climactic phase.

A deputation of Smith-Barry's own Cork and Tipperary tenantry went to him in early July to ask him not to co-operate with the 'syndicate of stranger landlords' who had prevented a settlement on the Ponsonby estate. When he refused, the tenants met with O'Brien and resolved to withhold rent from Smith-Barry and to levy themselves at 10 per cent to aid the Ponsonby tenants. On 4 September, the properties of the Tipperary tenants of Smith-Barry were declared confiscated and put up for sale. A deputation consisting of two of their leaders crossed to London to seek the advice of Parnell. The latter would not meet them, but conveyed to them, through J. L. Carew, M.P., the message that he would not advise any tenants to surrender their holdings. The letter from Carew conveying Parnell's stance was brought back by the deputation, which gave it to Redmond. The latter arrived late at a huge and enthusiastic meeting in Tipperary the following Sunday and showed the letter to Gill and the other parliamentarians present. With their agreement, Redmond duly communicated Parnell's view to the meeting and explained that any decision to allow their holdings to be sold (rather than come to terms with Smith-Barry) must be taken on their own responsibility. The effect of this news, Redmond recalled two years later, was that 'their ardour was somewhat dampened. Nevertheless, with a courage and heroism which would never be forgotten in the annals of Ireland . . . notwithstanding the advice of Mr. Parnell, they determined to allow their farms to go.'[114] At the meeting

Redmond lauded the tenants' action, 'which had sent a thrill of pride and of gratitude throughout the whole Irish race' and had exhibited 'the very highest type of heroism – self-sacrifice and chivalry'.[115] By October, a full-scale boycott of Smith-Barry, as well as of certain tenants who had bought back their holdings at the sheriff's sale, was in progress. The following month the wealthy town tenants, preparing for eviction, moved their stock and furniture to a new site outside the town, where they began the building of new wooden houses and shops. Thus was 'New Tipperary' born.[116]

O'Brien emerged from prison at Christmas full of enthusiasm for the new development. However, although it quickly caught his and the public's imagination, it became a very dubious asset to the Plan as a whole. Not only did it divert attention away from the struggle on other estates, but, more importantly, it proved a huge financial drain on the fundraising initiatives of 1889. In April 1890, Dillon returned from the Antipodes having raised about £40,000, while the Tenants' Defence Fund, set up at the October convention (Redmond was one of its four honorary secretaries), yielded £61,000 by the end of May. Yet the building of New Tipperary swallowed up between £40,000 and £50,000, leaving the almost 1,000 evicted families around the country in the same precarious position as before. The prospect of fresh evictions, once a key weapon against the Government in the battle for the sympathy of British public opinion, was now a source of dread to the Plan organizers.[117]

In the meantime, Redmond struggled manfully to promote the new association at county conventions. At Wexford in November 1889 he emphasized that it did not imply a winding down of the Plan, but rather an indication that the tenants on the remaining estates could henceforth rely on the support of a united party and people – a rather unrealistic proposition, given the evidence to the contrary. At Roscommon in the same month, he called on the tenants there, who had won their own demands, to stand behind the estates still in the conflict. His deficiencies as an agitator were evident when, at the first venue, he attacked the diehard landlord Colonel Charles Tottenham using a quotation from *Hamlet*. At the second, even more quaintly, he deployed lines from a Roman poet (to general applause, although he did not translate from the Latin) to exhort his listeners to solidarity with their fellows.[118] Nevertheless, when the preparations for the Limerick convention, scheduled for 3 December, brought Redmond into confrontation with Bishop O'Dwyer, he showed where his real strengths lay.

The practical matter at stake was whether the bishop, known to be hostile to the agrarian movement, would allow his priests to take part in the convention. He first wrote to ask whether there would be 'open or covert advocacy' of the Plan of Campaign at the convention. Redmond wrote back on 30 November enclosing a copy of the constitution of the association, 'from which his lordship will perceive that the Association does not involve or contemplate the advocacy of any particular combination amongst the Irish tenant farmers . . . it will be my duty to secure that the proceedings are conducted in accordance with the constitution'. Not satisfied, the bishop's secretary replied the next day 'to express his regret that you have not given him the assurance' that was the condition of his allowing his clergies to attend. His lordship was already familiar with the constitution, but

> The 'Plan of Campaign' has been condemned as sinful. That decree beyond yea or nay binds the conscience of every Catholic in Ireland under pain of mortal sin . . . You cannot then think the bishop is going beyond his clear duty when he asks . . . [for] an undertaking on the part of its chairman that he will not allow the 'Plan of Campaign' to be referred to in terms that are inconsistent with the loyal and obedient submission due to the teaching authority of the Church.

Adding cajolery to compulsion, the letter went on:

> His lordship is most anxious that he and his clergy should be able to join this Tenants' Defence Association, and he will take it as a personal favour on your part if you give him the assurance that he conscientiously requires . . . kindly send me as early as possible tomorrow, by telegraph, the one word 'Yes', and I shall then have the necessary permission sent at once to the clergy.

Redmond's reply was terse but diplomatic. 'Your letter just received,' he telegraphed on 2 December, 'I infer from it that the meaning of my letter of the 30th November has not been fully apprehended.' Repeating the points of that letter, he added:

> but you will perceive that it is impracticable for me as a layman to undertake in advance to prevent such references in speeches as might afterwards be construed by more competent judges to be inconsistent with the due submission to the teaching authority. I have undertaken what substantially meets the case, and I cannot undertake what is impossible, namely – the function of determining matters which I am neither authorised nor competent to decide.

The answer, by telegram just over two hours later, was a climbdown by the bishop: 'Thanks for the telegram, which is entirely satisfactory and sufficient.'[119]

Redmond had skilfully steered between annoying the bishop, thus jeopardizing clerical attendance at the convention, and being browbeaten into obeying a cleric who was, in nationalist terms, a maverick. The day after the convention, a *Freeman* editorial on the attendance of the priests brought a reply from the bishop himself, which claimed that he had 'previously received an explicit assurance from the convenors of it that they would abstain from any contravention of the Papal Decree condemning boycotting and the Plan of Campaign, and it was only on the faith of that assurance the clergy were allowed to attend.' Redmond was thus enabled to publish the entire correspondence, and readers were left to judge how far it bore out the bishop's account of what Redmond had promised. The paper congratulated Redmond on his adroitness in handling 'a difficult and delicate task'.[120]

V

With the bulk of his activities and responsibilities now centred in Ireland, Redmond moved residence during 1888 from London to Dublin, where he lived with his family at 15 Upper Fitzwilliam Street. His presence in the House of Commons shrank to insignificance in the next three years: he attended periodically for urgent divisions, but made few speeches. During these years of the Plan of Campaign, he added to his reputation as a rising intellectual of the party and a rival to Sexton as a crowd-puller to lectures on nationalist themes.

His lecture 'The Truth about '98' was published as a pamphlet by the Irish Press Agency with the aim of counteracting the literature being circulated in Britain by the Irish Loyal and Patriotic Union, which played upon fears of a repetition of the sectarian atrocities of the insurrection.[121] On 29 November 1886, he lectured at the Rotunda on 'Irish Protestants and Home Rule', a theme made highly topical by the recent controversies on the Home Rule Bill. He sought to refute two notions: that pro- and anti-Home Rule sentiment in Ireland reflected the existence of two nations (an idea gaining currency in Britain, especially among Liberal Unionists) and the fear that the Protestant nation would suffer persecution at the hands of an inevitably Catholic majority in a Dublin parliament. He outlined the history of the Protestant colony in Ireland from the seventeenth century, when it was required by England 'to enslave the Irish nation', to its own gradual development of the aspiration to freedom from English rule, an aspiration that at first excluded the Catholics from all political power. In time, for Grattan and his colleagues, the nascent sense of nationality had come to include the older community:

> Irishmen do not forget that Protestants won the Parliament of '82; Protestants organised the Society of United Irishmen, and filled its ranks both before and after it became a revolutionary body; Protestants gave the franchise to Catholics in 1793; Protestants led the rebel armies in 1798; Protestants gallantly, but vainly, defended Irish constitutional liberty in 1800.

It was true that there had always been 'an intolerant anti-Irish and anti-Catholic faction' that had opposed Catholic claims and driven the people into arms in '98. But he would not allow this group the status of a nation: 'these men have never risen above the tactics or the aspirations of a faction'. Focusing on the rare moments since the reign of Queen

Mary when the Catholic Irish had briefly recaptured power, he argued that Protestant fears of persecution were groundless:

> Irish Catholics are almost the only people in the world's history who have never persecuted for conscience' sake . . . when they had the

Figure 9. No.15 Upper Fitzwilliam St., Dublin, John Redmond's Dublin home between 1888 and 1890.

> supremacy in the past they never oppressed their Protestant fellow-countrymen, and . . . in matters in which they hold power today they make no distinction between men of different creeds

Any survey of this topic had to confront the tales, deeply embedded in the Irish Protestant folk memory, of a general and organized massacre of Protestants in 1641, which had been used to sway British voters in the July election. He took as his authority the highly reputable Protestant historian W. E. H. Lecky to assert that such stories were 'utterly and absolutely untrue', although some murders had occurred in what was fundamentally a defensive war for religious toleration.[122]

Inadequate though they might have seemed to his opponents, Redmond's efforts to engage with the concerns expressed by Protestants contrasted with the attitudes of many of his colleagues in the party. Healy was certainly not one who would offer any guarantees to the minority. What Healy's biographer, Frank Callanan, has called his 'attitude of complacent dismissiveness' to the unionist opposition to Home Rule, and the crudity of formulations such as 'the bigots who are fools enough to suppose that the Ministers of an Irish Parliament would dine off roast Protestant must be left to the care of the National schoolmaster' (as he wrote in a 1885 article), were hardly designed to allay fears.[123] However, although credit should be given to Redmond for realizing that there was a job of nation-building to be done, and for playing the part of a statesman in applying his mind to the problem, it must be allowed that his conception of political Protestantism in Ireland was static and outdated. There are no signs that he examined the evolution in attitudes towards the Union among Protestants during the nineteenth century. Above all, he shows no awareness of the distinctive position of the Ulster community within Protestantism as well as within the island. He does not seem to have asked himself why the descendants of those independent-minded Ulster Presbyterians who had supported the United Irishmen at the end of the eighteenth century had become, not merely reconciled to the Union, but its staunchest supporters: it seemed to him enough to remind them of the glorious history of their ancestors. In fairness to him, it is true that Ulster was not at this time putting forward claims for separate treatment within Ireland: that would come much later when it realized that it could not hold the entire island for the Union. But, underlying the appearances, there were in reality two Protestant communities: one mainly middle class or landed, affluent, thinly spread in the provinces outside Ulster; the other numerous, with a much stronger plebeian element, concentrated in the north-east, with a confidence in its identity, which owed much to a burgeoning economy increasingly integrated with that of industrialized England and Scotland. The approaches that might work to reassure the first were unlikely to impress the second. Redmond hoped to reconcile the 'Irish democracy' with the 'English democracy'; the existence of an 'Ulster democracy', which might not be reconcilable, was beyond his ken.

In early 1889 he took time out from his Plan responsibilities to deliver two talks in Dublin. The first was a public lecture on the career of Thomas Drummond, the reforming chief secretary of the 1830s whose efforts to give substance to the enactment of Catholic Emancipation had opened up places in the magistracy to Redmond's own grandfather and grand-uncle. Drawing a pointed contrast with the present Balfour regime, he called Drummond's career

> a lucid interval in the mad misgovernment of Ireland . . . the one solitary effort of English statesmanship, prior to the days of Mr. Gladstone, to give effect to the promise upon the faith of which the Union of 1800 was carried, and to rule Ireland as an integral portion of the United Kingdom by just and equal laws.

Nevertheless, Drummond's ultimate failure justified Redmond's contention that 'English government of Ireland, even when done with sympathy and honesty of purpose, is impossible.'[124]

At the Dublin lord mayor's banquet in April, replying to the toast 'Ireland a Nation', he went to new lengths to reassure Liberal allies that Home Rule did not mean separation. Buoyed by a string of further by-election victories for the Gladstonian Liberals – three in the previous five weeks – he quoted approvingly from a historian of federalism, who had recommended it as appropriate for situations in which there was a partial, but not total, community in origin, feeling, interest or identity between two peoples, adding: 'Most of us here tonight are believers in the principles of federalism . . . this is the position which we, as Irish nationalists, take towards the question of our relations with England and the Empire.' He singled out for attack the 'fallacy' of those Unionists who saw the Irish and English as sharing the kind of identity that would enable them to become 'fused together'.[125] Although he did not explicitly criticize the opposite 'fallacy' (that of complete independence), it was a new departure for a nationalist to express a positive wish, accompanied by an intellectual rationale, that Home Rule should not lead in the direction in which both its enemies and its more 'advanced' friends assumed it did, that of separation. In the light of his later stance during the split, it is significant that he made no attempt to set down the minimum requirements of a new Home Rule Bill, nor make any criticism of defects in the Bill of 1886. The speech was in harmony with Parnell's acceptance of that Bill as a final settlement of the Irish demand, a position from which he had not since departed. It was more than four years since the leader had uttered his famous 'ne plus ultra' speech at Cork, declaring that no man had the right to fix the boundary to the march of a nation; that statement was one which, it now seemed, Redmond would prefer to forget.[126]

Later that year, with the Tipperary agitation at its height, Redmond found time to support the temperance movement. His conviction that

Home Rule was near at hand gave him new hopes for its future. Addressing a Dublin branch of the League of the Cross, the Catholic temperance association supported by his father, he lamented the decline of the movement since its great days in the O'Connell era and predicted that immediately following the enactment of Home Rule, the country would see a temperance movement the like of which had not yet been seen, combined with drastic restrictive legislation on the drink trade. There was a certain sneer in the *Freeman* headline 'The Temperance Question – Mr. John Redmond Preaches a Crusade' and its leader felt that he carried his principle too far in advocating legislation of that kind; it did not believe in 'the soberising of a people by Act of Parliament'.[127] The speech triggered an unusually spirited correspondence in the paper, one letter-writer stating that he knew from intimate knowledge of English constituencies of the beneficial effects of pro-temperance speeches on support for Home Rule there; the speeches of Redmond, Biggar and Davitt had been particularly helpful in this regard.[128]

At the meeting, Redmond supported the project to erect a statue to Father Mathew, the 'apostle of temperance' who had led the Irish movement forty years previously. A few days later, however, Archbishop Walsh publicly opposed the idea as 'eminently unsuitable'. The following year, at public ceremonies to mark the centenary of Father Mathew's birth with the laying of the pedestal stone of the statue, the Irish Catholic clergy was notable by its absence (the English Catholic Church was represented), and Dublin witnessed the strange sight of the Protestant archbishop of Dublin and other non-Catholic clerics heaping praise on a Roman Catholic priest while his own Church looked the other way. Of the Irish Party, the only members present were two Protestants; Redmond, alone of the Catholics, had agreed to speak but was called away to the Tipperary trials then in progress.[129] It seemed that the temperance movement was too tainted with Protestantism for the liking of the Catholic hierarchy, who, if they could not control it, preferred to ignore it. Redmond later lamented the public apathy that had left the statue project short of money, saying that the episode illustrated forcibly the barriers raised by religious and political differences in getting united action on social problems.[130] It was another instance of that Gallican self-assurance as a lay Catholic that made him unafraid to differ with his clergy, and demonstrated both an independence of mind and an ecumenical awareness that marked him out from many of his co-religionist contemporaries.

VI

At the end of 1889, two events – both private, but one carrying vast though as yet unimaginable political implications – occurred, which between them would soon set Redmond's life on a new course. On 12 December, Johanna gave birth to a stillborn girl, and died the same day at their Dublin home. Redmond was in County Tipperary at the winter

Figure 10. The grave of Johanna Redmond at Glasnevin Cemetery.

assizes when the death took place, and returned home in the evening to be given the news. The *Freeman* reported that 'up till within the last day or two Mrs. Redmond was in the best of health – full of life and spirits and the good humour and brightness with which all her friends at all times associated her'.[131] It is possible – it can be no more than a surmise – that an accident involving the couple three months earlier may have given rise to the tragedy. They had been thrown from their car near Wexford by the shying of the horse, and Johanna had been reported as suffering shock.[132] Her funeral was attended by a large contingent from the party, as well as from the bar and other professions. Conspicuous among the wreaths was one from the people of Tipperary, 'with whose present struggle Mr. Redmond has so intimately associated himself'. The *Freeman* reporter noted 'the genuine and marked concern of all present for his sudden and heavy trouble'.[133]

The second of these fateful events came just before the year closed. On 27 December *The Times* reported that Captain O'Shea had instituted divorce proceedings against his wife, Katharine, naming Parnell as co-respondent. Parnell told the *Freeman* that he had reliable information that Edward Houston, the hirer of Pigott, had incited O'Shea to take these proceedings, which were based on a falsehood. That newspaper reflected most nationalist opinion in asserting that this was merely the resumption of the Unionist campaign to bring down the Irish leader. It declared that the public had total confidence in what Parnell said, and none in O'Shea.[134] The early weeks of the new year saw its columns filled with resolutions from representative bodies all over Ireland expressing unaltered confidence in Parnell's leadership and indignation at the continued intrigues against him. Davitt, who was assured by Parnell in vague terms that he would emerge from the case 'without a stain on his name or reputation', declared his 'unabated confidence' in the leader.[135] There the matter would rest until the case came forward the following November.

December 1889 saw another development, involving the Irish leader and the Liberals, which would play a highly significant role in later events. On 18 December, Parnell visited Gladstone at home at Hawarden, and the two spent much of the following day in conversation. The discussions were confidential, but it was understood that the talks ranged over the outlines of the next Home Rule Bill. From the tone of the speech that Parnell delivered at the Reform Club in Liverpool that evening, it could be inferred that he regarded them as highly satisfactory.[136]

Redmond's recovery from the blow of Johanna's death was slow. Although he was back at his legal work within a couple of months, mostly in cases involving the Tipperary tenants, and also involved in attempts at arranging arbitration on the Plan estates in County Wexford,[137] his withdrawal from public life was almost ostentatious. He made no comment when the report of the Special Commission in February 1890 included his name on a long list of M.P.s found guilty of criminal conspiracy to incite to boycotting and non-payment of rent, though acquitted on the graver charges of treason and complicity in murder. He did not attend the funeral of Parnell's old colleague Biggar in February, nor that of another party colleague, Matthew Harris, in April. Neither did he attend the grand opening of New Tipperary on 12 April, at which O'Brien and Davitt were the star attractions and speeches were made by a long list of Irish and sympathetic British M.P.s.

He took no part in the two major social events of the party that summer: the banquet given in May in honour of Dillon and the other members who had fundraised in Australia, and the wedding of O'Brien in London in June.[138] He made no public speeches at all until the autumn of 1890. His parliamentary attendance was patchy (although he took care to be present for vital divisions) and his contributions negligible.

Redmond's reclusiveness that year is undoubtedly explained, not only by his grief,[139] but by his need to arrange for the care of his three young children, all under six years of age at the time of their mother's death. He had no option but to leave them in the care of servants while he worked. A brief insight into his domestic circumstances in those months comes from a bizarre incident that took place at the end of June 1890. In Greystones, a coastal town in Wicklow, a young assistant was shot by a deranged man who entered her shop. In her efforts to escape her assailant she ran across the road into a house that happened to be occupied by Redmond's three young children with their nurse and cook; their father was absent that day in Westminster. She was pursued by the gunman, who fired through the kitchen window. The two terrified servants were required to appear as witnesses at the subsequent murder trial, the young woman having died of her injuries.[140]

Redmond's constituents in North Wexford, when he finally came to meet them, might legitimately have wondered about the quality of their parliamentary representation over the previous year. At a large meeting at Enniscorthy on 21 September, he drew on their sympathy: 'During the year that had passed circumstances which his constituents, with their usual indulgence and generosity, fully appreciated and understood had almost completely incapacitated him from the discharge of the duties of public life.' Doubtless reflecting his own emotions in the recent months, he described the four years that had elapsed since the 1886 election as 'like some hideous nightmare full of suffering, gloom and helplessness'. But he and the country were emerging from their nightmares. The Crimes Act was now in abeyance in most of the country and fewer men were in jail now than at any time since its passing into law; this he claimed as a victory for the people, who with 'courage, loyalty and patience' had kept their ranks unbroken. Belatedly replying to the Special Commission verdict, he asserted that the boycotting he had always advocated was peaceful and legitimate, and never anything 'which worked either through outrage or crime, or the fear of outrage or crime'. He admitted that it was 'a terrible and dangerous weapon, and he would go so far as to say that in a freely and constitutionally governed country it was a weapon that ought not to be used, and the constant use of which would be intolerable'. But anything the people had gained in the previous decade, he said, had been won in large part through the legitimate use of this weapon.[141]

The Irish Party and its prominent supporters at home were more than usually jittery that summer, whether because of unspoken fears about the impending divorce case or otherwise. Complaints about absence of members from Parliament had become an annual event; the previous year the *Freeman* had called it a 'grave dereliction of duty' when, despite the sending out of urgent whips, absentees had saved the Government from defeat by small majorities (in one case, a majority of two).[142] On 19 June 1890, seventeen members of the party, including Parnell himself, were missing (many were at Ascot races, while Parnell was ill) when the Government had a majority of four on a vital clause of a Local Taxation Bill. This time the criticism came from the archbishop of Dublin, who indignantly complained that Irish members had deserted their posts for several days past. Dr Walsh went on to state that if a satisfactory explanation was not forthcoming – 'I do not care who the absentees may be' – he would find it hard to place any further trust in the party.[143] The attack was so strong that the *Freeman's* London correspondent weighed in with a defence of the party, writing that any reflection on the honesty and capacity of the Irish Party as a whole was 'a matter of profound surprise and regret'.[144] The fact that the criticism was implicitly aimed at poor management of the party by its leader was not lost on members. In reality, Parnell's absences and remoteness from colleagues were becoming a severe test of their patience and loyalty, made worse by his seeming lack of awareness that anything was amiss.

The friction within the party extended beyond affairs of management to those of policy. Earlier in the session, Balfour had introduced a Bill for the biggest land purchase scheme yet, providing for state-backed loans of £33 million to enable tenants to buy out their holdings. Although Parnell attacked it, his objections to it were on matters of means rather than of end; he had always advocated tenant purchase in so far as it was compatible with his preference for the retention in the country of a resident landlord class.[145] The agrarian wing of the party, along with Davitt, was more fundamentally opposed, focusing on the sums to be paid to the landlords and labelling the Bill a 'Landlord Relief Bill'. Davitt in particular found it easy to get English audiences to listen to his denunciation of 'the buying out of the Irish landlords at the expense of the British taxpayer'.[146] The party's obstruction was partly responsible for the Bill's withdrawal in August, but during its course through the House certain of Parnell's comments caused confusion, to say the least, among his supporters. On 21 April, moving the Bill's rejection, he put his own proposal that the landlords should be granted a sum equal to a certain number of years' purchase (that is, of annual rent) to enable them to pay off debts and encumbrances, while the judicial rents of the tenants should be reduced by 30 per cent. The *Freeman* commented: 'It is certainly a curious thing to find the Irish leader bringing forward a scheme by which the landlords could be retained in Ireland.'[147]

But Parnell produced his biggest sensation on 11 July, when he broke a prolonged absence from the debates on the Irish estimates to attend the constabulary vote. He followed an impassioned harangue from Dillon with a calm invitation to Balfour to devote the last weeks of the session to bringing an end to the Plan of Campaign by extending the benefits of a previous Act to the tenants of the Plan estates.[148] The short speech left colleagues, allies and opponents alike mystified. Shortly afterwards, the *New York Times* published a story from its London correspondent, Harold Frederic, a close friend of Healy's, to the effect that there was 'consternation and disgust' among members at the way Parnell had 'coolly given away their whole case against Balfour'; the article speculated on his mental state and accused him of abusing his position as leader, which in any case it was difficult to see him retaining once the O'Shea case had come to trial. The *Nation* reprinted the report on 2 August, together with a letter signed by Sexton, Dillon and O'Brien indignantly denying its truth.[149]

Fresh events brought a temporary distraction from such rumours. On 18 September, in a transparent dodge to frustrate the stated intention of O'Brien and Dillon to go to the United States to raise funds for the evicted tenants, Balfour had them arrested on old charges connected with New Tipperary. Free on bail, on 10 October they failed to appear in court, eluded the police and escaped from Dalkey harbour to France in a small yacht. From there they sailed to the States. Meanwhile, Parnell continued to exasperate his colleagues when he announced at the last minute that he would not be attending the meeting of the party called for Dublin's City Hall for 6 October, which was regarded by all as crucial for the clarification of future policy. Justin McCarthy, who took the chair in his place, assured the meeting that 'our great leader . . . is in entire and active co-operation with everything we do' but the air of mystery and unease surrounding Parnell persisted.

Redmond, following his return to active politics, became heavily involved as defence counsel in a protracted series of trials at Tipperary, which arose from renewed agitation there, in particular from what Morley, who was present, called a 'deplorable, lawless, cowardly, unprovoked outrage' by the police on a meeting in the town on 25 September, in which the M.P. Henry Harrison and many others were batoned.[150] The trials continued right through October and did not finish until 19 November, by which time a chain of events was unfolding that would bring disaster to Parnell and destroy the Irish Party as a united political force.

If Redmond attempted during these weeks to see into the future, it would not be surprising if he saw in the man who often stood opposite him in court, the Dublin Unionist Edward Carson (lately nominated by Balfour for the Trinity College seat and for the post of solicitor-general),[151] a future political opponent. But he could not in his wildest fantasies have imagined that the man who often stood alongside him in court, his fellow-nationalist, Timothy Michael Healy, would within a few short months be his bitterest opponent and traducer.

7 The Rupture

> I am bound to him [Parnell] by the double ties of private friendship and political allegiance.
>
> Redmond in Dublin, 18 November 1890[1]

> If I were dead and gone tomorrow, the men who are fighting against English influence in Irish public life would fight on still; they would still be independent nationalists.
>
> Parnell at Listowel, 13 September 1891[2]

I

The hearing of Captain O'Shea's petition for divorce took place over two days, 15 and 17 November 1890. Neither Parnell nor Katharine O'Shea contested the evidence. A decree nisi of divorce was granted to Captain O'Shea, the jury having decided that adultery had taken place between Katharine and Parnell without the connivance of her husband. The nationalist and unionist press were predictably the first to take sides. The *Freeman* saw in it the opening of a new phase in the unrelenting campaign of Parnell's 'Unionist and Pigottist' enemies; the *Daily Telegraph* gleefully considered itself to be writing Parnell's political obituary.[3] Thus began a trauma that would shatter the unity of the Irish Party, see the death of Parnell within a year, and leave the nationalist movement split for a further eight years in a dispute which, in its rupturing of families and friendships and in the bitterness of its antagonisms, foreshadowed the Irish Civil War of some thirty years later.[4]

On the morning the verdict was announced in the press, Tuesday 18 November, Redmond left Carlow, where he had chaired a county convention of the Tenants' Defence Association the previous night, and hurried to Dublin, where he presided that evening at the fortnightly meeting of the league's central branch. An unusually large number of M.P.s were present, a majority of whom would later emerge as reliable supporters of the leader. It is possible that this was not accidental, and that Parnell had sent them to 'guide' the meeting.[5] Certainly, Redmond's movements at this time indicate that only exceptional circumstances could have brought him there. He had been immersed in the Tipperary trials until Saturday, had come to Dublin to deliver a speech at a league rally on Sunday, had gone to Carlow on Monday and was due back in Tipperary the day after Tuesday's crucial meeting. It is unlikely, had it been a routine gathering of the central branch, that he would have found the time in such a busy schedule to attend, let alone to preside.

While much of nationalist Ireland and Liberal Britain hesitated, Redmond had been swift in deciding on his position, and was now unequivocal in stating it. Any talk of Mr Parnell's leadership being prejudiced in the remotest degree by what had occurred in London was, he said,

> the wildest and most grotesque absurdity . . . The Irish Party are bound to their leader by ties of absolute confidence and unquestioning loyalty. If he was thinking of quitting, the Irish people would come as one man and entreat him not to desert them, but thank God no such danger ever existed . . . I am bound to him by the double ties of private friendship and political allegiance.

'These words,' said Alderman V. B. Dillon, 'would find an echo in the heart of every person in Ireland as they found an echo in every heart in that room.' Redmond's speech set the tone for the half-dozen that followed, giving the meeting the character of a rally for Parnell. The three M.P.s who would later be anti-Parnellites, including Healy, spoke at the end and were equally vehement in their declarations of loyalty. In a foretaste of the invective that would characterize the split, J. J. Clancy labelled as a 'traitor' anyone who would desert Parnell.[6]

Two nights later, a public meeting in Dublin's Leinster Hall, originally planned as a rally for the evicted tenants, turned into an even bigger pro-Parnell demonstration. More than 20 M.P.s, including Redmond, were on the platform to pledge allegiance to the leader. A cable was read from the delegates in the United States (signed by Dillon and O'Brien and three of the four others), which declared that 'the Irish Party stand a solid phalanx at the back of Mr. Parnell . . . [whose] statesmanship and matchless qualities as a leader are essential to the safety of our cause'.[7] The speech that, according to the *Freeman*, 'took the meeting by storm', was that of Healy, who castigated those in Britain calling for Parnell's removal as 'this howling pack' and said they must not abandon their leader 'within sight of the Promised Land': the question was one for the Irish Party and people alone to decide. It was a speech he would not be allowed to forget for many a year, given his change of position a week later.[8]

That same day the first break in the nationalist ranks occurred when Davitt (not an M.P. at this time), in his *Labour World*, called on Parnell to resign on the grounds that Liberal supporters in Britain would no longer accept an alliance with a party led by him.[9] His judgement was accurate. The first week of the crisis ended with Nonconformist chapel-goers throughout Britain, the grass-roots of the Liberal Party, hearing their clergymen denounce the adulterer Parnell. The Revd. Hugh Price Hughes told a crowded meeting at St James's Hall on Sunday that Nonconformists would not tolerate an alliance with the Irish leader.[10]

Figure 11. Parnell (seated, with hands folded) is re-elected as chairman of the Irish Party on 25 November 1890 in Committee Room 15, House of Commons. John Redmond was absent from the meeting. (*Illustrated London News*, 6 December 1890). *Courtesy of the National Library of Ireland.*

W. T. Stead, the former editor of the Liberal *Pall Mall Gazette*, had already conveyed the same message in a letter to Gladstone on 20 November: 'I know my Non-conformists well and no power on earth will induce them to follow that man to the poll, or you either, if you are arm-in-arm with him.'[11] The Irish Catholic bishops had made as yet no public comment on the crisis; the *Freeman* carried an editorial on the rising murmur in 'Pharisaical England' on the moral issue.[12]

Further court cases in Tipperary the following week kept Redmond away from the centre of the action, which now shifted to Westminster. The Irish Party was due to meet on Tuesday 25 November, the day of the opening of the winter session of Parliament, to elect its chairman. On Monday evening Gladstone, responding to the rising tide of Liberal disquiet, met Justin McCarthy, the vice-chairman, and told him that Parnell's retention of the leadership would mean the loss of the next election and the postponement of Home Rule beyond what years remained to him (Gladstone). However, sensitively couching his message in praise of Parnell's record of splendid service to Ireland, he failed to convey, and McCarthy failed to grasp, the stark implication that he (Gladstone) must resign if Parnell continued as Irish leader.[13] To remove any doubt, Gladstone that night wrote his famous letter to Morley, intended for the latter to show to Parnell before the meeting, in which he concluded

> ... [Parnell's] continuance at the present moment in the leadership would be productive of consequences disastrous in the highest degree to the cause of Ireland ... [and] would render my retention of the leadership of the Liberal Party, based as it has been mainly upon the prosecution of the Irish cause, almost a nullity.[14]

On Tuesday morning, neither McCarthy nor Morley could find the elusive Parnell. The Irish members, unaware of either Gladstone's oral or written message, proceeded unanimously to re-elect Parnell to the chairmanship (although, on their own evidence later, many members regarded this as an honorary action only and expected Parnell to resign after it.)

After the meeting, Morley read the letter to an unmoved Parnell, who assured him that the whole affair would soon blow over. That evening Gladstone, hearing of the party's action and of Parnell's obduracy, decided to release the letter to the press. News of it reached the ears of the Irish members that night. Only then did McCarthy tell his dismayed colleagues of his meeting with Gladstone, by which time it was too late to intercept the letter.[15] Members urged Parnell to resign, to no avail; thirty-one then signed a requisition to convene another meeting to reopen the leadership question. It was the beginning of the revolt against Parnell within the Party. The organiser of the requisition was the South Wexford M.P. John Barry, an instigator of the overthrow of Shaw as chairman in 1880; its signatories included Sexton, McCarthy and the Healy brothers, Tim and Maurice.[16]

When the party met next day, Barry moved that the proceedings be adjourned until Friday to give Parnell an opportunity to reconsider his position. Parnell refused to do any such thing, on the grounds that he had been unanimously re-elected the previous day. Members present, notably McCarthy and Sexton (Healy at this stage was ill in Dublin), urged him to retire in the interests of the Home Rule alliance, saying that Gladstone's letter had brought about a material change since the previous day. M.P.s who identified with the agrarian movement wanted at least a temporary withdrawal in the interests of the evicted tenants. The meeting finally agreed to adjourn until the following Monday. Meanwhile, the 'American' delegates were shifting their position in the wake of the Gladstone initiative: O'Brien cabled a recommendation that the party open negotiations with Gladstone, while Dillon was also perturbed by the letter.[17]

As resolutions of support for Parnell poured in from league branches all over the country, Redmond crossed to London on Thursday night, 27 November, shortly after Healy, who arrived reportedly looking 'exceedingly ill'. On Friday Parnell wrote his momentous riposte to Gladstone's letter, his 'Manifesto to the People of Ireland'. Going beyond a mere defence of his record or a denial of the right of the Liberals to dictate the Irish leadership, it took the fight to his opponents, throwing over completely in tone and content the Union of Hearts strategy he had himself so carefully cultivated since 1886. It spoke of 'the integrity and independence' of a section of the party having been 'apparently sapped and destroyed by the wire-pullers of the English Liberal Party', and described leading Liberals, including Gladstone, as 'English wolves howling for my destruction'. Most damaging of all to the Liberal alliance was his rewriting of the history of his meeting with Gladstone at Hawarden the previous December, including 'revelations' of the details he alleged the latter had given him of the Home Rule Bill he was preparing. These included provisions that the three key areas of the land question, control of the police and appointment of judges would not come within the remit of an Irish parliament for many years. Combined with this was the intention to reduce the Irish representation at Westminster from 103 to 32. Given these limitations on the powers of an Irish government, Parnell asserted that it would be 'the height of madness' to agree to 'disband the army which had cleared the way to victory' by consenting to such a reduction.[18] Most of the remainder of the manifesto contained what has been called 'an intemperate farrago of abuse and tendentious and improbable allegations'.[19] Parnell ended with a call for the party to maintain that independence of English parties which had 'forced upon the English people the necessity of granting Home Rule to Ireland', and was the only means to achieve that goal. And the Irish people throughout the world would agree with him 'that a postponement would be preferable to a compromise of our national rights by the acceptance of a measure which would not realise the aspirations of our race'.[20] Redmond, in company with another Parnell loyalist, J. J. O'Kelly, and McCarthy, listened that evening as Parnell read out the text. McCarthy, knowing that Gladstone would contest the Hawarden allegations, expressed his disagreement with the whole document, while the two Parnellites stayed silent, seemingly stunned by the magnitude of what their leader was prepared to do to escape his predicament.[21]

The manifesto was issued late on Friday night, 28 November, and was described by the *Freeman* the following day as 'one of the most remarkable documents ever penned by an Irish leader . . . [it] falls like a bombshell into the camp of his quondam apparent allies'.[22] That weekend, Gladstone denied each of Parnell's allegations concerning the Hawarden conversations. No formal proposals had been put forward, he said; they had merely discussed without prejudice a list of points concerning possible improvements to the 1886 measure, and Parnell had not objected to a single one of his suggestions. These matters aside, it was clear that the possibility of the two men working together again had been dealt a fatal blow by the publication of the proceedings of a confidential meeting. As Liberals reeled and Tories exulted, Monday morning's *Freeman* carried an address cabled by all but one of the delegates to America, which came out against Parnell and 'his further leadership'. They had read the manifesto with 'the deepest pain' and lamented his 'rash and fatal path'. The exception was Harrington, who clung to the hope that Parnell might voluntarily retire. It seems that Redmond entertained the same hope. Healy wrote to his wife on Sunday night: 'John Redmond said to Barry in the Club tonight that he was going to beseech Parnell to retire, but that he knew it would be useless, although he did not believe Parnell would have 20 supporters tomorrow.'[23] There is no corroboration for this statement regarding Redmond's intention that evening. As to whether he actually went to Parnell, Healy is again the sole source. The Liberal M.P. Professor James Stuart wrote to Herbert Gladstone, son of the statesman, that Healy had told him that Redmond had gone the same evening to beg Parnell to resign.[24]

Irish opinion, unable to absorb the suddenness of the rupture with the politics of the recent past – what Frank Callanan has called 'the sundering of the sentimental nationalist diptych of home rule, the intertwined portraits of Parnell and Gladstone'[25] – now began to reflect the disarray among its leaders. Archbishop Walsh the first member of the Catholic hierarchy to pronounce publicly on the crisis, in a press interview called the manifesto 'an act of political suicide'.[26] Davitt lamented 'Here we are now in splinters. Mr. Parnell's manifesto is a last desperate move. I don't see how he could have struck Ireland a worse blow.'[27]

After two weeks, the issues of the crisis were now laid bare; the fateful third week saw their resolution in the famous debates in Committee Room 15 at Westminster. Seventy-three members met there on Monday 1 December. The anti-Parnellites had chosen a Protestant M.P., William Abraham, to move a motion that would terminate Parnell's chairmanship. Parnell used his position as chairman to obstruct this; instead, they discussed an amendment from a Parnellite, Colonel J. P. Nolan, that the question of the chairmanship be postponed to give members a chance to consult their constituents, and that they meet next in Dublin. Sexton moved against this, and eloquently and at great length brought the subject back to the leadership issue. He wanted to know who the members were whose integrity had been 'sapped' by the Liberals, claiming that he and others had always safeguarded the party's integrity while Parnell had for long periods been absent from the scene. He declared that, although he had a love and regard for Parnell such as he could never feel for any other leader, 'no service by any leader entitles him to ruin his cause'.

Redmond spoke next. Putting his shock at the manifesto behind him, he made it clear that for him the principle of the independence of the party overrode all other matters, even Home Rule itself. He began with a statement of his credentials:

> I don't claim the same authority as Mr. Sexton from attainments or services, but I do claim the same authority as he has claimed for himself to speak here on behalf of the men who stood by your side, Mr. Parnell, when almost alone you created this movement (*hear,*

> *hear*). I claim the right to speak as one of those who, during the 10 years that have elapsed both in Parliament and in the country, and in America and Australia and throughout the world, have freely given the best years, perhaps, of my life in sustainment of the cause which Mr. Sexton served and you led.

He cautioned those members whom he saw as overly concerned with the Liberal alliance: 'in deciding a question of this kind, where we are asked to sell our leader (*loud cheers*) to preserve an alliance, it seems to me that we are bound to inquire what we are getting for the price that we are paying (*renewed cheering*)'. Parnell interjected, 'Don't sell me for nothing. If you get my value you may change me tomorrow (*renewed cheering*).' Redmond went on: 'it seems to me that in selling our leader in order to preserve the Liberal alliance, we are selling absolutely and irrevocably the independence of the Irish Party'. The Home Rule Bill being prepared by Gladstone, as described by Parnell in his manifesto, was, he said, shown to be 'a sham and a fraud on the nationalist aspirations'. The attitude taken by Gladstone was unworthy of a great man:

> My belief is that if he were a great man he would not be so precipitate in writing that letter. My belief is that if he were an honest man, and true in his denials of your manifesto, he would now, even at the eleventh hour, give such assurances as would ease the political situation. No; it seems to me, however, that his desire is that you should be trampled to the ground, and whoever tramples you, I will not take part in the transaction (*cheers*).

He disagreed completely with his 'friends' the agrarian M.P.s as to the implications of Parnell's continued leadership for the evicted tenants. If the party yielded to 'English clamour' and sacrificed its leader,

> then the source of supply on which these tenants have been depending for so long – the generosity of the Irish people in America – will be diverted from those tenants in a way which could not be possible under any other conceivable circumstances. Any man who has been in America, as I have, and knows America as intimately as I do, must be aware of the fact that your dethronement will rend the Irish people in America in twain.

He concluded by seeking to convince his hearers that his allegiance to Parnell was motivated by something more than personal friendship. His own public record, he thought, entitled him to believe that whatever course he took the people would accept that he was 'actuated by the highest motives of patriotism':

> It is true that I have a feeling of personal loyalty to you. I have said elsewhere, and I say here, that you have been my friend, and I think this is no time in which a man who has been once your friend should be against you. But I most solemnly think that while you remain my

> friend, and my personal attachment is the same to you as it always was, I declare most solemnly, and I know I will be believed, that in this consideration I am not allowing my personal attachment to you to weigh in the balance.

If those M.P.s who reversed their allegiance after the first week of the crisis could be taunted for years afterwards with their effusive support for Parnell at the Leinster Hall, Redmond too now gave a commitment that would long be hung around his neck:

> I recognise the obligation and the pledges which I took when in 1885 I was elected a member of this party, and if this party comes to a hostile decision to my view, then, before taking any steps to support Mr. Parnell if he chooses to go further, I will deem it my duty to resign my seat, and in the most formal way consult the wishes of my constituents.

Redmond was followed by Healy, whose arguments were calculated to embarrass Parnell's followers by contrasting their acceptance of the 1886 Bill with their support for the manifesto. The party had abated many of its demands, he said, when they accepted that Bill. They had done so to conciliate English opinion. Was that opinion now to be described only as clamour? The 1886 Bill had not granted immediate control over the police and judiciary either, and would have removed all Irish representation in the imperial Parliament. Raising the temperature of the debate, he then questioned the sincerity of Parnell's objections to Gladstone's proposals. He quoted damagingly from statements Parnell had made at Liverpool in December 1889, immediately after the Hawarden interview, when he had spoken glowingly of Gladstone and the Liberals. The *Freeman* account runs:

> Mr. Healy: ' . . . Either Mr. Parnell at Liverpool was false, or his manifesto was false (*hear, hear; no, no; shame*).'
>
> The Chairman: 'I will not stand an accusation of falsehood from Timothy Healy, and I call upon him to withdraw his expression.'
>
> Mr. Healy: 'Out of respect to the chair I will withdraw the accusation (*hear, hear*).'

Healy justified his about-face since Leinster Hall on the grounds that Ireland's hopes for Home Rule rested on the conjunction of Parnell's name with Gladstone's willingness to make a settlement. The Liberal leader's letter had changed everything. With Gladstone gone, Parnell's power would be rendered worthless. In an obvious tilt at Redmond, he concluded by stating: 'We cannot found our position upon sentiment, upon the claims of friendship, upon anything except the awful necessities that surround us in the presence of a trembling Irish cause.'

Parnell replied immediately to Healy's very effective speech. Reminding him of his Leinster Hall declarations, he taxed him with ingratitude, considering that it was he (Parnell) who had first discovered his genius, trained him and found him his first seat in Parliament, 'going past the prior right of my friend Jack Redmond'. Seeking to split his opponents, he said that he had sent McCarthy to Gladstone on Sunday to seek a written commitment from the Liberal leaders to rectify the objectionable points of the proposed Bill. He now stated that if Gladstone made two concessions – on control of the constabulary and on power to settle the land question – 'I should retire from public life as a matter of course'. He advised the members 'before you vote my deposition, to be sure you are getting value for it'. He ended with the affecting plea 'It is not an unfair thing for me to ask that I should come within sight of this "promised land".' The *Freeman* London correspondent wrote: 'Mr. Parnell's own speech was one of great power and declamatory effect. He spoke with an altogether unprecedented display of feeling, and towards the close his voice actually broke with emotion and the entire meeting was fairly carried away.'[28]

The debate lasted eleven hours, with telling points made by members on both sides. The following day, with acrimony increasing and references to the moral aspects of the divorce appearing in some anti-Parnellite speeches, it became clear that a majority was opposed to Parnell's continued leadership. After another marathon debate, a vote was taken and Colonel Nolan's amendment was defeated by 44 votes to 29.[29]

On Wednesday 3 December, Parnellite tactics were again in play. Clancy put forward a 'compromise' amendment that in view of the difference in recollection between Parnell and Gladstone regarding Hawarden, the party's whips be instructed to go to Gladstone, Morley and Harcourt to ascertain their views on the 'two vital points' of the police and land settlement; if they gave the required assurances, Parnell would retire. Although the chances of the Liberals playing along with this move seemed remote, the prospect of securing Parnell's retirement voluntarily, and thus of maintaining the party's unity, offered a ray of hope to his opponents. Sexton wished to know who would decide on the adequacy of the Liberal assurances. Would Parnell accept a majority decision of the party, and, if that decision judged them adequate, would he then retire? Healy, full of emotion, told Parnell that if he could meet the party on these two points, he would be the first to call him back 'to your proper place as leader of the Irish race (*loud and prolonged applause*)'. Parnell did not answer, but agreed to consider.[30]

On the same day, the standing committee of the Catholic hierarchy finally met to consider the situation. On Thursday morning, a vehement denunciation of Parnell signed by 4 archbishops and 20 bishops appeared in the papers. This combined moral condemnation – 'Surely Catholic Ireland, so eminently conspicuous for its virtue and the purity of its social life, will not accept as its leader a man thus dishonoured, and wholly unworthy of Christian confidence?' – with a warning of the political consequences for Ireland if Parnell remained leader.

Meanwhile, Parnell had hardened his position overnight. He now answered Sexton's questions by stating that he could not surrender to the party his responsibility to judge the Liberal assurances, a responsibility that devolved on him 'not because I am the mere leader of a Parliamentary party, but because I am the leader of the Irish nation'. In place of Clancy's resolution, he put his own two-part proposal. The party would commit itself to reject any Home Rule Bill that did not confer immediate control of the police on the Irish executive and full power to settle the land question on the Irish parliament; three delegates from each side of the party would be chosen to confer with Gladstone, Morley and Harcourt to ascertain whether they would embody these measures in the next Home Rule Bill. He would retire if the party, after consultation, decided that this was the case. This was setting the bar a good deal higher for the Liberals, who could not be expected to give such detailed commitments while in opposition, but Parnell justified it on the grounds that in Gladstone they were dealing with 'an unrivalled sophist' who had to be got to make his intentions clear. It also alienated the sympathy of the more moderate anti-Parnellites, and set the scene for the descent into bitter acrimony that followed.

Charging Parnell with insincerity in his promise to submit the matter to the judgement of the party, Healy accused Parnell of framing a new policy to appeal to 'the hillside men' (the Fenians), since his old policy, the Liberal alliance, had 'perished in the stench of the divorce court'. Addressing him as 'you, a Frankenstein, who having created this party, is able and determined to destroy it', he stated his readiness to take the fight against him to the country. Redmond tried to win back the advantage for Parnell by reproaching Healy with 'the worst-tempered and most hysterical speech that was ever delivered by a man in the position of a leading politician', following on the 'stirring of his better nature' the previous day. Parnell, however, was forced to cede ground and did not press his resolution to a vote. Instead, a modified version of the Clancy amendment was passed, resulting in the selection of a committee to arrange the meeting with the Liberal leaders. Redmond was one of the members – the others were Sexton, Healy and Leamy – deputized to conduct the interview.[31]

The deputation immediately ran into difficulties when Harcourt and Morley declined to meet it. The following day (Friday), Gladstone told its members that he could not discuss policy matters while they were linked to a 'difference of recollection' about Hawarden which he did not acknowledge to exist. The party reconvened in the afternoon to agree new terms of reference proposed by Redmond, and a fresh meeting with Gladstone was sought. The latter then refused to discuss Home Rule legislation until the Irish Party had disposed of the question of the leadership and 'the former relations' had been resumed.[32] Thus ended the Clancy initiative. Its failure brought the spotlight back to the question of the leadership. That night, Healy wrote apprehensively to his wife about the moment of decision, which he knew could not be long delayed, and the chances of defeating Parnell by majority vote: 'It will be a miracle if we succeed . . . If we fail the men most largely responsible for the mischief that will follow, as they backed Parnell all through are John Redmond and Dr. Kenny.'[33]

On Saturday, 6 December, the *Freeman* was steady in its support of Parnell, but the two nationalist weeklies were against him. O'Brien's *United Ireland* wrote: 'The path of duty is clear at last. Ireland or Parnell is now the issue'; the *Nation* declared: 'The leader whom we used to follow is no more.' The party gathered and listened as Redmond read the formal report of the deputation. The *Freeman's* London correspondent described the atmosphere:

> it was quite apparent from the demeanour of both sides that a crisis was at hand. There was an undercurrent of excitement that was with difficulty suppressed during the reading of the correspondence with Mr. Gladstone . . . The reading of the delegates' report was no sooner ended than the pent-up storm burst on the meeting with the swiftness and violence of an avalanche.

The storm came when Abraham tried to return to his original motion of Monday, a move that Parnell again obstructed by calling on one of his own supporters. In the uproar, Parnell lost both his composure and his control of the meeting for some time. Shortly afterwards, the exchange occurred that set the tone for the coming controversies in Ireland. John O'Connor said that if the party rejected Parnell's leadership, it would effectively place itself under that of Gladstone. The *Freeman* report continues:

> Arthur O'Connor: 'He is not a member of the Party.'
>
> Redmond: 'The master of the Party' (*cheers and counter-cheers*).
>
> Healy: 'Who is to be the mistress of the Party?' (*Cries of 'shame', noise, several members calling out remarks which could not be distinguished in the uproar*).
>
> William Redmond: 'They must be very badly off when they go to arguments like that.'
>
> A voice: 'It is true.'
>
> Arthur O'Connor: 'I appeal to my friend the chairman' (*noise*).
>
> Parnell: 'Better appeal to your own friends. Better appeal to that cowardly little scoundrel there (*noise*) that in an assembly of Irishmen dares to insult a woman' (*cheers and counter-cheers*).
>
> Arthur O'Connor: ' . . . whatever painful duty we have to discharge we should discharge it like gentlemen' (*cheers*).

When Abraham's turn came, he moved the termination of Parnell's tenure of the chairmanship of the party. When Parnell tried to rule the motion out of order, Arthur O'Connor signalled the end of anti-Parnellite patience, protesting that it was obvious that a partial chairman was helping a minority to postpone indefinitely the decision of the majority. McCarthy then intervened and invited all who thought like him to withdraw from the room. Redmond watched as forty-four members, many of them close colleagues, followed McCarthy to the next room, where they passed a resolution that they 'being an absolute majority of the whole number of the Irish Parliamentary Party' declared that Parnell's chairmanship was terminated. Twenty-seven M.P.s stayed with Parnell. Henceforth, the Parnellites would call their opponents 'seceders', while they in turn would be denounced as 'pledge-breakers' for not abiding by the view of the majority. Technically the Parnellites were in the right, since the view of the majority had not been expressed in a vote of the whole party, but that was the result of Parnell's partiality in the chair. Declaring Parnell's tenure of the chair terminated, the majority group elected McCarthy as its chairman, to exercise his functions jointly with a committee of eight.[34] Healy was its most prominent member, and two places were kept open for the absent Dillon and O'Brien.[35]

II

Redmond's decision to adhere to Parnell came at a greater emotional cost than that incurred by most of his colleagues who decided to break with him. For many members, their natural regret, even consternation, at the breach with a leader who had raised the Home Rule cause to unprecedented political significance was overwhelmed by the conviction that Parnell had become the chief danger to that cause. For Redmond, everything in his character and past behaviour seemed to point to an identification with the majority in following the path marked out in 1885–6. Not only was he temperamentally averse to the radical destructiveness embodied in Parnell's manifesto, but nothing in his utterances since 1886 had hinted at his having second thoughts about the adequacy of that year's proposed settlement. Despite his protestation that he was not allowing personal loyalty or sentiment to influence his judgement, it is difficult to see how anything but his attachment to Parnell could have made tolerable for him the wrench with his own recent past and led him to attach greater weight to Parnell's new-found misgivings about the Liberal alliance than to the short-term prospects of Home Rule.

That attachment was compounded of similarities of social background and – insofar as it is possible to discern ideologies in a party of pragmatists – a shared set of political beliefs. Both men held that a Home Rule Ireland must seek to include diverse elements within the nation. Redmond, despite his involvement in the Plan of Campaign, was, as we have seen, no agrarian radical; he did not wish the interests of the tenants to eclipse all others within the movement. Like Parnell, he could, from a tory-paternalist vantage point compatible with his gentry background, envisage the agricultural labourers as a needed counterweight to the influence of the tenants, and also hope for a role in the future for those resident landlords who would accommodate themselves to the new order. Equally, although a devout Catholic, he had shown himself well able to fend off unwelcome interventions by clerics in the political movement. He had too much respect for the Protestant tradition to identify with the tide of Catholic triumphalism, personified by Healy, which now engulfed the country.

But alongside shared political vision and the hunting parties at Aughavanagh, there was the spell which Parnell's personal magnetism had cast over him. Five years after Parnell's death he told a US audience:

> Here was a strong, still man, a man to be followed and trusted to the death by his friends, a man of grim and stern resolve, of unbending nature. He was unmoved by applause as by hatred and scorn . . . Never will [Ireland] be represented by a higher or stronger personality . . . [36]

At the unveiling of the Parnell monument in Dublin many years later he balanced this characterization by calling him 'one of the tenderest, gentlest, and most sensitive hearts I ever knew'.[37]

In the years after 1886, and especially in the year of his private grieving which immediately preceded the split, Redmond had been allowed to burnish his personal image of the matchless leader in a way in which others were not. His remoteness from the centre of the party's internal politics had shielded him from first-hand experience of the irritations – the mysterious disappearances, the failure to endorse fully the Plan of Campaign – which had revealed Parnell's inadequacies as leader and had so exasperated those, such as O'Brien, equally susceptible to his charisma.

Now the pull of conflicting loyalties affected Redmond deeply. He wrote to Father Furlong on 7 December: 'Nothing in the present heartbreaking crisis gave me greater pain than your telegram . . . I need not, I am certain, assure you that I have acted from a clear and strong conception of what is best for the country and from no other consideration whatever.'[38]

III

With a by-election pending in North Kilkenny, the arena of conflict was now transferred to Ireland. A large number of M.P.s of both factions arrived in Dublin on the following Wednesday morning, 10 December. Parnell proceeded to the office of the *United Ireland*, where he dismissed Mathias Bodkin, the editor, and installed Leamy in his place. That night, in the midst of 'a torrent of popular feeling' in his favour, he went from the Mansion House to the crowded Rotunda, where 'the fervour within rivalled that without', to inaugurate his campaign. Healy and his brother were attacked in O'Connell Street and had to have police protection. On the platform with Parnell were John and William Redmond and six other M.P.s, together with the lord mayor. Parnell

Figure 12. 'Under Which Flag?': anti-Parnellite cartoon (*United Ireland*, 6 December 1890). *Courtesy of the National Library of Ireland.*
As the split takes hold, Erin is faced with the choice of following a lone Parnell towards the clouds of dissension, or his opponents (from left, Tim Healy, Thomas Sexton, John Dillon, William O'Brien and T.P. O'Connor) towards the sunburst of an Irish Parliament.

offered a passionate vindication of his actions, saying that the independence of the party had to be defended against Gladstone's intervention, and portrayed himself emotively as the victim of 'a movement of mutiny' while he was 'crippled in strength' by illness. He promised to pursue the settlement of the land question, and made a pitch for the support of the labouring classes, to whom he would have more to say in the near future.

Redmond spoke next, giving his apologia for the position he had taken in Committee Room 15. He had never believed in the likelihood of Gladstone's retirement threat being carried out; as confirmation of this, he cited the latter's statements since Saturday that he was determined to carry on. (This, of course, ignored the fact that Gladstone now looked on the 'seceding' majority, with its new leadership, as the legitimate Irish party.) Making the best of the weakest points in the Parnellite case, he attempted to justify both Parnell's silence in the year since Hawarden and his breach now of that silence:

> I say for my part, I believe that if he had spoken at any time during the past year while hope still remained that at the head of an united

> party he would have been able to force the hand of Mr. Gladstone he would have been false to Ireland. If he allowed himself to be driven out of public life with this secret locked in his breast of the worthlessness of the Home Rule bill he would have been doubly false to the interests of his country.

Speaking of his part in the deputation to Gladstone, he told of having sat with the others for an hour in the latter's room:

> I said the Irish people honoured and loved him for what he had done in the past. I said to him our country was now standing on the brink of an abyss. I said to him you are the one man living who by saying a word, by stretching out a hand, can save our country. I asked him not to allow any official etiquette, or considerations of personal dignity or offended dignity, to stand in the way, and I asked him in God's name to tell us the truth what it was he proposed to give us, and he sat in his chair deaf to my appeal.

Gladstone's record in the 1885 election and in the whittling down of the 1886 Bill entitled him (Redmond), he claimed, to believe that there was small chance of the next Home Rule Bill being satisfactory if they abandoned their independence. He did not advert to the awkward fact of his own wholehearted acceptance of that Bill at the time. Finally, he seemed to clutch at straws when he asserted that none of the trouble would have happened if Dillon and O'Brien had not been absent from the country. 'I love, honour and trust them,' he said, calling for their return as soon as possible.[39]

While the Rotunda meeting was in progress, a group of anti-Parnellites led by Healy and Bodkin retook possession of the *United Ireland* office. The next morning, a furious Parnell led a group of supporters, including four M.P.s, one of them William Redmond (John's whereabouts are not known), in an attack on the locked office, whose door they battered down before recapturing it. After this, control of the paper remained with Parnell. Bodkin, however, managed to bring out one more anti-Parnellite issue of the paper, which gave a graphic account of the raid, describing Parnell's face as 'distorted with mad passion'.[40]

Before going to Kilkenny, Parnell travelled first to his own Cork city constituency. His rail journey there was marked by hostile receptions at stops along the way; his welcome in the city, however, was described by the *Freeman* as rivalling Dublin's in its enthusiasm. The pattern was already beginning to emerge of Parnell's support being concentrated in the cities and towns, with the rural areas predominantly against him.[41] At Kilkenny, the Parnellites were faced with the formidable organizational skills of Davitt, who devised the strategy of dogging Parnell's footsteps throughout the constituency, confronting him at every opportunity in order to subvert his principal strength, the regal mystique that had hung about his image for ten years. The rhetorical onslaught on the deposed leader was carried on principally by Healy and by the eccentric and unstable Dr Charles Tanner, a Cork Protestant M.P. who had made a speciality of violent abuse of the police during the Plan of Campaign.[42] Healy now employed a populist rhetoric that abandoned issues of high politics and fixed on the details of the divorce case – the more embarrassing and ridiculous, the better – and on offensive references to Katharine O'Shea, as well as on personal denigration of individual Parnellites. At Freshford, he told the crowd 'they should strike a blow for Ireland and for O'Brien and Dillon, and not for the man down at Brighton riding on a fire-escape'.[43] Anticipating that the Parnellites would try to paint their opponents as Liberal stooges, Healy contended that Redmond and two other Parnellites were the only M.P.s in the entire party who could be accused of ever holding place under a British Government (a weak reference to the clerkship Redmond had held in the House of Commons before becoming a M.P.) and, more tellingly, that Redmond, unlike Sexton, was a member of the National Liberal Club, that hotbed of Liberal intriguers and 'wirepullers'.[44]

Two factors weighed against the Parnellites from the start: the opposition of the vast majority of the Catholic clergy, and poor organization, which limited their campaign to rapid sorties led by Parnell himself from his base in Kilkenny town. Redmond, his most prominent supporter, was late in arriving in the constituency, having been detained in Tipperary at further Plan of Campaign trials. He ignored Healy's attacks, repeated his high regard for Dillon and O'Brien and strove for a high tone:

> I am not here . . . to say one harsh word of any man arrayed on the other side of this controversy. God forbid that any word of mine should add to the difficulties and dangers of the situation, and heavy will be the reckoning which must be made with any man on any side of this struggle who allows his temper to run away with his judgment . . . (*a voice – 'Healy'* [*hisses*]*; another voice – 'Down with him'* [*groans*]). For my part I give to every man opposed the same credit for just as pure motives as I claim for myself (*cheers*). There are men on the other side of this controversy, men I honour, and love, and respect. [45]

As the flying column of Davitt and Tanner pursued Parnell around the county, with Tanner sounding his rallying cry 'Tally-ho Mr. Fox!', the atmosphere became violent. In the village of Ballinakill, rival groups of supporters clashed and Davitt was hit with an ashplant. At Castlecomer on the same day, lime was thrown at Parnell, some of which hit him in the eye; the incident caused him to be laid up in his hotel all the next day. When he appeared on the balcony in the evening, the sight of him wearing a bandage over the injured eye was, according to the *Freeman*, more effective than any speech. The same newspaper complained that Tanner incited a crowd to throw mud at its reporters by calling out, 'Here comes the Fire Escape Journal', and demanded that Davitt dissociate himself from the 'disgraceful' doctor.[46]

At Kilkenny town the following evening, Redmond regretted the fact that the newspapers were under-reporting 'the blackguardism and ruffianism which had emanated from their opponents'. He was acutely conscious of the damage done to the cause by the violence:

> What a spectacle they presented to the nations of the world! They claimed for Ireland the right of self-government, and yet here in Kilkenny in settling among themselves a purely Irish matter – the election of a member for an Irish constituency – they could not apparently do so without conduct and language which would be disgraceful to the lowest dregs of the lowest slums of any city in the world.[47]

Those close to the realities were observing that while Parnell's support was strong among the numerically small upper classes, and among the poor of the towns, who did not have the vote, it was weakest among the large middle group of tenant-farmers.[48] Bishop Abraham Brownrigg wrote to Archbishop Walsh that 'the lowest dregs of the people, the Fenian element, and the working classes are all to a man with Parnell'.[49] The Church hierarchy was throwing its full influence into the scales, opening Church grounds to anti-Parnellite meetings, at which priests spoke from the platforms. Apart from moral disapproval of Parnell's conduct and fears for their own future influence if he were to succeed despite the condemnation of the hierarchy, the priests were concerned at the sudden apparent resurgence of the Fenians, and at Parnell's flirtation with them. Some of those alienated from Parnell since the Kilmainham treaty had come to flock under his banner, one such being the Cork Fenian P. N. Fitzgerald, who became the assistant director of his campaign. Parnell responded with ambiguous hints concerning a possible failure of the constitutional movement. 'If the young men of Ireland have trusted me,' he said, 'it is because they know that I am not a mere parliamentarian.' An unauthorized 'appeal to the hillside men' issued in his name was repudiated by him, but Redmond allowed himself to echo its rhetoric at Kilkenny when he declared that Parnell's fight 'was the same old fight that in the old dark days was fought by the brave Irishmen on the hill-sides'.[50]

Over the final weekend of the campaign he struggled, like Parnell and his other supporters, to keep attention on the issue of who had the right to decide the Irish leadership, but it was clear that the message was making little impression in the small towns where he spoke. At Johnstown on 19 December he referred to the influence of the priests, avowing that if the people were left to themselves, the anti-Parnellite candidate would not get more than 50 votes, and claiming that the clergy were divided.[51] But only one parish priest dared to defy his bishop's policy, drawing a distinction between public and private morality and urging his hearers to exercise independent judgement. Significantly, his was the only parish in which Parnell received a majority of the votes.[52] The election result, 2,527 votes for the anti-Parnellite Sir John Pope-Hennessy against 1,362 for Parnell's candidate, Vincent Scully, announced on 23 December, was a crushing blow for Parnell. He could only explain to his followers that they were faced with a conspiracy, hatched by a group that included Davitt, Healy, the Liberal newspaper magnate W. T. Stead and others, and pledge to fight on.[53]

The biggest casualty of the Kilkenny election was the myth of Parnell's kingly imperturbability. Some of Redmond's strictures about the language used in the campaign could have applied equally to Parnell. Personal abuse such as 'Gutter sparrows like Dr. Tanner!' and 'Hounds like Davitt!' injured not so much his opponents as his own reputation for self-control. Journalists covering the campaign noticed his dishevelled appearance and fevered, wild-eyed demeanour throughout, and wondered if he was going mad.[54] Coming so soon after the violence at the *United Ireland* office, none of this can have been comfortable for Redmond. It must have been a considerable relief when Timothy Harrington, the only member of the delegation to America not to have signed the anti-Parnell telegram in the wake of the manifesto, arrived back in Ireland and reached Kilkenny on the night before the vote. His declaration in interview that he placed his hopes in Dillon and O'Brien to resolve the conflict coincided perfectly with Redmond's sentiments and seemed to create a space for a moderate Parnellite position that would seek to prevent the party split from becoming irreparable.

IV

The weekend of Harrington's return, O'Brien was already on the Atlantic, having left New York with T. P. Gill on 13 December. Facing arrest if he landed in Ireland, he and Gill sailed for France and arrived at Boulogne on Christmas Day. Although both men had signed the anti-Parnell messages sent to Ireland since the latter's manifesto, their distance from the scene of conflict allowed them to hope that a final split could be averted, and they were horrified by the reports they received of the tactics and language used by Healy and Tanner in Kilkenny. Both cherished warm personal attachments to the deposed leader. Both were fearful of the damage a defeated and humiliated Parnell might inflict on the prospects for Home Rule and on the constitutional movement itself.[55]

There was every indication that Redmond, in common with Harrington and other Parnellites, believed that a compromise solution was still possible. Although he had alienated friends and risked his political future to stand by his beleaguered leader, his speeches showed that he did not embrace the ruthless logic, shared by Parnell and Healy, by which each sought the annihilation of the other. He had made a judgment that the interests of Home Rule required the preservation of Parnell's leadership; he now set himself to see whether the substance, if not the form, of this leadership could be maintained and reconciled with the re-unification of the party.

Parnell, though reluctant to enter negotiations in the bitter aftermath of Kilkenny, was persuaded to meet O'Brien. On 30 December, the Redmond brothers, Clancy and Dr Kenny accompanied Parnell to Boulogne. Redmond, in his later account to Barry O'Brien, noted that O'Brien was effusive in his greeting, while Parnell was 'extremely reserved and cold'.[56]

Before leaving New York, O'Brien and Gill had conferred with T. P. O'Connor and drawn up a set of proposals which they hoped might smooth the way to a voluntary retirement on Parnell's part. When the talks began, Gill outlined the New York proposals to Redmond, who passed them to Parnell. A meeting of the whole party was to be convened which would 'wipe out' the proceedings of Committee Room 15 and recognize the irregularity of the election of McCarthy. Parnell would then retire and McCarthy would be elected chairman by the whole party. Parnell was to continue as president of the National League, to have the power to nominate half of the party committee if he wished and to have his influence secured in all negotiations with the Liberals about Home Rule. The party would make a public declaration of gratitude to him and state the circumstances mitigating his behaviour in the crisis. Others were to be involved also: Gladstone was to be asked to acknowledge his mistake in publishing his letter so precipitately, while Archbishops Croke and Walsh would be asked to withdraw their denunciations of him. Thus Parnell's influence would remain intact in most respects.

F. S. L. Lyons has described these proposals as 'breathtaking in their bland readiness to overrule virtually every step taken by the majority with whom Dillon and O'Brien had hitherto publicly aligned themselves'.[57] Redmond would later defend his own support for them on the grounds that they constituted 'a sham retirement and not a reality'.[58] Parnell, in reply to these generous terms, stated that he could consider them only if O'Brien were to take over the chairmanship from him, and also turn down the chairmanship of the *National Press*, the new anti-Parnellite newspaper launched to compete with the *Freeman*. O'Brien asked for time to consult Dillon, and in the meantime Parnell returned to London, where he came up with a new and simpler proposal on 1 January. This discarded the various declarations; instead, O'Brien would ask McCarthy, acting as *de facto* chairman, to see Gladstone and seek a memorandum from him setting out his intentions as to the Home Rule matters raised by the deputation on 5 December. McCarthy would pass this to O'Brien, who together with Parnell would assess its adequacy. If they judged it satisfactory, Parnell would retire. To O'Brien's objection that this reduced McCarthy's role to one of messenger, and that he would accept only if the latter were allowed to remain as chairman, Parnell insisted that only O'Brien was acceptable to him as his successor.

This left matters deadlocked, with O'Brien promising to advance an alternative plan.[59]

At this point, Gill, acting as O'Brien's intermediary, evidently felt the indispensability of Redmond as a moderating influence on Parnell. He wrote to O'Brien on 2 January: 'Depend upon it, from this stage forward it is necessary [the word is triply underlined by Gill] to have Jack R present at everything.'[60]

Meanwhile, other anti-Parnellites were uneasy at the news that O'Brien was in talks with their *bête noire*. During the Kilkenny election, when the prospect of such talks was a mere rumour, Archbishop Croke had written to O'Brien:

> Parnell has hopelessly fallen. The bishops and priests and all good men are determinedly *against* him, and his future leadership, under any conditions, is absolutely impossible so far as they are concerned. How then can you touch him? What good can he do?[61]

Healy had also spoken in similar vein in Dublin on Christmas Eve:

> . . . a man who would sacrifice not only his 86 followers, but the millions of the Irish population to satisfy his purpose and ambition. I say we will have no dealings with him (*no, no*). We will have no compromise with him (*hear, hear*). We will have nothing with him except combat and we will give him nothing but defeat.[62]

At the request of Archbishops Croke and Walsh, Healy went to Paris with Barry to try in person to talk O'Brien out of his scheme. After a long conversation on 5 January he came away exasperated at what he saw as O'Brien's overestimation of Parnell's Irish support and the extent to which the latter seemed to have cast a spell over him, leaving him impervious to argument. O'Brien insisted in reply that his chief concern was to rescue the party and the Liberal alliance.[63]

Parnell returned to Boulogne, this time with Redmond and Harrington, on 6 January to hear O'Brien's new proposal.[64] This was that the Liberal assurances should be sought as Parnell had suggested, but the new chairman should be Dillon rather than himself. McCarthy should be allowed to join O'Brien and Parnell in assessing the Liberal proposals. Parnell at first rejected out of hand the idea of Dillon as chairman, but ultimately agreed when put under strong pressure by Redmond and Harrington to accept. The 'Heads of Agreement' document which Parnell then drew up was, with that exception, similar to his proposal of the previous week. The terms of the Liberal memorandum were to be kept secret until the introduction of the Home Rule Bill and to remain so unless the Bill did not measure up to the assurances given; if, however, the Bill was satisfactory, Parnell had the right to publish the memorandum after the Bill became law. The master tactician thus aimed at ensuring vindication, and the possibility of a comeback, for himself in the future no matter what the Liberals did. As to O'Brien's other points, Parnell, who had made known his true opinion of McCarthy's political gifts by calling him at Kilkenny 'a nice old gentleman for a tea-party', was adamant that there could be no role for the latter in assessing the Liberal assurances.[65]

When Dillon was cabled with the details, he at once cabled back his refusal, but agreed to come to Boulogne. His arrival there on 18 January coincided with efforts to get the required guarantees from the Liberals. Crucial to these efforts was the part played by Gill, who hastened back and forward between Boulogne and London and was instrumental in getting Morley to pass on the 'Heads of Agreement' to Gladstone. Harcourt urged Gladstone to stand firm by his position of 5 December that he could not discuss the details of Home Rule until the Irish cleared up the issue of the leadership. However, Gill induced Morley to try to persuade the Liberal leader into 'straining a point': Gladstone could deal officially with McCarthy as the elected leader of the Irish party while unofficially being 'thoroughly enlightened' as to his future sidelining.[66] Dillon was now keeping an open mind as to whether the whole venture might succeed, impressed as he was by the evident desire for peace of Sexton and McCarthy on the one side and of Redmond and Harrington on the other, and appalled by what he later called 'the outrageous attitude assumed by Healy's faction... and by the bishops.'

Finally, having agreed to look no further than McCarthy, the Liberal leaders on 28 January decided on the terms of the guarantees they would give to the Irish. The land question would be settled by the Imperial Parliament either at the same time as the Home Rule settlement or within a specified period afterwards, or the power to settle it would be given to the Irish legislature; the semi-military Royal Irish Constabulary would be transformed within five years into a civil force by the Irish government; the Liberal leaders would regard it as their duty to include the above in the Home Rule Bill as 'essential provisions'.

O'Brien and Dillon found these assurances highly satisfactory and invited Parnell to return to France to examine them. Their hopes were high that the whole matter could be settled within a week. Redmond had already cabled O'Brien and Gill, in advance of the transmission of the assurances, that Parnell wished to meet Gill in London, and told O'Brien to have 'no anxiety about [Parnell's] bona fides'.[67] Even the irreconcilable Healy and the bishops, once they heard that the assurances would be given, looked more tolerantly on the negotiations. Healy assumed that if Parnell showed bad faith, some or all of his followers would come over to the majority under a Dillon leadership. Everything now depended on Parnell and how he would view the assurances.

In the period since his previous visit to Boulogne, Parnell had kept up a punishing routine of travel from Brighton to Ireland each weekend, speaking at public meetings in a desperate effort to win lost ground. He was usually accompanied by Redmond, Harrington, Clancy and one or two other prominent supporters. At these meetings he maintained his position as strongly as ever on the implications of Gladstone's letter for the party's independence, and on the need to guard against a Home Rule Bill which would make inadequate provisions on the land, police and judiciary questions as well as on the retention of Irish members.

Just before returning to France, he travelled to Ennis in the west, a locus of Parnellite support. Redmond, who shared the platform, praised the numbers in attendance as a 'consolation and gratification' personally to Parnell. Speaking under the statue of Daniel O'Connell, he said that the last two months had witnessed one of the basest and meanest attempts ever on a man 'greater in many respects than the man under whose shadow they were assembled today'. Parnell was now sought to be dragged down by 'men whom he had created (*cries of 'Healy'*)'; and

> other men in England, though they were anxious that some Home Rule bill should be given, were anxious to make it as meagre as possible, and desired to get out of the way the one man of the Irish race who was strong enough to strike a bargain upon an equal footing with the greatest of the English statesmen (*cheers*).

Significantly, however, his choice of words implicitly left the door open for a voluntary withdrawal by Parnell: he warned against any attempt 'to drive Mr. Parnell against his will from his position'.[68]

Parnell arrived in Calais on 2 February in what was evidently an exhausted state, at the end of three continuous days of travel to and from Ireland. Not long into his discussions with O'Brien and Dillon, the latter brought up the question of the funds he would need as chairman to pay parliamentary salaries. Parnell suggested that these funds be lodged in both their names. Dillon's reply – to the effect that Parnell could use this control to cut off Dillon's supplies when he wanted – appears to have wounded Parnell deeply. Redmond wrote to O'Brien later that 'I am afraid John's interview with P. at Calais had a *very bad effect* . . .'[69] This row was not decisive, however, in the breakdown of the peace plan. That came later, after Parnell had returned to London. On 3 February he wrote to Gill that at Calais he had 'omitted to notice' that the assurances included no provision for the retention of the full Irish representation at Westminster in the event of the land question not being settled simultaneously with Home Rule; he was also concerned that the changes to the police force should be mandatory in the Home Rule legislation and not left to the discretion of the Irish executive.[70] Redmond and Clancy conferred at length with Parnell in London the next day; it seems that they tried, unsuccessfully, to prevail on him to accept the assurances.[71] Redmond, who had just received news that his mother was dying, had to leave urgently for Dublin that evening. Clancy wrote on his behalf to O'Brien, entreating him to have patience and not lose heart: 'We believe Parnell is sincere and is acting bona fide'. A little more concession, he wrote, would 'make things right'.[72]

On 5 February, Redmond wrote to O'Brien that he understood there would be no problem in getting a strengthened assurance on the police question, and that the issue of the land settlement was the only point in dispute, a matter about which he begged O'Brien 'to leave no stone unturned to bring about the small further concession . . . to put us all in accord'.[73] Even as he did so, Parnell's negative mood was deepening. Writing to Gill that day, he claimed to have formed an impression from a conversation with him the previous day that the Liberals were making 'new proposals and demands', aimed at excluding him (Parnell) from the assessment of the assurances, thus placing him in a 'humiliating and disgraceful position'. To make matters worse, he had received 'information of a most startling character' from a 'reliable source' that the Liberals intended to keep the Irish representation at full strength at Westminster, not temporarily (as leverage while Irish autonomy remained incomplete), as Parnell was demanding, but permanently, as a pretext, he claimed, for the Imperial Parliament to exercise a veto on legislation of the Irish body.[74]

To this letter, which Dillon called 'a most treacherous document', a bewildered Gill replied that evening, and wrote again on the two following days, that Parnell's impression must be founded on a misunderstanding, that he knew nothing of any new Liberal conditions and could not speak for anyone but O'Brien. Parnell, however, was unimpressed and disputed the accuracy of Gill's recollection of their conversation.[75] Redmond, detained in Dublin, was evidently contacted by Gill, as he cabled to the latter on 6 February: 'Impossible to start this morning wire nature of immediate danger can I do any good by telegram prevent any final decision till he consults friends reply Redmond League office.'[76]

He managed to cross to London that night and spent some time with Parnell in London the following day. Writing to O'Brien, he was still optimistic regarding the two amendments to the assurances sought by Parnell, and made light of the latter's new objections. However, he told O'Brien that his 'power for good' had been 'enormously lessened' by the publication of a statement in the press that O'Brien and Dillon had informed Gladstone of their satisfaction with the assurances already given.[77] Meanwhile Gill had brought Parnell's letter of 5 February with him to Boulogne, from where O'Brien wrote to Parnell on 8 February that he had read it with 'astonishment' and that there was 'not a shadow of foundation' for Parnell's claims.[78]

In the absence of movement from Parnell, breakdown now seemed inevitable. O'Brien, writing to Redmond the same day that there was 'not the smallest use in prolonging the agony', looked forward with dread to an outcome which would make Healy 'the happiest man in London'.[79] As O'Brien wrote to Parnell on 9 February lamenting 'the unspeakably sad and tragic turn of affairs',[80] Redmond also wrote to the latter urgently requesting a meeting:

> . . . Until you have seen me I would strongly urge you not to publish anything whatever. I have some good reason for believing that the Liberals won't agree to amend the memo in any respect even as to the Constabulary and that therefore, if you so choose, you will be in a position to break off on that ground, which I'm sure you see would be an infinitely safer ground than the 'new condition' which O'Brien never heard of and did not agree to . . .[81]

He was right; it was Liberal intransigence, as much as that of Parnell, which brought the end, when Gill carried the news to Parnell on 10 February that the Liberal leaders had refused 'to alter a comma' of the assurances. Parnell cabled to O'Brien and Dillon that he must stand by his 'Calais position'. With supreme insouciance, he wrote to O'Brien that he regretted that

> it is not possible for me to consider the National interests so safeguarded that I could feel there would be no danger to the cause in my now surrendering the responsibility which has been placed upon me and which I have accepted at the hands of our nation and our race.[82]

The *Freeman* on 11 February reported the failure of the negotiations. At the Euston Hotel just before returning to Dublin, Redmond gave McCarthy a memorandum which stated that Parnell and his followers had abandoned 'any hope of coming to a satisfactory and honourable understanding with the seceders'.[83] O'Brien and Dillon crossed on 12 February to England, where they were arrested and brought back to serve their 6 months' sentence in Galway Jail. Before leaving France they issued statements which condemned the 'shocking vindictiveness and brutality' of (unnamed) eminent opponents of Parnell who had shown 'an utter disregard of what was due to him', but which also rejected the 'outrageous charges and insults' levelled by Parnell at his former colleagues and the Liberal leaders.

If Redmond's services as a negotiator were little tested at the Boulogne discussions, thanks to the Liberal refusal to adjust the assurances, his efforts as adviser to Parnell were nullified by one whose attitude to the advice of his friends could be described, at best, as toleration. Dillon later wrote to O'Brien that Parnell, faced with the urgings of his followers to accept the assurances, had 'trampled on them all and routed them with slaughter'.[84] Parnell told Andrew Kettle (soon to be a Parnellite candidate in another by-election), 'I have a lot of poor weak men around me. In fact I have more trouble with them than with the other fellows.'[85]

It is doubtful whether more flexibility from the Liberals on their assurances would have made much difference to the outcome, given the strength of Parnell's drive to vindicate himself and his capacity to rely on his own resources. However, it is possible, had Parnell then fallen back on the later objections which had so astounded Gill and O'Brien, that Redmond and Harrington would have been forced to confront the likelihood of Parnell's bad faith and to reconsider their allegiance to him. As it was, the action of the Liberal leaders relieved them of this need, so that they emerged from the episode more tightly bound to Parnell than ever.

Undertakings of confidentiality prevented recriminations about the breakdown of the Boulogne negotiations until later in the year, when Redmond's role in particular would come under sustained attack. For now, he told the central branch on 24 February that the seal of secrecy placed the Parnellites at a greater disadvantage then the seceders, and if the truth were revealed it would show that Parnell had acted throughout with 'absolute forgetfulness of self'. Neither did any blame lie with O'Brien for the failure – nothing in his career, he said, reflected greater honour on him than the role he had played – but with 'a knot of persons who would have no fair settlement at all.'[86]

The positive legacy of Boulogne was the assurances given by the Liberals. These were published by McCarthy and Sexton following their party meeting on 12 February (all sides had agreed that they need not be kept secret). Given the lack of agreement, however, they rapidly became a political football. By 16 February the *Freeman* was referring to them as 'alleged assurances'. Parnell, back to his round of weekend meetings, told an audience at Roscommon on 22 February of 'Mr. Justin McCarthy's assurances, which he says that Mr. Morley says that Mr. Gladstone has given to him . . . these third-hand assurances . . .' He proceeded to open the rift wider than ever:

> We shall adopt an attitude of armed observation, until we see what solution is going to be offered to us . . . these seceders, bound hand and foot as they are, without their independence, and forming only an appendage and tail of the Liberal party, some say in receipt of English money, in repayment for the surrender of their independence . . .[87]

V

Polarization deepened as the anti-Parnellites set up the Irish National Federation on 10 March to rival the National League, of which Harrington continued as the chief organizer. A few days earlier, they had launched the daily *National Press*, the successor to the *Insuppressible*, which would pour forth an incessant stream of personalized invective against Parnell and, to a lesser extent, his leading supporters, over the coming months. This editorial policy, which diagnosed the O'Shea divorce case as the 'first cause of the evil', was decided on and sustained by Healy.[88] Sexton, nominally editor, had a managing role and was soon known to be unhappy with the paper's concentration on the 'moral question'. Both the paper and the organization enjoyed strong clerical support. The *National Press* reported: 'Every priest who has been prominent in the national movement was present at the [National Federation] meeting. The four archbishops blessed the infant in its cradle. Almost every bishop in Ireland concurred in its benediction.'[89] Healy's speech at the federation cast Parnell in role of would-be dictator of a Home Rule Ireland:

> I re-echo the sentiment that Home Rule, under Parnell, might indeed have been a curse rather than a blessing (*cheers*). We are teaching the Irish people the meaning of constitutional action; we are teaching them a lesson in self-government. They are learning the lessons at this present hour [that] . . . the majority in the end must rule (*cheers*). We will make that principle a potion which Mr. Parnell must swallow if it was gall and wormwood to him. I would never consent for one hour to remain in the party of which Mr. Parnell was the leader. I will never tolerate him. I will never consent to him in any shape or form.[90]

The anti-Parnellites were thus better prepared for their second electoral contest, the by-election campaign in North Sligo, which took place in the second half of March. With the constituency containing one district that had remained relatively immune to anti-Parnellite propaganda, and in which many of the priests were Parnellite under a bishop who insisted on remaining neutral, the contest was less one-sided than in Kilkenny.[91] Parnell campaigned as feverishly as before for his candidate, V. B. Dillon, on one day covering fifty miles to speak at three meetings. The *Freeman* marvelled at his 'energy and tireless exertions'.[92] Trying to make the primary issue that of leadership, he attacked his opponents: 'Can you make any of them a leader? . . . Can you select the foul-mouthed Timothy Healy? Can you trust in uncertain and wobbling Tom Sexton? And can you follow hysterical Davitt who never belongs to any one party for 24 hours altogether?'[93] Violence was again a feature of the campaign. Healy having been injured in an assault at Tipperary by O'Brien Dalton, a prominent Parnellite, his place in Sligo was taken by his brother Maurice, helped by Sheehy and Davitt.[94] Condemnation of the incident by leading Parnellites was mild. Fighting erupted when anti-Parnellites entered some of the Parnellite areas – Maurice Healy and his canvassers were stoned out of one such parish – and when Parnell held a rally in Sligo town.[95] The *Freeman* tried, to little effect, to counter Healy's cultivation of clerical support by digging up an 1882 allegation by Charles Bradlaugh, the embattled atheist M.P., that Healy had told him he shared his opinions on religious matters but could not reveal them in priest-ridden Ireland.[96]

The *National Press* reported on 23 March that at all the Catholic churches in North Sligo the previous day the priests had earnestly called on the electors to vote against the Parnellite candidate.[97] Redmond was on hand at the Sligo polling booths on 2 April to witness the arrival of large numbers of illiterate voters, led in groups by their anti-Parnellite priests.[98] This time, however, clerical intimidation was working in both directions, and Healy complained of the encouragement of mob behaviour by the Parnellite section of the clergy after the election. The result gave what the *Freeman* termed the 'West British Helot Party' candidate a majority of 768, a much narrower win than at Kilkenny, but nevertheless another decisive defeat for Parnell.[99]

Redmond criticized clerical intervention as damaging to the Home Rule cause, a contention that became self-fulfilling when the British press reported Parnellite speeches denouncing it.[100] At Rathmines on 20 April he criticized the action of Dr Thomas Nulty, bishop of Meath, in returning the Church dues paid by Parnellites elected as Poor Law guardians, as injurious to the true interests of religion as well as to politics. Parnellites fought back as best they could by seeking to distinguish between the political and the moral, and by pointing out what seemed to them the double standards of the bishops. At Wexford, to which Redmond finally returned on 10 May in answer to the constant anti-Parnellite taunt that he was afraid to face his constituents, he denied that by supporting Parnell they were condoners of sin or apologists for adultery. While they detested the sin laid at his door, they denied that his capacity for political leadership, tested over sixteen years, depended in any degree on the circumstances of his private life.[101] As Parnell and others had done, he made much of the sixteen-day delay in the issuing of the bishops' anathema following the divorce decision, using it as proof that their opposition to Parnell was a response to English pressure rather than to the moral issue.[102] On 8 June, at a meeting at Castlepollard, from which the priests at masses had warned people to stay away, Redmond stated that Archbishop Walsh had written no fewer than six letters in the ten days after the divorce decision, not one of which mentioned the moral issue.[103] None of this prevented Archbishop Croke on 3 June from calling Parnell 'a fallen man . . . a public, reckless and unrepentant sinner'.[104]

Through the thick of the controversy, Redmond did not, publicly at least, abandon all hope of a compromise settlement. Although he continued, along with Harrington, Clancy and a small number of others of the twenty-eight loyalists of Committee Room 15, to campaign vigorously for Parnell, it was evident that his approach was not identical to his leader's. While Parnell fought with frenetic energy for his political life, and accepted the prospect of a permanent split (declaring at Mullingar in May that 'he would rather be the leader of a good minority than of a rotten majority'), Redmond maintained as emollient an approach to his more moderate opponents as was possible in the circumstances. In an article written in March for the *Melbourne Advocate* (which had declared against Parnell), he affirmed that he fully recognized the honour and honesty of their motives, and had not accused them of anything worse than panic when Gladstone released his letter.[105] The following month, he deprecated the violence at the hustings by supporters of both sides, saying that it was 'to the discredit of Irishmen' that political controversy could not be carried on without it, as in England. He welcomed the fact that the National League of America had resolved to use its good offices to try to bring about reunion in Ireland.[106] At Wexford, he spoke of the 'terrible gravity' of the misfortune that had overtaken the country, which could be minimized only

> by full and free discussion, by toleration of the opinions of those who are opposed to us, and by recognising the fact, as I have done from the first, that good and true Irishmen are upon both sides of the controversy . . . I absolutely loathe the personalities, the insults and the scurrilities which have during the past few months brought discredit and disgrace upon our country, and I can truthfully claim that I have done my best to keep this controversy upon a high level.[107]

It was all the more difficult to maintain his equilibrium now that he was a prime target in the sights of the *National Press*. Healy's paper mixed cheap slander (Redmond's criticisms of priests were indistinguishable from the 'No Popery' cries of the Orangemen) with the more serious charge that he had broken his party pledge. It intoned: 'On Mr. Redmond the guilt of broken faith presses with double weight because he solemnly renewed that pledge . . . in the discussions in Committee Room 15.'[108]

To this Redmond replied that the seceders' action had released him from that pledge, since they had held a meeting 'without notice to him or his friends, summoned he knew not how' and constituted themselves a new party.[109] The paper landed some well-researched and damagingly accurate hits on his support for Parnell's new strategy. An anonymous contributor, 'JJD of Cornwall' (very possibly Healy himself), had preserved Redmond's speeches of 1886 on the Home Rule Bill in the House of Commons and at the Chicago convention and used them to good effect to point up the contradictions with his present stance. Regarding the retention of Irish members, he had said that if the Home Rule parliament was to do its work of binding together the nation, it could not stand the additional drain of representation in the House of Commons. Parnell had then thought it was 'not a vital question'.[110] Redmond and Davitt had repudiated at Chicago the post-convention speech of Finnerty, who said that nothing Parnell did could induce him 'to subscribe to the policy that Gladstonian Home Rule is to be accepted as a final settlement of all Ireland's troubles'. Was not Redmond now, in supporting Parnell, playing exactly the same role as Finnerty then? But, commented 'JJD', 'there were then no "English wolves". These grew up like mushrooms after the Divorce Court.'[111]

Later that year, on a platform with Parnell, he would account for his former position by claiming that the situation surrounding the 1886 Bill was

> one which made it well-nigh impossible for the Irish party . . . to reject a measure which every one of them knew was not in any respect a complete and satisfactory measure . . . the Liberal Ministry [had] said 'Take it in full settlement, take it with all its defects, or else we will resign, we will dissolve Parliament and your chance of getting anything will be gone'.[112]

Undoubtedly the biggest sensation Redmond caused in those months was his speech at the National League central branch on 21 April, when he stated that the Plan of Campaign was about to collapse for want of funds, and called on his opponents to join in saving the evicted tenants. As one who had 'never spared himself in the service of the Plan of Campaign tenants (*applause*)', he gave as his opinion that the continuation of the Plan until the tenants obtained their full terms was no longer possible. The two reasons were that, because of the split, sufficient support funds were no longer being raised, and the anti-Parnellite leaders had published not only the exact extent of the funds held, but also the liabilities and amounts paid out monthly in grants to the evicted. 'A more mad and suicidal policy' was never heard of, since the landlords could calculate 'with mathematical precision' the exact moment at which the tenants would be at their mercy. This was a specimen of the 'new kind of political sagacity and statesmanship (*laughter and applause*)' that could be expected from McCarthy and his cabinet. What must be done, he said, was that the only money now available for the Plan, the funds kept in Paris (exceeding £30,000), should be disbursed by Parnell and administered impartially by one person from each side of the split who knew the estates well and would not seek to make political capital from it. Most importantly, the funds should be used with a view to getting settlements on the estates as soon as possible.[113] This speech made it easy for Redmond's enemies to concoct a new charge against him of 'abandoning the Plan of Campaign tenants', although cogent arguments to prove him wrong were lacking. Healy's own attack was easy to fend off, since he had never involved himself in the Plan, and Redmond denied his right to criticize his sincerity.[114] Thomas Condon, an anti-Parnellite and Plan activist, could only bluster that

> there was sufficient manhood and national feeling in Ireland to prevent these tenants being trampled mercilessly out of existence as they would be if Mr. Redmond's programme was carried out . . . the gallant men of Tipperary were not going to follow the chicken-hearted advice of himself or those associated with him.[115]

Parnell still managed to combine parliamentary activity with his Irish campaign. Much of the spring session was taken up by Balfour's Land Purchase Bill, aimed at providing £33 million of state-guaranteed loans to enable tenants to buy their holdings. Parnell had opposed it, albeit half-heartedly, in 1890, in the interests of the Liberal alliance, but now switched to supporting the Government, which incorporated an amendment of his into the Bill that would allow a much larger number of the smaller tenants to purchase. The anti-Parnellites deserted their Liberal allies and supported the Bill, which passed its third reading on 15 June.[116] Parnell's attempt to win over the small tenants came too late to reverse their anti-Parnellism, and in any event the amendment was emasculated by the House of Lords.[117] The House had earlier witnessed the humiliation of Parnell by Maurice Healy. This arose from a challenge Parnell had unwisely issued that both should resign and recontest their Cork seats, a move from which Parnell had since backed away. To Liberal and Tory cheers, Healy challenged Parnell to keep his promise, while Parnell stared defiantly ahead.[118]

New depths of vituperation were plumbed on 1 June, when Healy opened up a new line of attack on Parnell, charging him with embezzlement of party funds. The infamous 'Stop Thief' editorial took up a call made by Archbishop Croke for an audit of party funds, and provocatively developed it: 'the burrowing adulterer . . . has for years been stealing the money entrusted to his charge'.[119] Over the following days Healy tauntingly logged the fact that no libel writ had been received, and rammed home the charge: 'His Grace nowhere suggested that Mr. Parnell pocketed the money. We did . . . He never suggested that Mr. Parnell was a thief. We say so.'[120] The *Freeman* called the allegation 'the figment of a diseased and distorted brain'.[121]

The death of the veteran nationalist M.P. The O'Gorman Mahon brought about the third and last of the by-elections fought by Parnell, in Carlow, in late June. Just before it took place, he and Katharine were married on 25 June near Brighton (the divorce having been made absolute in mid-May). The Catholic hierarchy responded by unanimous resolution: 'Mr. Parnell, by his public misconduct, has utterly disqualified himself to be their political leader . . . [he is] wholly unworthy of the confidence of Catholics.'[122] The marriage further isolated Parnell in Ireland, losing him the support of some of his followers and giving his enemies further ammunition for moral outrage. 'In the eyes of every Catholic in this country these wretched people had added sacrilege to adultery,' said M. J. Kenny M.P. at Tullow.[123] In the prosperous rural constituency of Carlow the Parnellites fought an uphill battle for their candidate, Andrew Kettle, a Dublin agrarian radical. Stones and bludgeons were in use on both sides.[124] Redmond, according to the *National Press*, 'passed a bad quarter of an hour' at Tullow and had to be rescued by the police when a crowd made a rush for him.[125]

The result was 3,755 votes for the anti-Parnellite against only 1,539 for Kettle. The upward trend, which might have been discerned between Kilkenny and Sligo, was devastatingly reversed. The *National Press* exulted: 'Faction is crushed. The men of Carlow have dealt it the death-blow . . . ' The *Freeman* lamented: 'the spirit of nationality is dead'.[126]

VI

Parnell had already scheduled a 'National Convention' for 23 July, an event which now took on added importance in the wake of his third successive defeat. 'Every man is wanted. Every man should be at his post', the *Freeman* exhorted a few days after the Carlow election.[127] Around the same time, in a letter smuggled from Galway Jail, O'Brien wrote to Gill of the 'splendid opportunity for reunion' opened up by the election result, not through further futile negotiations, but through a realization by Parnell's supporters that their cause was hopeless. Feeling unable to communicate directly with Redmond for fear of misunderstanding, he outlined to Gill the steps which should be urged on Redmond:

> The Dublin convention is plainly [organized] on the eve of our release to make Parnell's men nail their colours to the mast and make reconciliation impossible . . . If Redmond will write a letter suggesting that the convention be postponed, in view of the declaration of [the result] . . . in Carlow, until our release and until there be consultation as to some possibility of re-establishing union, it would be a decisive stroke . . . Of course, if Parnell declined, Redmond would have to write and give his reasons for declining to attend the convention. It would be easy for him to make an irrefutable case . . . If John Redmond shows that spirit, I am pretty confident that we would be able to enforce tolerant and even generous treatment from the other side – though, of course, Parnell's own follies have tremendously strengthened the party of no quarter . . .[128]

The convention was held in the Leinster Hall, its attendance swollen by members of the Gaelic Athletic Association, recent recruits to Parnellism who had held their own gathering the previous day.[129] The size and enthusiasm of the assembly reflected Parnell's one sizeable bastion of strength in Dublin. The *Freeman* reported 2,500 delegates present, with 24 M.P.s on the platform. Redmond, however, was notably not among them. It is not known if Gill had communicated with him on the lines suggested by O'Brien. Earlier that week, however, he had begun an appearance for the defence in two sensational, though non-political, murder trials at the Wicklow assizes. Eyebrows must have been raised when his curt telegram was read out amid the letters of apology: 'Wicklow Thursday – Detained here; heavy murder case; regret can't attend Convention.'[130] Although the excuse for the absence was cast-iron, it was the first instance of what was later interpreted as an attempt by Redmond to distance himself from Parnell.

At the convention, Parnell acted as if he were still the undisputed leader of the nation, endorsing a set of new policies on the land and labour issues and on amnesty for the men imprisoned for the dynamite outrages of the previous decade. He affected to have no hope for a good Home Rule Bill from the Liberals in the absence of his own indispensable leadership: 'No answer has been given to us. I know what it is going to be, I know it will be disappointment to the Irish people and their just hopes and expectations.' The strain of recent months was evident when he lost himself in a megalomanic rant, in which he likened himself to Napoleon in his final days:

> And if we are to be beaten, if in this Peninsular warfare we are to be beaten ('*never*') as we have been beaten at Kilkenny (*groans*), in Sligo, and in Carlow (*groans*), our spirits are not subdued, we live for the future; and then if we meet with a Waterloo at the general election ('*no, no*') we will meet with it as did the Old Guard (*loud cheers*) of the great Napoleon, proud and confident of our future . . . knowing well that we shall rise through defeat to victory . . .[131]

Dillon and O'Brien were released from prison on 30 July. In Galway jail, although both continued to be appalled at Healy's dominance of the anti-Parnellite forces, they had agreed that there was no question of siding with Parnell. O'Brien had argued for postponing a declaration until new peace proposals could be discussed (what Healy called 'another effort to revive the fatal Boulongdering which went on some months ago'[132]). This was in harmony with the news that Dillon told him he had received from his cousin V. B. Dillon 'that Redmond, Clancy, etc. are anxious to co-operate with us for peace, and ask us not to commit ourselves'.[133] However, with the dramatic shift in the balance against Parnell since Boulogne, Dillon was convinced that the priority was to fight Healy's influence from within anti-Parnellism, after which it might be possible to offer conciliatory terms to moderate Parnellites such as Redmond. Dillon's attitude prevailed, and the two released a statement immediately on their release, declaring against Parnell. Parnellites in general were reported by the *Freeman* to be 'much astonished and disappointed' at the rapidity of the declaration, and William Redmond and Leamy made immediate 'fervid speeches' in response the same day.[134]

A further blow to Parnell came on 31 July when Edward Dwyer Gray, the biggest shareholder in the *Freeman* company, who had been seeking a way since the Sligo election of reorienting the editorial policy of the paper, announced his opposition to Parnell, giving the latter's marriage as the grounds for his change of stance. The paper, under its editor Dr Edward Byrne, did not immediately adopt this policy, but modulated its tone. Its 1 August leader 'We are for Conciliation' pleaded: 'we deprecate excited criticism upon the action of theirs [Dillon and O'Brien], no matter how mistaken and unfortunate we believe it to be'.[135]

The conciliation looked for by the *Freeman* did not materialize. Although the speeches of O'Brien and Dillon at Mallow on 9 August were free of personal abuse,[136] Parnell was not long in rounding on them, using the Plan of Campaign débâcle against them. On 11 August, Harrington announced that for the first time in its nine years the

National League had made no grants in aid of evicted tenants, the funds having expired.[137] At Kells on the following Sunday, Parnell adopted a 'told you so' attitude. Allowing the Plan to go ahead was one of the political mistakes he had made, he said; he had never agreed with asking poor tenants to do what he was not willing to do himself. Looking to the Paris Funds was illusory – there was not enough money there to maintain the tenants of even one Plan estate for one year. The speech generated a newspaper controversy between Parnell and Dillon; ironically, the acquisition of new enemies allowed Parnell to debate the split's political issues for the first time.[138]

Redmond conspicuously made no public comment on any of these moves, maintaining a six-week period of silence in Ireland, which would prompt much speculation about his attitude. Such speculation intensified in early September when he was advertised as due to speak with Parnell at Westport, but did not turn up.[139] Taken together with his absence from the convention, this withdrawal gave birth to the story of Redmond's 'desertion' of Parnell, which after the latter's death was used by opponents to portray Redmond as a self-aggrandizing factionist posing as a Parnellite. O'Brien, Dillon and Healy would all make liberal use of the 'desertion' charge in the coming months and years. In 1895, the *Freeman* was still editorializing on how Redmond had 'cold-shouldered Parnell in the last months of his life' by staying away from the July convention and the Westport meeting.[140] The accusation was taken up after 1900 by the critics of Redmond's leadership of the reunited Irish Party to portray him and the party as unworthy inheritors of Parnell's mantle.[141]

Much of what lay behind the 'desertion' allegation had more to do with appearance than with reality. Behind the scenes in July, Redmond was busily co-operating with Parnell in the House of Commons in taking up the question of amnesty in relation to the cases of John Daly and James Egan, two men convicted of involvement in a bomb conspiracy in 1883. He had visited Daly in Portland prison at the time of the Carlow election but was refused a private meeting; having protested in the House, he was successful on his second visit in late July. On 3 August, he moved a motion for the amnesty of Daly in a powerful speech that advanced evidence that the conviction was the result of a police plot during Harcourt's home secretaryship. The speech was no ordinary one: the density of its factual material spoke of days of research and preparation.[142] Nor was there anything new in his absence from Parnell's public meetings: eight weeks had gone by between the Sligo election and the end of May during which the two men were equally busy but did not share a platform, a fact that reflected no more than an intelligent division of labour between Parnell and his chief supporter.[143]

However, it is not surprising that his public silence in August and the first half of September should have excited speculation. In the absence of any explanation from Redmond himself, we can only conclude that it reflected, not only a desire to keep himself open to possible fresh overtures from O'Brien, but a degree of unhappiness with the direction Parnell's campaign was taking. There had always been a plausible case that it was destructive of the Home Rule cause; it now seemed to be damaging Parnell himself. His friends had been pleading with him to take a break from his relentless campaigning, seeing it as both fruitless and injurious to his health. There is no evidence, however, that Redmond was considering a defection from Parnell in the manner of Dwyer Gray. His goal, an increasingly unrealistic one, remained an accommodation with the O'Brien–Dillon section involving a voluntary withdrawal of Parnell, which would allow the bulk of the party to reunite on honourable terms. At this time, neither he nor anyone else could know how short a time Parnell had left to live. After the latter's death, however, it was easy for his enemies to make the weeks of silence seem like an abandonment of a dying man.

Two considerations forced Redmond to end his moratorium. Firstly, no approaches were made to him by Dillon or O'Brien, during those six weeks, to reopen negotiations, leading him to conclude that they were now firmly in Healy's grip. Secondly, even if he was considering giving up the fight, there was no likelihood that the 'tolerant and even generous treatment' hoped for by O'Brien would be forthcoming from the Healy camp. On 6 August a depressed Gill had written to O'Brien from Nenagh that although relations between the two sides at local level were good, and only the clergy imported 'personalities' into the split, yet 'Among the Parnellites here what they most dread in leaving him [Parnell] is the alternative of being delivered over to Tim Healyism [Gill's emphasis]. . .'[144] Gill wrote of his horror at the 'black list' of Parnellites already published in the *National Press*; that day's edition contained another such list, as well as an 'atrocious' speech by M. J. Kenny. He urged O'Brien to speak out against such blackguardism, and not to find excuses for it by thinking of the 'gutter-sparrows' among the Parnellites, pointing out that no important Parnellite voice had 'striven to befoul or embitter the controversy' since his release.[145]

These unpropitious circumstances left only one avenue open to Redmond. Ironically, it was a speech of Parnell's, at Listowel on 13 September, which was the immediate occasion of his own return to the platform. In words which seemed as much a challenge to Redmond to declare himself, as an attack on Dillon and O'Brien, Parnell went beyond previous criticism of the management of the Plan to denounce its whole concept. It had been started, he claimed, not for the benefit of the tenants, but 'for the benefit of an English political party'. It was 'a false and a foolish motive' that had asked the tenants to leave their holdings 'because certain English members said it was necessary to show that the Irish people were fighting Balfour'. This was an incredible twist, given that his early doubts about the Plan had centred on the risk of its alienating the Liberals. Throwing contempt about with impartial abandon, he insisted on being one of the administrators of the Paris Fund, since he had made it grow and was not going 'to have it squandered and wasted without my knowledge by a parcel of idiots'.[146]

Redmond responded in Dublin the next evening. He spoke first of O'Brien and Dillon in mixed terms of sorrow and censure. No two men had stood in such esteem and affection, but he regretted to say that their position now was 'devoid of either courage, independence or political foresight'. If they had renewed their efforts of Boulogne, which had 'almost succeeded', their influence for peace would have been enormous, but they had instead put themselves in the 'humiliating position' of being tied to Healy, whose conduct and methods they 'despised and loathed'. (The charge of lack of courage would never be forgotten by O'Brien, who would return it with interest on Redmond on many occasions in the years ahead.) The two men should have stayed in the United States, where they would have gathered £80,000 to £100,000 for the Plan, he said, echoing Parnell while forgetting his own plea of December that they should return with all haste. The anti-Parnellites had turned the question of the evicted tenants into a partisan one, he claimed; his and others' efforts to act jointly with them had been 'rejected with insult', and tenants had been told to abandon Parnell or face withdrawal of their grants.

But having made clear that he was not about to abandon Parnell, and while repeating his own criticisms of the management of the Plan, he would not accept Parnell's strictures on the Plan *per se*: 'he knew nothing about it being started as an act of disloyalty to Mr. Parnell; but he did know that when it was started it received from him [Redmond] his whole and entire support'. He agreed with Parnell, however, 'that the Plan of Campaign was, in reality, more a political than an agrarian movement'. It was started 'as a great political engine wherewith to fight Balfour and to fight Coercion,' he said, and as such it might still have been useful if disunion had not destroyed it.[147] As an agrarian movement, it had its defects, but it also had its victories. It had reduced the rents, and might be said to have brought on the 1887 Land Act. Its 'terrible defect', however, was that it was too expensive, sometimes costing the organization four or five times the rents being withheld. Now that the figures had been announced, the duty of everyone involved was 'to wind up the whole thing as quickly as possible'. On the many estates where reasonable terms were available, the tenants should be allowed to accept them, he suggested. On those on which settlements were not possible, the tenants must be supported 'come weal or woe', but rigid economy must be enforced, new building, as at New Tipperary, stopped and all unnecessary legal costs ended at once. On those conditions, he would use his influence with Parnell to induce him to make a grant from the Paris Funds. It was in the interests of both sides, he asserted, to get the question 'out of the way', otherwise it would be left like a stone around the neck of the next Liberal chief secretary.[148]

Figure 13. Humpty-Dumpty': anti-Parnellite cartoon (*Weekly National Press*, 26 September 1891). *Courtesy of the National Library of Ireland.*

Leading Parnellites (clockwise from upper left, John Redmond, Tim Harrington, Patrick O'Brien and Dr Joseph Kenny) struggle vainly to restore Parnell to the leadership of a united party while an amused anti-Parnellite voter looks on.

Redmond's return to the fight triggered a virulent response from Healy. The *National Press* devoted several editorial columns to the speech on two successive days. In pinning their hopes on renewed negotiations, it claimed, the 'desperate and drowning Parnellites' had been clutching at a last straw to save themselves; Redmond's 'rage' was that a separate avenue of peace was not opened up for himself and some of the others:

> It is a notorious fact that Mr. John Redmond was anxious to slip out through the back door when he saw how the game was going . . . [and] to sneak back to the party he had deserted and betrayed. But he found the back door shut tight against him . . . It is, politically speaking, as the shriek of the lost soul.[149]

Redmond, together with his brother, Leamy, Clancy and others, shared a platform with Parnell for what would be the last time on 20 September at Cabinteely, County Dublin. Parnell's speech was calm and free from abuse. Redmond seemed, in the midst of a defiant championing of Parnellism, to hold out still the antennae of conciliation. Accepting that Dillon and O'Brien were now in the other camp, he said, 'it is only now that there is an opportunity of arguing the matter decently with those who differ from the men supporting Mr. Parnell'. He did not believe that they would be content to carry on their campaign by scurrility and intimidation. Two things were certain. Gladstone, when he introduced his Home Rule Bill, would know that the standard he must meet was that of Parnell rather than of 'the leaders of the seceders'; any measure of which Parnell did not approve would have no chance of acceptance as a final settlement. Second, those 'weak-kneed' politicians in Ireland who a while ago would have accepted a modest measure of Home Rule would now be forced 'for shame's sake, if for no other reason' to seek as large a measure as that demanded by Parnell. Parnell's action had prevented the situation of 1886 from ever arising again, he declared.[150] Unfortunately for Redmond's hopes for conciliation, O'Brien, speaking the same day at Westport, put the final nail in its coffin when he seemed to indicate that he was indeed relaxed about Healyite tactics against Parnell. In one of the phrases that would reverberate down the years of the split, he spoke of Parnell's opponents realizing that he could not be 'fought with sugar sticks'.[151]

On 22 September, the Parnellite cause suffered another hammer blow when the *Freeman*, following a meeting of the board of directors, appeared with the long-threatened change of editorial policy. Parnell immediately set himself to the task of replacing it with a new paper, but interrupted this to return the following weekend for a Sunday meeting at Creggs, a village seven miles from Roscommon town. Feeling ill on his arrival in Dublin, his supporters alarmed at his physical appearance, he disregarded the advice of Dr Kenny against travelling to Roscommon, and spoke in the rain without cover to a small crowd. No prominent Parnellites accompanied him to the meeting (a fact that became part of the posthumous cult of Parnell and later a weapon in the hands of new contenders for his legacy). However, there was no desertion, bleakly though Redmond and the others must have viewed the immediate prospects. On the same day Redmond was sharing a platform at Clonard, County Meath, with William, Clancy and J. L. Carew, in which he carried on the controversy with O'Brien.[152]

Following a meeting with the promoters of the new daily paper, to be called the *Independent*, Parnell left Dublin, once more against medical advice, to return to Brighton. O'Brien and Dillon announced the start of their autumn campaign of weekend meetings; Gill replied in the *Freeman* to allegations made by Parnell at Creggs about Boulogne. All such considerations were suspended with the announcement, on 7 October, of Parnell's death at Brighton the previous day.

VII

John and William Redmond, reported to be 'deeply affected' on hearing the news, went to the league offices in Dublin and met with a small group of colleagues. They then left for Brighton to arrange for the return of the remains. The tone of the *Freeman* was sorrowful, preferring to remember 'the bright days when Mr. Parnell was leader of a united nation' and calling for Irishmen to forget the 'rankling bitterness' of the months past. Addressing his followers, it declared hopefully, 'No principle is now at stake, no person now blocks the way.'[153] But the only remaining Parnellite organ, the weekly *United Ireland*, now edited by Leamy, was in no mood for conciliation:

> The greatest Chief that this land has known has been murdered by the men whom he dragged from obscurity. Murdered he has been as certainly as if the gang of conspirators had surrounded him and hacked him to pieces . . . Shall Ireland exact no punishment for what has been done?

It named O'Brien as 'dead Caesar's Brutus' and asked, 'Is Mr. John Dillon satisfied now?'[154] The *Freeman* deplored this appeal to the 'passions of desperate or ignorant men' and feared what might happen at the funeral. In the charged emotional atmosphere, Dillon was called a 'murderer' in the streets of the capital. Confounding fears of violence, however, the huge funeral procession through the city streets was a calm, dignified affair. The wreath from Redmond read 'To my beloved friend and honoured leader'. At Glasnevin cemetery, the scene, reported the *Freeman*, was 'inexpressibly touching'.[155] Margaret Leamy remembered later:

> The shades of the autumn night were closing in when he was laid to rest. Blurred by tears I can see them still – the faithful ones who stood there gazing down on the coffin of their Chief as it was

> lowered into the grave. The two Redmonds, overcome by emotion; my husband, Henry Harrison, Dr. Kenny; Tim Harrington and the rest – faithful unto death. And so the shadows darkened![156]

The following day Redmond and other Parnellites met at the National Club, in what Leamy told his wife was 'the most heartrending experience of all', 'like a family of bereft orphans . . . captainless and rudderless on a stormy sea'.[157] The uncompromising manifesto they issued that night, signed by twenty-eight Parnellite M.P.s, put paid to any hopes on the other side that the struggle might be about to end. In what the *Freeman* called a 'declaration of war', the manifesto stated that

> we propose to carry on the struggle until the principles for which [Parnell] lived and died have triumphed, and the national unity has been restored around a Parliamentary party pledged to work for Ireland under the flag of Independent Opposition and absolutely free from the control of any foreign power or party . . . But with the men immediately responsible for the disruption of the National party, who, in obedience to foreign dictation, have loaded with calumny and hounded to death the foremost man of our race, we can have no fellowship.[158]

For Redmond, the fateful decision to continue the fight followed logically from the decision to throw his support behind Parnell in Committee Room 15. The chief political issue of the split, inextricably bound up with the personal position of Parnell while he lived, had survived his death and lived on in the failure of the majority section to repent the great sin of discarding its leader at the behest of the Liberals. Clearly, no *rapprochement* was possible with Healy; equally, it seemed that Dillon and O'Brien had capitulated completely to Healy and were now beyond negotiation. Those, on the other hand, who had seen Redmond's chief concern as being to preserve Parnell's honour and who underestimated the depth of his engagement with the political issue, expected Parnell's death to remove the main obstacle to his rejoining the majority and were dismayed at his new-found intransigence. O'Brien many years later could only see his decision at that moment in such personal terms:

> He had only to say the word (it is quite certain Mr. Harrington would have gladly said it with him) to have united the country around Parnell's coffin in a spirit of generous justice to his genius . . . unluckily, Mr. Redmond failed wholly to rise to the opportunity of his life . . . the part he now took, when Parnell was no longer living, and when every motive of honour to his memory as well as to the country ought to have prompted him to complete the national appeasement he had strenuously laboured for at Boulogne, is one for which the most compassionate critic of Mr. Redmond's career will search in vain for an excuse . . . It was to be no longer a question of Parnell's leadership but of vengeance for his wrongs . . . He allowed himself to be steadily pushed to the front as the apostle of the new

> avenging war. Time will not soon wash out a still deeper stain. He allowed the principal force of the popular fury to be directed against Mr. Dillon and myself.[159]

Redmond had embraced the attitude of Parnell when the latter stated 'he would rather be the leader of a good minority than of a rotten majority'. Healy wrote of him now as the evil genius of discord, the only one of real ability among the Parnellites, who, like Lucifer, 'would rather rule in hell than serve in heaven'. From his own standpoint, he had fought hard for a reconciliation on terms consistent with the principles he believed in. If he could not have both, he would choose the principles.

VIII

On 21 October Redmond announced his resignation of his North Wexford seat and his candidacy for Parnell's seat in Cork city.[160] In the history of Irish elections, there can seldom have been a less evenly matched contest, or a greater test of character for a candidate. In Dillon, O'Brien and Healy, later joined by Davitt, he faced four powerful adversaries, all the while deprived of a print medium in which to answer the daily denunciations of two newspapers. The onslaught they launched against him was compounded of equal parts legitimate criticism, misrepresentation and outright falsehood. Its ferocity was a measure of the mixed bewilderment and anger of the 'lieutenants' at the impertinence of a relative upstart, a retiring member of the party's second rank, in perpetuating the split.

Where did Redmond find the strength to confront such odds? Some of it undoubtedly lay in the grim euphoria of beleaguerment which drew Parnellites close together during that time.[161] With things hardly capable of getting worse, nothing was to be lost in carrying on. The mere contesting of the seat, whatever the chances of victory, would be a defiant valedictory tribute to the dead leader. He told the league central branch on 20 October that there were three alternatives open to them: peace with their opponents; immediate retirement (which he bitterly said would be justified by the people's ingratitude to Parnell); or 'giving Ireland a chance to declare if she would drive the rest of them from public life as she had driven Parnell'. If it were to be the last, he would abide by it and retire with an easy conscience of having done his duty.[162]

It was O'Brien who opened the offensive. Bristling at the charge of having hounded Parnell to death, he took up Healy's suggestion to publish all the Boulogne proceedings 'to utterly destroy whatever remnant of influence these gentlemen still possess in Ireland'. His letter to the *Freeman* published on 16 October ('A first glimpse of the Boulogne negotiations – a hard nut for Mr. John Redmond and others') initiated a controversy that continued for six weeks in letters and speeches. The burden of his case was that Redmond and others had initially accepted that the basis of any accord must be Parnell's retirement from the chair, and had assured O'Brien that they would desert Parnell if he went back on the terms of agreement, but had failed to 'stand up for' either principle. These assertions missed the point that the whole endeavour was predicated on a voluntary retirement, and that since no agreement had been reached, the question of Parnell's bad faith never arose. His charge that they had failed to enforce the retirement was really a charge that they had not become anti-Parnellites.[163] O'Brien coupled the charge of lacking the courage to oppose Parnell with the opposite one of lacking the courage to support him in his final months. For months Redmond had shirked his duty, he claimed, at Cork on 1 November; at the July convention he had 'caught a diplomatic cold' and 'shrank from Mr. Parnell's side when the fight was hottest' – not, he hastened to add, from treachery, but because his heart was not in it and he wanted the fight to end, all of which only made his present course 'so grossly and horribly inconsistent to [*sic*] Parnell and the country'.[164]

Redmond's and Harrington's first reaction to the letter was one of surprise. They could only respond that no one had blamed O'Brien for the failure at Boulogne or suggested that he had not done all in his power for a settlement. But the letter said more about the compounded grief and guilt O'Brien was suffering than it did about Redmond. In the light of O'Brien's attachment to Parnell, it is understandable that he should answer the 'hounding to death' charge by quoting from a letter the leader had written to him at Boulogne expressing 'how deeply I feel the kindness and gentleness of spirit' shown to him by O'Brien throughout the negotiations.[165] The exchanges became increasingly bitter as the controversy continued. It sprang into life again in January, when Redmond told Gill that he was considering bringing a libel action against O'Brien for his 'shameful statements'.[166]

Dillon entered the fray at the Wexford convention of 22 October to select Redmond's successor. The suggestions that Redmond had made as to the winding up of the Plan of Campaign now became 'very false and cruel charges about the evicted tenants'. He claimed that Redmond's conduct amounted to an 'abandonment' of the tenants while he and O'Brien were in jail. In declaring the tenants ruined and advising them to make settlements, he had allowed himself to be made a 'cat's-paw' of the landlords. Ignoring Redmond's closely reasoned arguments concerning the uses of the funds, he asserted that the Paris Funds of £40,000 were there to support the tenants, but Redmond was 'party and privy to cutting off the supplies from these poor men'. To the 'abandonment' charge, Redmond replied that the record books of the Plan estates had been removed from the London office early in the split, leaving him unable to take any further part in the campaign.[167] Dillon went on to give his own version of the summer desertion charge: he asserted that Redmond 'never went near' Parnell from the end of July to mid-September, and that it was 'notorious in Dublin that he intended to desert'. He added the accusation that Redmond was advertised to speak at Listowel, Westport and Creggs but refused to do so.[168]

There were also the predictably barbed missiles from the Healy camp. Maurice stated that he had begun his career 'as a placeman in the British Parliament'; the Wexford electorate were glad to be rid of him, since he was 'perhaps the worst attending of any member of the Irish Parliamentary party, and perhaps neglected his Parliamentary duties more grossly and shamefully than any member of that party'.[169] The efforts he made in Cork to win the labour vote, when he met representatives of Parnellite workingmen, also left him open to attack. The *Freeman* reminded the voters of his Rathfarnham speech just before the split, when he elevated the solidarity of the national movement above the sectional interests of labour.[170] Late in the campaign, Davitt intervened in the same vein, saying that in all his speeches Redmond had never shown that he cared a 'thraneen' for the interests of artisans and workers; his Rathfarnham speech in fact had shown the opposite.[171] (Davitt had been similarly critical of Parnell's recent advances to the labour movement, which he had described as a 'death-bed conversion'.) Both comments referred to a league demonstration held on 16 November 1890 at which Redmond had opposed (without naming him) Davitt's efforts to set up a national labour organization. Redmond had vigorously warned against the 'formidable danger' of the doctrine that the interests of labour were not safe with the Irish Party. In England, he claimed, the labour question might be fought out as one political question among many, but in the completely different conditions of Ireland, where 'one great all-absorbing question' dominated all others, the national movement could not afford to be disunited. Praising the labourers as 'the most unselfish of all classes', he had contended that their interests could never be settled until Ireland had the power of making its own laws.[172]

Support for Redmond, as for Parnell in the previous elections, came from the marginal sectors of nationalism. Echoing the 'dregs' remarks made by the bishop at Kilkenny, the *Freeman* commented on the large crowd that greeted Redmond at Cork railway station: 'precisely the same class of people who formed until recently the backbone of Parnellism in Dublin are today ready to shout approval to the wild statements that are made in the name of Independence . . . How many of them are voters?'[173] He received campaigning support from the extremist members of the Cork Young Ireland Society, who later elected him their president,[174] and from Fenians such as P. N. Fitzgerald. His opponents also forecast that a section of local Tories would vote for him.

The Cork election campaign was one of the most violent of the century in Ireland. The *Freeman* carried daily reports of 'disgraceful Redmondite rowdyism'. Dr Tanner was predictably in the thick of the conflict. The windows of both headquarters were broken; each side accused the other of breaking up its meetings; William Redmond and

John O'Connor were injured in scuffles; and by 30 October, with a week left before the vote, 108 people had been treated in hospital for injuries.[175] A more sinister element was added on 27 October with an explosion at the Dublin office of the *National Press*. A huge crowd the following day heard Dillon and O'Brien condemn 'the conspiracy of violent intimidation and of murder'.[176] Redmond welcomed the entry of Davitt into the campaign on 30 October, as the latter had promised not to misrepresent his past record, and both subsequently did their best to calm passions.[177] The outcome gave 3,669 votes to the anti-Parnellite Martin Flavin, a local butter merchant, 2,157 to Redmond, and 1,161 to Capt. D. R. P. Sarsfield, the Tory candidate.[178] Back in Dublin, Redmond was greeted with a torchlight procession. At the National Club, he said that it had been 'a privilege' to pay this last compliment to his dead leader. He claimed that the election would have 'momentous and disastrous' effects on the prospects for Home Rule. The openings given to opponents of Home Rule were evident on the same day in the report of the speech of the prime minister, Lord Salisbury, at the London Guildhall: 'What we have seen has not made us think that a domestic Legislature will be distinguished by peace or order or an abstinence from blackthorns, or freedom from the curse of ecclesiastical domination.'[179]

A lull followed, during which both sides took stock. The link between Parnellites and their new-found Fenian friends was underlined in mid-November following the death, within weeks of his release from prison, of P. W. Nally, a Fenian who had served a sentence for his part in an 1883 conspiracy. Redmond appeared for his relatives at the inquest and attended the funeral at Glasnevin, in which Nally was interred in the 'Fenian Circle' with major figures of the Fenian past. Alongside him stood the veteran Fenian leaders James Stephens and John O'Leary, together with most of the prominent Parnellite M.P.s.[180] In the meantime, there was no sign of Redmond acting upon his threat to retire from public life. An amnesty meeting at Limerick on 22 November provided an opportunity to restore some semblance of harmony: Redmond, Davitt and other M.P.s from both sides were cheered impartially by the crowd as they called for the release of Daly and Egan.[181] However, Dillon and O'Brien refused to take part in such shared ventures. O'Brien did not think the prison doors would be forced open 'by enabling Mr. Redmond and his party to make some wretched capital out of the sufferings of these poor men'. The *Freeman* wanted no misunderstandings: 'the only condition upon which that union is possible is the voluntary – or if not voluntary, the compulsory – retirement of Mr. John Redmond and his Parliamentary friends from their extraordinary attitude of defiance of the expressed will of the country'.[182]

The death of the ex-whip and Parnellite M.P. for Waterford city, Richard Power, on 30 November, presented Redmond with another opportunity to regain a seat. Power had enjoyed strong support among the workers in the bacon and provisions trade living in the Ballybricken area of the city, a fact that offered Redmond a chance of winning the seat and may have caused him to postpone thoughts of retirement. Davitt proposed that the Waterford vacancy should not be contested and that a truce be called between the two sides until the general election. Redmond replied that he thought it 'a most reasonable' idea, if it meant 'that each party should be permitted unchallenged by its opponents to fill up from its own ranks any vacancy in a seat which had been held by one of its members'.[183] Davitt replied that he had spoken only for himself and did not see much chance of a truce being agreed to 'by the Stalwarts on both sides'; moreover, the writ had already been moved by Redmond's friends.[184]

The campaign opened with Redmond's arrival in the city on 11 December, a year to the day since Parnell's arrival in Kilkenny. He told the crowd at Ballybricken that he had read Davitt's letter 'with sympathy and respect' but was sorry to find that his proposal meant the vacancy would not be filled. However deplorable, the contest had to go ahead, he said. The anti-Parnellite originally selected was a local unknown, William Keane. However, the anti-Parnellite leadership and the *Freeman* begged Davitt to contest the seat. He held back at first, but changed his mind after an assault was made upon him by a small boy with a stick. Conflicting accounts of the cause of the violence were traded; the *Freeman* claimed that a Redmondite crowd was armed with bludgeons, while Redmond said that a crowd similarly armed had marched into the city from the surrounding county led by O'Brien, Davitt and Tanner.[185]

In a short campaign, Davitt and Redmond attacked each other's records. The former again brought up the Rathfarnham speech against Redmond, while the latter echoed Parnell's attack on Davitt at Kilkenny when he had called him a 'jackdaw': he had lived for the last ten years 'upon a fictitious reputation' and was 'a very thorn in the Irish Parliamentary party and a source of trouble, embarrassment and danger to their leader'. Davitt challenged Redmond to tell the artisans and labourers of Waterford what he had done in support of their 'just and reasonable strikes'.[186] O'Brien claimed that Redmond's support was largely dependent on the Tory voters, but also commented wittily on the incongruity of the sight of Redmond in the company of Fenians: 'Mr. John Redmond is not by any means the stamp of man to take to hillsiding (*laughter*), except in a Pickwickian sense, to take to the hillsides of Ballybricken for electioneering purposes.'[187] With the issue of Parnell's leadership removed, the anti-Parnellites struggled to accommodate themselves to the existence of the new minority voice within nationalism. The *Freeman* opined on 8 December: 'A division of parties in Ireland would not be fatal to the Irish cause or degrading to our national self-respect if the disputants could be persuaded to observe the common decencies of debate.' Four days later, the attempt to strike a calmer tone was foundering: 'had he the tongue of a Grattan, [Redmond] could not hide the hideousness of the policy which he now enunciates . . . of eternal dissension in the country'.[188] Dillon, similarly torn, called for all nationalists to meet as friends and 'discuss these matters like sensible men and patriotic Irishmen', then in the same speech said that he regarded these men as 'the worst and most dangerous enemies of our race'.[189]

A few days before the vote, the first issue of the new paper that Parnell had been planning just before his death, the *Irish Daily Independent*, appeared on the streets in time to lend support to Redmond's campaign, marking the start of a rivalry with the *Freeman* that would last more than three decades. The latter organ brought its full batteries to bear on Redmond in a comprehensive indictment on 21 December, an article entitled 'Who?' consisting of eighty-five questions, the answer to each of which was 'John Redmond'. Intended as the killer blow, it mixed fact:

> Who said at Birmingham on the 17th June, 1886, 'having given the closest attention to these methods, he was able to say that the scheme of Mr. Gladstone was entirely satisfactory to them, and that the Irish members accepted the late offer of the Government as a final settlement between the two countries'? . . . Who says he would not now accept that bill?

with misrepresentation: 'Who told the evicted tenants that he would stick to them to the end? . . . Who now tells the evicted tenants that they should crawl back to the landlords?', and invention:

> Who accepted the proposals made by Messrs. Dillon and O'Brien at Boulogne as satisfactory and promised that if Mr. Parnell would not agree to them he would no longer support Mr. Parnell? . . . Who has the patronage of the *Times*? . . . Who is the pet of Mr. Balfour and Lord Salisbury?[190]

It was all to no avail. Redmond received 1,755 votes to Davitt's 1,229, breaking finally the run of Parnellite defeats and giving Redmond the seat he would occupy for twenty-six years. Davitt claimed that Redmond had won by a combination of 'Terrorism and Toryism'. O'Brien portentously announced: 'Waterford has cut herself off for the moment from the Irish nation.' And in a foreshadowing of a second split, one which would soon beset the anti-Parnellites, the *Freeman* laid the blame implicitly at the door of Healy's paper. Men, it claimed, who had gone along simply to hear Redmond speak, on finding themselves branded as 'drunken rowdies . . . filled with porter' were driven by resentment to vote for him. Underestimating Redmond's motives, it indicted 'the bitter personal assailants of John Redmond in the Press' and the 'sneers and snarls' of 'the journal to which we refer' at Redmond's long silence during the summer, which had goaded him back 'into a position from which he was at the time anxious to escape'. Had he been 'treated with a little more consideration', it felt that he would gladly have thrown in his lot with the majority after Parnell's death.[191]

Answering Davitt in an *Independent* interview and at the league central branch, Redmond denied the charge of inciting violence, claiming that apart from the one violent incident he had 'never seen an election conducted in such perfect good humour' and that he had denounced the assault on Davitt and expressed regret to him. He had won the labour vote because the workingmen, having watched Davitt for many years, had concluded that he was 'an impractical theorist'; if they wanted labour reforms they would look to the 'thorough and comprehensive programme' adopted at the July convention. On the question of the next Home Rule Bill, he asserted, in a criticism of a recent speech of Davitt's, that 'we at any rate do not believe in the principle that half a loaf is better than no bread (*hear, hear*)'. An incomplete measure would fail and lead to its being revoked, he claimed.[192] At the National Club on 31 December, Redmond denied Dillon's charge that he delighted in the split. Citing the role he had played at Boulogne, he added: 'Day and night the sorrow, the humiliation of this contest has been pressing on me hard.'[193]

The aftershocks of Parnell's death and the tumultuous autumn campaigns continued into the first weeks of 1892. The letters and speeches of both sides took on a defensive tone, as each denied charges of vilification. At Naas on 3 January, Redmond called 'grossly slanderous' O'Brien's repetition of the charge that he had planned to desert Parnell.[194] O'Brien wrote emotionally to the *Freeman* on 18 January: 'Is Mr. Redmond really serious in picturing me as pursuing him with deadly personal animosity?'[195] He added that Redmond's statement, that to his (Redmond's) certain knowledge O'Brien had entered Galway jail just as strong a Parnellite as himself, was 'grossly offensive'. The continuance of 'these detestable personal recriminations' was repugnant to him, and he called for the whole matter of Redmond's and his own relations with Parnell to be arbitrated by two friends; he would pledge himself to retire from public life in the event of an adverse finding, if Redmond did the same.[196]

These exchanges were signs that the fight was losing some of its intensity. The split was beginning to settle into the war of attrition that would paralyse the nationalist movement for the next eight years. On 7 February, the day before Parliament opened, T. P. O'Connor thought he detected a 'stillness' in the political atmosphere. He interpreted this as a sign of a coming reconciliation, the Irish people being tired and 'a little ashamed' of the controversy.[197]

8 The Metamorphosis

> One calm, far-seeing brain, one dauntless, unpurchasable heart . . . Mr. Parnell taught Irishmen self-respect and self-reliance.
>
> Redmond in New York, 15 June 1892[1]

> . . . the word 'provisional' has, so to speak, been stamped in red ink across every page of this [Home Rule] Bill.
>
> Redmond speaking on the Second Home Rule Bill, House of Commons, 30 August 1893[2]

I

Twenty-four months had wrought a transformation in Redmond's life. Still struggling to accept the loss of his young wife, he had been propelled from a comfortable niche in the old party, in the second rank of Parnell's retinue, to the leadership of a fragment of that party. It is tempting to find in his personal grief the source of the energies that lifted him from comparative indolence and galvanized him from the start of the split. His opponents raged at and ridiculed his metamorphosis from the paragon of moderation of pre-split days into a pretender who now posed as a more stalwart nationalist than they. But they had underestimated him. His low profile in Parliament in the late 1880s, his background role in party affairs occasioned by his involvement in the Plan of Campaign and its associated legal work, his absence from the scene just before the great convulsion began, all caused them to forget the promise he had shown, when as a 25-year-old M.P. in his first year in Parliament he had not hesitated to challenge, with eloquence and courage, such giants as Gladstone and Forster.[3] They also obscured his more recent development into a political thinker and strategist, as evidenced by the thoughtful lectures he gave on Irish history and such contemporary topics as federalism.

During 1890 he had moved house from Fitzwilliam Street to the cheaper north side location of 7 Belvedere Place, just off Mountjoy Square and close to the street of his birth; this remained his Dublin home until the end of the split. On another street off the same square lived Healy, while Dillon lived in nearby North Great George's Street. Thus the three principal protagonists of the split all lived within a few minutes' walk of each other amid the decaying Georgian splendour of the capital, whose decline they blamed on the Union. There was no doubting which of them was the most popular figure in the streets. Dublin being a Parnellite city, Healy and Dillon had to keep their heads down, while Redmond and his brother were often greeted with the singing of the old '98 ballad 'The Boys of Wexford', a tune that became a staple of Parnellite bands at their public meetings and torchlight processions throughout the 1890s.[4]

Figure 14. No. 7 Belvedere Place, Dublin, John Redmond's Dublin home between 1890 and 1900.

Death continued to hover near. During the Kilkenny election the only child of William and Eleanor, two-year-old William Dalton Redmond, died. Katherine Tynan later remembered Eleanor as 'a sad woman, or a sick woman, Willie waiting on her with anxious and tender affection'. In February 1892 came the death of Redmond's mother. It seems that Eleanor may have taken on the mothering of Redmond's children at this time. A picture of Redmond in the role of father emerges from Tynan's recollections: at a picnic at Kilmurray Grove, the house of Margaret Leamy's father at the Glen of the Downs, County Wicklow,

> the luncheon tables spread in the open air on the lawns and John Redmond leading by the hand his little daughter Essie, her wild red curls coming from under her white sun-bonnet, her little freckled face uplifted while she told someone that she thought she liked gentlemen better than ladies. John Redmond was a tender father.

Given the fragility of life generally, and especially among children, it is not surprising that otherwise rational men could be superstitious. Redmond's superstitions are not as well logged as those for which Parnell was notorious, but, according to Leamy, he 'never passed a magpie without taking off his hat to it for luck'.[5]

A moment in family life at Belvedere Place in the mid-1890s is captured in an anecdote told by Margaret Leamy. At a party to entertain some important guests, Redmond's children staged a play written by Essie. It was a story of the Crusades, with eight-year-old William in the role of 'Sir Hubert', just returned from the Holy Land. Having given an account of his battles and victories, the boy ended with a declaration of how happy he was to be with his beloved wife again:

> Then it was his sister's turn to speak. Imagine the feelings of the audience when she said: 'I, darling, have not been idle during the seven long years of your absence. I have seven little children for you!' She drew aside a curtain, and there were discovered seven little children like steps of stairs, guests of the evening also. Roars of laughter greeted this, and Essie, who was a beautiful but quick-tempered little girl, stamped her foot, crying 'I don't know what you are all laughing at! We will play no more' and walked off in high dudgeon. For years we used to laugh over this.[6]

II

Of the thirty-one Parnellite M.P.s who returned to Westminster on 8 February for the 1892 session, Redmond was the only one elected on the programme set out in Parnell's manifesto and at the July convention. The others were living on borrowed time, knowing that they would soon have to submit themselves to their constituents' judgement or retire from politics. By this time, the Tory–Liberal Unionist governing coalition headed by Lord Salisbury and Arthur Balfour was nearing the end of its sixth year in office. Dissolution was at most a matter of months away.

Redmond's first actions as parliamentary Parnellite leader took up where Parnell had left off the previous year. He began by attending to the new (or more accurately, revived) Parnellite support base in 'advanced' nationalism, using that traditional bridge between constitutionalists and physical force men, the amnesty question. He moved an amendment to the Address calling for the amnesty of Daly, Egan and fourteen other Irishmen serving long sentences in British prisons for dynamite offences. His seventy-minute speech was an appeal, both eloquent and forensically detailed, which sought to establish three grounds for amnesty: that the men were political offenders; that the convictions were wrong, having been obtained under dubious circumstances; and that the treatment meted out to the men had been excessive.[7] Behind the scenes he sought from the home secretary, and was granted, permission to visit Daly and Egan as a legal adviser, a move that continued the efforts of 1891 and heralded many years of work on behalf of Fenian prisoners.[8]

A few days later, in a debate on a Sexton amendment criticizing the Land Purchase Act, Redmond followed Parnell in his receptiveness to Tory land legislation. While he agreed that there were serious defects that stood in the way of tenant-farmers taking advantage of the Act, he disagreed with Sexton's statement that the Act had failed to provide an acceptable basis for the establishment of a peasant proprietary: 'My opinion is that it does afford a basis, and a valuable basis . . . the machinery is there, and the defects can be removed, and when that is done an enormous boon to the tenant farmers of Ireland will result.'[9] Turning to the great question of the next Home Rule Bill, he stated that there existed 'the gravest anxiety' among 'large masses of the Irish people' who wanted further information, not as to the details of the Bill – 'that is a cry that we have never raised; that is a foolish and impossible demand' – but 'with reference to certain of its main features and proposals'. They knew from the speech of Morley a few days ago that it would be proposed to keep the Irish members at Westminster, but as to other matters, 'especially how far the Imperial Parliament is to retain the power of interfering with and controlling Irish legislation', they knew absolutely nothing. Anticipating the anti-Parnellite reply, he said:

> We are told we should simply trust to the admitted, recognised and honoured earnestness of the right hon. Gentleman the Member for Midlothian [Gladstone] . . . that we should not embarrass our friends . . . [but] the policy of patience, silence and confidence, which might have been safe when Ireland had a united Nationalist representation and a wise and powerful leader, is, as many of us know, both unsafe and unwise in the present circumstances of political life.[10]

They had been refused this information at the time of Committee Room 15 and afterwards, and Irish people had wondered why. Harcourt had caused the greatest anxiety, he claimed, when he had stated that, while the English people and the Liberal Party still adhered to Home Rule, neither he nor his colleagues were in favour of what he called 'Mr. Parnell's Fenian Home Rule'. Redmond quoted from a Parnell speech during the split, in which he had defined Home Rule as 'a Parliament with full powers to manage the affairs of Ireland without trenching on any Imperial prerogative or injuring any Imperial or English interest; but . . . supreme in regard to Irish questions'. If that was what Harcourt referred to, he said, he was wrong in calling it Parnell's Home Rule:

> There is not an Irish politician who will take that programme in his hand and say he will accept one whit less as a satisfactory solution . . . It is the Home Rule of O'Brien and Dillon and McCarthy, and I say it is monstrous on the part of the right hon. Member for Derby [Harcourt] to pretend that it is a Fenian Home Rule scheme. I also deny that the scheme has any connection with Separation. We are a constitutional party seeking, within the Constitution, to obtain the restitution of the Irish Parliament.[11]

He then alluded to the possible scenarios they would face if, as seemed likely, the Bill were passed by the Commons but rejected by the Lords. In a prescient passage, full of significance for future Irish debate on the Liberal alliance, he quoted recent utterances by Harcourt and Trevelyan, which, he said, had caused great unease. The former, responding to Lord Salisbury's threat that the Lords could and would throw out a Home Rule Bill, said that the Lords 'should be allowed to do their worst on the whole scope and tenor of Liberal reforms'. This had been taken in Ireland to mean that if the Bill were thrown out by the Upper House, it would be hung up while the Commons dealt with the other items of the Newcastle programme (the package of Home Rule plus British rural, religious and electoral reform agreed by the National Liberal Federation at Newcastle in autumn 1891). Trevelyan had listed a batch of reforms, which, he said, would be dealt with by the Liberal ministry immediately on its coming into power. Were these seven or eight measures to be passed simultaneously with the Home Rule Bill? Trevelyan's reply was equivocal: 'I never said it was to be done in the same Parliament, or anything of the sort.' Redmond commented: 'I feel myself in a worse position than before, because it now seems to be uncertain whether the Home Rule Bill is to be the first Bill, after all, to be submitted to the House of Commons and the House of Lords.' The best way to forestall a rejection by the House of Lords, he claimed, was by making the voters absolutely clear on what they were voting for:

> Sir, in asking for information, I deny that I am taking a course which will embarrass the Liberal Party in the future . . . Sooner or later

> these main features will have to be discussed in the constituencies, and if these main features were voted upon by the constituents the House of Lords would not dare for one instant to stand between Ireland and that Home Rule which the English electors want. In asking for information I am taking the most direct course to hasten the progress of Home Rule.[12]

Anti-Parnellites were not impressed with this reasoning. The *Freeman,* noting that *The Times* had praised the 'force and adroitness' of the speech, commented that the Tories owed much to Redmond, given his insistence on 'premature disclosure' of the Home Rule Bill so that it could be 'torn asunder'. Davitt, in a reply at the National Federation central branch, said that Redmond should search his conscience and ask himself why he was being lauded by the 'ancient enemies of Ireland'. His role, he claimed, was similar to that of Chamberlain in 1886, who had also demanded that Gladstone produce his Home Rule scheme before he judged the moment right, a demand that Parnell had praised Gladstone for refusing. Touching on Redmond's most vulnerable point, he asked how the next generation would regard men 'who six years ago accepted a Home Rule Bill from the only English Minister who ever brought forward one in Parliament, and now endeavour to embarrass the self-same Minister by calling upon him to produce his amended scheme that his enemies may go about picking holes in it?' Redmond and his friends, silent between 1886 and 1890 on the particulars of Home Rule, were now, he said, 'strutting before the House of Commons as the irreconcilables of Irish popular opinion'.[13]

Thus did 'Redmondism' make its entry onto the political stage, as Redmond sketched out the watchdog (his enemies would have said gadfly) role that he and his small band of followers would play in the nationalist movement for the rest of the decade. The Parnellite constituency to which he looked for support spanned a diverse range of groups, located mostly in the towns and cities. The constitutionalist majority comprised the adherents of the moderate Parnell of the later 1880s, typified by the Parnellites on Dublin Corporation who voted to present an address to Baron Houghton, the new lord lieutenant in 1892, as well as the rhetorically militant group centred on *United Ireland* and its editor Edmund Leamy. However, among the organizers and party workers on whom Redmond and his colleagues depended for the work of voter registration and electioneering, there was also a sizeable group of Fenians or quasi-Fenians, attracted by the militant rhetoric and beleaguered image of the Parnell of 1891, eager worshippers in the rapidly growing cult of a mythologized Parnell.[14] Among them moved the secret organizers of the IRB. There were also veteran Fenian leaders, such as O'Leary and Stephens, home from exile to live out their days in Ireland and keep alive the pure separatist doctrine, who maintained a critical friendship with the Parnellite movement but did not involve themselves in active political work.[15] As Matthew Kelly has pointed out, the militancy of William Redmond's oratory, though mainly focused on past rebellions, served to bond the separatists and constitutionalists.[16] By this constituency John Redmond would be seen as the truth-teller, coldly realistic about Liberal shortcomings and tendencies to backslide on Home Rule, a puncturer of the illusions fostered by the Union of Hearts. In the eyes of his opponents, he was the wrecker, at best a fool unable to cast off the spell of his deceased leader, at worst an egoist and unprincipled opportunist, and effectively a Tory ally by his creation of additional difficulties for the Liberal Government.

III

Redmond returned to Dublin to deliver a St Patrick's Day address at the Rotunda entitled 'The National Demand', in which he elaborated his Commons speech for an Irish audience. They now had three 'strenuous reasons', he claimed, for refusing to trust the Liberals. The first followed from Parnell's revelations about the Hawarden discussions:

> the large mass of the Irish people had never had any doubt upon this matter in trusting to the word of their own leader (*loud cheers*). He would show that every act of Mr. Gladstone and his friends, from that very day to this, corroborated the accuracy of Mr. Parnell's recollection of that conversation.

Second, recent speeches of prominent Liberals told of a 'distinct change of front going on amongst the Liberal party' on Home Rule. Their rising star, Herbert Asquith, had indicated at Edinburgh that, even with an Irish parliament in place, the imperial Parliament could still interfere with, revise or amend Irish legislation. In a retaliatory thrust at Davitt, he added:

> It was bad enough to have English politicians speaking in this way, but the necessity for defining their position was still more imperative when an Irish politician of the standing of Mr. Michael Davitt (*groans*) declared at Bandon that he and his friends would be satisfied to accept anything that could be got from the Liberal party.

The danger of Home Rule being hung up after a rejection by the House of Lords was his third reason for insisting that they 'enable the English electors to know before the general election what it was that they meant by Home Rule'. He proceeded to define the 'national demand', tracing its formulation since the days of Grattan. Its essence was contained in the speech of Parnell at the July convention: 'Everything was contained in the provision that the Irish Parliament should be supreme in the management of Irish affairs . . . [on this] there could be no compromise without disaster and dishonour (*cheers*).'[17]

The Liberal leadership, prudently anxious to assess the extent of their likely Irish support in the next Parliament, took seriously what Redmond had to say about their forthcoming Bill. Their concern is shown in the lengthy private correspondence that took place that spring between Redmond and the Liberal M.P. William Mather, preceded by a conversation between the two men, accompanied by J. L. Carew and two others, at the Reform Club on 30 March. It seems probable that Morley used Mather as an intermediary to sound out Redmond's views in detail, since it was Mather who drew up a memorandum on those views and sent copies to the participants for comment. The notes covered eight points relating to Home Rule legislation, including the provisions for the land and police questions already agreed by the Liberals at the time of Boulogne.

On the crucial point of the respective competencies of the imperial and the Home Rule parliaments, Mather noted Redmond's stipulation that the imperial Parliament, though its supremacy remained intact, must not 'repeal or review' individual Acts of the Irish Parliament, and his agreement that if a question of *ultra vires* arose, a Supreme Court should decide on it.[18] In his written comments on this memorandum, Redmond dealt in detail with the relationship which in his view must obtain between the two parliaments. He wrote that the imperial Parliament had no power to divest itself of its own supremacy, and hence the power that had brought Home Rule into being would remain untouched and capable of amending it or repealing it altogether; therefore, 'what we demand is that by international compact it should be secured to us, *that while our Statutory Parliament exists* it shall have supreme and sole control over all purely Irish affairs'.

But why not leave things as they were in colonial constitutions? There, the imperial Parliament could, in theory, interfere at any moment and override the authority of the local legislatures, but in practice never did. Why should Ireland not be satisfied with a similar arrangement? Because, he wrote, the colonies were a very different case from Ireland, in that they were 'at the other side of the world' and there was no inducement for Westminster to interfere in local matters of which they understood nothing. In Ireland, on the other hand, especially with Irish M.P.s at Westminster,

> it will be the interest of one section of Irishmen to endeavour in season and out of it, to appeal from the Irish to the Imperial Parliament. A power which in the case of the colonies is harmless because an absolute dead letter would in the case of Ireland be a constant source of danger.[19]

Mather, in his reply, wrote that Redmond's admission that a Supreme Court should decide on any question of *ultra vires* 'seems to meet almost any difficulty of the construction the Irish Parliament might put upon its powers were the Imperial Parliament to question that construction. It would give great confidence and assurance of smooth-working.' Such a court would be especially useful, he wrote, in the early life of the Irish parliament when questions might arise as to the interpretation of its powers and it might not be prudent to involve either the crown or the imperial Parliament. The Supreme Court could determine such questions 'without producing irritation or humiliation'. Mather went on to offer his thoughts on the other features they had discussed, including protection against religious ascendancy and the retention of the Irish members. The latter turned out to be a very complex matter, once examined in depth: for example, how to overcome the anomaly of having Irish members voting on English and Welsh matters while the power of English and Welsh M.P.s to vote on Irish matters had been removed? He also asked Redmond to suggest any safeguard that might allay 'the fears of the prejudiced and feeble-minded' as to the national majority taxing Ulster unfairly.[20]

Further letters were exchanged in the same friendly and constructive spirit. Redmond qualified his acceptance of the Supreme Court idea: it would have to be very carefully phrased to make it clear that there was no intention to leave the Irish parliament subject to a judicial tribunal in the management of Irish matters. His reply to Mather on Ulster's fears was brusque: 'I don't consider any special safeguards necessary at all'.[21] Mather felt that Redmond had touched on a crucial point in mentioning the possibility of a rejection by the Lords. He agreed that the way to avoid this was by getting a 'commanding majority' on a measure well understood by the country during the election; the Lords could not then plead the country's ignorance.[22]

The comprehensive and probing discussion ended in late May, when Redmond wrote an article on Home Rule for publication in the monthly *Nineteenth Century*, and Mather, in acknowledging it to be a 'most able and most valuable . . . thorough treatment of the Home Rule question in all the details essential to a settlement', begged him not to publish it as its effect at that time would be to damage Gladstone's position as the initiator of the legislation.[23] Redmond responded by delaying publication until October, after the general election.[24]

IV

Different views persisted among the anti-Parnellite leaders as to the best way of dealing with the Parnellites as the election approached, and were reflected in the uncertain tone of the *Freeman*. Just before the start of the Session, it had echoed O'Brien in calling for a truce, incurring the wrath of the *National Press*.[25] However, the latter paper's financial problems led Healy to accept a purchase offer from the *Freeman* Company. Healy drove a hard bargain and the result was a merger rather than a buyout. On 25 March three members of the *National Press* board, including Healy himself and the industrialist William Martin Murphy, were co-opted as members of the *Freeman* board of directors, while Dillon accepted the chair, but only on condition that Sexton and O'Brien also joined the board.[26]

The tensions within the new board, containing as it did members such as Dwyer Gray who were appalled at Healy's conduct of the anti-Parnellite campaign and who were, in turn, anathema to Healy, were not long in manifesting themselves.[27] At the extraordinary general meeting of shareholders held in May to ratify the changes, there were acrimonious exchanges when Dillon nominated Gray to the chair while Healy supported Murphy. The meeting continued over five days, attracting enormous coverage in the paper itself, and characterized by constant outbursts of acerbity on the floor. In an indication of the animosity between Healy and Gray, the old accusation regarding Healy's alleged conversation on religious belief with Bradlaugh, which the then-Parnellite *Freeman* had attempted to use against Healy during the Kilkenny election, was again brought into play by Gray at the meeting.[28] The real issue at stake was well articulated by Redmond's old friend, now implacable opponent, Father Furlong, at the Wexford anti-Parnellite convention on 24 May, when he alluded to the merger: if the new paper was to be a really national organ, he said, it could be so only 'by preserving the *National Press* spirit and the *National Press* vigour and by maintaining an uncompromising attitude of hostility towards the men who would bring destruction to Ireland if they had their way'.[29]

Inconclusive though the battle in the boardroom may have been, Healy's influence on the *Freeman*'s editorial policy and style was now, as the election approached, exactly what Furlong had called for. 'Redmondite rodomontade' took its place alongside 'Redmondite rowdyism' and 'Redmondite ruffianism' in the lexicon of the paper. Calling him 'the Only Possible Mr. Redmond' (an echo of 'the Only Possible Leader', the sarcastic title bestowed on Parnell by Healy in 1891), the paper taunted Redmond with not having contested the seat he had vacated in North Wexford. With Redmond announced as a speaker for an Amnesty rally at Enniscorthy on 8 May, it remarked waspishly that that issue was his only way of getting a hearing among the constituents whom he had betrayed, and that he should explain why it had taken the divorce court verdict to open his mind to the ill-treatment of Daly and Egan in prison.[30]

Early in the year, the neutral Gill had sent Redmond and Dillon copies of a seven-page, six-clause memorandum entitled 'Suggested basis for a modus vivendi', and had acted as a channel of communication between the two men.[31] He told the latter of his conviction that there was 'a strong feeling on Redmond's part' to come to 'some sort of arrangement' between the two factions.[32] The question of how the disunion in the Irish ranks might be prevented from damaging the chances of a Liberal return to power was also among the issues discussed by Redmond and Mather. At the original conversation, Redmond had expressed himself willing to work out a *modus vivendi* with the anti-Parnellites by which no Irish seats would be contested between nationalists. This would avoid the danger of Tories winning some of them, and also avoid the spectacle of bitter strife among nationalists which would injure the Home Rule vote in Britain. It was probably Mather's influence that brought immediate results on this point. T.P. O'Connor, one of the anti-Parnellites closest to the Liberal leadership, made a conciliatory speech at Liverpool in early April suggesting that the two nationalist factions assess their respective strengths in each constituency and come to an arrangement for proportional representation aimed at avoiding contests wherever possible.[33] Healy, speaking in Dublin, immediately shot down the idea. The 'factionists' must not be recognised as 'a separate party'; on the contrary, efforts must be renewed to 'put down the pledge-breakers'. To opt for peace now, he said, was to give in to blackmail and blackguardism. Ireland must get worse before she got better. They must face the music at the general election in order to 'find out the true dimensions of factionism'.[34]

Redmond ignored Healy's response and waited for the other anti-Parnellites to react. He wrote to Gill asking for news of what 'was going on in the happy family' [of anti-Parnellites] and expressing his 'great interest and satisfaction' at O'Connor's speech.[35] At a meeting of ward representatives in Dublin on 12 April, he welcomed the 'extraordinary change of spirit' heralded by it, in which 'he speaks of us as brother nationalists desiring to obtain justice for Ireland, but differing from him and his friends as to means and as to methods'.[36]

A fortnight later, no word had yet come from Dillon or O'Brien, prompting Redmond to say at Howth that the real leader of his opponents was Healy, backed up by certain bishops and certain clergymen.[37] At Drogheda on 26 April, he stated that he could not disguise the contempt he felt for the position in which Dillon had placed himself, given that everyone knew he detested the methods and distrusted the motives of Healy: 'He challenged Mr. Dillon to deny that he was constantly expressing in private warm approval of that suggestion of Mr. T. P. O'Connor.'[38]

In fact, said Redmond, if his information was correct, the idea had originated, not with T. P. O'Connor at all, but with Dillon himself. The same evening, Healy in Dublin reiterated his position: 'I am not prepared to recognise that pestilent evil, as I believe it to be – a second party in the Irish national representation (*loud cheers*).'[39]

The silence from the other leaders persisted. Thus it was that Redmond, addressing league members in Dublin on 4 May, felt

> justified in concluding that Mr. T.P. O'Connor had been repudiated, and his idea had been cast on one side by the 'seceders'. If that be so there was only one alternative . . . to fight it out at the general election . . . if it be war, there should be no mincing matters. If it be war it should be a thorough-going war (*applause*), it should be a war waged in every constituency in Ireland where they could get a foothold against every man who was not with their party . . .

Their resources, he said, though small, were greater in proportion to their needs than those of their opponents. This he deduced from Dillon's recent admission that, since the exhaustion of the Plan of Campaign funds, the anti-Parnellite party in the previous year had had to spend most of the £17,000 in its National Fund on the evicted tenants, leaving only £3,000 for political purposes.[40] The *Freeman* in turn accused him, in these 'callous and cold-blooded' comments, of glorying in his abandonment of the evicted tenants.[41]

A final attempt was made in late May to bring about an accommodation, this time mediated by Henry Labouchere, the Radical M.P. thought to be one of the 'wire-pullers' denounced in Parnell's manifesto. Clancy wrote to Redmond that Labouchere had met Carew and told him that Dillon, O'Brien, Sexton and O'Connor were 'not only willing but rampant for an arrangement as to seats'. Carew and fellow-Parnellites had insisted that the other side, as the larger party, should issue the invitation to a conference. Labouchere had replied that the Dillonite-Healyite divide made this impossible.[42] The attempt thus foundered for want of a mutually acceptable basis for negotiations.

With dissolution edging ever nearer, the election campaign was already being fought in Ireland. The *Freeman* ridiculed a call by Harrington at Newbridge on 3 June to 'leave the two parties precisely as they are':[43] such a proposition, implying that the Parnellites would have twenty-nine seats in the next Parliament, was 'so audacious' that it could only be a declaration of war. Dillon chose the venue of Bradford on 5 June to make a belated proposal aimed at limiting intra-nationalist strife: a 'board of conciliation' comprising the Dublin lord mayor (a Parnellite), Archbishop Croke and two others could avoid blood being spilt in certain places by allowing a minority of Parnellites to be returned.[44] Redmond read of Dillon's suggestion just before he left Ireland for New York in response to an invitation to address Parnellites there. According to the interview that he gave to the *New York Morning Journal* of 13 June, he at once made enquiries into it, and was told

> that Mr. Dillon's idea of such an arrangement was that the McCarthyite members should be permitted unopposed to obtain seats for 74 members, and that the Parnellite party should be permitted to obtain seats for some 10 or 12. This meant that while the McCarthyite party should not throw over any of its members and should not express any disapproval of Mr. Healy or his methods, we were to consent to some 20 of our members having summary vengeance taken upon them, and they themselves retired to private life.

So anxious had he and his colleagues been to avoid contests that they had made the 'fair and reasonable' proposal (encapsulated in Harrington's speech) that they would not contest seats held by the McCarthyites. This had been rejected by Dillon, 'who says the constituencies would revolt. What Mr. Dillon really meant was that Mr. Healy would revolt . . . he has satisfied himself that Mr. Healy would reject it, and he is not in a position to act without the permission of that gentleman'.[45] The same newspaper the previous day had carried an interview with Dillon, who outlined his reasons for rejecting the affront to democracy implied in Harrington's armistice terms:

> For the all-sufficient reason that there is no power on earth to induce the constituencies to agree to it. There are now 29 Parnellites. By far the greater number of these 29 constituencies condemn by overwhelming majorities the policy of their representatives, and could by no conceivable means be induced to re-elect them. They would most certainly revolt if we accepted such a proposal.[46]

Redmond's arrival in New York on 12 June received a cool greeting. The friendly *New York Herald* carried the improbable headline 'Redmond, M.P., Arrives on an Errand of Peace/To Harmonise Warring Factions in this Country'. The *New York Recorder* more accurately reflected local feeling when it announced 'He Should Not Be Here/Redmond Is Needed In Ireland, say National League Men'. It reported that there was no sign of the men who had escorted him to the Chicago convention in 1886, nor of those who had 'built up the great Parnellite platform', and that Redmond seemed to feel the disappointment. A lift was provided by the extravagant address of welcome presented by local nationalists of Waterford origin. Their pride in their native city 'was intensified on Christmas Eve 1891, when we heard across the flashing wires that the *Urbs Intacta*, true to its title, untouched by treason, untainted by dishonour, unintimidated by whiggery, had sent you to fill in Parliament the place of the lamented Richard Power.' Redmond put the Parnellite view of the Liberal alliance:

> it is our most earnest wish that the national forces in Ireland should be reunited. And, gentlemen, what we mean by union is the union of independence . . . It is possible to be in close friendly relations with an English party and be independent. That was the position in which the Irish National party was from 1886 down to the unfortunate crisis which arose in November 1890.

The *New York Press*, however, did not seem interested:

> Into the details of the dispute between the Parnellites and the followers of Mr. Dillon and Mr. McCarthy the American people have no wish to enter. It is an unseemly and unnecessary contest that they wish to have nothing to do with . . . The contemplated contest for Irish Parliamentary seats between Home Rulers in the face of an active and irreconcilable foe is worse than a blunder. It is a crime. It is treason to Ireland.

In his main address at the Academy of Music on 15 June, Redmond tried to strike a magnanimous note, even regarding Healy:

> We don't even ask that that man shall be driven out of public life who publicly boasted that he would drive Parnell into the grave or into a lunatic asylum. But we ask the same measure of forbearance on their side. Peace may yet be restored if Mr. Healy is not permitted to rule the destinies of his party . . . But if there is to be a policy of vengeance then we will fight it out.

A basket collection raised $2,000 (about £400).[47] Although the meeting was, as he claimed at Cork on his return, 'far larger than could be assembled in Ireland in any building' and he had never witnessed 'such earnestness, such enthusiasm and such devotion', his success in achieving the objective he had set for the visit ('to bring many men, at present holding aloof, to our side in this struggle') was decidedly limited.[48] The *New York Herald* called his address 'a calm, dispassionate, logical and eloquent statement of the case from the side of the Parnellites', but reflected the failure of most American sympathizers to grasp the depth of the split when it wrote: 'The Parnellites and the Healyites should stop their bickerings and come together at once.'[49] For the *Freeman*, the visit to New York was a 'gigantic political swindle'; Redmond had fraudulently hauled down the flag of faction and run up the flag of peace.[50]

His return launched him once again into the barbarities of electioneering rhetoric. At Inchicore, he promised that he and his colleagues would 'go to that Parliament, as I went eleven years ago, free and unfettered, hating the Tory party, and despising the Liberal party (*cheers*); prepared to take what we could get from either side; prepared to drag our rights from Englishmen, and not to beg for them (*loud cheers*).'

Even if the Independent nationalists returned only one man, 'the voice of that man alone would be able to prevent the treachery and betrayal by the acceptance in the name of Ireland of a Bill which was not a measure of our rights'.[51] A few days later, back in his own constituency, he was less optimistic about the working of democracy:

> I fear that the determination of the Liberal party has been so weakened by the exhibition of treachery on the part of large masses of the Irish people and large numbers of the Irish members . . . [as] to destroy the possibility of even a party of independence wringing from the Liberal party a full measure of our rights.

He dwelt on the plight of the Irishmen 'eating their hearts out' in English convict cells: 'They are our kith and kin (*cheers*). They are men who sacrificed everything that was most dear to them in an effort to benefit Ireland. What do we care whether their effort was a wise one or not (*cheers*), whether a mistaken one or not? (*cheers*).'[52]

At Ballybricken on 30 June, he returned to Davitt's criticisms of his own and Parnell's records on the labour question. Davitt, he asserted, had never done one-twentieth of the good to the labourers of Ireland that was done by 'the man who drafted the Labourers Acts, which gave decent dwellings to the labourers throughout the country. I mean Mr. Parnell (*cheers*).'[53] His own principles were plain, he said. He held the view that it was 'essential for the protection of labour that labour should be organised (*hear, hear*)'. He had seen a great example of the power of organized labour in New York, when he had been given an address by a group of workingmen who had told him that by their own power they had practically established an eight-hour day:

> I therefore am strongly in favour of the principle of trades unionism (*cheers*) . . . I would appeal to the labouring population of Waterford to strengthen their organisation, but at the same time I would appeal to them to act in that organisation with due regard to the general interests of the community, and with moderation, good sense and reason (*cheers*).

Adopting Parnell's stances of 1891 on labour's demands as his own, he continued:

> I am in favour of limitation, wherever it is possible, of the hours of labour (*cheers*) . . . Every reasonable demand made on behalf of the labour movement has my support – seeing that the rate of wages is a rate which will enable men to live, educate and bring up their families, seeing that the class of labour employed is a legitimate class, and I believe in the strict enforcement of this and the preventing of excessive employment of the young (*hear, hear*) . . . I am glad to know that with every demand made by the Labour party of Great Britain I have been in sympathy (*cheers*).[54]

Redmond's adversary this time in Waterford was his old Plan of Campaign colleague David Sheehy. The week before the vote, Sheehy was reported by the *Freeman* to be confined to bed following a brutal attack in the city. 'Redmondite ruffians' were also reported to be assaulting priests in the streets. O'Brien was the victim of a serious assault in Cork. The *Daily Independent* reported that Dr Tanner was implicated in an 'extraordinary scene' of violence at a Tuam meeting of the Parnellite Colonel Nolan. All over the country in the constituencies, the Parnellites complained of wholesale interference by the Catholic clergy to bring out the anti-Parnellite vote and intimidate Parnellite voters.[55]

Redmond was returned with a reduced majority on 7 July.[56] When the final results were published on 18 July, there were 72 anti-Parnellite to 9 Parnellite seats. Four of the Parnellite seats were in Dublin city and county. There were close results in four other constituencies, and a further Dublin seat would certainly have been won if the intervention of an anti-Parnellite had not split the nationalist vote and handed it to a Unionist. Because the Parnellite vote was spread thinly in the rural constituencies, the number of Parnellite seats won underrepresented that vote. In the 44 constituencies contested between them, Parnellite candidates received almost 70,000 votes to the anti-Parnellites'

110,000. A total of 279,509 votes were cast for the anti-Parnellites, giving a 4:1 ratio in the vote as against the 8:1 ratio in seats. In a proportional electoral system the Parnellites could have expected 15 or 16 seats. Not only did the result fall far of what Harrington's 'armistice' arrangement would have yielded; it was worse even than that offered by Dillon and rejected by Redmond in New York as a 'policy of vengeance'.[57] It seemed that Redmond had not only misjudged the extent of Parnellite support but had also erred in attributing to Healy alone the resistance to an undemocratic arrangement that would have left the Parnellites grossly overrepresented.

V

The election result left the new Liberal Government dependent on the anti-Parnellites for power. With the support of the small Labour Party and the anti-Parnellites, the Liberal majority was a mere 24, hardly the kind of 'commanding majority' for Home Rule that Mather had seen as a prerequisite for facing down the opposition of the Lords. Parnellite votes would increase that majority to 42, giving them, if not the balance of power, certainly the power to give the new Government many anxious moments.[58] In the debate on the address on 8 August, Redmond removed doubt as to his intentions by announcing that the Parnellites would vote to put the Liberals into power, so that 'the speediest and the freest possible opportunity will be given to [them] to redeem the pledges which they have given to the Irish people'. He understood these pledges to be twofold: first, that the effective settlement of the national question must be the first work of Parliament, and all other reform measures must wait ('Ireland blocks the way', in Gladstone's phrase of 1886); and second, that the settlement must be a final one. He voiced the concerns he had discussed in his correspondence with Mather, particularly the issue of how the supremacy of the imperial Parliament could be reconciled 'with the concession of a free and unfettered control of Irish affairs by an Irish Legislature'. On the evicted tenants question, he called for a short autumn session to pass into law the Parnellite Bill introduced in March, which all nationalists and Liberals had supported, and which proposed to give the Land Commission power to compel landlords to sell to the evicted tenants the farms from which they had been evicted. Finally, he appealed to the outgoing and incoming home secretaries to reconsider the case for amnesty initiated by Parnell and himself, particularly in the case of Egan, which was admitted on all sides to be distinct enough to merit review.[59]

Morley was formally installed as chief secretary on 13 September, and the following day all remaining proclamations in force under the Crimes Act were suspended.[60] But it was soon evident that there would be no autumn session for the evicted tenants. Instead, Morley announced on 28 September the setting up of a commission of inquiry into the matter (something for which Redmond in his Commons speech had said he saw no need); it was three weeks more before the five members of the commission were named. The *Independent* claimed that the workload would take two to three years, and concluded that the question was 'shelved indefinitely'.[61]

Within two days of his installation, Morley sought a friendly 'chat' with Redmond. Following a stiffly non-committal reply from Redmond,[62] the two men finally met, at Morley's 'urgent request' (according to Redmond), on 17 October at the house of Lord Chancellor Sir Samuel Walker in Dublin. The revealing conversation was recorded by Redmond in a twelve-page memorandum.[63] Having ranged over the matter of nominees to a vacant land commissionership (Redmond refused to suggest a name and advised Morley 'to shake himself clear of all placehunters, to give it to some undisputed man qualified for the position') and the commission on the evicted tenants, they turned to the immediate future:

> Redmond: 'How do you regard the prospects of this winter?'
>
> Morley: 'With grave misgiving. If I can't rule Ireland this winter with success it means destruction. I don't believe the talk about a revival of secret societies . . . though there may be a revival of Parnellism . . . At the same time I know there are forces behind you which you yourself cannot entirely control. They could make my task this winter an impossible one. Can you give me any hope on this point?'
>
> Redmond: 'It depends on yourself. If you are thorough you can disarm hostility. In the first place release the prisoners.'

A discussion followed on Redmond's argument that the Irish 'so-called Dynamiters' had received enough punishment, when compared with the Walsall (English anarchist) bombers, who had served relatively short sentences. Later Redmond brought the talk back to the prisoners issue:

> Redmond: 'Can you promise me anything about Amnesty?'
>
> Morley: 'All I can promise is that I will write to Asquith [home secretary] and press your views upon him . . .'
>
> Redmond: 'But after all *you* can decide it. If you demand it the Cabinet must agree.'
>
> Morley: 'That no doubt is so; but I cannot say anything more to you now . . .'
>
> Morley (later): 'Have you any suggestions as to securing a peaceful winter?'
>
> Redmond: 'Amnesty – Amnesty – Amnesty!'

Morley's nervousness about the Government's fragility in the light of nationalist disunion was evident:

> Morley: 'Could you promise us a united Nationalist Party?'
>
> Redmond: 'No. Reunion has been made impossible by insults and blackguardism of Healy and others.'

Morley: 'Yes – the misfortune of the thing is that the man (Healy) with most brains amongst the anti-Parnellites is – what shall I say? – without character –'

Redmond: 'A political savage –'

Morley: 'Yes, but you must remember the anti-Parnellites are not all of his way of thinking. The cleavage between you and the anti-Parnellites is no greater than the cleavage between the one section of the anti-Parnellites and the other. In fact the whole nationalist movement is in chaos.'

Redmond: 'That was inevitable from the destruction of Parnell.'

Morley: 'Perhaps so. Remember always I am as much a Parnellite as an anti-Parnellite and have been all this time.'

Turning to the Home Rule Bill, Redmond asked Morley to make public the 'understanding and agreement' that Dillon had claimed to have with Gladstone about the Bill.

Morley: 'Understanding and agreement with Dillon! There have been absolutely none.'

Redmond: 'But Dillon in a public speech has declared that there have been such . . .'

Morley: 'As to Home Rule . . . they know no more than you do.'

Redmond: 'That makes the position of affairs still more grave. Did you read Stead's article in this month's *Review of Reviews*?'

Morley: 'No.'

Redmond: 'Well he says we may get a London County Council for Ireland, but no more.'

Morley: 'There are of course two sections in the Cabinet. One of Stead's way of thinking but the other, to which of course I belong, would not remain in the Government a single hour if our Home Rule Bill only meant that.'

Morley promised to introduce a Bill that would be 'impossible for them to reject', but, mindful of Redmond's critical stance, asked: 'But do you really want Home Rule?'

Redmond: 'Certainly – genuine Home Rule.'

Morley: 'Then don't destroy our chances of giving it to you.'

Redmond: 'We don't intend to do so and we believe others are "embarrassing the Government" far more than we are [a reference to the promises made by Dillon in the name of the Liberals, about which Morley said he had protested to Dillon].'

The interview ended with a discussion of the issue of clerical interference in politics, still a live one for Parnellites as they struggled to come to terms with their electoral losses. The *Independent* had claimed moral victories in the two Meath constituencies, where its candidates had been defeated by 403 and 83 votes respectively, on the grounds that the winners, Davitt and Patrick Fulham, were 'the nominees merely of the clergy'.[64] The party had launched petitions to have the results overturned. Redmond told Morley that 'the people should be freed from the monstrous clerical intimidation which is prevalent all over Ireland.' Morley replied: 'It is horrible and almost incredible, but the time to defeat it is *when* you get Home Rule, not while trying to get it.' While Morley took 'the gravest view possible' of the likely damage to the Home Rule cause from publicity attending the petitions, he ruled out Redmond's suggestion that the way to avoid the exposure was 'not to defend the petitions and to let us have the seats'.

The hearing of the South Meath petition began on 16 November, with Healy acting for the respondents, and went on for twelve days, receiving massive newspaper coverage. The judgement found that Bishop Nulty and his priests had practised 'spiritual intimidation', which was 'gross, open, palpable and all-pervading'. The bishop's pastoral letter and sermons were largely to blame, and Nulty had turned his clergy into 'a vast political agency', which had canvassed in and out of the churches the idea that Parnellism was sinful.[65] The election of Fulham was therefore overturned. The London correspondent of the *Independent* wrote that it was difficult to convey to Irish readers the effect in England of the evidence given: 'Bishop Nulty can pride himself on having done more to arouse the fears and apprehensions of the English people than all the Tory orators put together.'[66]

The hearing of the North Meath petition was a repeat performance, beginning on 15 December and ending with the unseating of Davitt on 23 December.[67] In an article 'The Lesson of South Meath' for the *Fortnightly Review* in December, Redmond claimed vindication while attempting to limit the damage caused. He argued that while the petition had shown that the Parnellites would have won if not for clerical interference, it also showed that the law was strong enough to remedy this, and the fact that it was local Catholics who had financed the heavy costs of the petitions and that 100 of them had volunteered evidence showed that Catholics were determined not to have a clerical ascendancy and would 'defend civil liberty from the attempted aggression on the part of the Catholic priesthood'.[68]

The Parnellites strained every nerve to win the by-elections in the two constituencies, which took place in January and February of 1893. The boost a victory would have given was, however, denied them. Both elections resulted in repeat wins for the anti-Parnellites, though by even narrower margins than before. The *Independent* alleged that the results had been achieved by the same methods as previously, only used 'more insidiously'.[69]

The political game in Ireland in the autumn of 1892 was dictated, as it would be for the next seven years, by the need of each party to show the other in the worst possible light to fellow-nationalists. Parnellites accused their opponents of having a childlike trust in the Liberals' intentions to redress every wrong; O'Brien claimed that the demand for an autumn session was raised 'to hamper a friendly government'. 'We,' he said enigmatically, 'will give the evicted tenants an Autumn Session here at home.' The personal exchanges continued unabated. The *Independent* routinely called Dillon 'the melancholy humbug' and the *Freeman* the 'Fallen Journal'.[70] O'Brien spoke at Woodford of 'the perfidy of the Redmondites, and especially of Mr. Redmond himself' towards the evicted tenants.[71] Redmond in Dublin made light of the 'foul calumny', pointing to O'Brien's tendency 'to regard the whole world as divided into two classes: those who are scoundrels and traitors of the deepest dye – who are not fit to be permitted to live – and the other class is composed of those whose boots he is willing to polish (*laughter and applause*)'.[72]

The issue that dominated all others for the time being was the wrangle over the Paris Funds, which had been 'locked up' after Parnell's death by the joint action of the Parnellites and Katharine Parnell, pending agreement as to how it should be disbursed. With the general election over, the danger to the Parnellites of the funds being used to finance the campaign of their opponents was now past. Redmond and his colleagues, mindful of the fact that lawsuits were pending in the English and French courts, now wanted the funds placed at the disposal of the tenants. At Aughrim on 21 August he made two proposals. First, a new national fund should be set up, to be managed by a committee drawn equally from both sides, which would appeal to their brethren in all parts of the world. Second, the Paris Funds should be opened up to the evicted tenants on two conditions – that it be disbursed by an independent committee enjoying the confidence of both sides, and that the fund be used partly to rebuild houses battered down during evictions, so that, in the event of amicable agreements being reached, the tenants could return.[73] Dillon replied a few days later agreeing with the first condition regarding the funds, but saying the second 'looked hardly honest but rather like an obstructive and absurd condition', since it implied that his party had obstructed fair settlements. The Paris Funds, he said, should be used for the support of all the evicted, otherwise they would be starving these families into accepting settlements that would pauperize them.[74] On 1 September, Redmond claimed that his suggestion, which was aimed at preventing the fund from being dissipated solely on maintenance, had been 'rejected with insult' by Dillon.[75] It was difficult to see the practical difference between the two proposals, since Redmond had agreed with supporting tenants on estates such as Clanricarde who could not get a fair settlement. However, he conceded Dillon's point when he renewed his proposal at the Parnellite convention at the Rotunda on 10 October, making no mention of the use of the fund, except that it not be used for political purposes.[76]

The *Freeman* immediately found other objections in the way of agreement, indicating, not a change of mind on the part of Dillon, but Healy's control of the editorial policy of the paper.[77] The controversy raged on until Dr Croke intervened on 27 October, putting a modified proposal that was immediately accepted by Harrington on behalf of the

Parnellites.[78] On 29 October Healy and O'Brien moved a resolution at their parliamentary committee accepting the Croke proposal.[79] It seemed that the evicted tenants would at last get their share of the Paris Funds. Redmond proposed practical steps to put the agreement into effect before the next stages in the lawsuits were reached. On 4 November, however, the *Freeman* announced that the bankers had refused to release the fund even if the litigants settled their differences, and commented: 'So dies, and in somewhat a ludicrous fashion, the latest stalking-horse of the Redmondite faction.'[80] Further recrimination followed, with Harrington suspecting the hand of Healy behind the delay. There the matter would rest until July 1894, when the legal procedures were brought to an end and the fund finally became available.[81]

While these controversies raged, Redmond addressed questions of recruitment and organization. In line with the general decline in Parnell's support, the National League had suffered a catastrophic slump in membership during 1891, falling from 641 branches on 31 March to 212 on 31 December.[82] In order to locate and mobilize Parnellite support, Redmond turned to an idea first tried by Isaac Butt in 1874, that of a 'National roll'. On 15 November at the National League offices in Dublin, he unveiled his project of an 'Army of Independents in Ireland' (soon to be known universally as the 'Army of Independence'). This unarmed army would have 'a corps in every province, a brigade in every county' with insignia, a badge bearing Parnell's head and so forth. He explained that

> to a martial people like our countrymen . . . the inception and enrolment of an army pledged to carry out the principles of the greatest fighting leader under whom the Irish race has ever served in a constitutional battle would be the proper means to call forth the strength and mobilise the forces of the land.[83]

The *Freeman*, in Healy's best editorial style, ridiculed 'the Redmondite Salvation Army' with Field-Marshal Redmond, Brigadier O'Kelly and Major-General Kettle as its trustees. Chief Superintendent John Mallon of the Dublin Metropolitan Police reckoned that the establishment of the new organization 'indicates decadence in the Parnellite ranks' and suspected that the inspiration had come from Fenians associated with the Parnellites, who wanted to record their numerical strength.[84] However, Redmond had every reason to wish to draw on support from the Fenians, whose membership now outnumbered that of his own organization: the police figures for 1892 for the IRB and the National League were 11,051 and 8,076 respectively.[85] The martial trappings and verbal sleight of hand centred on the word 'Independence' in its title seemed designed to attract grass-roots Fenians to the new 'army'. In the end, Redmond's attempt to create a single body for constitutionalist and extremist rank and file was a failure. Enrolment went on with much publicity into the early months of 1893, and thereafter more quietly. At the end of 1893, it had 5,400 members in 25 branches outside Dublin, less than the surviving membership of the National League. After 1893 it was seldom heard of.[86]

VI

Just before the opening of the new parliamentary session, the most significant for Ireland's future since that of 1886, the amnesty campaign won its first victory with the release of Egan from Portland on 22 January 1893. Redmond's amendment to the Address was again on the amnesty theme; his speech included an extended consideration of what constituted a 'political' offender and of Great Britain's role as a sanctuary for such men from all over Europe. Given that dynamite had again intruded itself into Irish political life, in an explosion on Christmas Eve in Dublin which had blown a policeman to pieces, he may have regretted his overconfidence in the 1891 Commons amnesty speech in which he had declared 'the dynamite conspiracy is as dead as Julius Caesar'.[87] He now emphasized

> that the action of Irish Nationalists on this question has not been taken by way of sympathy with, or to condone, the use of dynamite. There is but one feeling on this matter throughout the length and breadth of Ireland, and that is, that the use of dynamite is not only unjustifiable, but an absolutely insane proceeding.[88]

This disavowal did not prevent the *Daily Chronicle* from calling the amendment 'Mr. Redmond's dynamite amendment'.[89] The response of Asquith was frosty in the extreme. He made it clear that there would be no further releases. Referring to Redmond's definition of a political prisoner, he asked if everyone was to be regarded as such who committed a crime from a political motive. If so, was the crime of the Phoenix Park murderers to be taken as political?[90] 'You have to look in these cases,' he said, 'not to the motive merely, but to the methods by which the crime is carried out.' Assassins and dynamiters put themselves 'outside the pale of political offenders' and would receive no consideration or indulgence from him.[91] Redmond called the speech 'extreme' and predicted that it would create 'a most bitter feeling in Ireland'. The *Independent* said that the debate had 'torn the veil' from the face of the Liberal ministry and their Irish allies.[92] The *Freeman* blamed Redmond for bad tactics in choosing an inopportune moment for his amendment, which had resulted in a House friendly to Ireland voting against amnesty by 397 votes to 81, tying the hands of any future minister who might want to show clemency.[93] This masked the fact, however, that Dillon and his colleagues were now vulnerable to the charge that they had falsely conveyed the impression of agreement between them and the Government on the amnesty as on the evicted tenant question.

Gladstone introduced the Home Rule Bill on 13 February. Putting aside the animosities of two years, Redmond concurred with Sexton's compliment to the prime minister. Speaking on the first reading, he said:

> The spectacle of this aged statesman who in 1886 was driven from Office by a large majority at the polls, and who during the seven years that have elapsed has maintained his position on this Irish Question, and who comes down at the end of seven years to repeat, with eloquence that age cannot wither nor custom stale, his plea for the freedom of a poor and long-suffering country, does seem to me to be a spectacle which must arouse emotions in the mind of every man in every Party.

But uppermost in his mind was

> the absence from this Assembly of the great Irishman who was the real father of Home Rule . . . who drove the Prime Minister and his Party from the paths of coercion in which they had so long strayed, and who taught them that in concession to Irish national sentiment were to be found alone Irish content and Imperial safety.

His speech was a welcome for the broad principle of the Bill, qualified by his well-known reservations on imperial supremacy and the crown veto. He was glad to hear that a limit of six years was to be fixed for (a phased-out) imperial control of the constabulary, and the land question subject also to a fixed term, but was adamant that, as long as those questions were reserved to Westminster, 'you should not touch either the number or the powers of the Irish Members in this House'.[94]

At home, the Bill attracted immediate criticism in Parnellite circles, particularly the provisions for cutting the Irish representation at Westminster from 103 to 80, and the financial clauses that seemed to presage what Clancy, in a very able analysis of the Bill, called 'financial destruction from the very start'. The *Independent* commented that a comparison of this Bill with that of '86 showed 'how wise, prudent and truly patriotic' had been the action of the Independent party in adopting an 'attitude of cautious reserve' to the Liberals.[95] When the Parnellite convention assembled at the Rotunda on 9 March, Redmond had the delicate task of allowing the venting of disapproval while ensuring that extreme supporters did not secure a rejection of the Bill. He said: 'It would have been easy for us to have torn these sections into shreds . . . but we have prepared to adopt a moderate, conciliatory, and, I will say, generous attitude towards the Bill and its authors (*hear, hear*).' While the Bill, even when amended, would fall short 'of the aspirations of other generations', they would take refuge in Parnell's dictum that no man could dare to set a limit to the onward march of a nation. They would go back to the House as friends of the Bill, seeking 'to mould it' to make it acceptable as 'a moderate concession of Irish liberty'. Making a virtue of necessity, the *Independent* boasted of the contrast between the robust debate of the convention and that of the 'Whigs', filled with its tame delegates and the 'clerical would-be rulers of Ireland'.[96]

The debate on the second reading began after the Easter recess on 6 April. Redmond's contribution a week later was a magnificent oratorical set piece, which dwelt mainly on the high constitutional aspects of the Bill while navigating skilfully between uncritical acceptance and rejection. Answering assertions made by his old adversary Chamberlain, he denied that he and his friends disputed imperial supremacy, or refused to compromise on what they regarded as Ireland's right: 'This Bill is offered as a compromise, and is accepted as a compromise.' As to whether they accepted it as a final and immutable constitution, he did not believe it would be so if passed into law: 'If Ireland shows, as she will show, a real capacity for self-government, this Constitution must develop.' Any clause put into the legislation saying it was a final settlement would not be worth the paper it was written on. They could not bind the future, 'with its new interests, its wider needs, and its higher aspirations'. He denied Chamberlain's implication that in refusing to accept it as a final settlement they would be accepting it in bad faith, and only for the purpose of pursuing designs hostile to the Empire. Interestingly, his view of just where the 'march of the nation' might lead was different from the standard assumption that it must tend to separation. His view agreed with that of Chamberlain in 1885, that a final solution lay in federalism. In an echo of his own 1889 speech on the subject, he asserted that the two countries were 'too closely allied for separation, too distinct ever to be merged into one country and one people'. Yet for even such limited autonomy, physical force was not to be ruled out in principle. Chamberlain had stated that

> no sane man now feared armed insurrection against the English Government . . . Well, Sir, I am bound to admit that with the advance of science armed insurrection against British rule in Ireland has become practically impossible. But if the right hon. Gentleman means that the spirit of insurrection in Ireland is extinct he is but a superficial observer, because there can be no question but that the spirit of resistance by every honourable means against the Union, and a desire to rule in Irish affairs, is as much alive today as it was at any period during the last century.

Their claim did not rest on grievances alone:

> If the government of my country by Englishmen were the best that could be devised by the wit of man I would be as strong a Home Ruler as I am today. Without exaggeration, I believe that Irish Nationalists would rather be badly governed by their own countrymen than live under the best English Government you could give them.

On the financial clauses, he had met no member of any political party in Ireland who thought that the government of Ireland could be successfully worked under the provisions of the Bill as they now stood.

Figure 15. 'A Soldier's Legacy': Parnellite cartoon (*Irish Weekly Independent*, 8 April 1893). *Courtesy of the National Library of Ireland.*

The Parnell myth as propaganda: as John Redmond's Parnellite party prepare to adopt a critical attitude to the second Home Rule Bill, Erin picks up the rifle of the fallen Parnell while gazing towards the objective of the Irish Parliament.

The opposition of Ulster Unionists to the Bill was as strenuously expressed as in 1886. In January, a huge meeting at the Ulster Hall in Belfast had listened to a fiery oration from the Revd R. R. Kane, the Orange Order leader.[97] Dark hints at possible armed resistance to the enactment of Home Rule in the province would be heard from some of that community's spokesmen during the year. In a lengthy passage, Redmond took an airily dismissive view:

> The very name of the Ulster question itself is a falsehood. There is no Ulster question (*Opposition laughter*) . . . There may be a Belfast question – there may be a question of a small corner of Ulster, but it is false to speak of this question as an Ulster question.

He repeated the demographic arguments of his 1886 speech to disprove that a majority in the province opposed Home Rule, and impugned the 'myth' of Ulster's uniqueness: 'I wish Ulster were as prosperous as Unionist members endeavour to depict her. Belfast is prosperous, and long live her prosperity; but as Belfast has grown in prosperity Ulster has declined.' Insisting as before on treating the issue as part of the whole historical question of Protestantism in Ireland, he demonstrated that his thinking had not evolved since his Rotunda lecture of November 1886. Although the great mass of Protestants were frightened, understandably, by the Bill, the 'bitter and violent agitation' against Home Rule was, in his view, the work of merely a small unreasoning minority concentrated in the Orange society. Generosity, tolerance and the glorious history of Protestant nationalism would be, as they had always been, the guidelines of Irish Catholics in dealing with their fellow-countrymen. His own recent experience argued that Protestants should be encouraged rather than alarmed: 'I and my comrades sit in this House as the result of defeating the unanimous opposition of the priests and bishops of Ireland'; when was such a spectacle afforded as 70,000 Catholic votes being recorded against such opposition? His final flourish came with the lines from *Macbeth* that Isaac Butt had quoted in 1876 while he, as a young lad, had listened in the gallery of the House.[98] The Irish case for self-government was in the physician's answer to Macbeth: 'Therein the patient must minister to herself.'[99]

The London press was almost unanimous in its praise for the speech. The *Westminster Gazette*, not known for praise of nationalists, called it

> in every way a remarkable speech, whether for its breadth of view, its moderation, its wealth of quotations . . . [it] carried us through Home Rule and beyond it to Federalism, and it is a very hopeful sign that this Imperial way of looking at the Home Rule question is permeating the minds of the Irish leaders. One conspicuous feature of Mr. Redmond's speech was its freedom from cant. In this Mr. Redmond is the lineal descendant of Mr. Parnell.[100]

The parliamentary diarist, Sir Henry Lucy, wrote:

> Today he strode into the front rank of Parliamentary debaters. His manner of delivery is excellent. He has a melodious voice, perfectly under control. His diction is pure, free from the gaudy colours which come natural to some of his countrymen, and yet, as was shown towards the end of his speech, capable of sustained flights of lofty eloquence . . . [His] oratorical style, as the House discovered, is based upon a substratum of solid knowledge, sound commonsense, and a statesmanlike capacity to review a complicated situation.[101]

Shortly afterwards, Gladstone revealed the cast of his mind on the Ulster question. Speaking in the House on 3 May, he commented that

> in 1886, in proposing the Irish Government Bill, . . . we did state that if the inhabitants of the north-east corner of Ireland, forming a very small and limited portion indeed of the general community, were resolutely desirous of being exempted from the operation of that Act, we should be prepared to entertain a proposal to that effect, and I believe we made that declaration with the general concurrence of those who are termed the Nationalist Party.[102]

Gladstone, in the 1886 debate, had indeed listed the partition option among a set of 'various schemes' that had been advanced on behalf of Ulster, none of which seemed to have enough merit, or support, to warrant inclusion in the Home Rule Bill, but which deserved 'careful and unprejudiced consideration'.[103] But he now went on to make what the *Independent* called the 'astounding statement' that Parnell had been willing in 1886 to allow the north-east corner of Ireland to be excluded from Home Rule if its people so desired.[104] When questioned the following day by T. W. Russell, the Liberal Unionist M.P. for South Tyrone, Gladstone claimed that he had used the words 'concurrence or acquiescence' to describe the nationalist attitude. While he understood Parnell's dictum of 7 June 1886 – 'No, Sir; we cannot give up a single Irishman' – to be 'an earnest deprecation' of such exclusion, he took him not to be opposed 'provided it were found it gave concord to Ireland instead of the present painful disagreement'.[105]

Possibly because the prime minister's intervention came in the course of debate on the Miners Bill, many nationalists may have missed it; the *Independent* lamented that they had left it to Russell to get an explanation, adding that no nationalist 'could submit to so degrading a misrepresentation of his opinions'.[106] It was another day before Redmond's response appeared, in an interview with the Press Association. Admitting that he and his colleagues were 'much surprised' by Gladstone's statement, he reiterated Parnell's 1886 maxim and said that if nationalists then had acquiesced in anything, it was in 'its instant and emphatic repudiation by their Unionist fellow-countrymen'.[107]

The partition idea was at this stage an expedient entertained only by some of the Liberal Unionists. The example of the partitioning, into loyal and secessionist entities, of the state of Virginia in the American

Civil War was raised by the Chamberlainite M.P. Jesse Collings at the start of the 1893 debate with the words, 'I think Ulster has a right to demand treatment of that kind.'[108] Of the nineteen Ulster Unionist M.P.s, only the three Liberal Unionists would consider such a proposal, and then only as a last resort. The Press Association reported:

> These Irish Liberal Unionist members state that they are in full agreement with their Conservative colleagues in strongly opposing the whole Home Rule Bill as it at present stands, but in the event, which they consider highly improbable, of such a Bill being passed, or becoming likely to be passed, then they reserve to themselves the right to claim that Ulster be exempted from its operation.[109]

The fact that the major protagonists on both sides began from the assumption of the island's continued political unity, and that all knew that in any case the Bill would not pass the Lords, relieved Redmond and other Home Rulers of having their resolve on the matter tested at that point, as it would be in 1914, and allowed nationalists to continue in comfortable denial of the insuperable differences that daily realities told them polarized the two parts of Ireland on the issue of self-government.

The Bill passed its second reading on 21 April by a majority of 43. The Independent nationalists put down their amendments for the historic Committee stage, which opened on 8 May. The first of these, William Redmond's motions to have the legislature designated a 'Parliament' and its assembly a 'House of Commons', were rejected by Morley and Gladstone. The *Independent* castigated Morley for opposing the symbolically important amendments and was able to accuse the McCarthyites of voting 'that there shall not be an Irish Parliament, and that there shall not be an Irish House of Commons'.[110] The *Freeman* deprecated the waste of an afternoon 'in a barren and absurd debate on a meaningless issue of words'.[111] The powers granted to the Irish legislature in Clause 2 raised the issue of the supremacy of the imperial Parliament. Here it seemed that Redmond's conversations with Mather had borne fruit. Gladstone successfully resisted a Tory amendment that would have had, notwithstanding anything in the Act, the imperial Parliament's power and authority 'remain unaffected and undiminished over all persons, matters, and things within the Queen's dominions'. In the long two-day debate, in which Chamberlain and fellow-Unionists protested that the clause as it stood offered only the theoretical and ineffective imperial supremacy that obtained in the colonies, the statements of Redmond were taken by all sides to be the definitive expression of the nationalist view on the matter. Chamberlain's concept of supremacy seemed to him, he said, to mean 'the exercise of the right of control and revision . . . day after day in every detail of Irish public affairs', with the imperial Parliament acting as a 'Court of Appeal upon every single act in every Irish matter of the Irish Parliament'. To his mind, it meant rather that

> Ireland was to be allowed in her own Legislature, free from the interference – the stupid, meddlesome, and ignorant interference of that House, to manage her own affairs subject to this condition: that the Imperial Parliament had the power, which, in his belief, it could not divest itself of by any Act . . . and of which they would have no right to complain if it were exercised to put down any intolerable acts of oppression, which they believed would not arise in Ireland.[112]

Gladstone responded that he had just heard

> what appears to me to be a rational, just, and constitutional account of the supremacy of the Crown, and as to the use of that supremacy in the government of Ireland . . . I accept the declaration of the hon. and learned Member for Waterford as being given in good faith. I hold the hon. and learned Member bound to his words.[113]

The progress of the Bill slowed to a crawl as the opposition used obstructive tactics that seemed to be tolerated by the Government. By the end of May only two of forty clauses had been dealt with. As Redmond's position became difficult, the *Independent* on 1 June warned: 'Every change that has been made in it is a change for the worse . . . The time has come for the Independent members to take resolute action on behalf of Ireland.' On 20 June, with Unionist obstruction continuing, one of the Parnellite ex-M.P.s, W. A. MacDonald, spoke critically at the National League's central branch of Redmond and the party for their support of the Bill thus far.[114] The crucial financial clauses, which nationalists hoped would be amended in Ireland's favour, were reached on 22 June. The revenue from customs – estimated at £2.36 million – was to be taken as the contribution of Ireland to the imperial Exchequer. Excise and postal duties would be collected by the Irish Government, giving it a starting surplus of £0.5 million each year.[115] In May, however, the Government discovered an overestimate of the excise duties, which implied a much lower surplus. Rumours began to circulate about a new Government scheme, which would restore the £0.5 million surplus, but would institute the original arrangements only after six years. In the meantime, the imperial Parliament would continue to fix and collect all taxes. Redmond warned Morley privately that such a provision, which would 'take from the future Irish Government the collection, even for a time, of all Irish taxes', would be 'unjust and humiliating in the last degree' and would cause his members to vote against the third reading.[116] Following a meeting between the two men, Redmond told Morley that his colleagues felt, if anything, more strongly on the subject than he did, and there was no hope of their supporting the scheme.[117] By 20 June, two days before Gladstone announced the scheme, Redmond was telling Morley that he 'very much regretted' that the Government was standing fast, as it involved a principle 'which as I told you it is impossible to expect Irish Nationalists to approve', but he did not repeat the threat to vote against the Bill.[118]

The progress of the Bill gathered speed in July when Gladstone announced a time limit on the remaining clauses, which would be taken in groups. Stormy scenes ensued in the House as Tories protested at the use of the closure.[119] The general drift of the changes, however, was in a negative direction from a nationalist point of view. On 10 July, Redmond moved an amendment to omit the clause reducing the Irish representation at Westminster to eighty members. It was a carelessly conceived move which would have left no reference to any representation at all. The Unionists saw a chance to discredit the Government by voting for the amendment. Spotting the risk to the Government at the last minute, owing to a chance remark by Chamberlain, the McCarthyites swung behind Gladstone when he stood by his clause, thus ensuring the amendment's defeat. Confusingly, Gladstone himself just before the vote said that he would leave the question to the House to decide, enabling the Parnellites to claim that their opponents had voted unnecessarily to disenfranchise twenty-three constituencies. The chaos within the forces of nationalism was starkly underlined as the rival newspapers screamed treachery at each other, with the *Freeman* alleging that it was Redmond's 'clumsy stupidity', or worse, that had almost wrecked the Bill's chances.[120]

There was further disunity when the financial clauses came up again on 25 July, when Redmond moved to have the control of taxation (except customs and excise) transferred immediately rather than in six years. Sexton argued in favour of the Government proposal on the grounds that it would leave the legislature £25,000 better off. This, said the *Independent*, was giving away 'the very essence of self-government'.[121] Redmond, interviewed by the journal *Black and White*, castigated the proposal to collect all Irish taxes 'and, if we behave ourselves, to give us a little pocket money to get along with'.[122] The Parnellite resistance could not prevent the passage of the clauses, although Redmond managed to extract a commitment to set up a Royal Commission to inquire into Irish–British financial relations.[123] After forty-seven nights of debate, the Committee stage ended on 27 July amid scenes of confusion and violence in the House when the closure rule was enforced.[124]

Back in Dublin at a second Parnellite convention on 9 August, Redmond used all his powers of persuasion to convince a sceptical audience not to bind him to vote against the Bill's third reading. Defective as it was in its details, he said, 'still like the toad, ugly and venomous, bears yet a precious jewel in its head',[125] it enshrined a principle against which they could not take the responsibility of voting. For the first time since the Union, the Lower House of Parliament, representing the masses of the English people, would have solemnly pledged themselves to destroy the Union and restore a freely elected parliament to Ireland. Even

Figure 16. John Redmond addresses the Parnellite convention at the Rotunda Round Room, Dublin, 9 August 1893, persuading the delegates not to bind him to vote against the Third Reading of the Home Rule Bill (*Irish Weekly Independent*, 12 August 1893). *Courtesy of the National Library of Ireland.*

though they knew the Bill was not going to pass into law, 'an enormous step will have been made along the road which we have been travelling'. Faced with an amnesty amendment stating that no Home Rule measure was acceptable that was not accompanied by the release of the prisoners, he appealed to its mover, the Fenian F. J. Allan, to withdraw it: it would be 'folly and madness' to bind themselves in this way.[126]

The debate on the third reading showed again the differences between the two nationalist sections. For Redmond on 30 August, the discussions in Committee and the ungenerous and unjust financial provisions had confirmed that the Bill could not, even if passed into law, 'afford either a full, a final, or a satisfactory settlement of this question . . . the word "provisional" has, so to speak, been stamped in red ink across every page of this Bill'. As long as they were not asked to accept it as a final settlement, as they had been in 1886, he had no objection in principle to the restrictions on the powers of the legislature, especially those that were inserted to offer security to their fellow-countrymen who imagined that their civil and religious liberty would be menaced by an Irish parliament. It was because they would 'at last have obtained from the Representative House of the masses of the British democracy a reversal of the Act of Union and the solemn affirmation of the principle of Irish self-government' that he would with a light heart, and in spite of all the Bill's defects, vote for the third reading.[127] Dillon, by contrast, the following evening hailed the Bill as a 'satisfaction of the National demand' and 'a great charter of liberty'.[128]

The Home Rule Bill passed its third reading on 1 September by a majority of 34. A week later, despite a valiant defence by the Liberal peers Lord Rosebery and Earl Spencer, it was thrown out by the House of Lords by one of its largest ever majorities.[129]

9 The Vacuum

> The men who struck down Parnell have had their chance. They have brought back nothing but disunion and disgrace and dishonour. We appeal to Ireland to give us our chance to see whether we cannot do better and nobler things.
>
> Redmond at the Rotunda, Dublin, 8 October 1894[1]

> [The policy of] carp, cavil and fault-find . . . living a kind of hand-to-mouth political existence, continually on the look-out for some pretext to denounce the Irish Nationalists.
>
> *Freeman's Journal* on Redmondite policy, 18 March 1895[2]

I

Ireland was quiet in the autumn of 1893. The weather, always a factor in Irish rural discontent, played a part: there had not been in nearly seventy years a season more favourable to agriculture, and the harvest had been saved in excellent condition. The year just passed, said an article in the *Independent* in January 1894, had been 'one of the most peaceful and prosperous this century'; the people as a whole had been 'never freer from distress and the evils which follow in its course'.[3] Increased opportunities were opening up to tenants to purchase their farms under the Land Purchase Acts. Those not in a position to purchase could look forward to the second round of judicial (downward) rent revisions due to begin in 1896. Political discontent over the defeat of the Home Rule Bill was muted by the fact that the action of the House of Lords had been generally anticipated. Most nationalists seemed prepared for the moment to trust in the alliance of the majority Irish Party with the Liberals to find a way out of the impasse. Their viewpoint was probably well expressed in the editorials in the *Freeman* which stated that none would blame Gladstone or the Liberals for the rejection of the Bill – they had played their part nobly – and the Irish Party must now be prepared, as a *quid pro quo* for the Home Rule Bill, to support the British democracy in realizing its own cherished projects. The only way to defeat the obstacle of the House of Lords was a Home Rule victory at the next election.[4]

With no seeming chance of a reunion of the party on terms that he could regard as honourable, Redmond could only wait for the disillusion that must follow what his judgement told him would be the failure of the Liberal alliance. The suspicion he had entertained and voiced for the previous two years that, apart from Gladstone, Morley and one or two others, there were few warm supporters of Home Rule among the Liberal leadership, and that most of them would be glad to shelve it and press on with the rest of the reform package for which their constituents impatiently waited, came to the fore in the wake of the defeat of the Bill. Such suspicions could only be strengthened by weak statements from Gladstone in Edinburgh on 27 September (in the next session it would 'reappear above the waves amidst which it has for the moment seemed to founder') and from Asquith on 17 October, which suggested there would be no early re-introduction of Home Rule.[5]

In seeking advantage for his party, Redmond had to steer between two conflicting pressures. Taking too extreme a course against the Liberals would tend to alienate popular British support for Home Rule and risk putting the 'coercionists' back in power, something that moderate nationalists, including Parnellites, would not tolerate. Chief among those advisers who warned him against taking this direction were T. P. Gill, the mediator at Boulogne, and James (J. J.) O'Kelly, a Parnellite close to the Liberals and to the Irish community in Britain, who had lost his North Roscommon seat by less than 100 votes, and who had been less critical than other Parnellites of the Home Rule Bill.[6] On the other hand, he had to consider the views of the Fenian activists who sustained him not only with their votes but with their willingness to work for the party.

In Dublin, the various Redmondite elements came into contact at meetings of the Amnesty Association, the National Club and the National League. Redmond, Harrington and the other M.P.s met the activists regularly at the offices of the *Independent* newspapers, where several of them were employed. Although the editor of the *Daily Independent* was Dr Edward Byrne, a constitutionalist who had resigned from the editorship of the *Freeman* when it changed sides in 1891, its manager was Frederick J. Allan, a member of the Supreme Council of the IRB, and the leading Cork Fenian P. H. Meade became a director of the company in 1894. Chief Superintendent Mallon reported that the fifty active IRB men he knew in Dublin were 'all either members of the National Club, the Nally Gaelic [i.e. GAA] Club, the Independent Labourers' Club . . . the Amnesty Association, or the staff of the *Daily Independent* and *Evening Herald*'. The newspaper's office was effectively the Dublin IRB headquarters.[7] Tension between the militants, centred on the National Club, and the moderates of the National League was chronic. Allan wrote to Redmond in September 1893 complaining of Harrington's seeming desire to pick a quarrel with the club: his words at a recent league meeting that 'These fellows will have to be fought sooner or later' had left 'a very irritable feeling upon a hardworking earnest lot of young fellows.'[8]

Fenianism in the 1890s was a fragmented phenomenon, paralysed by dissension and personal feuds, more a social outlet and badge of identity than a successful revolutionary incubus in the constitutional movement. Mallon doubted whether its leaders had an accurate idea of the numerical strength of the organization.[9] Most of these men, while looking forward to the day when armed insurrection would be feasible, disapproved of the dynamite policy espoused in the 1880s by O'Donovan Rossa and the *Irish World*.[10] Nevertheless, dynamitards were active in Dublin and some of those on the fringes of the Dublin Parnellite groups were strongly suspected by the police of being responsible for the sporadic dynamite outrages that had occurred since 1890. Following the explosions at the *National Press* in 1890 and on Christmas Eve 1892, an explosion broke over 300 windows at the Four Courts in May 1893, another bomb was found there a month later, and explosives were found at Aldborough barracks later in the year.[11] A compositor on the *Independent*'s staff was strongly suspected, with two other frequenters of the National Club, of responsibility for the Christmas Eve bomb. In November 1893 one of the three was shot dead, leaving the police with grounds to suspect that the murder was the execution of an informer linked with the bombing.[12] The trial on 12 January 1894 of two men charged with the murder was attended by Redmond, Harrington and Leamy but collapsed when the crown case broke down.[13] A month later, one of the men, another compositor, was again in court charged with possession of explosives on the night of the murder.[14]

At the Parnellite anniversary convention at the Rotunda on 9 October, Redmond placated his militant base by announcing a 'policy of fight' and threatening abstention from Parliament. He branded Dillon's acceptance of the Home Rule Bill as a full settlement as 'a piece of gross presumption and gross stupidity'. In Parnell's time, Gladstone had declared that Home Rule blocked the way of English reforms, but now 'Home Rule has been hung up by the Liberal party (*cheers*) and . . . English voters . . . are about to have it proved to them . . . mark you, by Irish representatives (*hear, hear and groans*) that Ireland does not block the way.' This, together with the unreasonable attitude on the amnesty question, 'inclined him to say that we Independent Nationalist members are under no obligation whatever to aid them by our votes in Parliament . . . in my opinion most of us can spend the coming month far more profitably here in Ireland (*loud cheers*) rallying our forces and organising our people'.[15] The following evening at the league central branch, he seemed anxious to justify his new course in constitutionalist terms. It was probable, he said, that when the Government went out of office, none of the three questions – Home Rule, amnesty or the evicted tenants – would have been settled:

> Unless Ireland has awakened from the lethargy which seems to have crept over her . . . unless the young men of Ireland have banded themselves together, there will inevitably come after that a period of national depression, which will only be broken, probably, by some outburst of violence which it is in the interest of all of us to avert

> (*hear, hear*) . . . I believe those of us who may seem to some English statesmen to be taking a somewhat extreme course . . . are the best and only real friends of the constitutional movement (*hear, hear*).[16]

Advice against abstention came from Gill, who wrote on 13 October that he approved of 'Ireland Stops the Way' as a slogan for agitation both in Ireland and in the House of Commons, and approved of the nine Parnellite M.P.s staying at home during the autumn to agitate and organize, as long as they paired correctly. But if by some chance their abstention without pairing led to the Government's overthrow, he asked, 'Where will you be? What do you expect to gain?' He disapproved of the offensive tone being used on Independent platforms in speaking of the Liberal Party 'and things and measures which the English democracy and working classes hold very dear . . . speaking in this way was one of the mistakes poor Parnell admitted to me and he tried and generally managed to avoid it in his later speeches'. In flattering words, he pointed to a vista of wider acceptance:

> In Ireland mark this – whatever growth of Parnellite strength has taken place during the year is *largely due to the impression created of the sagacity of your action in Parliament throughout the session*; to the *confidence* thus inspired in your *wisdom*, *discretion* and *skill* – your Parnellesque qualities, in short, a confidence which has been greatly heightened by the squabbling on the other side. Men who feared that in supporting Parnellism they were helping to *wreck* Home Rule have begun to feel that they are doing the contrary and that Parnellism is likely to furnish from its bosom a new leader to whose prudence and adroitness and courage they can trust the constitutional cause. Beware of upsetting that feeling for in my deliberate judgment there is where your *solid* basis lies.[17]

On 24 October, Gill wrote again. He saw nothing to be gained by the reintroduction of the Home Rule Bill. The right course was to get the necessary minimum of British measures (including a Bill to reform the register) passed to enable the Liberals to get a majority at the next election. Redmond should offer to help them pass provided an Evicted Tenants Bill was passed also and the general election held immediately afterwards. He should also address a series of meetings in England 'in a strongly democratic tone' and point out to the British democracy 'that we have no quarrel with them'.[18]

Whether or not in response to Gill's advice, Redmond, at Naas on 29 October, backtracked on his abstention threat. He announced himself willing and anxious to help pass the two Bills coming up in the winter session (due to open on 2 November) if the Government would only devote one week of the session to passing a reinstatement Bill for the evicted tenants. It was also perfectly reasonable that the 1894 session be given to English Bills, on two conditions: that the Bills be of the type that would help the Home Rule cause to win at the next election, and that Parliament be dissolved at the end of 1894.[19] In a letter to the American press on 2 November, which the *Freeman* called an 'audacious recantation' of a 'policy of wreck', he claimed that it was absurd to construe recent declarations as implying that they meant to throw out Gladstone and restore Lord Salisbury, but 'any paltering' with Home Rule 'may convert us from supporters into opponents'. They were determined not to allow a prolongation of Parliament with the indefinite hanging up of Home Rule, he wrote.[20] The following week he and his colleagues voted with the Government to defeat a hostile amendment to the Employer Liability Bill, although they abstained from voting on all 101 divisions on the Parish Councils Bill, the second major measure being put through in the winter session.[21]

Outside Parliament the rhetorical 'policy of fight' went on through the autumn as the small Parnellite band of M.P.s combined attendance at Parliament with a tour of their Irish support centres. Again the amnesty movement proved the perfect cover for parliamentary moderation. Although Redmond did not approve of Fenian methods in the present, he allowed an honoured place for them in the story of the movement. At Cork on 22 October he told an amnesty meeting that it was Fenianism that had opened Gladstone's eyes to the demands of Ireland, adding that 'it is easy to denounce the methods of the Fenian party. I have always thought those methods ill-advised . . . [but] in the past the National cause never gained anything except through the efforts of men similar to the men whose release we are now demanding.'[22] At Wexford on 26 November he castigated the 'wrong, foolish, short-sighted and ungrateful' stance adopted by the farmers since 1890, but praised the towns of that county, which 'in the old days, ran red with English blood' and which 'refused to bow their heads in submission to the orders of an English statesman'.[23]

At Tuam on 17 December and at Dunmore on the following day he made political capital out of recent events, reminiscent of the bad old coercionist days, which were deeply embarrassing to the anti-Parnellites. Evictions had begun in the autumn of 1892 on the DeFreyne estate in County Roscommon, the police had been used to protect the levelling and burning of houses, prosecutions had resulted from attempts to build shelters and two M.P.s had recently been brought to trial for unlawful assembly.[24] In January, there would be reports of jury-packing in a County Clare Whiteboy trial. Redmond castigated Morley for failing to stand up to the Dublin Castle administration, and the McCarthyites for seeking to suppress the truth about what was happening.[25]

As the winter session continued into 1894, further statements from leading Liberals seemed to confirm Redmond's fears that Home Rule was being hung up. Harcourt at Derby on 24 January scotched any idea that the Government would dissolve on the Home Rule question; it was determined to proceed with its Newcastle programme as a whole.[26] On 28 January, Redmond outlined to the Press Association the only conditions under which his party could agree to Home Rule being hung up for the 1894 session. He expected an Evicted Tenants Bill to be pushed through as a priority, followed by the Registration Bill, and a general election as soon as possible afterwards. In the meantime, one of his amendments to the Address would be a motion of censure on the Irish administration.[27]

In mid-February 1894, it seemed for a time as if Harcourt's policy might be thwarted and Home Rule saved from indefinite postponement. Since the House of Lords had mutilated the two reform Bills passed by the Commons, two options, in Redmond's estimation, presented themselves to the Government. It could compromise with the Lords, pass the Bills and proceed with the rest of the reform package, or it could seize the chance to fight the Lords, drop the two Bills and call a new Session for the sole purpose of passing Evicted Tenants and Registration Bills, then go to the country. The latter course would benefit both Ireland and the Liberal programme.[28] The outcome saw both scenarios partly realized. Compromise was reached on the Parish Councils Bill, allowing it to go through, but Gladstone won the Commons' support for rejecting the Lords' amendments to the Employer Liability Bill and voting to abandon it, thus bringing the two Houses into confrontation. However, with the Grand Old Man's vigour noticeably in decline, it seemed as if the fight would have to wait for another day. The *Independent*, lamenting that seventy-one Irish M.P.s had constituted themselves 'the tail of the Liberal party', remarked wryly on the use that Parnell might have made of the crisis to strike a blow for Ireland.[29]

On 4 March, the long-rumoured resignation of Gladstone was announced. The following day the longest parliamentary session on record came to an end, with nothing more to show for its labours than, as the *Independent* commented, a measure of self-government for English villages.[30]

II

The Queen's Speech for the new session, which opened on 12 March 1894, made no mention of Home Rule, but promised an Evicted Tenants Bill and a Registration Bill. During the debate on the Address, the new prime minister, Lord Rosebery, added a new phrase to the lexicon of Home Rule, and struck another blow at nationalist hopes, when he gave as his view 'that before Irish Home Rule is conceded by the Imperial Parliament England, as the predominant member of the partnership between the Three Kingdoms, will have to be convinced of its justice.'[31] Redmond responded that the Liberal leadership had passed 'into the hands of men of whom I must say that we have no strong faith in their devotion to the cause of Home Rule' (he excepted the chief secretary). 'That position,' he declared, 'is an absolutely intolerable one from the Irish point of view.' But the prime minister's statement had made things far worse, because it now seemed

> not merely that Home Rule is to be shelved and a Dissolution indefinitely postponed, but that after the next General Election, even if the Liberal party should obtain a majority in Ireland, Scotland and Wales, and in Great Britain, we are not to get Home Rule unless, forsooth, there should be a majority of English Members in its favour.[32]

The *Freeman* admitted that Rosebery had 'aroused some uneasiness' but was reassured when the latter, at Edinburgh on 18 March, explained that his 'predominant partner' remark had meant only that the English majority against Home Rule would have to be so reduced that the Liberals in the Commons would be enabled to defy the House of Lords. Dillon, who was in the audience to hear the gloss, was reported as 'firmly convinced that in Lord Rosebery the cause of Ireland had an honest and honourable champion, who would be false to no pledge which was given by the Government'.[33] However, in the first public sign of a crack in anti-Parnellite allegiance to the Liberal alliance, Healy declared that if the Irish Party were united, they would have heard 'no such speech as they had had lately from Lord Rosebery'.[34] The *Independent*'s London correspondent claimed that after Redmond's speech Healy had gone to Morley 'in a savage temper' and threatened that unless Rosebery retracted his statement about the English majority he would put the Government out of office.[35]

Healy's breaking of ranks coincided with his defeat in the long struggle between his and the Dillonite factions for mastery of the *Freeman* Board. In the previous year, he had objected to Dillon's attempt to co-opt a Parnellite onto the board who would aim to restore the paper's falling circulation in Dublin. A fierce controversy was then triggered in which Archbishop Walsh had to intervene to quell the public discord. A temporary victory for Healy in June 1893 led to Sexton resigning his parliamentary seat (a decision he rescinded a few days later in response to pleas). The animosity transferred itself to the National Federation in September 1893. Fresh newspaper controversy broke out again that month on the Paris Funds, this time with Davitt pitted against Healy and his acolytes. Financial trouble at the *Freeman* caused the smouldering quarrel to burst into flame again in late March 1894, with Healy launching bitter attacks on Dillon and Sexton. Finally, on 29 March, Healy was voted off the board.[36]

Meanwhile, the *Independent* newspaper group, consisting of the *Daily Independent*, the *Evening Herald* and the *Weekly Independent*, started on the small capital of £30,000 (compared to that of £180,000 for the *Freeman* group), was prospering. Redmond told the annual general meeting of the company on 2 April that, apart from capital liabilities, the balance sheet compared favourably with that of the *Freeman* company, whose advertising revenue and receipts had both fallen. Making an appeal for more capital – they needed a quarter more than the amount already invested – he said the papers 'are on the very verge of success . . . approaching a haven of safety and security'.[37] The following month the *Daily Independent* could report 'a substantial response' to the appeal for capital.[38]

The Registration Bill, the Budget and the Evicted Tenants Bill were all introduced within a week of each other in mid-April. Each gave the Parnellites further opportunity to make political capital against their opponents; each increased the discontent and instability within the majority group. The first was one of those reforms that Redmond had promised to support in order to conciliate Liberal opinion, on condition that they helped the Home Rule cause. However, hints by Government spokesmen that the reforms would include cutting the Irish representation at Westminster caused him to change his mind, and 8 of the 9 Parnellites abstained on 4 May when the Bill passed its second reading by a majority of only 14.[39]

The Government had the same majority a week later when all the Parnellites voted against the increase in taxes on beer and spirits, a measure which the *Independent* estimated later would add £121,000 to the taxation of Ireland in the case of spirits alone. By 26 May the paper could charge the McCarthyites with voting through a total of £1,000 per day from the pockets of Irish taxpayers to fund the expansion of the British navy (the major cause of the deficit that the Chancellor sought to redress).[40] Redmond told a deputation of Radicals and trade-unionists asking him to oppose the liquor duties and the Local Veto Bill (which would give greater local powers to close public houses on Sundays) that he looked on the measures from a purely Irish point of view, rather than on their own merits, and would vote accordingly against them.[41] His views on temperance now took second place to the need to oppose a Budget that added to Ireland's tax burden at a time when he believed, on the expert advice of Sir Joseph McKenna, former Buttite M.P. for Youghal, more recently M.P. for South Monaghan, that the country was already contributing some £4 million more than her fair share each year to the imperial Exchequer.[42] On 29 May, in a happy coincidence of timing for the Parnellites, the terms of reference were published for the Royal Commission on Financial Relations, which Redmond had extracted from Morley the previous year in the debates on the financial clauses of the Home Rule Bill. On 21 June Redmond attended its first sitting in London, when it began the protracted process of inquiring into the great question of the fiscal treatment of Ireland under the Union.[43]

The Evicted Tenants Bill proposed a Board of Arbitration with compulsory powers to reinstate tenants, with a fund of £100,000 to be provided from the Temporalities of the Church of Ireland. Tenants would be restored at their old rent but could apply to the Land Commissioners to fix a fairer one. The Bill was weaker than the failed measure of J. J. O'Kelly of 1892, the main difference being that the earlier Bill had provided for 'grabbers' (those who had taken the farms of some of the evicted) to be removed with financial compensation, while Morley's Bill now proposed leaving the grabbers in place and finding alternative farms for the evicted.[44] Dillon estimated that it could restore about 1,000 tenants to their homes, about two-fifths of the total.[45] It could be defended on the grounds that a more controversial measure was less likely to pass, as even the *Independent* admitted on its introduction.[46]

Nevertheless, its deficiencies were useful ammunition for Parnellites, especially in the light of Dillon's seeming confusion when he praised it as a 'great Bill' and in the same speech talked of half a loaf being better than no bread.[47] Redmond left it to Harrington and Clancy to criticize its details while he fought to prevent its being lost from lack of time, due to Harcourt's efforts to give the Finance Bill priority over all other measures. It was 19 July before the second reading was reached, when Morley announced the raising of the funding to £250,000. Tory obstruction forced the Government to guillotine the debate, and all nationalists voted with the Government for the third reading on 7 August, giving it a majority of 32. Given the certainty that it would not pass the Upper House, both nationalist parties were in agreement on the hollowness of the victory.[48] On 14 August, the Lords duly threw out the Evicted Tenants Bill by 249 votes to 30. 'So ends the dreary farce,' said the *Independent,* blaming the speeches of Government speakers, which had been 'half-hearted to the last degree'. The ending, though deplorable, had been foreseen for two years, it claimed. The one chance to settle it had been lost when the Government, with anti-Parnellite support, refused the Independent Party's demand to deal with it in autumn 1892. The intervening delay had destroyed the strongest argument in its favour, its urgency. The paper indicted the 'Whigs' for voting for £300,000 in extra taxation and getting nothing in return (even the Coercion Act had not been dealt with, in spite of Redmond's pressure on Harcourt in early summer to repeal it).[49]

The unpromising atmosphere of the early summer of 1894 generated new rifts within the anti-Parnellite bloc. The *Irish Catholic*, now a Healyite paper, published a stinging attack on McCarthy on 23 April for stating that the Irish Party were the masters of the situation and held the Government in 'the hollow of our hands', adding that 'Mr. Parnell in the days of his power was wont to avoid mere braggadocio'. If they had such power, why was so little being done with it? On 5 June at the National League central branch, Redmond asked, 'What good or what benefit can Ireland derive from the continuation of the present Parliament?' – a remark that the *Freeman* called 'the most fatuous and foolish of his utterances so far'. Three weeks later two anti-Parnellite M.P.s, one of them the member for East Wicklow, John Sweetman, put down a resolution at a party meeting calling for an early dissolution. Though defeated by 29 votes to 2, with some abstentions, the resolution was a sign of demoralization in the party that went beyond the personalized Healy–Dillon feud. On 5 July, McCarthy looked forward to a 'good working session' in the following year, in which his Liberal allies would 'reaffirm by resolution their faith in the cause of Home Rule', while the way would be cleared for a raft of English and Welsh Bills. The following month the *Independent* published a letter from Sweetman, originally written to the *Freeman* but suppressed by it, which called again for dissolution. It claimed that the people were beginning to have as little confidence in the Irish Party as in that of Butt before Parnell came to the fore, and that political apathy was general in Ireland.[50]

If Parnellite strategy made any sense now, it was to attract disillusioned moderates to a more robust form of constitutional action, while simultaneously co-opting Fenian support and preventing younger nationalists from being misled into extremism. In the second of these arenas, however, there were forces pulling the other way. The summer of 1894 was notable for the bizarre visit of O'Donovan Rossa, back home after twenty-nine years of exile. Sentenced to life imprisonment as a Fenian in 1865, released and sent to the United States five years later, he had refused to condemn the Phoenix Park murders and had been an advocate of the dynamite campaign of 1883–85. He was later expelled from Clan na Gael on suspicion of being a spy, and his relations with the other extremist groups in America were poor. He arrived in Ireland on 26 May and stayed for three months, during which time he toured the southern half of the country, speaking to large audiences. Early in June, a letter from Sir Joseph McKenna warned against the advisability of associating Rossa with the amnesty movement. This advice seems to have been followed for the most part. But although Redmond and his principal colleagues stayed away from the meetings, this was not true of the broad left wing of the Parnellite movement.[51] The *Independent* gave free advertising to the Dublin meeting on 26 June, and Rossa's arrival was greeted by what the paper called an 'immense turnout' comprising trades bodies and bands in a torchlight procession. At a packed Rotunda, F. J. Allan, in putting the resolution of thanks, said that 'they who had clung to the old faith through all the temptations of the constitutional movement must have been filled with hope and encouragement by the presence of a man like O'Donovan Rossa there that night (*cheers*)'.[52]

At his first meetings Rossa stuck to his avowed purpose, which was to tell of the horrors of his prison experiences, and not to interfere in 'politics', but as the tour went on his utterances began to do just that. At Listowel on 12 July, he branded the Morley regime as being as bad as Balfour's and commented on other current issues. At the unveiling of the memorial to the Manchester Martyrs at Birr on 22 July, he asserted that wherever Irishmen were gathered 'their pulses beat with the old desire for vengeance'; he had met some of 'the old stock who were inclined to put their trust in the devil for their salvation'. At his farewell lecture at the Rotunda on 18 August, with James Stephens on the platform, he referred to Davitt as a 'scoundrel' who went about lecturing in England to disarm the disaffection of the Irish there.[53] Possibly the most disrup-

Figure 17. 'Still Falling': Parnellite cartoon (*Irish Weekly Independent*, 3 February 1894). *Courtesy of the National Library of Ireland.*
A disconsolate John Dillon and William O'Brien contemplate the downward slide of the demoralised anti-Parnellite majority 'Whig' party, while the jackdaw Tim Healy, perceived chief agent of the party's misfortune, looks down.

tive effect of his visit was on Dublin Parnellite circles, beginning on 5 July with the announcement of his candidature for the city marshalship. This was at first thought to be a hoax, but soon assumed a serious form, and other candidates withdrew in his favour. Despite an attendance at a Phoenix Park support rally claimed in the *Independent* to be 30,000, the Dublin Corporation voted another into the post. An indignation meeting protesting at the corporation's action heard the Parnellite lord mayor, V. B. Dillon, castigated and the Dublin press of all hues branded 'rotten and corrupt'. At the farewell lecture, a speaker seconding the vote of thanks said that Rossa's candidature had shown that there was no difference between Tories, anti-Parnellites and Parnellites, and that he had 'awakened a new spirit' that they would not let die.[54]

Nothing better testifies to the difference between the conditions of late 1886 and those of 1894 than the fact that a figure so marginal in American Fenianism should now receive a hearing in Ireland at all, even among mainstream Fenians. After the defeat of the first Home Rule Bill, Parnell had been able to send emissaries, one of them Redmond, into the heartland of the American extremists to neutralize their opposition to constitutionalism. Now, following the defeat of the second, an ageing, possibly deranged, Fenian could cross the Atlantic to roam free for three months in Ireland, preaching his sterile doctrine of hatred and vengeance. That he could do so is an indication both of the atmosphere of general disillusion with political parties, resulting from the split and the failure of the Home Rule Bill, and of the absence of a commanding presence at the head of the constitutional movement to point a way forward.[55]

The question of what that way might be, and Redmond's efforts to remedy the leadership vacuum, became the central issue of the rest of 1894 and the first half of the following year. No longer were the Parnellites on the defensive, answering charges of wrecking the chances of a friendly Government. It was now the majority party that had to defend two years of what seemed like blind trust in the Liberals, with nothing to show in return. Further demoralization was added to that party's woes in September with the revelation in the *Independent*, under the heading 'The "Kept" Party', that it had received donations of £100 each from Gladstone and from Lord Tweedmouth, the Liberal treasurer, the second in response to a circular from McCarthy.[56] This supplied Healy with fresh material for his assaults on the leadership, until Edward Blake, a confidant of Dillon and McCarthy, claimed that Healy himself was the only man he had ever heard proposing that an appeal be made to members of the British Government for aid.[57] Another issue that told against the anti-Parnellites was their association with Liberal policies on education. When Bishop O'Dwyer of Limerick denounced T. P. O'Connor and Davitt for their role in helping Radicals to oppose Catholic candidates in the London School Board elections, the *Independent* found itself in agreement. 'Will anyone dare to say,' wrote the bishop, 'that, as compared with Mr. T. P. O'Connor's treachery and irreligion, Mr. Parnell's sin was not venial?' The paper saw the same Nonconformist influences that had been instrumental in overthrowing Parnell now working against the interests of Catholic education. Shortly afterwards, in its indictment of Davitt, it joined the charge of aiding his 'secularist friends' in London to that of undermining Parnell.[58]

A rally in Hyde Park on 26 August addressed by O'Brien and Dr Tanner and various Radical speakers (the official Liberals stayed away) opened a debate on how to fight the House of Lords. At the National League central branch on 4 September, Redmond identified the predicament of nationalists: 'We have no National leader . . . We have, I assert, no national representation in the House of Commons . . . the entire constitutional movement in Ireland seems in danger of sinking beneath a load of contempt and degradation and ridicule unless the Irish people will resent this.'[59] But the attempt to set up an agitation against the Lords as a substitute for Home Rule was, he claimed, an even greater danger: if persisted in, it would kill Home Rule. He quoted Lord Salisbury to the effect that the Lords would go on rejecting such Bills if they were 'smuggled in' by not allowing the electors to know the lines of a Bill in advance, whereas if a 'fair and square' issue of Home Rule was put before the electors, and if a majority declared in favour on that issue, then the House of Lords would pass the Bill. The Hyde Park demonstration, with 'the mock heroics and dismal hysterics of Mr. William O'Brien' was 'the most arrant humbug'.[60]

At the Parnell commemoration lecture on 8 October, he referred to the doctrine of the moment, that the people of Great Britain would rise up in a mighty agitation against the Lords. That talk, he asserted, was 'sheer midsummer madness . . . it means the postponement of the demand for Home Rule for this generation'. In an assessment which he would one day be forced to revise, he reminded his hearers of the position of the House of Lords in English history:

> It is an integral portion of the constitution of England . . . Most of the present holders of the titles in the House of Lords are the descendants of the men who wrung the charter from John on the plain of Runnymede . . . I say to abolish that portion of the constitution which is older probably . . . than the House of Commons itself . . . means a revolution greater than any that has taken place in the whole constitutional history of England . . . when I hear this ignorant and dishonest talk about abolishing the House of Lords, I feel bound to point out to my fellow-countrymen the vast magnitude of this question.

His remedy was to force an immediate dissolution, after which, for Home Rule to get another chance, 'there must be a decision by the constituents fairly and squarely in its favour'.[61] The *Freeman* contrived to avoid the point, calling the speech 'a panegyric of the House of

Lords'.[62] In an article in October's *Nineteenth Century* entitled 'What has become of Home Rule?', Redmond claimed that even to withdraw the Lords' veto could not be done 'without convulsing England from end to end'. But what of the objection that the Government would be risking defeat in going to the country on Home Rule alone?

> Than that such a condition of affairs should prevail after another general election – with Home Rule still postponed and a political gangrene, as it were, eating at the heart of Ireland – better any day a new Coercion regime. Such a regime would at least secure, while Home Rule was denied, that the whole strength of the Nationalist party in Ireland would be on the side of Ireland.[63]

The article appeared the day after a long-awaited speech on Liberal policy by Lord Rosebery at Bradford, in which the policy of Lords reform officially displaced Home Rule as the first item in the Liberal programme. The Lords issue, for Rosebery, 'included and represented' all other issues, including Home Rule; the *Independent* called it 'a piece of black treachery'.[64]

The Financial Relations Commission resumed sittings in London in early November. Redmond was recovering from illness, but still unable to examine witnesses when he attended. The *Independent* castigated the *Freeman* and O'Brien for sneering at his incapacitation. On 1 December it was announced that Redmond was sailing that day for the Cape under the orders of his physician, having been 'in delicate health' for the past month. He hoped to be back in mid-January with renewed strength. During his absence the Financial Relations Commission held a week of sittings in Dublin. The *Freeman* noted caustically:

> if he returns in time to vote on the report, not even his most ardent admirer will assert that Ireland's interests will have suffered by being left, for the interval, in the care of the 'Whig' Mr. Sexton and the 'Whig' Mr. Blake. In Irish financial affairs Mr. Redmond, the independent statesman, has always been compelled 'to say ditto' to Mr. Sexton.[65]

The extent of Redmond's control over the *Independent*'s editorial policy had come into question in mid-November when it carried an extraordinary personal attack on Morley in a leading article occasioned by his reception of a Dublin City Council deputation pleading the amnesty case. The City of Dublin, it said, had been insulted by

> this commonplace Englishman, who is evidently as mean as he looks . . . Having denied God years ago in his books, this latter-day friend of the Bishops denied the plain meaning of his Leinster Hall words with equal effrontery when he got into the Castle . . . He is tabooed by the class which people are accustomed to call better, because he has violated the canons of Society . . . He is a pariah to the middle class . . . Weak as a friend, impotent as a foe, Ireland will be the grave

> of [his] reputation . . . He is not worth his salt . . . The man is a fraud . . . a person of lath and plaster . . . a shoddy statesman . . .[66]

A letter from Morley to Redmond indicates that the latter had written to dissociate himself from the insult:

> I feel perfectly sure that you had no part or act in that very mischievous and offensive performance; but still I am not the less pleased to have your letter. To me you have always been the most honourable of opponents, so far as you have been an opponent. The worst of the article is its effect on English opinion.[67]

The most likely author of the article was James O'Donovan, the assistant editor recently appointed to help remedy defects in the editorial department, a man of very extreme views and a relative of O'Donovan Rossa, according to John Mallon.[68] The problem of controlling the Fenians at the newspapers was not easily dispelled. A letter from Allan to the *Weekly Independent* in March 1895, following the execution of a Kerry Moonlighter convicted of an agrarian murder, carried another bitter attack on Morley and went on to draw broader conclusions:

> But only lately . . . has he shaken off the last shred of shame and lied openly and unblushingly as only an English Minister can do . . . John Morley as a liar stands convicted! . . . [At the next election] the same waste of energy and enthusiasm will be witnessed . . . Should it not make, at least, thinking Irishmen pause once more to consider whether the farce of wasting Irish energy in the British Parliament has not gone on long enough.[69]

Redmond protested to the editor, M. A. Manning, who replied that he would no more hold himself responsible for Allan's or any other correspondent's views than would Dr Byrne (at the *Daily*) for the letters of John O'Leary, which he invariably published. Nevertheless, he added:

> As I have heard from you, and as I cannot for a moment forget that your feelings and opinions should guide me in such matters I will be a bit more exclusive for the future. This I write to you in the same spirit of confidence as you have written me.[70]

The same issue of the *Weekly Independent* carried a brief leader on a recent speech by Redmond, which must have been read with shock by his 'advanced' followers. Speaking at the Cambridge Union on 26 February, he declared that Home Rule was a middle course

> between separation from England which, he said, was undesirable and impossible (*cheers*) on the one hand . . . and this over-centralisation of government on the other . . . [and] would be the first step in the great system of decentralisation which he was convinced would one of these days end in the devolution to local assemblies of local affairs, and thus clear the way for the creation of that great Imperial Senate which, in future, he believed, would govern this Empire, and which would

> consist not merely of representatives of England, Ireland and Scotland, but of those mighty dominions throughout the world which had been won by Irishmen just as much as by Britons (*cheers*).[71]

His expression of such sentiments was not new – he had voiced them in Australia, and at home in 1889 and 1893 – but the explicitness of the reference to the undesirability of separation was unprecedented for him. The speech excited very little attention at the time – the *Freeman* ignored it, the *Daily Independent* published it without comment and the *Weekly Independent* regretted that it had received only a summarized report – and there were no defections, or even protests, from the Fenian grass roots. But his reported words would come back to haunt him at the time of the reunification of the Irish Party in 1900 and later. By then they were weapons in the hands of Arthur Griffith's *United Irishman* and others opposed to the whole parliamentary project, who alleged that he had flouted Parnell's legacy by setting an actual boundary to the march of the nation.[72]

III

Redmond's return from the Cape on 20 January 1895 was marked by a reception at the National Club preceded by a procession with the usual trappings. The *Independent* claimed that the overflow of people from the packed club amounted to 2,000; the police reckoned that not more than 500 were present outside. Redmond responded to the welcome with an attack on the 'feeble, discredited, and hatred-torn representatives of the factions' on the other side, whose fierce personal quarrels had become a public scandal. 'We are the only united political party in Ireland,' he boasted. Their first duty, he said, would be to 'arraign the Ministry' when Parliament met. They were at 'the eve of the end of the life of this useless Parliament . . . for Ireland so full of heartbreak and disappointment'. Though Ireland had held the balance of power, the result had been 'absolutely nil'. Their policy must be to force a dissolution as soon as possible, and 'to insist, as far as we can insist, that the Home Rule question shall be the one great issue to be submitted to the English electors at the next election'. But what if the Tories were returned to power? Many who could follow Redmond's logic yet blanched at such a prospect, among them a large section of Parnellites. He answered that he did not think the Tories would dare to resort to coercion again; rather they would 'deal with practical Irish questions'. He declared:

> It would be a question for us to consider whether if we cannot get Home Rule this year or next year confessedly from a Liberal Government, and when they won't give us anything else, whether it would not be better to have a Government in power that could give us and probably would give us something in the meantime (*loud cheers*).[73]

(The last passage may have been one of those which, according to the police reporter, were 'not well received'.[74]) The *Freeman* said the speech used 'flimsy sophisms to cover naked treason . . . [Redmond] frankly threw off all disguise, and avowed his alliance with the Coercionists'.[75] This criticism did not deflect him from his course. A few days later at Ballybricken, he continued his efforts to revive the spirit of 1885, promising to do all in his power to make it known that 'we care no more for Liberals than for Tories and that, of the two, many of us would prefer an open enemy to a false friend'.[76]

On 11 February, Redmond moved his amendment for the dissolution of the House. His speech traced seven stages in the decline of the Home Rule question, from 'the commanding position of pre-eminence and of urgency' to which Parnell had brought it to the present 'feeble cry that the cup of the Lords must be filled up'. No legislative benefit had accrued to Ireland from this Government, which was absolutely impotent, he declared.[77] Morley replied that 'no more mischievous

Figure 18. 'Next St. Patrick's Day': Parnellite cartoon (*Irish Weekly Independent*, 2 March 1895). *Courtesy of the National Library of Ireland.*
The young Parnellite party has high hopes for the general election of summer 1895.

blow' had been struck against Home Rule than by this amendment. Redmond, he said, had 'committed himself to a political paradox': this Government, which had passed a Home Rule Bill through the Commons, was to be ejected by the friends of Home Rule in the name of Home Rule, with the help of the party that regarded Home Rule as treason to the constitution and dangerous to the safety of the Empire. Morley also attacked Redmond's prediction that the Government's new Land Bill – the first reform item mentioned in the Queen's Speech – had no chance of becoming law.[78] For his part, Redmond could retort that it was the prime minister and the home secretary, not he, who had given such small odds for its passage.[79]

Redmond was generally vulnerable to the charge that, in playing Cassandra regarding the Liberals' intentions, he was helping to bring about the evils he predicted. The anti-Parnellites were eager to embrace assurances, such as that of Harcourt on 26 February, that Home Rule remained the primary policy of the Government, and the *Freeman* saw what it called the policy of 'carp, cavil and fault-find' as aimed at wrecking the efforts of the Irish Party.[80] Nevertheless, he could claim vindication of his stances on the amnesty and the House of Lords questions. Sexton and Healy had recently favoured the ventilation of the grievances of the prisoners, a change from the days when they denounced his party for doing the same for selfish motives.[81] As for the Lords issue, it seemed likely to be dropped, as little was heard of it now, he told the St Patrick's Day banquet in London, claiming that O'Brien had come around to his way of thinking. In support of his claim, he quoted Lord Salisbury's statement that 'a declaration of the people on the clear issue of Home Rule would compel the House of Lords to deal with it'.[82]

On 8 April, John Sweetman's discontent with anti-Parnellite policy came to a head when he announced his resignation to the electors of East Wicklow and sought re-election as a Parnellite. The anger of the *Freeman* was matched by the jubilation of its rival: the latter called it a 'thunderbolt' to add to the confusion of the 'Whigs'. The by-election was the chance the Parnellites had been waiting for to show the turn of the tide of nationalist sentiment in their favour. Redmond arrived for the Easter weekend selection convention, fresh from having voted with the Tories against the Government nominee for Speaker, leaving it with a majority of only 11. He immersed himself in the constituency for the next fortnight, personally supervising the intensive electioneering, everywhere hammering home the message of McCarthyite dereliction of duty to Irish interests, and appealing to local loyalty to Parnell's memory. The 1892 vote in East Wicklow had been divided three ways almost equally between anti-Parnellite, Parnellite and Unionist, with the then anti-Parnellite Sweetman coming 318 votes ahead of the Parnellite W. J. Corbet, who came last. Despite the high hopes of Redmond and his friends, however, the result was another, though narrower, victory for the anti-Parnellites, who won a majority of 62 over Sweetman.[83] (The constituency was, however, won by Corbet for the Parnellites a few months later.)

Clerical interference was again a feature of this and the subsequent elections of 1895. Redmond had met Archbishop Walsh in February and discussed the split with him in a lengthy chat after lunch at the Mansion House. Redmond's recollection was that Walsh himself suggested that he (Walsh) should make a declaration that the issue between the parties was a purely political, and not a moral or religious one. He had 'severely censured' two priests of his diocese who had claimed at the last election that it was a religious question, and had forbidden his priests to speak on politics in their churches.[84] A letter to this effect from Walsh duly appeared in the press on 9 March. In Cork on 17 March, Redmond challenged Archbishop Croke 'to have the manliness' to say whether he would take the same stance as Walsh.[85] In the meantime, Walsh had left the country on a long visit to Rome. When he returned in the middle of the Wicklow campaign, he astonished Parnellites with his contradiction of the 'rumour' he had heard that he wished priests to abstain from political involvement; he went further and exhorted them to be active in the election.[86] This was incompatible with the spirit, if not the letter, of his March statement. But Walsh denounced as 'a very shabby trick' the action of Wicklow Parnellites in posting a placard that quoted the March letter, reassuring voters that their archbishop saw no religious dimension to the issue, and added in large lettering 'SO VOTE FOR SWEETMAN'.[87] This tactic had been suggested to Redmond by the Parnellite parish priest of Aughrim.[88]

Redmond did not hide his disappointment at the failure to take East Wicklow. He blamed it on the 'continued power of clerical interference', alleging that Walsh privately used his authority to silence every priest on the Parnellite side and encourage those on the other. In Arklow, he claimed, every arriving voter was brought to the parochial house, spoken to and then brought to the polling booth. Because of this, the votes of the illiterate had gone against them by a factor of 20 to 1. The action of Dr Walsh, he said, 'deserves, in my opinion, the condemnation of every Irish Nationalist (*hear, hear, loud applause*)'. He had no objection to the claim that each priest had a right to decide on a purely political matter, but 'when he comes into the political arena as a citizen his influence must be the influence of a citizen and not what I may call the supernatural influence which he exercises as a clergyman'.[89]

With a general assumption in Parliament that its days were numbered, there was little time for recrimination, and optimism quickly returned. Mindful of the very slim anti-Parnellite majority in South Meath, Redmond persuaded John Howard Parnell, brother of the illustrious leader, to contest the seat for the party. At Warrenstown in that constituency on 9 June, he introduced the candidate and looked forward to the reversal of the verdicts of 1892 and 1893. To his already familiar indictment of the 'Whigs' and their political failures, he added the spectacle of his opponents 'tearing out each others' entrails', thereby 'lowering the tone of the national movement' and disgracing the name of Ireland. Irish political life was now in a worse state than in the days of Sadleir and Keogh, he alleged, with nationalist representatives seeking justiceships of the peace, magistracies and crown prosecutorships from the Government, and the saddest part was that the country was not roused by this, but rather looked on with apathy and indifference. (He did not say whether his remarks about place-hunting applied to both parties, but the *Freeman* had publicized the taking of magistracies by three Parnellite ex-mayors).[90] Answering the accusation that he wished to restore Balfour's rule, he put his five weeks of imprisonment in 1888 to good, if unhappily phrased, service, when he claimed that many of those 'who talk this way about me are men who were taking pretty good care of their own skins at the time that I was lying on the plank-bed under Balfour (*cheers*)'. Postponing the election, he said, would only damage the chances of Home Rule in the English constituencies. If Gladstone had been allowed to dissolve Parliament following the 1893 defeat of the Home Rule Bill (the claim that the aged leader had wanted to dissolve in '93, but had been prevented by his colleagues from doing so, was now a standard item in Parnellite lore), he would have come back with a Home Rule majority and the Bill would now be law.[91]

Thanks to a new twist in the Healy–O'Brien feud, a fresh by-election opportunity soon presented itself. A libel case involving O'Brien and P. A. Chance, a Healyite M.P., sparked a controversy that spilled over into the pages of the *Freeman* and the *Irish Catholic* during May, and led to O'Brien's declaring himself bankrupt and quitting Parliament. His resignation in June created a vacancy in one of the two Cork city seats.[92] Redmond arrived in the constituency in ebullient form on 21 June and campaigned vigorously. The by-election result was another narrow defeat for the Parnellites, but this time a moral victory was won. The vote on 27 June almost wiped out the anti-Parnellite majority in Cork city, reducing it from over 2,000 to 177.[93]

In the meantime the Liberal Government had resigned on 22 June after less than three years in office. Its defeat by 7 votes on the Estimates had come on a night when 40 of the 71 McCarthyites were absent from the House.[94] Redmond told a rally a few days later that he did not regret that the blow had come, although dissolution had been brought about in unfavourable circumstances by the very men who had denounced him for advocating it in favourable circumstances in 1893.

Buoyed by the Cork result, Redmond and his colleagues launched themselves immediately into the general election campaign. The party's manifesto stated that the lesson of the past three years was 'clear and emphatic': there must be a return to the Parnell policy of a nationalist representation 'absolutely independent of all English parties'.[95] In one speech after another he castigated the record of the Liberals in government and of the McCarthyites as their stooges, asking his opponents what had been gained by the overthrow of Parnell. The chief sensation of the campaign, however, was within the majority party. At the anti-Parnellite convention at Omagh on 8 July, Healy produced a letter that he claimed proved that the committee of his party had bartered four Ulster seats to the Liberals for £200 each.[96] This was a far more serious charge than that connected with the Tweedmouth and Gladstone cheques affair of the previous year. McCarthy's slowness to comment deepened the crisis, which soon became the dominant issue of the whole campaign in Ireland. Healy's agenda became clearer when the *Irish Catholic* denounced the party's selection conventions as 'rigged assemblies'. The real target was Dillon and his efforts to exert a Parnell-like centralized discipline over the party.[97]

Voting began on 13 July and continued until the end of the month. Within very few days it was evident that the results were disastrous for the Liberals. Among the casualties were Morley, who lost his Newcastle seat. The *Independent* again reflected the sentiments of the extreme wing of Parnellism, as it exulted: 'No honest Irishman can regret the defeat . . . [Morley was] the worst Englishman who came into Ireland since the days of Cromwell.'[98] The paper had earlier, in reporting Redmond's speech in Waterford which criticized Morley's refusal to award state grants to the Christian Brothers' schools, referred to Morley as the 'Agnostic Chief Secretary'. Redmond refrained from such personal attacks, acknowledging that Morley had called on his party to place Home Rule, rather than the Rosebery policy of Lords reform, at the front of its platform, but was powerless to influence it.[99] But the paper's criticism of Morley's appointment of 'ex-Nationalists' as magistrates was an echo of Redmond's own. In writing that his object was 'to denationalise Ireland', it gave early political expression to the new 'cultural nationalism' which looked with suspicion on the granting to Irish people of positions of power in their own country under British rule as an attempt to assimilate them to Anglicized ways of thinking.[100]

When Irish votes were counted, it was clear that no Parnellite break-through had occurred. The Independent party improved its position from 9 to just 11 seats. Keen disappointment was felt in Dublin, where, despite the McCarthyites' leaving a clear field to the Parnellites in the St Stephen's Green and South County constituencies, the latter failed to take either seat from the Unionists. There was the consolation of seeing the Parnell name again in Parliament, for South Meath, and they also won both seats in Roscommon, a rare oasis of Parnellism in rural Ireland. As in 1892, the seats won did not faithfully reflect the votes cast, although on this occasion a much greater number of seats went uncontested. In the 19 constituencies where electors had a choice, the total Parnellite vote was 43,755 (a small increase on 1892) compared to the anti-Parnellite total of 48,408 (a slight decrease on 1892).[101]

Three years of Redmondite agitation under Liberal rule had been unavailing in the face of clerical power, nationalist apathy and economic prosperity. In an uncharacteristically dark moment a few months later at Carlow, Redmond gave vent to his disheartenment as he surveyed the years just past:

> for my part, I can say to you that they have been the five most miserable years of my life, and looking back today over those five years it seems to me as if I had aged by 20 years – aye! by 40 years – it seems to me as if none of us would have the strength or the power to go through 5 years more of the same kind.[102]

However, negative moods never held him for long. He told his constituents in the same month: 'The first essential in a politician, after honesty of purpose, is, I would say, the quality of patience. All things come right to him who will but wait . . .'[103]

10 New Directions, Old Quarrels

> I am one of those who believe what promotes the welfare and tends to the prosperity of the Irish people will tend in the direction of strengthening their desire for self-government.
>
> Redmond at the first meeting of the Recess Committee, Mansion House, January 1896[1]

> The sort of union they [the Dillonites] would like [with us] is a union such as Byron, I think, has described the union of Ireland with England – the union of the shark with its prey.
>
> Redmond at Clonmel, February 1896[2]

I

The election results laid bare the Redmondites' failure to win back the rural nationalist electorate for Parnellism. Anti-Parnellite electors might be disgusted with the infighting in the majority party, might be disillusioned with the Liberals, might harbour a sneaking sympathy with Redmond's criticisms, but they had not translated their disenchantment into votes. Redmond's own county of Wexford was emblematic: its prosperous farmers now busily availed of the land courts and the Land Purchase Acts, forming an increasingly conservative middle class that was happy to shed the ambiguous legacy of Parnell and accept the hegemony of its Catholic leaders, lay and clerical.

While he waited for a change of heart in the nationalist electorate, the programme of the new Tory administration, based on reforming legislation as an alternative to Home Rule – the policy of 'killing Home Rule with kindness' – offered Redmond an opportunity to explore possibilities previously unavailable to nationalist politicians. For the next few years, without abandoning his links with the Fenians, he adopted a policy of co-operation with Irish Unionist figures and members of the landlord class for limited common goals. Two factors facilitated this development. Given his party's marginal position, he had little to lose in departing from orthodox nationalist paths. Second, the cultivation of contacts with the leaders of the Irish Protestant tradition was personally congenial to him, since it harmonized with his instinct that a complete Irish nation had yet to be built, and with his sense of the potential within that tradition for a return to the legacy of Grattan and self-government.

II

When the new Parliament assembled on 12 August 1895, Redmond was quick to dispel any impression that he would be a compliant ally of the Tory Government. The issue was the overturning of the (unopposed) election of John Daly as the member for Limerick city. The Redmondites opposed the Government's efforts to have Daly barred on the grounds of his conviction; however, a motion ruling him incapable of election was passed by a large majority against nationalist opposition. This incident aside, the return of the Tories to power was received with relative equanimity by both factions of nationalists. This was more surprising in the case of the anti-Parnellites, whose election rhetoric had conjured the spectre of a return to coercion and attendant evils. The *Freeman*, commenting on 1 August on news of gloomy forebodings among Irish-Americans at the prospect of a Tory victory, said that the Irish at home did not share such views. The Tories, it said, had learned that persecution and provocation did not pay: 'After all, when the worst has been said of him, the Tory is a teachable animal.'[3]

Redmond's amendment to the Address began by denying that the election had returned a verdict against Home Rule. Although the Liberals had been pressed to go to the country on that issue alone, the only one on which they were all united, Lord Rosebery had declared instead that the contest was to be on the question of the House of Lords and the Newcastle programme. As far as Ireland was concerned, Home Rule still held the field. He wanted a statement of the Government's policy on this and on the land question, the evicted tenants, the creation of a Board of Agriculture (something being sought by men of all political views) and the industrial development of Ireland:

> So far as they knew the policy of the Government, it was founded on the belief that, without Home Rule the Imperial Parliament had the will, the time, and the capacity to govern Ireland properly. This was their alternative policy to Home Rule – a just, a constitutional, and a competent government of Ireland from Westminster. Since the date of the Union there had been no such government of Ireland from Westminster (*cheers*) . . . this alternative policy never had such a good chance of trial as it had now . . . as far as he was concerned, the more they tested that alternative policy during their tenure of office the better pleased he should be.

He saw the possibility of 'some solid advantages' accruing to Ireland, which she could not have obtained from the Liberals, but, do what they would, they could not destroy 'that which was indestructible – namely, the passionate demand of the overwhelming majority of the Irish people for autonomy'.[4]

The new Conservative policy was represented in person by Horace Plunkett, the Tory member for Dublin South County since 1892, a 41-year-old landlord and a pioneer of the co-operative movement imbued with a mission to reform Irish agriculture,[5] and by the new chief secretary, Gerald Balfour. Plunkett gave his view that the Irish question was entering a new phase, and that 'opinion in the country as to the blessings of Home Rule was rapidly changing'; the Irish people 'were gradually being disillusioned from chimeras'. His party now had 'a real middle course' between 'wild and inadmissible proposals and barren denials'.[6] Balfour greeted Redmond's speech as 'one of those earnest and impressive utterances which the House is accustomed to expect from him'. On Home Rule, he could only state that their attitude would continue to be 'one of unchanging and inflexible opposition'. On the land question, he would bring in a Bill to deal with the judicial tenants, the protection of tenants' improvements and 'the promotion of a more rapid and effective working of the Land Purchase Acts passed by the Unionist Government in 1885 and 1891'. With the other matters raised by Redmond, he assured him he had 'the keenest possible sympathy'.[7]

As a short-term remedial measure for the evicted tenants, Redmond had suggested the framing of a short Bill re-enacting a clause in the 1891 Act to allow the voluntary reinstatement of some tenants through purchase, and Balfour had promised to consider it. The Liberals had proposed to bring in just such a measure before the general election, but in the Wicklow election of April Redmond had denounced the anti-Parnellites' willingness to accept it as a 'betrayal of the evicted tenants'. By 19 August Redmond had prepared such a Bill, and by 5 September, when Parliament was prorogued, it was in force. Redmond's belief that the landlords would act differently under a Tory than under a Liberal Government seemed confirmed when Smith-Barry, who had declared in the earlier debate that landlords would not reinstate their tenants under a voluntary scheme, announced on 18 November that certain farms had now been relet.[8]

There were signs too that movement on the amnesty issue might not be far off. In the Commons on 16 August Redmond expressed appreciation of the 'frank manner' of the new home secretary, Sir Mathew White-Ridley, in his stated willingness to reconsider the cases of the ten remaining prisoners. If they had been convicted under the Explosives Act, Redmond said, they would be due for release in two-and-a-half years. A matter of weeks could, he claimed, be critical for some of them who were broken in health and spirits, and would be no danger to society if released. He offered to supply the necessary information for a new investigation of the cases.[9] A sign that his pressure might be bearing fruit came when the *Daily Express* of 3 December commented: 'No Unionist will lament if Sir Mathew White-Ridley is able in some instances to take a merciful view.' Meanwhile, Redmond continued his visits to Portland prison (he told a Limerick audience that he had been Daly's 'trusted adviser and friend' for four years, sitting for hours with him in his cell) and nominated the former Fenian and ex-Parnellite M.P. Joseph Nolan as the candidate for the election caused by Daly's disqualification. At the selection convention in Limerick on 4 September, Redmond extolled Nolan as 'one of the "Old Guard" . . . [who] in the old days, when they despaired of success for Parliamentary methods, had the courage to take up other weapons and to follow other lines . . . ' and had later become one of Parnell's 'loyal and brave comrades'. Once again, by-election success would elude him by a narrow margin, Nolan being defeated by the anti-Parnellite by only 87 votes.[10]

Across the Atlantic in late September, 1,000 delegates gathered at Chicago, where Finnerty called for the formation of an army of young Irishmen to be ready to strike at the Saxon. The *Independent* commented that there was no need for the new movement since the constitutional movement at home was far from dead:

> The Irish people are desirous that constitutional agitation should get one more trial. If it fails, then it will be for all sincere Irishmen to sternly face the situation . . . We entirely agree with our contemporary *United Ireland* when it expresses its pleasure 'that our countrymen have not relinquished the physical force idea' . . . There is no use disguising the fact that some day or other the physical force idea may have to be put into practice in Ireland.[11]

The outcome of the Chicago convention was the so-called 'New Movement', rechristened the Irish National Alliance (INA), with William Lyman as president, which soon attracted support in Ireland, especially among the followers of the amnesty movement. Because of its identification with one side in the feud among American Fenians, and because it was an open rather an oath-bound movement, it was opposed in the United States by the Devoy faction and in Ireland by the IRB Supreme Council under Allan and Fitzgerald.[12] By mid-1896, it had branches in Dublin, Belfast and four other centres, and was reported to be 'at daggers drawn' with the IRB.[13] The strength of the amnesty movement in a locality was reckoned by the police to be a measure of the existence of the INA in that locality.[14] In spite of its violent rhetoric, Mallon, now assistant commissioner, wrote in March 1896 that 'the men in Dublin who are recognised promoters of the INA do not appear to favour outrage, or to be of the class which would commit them', and regarded the 'inner circle' of Allan's group as far more dangerous.[15]

In October 1895, Redmond sent James Egan on a lecture tour of US Fenian centres with the aim of raising funds among them for the 'old cause'. According to Mallon, the monies were to be forwarded to the *Daily Independent*, where Allan would have control of the fund under the supervision of Redmond and the party. Redmond also had a political message for the Irish-Americans, according to Mallon:

> Mr. Redmond M.P. has given instructions that those at the head of affairs in the New Movement will understand that he and his party are not opposed to them, but are glad that they showed a spirit of

> activity . . . [but] that the Independent party have not given up hope of obtaining good measures for Ireland, and to depart from constitutional agitation until it is first found to be a failure, would show that they were unworthy of holding so long to 'Independence', but if they (the Parnellites) receive no concessions from Parliament, then they will advise the people through the *Independent* what course they are to follow, and it is to be in a position to give effect to their directions that their American brethren are asked to subscribe.[16]

This was vague indeed, and in the style of the references Parnell had made, especially during the split, to the contingency of the failure of the constitutional movement.[17] Any trust Redmond may have placed in the American leadership of the INA does not seem to have been reciprocated, an unsurprising fact if they had read the Cambridge Union speech earlier that year.[18] These extremists, however, rejected the efforts of constitutionalists even in the amnesty campaign. An editorial in the INA official organ, the *Irish Republic* (New York), declared that

> we repudiate Mr. Redmond's apologies for whatever explosions may have been caused by Irishmen in England. We can assure Mr. Redmond that we are prepared to give England another dose of the same medicine; that between England and Ireland there is war to the knife, and the sooner men like John Redmond and John Dillon stand aside and stop their gabbling nonsense the more speedily will the Irish cause be brought to a settlement . . . the time has come when those who are not for an Irish Republic must be treated as royalists, advocates of British rule and opposed to Irish freedom.[19]

On Redmond's other flank, in the same week as the Limerick election, the internecine strife between Healyites and their colleagues took another turn when William Martin Murphy was nominated to stand against the officially selected party candidate in a by-election in South Kerry. To the *Freeman*, this was Healy's plot against the Irish Party at last in the open. McCarthy's manifesto for the election spoke of the incessant campaign against the party's unity having reached its climax at the Omagh convention with Healy's 'baseless falsehood' that 'I and the Committee of the Party had sold Nationalist seats for English gold'. The contest was a brief but lively affair, with prominent clerics involved on both sides, and Tanner and Healy on opposite sides, ensuring a brisk trade in physical and spiritual threats and invective.[20] The Tory *Standard* wrote that it was not unfair to regard the Kerry election as an example of what might be expected inside an Irish House of Commons, when men like Healy, Tanner and O'Brien had come to the fore: 'one might imagine that these gentlemen had deliberately set themselves to alienate all that section of the British public which, under Gladstone's influence, had been induced for a time to tolerate the idea of Home Rule'.[21] The trouncing of Murphy by 1,209 votes to 474 encouraged the party leadership to take the war to Healy, and in

November he was voted off, in succession, the executive of the National League of Great Britain, the council of the National Federation and the committee of the Irish Party itself.[22]

The annual Parnell commemoration demonstration fell on 6 October, and was notable for its changed atmosphere. The *Independent* remarked on the notable increase in the contingents from the country, while the *Freeman* noted the 'kindly feeling between Nationalists and Parnellites'. The Liberal *Daily Chronicle* called it the largest for three years and reported that the procession was 'largely of young men and boys'. In his address to the national convention the following evening, Redmond reviewed the political situation for the first time since the general election. The demonstration, he said, had been 'truly national', and thousands had come from every part of the country in a sign that the Parnellite cause was not dead or sleeping and that 'the nationalists of Ireland will never lay down their arms until they have achieved the independence of their country'. Despite Parnellite warnings since 1891, a 'mad and suicidal policy' had ended in the destruction of both Home Rule *and* the Liberal Party. The anti-House of Lords agitation had been 'a sham and a fraud' – where was it today? Home Rule had been set back for years, he said, 'by a policy of cowardice and folly never I believe before equalled even in this unfortunate country'. Worst of all, 'the recent election showed that there is still a large proportion of the Irish electorate either so blind as not to understand or so apathetic as not to care for the dangers which surround the national cause'.[23] Turning to the future, he was 'not in the least daunted' by the large majority against Home Rule. He repeated his House of Commons message to the new Government, who professed to believe 'that they can kill the sentiment of Irish nationality by a policy of kindness'. They could deal comprehensively with the land question, release the prisoners, restore the evicted tenants, legislate for the benefit of the artisans and labourers and give justice to the Catholics of Ireland in the sphere of education, 'but we tell them frankly that at the end of it all they will be confronted still by the demand for Home Rule'. The *Freeman* hit back the following day in a leader titled 'Redmondite Rodomontade', saying that those responsible for the ruin of Home Rule and of the Government pledged to bring it in were Redmond and his colleagues: 'he conceived the heroic idea of serving Home Rule by expelling a Home Rule Government to make room for a Government bitterly opposed to it'.[24]

In the elegiac mood of that autumn, anti-Parnellite Ireland mourned the passing not only of the Liberal Government, but of an entire set of hopes and assumptions first kindled during the excitement of 1886, and cultivated through the years of coercion in the warm glow of the Union of Hearts. In this atmosphere, the Independent Party's manifesto issued on 10 October conducted a post-mortem on the events of the split and the record of the Liberal Government:

> The policy of allying the fortunes of Ireland to those of the English Whig party was tried by O'Connell, who was a giant, and it failed disastrously; it has been tried again by political pygmies, and it has ended in disaster, as we predicted it was certain to do . . . Gladstone is gone, Morley is gone, and Harcourt, safely enthroned on a Welsh seat, smiles benignly on the ruins he has made, and wonders at the imbecility of the men who still believe in him.[25]

At Drogheda on 6 December, Redmond developed the theme of mourning by framing the history of the split within a religious paradigm of sin and retribution:

> At this moment [Ireland] presents the miserable spectacle of an apathetic, half-despairing, divided people, whose ears are tormented by the squalid wrangles of miserable personal disputes, the spectacle of a people who are looking for justice, who are asking for men to sketch out a programme for them and to lead them on the right path and who find only men whose highest ambition seems to be to crush one another and to expose one another's weaknesses to the world. Oh! It is a terrible retribution. It is a terrible punishment that has come upon Ireland. I have often said that I believe, in the case of a nation just as in the case of an individual, that every base and dishonourable act sooner or later will meet its punishment even in this world (*loud cheers*) and the base and dishonourable act of which Ireland was guilty in permitting Parnell to be sacrificed to a set of hypocritical Englishmen (*loud cheers*) has already been punished, aye severely punished by the disasters that have fallen upon Ireland.[26]

III

From such sombre reflections, Redmond turned with a certain relish to the practical initiatives that were now opening up. Chief among these was the proposal from Horace Plunkett that, since Home Rule was off the agenda for several years to come, a committee be set up, to be drawn from all Irish parties, aimed at extracting practical benefit from the Government's professed desire to enact material reforms for Ireland. Plunkett's letter outlining his invitation – he suggested that 3 or 4 M.P.s be nominated by the Irish Party, 2 by the Parnellites and 2 by the Unionists – appeared in the papers on 28 August. Having received negative comment from the nationalist press – the *Independent* was in favour in principle, but said such a committee was a practical impossibility – Plunkett repeated his call on 19 October. This time Redmond accepted: 'While I cannot take as sanguine a view as you do of the benefits likely to flow from such a proceeding, I am unwilling to take the responsibility of declining to aid in any effort to promote useful legislation for Ireland.'[27]

McCarthy's reply, no doubt influenced by Dillon's advice, seemed confused by contrast: although he did not believe material reforms could quell the desire for self-government, and although he accepted Plunkett's sincerity of purpose, he could not take part in any organization that had for its object the seeking of a substitute for Ireland's greatest need. Plunkett later commented that McCarthy, 'offering, as it seemed to him, to give convincing reasons why he should accept the challenge, declined to do so'. The pro-Government *Morning Post* on 14 December, commenting on the Parnellites' positive attitude to the Government's ameliorative measures, said that 'there is no denying the fact that Mr. John Redmond and his followers speak on Irish affairs with power which the anti-Parnellites have completely lost'.[28]

The Recess Committee held its first meeting in public at the Mansion House on 7 January 1896, with only the anti-Parnellites unrepresented. Redmond recorded his 'intense satisfaction' that despite the bitterness of political divisions it had been possible to form a committee of the most divergent political views and creeds to promote the common good of the country. His attitude in joining it was that whatever the final outcome, it must help to promote the Home Rule cause, since what tended to advance the prosperity of the people must also tend to strengthen their desire for self-government; on the other hand, if their recommendations were disregarded by the country's rulers, a 'new and unanswerable' argument would have been created for the ending of the present system of government. He concluded: 'Looking at this whole project now from the point of view of a Home Ruler, I see absolutely nothing to lose from assisting in it, and I see a great deal possibly to be gained (*hear, hear*).'[29] Between its opening and 1 February the committee met six more times, adopting a set of general principles for suggestions to the Government on a comprehensive scheme for the development of agriculture, industry and technical education in Ireland.

Just as unionists and (some) nationalists were coming together in common endeavour, international affairs were moving in directions that would tend to drive them further apart and undermine the chances of bringing about a genuine reconciliation in Ireland. In mid-December, a dispute regarding the boundary between Venezuela and British Guiana led to the sudden flare-up of a diplomatic row between Great Britain and the United States. An ultimatum from Lord Salisbury caused President Grover Cleveland to invoke the Monroe doctrine.[30] As the stand-off developed, with panic on the stock exchanges and Congress voting $100 million for war, frantic efforts went on behind the scenes to avert the threat of war. A cablegram from Joe Pulitzer of the *New York World* on 23 December was addressed to 'leaders of British thought and politics', asking them to 'check the war craze here' by sending a message of peace to the American people. Redmond, as one of its recipients, replied:

> In this, as in all other matters, I can speak only as a representative of Irish opinion. If war results from the re-assertion of the Monroe Doctrine Irish national sentiment will be solid on the side of

> America. With Home Rule rejected Ireland can have no feeling of friendliness towards Great Britain.[31]

This reply was too much for some Parnellites, and not enough for others. From four American supporters came a cable stating their welcome for Irish solidarity with the US, but the solicitor for Redmond's party, Bourchier F. Hawksley, cabled on 25 December: 'Hearty Christmas greetings but am shocked at cable you are reported to have sent World New York and protest with all my energy Hawksley.'[32]

The crisis was defused just before the end of 1895, helped by a pacific message from Gladstone to Pulitzer. In the meantime Redmond received a critical letter from Angus Maguire, a failed Redmondite candidate in the general election, who seemed to have great difficulty reconciling Redmond's message with the views he had expressed at the Cambridge Union. He had read the cable 'with great surprise and regret', he said, adding that he did not see how they could expect the English partner to give extended rights and liberty if it believed the Irish partner was 'longing for some disaster to overtake the firm'. Since 'the natural, almost the inevitable, future of Ireland is to remain a member of the British Empire . . . what damages the Empire damages us . . . I consider your statement very damaging to our Home Rule policy.'[33] Redmond's reply provides a rare opportunity to hear him reconcile the apparent contradictions in his rhetoric. He regretted Maguire's disapproval of the cable but thought he had misinterpreted its meaning. It was not a declaration of separation, 'which I agree with you in regarding as impossible under existing circumstances':

> It seems to me that the real *quid pro quo* which we can offer to Great Britain for the concession of Home Rule is the transformation of Ireland from a disaffected portion of the Empire into a well affected one, as happened in the case of Canada. Ireland, undoubtedly, is disaffected now. I think there is no use in trying to disguise the fact. On the contrary, I believe if England once thought that Irish disaffection had died out under the present system she would not be likely to trouble her head about Home Rule.[34]

Only a few days into the New Year, fresh excitements arose. Reports from southern Africa told of a raid by an irregular British force led by Dr Leander Starr Jameson, the administrator of the British South Africa Company territory and a friend of Cecil Rhodes, into the Boer republic of Transvaal, which had been repulsed with the loss of 240 lives. Jameson was in custody, Chamberlain, the colonial secretary, was appealing for clemency for the survivors, and the question being asked on all sides was whether the raid had British Government backing. Kaiser Wilhelm II had congratulated Paul Kruger, the Transvaal leader, and the Paris press was rejoicing at the British reverse.[35] At Enniscorthy on 6 January, Redmond reflected on these developments, saying that there had never been a new year 'so full of menace and of danger to England', which was 'without one friend throughout the whole wide world'. 'Before such a combination this boasted Empire must crumble like a pack of cards', he said. The situation made it ever more necessary for Ireland to be united, rather than hamstrung by subservience to an English party and personal quarrels. Ireland must be 'defiant and supremely selfish in the assertion of her nationality', otherwise opportunities for her to force her demands would be frittered away. Although he emphasized that he was not expressing 'either gratification or the reverse' at the British predicament, the spirit in which his remarks were received was evident from the 'loud and prolonged cheering' that greeted a heckler who called for 'Cheers for the Boers'. The *Independent* on 10 January asked, 'Is the British Empire a fraud . . . is it a bubble?'[36]

IV

The theme of 'Unity' was on all nationalist lips after the 1895 general election. In this sense the election marks a watershed between centrifugal and centripetal phases in the nationalist movement of the 1890s. Between 1891 and the summer of 1895, the tendency of the movement was towards ever greater disunity, with Parnellites and anti-Parnellites each investing their hopes in the elections of 1892 and 1895 to produce a decisive shift in their favour, and Healyites ever more boldly challenging their own leadership. After the second election, the stalemate between the parties, combined with disillusion with the Liberals and the prospect of indefinite Tory rule, pointed to reunion as the only remedy. Every politician felt compelled to respond to the 'Unity cry', even if only to explain their reasons for rejecting it. The demand at first seemed greater among rank-and-file anti-Parnellites, among whom Redmond's stock had risen considerably as their doubts grew about the capacity of their own leaders, and less among Parnellites, convinced as they were that events had vindicated their stance and that unity would come on their terms when the scales finally fell from the eyes of the electorate at large. The anti-Parnellite *Cork Examiner* on 30 December, for example, accepted many of Redmond's criticisms of the Liberals, but went on to say that there was no excuse for his not rejoining the majority party.[37] Redmond at Elphin on 11 January answered the call for unity by saying that 'there can never be union in Ireland around . . . a policy of subserviency to an English party . . . there will be unity soon but it will be the unity of men whose eyes have been opened to the truth'.[38] Later that year he emphatically rejected a recent assertion by T. P. O'Connor that 'so long as the Tories declare they are against Home Rule and the Liberals declare they are in favour of it then so long is the alliance between the Nationalists and the Liberals inevitable and absolute'. Ireland's impotence, said Redmond, derived from the fact that 'in a mad infatuation, the majority of Irish members insist on lying down in the mud with the Liberal party and clinging to its coat-tails . . . [to promote unity they must] repudiate this useless and degrading alliance with a faithless and a shattered English party'.[39]

Most of the opprobrium for the use of personal invective during the split fell, in later years, on the head of Healy. This was justified, but also inevitable, given Healy's isolation after 1900 when the party was reunited. Redmond, along with Dillon and O'Brien, largely escaped criticism on this score. Frank Hugh O'Donnell would later write of Redmond that 'none of the foul memories of the sweeping brush era soiled his name'.[40] O'Brien would write in 1900 that 'though a vigorous and uncompromising partisan of his own side during the era of dissension, he never forgot that he was an Irish gentleman'.[41] It would be a mistake to assume, however, that he was always above this form of political warfare. In Redmond's diagnosis of Ireland's political ills, the political and the personal were inextricably linked. When Dillon replaced McCarthy as chairman in February 1896, the close alliance with the Liberals continued, leaving the major political issue of the split unresolved. Redmond and his fellow-Parnellites could not but see this pursuit of a wrong policy as the result of the incompetence, the unfitness to lead, of those two men. Thus, try as he might to avoid the cruder forms of personal attack, Redmond could not altogether exclude it from his rhetoric. Healy's style of scabrous personal abuse shocked with its vulgarity and its imputation of the meanest of motives to his opponents. Yet much of it had a witty, even absurdist, quality that allowed it to be laughed off easily. In addition, his targets these days were more likely to be his own colleagues than Parnellites ('He is one whom no man and no party, whom no friend and no colleague, can ever trust,' said Redmond of him at Enniscorthy on 5 January.) It may be wondered whether Healy's scurrility was more wounding than the weighty attacks launched by Redmond, which mixed political criticism with denigration of personal capacity for leadership, of which Dillon was the most frequent target.

In June 1894, he had asked what the Irish people had to hope for from the discord-torn party of the anti-Parnellites. Having castigated the 'foul record' of Healy and the 'political ineptitude and moral cowardice' of Dillon, he spoke of the 'hysterical and treacherous temperament' of O'Brien, and referred to Sexton as 'a man who, as far as I know, never succeeded in attaching to himself for one year's length at a time one sincere friend'. These men, he said, could

> never be the nucleus to form a new party upon the lines of Mr. Parnell . . . whereas with all our defects . . . shortcomings in experience, in accomplishments, in abilities, still the little party which contains Mr. Harrington and others of our colleagues has got the grit [and] the courage [to be] the nucleus of a new development in Irish constitutional agitation.[42]

Figure 19. 'Is he not a man and a brother?': Parnellite cartoon (*Irish Weekly Independent*, 8 May 1897). *Courtesy of the National Library of Ireland.* Illustrating the hollowness of 'Mrs. Freeman's' calls for 'Unity' while John Dillon and Tim Healy keep up their own feud.

During the electioneering of July 1895 at Athlone, he said of Dillon:

> The fact of the matter is that for long years before the split Dillon was jealous of the power of Mr. Parnell . . . I know well the opinion Parnell had of John Dillon. He never trusted him, while he tried to

> use Dillon, and it was very little use he could make of him (*laughter*) . . . he was always embarrassed by the foolish sayings and unwise doings of this man . . . He said of him – 'Dillon is as vain as a peacock, and about as intelligent' (*laughter*). While for three years Dillon had had a position of unprecedented power in Parliament – with 71 members, his party were 'absolute masters of the Government of the British Empire' – the Liberals had given him nothing but 'their well-merited contempt'.[43]

Even had all political differences evaporated overnight, therefore, so much damage had been done by what the protagonists had said about each other that it was difficult to see reunion coming about except at the end of a long transitional period of truce and tentative co-operation. Another obstacle was the suspicion, voiced by Redmond in reply to calls for unity emanating from Dillon's camp, that the latter's immediate motive was to enlist Redmondite help in crushing the Healyite faction. He adverted to this at a Waterford convention in January, saying

> Unity must come from the masses of the people, not from the leaders . . . it is an open secret that at any time for the last four years either of these sections would have been delighted to have joined with us in order to defeat the other section . . . our answer is 'Compose your own quarrels before you preach to other people'.[44]

As early as April 1894, Labouchere had come to Redmond with a confidential offer, seemingly from the Healyite wing of the anti-Parnellites, under which he (Redmond) would re-enter the majority party as leader with the power to fill half of the Party Committee with his friends. Redmond's memorandum of the meeting with Labouchere concludes: 'He said he could give me no names – but that "Tim" was beaten and he and his friends wd. prefer to see me head of the Party rather than Dillon. I said the whole thing was impossible.'[45]

At Clonmel on 2 February, he pointed to the fact that Dillon had refused to share an amnesty platform with him as evidence that the other side did not want co-operation. Instead they wanted to swallow them: 'The sort of union they would like is a union such as Byron, I think, has described the union of Ireland with England – the union of the shark with its prey (*laughter and cheers*).'[46]

Early in 1896, what Healy's biographer has called the 'settled loathing' between him and Dillon found new expression. Healy's removal from executive positions was never likely to ensure his quiescence as a rank-and-file member of his party. On 22 April he declined to be a member of the party committee charged with drafting amendments to the Land Bill, and announced that he and his followers would not obey the whips but adopt an independent course in Parliament. The challenge was not taken up by Dillon, aware of the strength of the clerical and conservative Catholic forces supporting Healy. The result for the moment was a stalemate, with effectively three parties now competing for nationalist support.

It was in this context that on 20 May the Dillonites resolved that the restoration of unity was 'of supreme importance', and proposed a 'Convention of the Irish Race', representative of nationalist opinion at home and abroad, at which the Parnellites would be cordially received, treated fairly and given full representation. The resolution invited Redmond and his friends to co-operate 'in a common, earnest endeavour to make the coming convention an effective means of satisfying the widespread yearning of the Irish race for a thorough reunion'.[47] The *Independent* rejected the call as 'most condescending', while Redmond's denunciation of Dillon's obstruction of the Land Bill constituted an effective dismissal of such initiatives. The Parnellites issued a 'Manifesto to the Irish People' on 15 August describing the 'so-called convention' as having its origin in the desire of one section of Parnell's betrayers to humiliate and defeat the other. When it assembled on 1 September, the paper headlined its report 'The Comedy Convention – an Assembly of Asses', although it was kinder to the overseas delegates, who, it assumed, were not aware of the Dillonites' close ties to the Liberals. Only 43 M.P.s were present, most of them Dillonites, with 22 Healyites boycotting the event. Significantly, only one bishop attended, Croke and Walsh being absent. Redmond later claimed that the only proposal put forward that tended in the direction of conciliation was a resolution of two priests, which asked the convention to declare its independence of the Liberal Party and appoint a committee of arbitration drawn from representatives of the three sections 'to see whether it is possible for them after that declaration of independence to frame a common platform on which all could act'. The priests, he said, were interrupted and denounced, and their proposal 'trampled upon'.[48]

The prospects for reunion may have remained dim, but the chances for limited co-operation seemed to revive when Redmond and Dillon stood together on the same platform, for the first time since the split, at an amnesty meeting in Tipperary on 27 September.[49] The fraternal spirit of the meeting was not, however, reflected in the *Freeman*'s coverage. It accused Redmond of violating the 'decencies' of the occasion with a 'brutal' attempt to turn the amnesty movement to personal and partisan advantage.[50] The *Independent* challenged its rival to prove the charge by quoting the offending passages of his speech. From the *Freeman*'s reply it seemed that this was the opening paragraph, in which Redmond expressed how gratified he was 'that circumstances have so altered in Ireland that it has been possible for Mr. Dillon to stand by my side today on an Amnesty platform in the county of Tipperary'.[51] The *Independent* a few days later claimed to have information that Dillon had telegraphed the *Freeman* after the meeting suggesting an editorial attack on Redmond, and that his motive was his undisguised annoyance that Redmond had received a warmer reception. It published a letter on 3 October from 'One who was there', alleging that the reason for Dillon's anger was the inevitable comparison which people drew between the two most prominent politicians there, and that it was 'almost cruel' to place Dillon in such a position.

Such comparisons were not mere inventions of the *Independent*'s propaganda machine. Dillon's jealousy is understandable in the light of assessments such as those made by the Liberal *Saturday Review* in February, which quoted Morley as saying that Redmond had been the second best speaker in the House while Gladstone was still there, and that with the latter gone, it was difficult to know who was his superior. He had all the attributes for success in a popular assembly, the paper wrote, including 'a flexible and sonorous voice, a handsome person and a command of a flowing and dignified vocabulary'.[52] In a later issue, it added that Dillon was 'a dreary bore', and all of the ability was 'on one side'.[53]

V

The Land Bill of 1896 was the first of the major reforming achievements of constructive unionism, described by Gerald Balfour as an amending measure to remedy the defects of the existing Land Acts. Introduced on 13 April, it was greeted critically but positively by Redmond, the anti-Parnellites having dismissed it in advance as a farce. The clauses on tenure, said Redmond, were less satisfactory than those of Morley's Bill of the previous year, but they had one great virtue: the Government could pass them. The failure to reduce the judicial term for rent review from fifteen years was a 'great blot', while the Bill did not go far enough in leaving tenants' improvements free of rent. The clauses on evicted tenants incorporated almost the whole of the Bill brought in by the Parnellites on 26 February. The purchase clauses, he described as 'eminently satisfactory': they should 'enormously facilitate and increase the number of peasant proprietors in Ireland, and go a long way towards the settlement of the land question'. On the whole, the Bill was one for 'amending and passing, and not for obstruction and rejection', he declared.[54]

From the beginning, his anxiety was, not that it would be defeated, but that it would be lost for lack of adequate time. The intentions of the Dillonites in this regard were not reassuring, since they voted (with the Liberals) against taking time for Government business, and helped to obstruct other Bills that were being taken before the Land Bill. When they opted to vote with the Parnellites and the Government on 12 May on the English Education Bill's second reading, reflecting the Catholic demand for denominational education but unleashing a storm of criticism from their Nonconformist and secularist allies, the pressure on them to compensate by obstructing the Tories in other ways was increased. On 23 May, a letter from Redmond to the *Independent* detailed the attempts being made by Dillon 'and those few of his followers who have been attending here this session' to wreck the Land Bill, adding 'I am not able to explain this idiotic proceeding; all I desire to do is to call attention to it.'[55] On 28 May at the National League central branch he accused Dillon of trying to soothe the Radicals, having antagonized them with his reluctant vote for the Education Bill: 'We don't believe in turning the other cheek, as Mr. Dillon has done, to those insolent and insulting Nonconformists who would, forsooth, dictate to Ireland on the question of Christian education (*tremendous cheering*).'[56]

On the Land Bill, however, he was heartened by the independent attitude of Healy, whose speech on the second reading on 8 June he viewed as evidence that 'there are a large section of Irish nationalists who do not regard this Bill, taken as a whole, as a sham, a fraud, and a humbug' (a reference to Dillon's reported comments on the Bill, later partially withdrawn by him). Redmond's concern to expedite the Bill's passage remained, and he appealed to the Government to prove it was in earnest by giving it sufficient time. So anxious was he not to prolong unduly the Committee stage that his party was sparing in the number of amendments it submitted, which touched only on the Bill's principal defects, and in June and July he succeeded in getting the Government to drop some of its own amendments and managed to have the twelve-o'clock rule suspended at least twice to allow discussion to continue. On the second occasion on 20 July, he pleaded nervously that the question as to whether the Bill would pass or not now depended 'not upon days, but . . . almost upon hours'.[57] Finally on 29 July the third reading was passed without a division. Although both Dillon and Davitt had denounced it, neither voted against the Bill. Landlord interests in the Lords were waiting to oppose it, and inflicted a temporary defeat on the Government on 6 August, but by 14 August they had withdrawn their amendments and the Bill had passed all stages.[58]

In that month all of Redmond's ships came into port together. On 3 August the long-awaited report of the Recess Committee was published – 'a perfect storehouse of vital information', as the *Independent* called it – whose main recommendation was the establishment of a Ministry of Agriculture and Industry under the control of an elected council.[59] A week later, the Financial Relations Commission issued its final report, containing the almost unanimous conclusion that Ireland had been overtaxed for many decades past to the extent of almost £3 million per annum.[60] In addition to the Land Act, which admitted 50,000 tenants to the benefits of previous Land Acts, the fruits of the session just ending were an Act for the Housing of the Working Classes (to promote artisans' dwellings in towns), a Labourers Act (to increase the building of rural labourers' cottages), an Equivalent Grants Act (giving Ireland £80,000 per year against agricultural rates) and a Light Railways Act. The *Independent* commented that if the Independent Party were the allies of the Tories, as their enemies alleged, they would at least have something to show for it.

As if this harvest were not enough, news came on 19 August of the imminent release of John Daly from Portland.[61] Redmond had been to see the prisoners several times during the year; White-Ridley had already ordered the release of one on medical grounds, and wrote confidentially on 3 August that medical reports on the state of health of Daly and three others justified their release on licence.[62] (Daly was on the platform with Redmond and Dillon at the Tipperary amnesty meeting to declare his opposition to the dynamite policy.) After a short break for shooting in the seclusion of Aughavanagh, Redmond summed up the achievements of the session, describing it without hesitation as 'the most useful Irish session of Parliament that has been held since the death of Mr. Parnell'.[63]

At October's Rotunda convention, he called for urgent action on the two reports, both of which he saw as opening up enormous opportunities. The Financial Relations report, he asserted, 'contained the most significant and important fact which has occurred in the history of Ireland since the Union'; in the next session they must demand to know what remedy the Government proposed for Ireland's overtaxation. He drew prolonged cheering when he described the proposal at the heart of the Recess Committee report as, he ventured to say, 'the largest step in the direction of Home Rule which has been taken for many a long day'. It would disestablish a major component of the 'Castle' system of government, the public boards centralized under the 'autocratic control' of Dublin Castle officials, and replace them with a more democratic alternative: 'one great department consisting of a board of a limited number of members – three or five – who would be nominated, with a board acting with them which should be, so far as the majority of its members were concerned, elected by the people themselves'. This new department would concern itself with repairing the damage done to the industrial resources of the country by past British discrimination and refusal of state aid.[64]

VI

On 19 November 1896, Redmond embarked on his fourth journey to the United States, this time on a visit the *Independent* described as 'in no way political'. Described on a publicity brochure as 'The Favourite Lieutenant of the late Charles Stewart Parnell – The Foremost Irish Statesman of the Age – The Most Brilliant Orator in the British Parliament – A Finished Scholar and Distinguished Man of Letters', he was billed to deliver lectures in New York, Boston and other cities on the non-controversial subjects of '15 years in the British Parliament (replete with vivid Reminiscences)', 'Irish Wit and Humour' and 'Irish Ballad Poetry'. Evidently he had concluded from the failure of the 1892 mission that there was more to be gained by avoiding partisan politics, which were necessarily beyond the grasp of American audiences, and playing to his oratorical strengths.

The first lecture, at the Broadway Theatre on 29 November, was judged 'an unqualified success' by the *New York Herald*, which commented:

> He has the advantage of a winning personality. He is governed by a persistent intensity . . . although dealing to a great extent with his lifelong political opponents, Mr. Redmond showed that he was willing to pay them just tribute . . . The temper of those whom he addressed was tested as the lecturer made complimentary references to some of the leaders of English Toryism. A kind word for Balfour was too much for some of the enthusiasts present, but on the whole the interruptions other than cheers were hardly noticeable.

This lecture, based on his parliamentary reminiscences, was the only one of the three whose content was widely reported.[65] Redmond told the story of his first day in Parliament, and later described with dramatic effect two of the most unforgettable scenes in which Parnell faced the Commons: the first in the aftermath of the Phoenix Park assassinations, the second when the House cheered his vindication in the Pigott forgeries affair, and he had not acknowledged the ovation by a word or even by the inclination of his head. He ended with a clear-eyed appraisal of the House of Commons from an Irish nationalist point of view:

> he had always found Parliament opposed to his country. Parliament resembles in some respects a great public school. There is the rough fair play. Schoolboys are sometimes bigoted and cruel and so are the members of the House of Commons at times, but there is something like rough fair play among them. It is a place where true grit and perseverance like that of Parnell will succeed.[66]

The sobriety of these reflections form an interesting commentary, as much on the image he later acquired of one excessively wedded to the House and its ways, as on his remarks in Dublin just before the start of the 1896 session, when he played to the Fenian gallery:

> We do not go to Westminster with the idea that we are going as members of the Imperial Parliament. We do not recognise their Imperial Parliament. We go there against our will; we go as ambassadors from our own nation into the hostile assembly of an alien nation (*cheers*).[67]

The American press was generally favourable in its reviews of the tour – the *New York Times* felt that his lecture on Parliament made for 'a delightful evening' and found that 'his estimates of England's great men of recent years seem uncoloured by partiality or partisanship' – while differing amusingly on details. The *Boston Globe* found one of Redmond's chief characteristics to be 'his continual and never-failing gravity of countenance. He did not smile once last night', while another paper reported that 'many times during the hour and a quarter that he talked the audience was moved to laughter'. The *Albany Sunday Press* found 'no trace of any brogue in his speech', while a Chicago paper quoted a compatriot of his as remarking on his 'undiluted brogue', which 'has the beautiful rumble of the River Lee'. There was much comment on his appearance, a Rochester paper finding him 'an exceedingly handsome man. He is not yet forty years of age, and in the full flush of manly beauty. His smooth, clean-cut intelligent face, his pleasant, well-modulated voice and his distinguished appearance, made him the picture of the ideal orator.' The *New York Advertiser* noted that 'his nose is of the Roman type, very strong and prominent, and his eyes are keen, while his manner is decisive'; the *Boston Globe* reckoned his nose and chin were 'decidedly Napoleonic, in fact they bear the stamp of genius, the first slightly suggesting the eagle's beak, the latter being beautifully proportioned and modelled'. All were agreed on his oratorical virtues, the only criticism being that he tended to place what the *Globe* called 'a superabundance of emphasis' on a succession of sentences, which became a little monotonous after a while.

In Toledo, Ohio, he was asked for his views on the new cycling craze and on that other development in transport, the electric tram. Revealing that he had ridden a bicycle for several years, he told the *Toledo Commercial*:

> Often when Parliament was in session and I could get away for a few days, I have taken my bicycle and gone for a trip through the country. Our country roads are fine for riding, and it is delightful to spin along in the country districts and when you are tired put up at some quiet inn. You know Dublin is the centre of the bicycle market of Great Britain [*sic*] and the first pneumatic tyre was invented there.[68]

On the trams, running for the first time that year in Dublin, he had strong but conservative opinions:

> They should not be allowed to take possession of your best streets. They are, of course, a great convenience, but if a street is not especially wide, I regard them as very dangerous, and give a most unsightly appearance to a city. We have a few lines in Dublin, but they are restricted to the suburbs. We would never permit the overhead network of wires that is allowed in so many American cities.[69]

The tour continued until early February and covered much of the US and Canada. Redmond travelled over 12,000 miles to speak in almost 40 cities. It seems that the second and third lectures on the programme had to be abandoned; he complained later of having been wearied by speaking night after night on the same subject, which by popular demand was his experience of the British Parliament. In each state visited he asked for and was granted access to the state prison, and found a 'marked contrast' with the British system: the American prisons humanized rather than brutalized their inmates, he felt.[70] Struck by the abolition of capital punishment in Michigan, where the number of capital offences was lower than in any other state, he was, however, shocked by the lynching system in Kentucky, where there had been fifty cases in the last year alone, mostly involving 'negroes accused of crimes against white women', in which 'the accusation is the same as condemnation'. He found everywhere sympathy for Cuba (which had just been conceded home rule by Spain) and a desire for US intervention to secure its independence.[71]

On the last two nights he departed from the non-political programme to address a meeting in Boston on 1 February on the financial relations question, and a massive amnesty meeting – 'the vastest, most enormous meeting I ever saw assembled together under a roof in any city in the world' – in New York's Grand Central Palace on 2 February. He was escorted to the hall by 1,200 'stalwart Irishmen' of the New York 1st Irish Regiment. Letters and telegrams supporting the amnesty demand were read from a total of fifty-one state governors and city mayors.[72] Citing the historical role of Britain as a sanctuary for political offenders from continental Europe, he told the audience that the right of Americans to interfere in this question was similar to that of Englishmen in the case of 'the torture of the Armenians by the Sultan of Turkey'.[73]

VII

Following the legislative harvest of 1896, nationalists did not expect similar results from the 1897 session of Parliament. There was, however, hope that benefits might flow from the conclusions of the two landmark reports, those of the Financial Relations Commission and of the Recess Committee. The Redmondite amendments to the Address sought action on these two reports. The confirmation of Ireland's overtaxation had brought support from unexpected quarters. In late 1896 the *Daily Express*, Ireland's premier unionist organ, accepted the report's verdict and declared that the robbery should cease and that Ireland should be paid interest on its past overpayments.[74] While Redmond was in the US, public bodies all over the country took up the issue and a series of public meetings took place in Cork, Dublin, Limerick and other centres, which drew support from unionist and nationalist opinion alike. A remarkable feature of them was the leading role assumed by leaders of the Tory landed class. The Cork meeting was convened by the earl of Bandon, as lord lieutenant of the county, in response to a united call from all the political parties. Another magnate, Lord Castletown, spoke in what the *Independent* called 'the spirit of 1782 and the American revolution'.[75] A meeting convened by Dublin's nationalist lord mayor to consider the issue was attended by the county's lord lieutenant, the Catholic and Protestant archbishops, the heads of the Chamber of Commerce and other public bodies. At Limerick, Lord Dunraven presided at another broadly representative meeting.[76] Clues as to why these men took up an issue that was likely to place them in opposition to their Tory brothers across the water lie in figures released in September 1897 showing that revenue outflow from Ireland had continued to rise since 1895, with almost half of the total increase accounted for by Harcourt's imposition of heavier estate duties in 1894.[77] The downward pressure on rents in the wake of successive Land Acts compounded the sense of grievance. A letter to the *Independent* on 19 December by Standish O'Grady, the unionist landlord and scholar of the Celtic Revival, told of the desperation at Government policies, which drove increasing numbers of them towards the 'pit' of the Landed Estates Court, where their estates were sold at knock-down prices.[78]

A few days into the 1897 session, Arthur Balfour astutely played for time on the Financial Relations report by announcing to the House that the Government would appoint a second commission to complete the investigations of the first, which in their view had not been brought to a conclusion. Unimpressed, the Landlords' Convention on 28 January unanimously voted to seek an 'early and adequate' consideration of the report in Parliament. On 9 February, delegates from 27 of the 32 counties assembled at the Mansion House to appoint an 'All-Ireland Committee'. The day before Redmond returned from the US the committee declared the appointment of the new commission to be 'most unfair and unjust to Ireland'.[79] At the Cork and Dublin receptions, Redmond lost no time in welcoming the advent of a united Irish agitation on the financial issue, describing it as 'full of hope for Ireland' and even 'the most important event which has happened in the National politics of Ireland since the Union'. The chief danger he saw was 'lest men, by making extravagant demands or by wild talk should frighten or scare away those Irishmen who, differing from us on other questions, are willing on this one at any rate to do their duty to their country'. For that reason, he was willing to give way so that the matter could be brought before Parliament by a Unionist, whose motion he would be proud to second. He looked forward to a near day when the country would 'thunder at the doors of Parliament with an absolutely united body of 102 Irish members'. In Dublin he called for a conference of all Irish M.P.s to decide on the best course of parliamentary action, a call which was promptly endorsed by the All-Ireland Committee.[80] A week later his signature appeared, together with those of Colonel Saunderson, leader of the Irish Unionists, Plunkett and Healy, on a notice convening such a conference. Dillon did not sign but promised to advise his friends to attend. In the House on 22 February, in response to questions from Redmond and Dillon, Balfour pledged that the new commission would not be appointed until after the debate on the first commission's report had finished.[81]

The conference met on 9 March with sixty-three M.P.s present and Colonel Saunderson in the chair. The result was the appointment of a small committee to draw up a resolution to be moved in the House on the financial grievance. It was immediately noticed that the committee included no representative of Dillon's party. If this was by Dillon's deliberate choice, as gossip suggested, it implied a negative attitude to the venture on his part and a threat to the united action on which its success relied. Such suspicions were soon confirmed. When the committee drew up a very moderate resolution stating that the overtaxation of Ireland with respect to its taxable capacity demanded the immediate attention of Parliament, Dillon and his colleague Blake refused to accept it on the grounds that it did not refer to the new commission. Clancy, on behalf of the committee, was forced to withdraw the resolution. Redmond's anger at the loss of the chance of united Irish action in the House was acute; it found expression in an interview on St Patrick's Day in which he accused Dillon of having obstructed the work of the conference at every step. All Unionists, whether or not they favoured the new commission, were opposed to including reference to it in the resolution, so that by his insistence on such, Dillon had broken up the conference. The enemies of Ireland could now exult that the unanimity of the Irish members was a myth. 'I cannot conceive what Mr. Dillon's idea really is,' he said, branding his action as 'not only intensely stupid, but also intensely unpatriotic'.[82]

With the preferred option of a unanimous Irish vote now dead, Redmond's only course of action was to second Blake's nationalist motion when the debate came up on 29 March. Blake's speech was an elaborate review of the whole question, which Redmond followed with a few hard-hitting points. They were taking their stand, he asserted, on the seventh article of the Act of Union, which entitled Ireland to be treated as a separate entity within the United Kingdom for taxation purposes, and to have her contribution assessed in proportion to her resources. The question was whether Ireland paid more than her fair share of revenue by this standard. Although the commission had shown that this was the case, the answer given was that she also received more than her fair share of expenditure, because it cost more to govern her. The reason was obvious:

> The government of any country carried on against the will of the governed will always be wasteful, extravagant, and at the same time bad. If Ireland were self-governed do you imagine for one instant that the cost of the civil administration of the country would be as it is today double per head of the population in Ireland to what it is in England? Do you imagine that Ireland would find it necessary to spend £1.5 million a year on maintaining an armed police force about one half the size of the regular army of the United States, or to pay a Lord Lieutenant a salary of £20,000 a year, just double what the President of the U.S. receives?

Although she had never ceased to protest against the Union, Ireland, a poor, depopulated country made to pay much more than her fair share of taxation, today appealed to one article in the Treaty of Union 'to protect her against further spoliation'. If justice was refused to Ireland, he as a nationalist would have the consolation of knowing that they had 'torn to shreds the last rag of argument' in favour of the maintenance of the Union.[83]

An appeal couched in such terms could not hope to gain cross-party support, and the motion was lost by 157 votes to 317, with only two Unionists voting with the nationalists, although many more abstained. The main speech against it came from Hicks-Beach, now chancellor of the exchequer, but, as if in illustration of that Commons sense of fair play to which Redmond had alluded in his American lectures, the surprise of the debate was the brilliant defence of the Irish case made by the Tory M.P. Sir Edward Clarke, who, in the *Independent*'s view, shattered the chancellor's case 'with the deft skill of the trained advocate'. The paper had no hesitation in blaming Dillon for the overall débâcle: he was 'saturated with vanity', jealous of Redmond and had to be 'agin' Healy on all occasions, it declared.[84]

In May Redmond signalled a new form of agitation on the financial issue when he announced that his party would contest every item in the Estimates. That month he and three colleagues had themselves suspended from the House for persisting in raising the question of Ireland's taxation during Committee of Supply.[85] The British press condemned the episode as a return to the obstruction tactics of Biggar and Parnell, while the *Freeman* denounced it as farce, which brought contempt on the Irish representatives. While such parliamentary militancy boosted the morale of American supporters of Redmond – a jubilant Edward O'Flaherty wrote from New York that the suspensions were an honour – Redmond did not repeat it. Later that year in Waterford he defended his abandonment of the 'active policy of combat', which he himself had preached, when he said the Parnellites were voices in the wilderness and such a policy was 'only possible when the country itself is behind it'.[86]

The first parliamentary attempts to give reality to the proposals of the Recess Committee were as unsuccessful as those concerning the financial grievance, but in this case the setback would be short-lived. Gerald Balfour on 12 April introduced a Bill to establish a Board of Agriculture and Industry, which was immediately criticized by Redmond for its lack of the elective element proposed by the Recess Committee, and for its meagre funding of £150,000, which was only a fifth of Ireland's entitlement to Exchequer funding for the relief of agricultural depression; the money, moreover, was not to come from the imperial Treasury but was 'our own money which belongs to us already'. The Recess Committee itself later amplified these criticisms. Alongside this Bill, Balfour brought in a second one for Technical Instruction, to be funded with £80,000 from the Exchequer. Both Bills were withdrawn by the chief secretary on 2 June, following the landmark announcement by his brother on 21 May of the Government's intention to create in the next session a thoroughly democratic system of local government, to be followed by giving Ireland the full agricultural relief grant due to it.[87]

The agitation on financial relations did not die with the failure of the parliamentary initiatives. The announcement of the plan for local government and the payment of the relief grant diverted attention from it for a time, and the All-Ireland Committee was forced to make an emphatic declaration that the latter concession would in no way meet the claim for financial redress.[88] The fact that the Government had not appointed the new commission by the end of 1897 seemed to offer renewed hope for united Irish action in the following year. In December, Edward Carson, M.P. for Dublin University and rising star of Unionism, threw his weight behind the agitation, and the committee held a very representative and largely attended public meeting, which listened to a masterly oration by The O'Conor Don, who was followed by Dillon, Healy, Clancy, the Unionist historian and second member for the university W. E. H. Lecky, and the grand master of the Orange Order, Reverend R. R. Kane. On this occasion Redmond was elsewhere, stealing a march on his rivals by delivering an early commemorative lecture on 1798 in his constituency.[89]

11 Commemoration and Conciliation

> . . . while I believe the constitutional movement may be, and will be in the future, of great value to Ireland, I believe that the salt of the public life of Ireland is to be found in the ideals of those men who believed in the ideals of '98.
>
> Redmond at 1798 commemoration in Wexford, 28 May 1898[1]

> Wherever . . . a Protestant, an anti-Nationalist, or a landlord, or others who have been opposed to you, come forward with a declaration that they are willing to devote their labours to the service of the country and to the government of local affairs, then I would entreat of the people . . . to judge every man upon his merits absolutely, irrespective of his creed or politics.
>
> Redmond at Irish Independent League, Head Branch, Dublin, 31 May 1898[2]

I

During Redmond's absence in the US in late 1896, the tensions within Dublin Parnellism sharpened. Harrington's feud with the extremists, which in February 1896 had led to an attempt, averted only by police action, to burn down both the *United Ireland* and *Independent* offices by Fenians barred from the National Club, worsened as he explored possibilities for reconciliation with the Dillonites and Healyites.[3] In December, at the National League central branch, he welcomed the remarks of Healy (at a Wexford convention of his supporters) that admitted that the Liberals had done nothing for Ireland, that Dillonism was discredited, that Redmond's policies in Parliament were 'sensible', and that he would support his initiatives on the Financial Relations report in the House.[4] Harrington stated the conditions for unity as the pursuit of an 'absolutely independent' policy and the recognition of Redmond's leadership of a reunited party, but his overriding wish was to draw Parnellism away from its Fenian connections and back into concord with its natural allies in the constitutional movement.[5]

These cracks became an open rift in the wake of a public letter from Archbishop Walsh that appeared in the press on 16 January 1897, in which he declared himself now 'absolutely neutral in politics' and identified the question of 'Leadership' as the main cause of 'the present sad state of things in Ireland'. Harrington's response was to publish an editorial in *United Ireland* on 23 January to the effect that, although human motives and the fact that they had 'too much to forgive' drove them to continue the split, 'if our opponents are willing to cry "*peccavi*" ["I have sinned"] even now at the eleventh hour, when they see they cannot wipe us out, theirs is the surrender and ours the right of adopting a conciliatory attitude for Ireland's sake'.[6] The fact that the Parnellites could not overcome the other factions and 'the whole ecclesiastical body in Ireland who have taken sides in this struggle against us' made reunion an imperative, it suggested. The article was short on concrete proposals, and seemed merely to hint at some mechanism by which Dillon could be allowed to stand aside (assuming he so wished) without excessive loss of face. On the same day, the *Independent* countered with a blast against any rumour that the Parnellites had the remotest intention of contemplating union with 'the men who betrayed Parnell and deserted to the English flag', who were now 'beaten to the ropes'. It asked:

> Is there one solitary reason why we should forgive the renegades who still boast that their treachery was patriotism? . . . The deserter in the field of battle is never allowed back to the fighting ranks. A slightly different treatment is meted out to him . . . To save [the Home Rule movement] from collapse, it is essential that the chief betrayers of Parnell should be forced to leave the cause to men with clear heads and honest hearts . . . In Heaven's name, what have we been fighting for these years, if it is even remotely possible that we will take Mr. Dillon and Mr. Healy to our bosoms now?[7]

Given that Byrne, the paper's editor, was with Redmond in the US, Harrington implied that the *Independent* had been hijacked in Redmond's absence by the extremists: 'The position taken up by the *Independent* is absolutely at variance with all Mr. Redmond's speeches and actions, and we prefer to be led by his practical common sense rather than by the hysterical attempt at mock heroics in the *Independent*.'[8] The latter in turn accused Harrington of the unauthorized use of Redmond's name in connection with his reunion schemes.

The addresses of welcome that greeted Redmond at Cork on 13 February spoke of 'strange events' and 'efforts to sap the integrity of the Independent party', while the Fenian P. H. Meade, now mayor of Cork, trusted that he would 'never lower the flag'. His response made no mention of deserters or their punishment; he was rhetorically closer to Harrington than to the *Independent* when he told his welcomers:

> We are upon the right road; the others are upon the wrong road . . . Well, when they are convinced of their error, let them turn back off the false road and come upon the true one. We must fix their eyes on the goal before us, quarrelling with no one . . . but respecting and defending ourselves, determined to pursue our own policy and maintain our own principles to the end.[9]

In Dublin, where thousands lined the quays and bridges from Kingsbridge station to the National Club, he declared that he would condemn strongly any Parnellite 'who ventures, either directly or indirectly, to say one disrespectful word of my friend and your honoured member Mr. Harrington'. Freedom of thought was an essential principle of their party, and the latter had spoken simply for himself. But his candid opinion was that 'the proposal made by Mr. Harrington is an impracticable and impossible proposal (*cheers*) . . . because it has been repudiated in all its essential principles by the *Freeman's Journal* acting for our opponents'.[10] In addition, the time was not right for such a move; it would be wiser, he suggested, to await the outcome of the Healy–Dillon struggle before making any advances to unity with one or other faction.

Events were tending in the direction of yet another split, this time, ironically, the result of efforts to heal previous splits. Harrington did not recant, but at the league central branch on 23 February pointed to the apathy in the country and the difficulties in raising funds as grounds for urgent moves towards reunion.[11] Redmond convened a conference of 'well-known Parnellites' for 20 April, during the Easter recess, 'to consider the position and prospects of the Parnellite party'. Optimistic Dillonites assumed that it would discuss the unity proposals, but were astounded to hear instead that it had resolved to set up a new organization, the Irish Independent League (IIL), with a seven-point programme: self-government; civil and religious liberty; independence of all British parties; manhood suffrage; immediate financial redress for Ireland; amnesty; and land law reform.[12] At a public meeting in the Rotunda that evening, Redmond explained the move by saying that the National League, a mainly agrarian movement, had achieved valuable benefits in the past but was now practically defunct, having been deserted by the bulk of the farmers, 'forgetful alike of gratitude and of wisdom', when it took its stand on the side of national principles.[13] The new organization was intended to appeal to a wider constituency in Ireland and across the Atlantic 'to give us such an organised force at our back as will enable us effectually to stem the influence of British opinion in this country'.

There was to be a hardening of the demand for self-government. The moderation of 1886 and 1893, when nationalists were willing to compromise on the national demand for the sake of an immediate settlement, had been 'spurned by England'. Gladstone's successors had abandoned Home Rule for a vague 'Federalism all round' policy that would have them wait for decades until all parts of the UK were prepared for it. It was now time, he said, to revert to the full historic demand, which was for the repeal of the Act of Union and the restoration to Ireland of an 'absolutely independent, separate and co-ordinate Parliament', with no English veto over Irish-made laws, save that of the crown. (On further explanation, this seemed identical to the formulation of the national demand he had pursued in 1892 and 1893.) On the financial relations issue, they would revert to the tactic of insisting on divisions on every vote in Supply. As for manhood suffrage, if enacted as in the US, it would result in the Parnellite party no longer being in a minority.[14]

Over the following months branches of the new organization were established in Dublin, Kilkenny and Wicklow, and later in Limerick and Cork. Predictably, it was derided by both sections of the anti-Parnellite press. Healy's *Daily Nation* approvingly quoted the *Spectator*'s comment: 'When in doubt call a Conference and found a new association. That appears to be the rule on which the Irish patriot now acts.'[15] Assistant Commissioner Mallon's assessment was that 'the new organisation will be as short-lived as the Irish Army of Independence established by the same party a few years ago. Most people are laughing at the whole thing as a good joke'.[16]

There was trouble at some of the Dublin meetings to convert National League branches to branches of the IIL. It took a police presence to quell what the *Independent* called 'some unease' at the 19 May meeting to set up the Usher's Quay branch; it had been the same at all similar meetings of the new league, Mallon claimed. There was a heavy Fenian presence on its provisional central executive: a police report listing 107 members pointed out that 36 were members of the IRB and 16 of the INA. The IIL enjoyed an initial growth spurt in the summer; after that progress was slow, and by the end of 1897 only twenty-six branches had been established outside Dublin.[17]

In the meantime, Harrington, whose amendment to leave the National League unchanged had been defeated at the April conference, announced on 11 May that he was severing himself from the party, and issued a circular to the clergy calling for funds to support a 'policy of reunion'. He began to appear on Dillonite platforms, and the National League, now one of four (constitutional) nationalist organizations in Ireland, continued a skeletal existence under his leadership.[18] Behind the scenes, he had been given undertakings by both Dillon and Healy that they would accept Redmond as the leader of a reunited Irish party, but he believed that the latter had come to an understanding with Devoy in the US, which prevented him from agreeing to such an arrangement.

It is not known whether in fact Redmond made any explicit commitment to Devoy during his US visit. It is probable, however, that the two men met, since Devoy attended the New York amnesty address by Redmond on 2 February, as evidenced by a letter from Allan to Redmond mentioning that Devoy had written to him to say 'that the New York meeting was one of the grandest he has ever seen – having regard to its representative character as well as to its size'.[19] The sudden shift to a militant tone so soon after the American visit suggests that some understanding was reached between them. There is also Allan's anxiety the following winter to reassure Devoy by letter that Redmond's lectures on 1798 were in conformity with republican orthodoxy.[20] An arrangement, if it existed, is likely to have involved at least an undertaking by Redmond to insist on the breaking of the Liberal alliance and adherence to the principle of independent opposition as a precondition for reunion, in return for which Devoy would throw the fundraising resources and political support of Clan na Gael behind the Redmondites.

Another intriguing possibility, regarding the funding of the Redmondites from a very different source, is raised by Mallon's secret report in June 1896 that his informant had told him that Redmond had received a large sum of money from Cecil Rhodes to maintain his party, 'and that a further and much larger sum is expected from that gentleman'.[21] Rhodes and his Chartered Company were widely suspected of being implicated in the Jameson raid (Harcourt in the Commons had suggested as much), but Redmond had stated in an interview that while he 'entirely disapproved' of the raid, he had 'no particular sympathy' with the attacks on Rhodes in the British press. The latter had, he said, been a good friend to Ireland and a close friend of Parnell in his hour of trial (a reference to the £10,000 donated by Rhodes to Parnell in 1888 and 1891 in return for the latter's adherence to the principle that some Irish members should be retained at Westminster under the next Home Rule Bill).[22] Rhodes's hopes for a future federal imperial Parliament harmonized very well with the sentiments expressed by Redmond at the Cambridge Union. Redmond's stance was criticized by the *Freeman* and weakly defended by the *Independent*, which wrote that his offence seemed to be 'not joining with the horde of Britishers who are never happier than when they are barking at the heels of some great man in trouble'. It also put him in trouble with John O'Leary, who wrote to the *Independent* of his 'absolute amazement' at the view expressed, and felt he represented a considerable body of nationalist opinion in saying so.[23]

The sensational revelation that Dillon had privately agreed to surrender the chair of a reunited party to Redmond if his followers consented, and that Healy was favourable to the idea, was made by Harrington in an interview with the *Independent* on 12 May. It was a pity he had not revealed this earlier, commented the paper, when it would have saved misunderstanding.[24] It soon began to appear that Dillon's followers did not consent. When a small number of Dillonites passed a pro-unity resolution favouring Harrington's efforts, they made clear that their support implied no such change of leadership.[25] Although nothing more was heard of the offer for a considerable time, it did serve to point to the increasing acceptance among nationalists of all shades that Redmond was the best qualified candidate to lead a reunited party, whenever it might emerge. It was evident that autumn that Dillon's thoughts were still on giving up the chair, when he said in an interview: 'As for myself, I would resign tomorrow if I could see any use in resigning.' The *Independent* commented sardonically: 'He might try it just as an experiment.'[26]

Towards the end of 1897 the prospects for removal of one of the obstacles to unity were improved when statements from Liberal leaders made it easier for Dillon, if he so wished, to abandon the Liberal alliance. At Manchester on 23 November, Herbert Gladstone, son of the great statesman and Liberal M.P. for Leeds, gave as his opinion that the Home Rule question must remain in suspension for the moment and that his party would be relieved of a great responsibility if the Tory policy of killing Home Rule with kindness were to succeed. The National Liberal Federation had earlier declared that electoral reform, not Home Rule, was to be the first plank in the new Liberal platform.[27] At Waterford on 7 December, Redmond begged Dillon to see the change in the Liberal position and acknowledge that the Liberal leaders had violated the primary condition of the alliance. He again rejected Harrington's proposals as containing no provision for the abandonment of Dillon's 'suicidal policy', while the idea of his own election to the chair of a united party under such conditions was 'a wretched sop', which would barter away Parnellite principles and policy for 'a doubtful honour for myself'. He added: 'No, let there be a reunion of principles . . . first of all let the people throughout the country come to a united idea (*hear, hear*). Then let the various sections in Parliament give their views.'[28]

II

The later 1890s was the period when the energies of Irish nationalists were increasingly turned from the paralysis of the political arena to the cultural sphere, where the search for an identity for a future self-governing Ireland was beginning. Leamy's *United Ireland* had laid out the agenda for this search just as the debate on the second Home Rule Bill got under way:

> in an article at which the London *Times* professed to take alarm, we said that 'Ireland a Nation' meant not merely a Parliament in College Green, but national thought, national life in its widest and truest sense, and the national individuality of the people of this island stamped on the history of the world.[29]

The National Literary Society was founded in 1892 under the presidency of Douglas Hyde, and embraced an uneasy coalition of scholarly revivalists of the Irish language, literature and folklore and a neo-Fenian group intent on making 'national and legendary heroes' known to a wider audience. The second group was centred around W. B. Yeats, who staged his play *The Countess Cathleen* the same year; the membership included John O'Leary and Maud Gonne.[30] In spite of Hyde's attempts to keep the movement above political controversy, Gonne lost no time in using the auspices of the society to spread a radical political message. In April 1893, for example, she was lecturing at Loughrea on the French invasion of the west coast in 1798.[31]

Hyde's presidential address to the society on 25 November 1892, entitled 'The Necessity for De-Anglicising Ireland', later printed as a pamphlet, became the seminal thesis of cultural nationalism and led to the foundation of the Gaelic League in 1893. Redmond was aware of these developments and showed what seems to have been a modest interest in them. He had talked at length with Hyde in March 1892, and was present with Leamy and other colleagues at a Dublin lecture given by Hyde in January 1894 on 'The Irish Language and Literature: Its Characteristics and Value'.[32] Further public meetings took place to popularize the revival of Gaelic as a spoken language. In the House in June 1896, Redmond took up the issue of the study of Gaelic in intermediate and university courses, asking the chief secretary to reverse the recent reduction in marks for the subject.[33]

The Redmondite press adopted a positive attitude to the movement from the outset. Prominent space was given to a long letter from a John O'Mahony in January 1895, entitled 'Shall Irish History be Taught in Our Schools?', which gave an overtly political meaning to de-Anglicization. Having stated that he personally was an 'out and out rebel' who did not agree with parliamentary agitation, the writer went on:

> We Irish youths must roll up our sleeves and kill West Britonism. We must form throughout our land literary clubs to teach our Irish history; also Gaelic football clubs, and in every manner we can consolidate and unite our boys, and let our watchword be – 'England's difficulty is Ireland's opportunity'.[34]

A leader in the *Independent* on 13 February 1895 endorsed a circular issued by the Gaelic League. In June 1899 the paper began a small contribution to the Gaelic revival with a special supplement entitled 'Our Mother Tongue' carrying articles on and in the language with pictures of the Gaelic League's leading personalities. This was followed in September by the introduction of a weekly reprinted article, complete with translation, from *An Claidheamh Solais* ('The Sword of Light'), the Gaelic League organ.[35] A few months later the *Weekly Independent* introduced a 'Gaelic department', consisting of a half-page of material in the Irish language.

The Gaelic League for a long time appealed to a diverse audience. The readership of the *Independent* seemed to find no contradiction between Gaelic revivalism and the toleration policy towards unionists being promoted by Redmond in 1899.[36] In September the inaugural meeting of the league's Dublin central branch was presided over by Lord Emly, and a still unpoliticized Patrick Pearse delivered a paper to the branch on the eleventh-century hero Brian Boru.[37] However, the police noted how extremists of various hues used the literary clubs as recruiting grounds. Redmond's future nemesis, James Connolly, read a paper to the National Literary Society in Dublin in November 1896 on the Marxist theme 'Irish Revolution – Utopian and Scientific'.[38]

The year 1897 was the year of the queen's jubilee, when Victoria celebrated her sixtieth year on the throne. It was also the year of preparation for the centenary of the 1798 insurrection, when many ghosts could be expected to walk. The double challenge for constitutional nationalist politicians was to stand aloof with dignity from the royal celebrations, while not overly offending British opinion, and at the same time pay homage at the shrines of the revolutionary tradition without encouraging illegality or violence. At the IIL head branch in Dublin a week before the jubilee celebrations in June, Redmond set out the Parnellite attitude. He was characteristically even-handed as he acknowledged the massive advances made during Victoria's reign in the population and prosperity of the Empire, as well as in the arts and sciences, adding:

> For my part I do not for a moment pretend to deny that if I were an Englishman I would be very proud of celebrating the sixtieth year of this reign. But, gentlemen, we in this country cannot be expected to – and whether we are expected or not we will not – share in this feeling of jubilation . . . I don't believe in giving unnecessary offence to any man, less than all to any woman; . . . but I do think that . . . it would be a monstrous thing if this great historic occasion would be allowed to pass without there being placed upon record for all time to come the feeling that we have, as Irishmen, with respect to the treatment of our country.[39]

In the House on 21 June, he moved his amendment to the congratulatory address:

> And we further represent to Your Majesty that this House deems it its duty to place the fact upon record that while the sixty years of Your Majesty's reign have witnessed the extension of representative government to all the great colonies, and the growing prosperity and contentment of the subjects of the Empire generally, Ireland has suffered during that period from famine, depopulation and poverty.[40]

He told the House: 'Ireland today stands apart altogether from your Jubilee celebration, and when you ask her to share in your joy and triumph she answers you by saying "First restore to me my liberty".'[41] The prospect of a united nationalist protest on the jubilee was aborted when the Dillonites walked out rather than support Redmond's amendment, but returned to vote against the substantive Address motion. Dillon afterwards told the *New York World* that he had done so because the amendment was not extreme enough.[42]

Not all was as it seemed in regard to these protests. Stories circulated in the British press of Irish M.P.s competing to get the best seats at the jubilee ceremonies.[43] The celebrations in Dublin passed off peacefully for the most part, with the police reporting enormous and orderly crowds of sightseers on streets decked with flags, decorations and illuminations. A

Figure 20. 'Victoria Must Learn the Truth': Parnellite cartoon (*Irish Weekly Independent*, 26 June 1897). *Courtesy of the National Library of Ireland.* John Redmond asks England, Wales and Scotland to wait with their loyal addresses while he informs Queen Victoria why the Irish people cannot join wholeheartedly in her 60th Jubilee celebrations.

few incidents marred the occasion. Extremists hoisted a black flag on the City Hall. Clashes took place between the police and stone-throwers attacking the Orange Hall close to the National Club in Rutland Square, resulting in fifty-one arrests. The police also intervened when a group of students sallied forth from Trinity College to break up an anti-Jubilee meeting being addressed by Maud Gonne near the front gate. Baton charges on the streets of Dublin on subsequent evenings left 200 people in hospital, according to the *Independent*.[44] Redmond's measured approach to the celebrations brought forth a conciliatory response from the *Daily Express*, which wrote that the nationalist leaders had taken a 'right and dignified course', and also that the time had come for the remission of the sentences of the remaining prisoners.

In the meantime, preparations had already begun for the following year's '98 commemorations. On 4 March a meeting in Dublin City Hall, chaired by O'Leary, resulted in the setting up of the 1798 Centenary Committee, a group that included all the leading Fenians of the IRB persuasion. Meade threw down an implicit challenge to all constitutionalists who would wish to associate themselves with the commemorations when he proposed

> that this meeting of Irishmen recognises in Theobald Wolfe Tone, the United Irishmen, and the men of '98, patriots of the purest and noblest type that Ireland has ever produced; that their memory should be revered and cherished by their countrymen as apostles of Irish union and champions of the noble cause of liberty . . . It was the urgent duty of Nationalist Ireland to show to the world that they did not fear to speak of '98 (*applause*).[45]

Members of Parliament were not to be invited to join the committee, a decision that Allan explained to Redmond as aimed at facilitating Fenian control of the movement:

> We have nearly three-quarters majority of the provisional committee now and so long as the other side [the anti-Parnellites] don't suspect us, we can get the control of the executive, but if after refusing several of their members we elected you, they'd probably go back to their original claim of an executive composed of half anti-Parnellites and half Parnellites, which would spoil us.[46]

Allan made the preoccupation of Fenians clear to Redmond:

> Of course the not unnatural fear on the part of many members of the Committee is that some speakers like the Lord Mayor may possibly speak in a half apologetic way for the men of '98 and so throw a damper upon the whole proceedings, as well as ruin us with the men in America.[47]

Soon afterwards, an American group, the '98 Centennial Association, was reported to be organizing a 'pilgrimage to Erin' for the coming year. No doubt in order to match the prevailing mood, the organizers of the annual Parnell demonstration announced that the music this year would feature national and martial rather than funereal airs.[48]

At a public meeting on 16 June to found a branch of the IIL in Newry, Redmond referred to the approaching centenary. As in the lectures he had delivered on the subject in the 1880s, his analysis of the '98 insurrection eschewed the 'Catholic' interpretation then in vogue among nationalists and emphasized the leading role played by Protestant Irishmen, to whose 'standard of liberty' Catholics had thronged. There was nothing in the history of the rebellion of which any Irishman should be ashamed, he claimed, adding that it was a rising against intolerable persecution and oppression, and although deeds of cruelty had been perpetrated by both sides, yet it was 'studded with incidents of the greatest heroism and public virtue'. He went on to clarify the extent of his differences with the contemporary physical force elements:

> Times are changed. I suppose in existing circumstances the possibility of such a rising at the present time or in the future is remote; but I have often said, and not merely on Irish popular platforms, but in my place in the House of Commons, that I believed that if the Irish people of today had a chance of success, that the system of government under which they are groaning at this moment would justify an uprising tomorrow (*cheers*). If we are working upon other lines, if we are endeavouring within the lines of the Constitution to win Irish freedom, I have no hesitation in saying that this is a mere question of expediency, and that we would be morally justified tomorrow in using physical force, if we had it at our command, to shake off the yoke under which we are suffering (*cheers*).[49]

Redmond gave two lectures on the insurrection in advance of the centenary year, one in the Mansion House on 22 November on 'Wexford in '98' attended by both Parnellites and Fenians, the second in Waterford on 8 December. At the Dublin meeting, which, according to Mallon, was a financial success and where the audience included 'the worst men in Dublin', Redmond received the Fenian embrace from O'Leary, who proposed a vote of thanks for the 'very eloquent and exhaustive lecture':

> While he was little in love with the methods of the present day, he was strong in the hope in a rising generation other and better than the present or the immediate past. He was confident there would always be found men in Ireland ready to live, and if needs be die, that Ireland may be free.[50]

Mallon reported in late November that 'persons of moderate views' in Dublin were anxious about the coming year, none more so than the lord mayor-designate, Daniel Tallon, a moderate Parnellite who had denounced those who had raised the black flag on the City Hall.[51]

In December, Redmond received a request signed by a long list of New York members of the Centennial group asking him to lecture there, an invitation he promptly accepted. He sailed on 29 December and, just over a year after his last appearance at the Broadway Theatre, delivered his '98 lecture there on 9 January, with a member of the Emmet family in the chair. A week later, an audience of 3,000 listened to the same lecture in Boston. He made it known that he had met members of the Tone, Emmet and Mitchel families, along with survivors of the '67 movement. Having thus secured his '98 credentials ahead of the competition, he was back in Ireland by 2 February in time for the opening of Parliament.[52]

III

The fortunes of the three Parnellite newspapers, the *Daily* and *Weekly Independent* and the *Evening Herald*, followed a course roughly parallel to those of the Parnellite party itself in the mid-1890s. The problem of under-capitalization reported by Redmond in 1894 was remedied to some extent, partly through the purchase of shares by the staff, but at the end of that year the company was still short by £3,000 of the minimum figure of £40,000 considered necessary to fund the business. At the same time, the struggle for solvency was being won. Redmond could report to the 1895 AGM that expenditure was down while receipts were steady for 1894 over the previous year.[53] Thomas Baker, the Secretary of the company, wrote to Redmond in August that recently enacted staff and salary changes had cut costs, bringing them 'a step nearer to that corner which we want to turn'.[54] The chairman's report for 1895 showed a further improvement in performance: there was still a net loss, but it had been cut to 'infinitesimal' proportions in the second half of the year, and receipts had increased by £6,000 over the 1894 figure. The 'period of anxiety and trouble' was now ended, according to Redmond.[55] The improved circulation may have reflected a revival of interest in politics brought about by the general election.[56]

This positive trend began to reverse itself, however, in the aftermath of the general election. With the failure of the Redmondites to increase significantly their parliamentary strength, and with no prospect of an end to the split, political apathy in the country deepened, and the effects on the newspapers were soon apparent. In early May 1896, Baker wrote to Redmond of a 'dire state of affairs': cash in hand could not nearly meet that week's urgent bills and staff wages, making a loan essential.[57] The problem was that the collection of revenues lagged chronically behind the deadlines for meeting expenses.[58] The following month Baker again wrote of the knife-edge that the papers walked from week to week: 'Is there any kind Christian (Jews or Pagans not objected to) friend who will come forward with assistance in this most deserving case?'[59] Even more seriously, Baker told Redmond of an 'alarming' falling off in the circulation of the papers in the three months since March, a trend he attributed only partly to the prevailing apathy. Despite changes in the editorial staffs, which he had regarded as very satisfactory in early May, the papers were sometimes late with important news: 'The public will buy the paper that gives the earliest and the most news irrespective of politics and to my eye the *Freeman's Journal* seems to be doing both and if it continues to hold the lead we will fall back more and more.'[60]

The *Independent* papers fought back by introducing illustrations (in March 1896) and innovations such as articles catering to the new mass tourism market in Ireland, and maintaining a more attractive layout and a clearer typeface than the *Freeman*. Despite the alarms of 1896,

Redmond reported to the 1897 AGM that the company was now in a 'thoroughly sound and solvent condition'. Electric lighting had been installed, a measure that would pay for itself in a few years, and new linotype machinery had been purchased. The actual net loss was now, he claimed, 'a mere bagatelle', which would be covered by the receipts of a single day. In addition, Redmond had heeded Baker's pleas to look for a sympathetic investor. He had brought back with him from his American tour one Louis Stuyvesant Chandler, whom he described to the AGM as 'a young American gentleman of high commercial standing . . . half an Irishman by blood and a thorough Irishman by sympathy' who had invested largely in the company. Chandler was to join the board, replacing Dr Fitzgerald who had not attended for three years.[61] Baker told Redmond before the AGM that £7,000 in new capital had been obtained in the previous two years, although he added soberly that much of it had gone to pay unpaid bills and salaries, and more was still needed, since outgoings always ran ahead of receipts, although the two were now about even.[62]

Even as these optimistic reports were being delivered in the summer of 1897, matters were taking another turn for the worse. Advertising revenue fell and circulation failed to improve in the second half of the year.[63] The launch that year of the *Daily Nation* by Healy, which had been expected to hurt both the existing dailies, may have taken advertising; however, the main cause of the malaise was internal. It must have been a rude shock for Redmond to receive from Baker in late July an eight-page memorandum containing a comprehensive critique of the operation of the company at all levels. Seeking to account for 'the waterlogged condition into which the papers seem to have fallen', Baker criticized each layer of management in turn. The board held weekly meetings, but it was only on the rare occasions when Redmond himself was present that any effective work was done, he complained. Although the board was 'Parliamentarian in complexion', some of the principal employees were 'ostentatiously the opposite'; the opposing element managed to identify the papers with its projects and use them 'to further the propaganda of hostility to Parliamentary action'. There was criticism of two of the editors. Dr Byrne, although a man of great journalistic experience and safe judgement, and a capable writer, had no business leanings and had become 'a standing model of irregular attention to the details of his office', allowing a 'widespread spirit of indiscipline' to infect the *Daily Independent*. But Baker's harshest criticism was reserved for Allan, the manager of the company. The latter was 'at the head of the anti-Parliamentarians' and had much influence over the majority of the staff, 'many of whom actively aid him in his outside undertakings'. The diversion of Allan's attention to 'other affairs' caused him to overlook important matters, and had sometimes led to violations of the board's standing orders. Complaining of Allan's 'unrestrained freedom of action', he concluded that 'the general result is a loose tone amongst the staff with a few exceptions'.[64]

A week later, Baker sent another memorandum, this time to Carew, detailing the great dissatisfaction felt among the editorial staff about the 'Parliamentarian' members of the papers' staff. His proposal was for a managing director to remedy the board's failings, and a working editor to take control of both editorial and management departments and 'work at it consistently'. Unrealistically, he seemed to think that Redmond would be available for the first job:

> Now if Redmond would take the control of the place into his hands and stick to the work for a few months continuously he would be the salvation of the papers and of those connected with them whose present liberty of action does more harm than good to them personally. This arrangement was suggested to him months ago by myself but he did not seem to take to it at all.[65]

In October, Byrne was declared bankrupt and the board was forced to dismiss him, O'Donovan taking his place as editor.[66] At the dinner on 12 December 1897 to celebrate the birthday of the *Independent* company, Redmond said he believed that the papers had 'done something to elevate Irish journalism' and that

> whether their Parliamentary party failed or disappeared, there would be a great future and a great work for these papers . . . There was, under the present conditions, room for two Nationalist journals in Dublin, and if they got Home Rule there would not only be room for them but there would be a necessity for them . . . above all, for a journal such as theirs . . . to hold up the banner of civil and religious liberty and give voice to the views of a large body of Catholic opinion in this country.[67]

He did not deny that they had 'to some extent, been recently hampered', but gave an implausible victim-of-its-own-success explanation for this: 'the fact that our increased business, our increased circulation, and increased advertisement connection have made it difficult with the machinery at our command to produce a paper such as we would wish'.[68]

Redmond took no immediate action on Baker's criticisms of Allan's managerial style. Only seven months later, when Allan wrote to say that he had learned of suggestions made to the board that he was neglecting his work at the paper for the sake of the '98 movement, did Redmond communicate the substance of the memorandum. Allan wrote back on 18 February 1898 that he was 'very sorry indeed to learn, for the first time, that the directors think there is "looseness somewhere in the business part of the concern"'. If they thought this, he said, it was their duty to go fully into it; they would find that the company 'was never running more smoothly or more economically', and something else must be responsible for the undisputed fact that 'circulations are dribbling away'.[69] By this time, Baker was writing to Redmond with greater urgency of tone than ever. On 9 March he told him that the situation was one 'demanding immediate action if the concern is to be rescued from a condition of things which can only have the one end'. He begged Redmond to look in London for 'a first class *Newspaper* man (not a journalist)' and place him in supreme authority over the papers. The longer delayed the necessary changes, he said, the more thorough they would have to be 'when procrastination has reached the full length of the tether'.[70] He wrote six times that month, including three times in one day, informing Redmond of the gravity of the financial situation. The accounts for 1897 showed a loss of £1,143 for the first half, rising to £1,903 for the second.[71] They had been exceeding their overdraft limit for weeks, he said; the bank was now drawing the line and he did not know where that Friday's pay cheques would come from.[72]

Redmond's response was to do finally what Baker had begged him to do the previous year – take over the post of managing director himself. The outcome was hardly the 'salvation' for which Baker had hoped. At the April 1898 AGM, Redmond blandly announced 'steady and continuous progress' and a strategy aimed at spending the company's way out of crisis. It was essential, he said, to enlarge the papers; to do this they would purchase at huge cost the latest 'two-decker' machine, which would give them 'the finest and best printing press in Europe'. The new Goss machine, made to order in Chicago, was duly installed and the first twelve-page issue of the *Daily Independent*, with one page printed in two colours, appeared on 24 August to great fanfare. The paper would now be in a stronger position, said the editorial, to cater for the public as 'an up-to-date, vigorous, enterprising journal', able to increase its size on occasions of pressure. Despite the hubris, however, the twelve-page format did not appear again. After September, it reverted permanently to its original eight-page size.[73]

By October 1898, Baker was involved in negotiations for a takeover with Alfred Harmsworth, the proprietor of the *Daily Mail*. Although Harmsworth was attracted by the idea of buying the company, he told Baker it would be impossible 'to connect ourselves with a paper of such divergent political views as those of the *Independent*'. Instead, he gave him a letter of introduction to another magnate, Keary: '[Baker] has what I consider a very good business proposition to put before you. The papers he represents *can be made to pay at once by good management*. This I am sure of. Only £5,000 is wanted.'[74] Baker was, however, put off any thoughts of a deal with Keary on discovering the latter's links with T. P. O'Connor, telling Redmond that it would be a very serious move 'to give ourselves so completely to our political opponents'.[75]

In January 1899 the search for a buyer ended when the Harmsworth brothers purchased the company. Shortly afterwards, the company was forced to raise fresh capital. A syndicate consisting of debenture shareholders, the biggest being the English Linotype Company, and including Carew (defeated Redmondite candidate in Kildare), the elderly Dublin Parnellite Alderman Meade, and J. Rochfort Maguire, ex-Redmondite M.P. for West Clare (and associate of Cecil Rhodes), bought out the Harmsworths and took over control. The *Daily Nation* crowed that 'English dictation is supreme in the office'. An accountant from Harmsworths had gone over the books and recommended savings of £3,000 a year.[76] The new managing director, J. R. Hosker of Glasgow, began to implement the cuts immediately. The *Daily Independent*'s London correspondent, J. J. O'Kelly, and Allan were the most prominent of those given notice of dismissal. In addition, up to twenty reporters and printers, including some of the hard men suspected by the police of past murders and bomb outrages, were fired. Mallon reported that the discharged men were 'hovering in public houses around Dame St. and Andrews St.' By late February the new management had asked for and been granted police protection for the premises. Mallon estimated that almost 100 persons had been let go, and it was 'not pleasant to have so many ill-conditioned, drunken, idle fellows loafing about'. The *Daily Nation* kept up a daily commentary on these events; Mallon had no doubt that Healy was the author of the articles and his informant was Allan.[77]

The *Daily Nation* asked caustically whether Redmond was not still drawing his managing director's salary of £500 a year (Sexton's was £800 at the *Freeman*). It published a letter from a disgruntled 'Parnellite' remembering that Redmond had assured them two years ago that the company was on the high road to success. He had become managing director, but the liabilities of the company 'spells £7,000 of a loss for his year's management': 'To pay a gentleman £500 a year to spend £7,000 is too much of a practical joke outside an asylum.'[78] Following the formal dismissals at the meeting of shareholders on 2 March, Mallon reported that up to 200 of those laid off and their sympathizers were 'lolling about all day'; he must have been asked to assess the personal risk to Redmond, for he wrote, 'As far we can gather John Redmond is in as much danger of personal violence as anyone in the community.'[79]

Thus ended the period of overt Fenian influence at *Independent* newspapers, although the retention of O'Donovan as editor of the *Daily Independent* ensured that an 'advanced' editorial tone was available when required.[80] In general, however, until the start of the Boer War in late 1899, the paper became less nationalist in tone and carried reports of appeal to the unionist middle classes on military displays, the Horse Show and the lord lieutenant's garden parties, possibly in deference to Redmond's policy of conciliation. The troubles at the newspapers did not end with the new regime. The new manager replacing Allan, H. F. Patterson, was soon in conflict with O'Donovan, who accused him of bossing him (he had said he would 'stand no nonsense from any member of the staff') and appointing a subeditor responsible to himself. Patterson justified his action to Redmond on the grounds that O'Donovan possessed 'neither the training nor the style necessary for giving character and force to an organ such as the *Independent*'. Furthermore, he did not think O'Donovan had 'done his work properly or conscientiously as editor'. Patterson also ran foul of Baker, who told Redmond that 'in his reforming zeal', he was showing indifference to local conditions. Patterson was soon demanding that 'the relative positions of Mr. Baker and myself must be clearly defined and determined . . . Two men cannot drive a coach together.' The matter came to a head in mid-July 1899 when the board decided that supreme editorial control rested with O'Donovan.[81] Two months later Carew took over as managing director, and Patterson seems to have resigned shortly afterwards.[82] The following March, in spite of claims of rapidly rising circulation figures, there were large outstanding debts and a court application for the company to be put in receivership was under way.[83]

IV

Two actions undertaken in the pivotal year 1898, one by Redmond, the other by William O'Brien, had a combined effect that would change radically the political climate and create the conditions in which the long dispute within nationalism could be resolved. The commemoration ceremonies planned for the year offered the potential both for lifting the cloud of apathy sapping nationalist enthusiasm and for sinking party differences on a common platform. One of the first actions aimed at taking advantage of this favourable prospect was the decision, in January, of O'Brien (out of Parliament since 1895), Harrington and six others to set up the United Irishmen's Centennial Association to ensure, as they stated in a letter to the press, that the celebrations would be 'truly National' and would exclude nobody, an implied criticism of the Fenian-dominated Centenary Committee.[84] Such a body could be expected to appeal not just to the broad anti-Parnellite masses but to the 'municipal' right wing of Parnellism.

At the opening of Parliament, Redmond made his own effort to guide the hand of history when he framed an amendment to the Address which reflected the hardening of the demand for self-government adopted by the IIL. Making use of the ambiguous term 'independence', it was extreme enough to make it impossible for the Liberals to support, while sufficiently within the definition of Home Rule to make it difficult for Dillon to oppose. Redmond's speech drew on the '98 legacy to harden his tone further, telling the House of

> the plain truth that Irishmen today hate English rule (*cheers*) . . . the spirit of revolution against that foreign interference in purely Irish affairs is alive in Ireland today . . . with the great bulk of the Irish people themselves at this moment, the question even of an armed insurrection against the system of government, which you insist on maintaining, is a mere question of expediency, and the chance of success (*cheers*).[85]

By driving a wedge between its two partners in this way, Redmond hoped to speed up the slow demise of the Liberal alliance; what the *Independent* called the 'evasions and insincerities' that had saved the appearances of Liberal fidelity to the Home Rule policy in the past would no longer be enough to secure Irish loyalty. In the event, Dillon, although he spoke against the amendment, broke with the Liberals to vote for it.[86] Predictably, the Liberal press was incensed, as was Harrington, who could only see it as a blow struck against, rather than for, unity.[87] The *Saturday Review* commented that 'Mr. Redmond's performance in manoeuvring Sir William Harcourt into a position where he was bound to vote against Home Rule was a triumph of Parliamentary craft.' The verdict of skilled parliamentarians was, it said, that Harcourt's disappearance into the Government lobby marked the 'the close of an epoch that had lasted 12 years'.[88]

At the IIL head branch on 8 March, Redmond defended his amendment. He denied that the demand for an 'independent' Parliament went beyond what Parnell had sought. It had had the useful effect of clearing the air by proving beyond doubt that the Liberals were not prepared to put Home Rule in the front of their programme. The people, he asserted, had long ago had enough of the Union of Hearts, and it was his duty to 'break the idols of clay before which so many Irish representatives bow down in adoration'.[89] The tactic was soon seen to bear further fruit when Dillon voted for an amendment of William Redmond's against the Liberal 'Home Rule All Round' policy, and declared that Ireland could win Home Rule 'without any English party' if the eighty nationalist members were united in Parliament, a move hailed by the *Independent* as a 'complete reversal' of Dillon's whole course of conduct since 1890. The Liberal *Daily News* was grief-stricken as it lamented Dillon's 'amazing folly' in this further defection.[90]

Aware that for the first time he was winning the argument over the Liberal alliance, and boosted by the knowledge that the anti-Parnellite leaders had been prepared to offer him the leadership, Redmond began to face the possibility of his being called upon to assume that role. The evidence for this is the bold strategy on which he now embarked, aimed at forging a broad coalition of diverse groups. In doing so, he made full use of the opportunities offered to him by that year of 1898. His parliamentary engineering of a coming together on Home Rule policy reduced his differences with the nationalist mainstream. On his left flank, the commemoration ceremonies gave him the chance to reinforce the militant message of the IIL. With his long record of lecturing on the insurrection, he held, among constitutionalists, what amounted almost to a copyright on it, at least on its Wexford aspects. On his right, the epoch-making Local Government Bill introduced by Gerald Balfour, which replaced the landlord-dominated grand jury system with a broadly democratic system of local representation, gave him an opportunity to reach out to landlords and other unionists. Such a 'conciliation' démarche was a logical development of the readiness he had shown to work with constructive Unionists in the Recess Committee and on the financial relations question. It demanded a degree of skill to bring these two themes, so disparate and seemingly contradictory in their tendency, into a coherent whole.

Redmond's welcome for the Bill was unstinting and full of awareness of the possibilities that it opened up. At the second reading debate on 21 March, he hailed its positive reception by Unionist M.P.s as 'a change of spirit which I hope will yet bring them completely into line with their fellow-countrymen of all sides in the furtherance of the welfare of our common country'. While the measure was, of course, no substitute for Home Rule, he said, 'I hope I am not alarming honourable gentlemen opposite when I say that I for one welcome the Bill as a step in that direction'. His tone changed when he turned to criticize Dillon's cold reception of the Bill. The latter had – inappropriately for a second reading speech – delivered a detailed clause-by-clause critique, prefaced with a declaration that he would vote in favour. Redmond poked fun at 'the habit into which I am afraid the honourable gentleman is rapidly falling of speaking against a motion and voting for it (*loud laughter*)'. Dillon and Davitt, together with some Radical M.P.s, had focused their animus against the agricultural relief clauses of the Bill, on the grounds that half of the relief grant was to go as a 'ransom' (Dillon's word) to the landlords. To this objection, Redmond replied that the grant was merely equivalent to those which England and Scotland had received since 1896, and, at £150,000 a year, far less than the £750,000 to which Ireland was entitled under the scheme. Turning to Dillon's criticisms, he made plain the rift between the two men on agrarian policy, which had first become apparent during the Plan of Campaign. Although Ireland in the past had suffered grievously from the system of landlordism, which, in its origin and history, was such that nothing but evil could flow from it,

> the hatred of a system by some honourable members from Ireland – they are, I think, very few – seems to have degenerated into a hatred of individuals, but I believe that even at the worst time that was not the general feeling of the bulk of the Irish people. After all, these landlords are Irishmen (*hear, hear*). They are mostly men of education and ability, and while we have waged war against a system I believe the great bulk of the Irish people never at any time desired to drive any class of their fellow-countrymen from the shores of Ireland (*hear, hear*). So far from desiring to ruin them individually I don't hesitate to say that I believe it would be a wise and blessed thing for Ireland to agree to any financial arrangements by which the landlords could transfer their estates to the people . . . [and be enabled] to remain in Ireland and take their proper place among the people. For my part . . . I don't grudge the Irish landlords this paltry £350,000 a year or whatever it may be that they will obtain in relief of their rates under the Bill.[91]

Redmond developed this theme in later speeches. At the IIL head branch on 15 April, he spoke of the upcoming elections for the new county councils, and his hopes for the financial relations agitation. Clearly fearing a swamping of the councils with the type of agrarian radicals who believed that the only relief the landlords deserved was the price of a one-way ticket to Holyhead, he stressed the need for the IIL to do its utmost 'to fight the battle for freedom of thought' in the elections; it would be disastrous for Ireland, he said, if narrow or sectarian ideas were allowed to influence them. Demonstrating that his attachment to the doctrines of Davis was more than one of lip service, he stated his belief in the centrality of the assent of the Anglo-Irish to a Home Rule settlement. The question of whether the movement to remedy the financial grievance would succeed had, for him, always been secondary to the hope that they would be able to show those fellow-countrymen who had 'held aloof from the National movement' in the past that they could not win justice under the Union. Something akin to what had happened in the 1782 movement in the English colony in Ireland was happening among the present generation of Irish unionists; the moment they realized they had been betrayed, they would 'throw in their lot with Ireland'. He continued: 'And let there be no mistake about it, the moment Ireland makes a united demand for self-government you will have a Parliament sitting in Dublin within six months.'[92] Reciprocation of such conciliatory sentiments came on the same day when, at the Conference of Grand Jurors and Peers, The O'Conor Don seconded the motion of the marquis of Londonderry to 'co-operate towards the good government of the country under the proposed new law'. Calling for trust in their fellow-countrymen, 'who would have their elective rights thoroughly', he said that they should not attempt by any indirect means to take from the people the power and the responsibility that the legislation would confer on them.[93]

Meanwhile, the '98 commemorations got under way with a 'monster' meeting in the Phoenix Park on 13 March, organized by the Centenary Committee. John O'Leary was accompanied on the platform by some Parnellite M.P.s and W. B. Yeats. The police were agreeably surprised; Mallon wrote that the meeting came off 'without the slightest unpleasantness . . . if the demeanour of the people be the same at all other meetings of the kind proposed to be held during the current year, there will be nothing to complain of'.[94] O'Brien's association, which had by now attracted INA members into its ranks, held a separate meeting on St Patrick's Day in Dublin. Up to the end of 1897 the police had counted 22 centennial clubs in Dublin City and 137 in the provinces, with a total membership of 11,395. By mid-May the corresponding figures were 28 and 283, with a total of about 30,000 members.[95] These local associations were affiliated to one or other of the rival national commemoration bodies. A conference in Dublin on 23 April chaired by John O'Leary succeeded in overcoming all controversies and amalgamating the two into a single organization.[96] A week later came the news that the planned 'pilgrimage' of Irish-Americans to Ireland had been called off, due to the outbreak of war between the US and Spain over Cuba. The intending visitors felt it their prior duty to make themselves available for military service at home.[97] This was no doubt welcome news to the police, but it may also have averted a threat to the newly won unity of the commemoration bodies. The presence of large numbers of Irish-American extremists at the '98 ceremonies could only have generated fresh controversies.

Nationalist opinion was divided on the Spanish–American war, with most Redmondites and Fenians enthusiastic in their support for the US, while clericalist Healyites hoped for a victory for Catholic Spain and Dillonites wavered. Redmond received a letter of thanks from President William McKinley in March for his message of condolence sent 'on behalf of the Irish people' for the loss of 255 lives in the explosion on the warship *USS Maine*, the event that triggered the war when an investigation attributed it to Spanish forces.[98] Redmond's new Parnellite ally in the US, John O'Callaghan, the publisher of the *Boston Globe*, made use of reported pro-Spanish statements by O'Brien and the *Freeman* to damage the 'Whigs' in America. O'Callaghan wrote to Redmond: 'I have rubbed "We hope Spain will win" in hard . . . [they are] knocked into a cocked hat here, on account of it. It is the worst blow they have got yet.'[99] By contrast, he wrote on 13 May, the attitude of the *Independent* had won friends 'by the thousand' and Redmond's cable of congratulations following the US victory at Manila harbour was 'just in the nick of time'.[100]

Redmond spoke at Wexford on 29 May, where 'this very night 100 years ago our brave forefathers rose against intolerable oppression', paying homage to the fighters of the past, while ruling out any return to their methods:

> For now, fellow-countrymen, that times are changed I for one will not tonight here on this peaceful and secure platform talk any cheap sedition, because I regard the man who talks about guns, drums and swords and is not prepared himself to take the lead as a man guilty of dishonourable conduct (*hear, hear*). But I do say that we are here tonight to maintain the tradition of the men of '98 (*cheers*) and let our enemies know that all that is wanted are the means to do [so], and we have the will to follow on the same lines if we saw but a chance of success lighting on our cause.

Every concession that Ireland had won, it had done so 'by the force of the revolutionary idea that stands at the back of the Nationalist movement', and while he believed that the constitutional movement 'may be, and will be in the future, of great value to Ireland', he believed that 'the salt of the public life of Ireland is to be found in the ideals of those men who believed in the ideals of '98'. There was more talk of 'the spirit of undying hatred of English rule' later in the day at Vinegar Hill, where he also denounced the idea of an Anglo-American alliance, from which the US would have nothing to gain.[101]

At the head branch two days later he joined the themes of '98 and local government. Of three conceivable ways to win self-government, he said, two – force of arms and the force of a semi-revolutionary movement such as that created by Parnell, which had never had a fair trial – were ruled out. The county council elections were the first step of a third way, if they were used to bring together 'Irishmen kept asunder in the past', as Davis – whose 'noble lines' he now quoted – had advocated. In the key passage of a speech that would have huge implications for his own political future, he urged:

> Wherever throughout the country a Protestant, an anti-Nationalist, or a landlord, or others who have been opposed to you, come forward with a declaration that they are willing to devote their labours to the service of the country and to the government of local affairs, then I would entreat of the people to think well before they reject that offer, and rather to judge every man upon his merits absolutely, irrespective of his creed or politics.

'If that were done,' he said, and 'so-called religious interference' kept out of the elections, it would be 'the longest step towards Home Rule for a generation'.[102]

The Irish unionist press hailed the speech. The *Daily Express* expressed appreciation of 'the truly patriotic and statesmanlike spirit in which it is conceived'. His words '"Wherever a Protestant . . .",' it wrote, 'deserve to be blazoned far and wide in Ireland'. If the new voters acted in that spirit, they would be met in corresponding spirit by the classes who had formerly held the power in county government. The *Irish Times* called Redmond's advice 'good and generous' and his position 'more worthy of Ireland' than Dillon's, although it appeared to misinterpret the speech as giving the unionist minority a veto on Home Rule.[103] Not all were so impressed. The *Freeman* was predictably scornful, calling Redmond a 'Tory in disguise'.[104] Harrington saw in it a departure from Parnellism into 'a cross between Irish Toryism and sham advanced Nationalism', forgetting that Parnellism itself was arguably a similar hybrid.[105] There were some meeting points between the two apparent extremes: O'Leary's 'pure' brand of Fenianism shared the landlords' distaste for and fear of agrarian agitation (O'Leary was himself a landlord). Nevertheless, Redmond's attempt to construct an alliance between constructive unionism and 'advanced' nationalism is indeed reminiscent of the prototype flying machines being invented and tested at that time, ungainly objects, all wing and little fuselage, which flew a few yards before crashing to the ground. Would Redmond's creation fly?

Only a month later the policy was under test on Dublin Corporation, where some Parnellite members had entered into a pact with the Unionists to elect the widely respected Sir Robert Sexton as the next lord mayor. The *Independent* was loud in its objections: allowing a fair representation of the minority on the new Councils was 'a very different thing from handing over . . . the chief municipal office in the country to the most prominent Unionist in the capital, while the battle for national self-government is still being fought'.[106] Controversy ensued, in which Harrington alleged that two years previously, in Dr Kenny's hearing, Redmond had supported the idea of Sexton as lord mayor.[107] On 13 September, Redmond was forced to clarify the limits of the 'toleration policy'. The Corporation would for the first time become a truly representative body, he said, its powers and dignity enormously increased, and the mayoralty must therefore be bestowed on one who would represent the national sentiment of the people. Unionists had made very fair promises about forgiving and forgetting, and if they held to these, and 'if they cease to be West Britons and declare themselves to be Irishmen (*applause*) why they will find that there will be no honour too great for the Irish people to bestow on them'.[108]

The commemoration ceremonies continued apace with meetings held all over the country. The Centenary Committee completed arrangements in June to erect a memorial to Wolfe Tone at St Stephen's Green, and shortly afterwards opened a public fund to finance the project. At the launch of the fund, Dillon and the Belfast anti-Parnellite Joe Devlin spoke alongside Parnellite M.P.s and were joined by Maud Gonne.[109] The year's commemorative events culminated in the laying of the foundation stone of the memorial on 15 August, with a huge procession including M.P.s of all factions, which wound its way from O'Connell Street to the Green, the Nationalist members of the Corporation attending in their robes. Also on the platform were William Rooney of the Gaelic League, reflecting the increased politicization of that body, and W. B. Yeats. Keynote speeches were delivered by Redmond, Dillon and O'Leary. The *Independent* praised the Unionist employers of the city, whose toleration 'and even appreciativeness' had made the day a holiday.

Redmond's oration at the event was noticeably lacking in the force that might have been expected from one with such impeccable '98 credentials. He was clearly uncomfortable on a platform assembled to pay homage to the most prominent of the insurrection's revolutionary leaders – references to Tone were rare in his oratory before and after 1898 – rather than to the nameless masses who had perished in it. The gestures he made to Fenian sentiment were thus both hyperbolic and unconvincing. Departing from his usual depiction of 1798 as the rising of a population goaded beyond endurance, he suggested that the movement was more than that: it was 'rather . . . the result of a deliberately, cautiously and ably planned effort to achieve National liberty (*cheers*) . . . the purest movement for liberty that illumines the annals of any country since the world began'.[110] The conflict with his oft-stated position that Pitt's Government had provoked the insurrection to give it an excuse to abolish the semi-autonomous Grattan's parliament was obvious. Worse, his extolling of a movement that had aimed at sweeping away that Parliament would scarcely appeal to those unionist fellow-Irishmen who, if they were ever to come over to the Home Rule camp, would only do so as the heirs of Grattan. The remarks he addressed to the foreign 'allies' who would rally to the cause – 'if ever the day should come – and which of us would not be glad to see it, when in the complications of the world Ireland would once again have an opportunity of striking a blow for liberty' – would one day seem suffused with irony.[111] For the moment, as if to give pause to those who hankered after a re-enactment of 1798, there came the news from Omdurman in the Sudan, where the small force of Sir Herbert Kitchener had demonstrated the efficacy of the Maxim gun by slaughtering 20,000 of the Mahdist army for a loss of 48 British and Egyptian soldiers.[112]

Following the August climax of remembrance, Redmond was impatient to redirect attention to the constitutional movement. No one who had honoured Tone, he said at the IIL head branch on 13 September, could fail to honour the memory of Parnell, who had fought 'in altered times . . . with altered weapons'. For the first time he talked of a national memorial to the dead chief, expressing the hope that a future anniversary would see the laying of its foundation stone.[113] Some of his hearers were quick to see that such a project, given the limited resources available, could only damage the prospects of the Tone monument fund. Even more pointed was his delivery of a lecture entitled 'From Swift to Parnell: Four Great Leaders of Irish Public Opinion' at the Antient Concert Rooms in October.[114] Although he took care to preface it with the remark that 'no survey of the principal leaders could be considered complete which omitted Wolfe Tone and the other leaders of movements founded on force', his choice of three great Protestant Irishmen, Swift, Grattan and Parnell – the fourth was O'Connell – showed his continued concern to appeal to the more open-minded Irish unionists. This lecture was no once-off academic venture: it became the focus of a national campaign as Redmond toured the country, delivering it in Cork and at least six other urban centres.

At the Parnell anniversary convention on 10 October, he returned to the impending revolution in local government. The main stumbling block to self-government, he said, was the division of the country into two opposed camps on the issue. Overcoming that division had been the ideal of Davis and of Butt. The latter had been succeeding until the land question had intervened, driving the landlords away. That question had now, he asserted, been more or less removed by successive Land Acts. He asked:

> Is there a possibility, however small, in the near future of obtaining through the instrumentality of these county councils a return to the ranks of Ireland of any men whose forefathers stood with Grattan

> one hundred years ago, but who since that day, for one reason or another, stood aloof from the Nationalist movement? . . . Ah, I say to you, if there is but the remotest chance it would be criminal folly on our side to cast it aside (*applause*).

He criticized O'Brien's recent speech in the West, which seemed to suggest that the best way to work the county councils for Home Rule was to run the elections on the narrowest sectional lines, disregarding the competence and fitness of candidates. (O'Brien had recently promised to 'make these 32 parliaments more obnoxious to the English garrison than any National parliament could possibly be'.) This was a 'mischievous' policy guaranteed to ensure the failure of the councils and prove that the Irish were incapable of ruling themselves. A case in point was that of The O'Conor Don, who had been driven from public life because he refused to stand as a Home Ruler. But he was a capable administrator, said Redmond, who had done 'incalculable service' to the country on the financial relations issue and was eminently qualified to serve on a county council. The O'Brien policy, which would have him shunned, was a disastrous one. The proper way to proceed was to insist on nationalist majorities wherever possible, but subject to that, to seek 'the best, the most qualified, the best fitted men' and welcome them into the ranks.[115]

At the Trinity College Philosophical Society in November, he spoke in Burkean tones on 'The Democratic Tendencies of the Age'. He told the audience that the Local Government Act gave a great opportunity to 'the well-to-do and cultured classes': if they came forward as patriotic Irishmen, they would get a welcome and a place in public life. If they failed to do so, they would have only themselves to blame if they were swamped by 'the rising tide of Irish democracy'. The mostly unionist students responded warmly, carrying Redmond on their shoulders across College Green to the old parliament building, where he addressed the crowd from an improvised rostrum. From there they chaired him to Jury's hotel for the society's banquet.[116]

In making such overtures to the class that was about to lose the power in the counties it had held for two centuries, Redmond was a lone voice among leaders of nationalist opinion. It is not known whom he consulted within his own party, but that rural supporters, at least, were unenthusiastic was signalled by the appearance in September of Roscommon's two leading Parnellites on a platform with O'Brien, active again in agrarian agitation in the west of Ireland. More vocal opposition would surface in the party in the following year, kindled by Redmond's premature announcement of the end of the land question.

The day before Redmond spoke of Davis at the Parnell convention, Dillon chose Glasgow as the venue to launch a fresh initiative on the unity issue by proposing a small conference with the Parnellites. Redmond's reply was predictable: as soon as Dillon and his colleagues broke with the Liberal alliance, and Dillon and Healy composed their differences, and if they proposed terms that were 'honourable and safe', he and his followers would not stand in the way of reunion. He claimed that the '98 celebrations had done something to bring the people together on Parnellite principles, a unity that he saw as the only basis for party reunion. It seemed as if the new climate of goodwill among nationalists presaged an end at last to the eight-year-old split. But the space that was now opening for a move to reunion presented Redmond with a dilemma: how long could he pursue his overtures to the Anglo-Irish tradition, a policy that evoked little sympathy from fellow-nationalists, even within his own party, if he were to involve himself in conciliation moves with those same fellow-nationalists? The day might not be far off when he would have to choose between two contrary forms of conciliation.

Redmond's efforts to escape the tight situation in which he found himself after 1895, and to build a new coalition around a broad and generous definition of Irish nationality, prompt a questioning of recent assessments of the man. Matthew Kelly writes of Redmond 'clearly lacking the charisma, political instinct and daring of his predecessor [Parnell]'.[117] Whatever about charisma (and Parnell's was unique), Redmond's actions were those of a resourceful politician who constantly probed the limits of what was possible in the conditions of his day. Whether viewed as an expedient of sheer survival or as a noble venture to lead his country in more positive directions, they called for audacity and nerve. And in their most successful manifestation, his relentless attempt to prise the majority party from the Liberal embrace, they displayed political abilities of a high order.

Redmond's links with the Fenians throughout the 1890s likewise call for a re-examination of Michael Laffan's claim that 'he had no taste or talent for appealing to the hillside men'.[118] If the latter term is taken to mean 'agrarian agitators', the claim is certainly true; if it is understood in its more usual sense of 'physical force men', it is not. Laffan quotes Oliver MacDonagh's contrast between Parnell and Redmond: 'Parnell first outmanoeuvred, then tamed and deployed the forces of violence; Redmond first underestimated them, then allowed them to seize the initiative.'[119] The second half of the statement has validity when applied to the period after 1907 when the IRB reorganized; it has none for the decade of the split. Ironically, it may have been Redmond's very closeness to the Fenians during the '90s, when their weaknesses were most apparent to him, which led to his complacency about them after 1907, when his contacts with them had ended. In the earlier decade, he simply continued Parnell's policy of neutralizing, or co-opting for constitutional action, the energies of the men of violence, using the amnesty movement as well as all the formidable powers of his rhetoric in and out of Parliament. He did this for about as long as Parnell had done, if the latter's quiescence between 1886 and 1890, while he nurtured the Liberal alliance, is taken into account. Whether either man 'outmanoeuvred' the Fenians, in the sense of diverting them from an insurrectionary course on which they might otherwise have embarked, is open to question. We cannot know what the Fenians might have attempted, at key junctures such as the aftermaths of the failures of 1886 and 1893, if constitutional leaders had not redirected nationalist anger. Did either Parnell or Redmond perform a great national service by saving Ireland from a bloody uprising during those decades? It is possible, but there were enough other forces, whether Government repression, internal disunity, or the nature of Fenianism itself, which were well capable of immobilizing the movement.

12 Stumbling towards Unity

> . . . he was beyond comparison the best fitted of his Parliamentary co-religionaries for the great duty devolving upon the leader of the new united party.
>
> William O'Brien, 1910[1]

> . . . it should be clearly understood that after the verdict of the people in these elections no party can exist in future which tolerates within its ranks any action which interferes with its unity and efficiency either in or out of Parliament, or tends to lower or degrade it in the eyes of the world.
>
> Redmond in letter to press following general election, October 1900[2]

I

The 1898 commemorations, helped by the waning of bitterness with the passage of time, had intensified the public mood favourable to reunion. Although this mood accorded with his natural inclination to reconciliation, Redmond had set down preconditions of policy which must be met before he could yield to it. As we have seen, he had already taken Parliamentary action to bring about the fulfilment of some of these preconditions. Now others would act in their own ways to increase the momentum towards a resolution.

The organization founded by O'Brien at the meeting in Westport on 23 January 1898 had broader purposes than the centennial commemoration. Its immediate aim was to revive a popular agitation against local land-grabbers and for the redistribution of the large depopulated tracts of grazing land in the interests of the poorer tenants of the west of Ireland. But O'Brien also saw the new movement, which he now called the United Irish League (UIL), as having national political potential: it would inject new life into the languishing grass-roots nationalist movement by appealing, as he hoped, to rank and file nationalists of all factions. His overriding purpose was, in short, to bypass the leaderships of the divided parliamentary groups and bring about a practical reunion from the bottom upwards.[3]

O'Brien told Dillon that he had come to the conclusion 'that the party can only be saved or united from the outside – that is to say by creating a healthy public organisation which at the right time would be in a position to cope with parliamentary mutineers and cranks'.[4] Despite his public professions that the UIL would stand equidistant from all sections, it is clear from his comments to Dillon that he had far more confidence in the latter than in either Redmond or Healy, whom he lumped together as equal obstacles in the path of unity. Much of the correspondence between O'Brien and Dillon in 1898 centred on the – unsuccessful – efforts of the former to attract the latter into a closer involvement with the organization of the UIL. His idea, O'Brien wrote, was 'to attract the rank and file of the Parnellites and Healyites . . . to a fight under a common flag, and to put their leaders in the dilemma either that they must join in or efface themselves.' If Dillon had seen his way to throw himself into the new movement, as he had done in the Plan of Campaign, 'Redmond and Healy would have been left without any platform, or anybody to attend to them'. And he was utterly opposed to Dillon's October 1898 offer of a peace conference:

> I thought we were all fully agreed that in the temper of Healy, Redmond and their followers, it was hopeless to look for unity by any conference within the party . . . [and] that unity could only come gradually by the formation of an outside public opinion which a general election alone could enable to enforce its will.[5]

The fact that Redmond, unlike O'Brien and Healy, wrote no memoir of the period of the split, combined with the understandable desire, in its aftermath, of all sides to forget, has left an imbalance in the subjective historical record and meant that the case for 1890s 'Redmondism' has never been put. The portrayal in the anti-Parnellite press, and in O'Brien's later memoir *An Olive Branch in Ireland*, of Redmond as an incorrigible enemy of unity has been accepted too uncritically by subsequent writers on the period, who have tended to write from the points of view of either O'Brien or Dillon. For example, Philip Bull cites a speech by Redmond in Cork in February 1898 as expressing 'unrelenting hostility towards reunion',[6] a judgement that cannot be reconciled with the latter's repeated statements of (conditional) support for reunion or with his encouragement of parliamentary co-operation and joint action with anti-Parnellites. In the Cork speech, Redmond set out the reasons why unity with the majority was not possible under present circumstances: the anti-Parnellites were 'like a dismantled ship' with no rudder and no captain (other than a nominal one), while the first and second mates had parties of their own; the ship was drifting and the captain was looking out for a rescue party. If there was hostility in the speech, it was a response to the comments of Dillon and the *Freeman* on his recent 1798 lecture in New York:

> They have not hesitated to attribute the lowest and the basest kind of motives to me as animating me on my trip to America . . . [it] strikes me as rather a curious and rather a stupid attitude to adopt on the part of a man who is posing at this moment as the great apostle of unity and conciliation in Ireland.[7]

The demoralized state of the majority party was no invention of Redmond's. Dillon was writing to O'Brien in mid-1898 that he was 'very sorry to say that an increasing number [of members] are prepared to throw themselves into oceans of whiskey and into nothing else', naming five M.P.s whose drunken behaviour had shocked him.[8] Even before that he had made up his mind to resign the chair when the year's session came to an end. Although he told O'Brien in April that he would do so to facilitate reunion and would suggest 'that a general convention should be called by some non-partisan body, and that at that convention the means of restoring union should be considered', he pointed out that this was not the course of action he would have chosen unless forced to do so by the 'inexorable logic of circumstances'. The decision that it was pointless to launch a parliamentary fund appeal for that year, the collapse of the National Federation, the persistent advice of his colleague Blake, all were factors that had 'forced on me the conclusion that I am not bound to continue labouring in what has become a hopeless position'.[9] Dillon's despondency regarding the failures of his own leadership seemed to paralyse his will. To the frustration of the more imaginative O'Brien, he was incapable of embracing wholeheartedly the UIL, which offered, in its founder's view, the prospect of 'fifteen or twenty young fellows, divorced from all the bitterness and failure of the last few years, springing up to infuse new blood into the party and stand no nonsense in the way of mutiny'.[10]

By the date of Dillon's Glasgow initiative, O'Brien's programme was showing results. The UIL had begun to spread beyond Mayo; more significantly, it was attracting the support of grass-roots Parnellites as well as federation members. In mid-August local Parnellites listened to O'Brien speak at the first UIL meeting in County Clare. The following month, O'Brien was joined on the platform at Elphin by two leading Roscommon Parnellites, the M.P. J. P. Hayden and John Fitzgibbon, who had already founded a local branch of the league.[11] The excitable O'Brien proceeded to endanger the whole project by cabling US supporters that the two Parnellites 'have united heartily with myself in insisting that there shall be no more dissension. Thank God!' The *Independent*, which had so far reported the UIL meetings neutrally, commented that O'Brien 'belongs to the hysterical order of politicians, and few people take him seriously nowadays'.[12] Hayden and Fitzgibbon felt compelled to tell the Parnellite convention that they had been misrepresented. By mid-October, however, O'Brien had retracted and the *Independent* could say that 'he now defines the participation of Parnellites in the United Irish League movement in terms to which no exception can reasonably be taken'.[13]

As with Redmond's supposed hostility to reunion, historians have taken at face value the anti-Parnellite propaganda that the growth of the UIL and its attraction of rural Parnellites left him by late 1898 in an increasingly isolated position. This was certainly the hope of his opponents, as is shown by Davitt's letter to O'Brien on 28 September: 'Their [Hayden's and Fitzgibbon's] adhesion to the movement of the UIL will mean the end of the split and the elimination of Shoneen [a derogatory term for a Catholic unionist] Redmond. The proposed meeting in Castlerea will rivet the attention of every honest Parnellite in Ireland.'[14] There is no doubt that a number of local Parnellite activists left the party to become full-time UIL officials. Yet there is no overt evidence that Redmond saw these developments as a threat to his own position or that of his party. The Castlerea meeting on 30 October heard speeches on the agrarian issue not only from the two Roscommon Parnellites but from the veteran Parnellite Pierce Mahony and most significantly of all from William Redmond, whether in attendance on his own initiative or to report back to his brother, we do not know.[15] Two weeks later the *Independent* hailed the 'very successful' UIL demonstration in Galway, at which the Dublin Parnellite M.P. William Field had joined O'Brien and Dillon, and a local Parnellite band had played.[16] Thus, as Redmond prepared to launch his nationwide lecture tour to pay homage to the ghost of Davis, his own paper was showing a relaxed, even affirmative, approach to the growth of the new movement. He told an interviewer from the *Pall Mall Gazette* at the end of the year, when asked if there was a prospect of a new land war:

> Land war! There will be no land war. No League or organisation could bring it about. I know there is a movement in the West to divide the grazing lands in order to relieve periodical distress. The principle has been accepted by Mr. Balfour in his speeches and by the Congested Districts Board. It was part of Mr. Parnell's programme. It is a most admirable object.[17]

However, pressure was building on him to respond more actively to Dillon's offer of a unity conference. Local bodies around the country passed resolutions in support of the idea, and in November the Parnellite chairman of the Limerick Board of Guardians, John McInerney, wrote to Redmond enclosing such a resolution. The *Independent* described it as 'vague, admirable in spirit' but added that the board's proposal of a plenary gathering of all nationalist M.P.s would surely result in a re-enactment of the scenes of Committee Room 15.[18] Redmond replied to McInerney by relaying a suggestion he had received from Patrick White, a prominent Parnellite, for a small conference consisting of five representatives from each of the three factions. He (Redmond) had agreed to this, but was now told by White that Dillon had turned down the idea, as he was unwilling to recognize the Healyites as a separate faction. Since any reunion that would pit Parnellites and Dillonites together against Healyites would only 'recommence the squalid personal conflicts' of the past, Redmond felt bound to decline to enter talks until either Dillon could speak for the Healy section, or the latter was represented separately.[19]

Redmond's insistence on separate recognition for the Healy faction showed a striking capacity to elevate political above personal considerations. Few, if any, of the split's protagonists had less reason than he to show magnanimity to Healy. On the other hand, Healy had moved closer to his own political position, being critical of the failures of the Liberal alliance and more inclined than Dillon to welcome the reforming legislation of the Tories; his separate inclusion would strengthen the prospects for a reunion based on the principle of independent opposition. Redmond told his IIL head branch on 6 December of the 'wise and statesmanlike' declaration of Archbishop Walsh, who had spoken of the folly of seeking to make peace between only two of the three sections. He did not care about the exact numbers or proportions making up a small conference, he said, as long as all sides were represented.

II

The interwoven themes of reunion, the growth of the UIL, the local government elections and Redmond's policy of 'toleration' towards unionists continued to dominate Irish politics in the early part of 1899. O'Brien's hope of attracting Parnellites away from Redmond bore limited fruit in January when J. J. O'Kelly, M.P. for North Roscommon, broke a long silence to dissent in the most public and vehement way possible from the policy of toleration. O'Kelly had more than a political motivation, however, since, as noted earlier, his long and leisurely tenure of the post of London correspondent of the *Independent* was being brought to a close by the cost-cutting measures implemented that year at the paper.[20] At a mainly Parnellite meeting at Elphin on 23 January to prepare for the coming elections, he (in language typifying the acceptance by many nationalists of contemporary notions of racial superiority)

> called upon the manhood of North Roscommon to stand to their guns and to vote for no man in these elections who had not a record of patriotism behind him (*cheers*) . . . Some people were advising them to vote for landlordism and landlords' agents (*cries of 'never'*). He could tell them that if they did so they would sacrifice everything that was won for Ireland in the struggle of the last twenty years. The landlords were trying to regain their position in the country, and they were trying to do it in two ways. First of all, they were preaching toleration. What toleration did the landlords show them or their fathers? He was old enough to remember the famine graves of '47 and '48 . . . his advice to the people was not to elect one of these men on any pretext whatsoever (*cheers*) . . . When the South Carolina niggers were set free they had sense enough to elect men of their own class. He did not want to insult them by comparing them with niggers, but he would say that if the men of Roscommon were going to cast their votes for landlordism in the coming elections, they would be worse than the South Carolina niggers (*cheers*).

There was more in the same vein soon afterwards at Strokestown, with pointed references to 'some men' who had been advising the people 'to put some landlords back'.[21]

Redmond continued to push toleration in small and large ways. In January he launched a subscription fund for the family of the late Reverend R. R. Kane, who, though

> a strong opponent of many of our religious and political principles . . . was an honest and manly opponent, and was a brother Irishman . . . I sincerely hope the day is not far distant when the growth of a better feeling between North and South, between Catholic and Protestant, may lead to a really united Ireland.[22]

The test case of the policy was the candidature of The O'Conor Don for a seat on the Roscommon County Council. The *Freeman*, along with O'Brien, Dillon and Davitt, kept up a continuous fire against him (O'Brien calling him 'neither fish nor flesh, nor even a good Redmondite herring').[23] The *Independent* accused O'Brien of going beyond the 'proper' – agrarian – objects of the UIL to use it as 'an electioneering machine pure and simple' in defiance of the understanding reached with Parnellite leaders in the West. The *Freeman* two months earlier had claimed that the league 'has done much to crush the Redmondite programme and policy'.[24] However, John Fitzgibbon, in spite of his early support for the UIL, threw his weight behind The O'Conor Don, condemning the other side's 'policy of the sweeping brush against those who happened to differ from them in either religion or politics'; he for his part would hold to his own and his leader's 'more broad-minded and tolerant views'.[25] The election result on 10 April returned The O'Conor Don by a margin of 489 votes to 192; in Limerick Lords Dunraven and Monteagle were elected at the head of the poll; in other parts of the country a sprinkling of landlords and peers achieved places in the democratic ranks.[26]

Whether an indication that deference was not yet dead in the Irish countryside, or, more likely, that the argument of Redmond, that it would be foolish to waste the administrative talents and abilities of these men, had struck a chord, it was clear that the electors were exercising their own judgement. The *Independent* hailed the results as a vindication of the policy of toleration against that of the 'Mad Mullah of the West'.[27] But in an angry letter to the *Freeman* entitled 'The Toleration Humbug', Davitt warned the new councils against co-opting anyone to their ranks except 'Nationalists and Democrats', remarking that 'it is a Celtic tendency to be too gracious towards defeated foes before they have surrendered their arms'.[28] Despite this advice, the Wexford County Council two weeks later co-opted two Unionists, Lord Fitzgerald and Captain Bryan.[29] That the election results enhanced Redmond's status among prominent nationalists abroad was shown by the endorsement of the veteran Newcastle upon Tyne Home Rule M.P. Joseph Cowen in May and that of John Devoy in July.[30]

With the release of the last of the dynamite prisoners in March (and the last Invincibles in June), the Amnesty Association was able to wind up its affairs.[31] The benign mood intensified in the summer: the *Independent* detected a new spirit in unionism after the *Evening Mail* and two Belfast papers condemned rioting that took place on 5 June when O'Brien brought the UIL to the northern city. The loyalist firebrand, William Johnston, M.P., and the Orange Order chief called off a counter-demonstration. The Redmondite organ felt it a 'double pity' that O'Brien had left Mayo and carried his agitation into Belfast: were not Leinster, Munster, Connacht and the nationalist parts of Ulster wide enough for his statesmanship?[32] The conciliation contagion even touched nationalist commentary on the Ulster 12 July Orange celebrations. The *Independent* wrote that although the demonstrations still had 'elements of the ridiculous', a new spirit was evident in

> the tolerant tone of a great number of the speeches, so far as the Catholic countrymen of the Orangemen are concerned. The bitterness of times not so far distant has distinctly toned down . . . which is distinctly encouraging to the hopes of those who wish to see Ireland progressing on those lines of true union of which Thomas Davis was the most illustrious exemplar and in some sense prophet.[33]

III

While the quiet revolution in local government went ahead in early 1899, moves continued to heal the split. Dillon had now withdrawn his original proposal for a small conference and given his backing to the Limerick resolution, rejected by Redmond as unworkable. The stalemate was broken when, on 7 February, just before Parliament reconvened, Dillon carried out his long-held intention to resign the chair of the majority party. The following week the Redmondites met and authorized their secretary, Pat O'Brien, to write to Sir Thomas Grattan Esmonde, the acting chairman of the anti-Parnellites, with a view to opening negotiations.[34] It was six weeks before they received a reply. A letter from Dillon in the press explained the long delay, which involved the illness of Esmonde and the time needed to convene the anti-Parnellite members.[35] The reply stood by the Limerick requirement that the basis for unity must be worked out at a full conference of all M.P.s, and gave the Redmondites three days' notice of the convening of this conference, to be held on 4 April. As the delegates gathered, a letter from Pat O'Brien appeared in the press explaining his party's refusal to attend. No longer rejecting a full conference as such, they merely asked for 'an interchange of opinion' between representatives of the different sides 'to ascertain whether any basis of agreement can be arrived at', as a preliminary to a full unity conference.[36] Apart from Harrington, who presided, only O'Kelly broke party ranks to attend the conference, which included fifty-three of both sections of anti-Parnellites.

At the conference, Esmonde, seconded by Healy, favoured granting the Redmondite demand for a preliminary meeting of committees of both parties to discuss the terms of reunion. Dillon and the majority opposed this, suggesting instead that a general conference be first convened, from which difficult matters relating to any scheme of reunion could be referred to a smaller body comprising representatives of each party. Dillon then outlined a five-point programme, which F. S. L. Lyons has described as 'scarcely distinguishable from that adopted by the Parnellites at the general election of 1892'. It advocated that the reunited party should be based on the principles and constitution of the original Parnellite party of the 1885–90 period, that it should be 'absolutely independent of all English political parties', that its main objective should be a measure of Home Rule as ample as those of 1886 and 1893 and that it should fight for redress of all Irish grievances, including those relating to the land, labour, taxation and education questions. The conference adopted this without dissent, and went on to accept Dillon's generous suggestion that a Parnellite be elected chairman of the reunited party. 'Past public service and capacity for future public service, absolutely irrespective of the course any adherent may have felt it his duty to take at or since the division of 1890' were to be the sole criteria for membership.[37]

Despite the lack of courtesy shown to them in regard to the convening of the conference, this was a programme that could hardly be rejected by any reasonable Redmondite. But how could the conference find a way to allow the absent Redmondites to engage with the majority without loss of face? Agreement could not be reached on the appointment of a committee to meet them, and the conference settled for an invitation to the Redmondites to reconsider their position and attend a further general conference.[38] This the latter declined, holding out for substantive negotiations to take place at a small conference representative of all sections.[39] Stalemate returned, the one difference being that a major advance had been made in laying down a policy blueprint for a reunited party.

On 1 May the nationalist press published a letter from the veteran Young Irelander and ex-premier of New South Wales, now living in Nice, Sir Charles Gavan Duffy, which hailed the results at the local government polls, including the success of the toleration policy. On the reunion issue, Duffy believed that the quarrel could be settled, but that the recent proposals for a general conference had failed because 'a crowd cannot negotiate'. It needed just 'three Irishmen' to meet to reach an agreement.[40] The *Independent* took up the theme a few weeks later when it launched a poll entitled 'Wanted: 3 Men in Ireland'. Readers were invited to enter on a coupon the names of the three men considered to be best fitted to reunite the Irish Party and a £50 cash prize was offered for the correct choice and order of names as determined by majority vote. The campaign ran for forty-five days, and the result, perhaps predictably in view of the paper's readership, showed

Redmond in first place. Esmonde was second, well ahead of his fellow-anti-Parnellites Healy, who came in sixth place, Dillon, who was ninth, and O'Brien, fourteenth.[41] The result may have reflected in part the growing acceptability of Redmond to the anti-Parnellite electorate in the light of his disengagement from the Fenians, a development made possible by the recent changes at the *Independent* newspapers and the end of the amnesty movement.

A fresh effort to break the impasse was triggered in July by a letter from Father John Fitzpatrick, an Irish priest resident in Nice, to the leaders of the three sections, appealing to them to ask Gavan Duffy to arbitrate between them. Redmond had already made the same suggestion in May, winning immediate assent from Healy but a refusal from Dillon. He now reverted to his original proposal, writing to Dillon and Healy to ask each 'if you would be willing to get your Whips to convene a meeting of your party for the purpose of appointing a small number of representative men to confer with a few of my friends to discuss the basis on which a reunion could be brought about'.[42] Healy's reply was favourable.[43] That of Dillon, however, was again negative. Since he was not now at the head of any party or section, he said, he could only confer in his capacity as an individual. In his judgement, the people, disgusted by past failures, had taken the task of reunion into their own hands, and M.P.s could best promote it 'by co-operating individually with the people' in this task.[44] Redmond's reply to Father Fitzpatrick regretted that Dillon's answer, 'declining both my suggestion and your own, dashes our hopes and leaves things in the same plight as before'.[45]

Dillon's stance implied that he had finally been converted to the O'Brien approach to reunion, a fact that is confirmed by his letter to Davitt in August: 'To me it is quite clear that the time for negotiations has gone by – and that the only safe way in which we can now look for unity is for all to unite without reference to the past on the platform of the United League.'[46] The *Independent* took a more cynical view, claiming that Dillon had backed away from the prospect of unity as soon as it became a real possibility, and that his action had startled and shocked many members of his own party. Redmond probably concurred with the paper's editorial when it said that now 'the game is to boss the country through Mr. O'Brien's organisation, and Mr. Dillon, who treated it coldly for a long time, has evidently fallen in with Mr. O'Brien's plans'.[47] For his part, Dillon was sceptical of Redmond's sincerity, as he confided to Davitt:

> I agree with you that Redmond's continued approaches are a sign that he feels himself in a tight corner. But you will observe that he is getting up an invitation to visit Boston – and whenever he thinks of going to America his game always is to pose as an apostle of unity.[48]

Redmond had been consistent in his approach to unity negotiations since October 1898, whereas Dillon now seemed ready to abandon all notion of reunion brought about by parliamentarians rather than accord separate recognition to Healy's faction.

Although disillusion with the Liberal alliance had become the consensus view of all sections, other political differences during the parliamentary session of 1899 lent an air of unreality to the talk of reunion. There was some co-operation in the House in opposing a Bill to create a monopoly in the Irish railways, and in supporting another to enlarge the boundaries of Dublin city by taking in the affluent, and largely unionist, townships of Pembroke and Rathmines.[49] But the controversies over the toleration policy had sharpened the distrust of Redmond on the part of Dillon and his friends. When Redmond put his Home Rule amendment to the Address for the second consecutive year, he was denounced by the *Freeman*. The Liberals, under their new leader Sir Henry Campbell-Bannerman, voted against it as before, while this time the Dillonites abstained rather than support it, earning the condemnation of the *Independent*.[50] The approach of the majority party to the financial relations agitation remained as lukewarm as ever. Dillon stayed away from the joint meeting of the All-Ireland Committee with peers and M.P.s on 2 February, his disenchantment evident in the *Freeman's* expressed view that the committee had discredited the cause of financial reform by using it as a lever to secure advantages for landlords.[51] At the meeting of the committee in London in March, chaired by Moreton Frewen, a Cork pro-Home Rule landlord, Redmond called for sterner measures than the parliamentary debates, which had failed to move the Government; the Irish M.P.s should oppose every stage of the Budget and every increase of taxation, he said.[52] Two months later, little had happened, and the *Independent* called the neglect of the issue by Irish M.P.s 'simply scandalous'.[53]

The respective responses of Redmond and Dillon to the one major piece of Tory reforming legislation that year were in character. The Agriculture and Industries Bill, which had passed both Houses by August, was the Government's response to the report of the Recess Committee; its centrepiece was the founding of a Department of Agriculture and Technical Instruction. Speaking on the second reading, Redmond welcomed the 'enormous good' that would come from it and paid tribute to its instigator, Sir Horace Plunkett, the convener of the Recess Committee, at the same time ridiculing the notion that the measure would kill the desire for Home Rule.[54] Dillon, though indicating at the start that he would vote for the Bill, greeted it with the same mixture of negative criticism and suspicion of Government motives as he had the 1896 Land Bill and the Local Government legislation, an attitude supported by the *Freeman*, leading the chief secretary to describe him as being 'willing to wound but afraid to strike'.[55]

Underlying the continuing differences was the parliamentary paralysis of nationalism, which expressed itself in the poor attendance of M.P.s of all sections, and which reached its nadir that year. Davitt kept

O'Brien informed of this, deepening the latter's disillusion with the parliamentarians, while the *Freeman*, in a blistering attack, pointed out in May that only 15 of the 82 nationalist M.P.s had been in attendance so far in the session.[56] The level of abstention can be attributed to the continuing plunge in the financial fortunes of the majority party, itself a measure of apathy in the electorate. Lyons has estimated that total receipts in 1898 amounted to £1,800 (of which only £146 was collected at home, and less than £8 in the US) and were scarcely better in 1899 at £2,020. The implications for parliamentary attendance are evident from Lyons's calculation that an M.P. who had been paid a minimum of £200 per annum from party funds to sustain him at Westminster before 1895 could expect to receive at most £90 in 1898 and about £68 the following year.[57]

It was only in July that an issue appeared on the horizon that had the potential to unite all nationalists. Unfortunately, it also had the potential to do serious damage to the harmonious spirit generated by the toleration policy and to undermine any moderate unionist sympathy for Home Rule. This was the crisis in the Transvaal, precipitated by the intervention of the British Government on behalf of the Uitlanders against the Boer republic. The crisis became full-blown warfare in October, by which time pro-Boer demonstrations were taking place on the streets of Irish cities. Redmond had left for the US before news of the first fighting arrived, but was unequivocal in stating in Dublin on 8 October that the sympathies of nationalists would be with 'the gallant little republic of South Africa' and that war, if it came, would be 'an unjust war, a war of aggression and aggrandisement . . . a crime against humanity and human liberty'.[58] When Dillon moved an amendment in the House against the war, William Redmond spoke in support and three days later had himself ejected for protesting against the grant of £10,000 required for the army.[59] On 25 October Davitt announced his intention to resign his seat and walked out of the House in protest. He would shortly leave on a three-month visit to South Africa.

As crowds hungry for war news gathered nightly at Trinity Street outside the *Independent* offices and cheered news of British reverses, posters appeared in nearby Trinity College calling on students 'to discourage the nightly exhibitions of pro-Boer sentiment manifested in Trinity St., SHOW YOUR WORTH – Come in your Thousands and Vindicate the Honour of your Country, for True Patriotism and Loyalty . . . GOD SAVE THE QUEEN'.[60] The old antagonist of nationalists in the Plan of Campaign years, Smith-Barry, now an M.P. for an English constituency, drew his own conclusions: 'In the light of recent events in the Transvaal, and the speeches of leading Irish nationalist members, it was evident that had Home Rule been given to Ireland it would have had to be taken away at a cost of much trouble, money and blood.'[61] A sorrowful response came from the pro-Home Rule Moreton Frewen, as he told William Redmond that he should have asked himself whether his attitude to the war helped or hindered the Home Rule cause: 'I believe that the Home Rule movement, because of the attitude of a group of Irish leaders, has been dislocated and dissipated, and that, having been in full sight of the promised land, we have again to commence our wanderings in the wilderness.'[62] That point had been anticipated by Davitt a month earlier:

> They had been told by some few croaking Nationalists in Ireland and some Liberal papers in England that they imperilled Home Rule because of their warm sympathy for the Transvaal in this trouble. If Home Rule could be killed by sympathy with justice, with liberty and with right, let it die (*hear, hear*).[63]

IV

The surprising *rapprochement* between Redmond and Healy had continued to blossom as the two men met twice during the summer. Healy's friend Arthur O'Connor brought Redmond to meet Healy, who later remembered: 'As if nothing had happened, Redmond's salute was "Hallo, Healy, old boy!" and we shook hands.' Healy wrote to his brother on 1 August: 'I had two interviews with Redmond . . . He is anxious for a settlement, because he sees he will otherwise be wiped out. The "Bounders" [Dillonites], knowing this, are not anxious for unity.'[64] Healy had written in May to Moreton Frewen that he had no ambition to lead a reunited party, but that of the other candidates, most of his friends would prefer Redmond to Dillon. But because of Redmond's record of opposing clerical interference in politics 'the priests would not easily reconcile themselves . . . For myself however I never thought his anticlericalism more than skin-deep.'[65] He remembered that 'I had to conceal from the Dillon party my friendly relations with Redmond, and pretend to be hostile to the projects of reunion. I therefore treated them in a grudging spirit, while at the same time I was caucusing with Redmond and his friends.'[66] In early August he suggested to Redmond a way out of his difficulty. Remembering that the 4 April conference had set up a standing committee to 'receive proposals tending to the restoration of unity', he suggested that Redmond formally put his own proposal, accepted by Healy but not by Dillon, before that body.[67] Redmond took this advice and wrote to the conference secretaries urging the appointment of a small committee, which would meet his 'friends'.[68] To the dismay of Dillon, the secretaries responded by agreeing to summon a new meeting of the conference for 23 November, at which a committee would be chosen.

With reunion for the first time a realistic possibility, Redmond turned aside to the campaign to raise a Parnell memorial in Dublin, which he had foreshadowed the previous year. The Lord Mayor's appeal for funds took care to advance the project as one which could unite all nationalists. Now that the memory of Parnell's last year had come to assume less prominence in the context of Parnell's overall career, and that the essence of the Parnellite case had been conceded by the anti-Parnellites, it was always likely that the project would be non-controversial among mainstream nationalists. The newly elected local bodies all over Ireland were unanimous in support. Opposition came from Dublin Fenian elements who, with a demonstration in the Phoenix Park in August, showed their determination to go ahead with their Wolfe Tone memorial.[69] More surprisingly, although Dillon and Blake had joined the executive of the Parnell memorial committee, the *Freeman* followed O'Brien, suspicious of all moves by the parliamentarians to come together, in also criticizing the idea.[70]

The foundation stone was laid on 8 October amidst scenes of enthusiasm, the *Independent* claimed, 'the like of which has seldom been equalled and rarely, if ever, surpassed' in the capital. Redmond's oration spoke of interpreting the desire of the people 'round the base of his monument, to blot out as far as may be the memory of past dissensions, and the endeavour once more to take up unitedly the great work to which he devoted his life, namely, the achievement of the liberty of Ireland'. A small group of supporters of the Wolfe Tone project staged a counter-demonstration; the *Independent* called it a 'miserable display' of hostility and warned that movement that if it countenanced the smallest attempt to interfere with the success of the Parnell project, a 'grave blow' would be struck at its own prospects.[71] The strength of the paper's language pointed to the continued pulling away of the Redmondite movement from the Fenian alliance as constitutionalist reunion loomed. For Redmond the Parnell memorial was a means of simultaneously vindicating and bidding goodbye to his own stance of the past decade, of slipping off the ties that had bound him to the 'Parnellism' of the 1890s while making the full legacy of Parnell – or a mythologized version of it – the property again of all nationalists. On 12 October he sailed to New York with Daniel Tallon, now lord mayor of Dublin, *en route* to Boston and other north-eastern cities. Their purpose was to raise funds for the twofold object of financing the Parnell monument and buying the Parnell family home and demesne at Avondale. After a six-week tour involving ten public meetings they returned with £6,000, enough to buy Avondale and begin work on the monument.[72] During the visit, Redmond had discussions with a number of American sculptors regarding the design and cost of a statue.[73]

Redmond was in the US when the anti-Parnellite conference met on the appointed day of 23 November. Dillon and most of his associates stayed away, and the meeting was attended by only nineteen, predominantly Healyite, members. With Harrington in the chair, it addressed its task and appointed a six-man committee to negotiate with the Redmondites. Together with Harrington, Healy, Esmonde and Blake, it cleverly chose Dillon as a member, putting him in the awkward position of having to choose between being swept along by what his suspicions told him was a Healy–Redmond axis or else appearing to be an obstacle in the path of unity. The move also acted to prise away some of his own supporters: his close confidant Blake told him that he might feel bound 'however reluctantly' to act on the committee, and Dillon replied that this would be 'a very great misfortune'.[74] As the Redmondite response was awaited, O'Brien, in his *Irish People* organ, preached to the nation that it was now too late for a conference of discredited M.P.s to do any good – the restoration of unity must be left to 'the people'.[75]

Redmond did not return directly to Ireland with Tallon but was reported on 11 December as having continued on to Liverpool *en route* to Paris on private business. His personal life was about to enter a new phase. His eldest daughter Esther was now fifteen, William was thirteen and at Clongowes, and young Johanna was twelve. On 16 December, almost exactly ten years after the death of his first wife, he was married to Ada Beesley of Leamington in a private ceremony at the Servite Fathers church in Fulham.[76] Shortly afterwards the family moved residence from Belvedere Place to Leeson Park on the south side. He cannot have failed to wonder if the symmetry would hold: as Johanna's premature death had not only pitched him into private grief but heralded a decade of political turmoil, did the new marriage portend a return to happiness in the public as well as personal sphere? Stephen Gwynn wrote of Ada's effect on Redmond's well-being:

> His friends found friendship with him easier and not more difficult than before this marriage, and were grateful for the devoted care which was bestowed upon their leader. She accompanied him on all his political journeyings, whatever their duration, and gave him in the fullest measure the companionship which he desired.[77]

The unity ball was now in the Parnellite court, and on 3 January 1900, Redmond's members met and nominated a committee of their own – consisting of Redmond, Hayden and Pat O'Brien – to meet the committee chosen by the November gathering.[78] At long last, on 17 January the two groups met at the Mansion House, though Dillon and Blake were absent, the latter only in deference to the views of the former. The cordial meeting, chaired by Harrington, agreed that the political situation required that all sections be consolidated into a single party, and that the programme adopted at the April conference should be that of the reunited party. It also agreed to invite nationalist members of all sections to meet in London on 30 January, the opening day of the new parliamentary session.[79] Harrington, who had worked harder than anyone else for this moment, wrote to members:

> if I may judge the spirit that will prevail at the forthcoming meeting on the 30th by the excellent feeling of concession and deference for one another's opinions which I have observed . . . the dismal chapter of the last ten years of Irish history will be brought to a speedy and happy end.[80]

The decisive moment had arrived for Dillon and his followers. Blake could no longer bring himself to stay aloof from the process and welcomed the outcome of the 17 January meeting in a letter to the press, thereby placing Dillon in a critical dilemma. O'Brien and the other UIL leaders were thrown into disarray by the sudden prospect of reunion without the clean sweep that they regarded as essential to reform the party. In his view it was 'a thoroughly dishonest attempt, under terror of the popular movement, to tide over the general elections, and befool the country with an utterly unreal mockery of unity which could not last a month after the general elections'.[81] Pressure mounted on Dillon to boycott the 30 January meeting, which Davitt called 'the Healy–Redmond snare'.[82] The *Freeman* mocked 'the pathetic tableau of Mr. John Redmond and Mr. Timothy Healy under the limelight weeping on each other's necks'.[83] But the effect of Blake's desertion was ultimately decisive, as Dillon told T. P. O'Connor, who had warned him against attending:

> If we were to remain away from the meeting on the 30th, what would be our position during the session? Would we not hand over the whole parliamentary position absolutely into the hands of Redmond and Healy? . . . It appears to me that the inevitable and logical consequence of remaining away from the meeting – specially after Blake's letter – would be to abandon attendance in parliament and remain in Ireland. This is of course what O'Brien is working for. But it is a course I am resolved not to take.[84]

O'Connor's advice in reply was that, if Dillon must attend, he should insist that the reunited party adopt the UIL as its organization; if this was not done, he should immediately break with it.[85]

While this flurry of correspondence passed between the anti-Parnellite leaders, Redmond coolly turned his back on political intrigue to deliver a lecture in Dublin on 'Irish Ballad Poetry'. Members of his little party were in the audience as he defended the national poet Thomas Moore against the charge of a lack of national spirit, extolled the poetic virtues of Clarence Mangan and dwelt at length on the writings of Davis, 'the truest, tenderest and bravest of the Young Ireland poets'.[86]

A total of fifty-four M.P.s turned up at Committee Room 15 on 30 January, among them Dillon and some of his followers, and Harrington again took the chair. Dillon attempted to raise the question of the attitude to the UIL, but Harrington ruled it out of order, taking the line that it was best to avoid details that might provoke controversy. When Dillon persisted, it was Blake who ended the argument by stating his view that such matters should be left until after the formal reunion of the party. The motion for this was proposed by Redmond, who 'expressed his desire to avoid all topics of irritation or controversy', and passed unanimously.[87] The following day both newspapers hailed the fact that unity had been achieved, the *Freeman* in somewhat more qualified tones than the *Independent*.

The reunited party met again on 6 February in Committee Room 16 to consider the election of a sessional chairman. According to the April programme, it was already agreed that a Parnellite should be chosen. The obvious candidates were Redmond and Harrington (the latter still generally accepted as coming within the definition of 'Parnellite'). The two men became the centre of a complex web of lobbying carried on by four of their erstwhile adversaries, two of them, Dillon and Healy, present at the election, the other two, O'Brien and Davitt, absent in Ireland but following events closely. Healy was known to back Redmond; on the other hand, Dillon's antipathy to Redmond was sufficiently strong for him to support Harrington. However, both O'Brien and Davitt had been stung by the recent defection of Harrington from the campaign to advance the UIL and his willingness to ignore the league in the push for a party reunion. O'Brien's judgement was that Redmond, having seen something of the power of the league in damaging his own organization, would show a healthy respect for it and would be less likely than Harrington to resist or obstruct its programme. Davitt wrote to Dillon two days before the meeting that

> O'Brien is most strongly for Redmond as chairman as against Harrington . . . [he] looks on Harrington as a treacherous 'friend' of the U.I.L . . . Healy, in desperation intends to down you by supporting Redmond. O'Brien is of opinion that your best plan is to turn the tables on Tim by proposing Redmond for the chair. I offer no opinion against this view. I have no confidence in Redmond, but I have less in Harrington. Undoubtedly, however, the election of Redmond would be more acceptable to the country than that of Harrington.[88]

An hour before the meeting convened, Redmond and his colleagues conferred with Healy, who reckoned that in a full party vote Redmond would be in a minority of five. Just then, a telegram arrived from O'Brien urging his friends to vote for Redmond rather than for Harrington.[89] Dillon reluctantly swallowed his objections to Redmond, whose election was moved by Blake and seconded by Healy. Redmond, at the age of forty-three, was then elected unanimously by the sixty-five M.P.s present, to his own great surprise, as he confided to Gill:'My unanimous election astonished me and especially when I heard William O'Brien had wired strongly to all his henchmen to support me!'[90] O'Brien ten years later wrote that in view of the pledge to elect a Parnellite to the chair, 'it seemed scarcely debatable that their choice must fall upon Mr. Redmond'. Whatever the assessment to be made of his behaviour since Parnell's death,

> he was beyond comparison the best fitted of his Parliamentary co-religionaries for the great duty devolving upon the leader of the new united party and need not fear comparison with any existing Irishman for the dignity with which he would be sure to support a great

> position, the charm of his Parliamentary eloquence or the easy affability which is often the accompaniment of accommodating opinions, but which is perhaps of more practical value in the conduct of a parliamentary party than intense conviction or the gifts for courageous action which electrify nations.[91]

V

Redmond demonstrated some of those 'accommodating opinions' in his first statements as party chairman when he indicated a move away from old stances to positions more representative of the views of the majority of the new party. There would be no further efforts to enlist Unionist co-operation in Parliament on the financial relations question: he told the House on 9 February that, although the sympathy of the Unionists on the issue was on the record, he regretted that they would not follow his party in its new approach, which was to make it 'a troublesome, and if possible, a dangerous question for every English party'.[92] And the party's manifesto published on 12 February asserted that 'the Land question is still unsolved', an explicit reversal of Redmond's 1898 statements that had attracted criticism from the Dillonites. The manifesto leaned even further in the direction of the UIL by adopting compulsory purchase as the only way to establish an 'occupying proprietary'.[93]

However, even amid trenchant criticism of the Government's war policy, Redmond's conciliatory instincts found expression. Speaking in the Address debate on 7 February, he admitted there was truth in the charge that Irish nationalist opposition to the war was motivated by anti-English sentiment, right or wrong. But he insisted that Irish sympathy with and admiration for the two Boer republics was also based on the merits of the issue. Striking an appropriate note for a sceptical audience, he found precedents for his attitude within the British tradition, in the opposition in Parliament of the great Irishman Burke to the war against American independence:

> Go back to the history of that war. Who led the Opposition; who inspired, who planned, who worked through steadfast years in opposition to that luckless war? An Irishman, and in doing so he poured forth a wealth of political wisdom which has been the nourishment of your wiser statesmen ever since, and which if it could be only understood and acted upon by your statesmen of today would induce you even now to retrace your steps . . . Yes, Burke and Sheridan and Grattan and the mighty Irishmen of that day took precisely the same stand in that eventful controversy that we their humbler countrymen take today upon the question of this war . . . In crises like this your best advisers have always been Irish statesmen and Irish soldiers. But you have always distrusted their advice, whether in the case of the present war or in other struggles.

And, though the cause was abhorrent, he had to

> candidly admit that in one sense I cannot but rejoice that so many Irishmen are fighting in this cause . . . I, as an Irishman, cannot help feeling a thrill of pride at the record of the heroism of the Irish lads from Mayo and Roscommon, who have suffered so terribly in this war.[94]

The papers were full of reports of the courage of the Dublin Fusiliers and the Connaught Rangers; Redmond quoted a newspaper estimate of 120 Irishmen killed or wounded to 56 Englishmen so far. On 8 March came the double announcement that the queen, in tribute to 'my brave Irish soldiers', had ordered that in future the shamrock could be worn by all Irish regiments on St Patrick's Day, and that she would shortly visit Ireland. Redmond, on the advice of Healy and Blake, reacted with a short statement that the Irish people would 'receive with gratification' the first announcement as a 'graceful recognition of the valour of their race'. They would, moreover,

> treat with respect the visit which the venerable Sovereign proposes to make to their shores, well knowing that on this occasion no attempt will be made to give that visit a party significance, and that their chivalrous hospitality will be taken in no quarter to mean any abatement of their demand for their national rights.[95]

Redmond soon had to backtrack on this moderate statement when he became aware that a group of nominal Home Rulers in Dublin Corporation led by Lord Mayor Sir Thomas Pile, intent on voting with their Unionist colleagues in favour of presenting a loyal address to the queen, were using his speech to bolster their case. A letter to the press on 14 March claimed misrepresentation and removed ambiguity. In speeches in London on 16 March and in Liverpool a week later, he hardened his position considerably, saying that it was difficult to believe that English statesmen could be so blind to the lessons of history as to imagine that the serious grievances under which the Irish people groaned could be mitigated by a royal visit or a British celebration of St Patrick's Day; if these grievances were not addressed, the expressions of goodwill towards Ireland they had seen would do more harm than good.[96]

The 8 March speech was too much for Dillon, who poured out his repugnance in a long letter to O'Brien. He had

> never felt more disgusted and humiliated than by his [Redmond's] crawling statement in the House on the Queen's visit . . . And this is the gentleman who is planted on our necks . . . a man whom no National instinct, nor even sense of the danger to his own position, can prevent from falling on his hands and knees to crawl before the combined snobbery of Great Britain and Ireland.

It was clear that, after five weeks, Dillon was far from reconciled to the terms of the February reunion:

> Redmond has probably told you of my attitude. But for your interference he had no more chance of being elected [than] I had of being elected Lord Mayor of London. I considered then that your support of him was a very great mistake, and I will confess that everything which has occurred since has confirmed me in that view. He and I are on perfectly good terms – so far as personal intercourse goes – but our relations are not [founded on] any deception on my part, for I told him frankly that I was totally opposed to his election, and that I was convinced he could not have been elected but for your active support. Having acquiesced in his election I shall give him fair play so long as I remain a member of the Party. But more than fair play I cannot give him, for I have no faith in him.[97]

Redmond's speech also seems to have provoked O'Brien into a sudden, though short-lived, move against his leadership. O'Brien told Jeremiah McVeagh, the UIL official (later M.P. for South Down) responsible for organising the St Patrick's Day banquet at the Hotel Cecil, London, that Redmond's expression of 'gratitude for the Shamrock' made it impossible to co-operate with him any longer, and urged him to 'Postpone the banquet and you will smash Redmond!'[98] More a momentary expression of anger, however, than a serious attempt at a coup, this outburst was not followed up by O'Brien, whose overriding concern in those months was to give Redmond 'a fair trial' regarding his attitude to the UIL.

The question of the precise relationship between the reunited party and the UIL was the dominant domestic issue of the first months following the reunion. In reality, that reunion had merely papered over the cracks. The mutual antipathy between Healy and his former anti-Parnellite colleagues was as much alive as ever, with the issue of the status of the league forming the battleground between them. The *Daily Nation*, employing Healy's trademark mixture of wit and low vituperation, kept up a constant barrage of attacks against what it saw as O'Brien's agenda of using the league as a personal instrument to dictate to the party. Dillon, the *Freeman* and O'Brien's own *Irish People* counter-attacked, branding Healy as the perpetuator of faction. The *Independent* took a moderately pro-Healy, anti-O'Brien slant. Over this mess of antagonisms, the control of a chairman concerned above all with healing old wounds was tenuous indeed.

The animosities of the split lived on in the February South Mayo by-election to fill the vacancy created by Davitt's resignation. There John O'Donnell, a founder of the UIL and protégé of O'Brien, faced opposition from the candidature of John MacBride, absent in South Africa at the head of the small band of Irishmen he had recruited to fight for the Boers. The latter received support from an unlikely coalition of

Redmond's former Fenian and separatist associates, among them MacBride's wife-to-be, Maud Gonne, and Healy's retinue. The contest was played down by the nationalist press, and the prior claim of O'Donnell was recognized in his victory on a low poll, which gave him 2,401 votes to MacBride's 427.

Redmond was from the first anxious to signal his approval of the UIL, though he was far from accepting anything that would detract from the primacy of the party. Harrington advised him to comply with O'Brien's wishes by encouraging party members to help in organizing the league, while aiming to make it the national organization of the party as the National League had been for the pre-1890 party. The UIL's programme was sufficiently elastic, he thought, to make it adaptable to different local circumstances, but making it a national organization would involve playing down its radical agrarian aspects in the rich farming areas of the east, 'where they look with suspicion upon the grazing agitation conducted by the League'.[99] Taking Harrington's advice, Redmond wrote in reply to an invitation from a Tipperary UIL branch that he was willing to give what help he could to spread the league into areas not yet organized. He called the league 'the strongest of existing nationalist organisations' and added that a national conference, representative of all 'the elements that have hitherto made up our great national gatherings', should be held as soon as possible to establish it as 'the National organisation'. He suggested Whitsuntide (early June) as a date for such a conference. In doing so, he touched on a sensitive issue for O'Brien. An early convention would, the latter feared, allow a Redmond–Healy alliance to dominate an incomplete league organization, leaving the party unreformed; the later the convention was held, the stronger the position of the league to exert its purgative influences on the party. His disquiet was reflected by the *Freeman*, which, while it welcomed Redmond's 'unqualified approval', called the setting of a date for a convention 'premature' until the league had been completely organized throughout the country.[100] The two men had already agreed that no such date would be set until the Munster UIL had held its provincial conference at the end of April. Anxious to placate O'Brien, Redmond assured him on 12 March that the mention of Whitsuntide had been added to the letter without his knowledge by Clancy, to whom he passed it for handing to the press; he was 'greatly distressed' that O'Brien should think that he had gone back on their understanding.[101] O'Brien told Dillon on 26 March: 'Unless Redmond at once carries out his solemn promise to throw himself genuinely in the work of the League and gets his friends to do likewise it would be impossible for us to touch the Convention.'[102] He then demanded of Redmond that the convention be deferred until the indeterminate date of Davitt's return from South Africa; neither was he happy about the inclusion of elements other than the league in the convention.[103]

Harrington urged Redmond on 30 March to resist O'Brien's demands as undermining his position as chairman:

Figure 21. 'For the Old Land: Unity and Organisation' (*Irish Weekly Independent*, 28 April 1900). *Courtesy of the National Library of Ireland.*
John Redmond, on right, newly elected chairman of the reunited Irish Party, holds up the flag of Unity and Organisation, helped by Tim Harrington and Tim Healy, on left. The persistence of the tensions of the split and the Independent's anti-Dillon and anti-O'Brien bias are evident in the fact that Dillon is seen looking the other way and O'Brien is nowhere to be seen.

> With every desire in the world to go to the utmost reasonable extent of concession and conciliation I must confess I do not see my way to put either myself or you completely under the feet of William O'Brien . . . No one has attempted to oppose his organisation. We have all been using our influence to keep anyone back from attempting any other organisation lest he might get reasonable grounds of offence, and the only acknowledgment we receive for our pains is to be told that there is no other organisation possible but the League . . . The men organising the UIL have evidently got instructions to oppose the Convention and to belittle the Party; and I tell you frankly in my judgment you will have to make a stand against it instead of appeasing this insane savagery any further.[104]

Advice to the contrary came from an Ulster priest, Reverend J. J. McCartan, urging him to 'beware of your Parliamentary friends' who were resisting the league; O'Brien was the 'soul of honour' and the league would 'either unite the country or throw it back another decade, accordingly as it is supported or thwarted by the Parliamentarians'. If the party gave no assistance, then forced a convention, a fiasco would result. He offered a positive incentive:

> If you throw yourself earnestly into the movement and organise your country on a fighting policy, which you always preached, how can it be said, with the leader of the Irish parliamentary party at its head, that it is *O'Brien's* movement? It will be *your* movement if you *wish*, and you can then summon your united country to a convention, and receive there a mandate which will give you more real authority than you can ever derive from the present party.[105]

By the time he received these counsels, Redmond was already meeting O'Brien halfway. He wrote diplomatically on 29 March reciting the steps he was taking to speed up the organization of the league and hoping that O'Brien would now drop the suggestion of the distant date.[106] Thereafter, he stepped up his active promotion of the league, pledged himself publicly to it and promised that the convention would be summoned by a joint committee of the league and the party with each having equal power to decide its composition. While Dillon remained strongly opposed to an early convention and sure that it would be used to secure Redmond's election as president of the league,[107] O'Brien's attitude changed within a week. He told Dillon that in view of Redmond's concessions there was now nothing to fear in a convention:

> To reject an invitation under these circumstances would be to proclaim ourselves irreconcilable to any terms of agreement with the Party. The result would be a horrible shock to the country and the beginning of a new civil war in which we would be hopelessly in the wrong . . . If Redmond behaves really well (and we will have ample opportunity of testing him) I see no very killing difficulty about his getting the honour, if he cares for it . . . to found our position on

> mere opposition to Redmond would be to play Healy's game completely and divide the country fatally.[108]

Addressing his constituents on 22 April, Redmond saw around him the faces not just of his old supporters but of 'those earnest, enthusiastic and patriotic men who differed from me in the past', and echoed the new O'Brien orthodoxy that the M.P.s had been compelled to reunite by the prior reunion of the people. He commended the UIL as 'the only organisation at the present moment which has any nationality or reality . . . every national object upon which Irishmen have got their hearts [set] is in its programme'. Their first duty must be to force the Government to introduce the compulsory purchase of land as 'an absolute necessity', he said, while careful to add that if the landlords joined with them they could ensure that this was done in a way which 'will not ruin a single landlord'. He added:

> I believe in conciliation, and I believe that in every sense of politics – in the spirit, as was once said by Parnell, of compromise – and if these men will join with us . . . I, for one, would not regret that they got terms a great deal better than they deserve from their past history.[109]

The spirit of compromise burst into bloom in earnest at the Munster UIL Convention on 26 April when Redmond shared a platform with O'Brien. The latter hailed his adhesion to the league's land policy, called his speech 'statesmanlike' and declared that he was proud to call himself a follower of Redmond.[110] On 3 May the joint committee met and fixed 19 June as the date for the convention.[111] Dillon's bitter suspicion that the convention was a Healy plot with Redmond as accomplice was slower to evaporate. Although he shared a platform with Redmond at Manchester on 13 May, it was only three days before the National Convention that he indicated a change of mind to O'Brien, when he told him that he would second Redmond's nomination for the presidency if desired.[112]

Attention now turned to the issue of which organizations would be represented at the convention. Would Healy's People's Rights Association (PRA) be allowed a separate presence there, as they demanded? Healy argued against calls within the association for a boycott until it became clear whether they were to be excluded.[113] Harrington and others called for representation to be given to all nationalist organizations.[114] However, the joint committee decided on 6 June to exclude all four of the 'split' organizations, the National League, the National Federation, the Independent League (all now, for practical purposes, dead) and the PRA. The parliamentarians on the committee had been outvoted by the UIL members. Redmond announced his 'deep regret' at the decision but said that in practice it need not mean the exclusion of any significant number of men, since most were entitled to be present in some other capacity (the elected local bodies, clergy and many other non-political associations had been invited). The question now was whether, because of a theoretical exclusion, they were to abandon the convention. He would, he said, take no responsibility for such a course. He addressed himself 'to Mr. Healy in a special manner . . . I ask him now to aid me in averting a National calamity'.[115] Healy's reply protested against the equal position of the league and the party on the joint committee and listed other steps in the 'downward path' of the party's capitulation to O'Brien. Calling the decision a carefully contrived plan to pack the convention, he warned Redmond that 'Mr. O'Brien intends either to make you his victim, or his slave'. The next day Healy announced that his group would boycott the convention.[116]

VI

> The greatest representative assemblage of Irishmen held here since the Union . . . since the portals of the 'Old House' in College Green were closed one hundred years ago there has been no assembly so well entitled as this one to style itself the Parliament of the people of Ireland.

With these words Redmond welcomed the delegates to the National Convention, which opened at the Rotunda on 19 June. A wide spectrum of nationalist opinion was represented, but, with the exception of labour organizations, the only political body recognized was the UIL. Anticipating controversy, Redmond called for a broad understanding of the meaning of unity: 'By unity I don't mean a dull uniformity of thought and opinion on everything . . . [but] a unity in essentials . . . in principles . . . consistent with the most generous toleration of one another's differences upon minor points.' When O'Brien, referring to the absent Healy and his confederates, stated that 'the League has succeeded in separating the wheat from the chaff (*cheers*)', Harrington pleaded for 'tolerance and gentle words', the methods used to end the split, to be applied at the convention to those still outside. John Fitzgibbon pointed to another incipient source of discord among nationalists when he spoke of the difference between the Land League and the UIL: the former had embraced all social classes of nationalists including the large grazier, but that category of farmer was an enemy of the new movement. They should not elect to the county councils 'men who while sympathising with the movement would do nothing but obstruct the splitting up of the farms'.

When discussion reached the UIL's draft constitution, there was controversy on the size of the parliamentary party's *ex officio* representation on the 100-man Provisional Directory, the governing body of the league. While the parliamentarians, represented by Blake, argued for parity of representation, O'Brien wanted it limited to ten. The latter declared that it was impossible that the party ever again be 'the predominant and supreme authority', but reminded delegates that there was no ban on the election of party men to the directory if they worked for the league. Redmond expressed himself as certain that league bodies would be proud to elect those M.P.s to the governing body who showed by their record that they were ready to work for it. 'I am not a bit uneasy as to the Party not having its fair and legitimate weight in the conduct of the movement in future,' he concluded.[117]

In the long battle fought between O'Brien and the parliamentarians, the outcome of the June convention represented a partial victory for each side. The league had now been endorsed by a national assembly as the sole national organization, while its constitution guaranteed the independence of the local league bodies in each constituency in the selection of candidates for Parliament. M.P.s would in future face critical scrutiny regarding not just their parliamentary performance but their attitude to the league. On the other hand, O'Brien's original mission to create a new party from the ground up had been thwarted by the reunion. Instead, the league could be said to have been 'captured' by the existing party. Redmond was now its national president. Not yet completely established on a nationwide basis – the number of branches increased from 409 on 31 January 1900 to 758 by 1 November in that year, but there were still no provincial directories in either Leinster or Ulster[118]– it was unlikely to remain the kind of organization O'Brien had envisaged in its early days. An undated letter written by Redmond to Harrington a few months earlier had indicated his pragmatic approach to the league's expansion and his confidence that it need not always be a personal vehicle for O'Brien: 'As for the League we can make it *our* organisation and I certainly would be glad to see Dublin organised before the Convention. You don't imagine that if we had branches of the League in the wards of the City that they would be the creatures of anyone.'[119]

In the interim between the convention and the expected general election, Redmond set out to enlarge the appeal of the party. In particular, he sought to attract the support of the large constituency that had lost interest in politics during the split and had switched its energies to the cultural nationalism of the Irish-Ireland movement. In a series of speeches in and out of Parliament he endorsed the viewpoint and aims of the Gaelic League. Before the convention he had praised the work of the Christian Brothers in the national education system in teaching the youth of Ireland the history of their own country and in stemming the process of Anglicization, at work since the Union, which he called 'an unmixed evil'.[120] In the House in July, he regretted that the *Report of the Board of Intermediate Education* – the body responsible for secondary education – contained no reference to the Gaelic language. It was 'monstrous', he declared, that Gaelic should be placed on a lower level than the continental languages in the examination system.[121] He called for new provisions for the 70,000 children in exclusively Gaelic-speaking households: these children should be taught to read and write in their own language, and should be taught English through the medium of Gaelic. This was asking for less than what the Welsh already had, he said, adding,

> this wanton attempt to destroy the Irish tongue must seem an outrage and a sacrilege. The injury to Ireland is a material and a moral one at the same time. This system undoubtedly debases the intellects and stunts the minds of the young children of Ireland . . . it deprives them of all knowledge of a glorious past . . . it places upon them the humiliating badge of inferiority.[122]

In Limerick on 2 September, his deprecation of Anglicization was even stronger. He saw an Ireland facing cultural extinction, a country whose population was diminishing daily and in which those who remained became denationalized and demoralized:

> it must, to every thoughtful man, be a sad thing to see how rapidly English tone, English fashion, English feeling, and mind you, not the highest English tone, not the highest English feeling or thought, but the lowest and most vulgar English tone, and feeling, and thought are spreading amongst the masses of our people (*cheers*) . . . The Irish language is almost dead; Irish literature is neglected; Irish history is not taught in our schools; Irish music is forgotten, the songs of the London music halls are imported into our capital (*cheers*) – and are sung in our streets, aye, and even sometimes in our drawing-rooms . . . It is lowering the tone of Ireland. It is ruining the old prestige, the honour of our race.[123]

He voiced similar sentiments when he attended a Douglas Hyde lecture in Dublin in October. He claimed to know of 'no living Irishman who deserved the name of Irish patriot more than Dr. Hyde' and promised to aid the Gaelic League in and out of Parliament, assuring it of the wholehearted support of his colleagues.[124]

To the labour movement, he reiterated the position of his Rathfarnham speech of November 1890:

> I believe that the labour interest in Ireland can only protect itself properly and obtain any benefits for its class by belonging to a great united Irish party . . . I say that inside that united pledge-bound party there ought to be the most generous representation given to the labour interest in Ireland (*cheers*).[125]

For those nationalists who had lost faith in constitutional action during the split, he had persuasive words at Galway on 22 September. He had never desired

> to quarrel with men who had expressed the view that more could be gained by force than by constitutional agitation. He had never found himself in a position in which he could take the responsibility of

> advising his fellow-countrymen, as Ireland was situated today, to go outside the limits of constitutional action (*hear, hear*). As they were at this moment in Ireland an unarmed people, it was his opinion that it was incumbent upon them to look to the constitutional movement of the immediate future to obtain for Ireland any mitigation of her state of oppression and slavery.[126]

At Belfast on 14 September he used a UIL platform, shared with Dillon, to address himself to Ulster Protestants. He spoke of the 'mingled pleasure and pain' that his visits there always caused him, since the city, the 'centre of national sentiment' a hundred years previously, had become 'one of the remaining – the sole remaining – obstacles which stand between Ireland and the achievement of her National rights . . . are we, the Nationalist party in Ireland, to any extent responsible . . .?' The national cause was not and never had been 'merely a Catholic cause', he asserted. He repeated his wish to see a land purchase scheme that 'would not injure a single landlord in Ireland'. He wished his words and protestations would be accepted by their Protestant fellow-countrymen:

> Home Rule as we mean it does not mean the wrong of any class or of any creed . . . [Davis's dream of an Irish nation] may seem far from realisation . . . but the moment when our Protestant fellow-countrymen in the North of Ireland will join hands with us for our common country –
>
> *A voice*: It never can be done, sir –
>
> But still I for my part will never abandon the hope that that day will come (*cheers*).[127]

If his understanding of Ulster unionism had evolved since 1886, there was little sign of it here. Conciliatory overtures aimed at landlords were unlikely to impress the Protestant democracy of industrial Ulster. Assurances of religious toleration were less likely to register than the presence of the massed ranks of Catholic clerics at the UIL convention and the prominent role in the movement played by several bishops. Those unionists who took an interest in the sayings of nationalists were more likely to have their attention held, not by the gentle words of Davis echoed by Redmond, but by the harsher language of ethnic resurgence spoken by Dillon, as at Oughterard in County Galway on 19 August:

> The first work [for the UIL] was that of winning the land of Ireland for the people and of driving from the possession of the land the breed of Cromwell and the exterminators who for ten generations had endeavoured to depopulate the country and destroy their race, but who, under the blessing of God, would yet be defeated in that foul endeavour, for the old Celtic race would yet win back the land which God gave to their fathers before these strangers came amongst them (*applause*).[128]

VII

The June convention of 1900 brought about no lessening of the strife between O'Brien and Healy; the newspaper and platform war between them raged unabated. Healy refused to recognize the outcome of the 'bogus' and 'rigged' convention or to dissolve the moribund PRA. He kept up a withering fire on O'Brien as the would-be dictator of the party. Alluding to recent UIL public meetings, which had gone ahead despite being proscribed by the authorities, the *Nation* wrote that O'Brien was chagrined that he had not been imprisoned as he had been 'long looking for a martyr's crown on the cheap'.[129] O'Brien responded by hinting that Healy should resign or be expelled from the party: anyone who, 'despite every offer and conciliation', continued to calumniate the National Convention and assailed the only national organization of the people to keep alive dissension on the eve of the general election, 'must step down and out'.[130] Healy, as F. S. L. Lyons has written, had fallen into the trap narrowly avoided by Dillon earlier in the year, that of failing to accept a *fait accompli* unpalatable to him and thus courting isolation.[131] Redmond, speaking at the founding of a league branch in Dublin, pleaded for an end to 'those horrible personalities' that continued in the newspapers and were 'disgracing the public life of Ireland'.[132] The plea fell on deaf ears. The stage was being set for the final showdown between Healy and his enemies.

Since May a liquidator had been engaged in winding up the *Independent* company, whose debts now amounted to £26,000, a sum equal to almost twice the value of the company's goodwill and assets.[133] Redmond was anxious to avert a hostile buyout by the *Freeman* company at the bankruptcy court, and, according to Healy, pleaded with him to encourage William Martin Murphy, to step in with a better offer.[134] The long negotiations bore fruit in August when Murphy and other large shareholders outbade the *Freeman* to buy the company. The daily paper was amalgamated with Healy's organ. The first issue of the *Irish Daily Independent and Nation* appeared on 1 September. Redmond wished it well and saw ample room for a 'friendly rivalry' between the two organs of nationalist opinion.[135] The *Evening Telegraph*, evening companion of the *Freeman's*, had signalled its attitude to the new paper: 'It gathers everything that is rotten in Irish public life into one bunch, and that is something to be grateful for.'[136] Murphy being a kinsman and political adherent of Healy's, the paper took a moderately Healyite stance, supporting party policy while opposing what it saw as the 'uncontrollable egotism and vindictiveness of Mr. William O'Brien'.[137]

With parliamentary dissolution expected at any time, the argument turned on the degree of freedom each constituency was to have in selecting its candidate. On 7 August in Dublin, Redmond set out what he understood to be the policy agreed at the convention: 'This organisation must not be used either to promote opposition to a member whose constituents are satisfied with him on the one hand, or to force down the throats of the constituents any member who may have lost their confidence by his action in the past.'[138] Two weeks later, a meeting of the Provisional Directory with the returned Davitt in the chair, held while Redmond was holidaying at Aughavanagh, passed a resolution that called on constituents to choose only members of the UIL as candidates for election.[139] At Limerick on 2 September, Redmond called the doctrine that none except league members should be eligible for election 'unconstitutional and absurd': the Provisional Directory had never meant to lay down such a 'preposterous' rule.[140] Later that week Healy announced in the press that league organizers had descended on his constituency of North Louth with the aim of forcing him to join the league or raising an alternative candidate. He declared that if Redmond asked him not to stand for re-election it would give him 'the greatest pleasure' to comply; otherwise he would stand, and would take no pledge other than the 1885 party pledge.[141] The next day at Thurles, Redmond protested 'with all the vehemence in my power against these old quarrels in the anti-Parnellite party being allowed today to interfere with the progress of this movement'. If Healy did not like the league, let him give it a fair chance and stop his attacks on it. If he had the power to order Healy to retire he would not use it; he did not want to see 'an able and astute politician' driven out, he declared, adding, 'I have no sympathy with the policy of the sweeping brush whether applied by him in the old days to some of us, or applied by other people today to him.'[142]

Dillon further stoked these tensions by stating his view in Belfast on 14 September that the choice of the constituents needed to be 'guided'. Speaking of a 'crisis' in the national movement, he proposed that the test of fitness of a candidate should include acceptance of the mandate of the June convention and loyalty to the league.[143] The *Independent* also wrote of a 'momentous crisis', caused by an attempt to subject the public life of Ireland to a 'shameful despotism'.[144] The reports coming from Dublin, Cork, Mayo, Louth and Tipperary indicated that Redmond's efforts to calm the dispute had failed. Rival selection conventions were being held amid turbulent scenes. Healy called UIL candidates 'tipplers and tricksters'. In Louth, O'Brien and Healy, standing on the same brake at a three-hour public meeting, tried to shout each other down.[145]

Lord Salisbury dissolved Parliament in September 1900. Redmond told T. P. O'Connor, the president of the United Irish League of Great Britain, to issue no general instruction to Irish voters there to vote for the Liberals; such support would be given only when that party had unequivocally declared for Home Rule.[146] The general election in October left the relative positions of the major British parties almost unchanged. The Conservatives won 333 seats, the Liberal Unionists 66 and the Liberals 184. The nationalist electorate gave its verdict on the 'crisis': most of the Healyite candidates were defeated, among them

Maurice Healy, ousted by O'Brien himself, and William Martin Murphy. The principal survivors were Healy himself and Redmond's former Parnellite colleague, now Healyite and financial backer of the new *Independent*, J. L. Carew. The first elected Irish Parliamentary Party since reunion was returned with eighty-two members, the vast majority of whom had promised loyalty to the league. On the face of it, O'Brien had won a resounding victory. However, as Philip Bull has pointed out, it was a hollow one. Only 6 of those actively involved in building the league before the reunion were elected; 49 members of the old party were returned, despite the fact that a significant number of them were obvious candidates for the purge that the league had set itself to carry out.[147] Redmond wrote to Blake:

> while I did not personally approve of the policy of making peace with a hatchet, it is, at least, very satisfactory that the country has pronounced its opinion in such a decided way . . . I think if things are allowed now to settle down, that we have a very fair chance of a strong movement, and a united party, but if a policy of expulsion be adopted, I have very great fears of the consequences.[148]

But for O'Brien and Dillon the fight with Healy was not over. In a speech at Westport on 8 November, which the *Independent* called a 'declaration of war', O'Brien described Healy's presence in the Irish Party as like 'a poisoned bullet in the body of a man' and told of his wish that the forthcoming convention should direct his exclusion from the party.[149] A letter to Redmond the following day gave the same unmistakeable message.[150] Redmond's reply was to ask him if he could not achieve his object by proposing a test for membership rather than 'exclusion of individuals practically by name'.[151]

Redmond's adherence to the league meant that he was now out of favour (privately, though not publicly) with Healy. The latter had already reproached him for his visit to Cork in July in the company of O'Brien, which, although Redmond denied it, he saw as effectively a scheme to oust Maurice from his seat. He wrote bitterly to his father on 19 November: 'It is years since I have taken any satisfaction in being in the House . . . Hence I am faintly amused at their talk about expelling me. If Redmond had a spark of courage he could have foiled the whole game . . . I never go near him . . .'[152]

The second convention of the year, held to give the league a permanent structure and also formally to constitute the united parliamentary party and elect its officers, opened at the Rotunda on 11 December. The reporter from the *Freeman* captured the tone of the gathering in comparing the receptions given to Redmond and to O'Brien: for Redmond it was 'a cheer of unmistakeable heartiness', for Dillon 'it shrilled higher' but for O'Brien 'a mighty and vehement volume of cheers, renewed again and again and again, made the roof ring forth a welcome of which there was no escaping the significance'. Opening the proceedings, Redmond declared that the character of the June convention had passed two crucial tests – that of the ballot box and that of finance, the appeal of June having raised almost £11,000 – which gave the final answer to those who had called it a 'rigged assembly'. He claimed for the present convention that it was 'a sovereign and supreme body' entitled to make decrees for the conduct of a national organization in Ireland, but for that reason its power should be used 'sparingly, with extreme caution, wisely, moderately, after full and calm deliberation', otherwise its decrees would lack 'moral weight and force'.

The temperature rose when O'Brien introduced his motion for the non-admission to the party of Healy and Carew, as 'active and unscrupulous foes of the National organisation at the late election'. As he answered the charge that this was a personal matter between Healy and himself, interruptions took place that soon became uproar, and a 'hand-to-hand scuffle' broke out in the gallery. Redmond stood up, rang the bell and called for order: 'I appeal to you in the name of your country not to allow that excitability which our enemies say is one of the curses of the Irish temperament (*hear, hear*) betray any signs of heat which would be fatal to the object of this Convention.' O'Brien continued with an impassioned attack on Healy, which raked over all the dissensions of the previous decade within the anti-Parnellite party: 'He knew of no case in history where a man was borne with so long, who was so much petted, so much cringed to, to see if anything would appease him as Mr. Healy . . . Parnell's little finger was worth more to Ireland than Mr. Healy's whole body.' An incandescent Harrington rose to answer, asserting that O'Brien's motion was resurrecting old disputes in which he and Redmond had sworn never to take sides; they were none of the business of the convention. Amid 'fierce uproar' he declared that he would not be O'Brien's instrument in driving out any other man. Redmond several times more called for order, to no avail. A Healyite priest, Father McNeece, moved an amendment to remove the exclusion clauses and to call for the chair to enforce 'unity and discipline' in the party. The 'intense and prolonged disorder' during his speech forced him to sit down.

Before the vote, Redmond stated that he would not enter into any questions arising from the pre-reunion period. He had entreated Healy to attend in June, bow to the authority of the convention and not thwart the General Election Fund: 'I am sorry to say that my advice fell upon deaf ears.' He now had to recognize the verdict passed by the people on such conduct, and the fact that the overwhelming majority of this convention supported O'Brien's motion. Nevertheless, he would vote against it, while accepting the decision of the convention. The McNeece amendment was defeated by a huge majority, and the O'Brien motion carried by a similar majority. Almost exactly ten years since Healy had led the revolt against Parnell in Committee Room 15, all the former Parnellites were found in the minority in both ballots, voting against the expulsion of their erstwhile bitterest foe.[153] The Parnell split had proved easier to end than the split among Parnell's opponents.

A short while later, Healy wrote to a constituent: 'Indeed I find so much fun in poor William O'Brien that I forgive him all his incantations.'[154] At the opening of the new Parliament he declared: 'The right honourable gentleman [O'Brien] stated that the United Irish League has deposited a united Irish party in this House. As a matter of fact it has deposited two parties, of which I am one.'[155]

13 Epilogue

> Redmond was not only a great orator but possessed elements of statesmanship of a high order. The fact that he was given no chance to apply his qualities in the rebuilding of his native land is one of the myriad tragedies of Irish history.
>
> David Lloyd George, 1938[1]

> The World War came, and though it found the vast majority of the Irish people denationalised through the spineless policy and vitiating doctrines of Redmond and his followers in the British House of Commons and in Ireland itself, the year 1914 also found a minority in whom had been developed by the Gaelic League, Sinn Fein, the Volunteers, and in a special manner by the Irish Republican Brotherhood, a more virile nationalism than had existed in Ireland for over a century.
>
> John Devoy[2]

The seventeen remaining years that Redmond spent as chairman of the Irish Parliamentary Party, which include the events for which he is best known and on which his reputation rests, obviously require a further volume. This long period spent as democratically elected leader of the Irish majority may conveniently be divided into four phases. The first, which lasted from 1901 until 1904, was centred on the efforts to win from the Tory–Liberal Unionist administration a final settlement of the land question, which would give the Irish tenants ownership of their holdings. The second stretched from 1905 to 1911, and involved the putting into place of the conditions in which a third attempt could be made to win a Home Rule Bill for Ireland, and the final success of that attempt. The third phase, from the spring of 1912 to the autumn of 1914, saw Redmond's successful piloting of the Home Rule legislation through the House of Commons, combined with his efforts, in an increasingly militarized atmosphere in Ireland, to come to terms with the implacable opposition of the Ulster Unionists to Home Rule. The fourth, which began with the outbreak of the Great War and the signing into law of the Home Rule Act, and ended with Redmond's death in March 1918, was taken up with the consequences of his call to Irishmen to join the British forces in the war, and with his increasingly futile attempt to safeguard the Home Rule victory while preventing the permanent partition of the island.

I

The key to Redmond's longevity as national leader lies in the combination of his personal characteristics and his political strengths and weaknesses. Of the prominent men who might have become leader in 1900, there was no one but Redmond who combined high ability with so little ego. It is inconceivable that O'Brien, with his bursts of manic energy punctuated by long periods of exhaustion, or Healy, with his acid tongue and inability to work with colleagues, could have allowed the divisions of the split to heal. The 'accommodating opinions' and cool, sanguine temperament of Redmond, on the other hand, gave him the tolerance needed to work with people to whom he had been opposed for a decade. His personal reserve gave him a certain resemblance to Parnell, but he did not exhibit the same forcefulness or create about himself the same mystique; according to the testimony of those who served under him in the party, he commanded not by awe but by kindliness, courtesy and tact. There were none of the bewildering disappearances that had characterized Parnell in his later years. Redmond won all-round admiration for his scrupulous attention to work and punctilious attendance at Parliament.

Aside from personal factors, Redmond's political prestige stood high at the time of his election. He was seen to have won the argument within nationalism over relations with the Liberal Party. His qualifications for leadership were seen as his judgement and oratorical powers as a parliamentary performer. These traits would continue to win him general acceptance as the best possible representative of the Home Rule cause at Westminster. They helped to overcome the distrust felt by many former opponents, especially those close to Dillon, who saw him as unsound on the agrarian issue. The error of his premature declaration that the land question had been solved was remembered, as were his friendly relations with unionists in the 1890s. His inclusive and high-minded Parnellite nationalism, and his tendency to appeal to reason rather than emotion, left Irish audiences with feelings of admiration but without the fire generated by ethnic demagoguery. This lack of a fanatical personal following made him less assertive of his own political ideas and more accommodating to the views of others.

In his first years as leader he restored the party's morale and the confidence of the nationalist public in it by reviving its effectiveness as a fighting force in the House of Commons. With no prospect of Home Rule legislation from the Tory–Liberal Unionist administration, and no worthwhile land measures in its legislative programmes for 1901 or 1902, the UIL's land policy became the priority of the party for the time being: a scheme of compulsory sale which would greatly accelerate the transfer of the land from the landlords to the tenants. The Irish Party created trouble in the House by returning to something like the old obstruction policy, holding up Government business and staging occasional theatrical displays in which members had themselves suspended. This had the desired effect on the grass roots and in Irish-America, and the party's coffers began to fill up once again. At the end of the 1901 session, there was general nationalist satisfaction with the party's performance under Redmond's leadership, while his personal status in the House rose to new heights. With the Liberal leadership weak and divided over the Boer war, he was increasingly spoken of as the real leader of the opposition.

In tandem with the party's militancy in the House, the league stepped up its programme of agitation in the countryside. The Government's response was to revive coercion in late 1901. League workers and M.P.s were arrested and jailed and public meetings held under league auspices were banned. By the end of 1902, ten M.P.s had been imprisoned.[3] But the agitation ran its course by mid-1902 when the leadership backed away from an extended campaign of boycotting for fear of the suppression of the organization.

When, in September 1902, Captain John Shawe-Taylor, a County Galway landlord, invited representatives of the tenants and landlords to meet in conference to reach agreement on a programme of land purchase that could be put to the Government, it was always likely that Redmond would respond positively, given his previous openness to conciliation with the landlords. (O'Brien, seeking an alternative to agitation, also accepted a place at the conference.) The result was the Land Conference, held at Christmas 1902 in Dublin and chaired by Lord Dunraven, whose report formed the basis of Wyndham's great Land Purchase Bill of the following year. The scheme agreed upon did not advocate compulsion, but rather a system of incentives to voluntary sale. The British Treasury was to enable tenants to purchase by providing loans, the repayments on which should be significantly lower than their rents. For the landlords, the price received should yield, when invested, an income equivalent to their net second-term rents. The gap between what the tenant could afford to pay and what the landlord could afford to accept should be bridged by a 'bonus' payment to the latter. In addition, there should be special measures to solve the problems of the western congested districts and of the remaining evicted tenants.

The report was immediately criticized by Davitt, and by the *Freeman's Journal*, now under Sexton's management, as too generous by far to the landlords. Nevertheless, the party and the UIL directory endorsed the report by overwhelming majorities. Wyndham's Bill, the first legislative fruit of the conciliation policy, appeared in March and was welcomed with reservations by the National Convention. The only dissenting voice was that of Davitt, Dillon being absent. After the Bill became law in late 1903, Dillon threw his weight behind Davitt and the *Freeman*, unleashing a fierce assault against the Act and the conciliationist landlords. These attacks posed a critical dilemma for Redmond.

The conference initiative represented a new method of winning Irish reforms based on a *rapprochement* between open-minded nationalists and moderate Unionists. He was in agreement with O'Brien in seeing its 'infinite possibilities', even hailing the Land Act as leading the way, via the reconciliation of classes, to an early concession of Home Rule. In autumn 1903, O'Brien urged him to confront what he regarded as a revolt against party and league policy. However, as Paul Bew has written, he 'refused all the options which would have brought on a critical test of strength'.[4] His stated reason (to O'Brien) for doing so was his horror of another party split. The goal of keeping the party united in the pursuit of Home Rule took precedence over all 'subsidiary' issues. Faced with a choice between an innovative policy that carried with it the certainty of party dissension, and a return to the traditional rigidities of Dillon's approach with a united party, he opted for the latter. No doubt remembering his own position in the 1890s, he stated in 1905 in a maxim that O'Brien would later call 'words of immortal unwisdom'[5]: 'I hold in the strongest possible way that it would be better for the cause of freedom for Ireland for the National Party to be united in an unwise or short-sighted policy rather than be divided with one section taking a far wiser course.'[6]

There is no reason to doubt that the experience of the split had marked him deeply: he would repeat often that the maintenance of unity had been his guiding principle since his election. But behind these professions lay a pragmatic awareness of his inability, had he so wished, to win over the party and league to the conciliation policy. When O'Brien, incensed, resigned from all his positions in the movement in November 1903, he left Redmond in an even weaker position. Although the latter tried to disguise his capitulation as allowing 'room for differences of opinion' on 'non-essentials', it was clear that party unity meant unity on Dillon's terms.

The conciliation policy was effectively abandoned in the 1904 session. Its enemies had succeeded, not in holding back land sales, but in ensuring that the Land Act would not yield a political dividend in the direction of co-operation between nationalists and unionists. There was no more talk of conferences; instead, the party returned to traditional modes of parliamentary confrontation. Redmond focused his attacks on the deficiencies of the Act – its failure to solve the critical shortage of land for smallholders in the West – and on the perceived breaking of pledges on Wyndham's part regarding its implementation, although he never identified himself fully with the Dillon/*Freeman* criticism of the Act as a vehicle for landlord greed. From that time, however, dates the effective birth of a joint leadership of Redmond and Dillon. The two maintained a constant and stiffly courteous contact by letter, the lugubrious Dillon bombarding Redmond with advice on tactics, draft resolutions and warnings of one or another danger to the party or the cause. This arrangement suited the bipolar division of the party's activities. While both men combined annual speaking tours in Ireland with faithful attendance in Parliament, it was Redmond who was the effective ambassador for the cause at Westminster and Dillon who was in touch to a greater extent with developments at home.

When the Land Conference landlords in August 1904 regrouped themselves as the Irish Reform Association to publish a plan for administrative devolution, Redmond's rhetorical response was one of welcome for a sign of movement, albeit inadequate, in the direction of Home Rule. In practice, however, he followed Dillon's advice. The scheme and its author, Under-Secretary Sir Antony MacDonnell who had been appointed by Wyndham, were denounced by the Ulster Unionists, who saw in it a sinister plot to undermine the Union. Despite Wyndham's disavowal of the scheme, Redmond believed him to be in sympathy with it and condemned him for a failure to stand up to the 'Orangemen'. The involvement of MacDonnell, and Wyndham's relations with him, became the subject of intensive Parliamentary inquiry early in the 1905 session. Redmond and Dillon were happy to 'sit tight' and ally themselves with the Ulstermen to weaken the Government, efforts that were successful when Wyndham was forced to resign in March 1905. Further efforts by Redmond inflicted a defeat on the Government in July 1905. The Government limped on for a few more months until internal divisions over the free trade controversy brought about its downfall in November. O'Brien, who had built a power base for himself in the Cork area, re-emerged in 1905 to renew his criticisms of those who had undermined the Land Conference policy, and make proposals for further conferences, but his efforts only drove Redmond and Dillon closer together.

II

The Liberal landslide of January 1906 ushered in a fresh set of challenges for the joint leadership of Redmond and Dillon. Told that the new Government could not introduce a Home Rule Bill in the next Parliament, they had accepted a promise of an 'instalment', namely, a devolution measure capable of subsequent enlargement to full Home Rule. The Irish vote in Great Britain had not been pledged *en bloc* to the Liberals at the election. Yet, given the abandonment of the conciliation policy, it was clear that Home Rule legislation in the future would come only through an alliance with a Liberal Government. Redmond was accordingly most anxious to cultivate the friendship of the mass of new Liberal and Labour M.P.s who represented the advancing 'British democracy'.

This concern was evident in the 1906 session when, in a superb display of parliamentary skill, he defended the interests of Catholic primary schools in England and Wales, which were threatened by the Liberals' Education Bill with secular management and the imposition of non-denominational religious teaching. Since the Tories also opposed the Bill, the greatest delicacy was required of Redmond in keeping his distance from them while striving for amendments to the obnoxious clauses. Having won those amendments in consultation with the English Catholic bishops, he was able to support the Government at the end of the year in rejecting the more radical amendments made by the House of Lords. His adroit navigation of the issue won the gratitude of the English Catholics, without alienating the support of the pro-Home Rule Liberal Nonconformist grass roots.

In autumn 1906 attention turned to the Government's 'instalment'. Redmond made it clear that he would support only 'a bold and statesmanlike' scheme; Dillon similarly talked up expectations. However, the Irish Council Bill, introduced on 7 May 1907 by Chief Secretary Augustine Birrell, fell short of what the Irish leaders wanted, and nationalist opinion, its expectations raised by the leaders' pronouncements, was immediately dismissive. At the National Convention called to consider it, Redmond's resolution urging rejection of the Bill was passed overwhelmingly, and had the immediate effect of killing it. Disappointment was widespread, and two M.P.s resigned, one recontesting his seat for Arthur Griffith's new Sinn Féin party. To restore morale, and to repair the damage done to his own position – he was widely believed to have favoured privately conditional acceptance of the Bill – Redmond embarked on an extensive speaking tour of Ireland in the autumn. Vulnerable to the charge of having placed excessive trust in the Liberals, he found himself the target of criticism uncomfortably similar to his own strictures against the anti-Parnellites in the 1890s, and faced calls for the party to oppose the Government and hasten a general election. In rejecting this course on the grounds that the Liberals were about to enact important reforms (Bills for a university and for the evicted tenants), Redmond could claim consistency with his former position: he had opposed the Liberal Government in 1895 only when all hope of reform had vanished.

The growing antagonism between the Liberal Government and the House of Lords in 1908 and 1909 forced Redmond to reassess the attitude he had taken in 1894 to the role of the latter. The Lords blocked first the Old Age Pensions Bill and the Licensing Bill, and then the 'People's Budget' of 1909, an action that made a general election unavoidable. Curtailment of the powers of the Upper House now became, in the words of Prime Minister Asquith, 'the dominating issue in politics'. Redmond had to accept that the removal or modification of the Lords' veto was a prerequisite to the passing, not merely of progressive social legislation, but of a Home Rule Bill, rather than a distraction from the latter goal. Having accepted this, his task became one of holding the Liberals to their commitment to Lords reform as well as to Home Rule. In 1909, Redmond's concern was to obtain an official declaration of intention to make Home Rule part of the Liberal programme. Without such a declaration, he told Morley, he would ask the Irish voters in Britain, not only not to support, but to vote against Liberal candidates. Asquith must also tie the issue to that of the House of Lords by asking that his hands be free to deal with Home Rule. The latter complied, surprising a sceptical Ireland with his statement at the Albert Hall in December that only a system of full self-government in regard to purely Irish affairs would solve the Irish problem.

The general election of January 1910 returned the Liberals and Tories with almost equal numbers of seats, giving the nationalists and Labour, separately or together, the balance of power. The conjunction he had awaited so long had finally materialized: Redmond was suddenly the pivotal figure in British politics. The smallness of the Liberals' victory tended to weaken their resolve to introduce a Bill to reform the House of Lords' veto. Redmond's task that year was to prevent back-sliding on the Liberal commitment, a task that required unrelenting pressure and was made even more difficult when Edward VII's death in May brought about a new atmosphere of bipartisan harmony in British politics. Talk of a constitutional conference filled the air, pointing to the danger of the Lords issue being settled by compromise, with unknown consequences for Home Rule. The conference met in June and July, then adjourned until the autumn.

In August, Redmond travelled with Belfast nationalist Joe Devlin to the US, where he found that the prospect of Home Rule had revived the enthusiasm of Irish-Americans, and was able to raise $100,000 among them. The resumed conference reached deadlock in November, making another general election unavoidable. The Unionists appealed to the electorate to end Redmond's stranglehold on the Liberals, reviling him as the 'Dollar Dictator'. However, the result, in December, left the parties with practically unchanged strengths. Asquith in 1911 passed the Parliament Bill to limit the power of the Lords. The latter were compelled to accept the end of their own absolute veto. The way was now clear for a Home Rule Bill with a good chance of success: under the conditions of the Parliament Act, it must pass the Commons three times before the Lords' veto became inoperative. His skilful use of his opportunities and undeviating application of pressure on the Liberal leaders won Redmond general praise not just as nationalist leader but, among British democrats, as the foremost proponent of a democratized Parliament.

III

When Birrell introduced the third Home Rule Bill in April 1912, Redmond greeted it as 'a great measure', spoke of the good relations between the Irish and British peoples and hoped that the Bill would allow Ireland to take her place in 'that great sisterhood of nations that makes up the British Empire'. It was already clear that fiscal autonomy would not be part of the legislation, a fact that excited criticism from O'Brien, Healy and extreme nationalists. The more politicized of the Irish-Irelanders also attacked the Bill in terms that carried echoes from the 1890s when Parnellites had attacked Morley as a 'denationalizing' influence and certain Home Rulers as 'West Britons'. It was also clear that the Ulster Unionists, led in the House by Edward Carson, would use every means available to resist the Bill. Their campaign against the Bill became increasingly vociferous as the committee stage progressed. Unconstitutional methods were spoken of: some Unionists talked of giving allegiance to the kaiser rather than to a Home Rule government, while Carson forecast that many army officers would refuse to obey orders to quell a revolt in Ulster. At a huge rally at Blenheim in July, the new Conservative leader, Andrew Bonar Law, stated that there was 'no length of resistance' to which Ulster could go which he would not be ready to support. In September, the Ulster Unionist Council (UUC) organized the signing of the Solemn League and Covenant throughout Ulster by more than 200,000 men (a similar number of women signed an equivalent document). Couched in quasi-religious terms, their pledge was 'We will not have Home Rule'.

These developments exposed the shortcomings of Redmond's engagement with the Ulster Protestant community. His understanding of its objections to Home Rule, in common with that of most other nationalists, had not advanced since the previous attempts at Home Rule legislation. He could only see those objections as emanating from the fears of an élite minority at the loss of its privileges. Fearing that Asquith and other ministers, taken aback by the unconstitutional rhetoric of the Ulster Unionist leaders, might waver, Redmond professed to see nothing in the threats of the Ulstermen beyond the usual wild talk, and was adamant that no concessions should be made on the Bill. Nevertheless, in his speeches during the autumn recess, he was as conciliatory as his nationalism would allow him to go as he attempted to answer the objections and fears of Ulster. Emphasizing his desire to meet those fears, he held out the offer of enlarged representation and other safeguards in a Home Rule Parliament.

So far, Unionist talk of the exclusion of Ulster had been used as a tactic to wreck the Bill. However, during the session of 1913, Carson moved to an acceptance that Home Rule could not be prevented for the rest of the island, and that Ulster must seek separate treatment. His first proposal, that the entire nine-county province of Ulster be excluded from Home Rule, could only be rejected out of hand by Redmond. But with leading Liberals such as Winston Churchill and David Lloyd George increasingly amenable to the idea of some form of exclusion, Redmond found himself in an awkward position. In September, the Liberal Lord Loreburn's letter to *The Times* calling for a conference to arrive at a compromise, coincided with, if it did not cause, a general shift of sentiment in favour of a negotiated settlement. Bonar Law told

Churchill that the Tories would negotiate if the Liberals would consent to Ulster's right to decide by plebiscite.

In the meantime, the paramilitary Ulster Volunteer Force (UVF) was set up and drilling began, along with a campaign to subvert army discipline, and the UUC set up a 'Provisional Government' of Ulster with Carson as chairman. At Limerick in October, Redmond again condemned the violent threats of the Unionists as mere bombast, and said that nationalists could never accept the 'mutilation' of the nation. The two-nation theory was to him 'an abomination and a blasphemy'. However, he allowed that there could be diversity of treatment in the government of Ulster to take account of concerns with civil and religious liberty, hinting at 'Home Rule within Home Rule'. In November, Asquith told Redmond that Carson and Bonar Law were demanding the total and permanent exclusion of 'Ulster' (the limits of that entity to be defined by agreement) as the basis of a settlement. Lloyd George had suggested an alternative plan within the Cabinet: the disarming of Ulster's opposition by temporary exclusion. Redmond did not reject this, but replied that any such proposal must come from the other side. At the end of the year, the growing restiveness of nationalists watching events in Ulster found expression in the formation of the Irish Volunteers, who were soon enrolling and drilling in large numbers throughout the country.

In late 1913 and early 1914, taking guidance from Devlin, Redmond was still giving Asquith an unrealistically sanguine view of the situation, telling him that nobody in Ulster believed that an organized rebellion was likely. However, in late February, alarmed at the probability of sectarian clashes, he asked for a mass nationalist rally in Derry to be called off. In March, Redmond and his colleagues told the Cabinet that, as 'the price of peace', they would concede county plebiscites in Ulster, with exclusion to be for three years. The White Paper that appeared on 9 March adopted this scheme, but with the time limit increased to six years. Carson rejected the offer as a 'sentence of death, with a stay of execution'. The atmosphere of crisis intensified: civil war was now spoken of by Unionists as a certainty if the Government imposed Home Rule on Ulster. The Curragh incident in March, in which army commanders pledged not to obey orders to suppress Ulster's opposition, and the gun-running at Larne and other ports in April, which made the UVF a formidable force, brought about a tense stalemate as the Home Rule Bill went through its final stages.

In June 1914, Redmond agreed to endorse the Irish Volunteers on condition that they accept democratic control by taking nominees of his party into their organizing committee. This put him at the head of an organization enrolling 15,000 recruits each week. During the summer, while the Government's Amending Bill, based on its March proposals, was in the House of Lords, Redmond came under pressure to make further concessions. In late July, he and Dillon accepted invitations from

George V to Buckingham Palace to negotiate a settlement with the other party leaders. With the nationalist leaders standing firm against a block vote for the excluded area, the conference reached deadlock on 24 July. Because of the likely outbreak of war in Europe, the Amending Bill was postponed on 30 July.

On 3 August the United Kingdom was at war with Germany. Redmond made his famous speech in the Commons that day, pledging the sympathy of the Irish democracy for the war effort and offering the Irish Volunteers for the defence of Ireland. He hoped that out of such joint action by Catholic nationalists and Protestant unionists would spring a result beneficial for Ireland. With Home Rule not yet signed into law, further consultations went on between Redmond and the Cabinet during August. Finally, on 18 September, Redmond's thirty-three years in the House of Commons reached a triumphant climax when the Home Rule Bill was placed on the Statute Book, albeit together with a suspensory measure to postpone its operation until the end of the war. Two days later, passing through Woodenbridge, County Wicklow, he spoke to Volunteers on parade and went further than in his 3 August speech, this time calling on them to enlist and go 'wherever the firing line extends'. The result was an immediate split between the 160,000 'National' Volunteers who supported his position and the 12,000 'Irish' Volunteers, led by such as Pearse and Eoin MacNeill, who opposed him.

IV

As Redmond began an intensive recruiting campaign in Ireland that autumn, he was anxious that the Government sustain Irish enthusiasm by keeping to its commitment to turn the Volunteers into a home defence force, and by forming an Irish Army Corps with distinctive badge and insignia. (The UVF had been given its own division, the 36th Ulster.) However, his lobbying of the Cabinet on these matters was obstructed by Lord Kitchener at the War Office, despite repeated promises by Asquith. Redmond's dealings with Sir Laurence Parsons, the commander of the 16th (Irish) Division, were similarly frustrating when he sought commissions for young Catholic Irishmen: Parsons staffed his division mainly with Protestant officers. Redmond's own son, William, had to enlist as a private.

Although he was now, in theory, the prime minister of an Irish government-in-waiting, his real power to influence events was no greater than ever. Home Rule remained a mirage. The obstructions erected by Kitchener and Parsons, and the likelihood that the war would last much longer than originally predicted, were factors he had not foreseen. By the spring of 1915, Dillon was convinced that Redmond's Woodenbridge speech had been an error of judgement and was worried at the discrediting of the Irish Party. He told Redmond that he would take no further part in recruiting. While recruitment was slower than in the first months of the war, it proceeded at a steady pace, despite news of the disasters at Gallipoli and the Dardanelles. By the end of 1915, 28,000 of the National Volunteers and 40,000 others had enlisted. But Redmond was increasingly estranged from Dillon and many others of his colleagues. His brother William and others close to him were on active service. Political developments added to his isolation. In May, he was offered a Cabinet seat in the new coalition Government, but felt obliged to refuse, in line with his party's traditional practice. In doing so, he deprived himself of all power while having to accept responsibility for the Government's mistakes. Carson joined the Cabinet as attorney-general. The symbolism of the appointment of the ardent Unionist James Campbell, who had talked of civil war, to the top legal position in Ireland, angered nationalists and embarrassed Redmond. He had protested vigorously, but in private, to Asquith; his patriotic refraining from public criticism in time of war was seen as acquiescence in Government actions. When he visited the Western front in November, he had the consolation of seeing a battalion of Ulstermen fighting next to the Dublin Fusiliers.

The IRB, reorganized since 1907, had secretly resolved at the outset of the war to stage an insurrection as soon as possible. Redmond's advice to Birrell underestimated the dangers from extremists, although the latter told him in December 1915 that the Irish Volunteers had increased their membership and that their meetings were 'centres of sedition'. Meanwhile, the propaganda of the constitutional separatists around Sinn Féin was having increasing effect, especially with rumours of conscription in the air. Redmond was in London at Easter 1916 when news came of the rebellion in Dublin, and was shocked at the messages he received from Dillon who, trapped in his house by the fighting, warned him to stay where he was. In the Commons he expressed his 'feeling of detestation and horror' at an insurrection that he regarded as a German plot and 'treason to the cause of Home Rule'. Following the surrender of the rebels, having accepted the first executions he urged Asquith repeatedly to exercise leniency. However, the imposition of military rule in Dublin under General John Maxwell took the situation far beyond his power to influence. The phasing of the fifteen executions over nine days caused revulsion among a population initially hostile to the insurrection and brought a wave of sympathy for the rebels.

In the aftermath, Asquith, seeing an opportunity to make a fresh effort at reaching agreement, asked Lloyd George to initiate negotiations with the Irish Party and the Unionists. The silence needed to give them a chance of success further damaged Redmond's standing in Ireland, being seen once more as acquiescence in the excesses of military rule. The talks revolved around a set of proposals that involved putting Home Rule into immediate operation while excluding six counties and keeping the full Irish representation at Westminster. The crucial clause was the time limit: the provisions would stay in force for the rest of the war and one year afterwards, and thereafter only until Parliament made permanent arrangements. Carson and Redmond (acting through Devlin) managed with great difficulties to win acceptance from their respective constituencies; much depended on the 'creative ambiguity' of the proposals. However, pressure from southern Unionists in the Cabinet forced the Government to make the partition clause permanent, causing the initiative to founder in late July amid bitter recriminations from an angry Redmond. The affair damaged and demoralized the Irish Party, and accelerated the decline in Redmond's authority among nationalists and the shift in sentiment towards Sinn Féin. Throughout late 1916 he struggled desperately to save the constitutional movement, calling for the withdrawal of martial law, a general amnesty and an imperial conference to settle the Ulster question. Though Irish sentiment was now against the war and recruitment was down, he opposed all suggestions of conscription for Ireland.

In the first half of 1917, Redmond was constantly vilified in much of the nationalist press as having been duped into consenting to partition. All was still not lost, however, if Home Rule could be brought into effect and he could begin to wield power. In May, the new prime minister, Lloyd George, offered Redmond a chance to assemble a convention of all Irish parties to try to negotiate a scheme for self-government. Redmond's acceptance took him back to the conciliation policy under which he had co-operated with moderate Unionists in the 1890s and in the Land Conference. The Irish Convention began in July in Dublin under the chairmanship of Sir Horace Plunkett. There were 95 delegates, of whom almost half, at Redmond's insistence, were Unionists, including 19 representing the Ulster viewpoint. Dillon refused to attend; Sinn Féin, not yet reorganized into the formidable force it later became, boycotted it. With support draining from the constitutional movement, there was an air of unreality about the proceedings. Redmond, though showing all his skills as a negotiator, was absent for long periods through illness. By late November, it seemed that a breakthrough was at hand. Lord Midleton, the moderate representative of a southern Unionist community shocked by the rise of separatism and reeling from its human losses in the war, proposed a Home Rule settlement without partition, in which the Irish Government would have full control of internal taxes, but not of customs, and with safeguards for Ulster. Opposition came, not only from the Ulster delegates, but from a majority of the nationalists led by Bishop O'Donnell who held out for full fiscal autonomy.

When the convention assembled in early January 1918, Redmond gave notice of an amendment that supported the Midleton plan on the strict condition that the Government commit itself to the deal and give it legislative effect (implying its imposition on Ulster, if necessary). With the Ulster delegates seeming to waver, all sides now felt that a deal was imminent. However, before the decisive debate on 15 January, Devlin and Bishop O'Donnell told Redmond of their opposition to his amendment in the absence of agreement from Ulster to 'come in'. Rather than divide the nationalists, he withdrew it. Nationalists were now seen as the obstructors of agreement, allowing the Ulstermen to revert to their partition demand, and the Midleton plan failed to win unanimity.

Redmond's failing health kept him bedridden for much of February; his illness now required an operation. On 26 February, he told Dillon of his wish to resign the party chair. A few days later, he underwent a successful operation. However, serious heart trouble complicated his recovery and he died on 6 March 1918, not yet 62 years old. The Home Rule cause to which he had sacrificed himself effectively died a month later when the Government agreed to implement the convention's majority report but linked it with the introduction of conscription.

The trajectory of Redmond's career is a tragic one, showing a long and difficult climb to the summit of success, followed by a relatively rapid and catastrophic collapse of authority initiated by the prolongation of the Great War and accelerated by the events of 1916 and their aftermath. The political tragedy was paralleled by the personal, with the death of his eldest daughter from illness, followed shortly afterwards by that of his brother William at Messines on the Western Front in June 1917. Like the hammer blows that presage the hero's doom at the end of his contemporary Gustav Mahler's sixth symphony, the loss of four by-elections in his last year tolled his fate in an eerie echo of Parnell's final electoral reverses. He did not live quite long enough to see the conscription crisis, or the eclipse of the party he had led, or the descent into violence that followed, but he could see at the end the wreckage of his hopes for an Ireland at once united and self-governing within the Empire, and the resurrection of forces that he had, too optimistically, assumed were part of Ireland's past. The Redmond legacy lived on only in the Waterford constituency, which he had represented. His son, Captain William Archer Redmond, DSO, M.P., TD, sat in the Dáil for that constituency until his death in 1932, to be followed by his widow until 1951.

Notes and References

Unless otherwise stated, all references to NLI Mss. are to the Redmond Papers at the National Library of Ireland

1. The Tradition

1 Engraved on pedestal of the Redmond monument, Redmond Square, Wexford Town.
2 Hansard, 171 (2nd series), 804, 12 Jun. 1863; 969, 16 June 1863.
3 ibid., 172 (2nd series), 242, 6 Jul. 1863.
4 Brian M. Walker (ed.), *New History of Ireland – Vol. VIII: Parliamentary Election Results in Ireland 1801–1922* (Dublin: 1978).
5 *Irish Builder*, vol. 9 (1 Apr. 1867), p. 87.
6 ibid.
7 Pedigree in Redmond family documents, NLI Ms. 15,276 (3).
8 L. G. Redmond-Howard, *John Redmond – The Man and the Demand* (London, 1910); Denis Gwynn, *The Life of John Redmond* (London, 1932), pp. 34–6.
9 Pedigree; Hilary Murphy, *Families of County Wexford* (Dublin, 1986), pp. 199–202.
10 Pedigree; Gwynn, *Life of John Redmond*, pp. 34–6.
11 Murphy, *Families*, pp. 200–01; Kevin Whelan, 'The Catholic Community in 18th Century Wexford', in T. P. Power and K. Whelan (eds.), *Endurance and Emergence: Catholics in Ireland in the Eighteenth Century* (Dublin, 1990), p. 148.
12 Gwynn, *Life of John Redmond*, p. 34.
13 Whelan, 'The Catholic Community', pp. 144–8.
14 ibid., p. 148.
15 Jarlath Glynn, 'The Catholic Church in Wexford Town 1800–1858', *The Past* (Organ of the Ui Cinsealaigh Historical Society), no. 15, (1984), p. 21.
16 ibid., p. 22; Redmond family tree and commentary, in possession of the Ryan family of Ballytrent.
17 Glynn, 'Catholic Church', p. 31.
18 Redmond-Howard, *John Redmond*, p. 7.
19 Redmond family tree and commentary.
20 David Goodall, 'The Freemen of Wexford in 1776', *Irish Genealogist*, vol. 5, no. 4 (Nov. 1977), pp. 448–63. A local newspaper reported on the celebrations of the triumphant Catholics and reformist Protestants: 'To general applause, a Catholic, Mr. Meyler, rose and gratefully proposed the toast of "The Protestant Boys". Not to be outdone, a Protestant, Mr. Nathaniel Hughes, leapt to his feet and proposed "The health of the Pope of Rome, and long life to him!"', *Wexford Herald*, 17 Apr., 1830.
21 Glynn, 'Catholic Church', pp. 23–4.
22 Oliver MacDonagh, *O'Connell: The Life of Daniel O'Connell 1775–1847* (London, 1991), pp. 409–10.
23 *Watson's or the Gentleman's and Citizen's Almanack for the year 1831*, p. 118, and for subsequent years to 1838.
24 Walker, *Parliamentary Election Results*.
25 Redmond family documents NLI Ms. 15,276 (1).
26 ibid.
27 *Watson's Almanack for the Year 1833* (Dublin, 1833), p. 89.
28 *Thom's Almanac and Official Directory of the United Kingdom of Great Britain and Ireland* for the years 1845–69.
29 ibid.
30 *Dublin Almanac and General Register of Ireland for the year 1837* (Dublin, 1837), p. 240.

31 Redmond-Howard, *John Redmond.*
32 *Thom's Directories*, 1862–69.
33 *Freeman's Journal*, 28 Mar. 1884; hereafter *F.J.*
34 Kevin Whelan, *The Tree of Liberty: Radicalism, Catholicism and the Construction of Irish Identity 1760–1830* (Cork, 1996), p. 21.
35 Redmond family documents, NLI Ms. 15,276 (3).
36 ibid. *Who Was Who 1897–1916.*
37 Brian Cleary, 'The Battle of Oulart Hill: Context and Strategy,' in Dáire Keogh and Nicholas Furlong (eds.), *The Mighty Wave: The 1798 Rebellion in Wexford* (Dublin, 1996), pp. 80, 87.
38 Redmond-Howard, *John Redmond*, p. 6.
39 ibid. p. 8.
40 Glynn, 'Catholic Church', pp. 33–4.
41 Walker, *Parliamentary Election Results*. He defeated his 21-year-old half-brother Walter, the son of his father's second marriage, by 321 votes to 51.
42 Redmond-Howard, *John Redmond*, p. 8.
43 David Thornley, *Isaac Butt and Home Rule* (London, 1964), pp. 126–31.
44 Frank Hugh O'Donnell, *A History of the Irish Parliamentary Party*, 2 vols. (London, 1910), vol. I, p. 61.
45 Conor Cruise O'Brien, *Parnell and His Party* (Oxford, 1957).
46 O'Donnell, *History*, vol. I, p. 78.
47 Editor and co-proprietor (with his brother, T. D. Sullivan, a Home Rule M.P. from 1880 and author of the unofficial national anthem 'God Save Ireland') of the *Nation*, kinsman of the Healys, a superb orator and author of the seminal nationalist history *The Story of Ireland*, Sullivan represented the pragmatic centre of Butt's party. In earlier days, as a member of Dublin Corporation, he had secured the site for the Grattan Monument in College Green, donating the entire sum of £400 subscribed by admirers when he underwent a spell of imprisonment in 1868. *The Catholic Encyclopaedia*, vol. 14 (New York, 1912).
48 Thornley, *Isaac Butt*, p. 167.
49 Warre B. Wells, *John Redmond – A Biography* (London, 1919), p. 32.
50 Stephen Gwynn, *John Redmond's Last Years* (London, 1919), p. 7.
51 Denis Gwynn, 'John Redmond', *Studies*, vol. 45 (Winter 1956) p. 389.
52 *Wexford Independent*, 3 Nov. 1880.
53 *Nation*, 22 May 1880.
54 Hansard (3rd series), 218, 169, 20 Mar. 1874.
55 ibid., 221, 741 (3rd series), 25 Jul. 1874.
56 ibid., 237, 134 (3rd series), 17 Jan. 1878.
57 *Wexford Independent*, 6 Nov. 1880.
58 R. Barry O'Brien, *The Life of Charles Stewart Parnell*, 2 vols. (London, 1899), vol. I, p. 62.
59 Ford to Butt, 6 Jan. 1875, Butt Papers, NLI Ms. 10415 (5).
60 *Dublin Evening Mail*, 16 May 1865; *Wexford Independent*, 11 Apr. 1868.
61 Thornley, *Isaac Butt*, pp. 188–9.
62 See chapter 2.
63 O'Donnell, *History*, vol. I, p. 78.
64 Norman D. Palmer, *The Irish Land League Crisis* (New Haven, 1940), p. 145.
65 Hansard (3rd series), 215, 776, 21 Apr. 1873.
66 ibid., 228, 721 (3rd series), 28 Mar. 1876.
67 Redmond-Howard, *John Redmond*, p. 8.
68 Hansard (3rd series), 229, 542, 12 May 1876.
69 ibid.
70 ibid., 545.
71 Quoted in Redmond-Howard, *John Redmond*, p. 8.
72 *Wexford Independent*, 3 Nov. 1880.
73 *Nation*, 6 Nov. 1880.

2. Beginnings and Bereavements

1 Quoted in John J. Horgan, *Parnell to Pearse – Some Recollections and Reflections* (Dublin, 1948), p. 55.
2 From collection of verse in private journal kept by John Redmond, now in the possession of Father Matt Glynn, PP, Tagoat, Co. Wexford.
3 Baptismal certificate from register of St Mary's Metropolitan Parish, kept in the Pro-Cathedral, Marlborough Street, Dublin, in Redmond family documents, NLI Ms. 15,276 (3). Many publications give incorrect dates for Redmond's birth, including the first biography written by his nephew, L. G. Redmond-Howard, the first two posthumous biographies, by Warre B. Wells and Stephen Gwynn, all of which place it in 1857, and *Who Was Who 1916–1928*, which gives 1851.
4 The place of birth is given in J. G. Swift MacNeill, *What I have Seen and Heard* (Boston, 1925), p. 201; see also *Thom's Dublin Directories*, 1853–56. The Georgian houses, by then tenements, were demolished in the 1980s; the street was rebuilt as Sean O'Casey Avenue.
5 Redmond-Howard, *John Redmond*, p. 9.
6 ibid, p. 11.
7 Joseph Lee, *The Modernisation of Irish Society 1848–1918* (Dublin, 1973), p. 17.
8 *Irish Daily Independent*, 17 Nov. 1897.
9 Redmond-Howard, *John Redmond*, p. 17.
10 ibid., pp. 4–5.
11 ibid., p. 13.
12 ibid., pp. 11–16.
13 ibid., pp. 13–14.
14 Alexander Melville Bell (1819–1905), the Edinburgh-born elocutionist and father of the inventor Alexander Graham Bell.
15 Redmond-Howard, *John Redmond*, p. 15.
16 ibid., p. 16.
17 ibid., p. 14.
18 Quoted in John J. Horgan, *Parnell to Pearse – Some Recollections and Reflections* (Dublin, 1948), p. 55.
19 Redmond-Howard, *John Redmond*, p. 18.
20 *Dublin University Calendar*, vol. I (1876), p. 71; S. Gwynn, *Last Years*, p. 5.
21 Memoir by John Gannon, *Clongownian*, vol. 8, no. 2 (June 1918), pp. 137–8.
22 Memoir by Father Robert Kane, *Clongownian*, vol. 8, no. 2 (June, 1918), p. 138.
23 M. J. [Mary] Redmond to Butt, 21 Jan. 1873, NLI Ms. 8695 (2).
24 Butt to M. J. Redmond, 26 Jan. 1873, NLI Ms. 8705.
25 M. J. Redmond to Butt, 12 Apr. 1873, NLI Ms. 8695 (14).
26 *F.J.*, 19 Nov. 1890.
27 S. Gwynn, *Last Years*, p. 5; D. Gwynn, *Life of John Redmond*, p. 82. The quoted lines refer to Macbeth asking the physician: 'Canst thou not minister to a mind diseased . . .' 'And he remembered well the effect produced upon that House when Mr. Butt went further, and recalled the answer of the physician, who said – "Therein the patient must minister to herself." That was their case for Home Rule.' Hansard (4th series) 11, 234–52, 13 Apr. 1893.
28 Terence Denman, *A Lonely Grave – The Life and Death of William Redmond* (Dublin, 1995), p. 22.
29 Thornley, *Isaac Butt*, pp. 305–7.
30 Michael Davitt, *The Fall of Feudalism in Ireland* (London, 1904), p. 123.
31 F. S. L. Lyons, *Charles Stewart Parnell* (London, 1977), p. 92.
32 The latter's title had been won with the St Patrick's Irish brigade which had fought for Pope Pius IX against the forces of Italian unification in the 1860s.
33 *Nation*, 3 Jan. 1880.
34 Redmond to Father Patrick Furlong, 29 Dec. 1880, NLI microfilm P 8531.
35 *Nation*, 20 Mar. 1880.
36 *Wexford Independent*, 17 Mar. 1880.
37 Cruise O'Brien, *Parnell*, p. 24.

38 The politics of the issue did not run along as clear a Whig–Parnellite divide as the Parnellite press suggested: O'Clery had testimony from Col. J. P. Nolan, a party whip, of an excellent attendance and voting record with the party, while a leading O'Clery supporter, Father Joseph Murphy of Ferns, could point to evidence that Garret Byrne had in the past shown no interest in helping the Home Rule cause while living in Liverpool.
39 The fullest and most coherent account of the meeting and riotous scenes, albeit written with a pro-O'Clery bias, is in the *Wexford Independent*, 31 Mar. 1880. Vinegar Hill is the site of a famous battle fought in the 1798 insurrection.
40 *Wexford Independent*, 3 Apr. 1880.
41 Barry O'Brien, *Parnell*, vol. I, p. 213.
42 *Nation*, 3 Apr. 1880.
43 *F.J.*, 17 Aug. 1880.
44 Registry of Deeds, Transcripts vol. 40, no. 42, 28 May 1879. The seven properties, which included Wexford County Court House, the land on which St Peter's College was built and the offices of the Provincial Bank of Ireland, yielded a net yearly rental of about £200 (worth £13,500 in 2005). Redmond paid £1,500 for these leaseholds, which were to stay in his possession only during the lifetime of his father. On the latter's death in November 1880, Redmond inherited all his property. Copy, Will of William Archer Redmond, 31 Oct. 1880, in Redmond family documents NLI Ms. 15,276 (1).
45 T. M. Healy, *Letters and Leaders of My Day*, 2 vols. (London, 1927), vol. 1, p. 102.
46 Redmond-Howard, *John Redmond*, p. 20.
47 All the extracts which follow are from Redmond's private journal; see note 2 above.
48 Redmond-Howard, *John Redmond*, p. 10.
49 Esther Redmond returned to London from India on 10 Sept. 1879, and died there of bronchitis on 30 August 1880: personal communication from Reparatrice Sisters, London. William Redmond, in a lecture given in Sydney on 10 May 1883, spoke of having a sister who devoted herself to religious life and 'died in the service of God in far-off India'. *F.J.* (Sydney), 19 May 1883.
50 Quoted from Lady Gregory's diary in John Kelly, 'Parnell in Irish Literature', in D. George Boyce and Alan O'Day (eds.), *Parnell in Perspective* (London, 1991), pp. 256–7.
51 Anna Kinsella, '1798 Claimed for Catholics: Father Kavanagh, Fenians and the Centenary Celebrations', in Keogh and Furlong (eds.), *The Mighty Wave*, pp. 139–55; Kevin Whelan, *The Tree of Liberty*, p. 173.
52 See Chapter 4.
53 *F.J.*, 18 Nov. 1886.
54 Malcolm Campbell, 'John Redmond and the Irish National League in Australia and New Zealand, 1883', *History*, vol. 86, no. 283 (July, 2001), 348–62.
55 For a more extended treatment of Redmond's rhetoric on 1798 in 1898, see Chapter 11. For a critique of modern attempts to idealize the insurrection to suit political purposes in the bicentennial commemorations of 1998, see Tom Dunne, *Rebellions: Memoir, Memory and 1798* (Dublin, 2004).
56 See Chapters 4, 6.
57 Cruise O'Brien, *Parnell*, p. 54.
58 *Wexford Independent*, 3 Nov. 1880. Redmond wired his mother: 'Father is in Heaven died in my arms yesterday funeral tomorrow Wexford High Mass Howe St. will write back soon'. Redmond family documents, NLI Ms. 15,276 (3).
59 Healy, *Letters and Leaders*, vol. 1, p. 102.
60 *Wexford Independent*, 10 Nov. 1880.
61 ibid.
62 Healy, *Letters and Leaders*, vol. 1, p. 102.
63 Redmond to Furlong, 22 Dec. 1880, NLI microfilm P 8533.
64 Private journal of John Redmond.

3. Passion and Pragmatism

1 Newscuttings of John Redmond's visit to America, Nov. 1896–Feb. 1897, NLI Ms. 7423.

2 Hansard (3rd series), 259, 853, 11 Mar. 1881.
3 Redmond to Furlong, 4 Jan. '1880' [1881], 6 Jan. 1881, NLI Ms. 28,894 (A).
4 *F.J.*, 2 Feb. 1881.
5 Redmond to Furlong, 29 Dec. 1880, NLI microfilm P 8531.
6 Redmond to Furlong, 22 Dec. 1880, NLI microfilm P 8533.
7 Cruise O'Brien, *Parnell*, p. 32.
8 Healy, *Letters and Leaders*, vol. 1, p. 200.
9 S. Gwynn, *Last Years*, p. 10.
10 Redmond to Furlong, 'Wednesday' [2 Feb.], NLI Ms. 28,894 (A).
11 D. Gwynn, *Life of John Redmond*, p. 33.
12 Barry O'Brien, *Parnell*, vol. 1, pp. 277–84.
13 Hansard (3rd series), 258, 69–72, 3 Feb. 1881.
14 A further five Irish members not at first in the chamber came in later to move Parnell's motion in succession and were also suspended.
15 Hansard (3rd series), 258, 85, 3 Feb. 1881.
16 *F.J.*, 4 Feb. 1881.
17 Lyons, *Parnell*, p. 147.
18 Cruise O'Brien, *Parnell*, pp. 59–61.
19 Redmond to Furlong, 8 Feb. 1881, NLI Ms. 28,894 (A).
20 Redmond to Furlong, 26 Feb. 1881, NLI Ms. 28,894 (A).
21 Barry O'Brien, *Parnell*, vol. 1, pp. 285–6.
22 Redmond to Furlong, 8 Feb. 1881, NLI Ms. 28,894 (A).
23 Hansard (3rd series), 258, 277–9, 7 Feb. 1881.
24 Redmond to Furlong, 8 Feb. 1881, NLI Ms. 28,894 (A).
25 Cruise O'Brien, *Parnell*, p. 64.
26 *Nation*, 26 Feb. 1881.
27 Redmond to Furlong, 26 Feb. 1881, NLI Ms. 28,894 (A).
28 Barry O'Brien, *Parnell*, vol. 1, p. 286.
29 Hansard (3rd series), 259, 171–6, 3 Mar. 1881.
30 ibid., 259, 186, 3 Mar. 1881.
31 *F.J.*, 4 Mar. 1881.
32 Hansard (3rd series), 259, 851–3, 11 Mar. 1881.
33 William O'Brien, *Recollections* (London, 1905), p. 253.
34 Redmond to Furlong, 26 Feb. 1881, NLI Ms. 28,894 (A).
35 ibid.
36 Redmond to Furlong, 25 Apr. 1881, NLI Ms. 28,894 (A).
37 *F.J.*, 13 Apr. 1881.
38 ibid., 23 Apr. 1881.
39 ibid., 3 May 1881.
40 ibid., 6 May 1881.
41 ibid., 6, 7 May 1881; *Nation*, 14 May 1881.
42 Redmond to Furlong, 9 May 1881, NLI Ms. 28,894 (A).
43 ibid.
44 Redmond to Furlong, 10 May 1881, NLI Ms. 28,894 (A).
45 *F.J.*, 11 May 1881.
46 Barry O'Brien, *Parnell*, vol. 1, p. 296.
47 Cruise O'Brien, *Parnell*, p. 67.
48 Redmond to Furlong, 'Monday' [23 May], NLI Ms. 28,894 (A).
49 ibid.
50 Hansard (3rd series), 261, 327–32, 12 May 1881.
51 Redmond to Furlong, 15 Jun. 1881, NLI Ms. 28,894 (A).
52 Hansard (3rd series), 264, 1627, 11 Aug. 1881.
53 ibid., 265, 264–8, 18 Aug. 1881.
54 ibid., 265, 292–6, 18 Aug. 1881.
55 ibid., 265, 394, 19 Aug. 1881.
56 O'Brien, *Recollections*, p. 328.
57 ibid., p. 304.

58 Cruise O'Brien, *Parnell*, p. 71; *F.J.*, 26, 27 Sept. 1881.
59 *F.J.*, 3 Oct. 1881.
60 O'Brien, *Recollections*, p. 339.
61 *F.J.*, 10 Oct. 1881.
62 Healy, *Letters and Leaders*, vol. 1, p. 135.
63 *F.J.*, 10 Oct. 1881.
64 ibid., 11 Oct. 1881.
65 Healy, *Letters and Leaders*, vol. 1, p. 136.
66 ibid., p. 137.
67 Cruise O'Brien, *Parnell*, p. 73.
68 O'Brien, *Recollections*, p. 331.
69 ibid., pp. 367–8.
70 ibid., p. 352.
71 *F.J.*, 14, 19, 21 Oct. 1881.
72 *F.J.*, 25 Oct. 1881.
73 Cruise O'Brien, *Parnell*, p. 74.
74 Redmond to Furlong, 5 Nov. 1881, NLI Ms. 28,894 (A).
75 O'Donnell, *History*, vol. 2, p. 46.
76 *F.J.*, 15 Nov. 1881.
77 ibid., 17 Nov. 1881.
78 ibid., 16 Nov. 1881.
79 ibid., 6 Dec. 1881.
80 ibid., 8 Dec. 1881.
81 O'Donnell, *History*, vol. 2, p. 46.
82 *F.J.*, 17 Dec. 1881.
83 Roy Foster, *Charles Stewart Parnell: The Man and His Family* (Brighton, 1976), p. 203.
84 *F.J.*, 27 Feb. 1882.
85 ibid., 13 Dec. 1881.
86 Lyons, *Parnell*, p. 192.
87 Denman, *Lonely Grave*, p. 24.
88 Hansard (3rd series), 266, 355–9, 9 Feb. 1882.
89 ibid., 266, 389–401, 10 Feb. 1882.
90 ibid.
91 ibid.
92 ibid., 266, 1437–442, 1444, 23 Feb. 1882.
93 *F.J.*, 14 Mar. 1882.
94 ibid., 15 Mar. 1882.
95 ibid., 18 Mar. 1882.
96 ibid., 14 Mar. 1882.
97 ibid., 20 Mar. 1882.
98 ibid., 28 Mar. 1882.
99 ibid., 31 Mar. 1882.
100 ibid., 1 Apr. 1882.
101 ibid., 3 Apr. 1882.
102 ibid., 4 Apr. 1882.
103 ibid., 3 Apr. 1882.
104 ibid., 10 Apr. 1882.
105 ibid.
106 ibid., 12 Apr. 1882.
107 Between 27 February and 2 May the total of his parliamentary questions amounted to eighty-one, placing him among the seven most active members of the party in this session (the others being Healy, Sexton, Biggar, O'Donnell, A. O'Connor and Callan). See Hansard, 275, General Index for the 1882 Session.
108 *F.J.*, 21 Apr. 1882.
109 Cruise O'Brien, *Parnell*, pp. 76–7; Lyons, *Parnell*, pp. 196–204.
110 Healy, *Letters and Leaders*, vol. 1, p. 152.
111 *F.J.*, 27 April 1882.

112 ibid., 1, 2 May 1882.
113 ibid., 3 May 1882.
114 Healy, *Letters and Leaders*, vol. 1, p. 156.
115 *F.J.*, 6 May 1882.
116 ibid., 8 May 1882.
117 ibid., 10 May 1882.
118 ibid., 25 May 1882.
119 Brief autobiographical note by Redmond (written in late 1880s), Redmond Papers NLI Ms. 15,273.
120 ibid.
121 ibid.
122 Barry O'Brien, *Parnell*, vol. 1, p. 358.
123 Lyons, *Parnell*, p. 212.
124 Redmond Papers NLI Ms. 15,238 (4): cutting from *Irish Daily Independent,* 18 Oct. 1893, 'A stale calumny exposed'. Redmond also repeated his explanation in the House of Commons on 1 Aug. 1888. See Hansard, 329, 1135–7.
125 Lyons, *Parnell*, p. 208.
126 O'Brien, *Recollections*, p. 428.
127 Lyons, *Parnell*, p. 211.
128 Hansard (3rd series), 269, 996–1002, 18 May 1882; Lyons, *Parnell*, p. 225.
129 ibid.
130 Lyons, *Parnell*, p. 216.
131 Hansard (3rd series), 269, 1652–1657, 25 May 1882.
132 Apart from putting sixteen questions, he spoke twenty-six times on the Coercion Bill during this period. See Hansard 270 and 271.
133 Hansard, 271, 1124–6, 30 June 1882.
134 *F.J.*, 3 July 1882.
135 ibid., 12 July 1882.
136 ibid., 1 Aug. 1882.
137 Lyons, *Parnell*, p. 226.
138 *F.J.*, 7 Aug. 1882.
139 ibid., 16, 17, 18 Aug. 1882.
140 Lyons, *Parnell*, pp. 226–34; *F.J.*, 25 Sept. 1882.
141 Cruise O'Brien, *Parnell*, p. 85.
142 Lyons, *Parnell*, pp. 229–30; *F.J.*, 18 Oct. 1882.
143 Lyons, *Parnell*, p. 238.
144 O'Brien, *Recollections*, pp. 235–7; Police Reports of Land League and National League proceedings, NAI INL 3/714, Box 3; *F.J.*, 13, 16 Nov. 1882.
145 Healy, *Letters*, vol. 1, p. 200. Healy seems to be confusing these years with a later period in the 1880s, when Redmond became relatively inactive.
146 O'Brien, *Recollections*, p. 252.
147 Katherine Tynan, *Twenty-Five years: Reminiscences* (London, 1913), pp. 89, 123.
148 Katherine Tynan, *Memories* (London, 1924), p. 61.
149 Barry O'Brien, *Parnell*, vol. 1, p. 366.
150 Parnell to Redmond, 1 Dec. 1882, NLI Ms. 15,237 (1).
151 Quoted in *F.J.*, 28 Nov. 1882.
152 Denman, *Lonely Grave*, pp. 24–5; *F.J.*, 28 Nov. 1882.
153 NLI Ms. 15,186 (3).

4. The Mission

1 Quoted in Campbell, see note 3.
2 *Freeman's Journal* (Sydney), 17 Mar. 1883.
3 For a recent account of the Redmonds' visit, see Campbell, 'Redmond in Australia and New Zealand'.
4 *F.J.* (Sydney), 10 Feb. 1883.
5 *Weekly Freeman's Journal*, 22 Mar. 1884.
6 *F.J.* (Sydney), 17 Feb. 1883.

7 ibid.
8 *Sydney Morning Herald*, 16 Feb. 1883.
9 *F.J.* (Sydney), 17 Feb. 1883.
10 ibid.
11 ibid., 24 Feb. 1883.
12 Barry O'Brien, *Parnell*, vol. 1, p. 370.
13 Campbell, 'Redmond in Australia and New Zealand', p. 350.
14 *F.J.* (Sydney), 24 Feb. 1883.
15 ibid.
16 Quoted in *F.J.* (Sydney), 3 Mar. 1883.
17 *F.J.* (Sydney), 10 Mar. 1883.
18 ibid., 3 Mar. 1883.
19 ibid., 10 Mar. 1883; Campbell, 'Redmond in Australia and New Zealand', p. 353.
20 *F.J.* (Sydney), 8 Sep. 1883.
21 *F.J.* (Sydney), 17 Mar. 1883. This account of the meeting was reprinted by the *Freeman* from the *Sydney Morning Herald.*
22 *F.J.* (Sydney), 24 Mar. 1883.
23 ibid.
24 ibid.
25 ibid., 31 Mar. 1883.
26 ibid., 14 Apr. 1883.
27 ibid., 31 Mar., 14, 28 Apr. 1883.
28 ibid., 28 Apr. 1883.
29 ibid., 19 May 1883.
30 ibid., 26 May 1883.
31 ibid., 9 Jun. 1883.
32 ibid.
33 ibid., 16 Jun. 1883.
34 Quoted in *Nation*, 18 Aug. 1883.
35 Quoted by Campbell, 'Redmond in Australia and New Zealand', pp. 355–6.
36 *F.J.* (Sydney), 30 June 1883.The Melbourne lectures on Home Rule and the Land League were published in John Redmond, *Historical and Political Addresses* (Dublin and London, 1898).
37 ibid., 21 July 1883.
38 ibid., 4, 11 Aug. 1883.
39 ibid., 25 Aug. 1883.
40 ibid., 8 Sept. 1883.
41 ibid., 3 Nov. 1883.
42 Letter of 7 March reprinted in ibid., 14 Apr. 1883.
43 Quoted in ibid., 10 Nov. 1883.
44 Quoted by Campbell, 'Redmond in Australia and New Zealand', pp. 358–9.
45 *F.J.* (Sydney), 10 Nov. 1883.
46 ibid.
47 ibid., 17 Nov. 1883.
48 ibid., 24 Nov. 1883.
49 See chapter 2.
50 *F.J.* (Sydney), 8 Dec. 1883.
51 Campbell, 'Redmond in Australia and New Zealand', p. 360.
52 Lyons, *Parnell*, p. 248.
53 *F.J.* (Sydney), 8 Dec. 1883.
54 See chapters 6 and 8; see also Michael Wheatley, 'John Redmond and Federalism in 1910', *Irish Historical Studies*, vol. 32, no. 127 (May 2001), pp. 343–64.
55 S. Gwynn, *Last Years*, p. 15.
56 Hansard (3rd series), 305, 960–74, 13 May 1886. That such sentiments formed a not insignificant current of opinion within moderate nationalism is shown by the Dublin *Freeman's Journal's* celebration of the appointment of the earl of Dufferin, 'the brilliant, versatile and able Irishman', as viceroy of India, ('the almost absolute

ruler over 200,000,000 people', it exulted). The prejudice of the English press might ignore his nationality, but 'no jealousy can conceal the fact, however, that Ireland has supplied a proportion of the greatest men to the English Empire largely in excess of her size and population'. See *F.J.*, 12 Sept. 1884.

57 Lyons, *Parnell*, pp. 247–8, 355.
58 *Irish World*, 2 Feb. 1884.
59 ibid., 9 Feb., 1884.
60 ibid., 19 Jan. 1884. By 2 February Ford's paper was claiming that the fund had reached $2,000.
61 *F.J.*, 23 Jan. 1884.
62 Lyons, *Parnell*, p. 111.
63 *Irish World*, 16 Feb. 1884.
64 J. P. Ryan to John Devoy, 12 Feb. 1884, reprinted in *Devoy's Post Bag*, vol. 2: 1880–1928, eds. William O'Brien and Desmond Ryan (Dublin, 1953), p. 238.
65 *F.J.*, 9 Oct. 1906.
66 Newscuttings of visit of Redmond, Davitt and Dillon to first Convention of United Irish League of America, Boston, Oct. 1902, NLI Ms. 7432.
67 Newscuttings of visit to second Convention of United Irish League of America, New York, Aug.–Sep. 1904, NLI Ms. 7435.

5. At Parnell's Command

1 *A Diary of Two Parliaments*, (2 vols., London, 1886), vol. II: *The Gladstone Parliament* 1880–85, p. 439.
2 Hansard (3rd series), 305, 960, 13 May 1886.
3 *F.J.*, 21 Oct. 1882.
4 ibid., 27, 29 Feb., 3 Mar. 1884.
5 *Weekly Freeman's Journal*, 15 Mar. 1884.
6 *F.J.*, 11, 14, 17 Mar. 1884.
7 ibid., 11 Mar. 1884.
8 ibid.
9 *Weekly F.J.*, 15 Mar. 1884.
10 Tynan, *Memories*, p. 62.
11 Redmond to Furlong, 9 Oct. 1885, NLI Ms. 28,894 (A).
12 *F.J.*, 11 Nov. 1884; 9 Jun. 1885.
13 William O'Brien, *Evening Memories* (Dublin and London, 1920), p. 76.
14 Denman, *Lonely Grave*, p. 35.
15 *United Ireland*, 24 Jan. 1885.
16 *F.J.*, 17 Sept. 1884.
17 ibid.; *Irish Times*, 17 Sept. 1884.
18 *F.J.*, 2 Dec. 1884.
19 ibid., 22 Sept., 19 Dec. 1884.
20 *Weekly F.J.*, 18 Apr. 1885.
21 ibid.; *F.J.*, 13 Apr. 1885.
22 Denman, *Lonely Grave*, pp. 33–4.
23 *Weekly F.J.*, 15 Feb. 1884.
24 Tynan, *Twenty-Five Years*, p. 123.
25 Memoir by Mrs. Wm. O'Brien of John and William Redmond, NLI Ms. 8507 (2).
26 *F.J.*, 20 Nov. 1885.
27 F. G. Sullivan to Redmond, 18 Oct. [1885], NLI Ms. 15,237 (1).
28 *F.J.*, 23 Oct. 1884.
29 ibid., 5 Dec. 1884, 7 Mar. 1885.
30 ibid. 27 Oct., 3 Nov. 1884.
31 Cruise O'Brien, *Parnell*, p. 86.
32 Lyons, *Parnell*, pp. 265–7.
33 *Weekly F.J.*, 19 Apr. 1884.
34 ibid.
35 ibid.

36 *F.J.*, 14 May 1884.
37 ibid., 25 Oct. 1884.
38 Hansard (3rd series), 293, 204-8, 24 Oct. 1884.
39 *F.J.*, 27 Oct. 1884.
40 ibid., 8 Nov. 1884.
41 ibid., 8 Dec. 1884.
42 Lyons, *Parnell*, p. 263.
43 *F.J.*, 22 Sept. 1884.
44 See, for example, *F.J.*, 26 Sept., 4 Oct. 1884.
45 Charles Wentworth Dilke (1843–1911), a leading partisan within the Liberal Party in the cause of franchise reform, legalisation of trade unions, improvement of working conditions and universal schooling. His fate foreshadowed that of Parnell, of whom he was a near contemporary, in the effective ending of his political career by a well-publicized divorce case in 1886.
46 Jacinta Prunty, *Dublin Slums 1800–1925: A Study in Urban Geography* (Dublin, 1998), p. 144; Mary E. Daly, *Dublin – The Deposed Capital: A Social and Economic History 1860–1914* (Cork, 1985), p. 287.
47 *F.J.*, 1 Nov. 1884.
48 Daly, *Dublin – The Deposed Capital,* pp. 284–6.
49 Redmond family documents, NLI Ms. 15,276 (1).
50 Quoted in Redmond-Howard, *John Redmond*, p. 19. The law student was W. M. Cook, who told the anecdote to W. T. Stead for a character sketch of Redmond in 1901.
51 Hansard (3rd series), 289, 1020-36, 20 Jun. 1884.
52 ibid.
53 Healy, *Letters and Leaders*, vol. 1, p. 201.
54 Elizabeth Malcolm, *'Ireland Sober, Ireland Free': Drink and Temperance in Nineteenth-Century Ireland* (Dublin, 1986), p. 261.
55 *F.J.* (Sydney), 24 Nov. 1883.
56 *F.J.*, 18 Mar. 1885.
57 In a speech at Enniscorthy in September 1890, Redmond said that 'the money that was spent on drink in Ireland every year was as great as the entire rental of the whole country. Let them think of that . . . what did Ireland get from the 12 or 13 millions of pounds spent every year on drink? They got some seven-eighths of the crime of the country, about half of the lunacy, the greater portion of the disease, and the greatest portion of the wretchedness of the poor . . . So long as it was not considered a disgrace for a man to drink to excess, so long as people only treated with a shrug of indifference the meanness and selfishness of the man who gratified his appetite for drink at the expense of his family, it was impossible for any legislative effort to stem the tide of drink . . . He wanted to see the day when a man who robbed his family for drink would be regarded by the public with the same abhorrence as the thief or the land-grabber... (*cheers*).' *People* (Wexford), 24 Sep. 1890.
58 *F.J.*, 11 Nov. 1886.
59 ibid., 6 Nov. 1884.
60 Malcolm, *Ireland Sober*, p. 273.
61 John Spencer, 5th Earl Spencer (1835–1910), twice lord lieutenant of Ireland, 1868–74 and 1882–85, strong adherent of Gladstonian Home Rule for Ireland from 1886 onwards.
62 Lyons, *Parnell*, pp. 269–74.
63 *F.J.*, 16 May 1885.
64 Lyons, *Parnell*, p. 276.
65 ibid., p. 279.
66 *F.J.*, 21 May 1885.
67 ibid., 9 Jun. 1885.
68 ibid., 13, 15, 16, 17 Jun. 1885.
69 ibid., 18 Jun. 1885.
70 ibid., 14 Aug. 1885; Lyons, *Parnell*, p. 283.

71 ibid., 24 Aug. 1885.
72 Redmond to Furlong, 18 Apr. 1885, NLI Ms. 28,894 (A).
73 Redmond to Furlong, 5 May 1885, NLI Ms. 28,894 (A).
74 Redmond to Furlong, 30 Sept. 1885, NLI Ms. 28,894 (A).
75 *F.J.*, 2 Jun., 7 Jul. 1885.
76 ibid., 24 Aug. 1885.
77 Redmond to Furlong, 30 Sept. 1885, NLI Ms. 28,894 (A).
78 T. M. Healy to Redmond, 1 Oct. 1885, NLI Ms. 15,196.
79 Redmond to Furlong, 5, 9 Oct. 1885, NLI Ms. 28,894 (A).
80 F. G. Sullivan to Redmond, 18 Oct. [1885], NLI Ms. 15,237 (1).
81 *People*, 24, 28 Oct. 1885.
82 ibid., 31 Oct. 1885.
83 Redmond to Furlong, 27 Oct. 1885, NLI Ms. 28,894 (A).
84 *F.J.*, 4 Nov. 1885.
85 Healy to Redmond, 3 Nov. 1885, letter in possession of M. J. O'Connor, Solicitors, Wexford.
86 Healy, *Letters and Leaders*, vol. 1, p. 230.
87 ibid., p. 235.
88 Lyons, *Parnell*, p. 306.
89 Healy, *Letters and Leaders*, vol. 1, p. 191.
90 Lyons, *Parnell*, pp. 306–7.
91 *F.J.*, 6 Nov. 1885.
92 Cruise O'Brien, *Parnell*, pp. 130–1.
93 *F.J.*, 30 Oct., 2, 5, 7 Nov. 1885.
94 ibid., 2 Nov. 1885.
95 ibid., 19 Nov. 1885. Redmond went on to defeat Stopford in North Wexford by 6531 votes to 917.
96 ibid., 23 Nov. 1885; Lyons, *Parnell*, pp. 301–02.
97 *F.J.*, 23 Nov. 1885.
98 ibid., 24 Nov. 1885.
99 ibid., 1 Dec. 1885; Lyons, *Parnell*, p. 319.
100 *Nation*, 12 Dec. 1885.
101 *F.J.*, 5 Dec. 1885.
102 ibid., 14 Dec. 1885.
103 ibid., 12 Dec. 1885.
104 ibid., 14 Dec. 1885.
105 ibid., 16 Dec. 1885.
106 ibid., 21 Jan. 1886.
107 ibid., 3 Dec. 1885.
108 ibid., 12 Jan. 1886.
109 ibid., 23 Oct. 1884.
110 Lyons, *Parnell*, p. 255.
111 *F.J.*, 27 Aug. 1885.
112 ibid., 5 Sept. 1885.
113 ibid., 8 Sept. 1885.
114 Cruise O'Brien, *Parnell*, pp. 128–30.
115 *F.J.*, 9 Sept. 1885.
116 According to Lyons, the Whig M.P. George Errington was the agent of the Foreign Office at the Vatican in this affair; the sum of £40,000 was collected by the end of 1883. For an account of the episode, including Parnell's strange behaviour at the presentation to him of the money, see Lyons, pp. 244–7.
117 *F.J.*, 12, 14 Dec. 1885.
118 ibid., 9 Sept. 1885.
119 ibid., 18 Dec. 1885.
120 ibid., 16, 19 Jan. 1886.
121 ibid., 27 Jan. 1886.
122 Lyons, *Parnell*, p. 341.

123 *F.J.*, 22 Feb. 1886.
124 ibid., 17 Feb. 1886.
125 Lyons, *Parnell*, pp. 321–33.
126 *F.J.*, 9 Feb. 1886.
127 ibid., 6 Feb. 1886.
128 ibid., 8 Feb. 1886.
129 ibid., 25 Feb. 1886.
130 ibid., 8 Mar. 1886.
131 ibid., 15 Mar. 1886.
132 See, for example, ibid., 5, 9 Mar. 1886.
133 Redmond to Furlong, 22 Mar. 1886, NLI Ms. 28,894 (A).
134 Healy, *Letters and Leaders*, vol. 1, p. 251.
135 Cruise O'Brien, *Parnell*, pp. 185–6.
136 *F.J.*, 9 Apr. 1886.
137 Cruise O'Brien, *Parnell*, p. 187.
138 Redmond to Furlong, 22 Mar. 1886, NLI Ms. 28,894 (A).
139 *F.J.*, 21 Apr. 1886.
140 Hansard (3rd series), 305, 960–74, 13 May 1886.
141 Johnston, known as 'William Johnston of Ballykilbeg', Orange campaigner for land reform, temperance and female franchise, and loyalist hero since his dismissal from the fisheries inspectorate by the Tory Government in 1879 for violent speeches against the Land League and Home Rule, had declared at Dungannon the previous week 'With the Bible in one hand and the rifle in the other we will fight against being handed over to these . . . Fenians, Invincibles and the associates of James Carey.' *F.J.*, 7 May 1886.
142 Hansard (3rd series), 305, 960–74, 13 May 1886.
143 *F.J.*, 14 May 1886.
144 ibid., 17 May 1886.
145 Rt. Hon. Sir Richard Temple, *Letters and Character Sketches from the House of Commons* (London, 1912), p. 72.
146 Hansard (3rd series), 305, 1198–204, 17 May 1886.
147 Redmond to Furlong, 13 May 1886, NLI P 8533.
148 Redmond to Furlong, 24 May 1886, NLI P 8531.
149 *F.J.*, 28 May 1886.
150 Lyons, *Parnell*, pp. 346–7; O'Brien, *Evening Memories*, p. 125.
151 *F.J.*, 1 Jun. 1886.
152 ibid., 2 Jun. 1886.
153 O'Brien, *Evening Memories*, p. 132.
154 *F.J.*, 8 Jun. 1886.
155 ibid., 16 Jun. 1886.
156 ibid., 18 Jun. 1886.
157 ibid., 18 Jun. 1886.
158 ibid., 26 Jun. 1886.
159 ibid., 12 Jul. 1886.
160 Lyons, *Parnell*, p. 352; Walker, (ed.) *Parliamentary Election Results.*

6. The Land and the Law

1 *Irish Times*, 20 Aug. 1886.
2 F.J., 17 Aug. 1886.
3 O'Brien, *Evening Memories*, p. 154; *F.J.*, 21 Sept. 1886.
4 *F.J.*, 27, 29 Feb., 3 Mar. 1884.
5 ibid., 31 May 1884.
6 ibid., 26 Jan. 1885.
7 O'Brien, *Evening Memories*, pp. 139–40.
8 *F.J.*, 20 Jul. 1886; Lyons, *Parnell*, pp. 355–6.
9 *F.J.*, 9 Aug. 1886.
10 O'Brien, *Evening Memories*, p. 139.

11 ibid., pp. 141–5.
12 ibid.
13 *F.J.*, 20 Aug., 7 Sept. 1886.
14 Redmond, *Historical and Political Addresses*; *Home Rule: Speeches of John Redmond, M.P.*, (edited and with an Introduction by R. Barry O'Brien), (London 1910), pp. 17–25.
15 *F.J.*, 7 Sept. 1886.
16 John Sadleir, M.P. for Sligo, and William Keogh, QC, M.P. for Athlone, both members of the Independent Irish Party formed in September 1852 to win the repeal of an anti-Catholic law and the adoption of the Tenant League programme. With their party holding the balance of power in the House of Commons, they earned the denunciation of nationalists when they broke their pledge of independence by accepting office in December 1852 in Lord Aberdeen's incoming Whig administration, Sadleir as a junior lord of the treasury, Keogh as solicitor general for Ireland.
17 ibid., 6, 14 Sept. 1886.
18 ibid., 9, 22 Sept. 1886.
19 ibid., 23 Sept. 1886.
20 ibid., 18, 20 Oct. 1886.
21 *United Ireland*, 23 Oct. 1886.
22 O'Brien, *Evening Memories*, pp. 155–9.
23 John Morley, *The Life of William Ewart Gladstone*, 2 vols. (London, 1908), vol. II, p. 458.
24 O'Brien, *Evening Memories*, pp. 177–87.
25 ibid., pp. 165–6; *F.J.*, 28 Oct., 10 Nov. 1886.
26 *F.J.*, 10 Nov. 1886.
27 Police Reports of Land League and National League proceedings, NAI 3/714, Box 3: speech at Kildare 27 May 1888.
28 *F.J.*, 15, 24 Sept. 1891; *National Press*, 16, 24 Sept. 1891; see Chapter 7.
29 *F.J.*, 6 Dec. 1886.
30 ibid., 13 Dec. 1886.
31 ibid., 17, 20 Dec. 1886.
32 ibid., 20, 31 Dec. 1886.
33 ibid., 3 Jan. 1887.
34 ibid., 17 Jan. 1887.
35 ibid., 20 Jan. 1887.
36 ibid., 2 Feb. 1887.
37 ibid., 21 Feb. 1887; for Redmond's own account of the Coolgreaney meetings, see his House of Commons speech in Hansard, 311, 1164–8, 3 Mar. 1887.
38 Hansard (3rd series), 311, 1160–70, 3 Mar. 1887.
39 ibid.
40 *F.J.*, 7, 9 Mar. 1887.
41 ibid., 21 Mar. 1887.
42 ibid., 14 Mar., 7 Apr. 1887.
43 Hansard, 312, 1712–29, 28 Mar. 1887.
44 Temple, *Letters and Character Sketches*, p. 274.
45 *F.J.*, 18 Jun., 9 Jul. 1887.
46 Temple, *Letters and Character Sketches*, editor's Introduction pp. xxiv–v.
47 O'Brien, *Evening Memories*, p. 75.
48 *F.J.*, 12 Apr. 1887.
49 ibid., 9 May 1887.
50 W. S. Blunt, *The Land War in Ireland–Being a Personal Narrative of Events* (London, 1912), p. 277. Blunt notes that this reason, given by Davitt when Blunt visited him at home in the summer of 1887, conflicts with that given in *The Fall of Feudalism in Ireland*, written by Davitt almost twenty years afterwards. See also Davitt's speech at Rathkeale on 29 Jan. 1888: 'I have not been very enthusiastic about advocating the Plan of Campaign, simply because I think it too moderate. In some instances it has given recognition to dangerous principles of tenants being satisfied that their rents

are fair when 10 or 20% is knocked off.' Police Reports of Land League and National League proceedings, NAI INL 3/714, Box 3.

51 *F.J.*, 8 Jun. 1887.
52 ibid., 9 Jun. 1887.
53 ibid., 13 Jul. 1887.
54 ibid., 16 Jul. 1887.
55 ibid., 18 Jul. 1887.
56 ibid., 23 Jul. 1887; Blunt, *Land War*, p. 284.
57 *F.J.*, 31 Aug. 1887.
58 ibid., 4 Jul., 3, 16 Aug. 1887. The Home Rule wins were, respectively, at Spalding, Bridgeton and Northwich.
59 ibid., 10 Sept. 1887.
60 T. D. Sullivan M.P., the current lord mayor of Dublin, told a Dublin meeting that the three shot at Mitchelstown were as much martyrs as the Manchester Martyrs of 1867, in whose honour he had composed the anthem 'God Save Ireland'; see *F.J.*, 28 Sept. 1887.
61 ibid., 13 Oct. 1887.
62 ibid., 12, 26 Sept. 1887.
63 ibid., 19 Oct. 1887.
64 ibid., 24, 25, 27 Oct. 1887.
65 ibid., 1 Nov. 1887.
66 Joseph V. O'Brien, *William O'Brien and the Course of Irish Politics 1881–1918* (Berkeley, 1976), pp. 54–7.
67 *F.J.*, 25, 26, 29 Oct., 21 Nov. 1887.
68 ibid., 11, 16, 24 Nov., 17 Dec. 1887.
69 ibid., 9 Jul. 1888.
70 Registry of Deeds, Transcripts vol. 48, no. 96, 21 Jul. 1886.
71 Cruise O'Brien, *Parnell*, p. 139, n. 3. Eight M.P.s were named at the commission as receiving payments from Parnell; the payments made to five of them, including Redmond, were, in Cruise O'Brien's view, 'probably' subsidies. The money paid by Parnell came ultimately from the 'Paris' funds. For Special Commission and 'Paris' funds, see below, this chapter.
72 *F.J.*, 28 Sept., 8 Oct., 2, 7 Nov. 1887.
73 In December he appeared for a group of Moonlighters in County Clare; in January he unsuccessfully defended J. R. Cox, M.P. for East Clare, on an incitement charge. See *F.J.*, 12 Dec. 1887, 30 Jan. 1888.
74 *F.J.*, 10, 27 Oct., 5 Nov. 1887.
75 ibid., 3, 5, 9, 22 Dec. 1887. The three were T. D. Sullivan, David Sheehy and Edward Harrington, the last, as in the case of Walsh, on a charge of reporting a meeting of a suppressed league branch in his newspaper, the *Kerry Sentinel*.
76 ibid., 7 Dec. 1887.
77 ibid., 1 Feb. 1888. He quoted one magistrate as saying that he represented the crown in court.
78 J. V. O'Brien, *William O'Brien*, pp. 58–9; *F.J.*, 3, 14 Feb. 1888.
79 *F.J.*, 21 Jan. 1888.
80 ibid., 29 Feb. 1888.
81 For a detailed narrative of the origins of the Special Commission and the Pigott episode, see Lyons, *Parnell*, pp. 374–8, 388–424; see also *F.J.*, 25 Jul., 16 Aug., 18 Sept., 16 Oct. 1888.
82 *F.J.*, 16 May, 8 Jun. 1888.
83 ibid., 22 Nov. 1887.
84 ibid., 9 May 1888; Lyons, *Parnell*, pp. 384–5.
85 *F.J.*, 20 Feb., 24 May, 18 Jun. 1888. The wins were at Dundee, West Southwark, Edinburgh West, Southampton and Ayr.
86 ibid., 8 Feb. 1888. Harcourt spoke of the Plan being vindicated by the rent reductions awarded by the courts.
87 Lyons, *Parnell*, p. 386.

88 ibid., pp. 383–4.
89 *F.J.*, 30 Apr. 1888. Blunt reported that when he had visited Archbishop Croke at his palace in July 1887, the latter had poked fun at Persico, saying that if he came to Thurles, 'he'd open his eyes for him, or shut them too, if he liked it better.' He was not much more reverent about the Pope, and gave Blunt an amusing account of his interview with Leo XIII: '"There's revolution," says I, "and revolution, revolution with guns against law and order, and a moral revolution against injustice. It's the latter we're having in Ireland". See Blunt, *The Land War*,' p. 281.
90 ibid., 5, 8, May 1888.
91 ibid., 18 May 1888.
92 ibid., 21 May 1888.
93 ibid., 4 Jun. 1888.
94 Police Reports of Land League and National League proceedings, NAI 3/714, Box 3: speech at Kildare, 27 May 1888.
95 ibid., speech at Ashford, 21 May 1888.
96 ibid., speech at Wexford, 27 May 1888.
97 *F.J.*, 26 Mar. 1888.
98 ibid., 4, 12, 14 May, 21, 29 Jun. 1888.
99 Police Reports, speech at Dungloe, 19 Jul. 1888.
100 ibid., speech at Scarawalsh, 22 Jul. 1888.
101 *F.J.*, 17 Aug., 15 Sept. 1888; *Irish Times*, 15 Sept. 1888.
102 *F.J.*, 6, 27 Sept. 1888.
103 S. Gwynn, *Last Years*, p. 18.
104 *F.J.*, 28 Sept., 2, 31 Oct. 1888; Margaret Leamy, *Parnell's Faithful Few* (New York, 1936), pp. 123–4.
105 Redmond to Furlong, 15 Nov. 1888, NLI Ms. 28,894(A).
106 *F.J.*, 23 Jan. 1889.
107 See, for example, *F.J.* 11 Dec. 1888, 31 May, 27 Jul., 25, 26 Sept., 2 Oct., 30 Nov. 1889, 19 Mar., 16 Jul., all of Oct. 1890; See also Leon O'Broin, *The Prime Informer – A Suppressed Scandal* (London, 1971).
108 *F.J.*, 13 Jul. 1891; Horgan to Redmond, 20 Nov. 1889, Redmond to Horgan, 21 Nov. 1889, NLI Ms. 15,237 (2), P 8434. Healy's fee exceeded Redmond's by 50 guineas due to his demand for a 'special fee' for 'acting off his circuit', since the trials were held in Wicklow rather than in the province of Munster where Healy normally appeared.
109 Lyons, *Parnell*, pp. 432–3. Parnell was able to promise £10,000, which he expected shortly to receive from Cecil Rhodes, the British colonial statesman and South African diamond millionaire.
110 See correspondence re. Garrynisk estate (1889) in NLI Ms. 15,237(2), P 8434; re. Tottenham estate (1890) in NLI Ms. 15, 238(1).
111 Lyons, *Parnell*, p. 433; *F.J.* 19 Jun. 1889.
112 *F.J.*, 11 Jul. 1889.
113 ibid., 20 Jul. 1889; Lyons, *Parnell*, pp. 433–4.
114 See letter of T. P. Gill, *F.J.*, 25 Aug. 1891, and report of Redmond's speech at Cork, *F.J.*, 26 Oct. 1891. Both recollections were published when the controversies of the Parnell split were at their height and the inception of New Tipperary had become a burning issue. Redmond was defending himself from the charge that he had gone to the 8 September meeting as Parnell's representative and told the people to let their farms go.
115 *F.J.*, 4 Jul., 10 Aug., 5, 9 Sept. 1889.
116 ibid., 5 Oct., 15 Nov., 3 Dec. 1889.
117 Lyons, *Parnell*, p. 435.
118 *F.J.*, 12, 14 Nov. 1889.
119 ibid., 6 Dec. 1889, for the full correspondence. See also Emmet Larkin, *The Roman Catholic Church in Ireland and the Fall of Parnell 1888–1891* (Liverpool, 1979), pp. 43–6.
120 *F.J.*, 6 Dec. 1889.

121 ibid., 18 Nov. 1886.
122 Redmond, *Historical and Political Addresses*; *Home Rule: Speeches*, pp. 26–41; *F.J.*, 30 Nov. 1886.
123 Quoted in Frank Callanan, *T. M. Healy*, (Cork, 1996), pp. 111–12.
124 *F.J.*, 19 Feb. 1889. This lecture was published in *Redmond, Historical and Political Addresses.*
125 *F.J.*, 24 Apr. 1889. The Home Rule wins were at Kennington, Gorton and Rochester.
126 Yet only a month later Parnell felt compelled to make an overture to his more extreme supporters with one of his classic balancing speeches, to a deputation of nationalist Irish town councillors in London, in which he adverted to the possibility that their constitutional movement might not achieve its goal and that 'the most advanced section of Irishmen, as well as the least advanced' had always understood that the parliamentary movement was to be a trial. See *F.J.*, 24 May 1889; Lyons, *Parnell*, pp. 443–5.
127 *F.J.*, 8 Oct. 1889.
128 ibid., 9 Oct. 1889.
129 ibid., 13, 14 Oct. 1890.
130 ibid., 6 Jun. 1891. The statue to Father Mathew now stands in Dublin's O'Connell Street.
131 ibid., 13 Dec. 1889.
132 ibid., 19 Sept. 1889. They were returning from a visit to William, who was again under arrest.
133 ibid., 16 Dec. 1889.
134 ibid., 30 Dec. 1889.
135 Lyons, *Parnell*, p. 463; *F.J.*, 22 Jan. 1890.
136 *F.J.*, 20 Dec. 1889.
137 NLI Ms. 15,238 (1).
138 His absence from the latter event was particularly conspicuous. O'Brien's wedding, to Sophie Raffalovich, a Russian Jewish heiress with an interest in the Irish question whom he had met in Paris, was attended by practically the entire Irish Party, and was the last time the undivided party met together before the Divorce Court revelations that brought about the split.
139 Among the Redmond family documents is an envelope containing a lock of hair and a flower wrapped in a sheet of House of Commons notepaper, on which is written 'My darling wife's hair and flower she gave me the first time I met her in Sydney.' Redmond family documents NLI Ms. 15,276 (1).
140 *F.J.*, 27 Jun., 7 Jul. 1890.
141 *F.J.*, 22 Sept. 1890.
142 ibid., 13 Aug. 1889.
143 ibid., 20 Jun. 1890.
144 ibid., 21 Jun. 1890.
145 Lyons, *Parnell*, p. 436.
146 *F.J.*, 29 Jan. 1890.
147 ibid., 22 Apr. 1890.
148 ibid., 12 Jul. 1890.
149 Lyons, *Parnell*, pp. 437–9.
150 *F.J.*, 26, 30 Sept. 1890.
151 ibid., 21 Apr. 1890.

7. The Rupture

1 *F.J.*, 19 Nov. 1890.
2 *F.J.*, 14 Sept. 1891.
3 *F.J.*, 18 Nov. 1890; *Daily Telegraph* quoted in *F.J.*, 18 Nov. 1890.
4 The story of the eleven months during which Parnell struggled, against increasing odds and an ever-deepening split in the Irish Party, to retain his leadership of the nationalist movement has been told several times. Conor Cruise O'Brien's *Parnell*

and His Party gives a full account of the three weeks following the divorce decree, culminating in the party split in Committee Room 15; F. S. L. Lyons's *The Fall of Parnell* (London, 1960) and Frank Callanan's superbly comprehensive and analytical *The Parnell Split* (Cork, 1992) record the bruising confrontations, rhetorical and physical, of Parnell's last campaign in Ireland.

5 Cruise O'Brien, *Parnell*, pp. 285–6.
6 *F.J.*, 19 Nov. 1890.
7 The four M.P.s fundraising in the US with Dillon and O'Brien were T. P. O'Connor, T. P. Gill, Tim Harrington and T. D. Sullivan. The one who withheld support from Parnell in the message read at Leinster Hall was Sullivan. Ten days later, when the delegates reversed their position in response to Parnell's manifesto, the one dissenter was Harrington.
8 *F.J.*, 21 Nov. 1890.
9 Quoted in *F.J.*, 21 Nov. 1890.
10 *F.J.*, 24 Nov. 1890.
11 Quoted in Robert Kee, *The Laurel and the Ivy: the story of Charles Stewart Parnell and Irish Nationalism* (London, 1993), p. 559.
12 *F.J.*, 21 Nov. 1890.
13 Callanan, *Parnell Split*, pp. 18–19.
14 *F.J.*, 26 Nov. 1890.
15 Callanan, *Parnell Split*, p. 19; Kee, *The Laurel and the Ivy*, p. 561.
16 Cruise O'Brien, *Parnell*, pp. 293–300.
17 ibid., pp. 302–03.
18 *F.J.*, 29 Nov. 1890; Cruise O'Brien, *Parnell*, p. 309; Callanan, *Parnell Split*, pp. 23–4.
19 Callanan, *Parnell Split*, p. 24.
20 *F.J.*, 29 Nov. 1890.
21 Callanan, *Parnell Split*, p. 25.
22 *F.J.*, 29 Nov. 1890.
23 Healy, *Letters and Leaders*, vol. 1, p. 330.
24 Callanan, *Parnell Split*, p. 30.
25 Callanan, *Parnell Split*, p. 26.
26 *F.J.*, 1 Dec. 1890.
27 ibid.
28 ibid., 2 Dec. 1890.
29 ibid., 3 Dec. 1890.
30 ibid., 4 Dec. 1890.
31 ibid., 5 Dec. 1890.
32 ibid., 8 Dec. 1890; Callanan, *Parnell Split*, pp. 49–51; Cruise O'Brien, *Parnell*, pp. 340–1.
33 Callanan, *Parnell Split*, p. 50.
34 *F.J.*, 8 Dec. 1890.
35 ibid., 9 Dec. 1890.
36 *New York Sun*, 30 Nov. 1896, in news cuttings of 1896 US tour, NLI Ms. 7423.
37 *F.J.*, 2 Oct. 1911.
38 Redmond to Furlong, 7 Dec. 1890, NLI Ms. 28,894 (A). William wrote more revealingly to the same correspondent at Christmas: ' Not to be on the side of so true a friend and Nationalist as yourself is to me the greatest pain . . . I could not abandon Parnell even for Gladstone and as one who has lived and worked for the cause in England I honestly believe that to throw Parnell over would injure more than anything else our chances of a *real* Home Rule settlement . . . I hate the Divorce, but when the Party deliberately elected Parnell in face of it, I cannot consent to throw him over at any suggestion from England. I may be wrong but God knows I believe I am right and as nearly all friends like yourself are on the other side I am nothing but trouble for myself for the course I have taken.' William Redmond to Furlong 26 Dec. 1890, NLI Ms. 28,894 (A).
39 *F.J.*, 11 Dec. 1890.

40 ibid., 12 Dec. 1890; *Suppressed United Ireland*, 15 Dec. 1890.
41 *FJ.*, 12 Dec. 1890.
42 In January 1888 at Owenduff, County Mayo, he called the police 'bastards' sons' and 'bastards' spawn'; at Achill he called them 'offspring of prostitutes'; in September 1888 he 'said the police were the lowest creatures on the face of the earth, he knew them to make prostitutes of their sisters for the purpose of obtaining promotion and position . . .' Police Reports of Land League and National League proceedings, NAI 3/714, Box 3.
43 *FJ.*, 13 Dec. 1890. The reference was to evidence given in the divorce court as to the method of Parnell's exit from Mrs O'Shea's house on one occasion when her husband returned unexpectedly.
44 ibid.
45 ibid., 15, 16 Dec. 1890.
46 ibid., 17 Dec. 1890. Contrary to the efforts by Healy and others afterwards to deny that the material thrown at Parnell was lime (Healy alleged in *Letters and Leaders*, vol. 1, p. 345, that it was flour and suggested that Parnell wore the eye bandage merely for effect), a letter from William Redmond to O'Brien dated 26 Dec. 1890 says emphatically, 'I *was there* and *I saw* the man's eyes filled with lime. I took some of it as it came from his face and it was lime.' NLI Ms. 10,496 (13).
47 ibid., 18 Dec. 1890.
48 Callanan, *Parnell Split*, p. 68.
49 Quoted in Lyons, *Parnell*, p. 543.
50 Lyons, *Parnell*, pp. 538–40; Callanan, *Parnell Split*, pp. 66–7, 249.
51 *FJ.*, 19, 20 Dec. 1890.
52 ibid., 18 Dec. 1890; Callanan, *Parnell Split*, pp. 67–8.
53 *FJ.*, 24–25 Dec. 1890.
54 Callanan, *Parnell Split*, pp. 69–73.
55 Gill had cabled McCarthy from the US in November 1890 to add a personal expression of grief to the message of the five delegates calling for Parnell's resignation, saying that he would 'follow Parnell to the death' but could not follow him to what seemed to him dishonour. Gill cable to McCarthy, undated [29 or 30 Nov. 1890], Gill Papers, NLI Ms. 13,507 (20).
56 Barry O'Brien, *Parnell*, vol. 2, p. 310.
57 Lyons, *Parnell*, p. 551.
58 *FJ.*, 5 Nov. 1891.
59 Lyons, *Parnell*, pp. 554–8.
60 Gill to O'Brien, 2 Jan. 1891, Gill Papers, NLI Ms. 13,507 (2).
61 Croke to O'Brien, 19 Dec. 1890, quoted in Lyons, *Parnell*, p. 553.
62 *Insuppressible*, 27 Dec. 1890.
63 Callanan, *Parnell Split*, pp. 83–5.
64 The account which follows is based on those in Lyons, *Parnell*, pp. 559–71; Callanan, *Parnell Split*, pp. 80–109, and on the controversy between O'Brien, Redmond and Harrington and Gill which appeared in the *Freeman's Journal* in the month after Parnell's death: see *FJ.*, 16, 17, 30 Oct.; 4, 5, 9, 11, 12, 13, 14, 16, 17, 18, 25 Nov. 1891.
65 Although Parnell, in a telegram to O'Brien, seemed to soften his objection to McCarthy as a judge of any assurances, telling him that he would be 'most glad if Justin would share in our mutual consultations' but 'as regards definite judgment' would 'prefer' the original arrangement, he later wrote to O'Brien that he was 'unable to see how I can in any way admit that Mr. McCarthy is a free agent or can be an independent judge, knowing as I do how completely he has delivered himself over to Gladstone and how willing he is to accept as satisfactory any statement or assurance by the former.' Parnell telegram to O'Brien, 11 Jan. 1891, Gill Papers, NLI Ms. 13,507 (5); Parnell to O'Brien, 16 Jan. 1891, ibid., NLI Ms. 13,507 (7).
66 Gill to Morley, 12 Jan. 1891, Gill Papers, NLI Ms. 13,507 (5).
67 Redmond to Gill, Redmond to O'Brien, both 27 Jan. 1891, Gill Papers, NLI Ms. 13,507 (9).

68 *F.J.*, 2 Feb. 1891.
69 Redmond to O'Brien, [misdated 7 Jan.] 7 Feb. 1891, Gill Papers, NLI Ms. 13,507 (3).
70 Parnell to Gill, 3 Feb. 1891, Gill Papers, 13,507 (11).
71 Callanan, *Parnell Split*, p. 101.
72 Clancy to O'Brien, 4 Feb. 1891, Gill Papers, NLI Ms. 13,507 (11).
73 Redmond to O'Brien, 5 Feb. 1891, Gill Papers, NLI Ms. 13,507 (12).
74 Parnell to Gill, 5 Feb. 1891, Gill Papers, NLI Ms. 13,507 (12).
75 Gill to Parnell, 6, 7 Feb. 1891, Parnell to Gill, 6, 7 Feb. 1891, Gill Papers, NLI Ms. 13,507 (13), (14).
76 Telegram Redmond to Gill, 6 Feb. 1891, NLI Ms. 13,507 (13).
77 Redmond to O'Brien, [misdated 7 Jan.] 7 Feb. 1891, Gill Papers, NLI Ms. 13,507 (3).
78 O'Brien to Parnell, 8 Feb. 1891, Gill Papers, NLI Ms. 13,507 (14).
79 O'Brien to Redmond, 8 Feb. 1891, quoted in Callanan, *Parnell Split*, p. 98.
80 O'Brien to Parnell, 9 Feb. 1891, quoted in Barry O'Brien, *Parnell*, vol. II, pp. 323–4.
81 Redmond's letter continued: 'If the negotiations are broken off on the ground of the assurances being in your view defective, I feel sure O'Brien would not say or do anything hostile, but I fear if your letter to Gill be published and made the pretext for the rupture, he would be driven to action which would be regarded as hostile . . . ' Redmond to Parnell, 'Monday night' [9 Feb. 1891], Harrington Papers, NLI Ms. 8581(2).
82 Parnell to O'Brien, 11 Feb. 1891, Gill Papers, NLI Ms. 13,507 (15).
83 *F.J.*, 11 Feb. 1891.
84 Dillon to O'Brien, undated letter from Galway Jail, O'Brien Papers, NLI Ms. 8555 (1), quoted in Callanan, *Parnell Split*, p. 101.
85 Andrew J. Kettle, *Material for Victory*, ed. L. J. Kettle (Dublin, 1958), quoted in Callanan, *Parnell Split*, p. 101.
86 *F.J.*, 25 Feb. 1891.
87 ibid., 23 Feb. 1891.
88 *National Press*, 7 Mar. 1891; hereafter *N. P.*
89 ibid., 11 Mar. 1891.
90 ibid.
91 Callanan, *Parnell Split*, pp. 113–14.
92 *F.J.*, 26 Mar. 1891.
93 ibid., 30 Mar. 1891.
94 O'Brien Dalton struck Healy hard in the face, driving fragments of his spectacles into his eye. See Callanan, *Parnell Split*, p. 112.
95 Callanan, *Parnell Split*, pp. 112–14.
96 *F.J.*, 1 Apr. 1891.
97 *N.P.* 23 Mar. 1891.
98 *F.J.*, 3 Apr. 1891.
99 ibid., 4 Apr. 1891.
100 ibid., 8, 10 Apr. 1891.
101 ibid., 11 May 1891.
102 Parnell himself, at Belfast on 22 May, admitted that Archbishop Walsh had written a letter the day before Gladstone's which advocated that he retire, but only on grounds of political expediency. This was the letter to Dr Kenny in which Walsh had said Parnell's re-election by the party made it easy for him to 'do the right thing' by 'a bold manly act'; ibid., 23 May 1891; Lyons, *Parnell*, pp. 483–4.
103 *F.J.*, 9 Jun. 1891.
104 ibid., 4 Jun. 1891.
105 Quoted in *F.J.*, 6 Mar. 1891.
106 ibid., 13 Apr. 1891.
107 ibid., 11 May 1891.
108 *N.P.*, 14 Apr. 1891.
109 *F.J.*, 24 Apr. 1891.
110 *N.P.*, 14 Mar. 1891. This was not quite fair to Redmond, who had been the only member of the party in the 1886 Home Rule Bill debate to say that 'he did not regard

as entirely palatable the idea that for ever and a day Ireland's voice should be excluded from the Councils of an Empire which the genius and valour of her sons had done so much to build up, and of which she was to remain a part'. But it was true that he had looked at the issue in a pragmatic light. See Hansard, (3rd series), 305, 960–974, 13 May, 1886.

111 *N. P.*, 17 Mar. 1891.

112 This was at Cabinteely, County Dublin on 20 September. *F.J.*, 21 Sep. 1891.

113 *F.J.*, 22 Apr. 1891.

114 ibid., 24 Apr., 1891.

115 *N.P.*, 1 May 1891.

116 *F.J.*, 22 May, 16 Jun. 1891.

117 For a detailed treatment of Parnell's position on Balfour's Land Bill, and on land policy generally, see Callanan, *Parnell Split*, pp. 282–7.

118 *F.J.*, 16 Apr. 1891; Callanan, *Parnell Split*, pp. 115–17.

119 *N.P.*, I Jun. 1891.

120 ibid., 5 Jun. 1891.

121 *F.J.*, 2 Jun. 1891.

122 *N.P.*, 2 Jul. 1891.

123 ibid., 29 Jun. 1891.

124 *F.J.*, 6 Jul. 1891.

125 *N.P.*, 29 Jun. 1891. By this time, Healy's dominance of the anti-Parnellite forces had raised a crop of imitators on platforms and in newspaper offices all over the country. His relentless vulgarization of the issues of the split in the *National Press* had largely achieved its aim of demystifying Parnell's image; 'Kitty O'Shea' had become a household name and ribald jokes about the couple abounded. Helped by Healy's ceaseless wordplay on the unfortunate candidate's name, the kettle became a symbol of popular opposition to Parnell, hung everywhere on trees and houses. Near one village, an effigy of 'Kitty O'Shea' holding a kettle was hung from a tree; at Rathvilly, women and children banged on kettles, keeping up a din that made it impossible for the Parnellites to be heard. *F.J.*, 2 Jul. 1891; Callanan, *Parnell Split*, pp. 129–32.

126 *N.P.*, *F.J.*, 9 Jul. 1891.

127 *F.J.*, 13 Jul. 1891.

128 O'Brien to Gill, undated, probably 10–11 Jul. 1891, Gill Papers, NLI Ms. 13,507 (20).

129 Squads of young men marching with hurley sticks on shoulders were a frequent sight at Parnellite public meetings during the split. The GAA in 1891 had greatly shrunk in size from its 1889 peak, at first because of the opposition of the Catholic clergy due to its perceived 'Fenian' tendencies, and then because of the Parnell split. The number of branches fell from 777 in 1889 to 339 at the end of 1891, with some counties having no branches by then. Of the surviving branches, 273 were reckoned by the police to be under 'Fenian', and 66 under clerical, control. In assessing the status of these branches, the police used the terms 'Parnellite', 'Fenian' and 'Extremist' interchangeably. NAI CBS 3/716, Box 4, 4467/S.

130 *F.J.*, 24 Jul. 1891.

131 ibid.

132 *N.P.*, 21 May 1891.

133 Dillon to O'Brien, 'Tues', quoted in Callanan, *Parnell Split*, p. 145.

134 *F.J.*, 31 Jul. 1891. Yet it seems that, the day after their release, Dillon and O'Brien sent a note to Redmond asking him to call to Dillon's house in North Great George's Street that evening. There is no record of Redmond having responded. Callanan, *Parnell Split*, p. 145.

135 *F.J.*, 31 Jul., 1 Aug. 1891.

136 Dillon said that the action that separated him from Parnell was 'the most painful act of my political life'. *F.J.*, 10 Aug. 1891.

137 ibid., 12 Aug. 1891.

138 ibid., 17, 18, 19, 21, 25 Aug., 10, 14 Sep. 1891.

139 ibid., 7 Sept. 1891.

140 ibid., 8 Oct. 1895.

141 *Gaelic American*, 7 Sep. 1907; Arthur Griffith's reminiscence of Parnell in *Sinn Fein*, 7 Oct. 1911, see also Richard P. Davis, *Arthur Griffith and Non-Violent Sinn Fein* (Dublin, 1974), p. 37.
142 Hansard, (3rd series), 356, 1141–51, 3 Aug. 1891. Redmond's interest in Daly's case was not new: he had spoken on the matter during his 'comeback' speech at Enniscorthy on 21 September 1890. O'Brien and others on the anti-Parnellite side had also done so in the summer of 1890.
143 Excluding by-election meetings, of the 21 major speeches delivered by Redmond in the 10 months between the Rotunda meeting of 10 December 1890 and Parnell's death, 10 were from platforms shared with Parnell.
144 Gill to O'Brien, 6 Aug. 1891, Gill Papers, NLI Ms. 13,507 (17).
145 ibid.
146 *F.J.*, 14 Sep. 1891. It was at this meeting, and at towns where his train stopped along the way there, that Parnell seemed to have a premonition of death, saying several times: 'If I was dead and gone tomorrow . . .'
147 This was historically inaccurate. The Plan, as described in Chapter 6, was initiated in October 1886, nine months before the passing of the Coercion Act.
148 *F.J.*, 15 Sept. 1891.
149 *N.P.*, 15, 16 Sept. 1891.
150 *F.J.*, 21 Sept. 1891.
151 ibid.
152 Callanan, *Parnell Split*, pp. 179–81; Lyons, *Parnell*, pp. 599–603; *F.J.*, 28 Sept. 1891.
153 *F.J.*, 8 Oct. 1891.
154 *United Ireland* 8 Oct. 1891. Redmond was in England making arrangements for the funeral when the article appeared, and thus was not in a position to repudiate it. At a league branch meeting on 16 October he said that 'he did not approve of calling any man a murderer, but when he was asked to repudiate an article in *United Ireland*, he would say he was no more responsible for *United Ireland* than Mr. Dillon and Mr. O'Brien were responsible for the *National Press*'; see *F.J.*, 17 Oct. 1891.
155 *F.J.*, 12 Oct. 1891.
156 Leamy, *Parnell's Faithful Few*, p. 101.
157 ibid., pp. 112–13.
158 *F.J.*, 13 Oct. 1891.
159 William O'Brien, *An Olive Branch in Ireland* (London, 1910), pp. 58–62. This book appeared when O'Brien's estrangement from Redmond, healed in 1900, had become final, in the wake of the former's second resignation from the reunited Irish Party. The criticism of Redmond's role in fostering the split was part of a comprehensive indictment stretching through the 1893 Home Rule Bill to Redmond's part in the failure of the conciliation initiatives that followed the Land Conference of 1902–03. The common thread running through all of these failures was, in O'Brien's view, lack of courage on Redmond's part in not resisting whatever influence was currently bearing on him. Ironically, during 1900, when Redmond was co-operating with O'Brien, Healy was accusing Redmond of a failure of courage in not standing up to O'Brien. Healy, *Letters and Leaders*, vol. 2, p. 452.
160 A Wexford supporter, W. J. O'Neill of Curracloe, wrote that Redmond's retirement 'causes me and your many friends great sorrow. We are proud of you for the way you have borne yourself all through. You acted like a true man – and may God bless you for it.' 22 Oct. 1891, NLI Ms. 15,238 (1).
161 Callanan, *Parnell Split*, p. 169; Leamy, *Parnell's Faithful Few*, p. 59; Tynan, *Twenty-Five Years*, p. 336.
162 *F.J.*, 21 Oct. 1891.
163 ibid., 16 Oct. 1891. For the rest of the controversy, which also involved Harrington and Gill, see *F.J.*, 17, 30 Oct., 2, 4, 5, 9, 11, 12, 13, 14, 16, 17, 18, 25 Nov. 1891.
164 ibid., 2 Nov. 1891. The reason for his absence from the convention was, as recounted above, his involvement in a murder trial in Wicklow.
165 ibid., 16 Oct. 1891.

166 Redmond to Gill, 14 Jan. 189[2], Gill Papers, NLI Ms. 13,492 (12).
167 *F.J.*, 26 Oct. 1891.
168 ibid., 23 Oct. 1891. In the cases of Listowel and Creggs, as we have seen, Redmond had other speaking engagements, next day (in the case of Listowel) or the same day (in the case of Creggs), at which he was fighting the Parnellite case (although of course he may have chosen those venues in order to avoid joining Parnell's platforms). Regarding Westport, there is no evidence for the assertion that he refused to speak there.
169 ibid., 24 Oct. 1891. The *National Press* of 20 May 1891 published the House of Commons voting records showing that the Parnellites had practically abandoned Parliament since the onset of the split. Of 237 divisions since November 1890, Redmond had voted in 9, Parnell in 2, Clancy in 17, while on the other side Healy had voted in 110, Sexton in 132, McCarthy in 136. The highest figure was for Healy's kinsman, Donal Sullivan, who voted 204 times.
170 *F.J.*, 30 Oct. 1891.
171 ibid., 6 Nov. 1891.
172 ibid., 17 Nov. 1890. Davitt had reason to attack Redmond on this point, since the Rathfarnham speech was in line with Parnell's concern to thwart Davitt's efforts to promote the Democratic Labour Federation in Ireland in 1890. The accusation that Redmond cared nothing for the workers, while understandable electioneering rhetoric, was wide of the mark, however, as a reading of the Rathfarnham speech will confirm. Redmond's attitude might be termed a precursor of the 'Labour must wait' motto of de Valera in later years.
173 *F.J.*, 22 Oct. 1891.
174 The gesture was made 'as a slight token of the love and admiration we hold for you . . .', Cork Young Ireland Society to Redmond, 30 Nov. 1891, NLI Ms. 15,238 (2).
175 *F.J.*, 28, 30, 31 Oct., 5 Nov. 1891.
176 ibid., 28 Oct. 1891.
177 ibid., 31 Oct. 1891.
178 ibid., 9 Nov. 1891. Dillon later reckoned that about 300 Tory votes had gone to Redmond.
179 ibid., 10 Nov. 1891.
180 ibid., 10, 12, 16, 17 Nov. 1891. The inquest jury found that the prisoner had been weakened by 'very harsh and cruel treatment' in Millbank prison for refusing to give evidence for *The Times* at the Special Commission.
181 ibid., 23 Nov. 1891.
182 ibid., 24 Nov. 1891.
183 Redmond to Davitt, 7 Dec. 1891, NLI Ms. 15,179.
184 Davitt to Redmond, 8 Dec. 1891, NLI Ms. 15,179.
185 *F.J.*, 14 Dec. 1891; *Irish Daily Independent*, 29 Dec. 1891, hereafter *I.D.I.*
186 ibid., 16, 17 Dec. 1891.
187 ibid., 15, 22 Dec. 1891.
188 ibid., 8, 12 Dec. 1891.
189 ibid., 14 Dec. 1891.
190 ibid., 21 Dec. 1891.
191 ibid., 26, 31 Dec. 1891.
192 *I.D.I.*, 29, 30 Dec. 1891.
193 *F.J.*, 1 Jan. 1892. A letter from a Wexford neighbour, Edmund Doyle of Broadway, at Christmas 1891, exemplifies the conflicting pressures on Redmond. Doyle pleaded with Redmond to use his 'present triumph' to do the greatest service an Irishman could render: 'You have proved your loyalty to your chief, use your influence now to heal the dissentions [*sic*] among our countrymen.' NLI Ms. 15,238 (2).
194 ibid., 4 Jan. 1892.
195 ibid., 18 Jan. 1892.
196 ibid., see also Dillon's reply to Redmond, ibid., 14 Jan. 1892, and Redmond's speech at National League, ibid., 27 Jan. 1892.
197 *F.J.*, 8 Feb. 1892.

8. The Metamorphosis

1 Newscuttings of John Redmond's visit to New York, 12–17 June 1892, NLI Ms. 7418.
2 Hansard (4th series), 16, 1504, 30 Aug. 1893.
3 Healy wrote in his memoirs: 'After Parnell died, Justin McCarthy, nettled by [Redmond's] assumption of leadership, asked me "Do you remember, while we were united, that any of us ever dreamed of consulting John Redmond about anything?" I answered "Never". Yet in 1891 he fell easily into the role of guerrilla leader.' Healy, *Letters and Leaders*, vol. 1, p. 200.
4 The chorus runs: 'We are the boys of Wexford / Who fought with heart and hand / To burst in twain the galling chain / And free our native land.'
5 Tynan, *Memories*, pp. 61–75.
6 Leamy, *Parnell's Faithful Few*, pp. 121–30.
7 Hansard (4th series), 1, 236–250, 11 Feb. 1892.
8 E. Leigh Pemberton to Redmond, in Letters 1892–1898 re. Fenian prisoners in Portland, NLI Ms. 15,222. There were limits as to the type of prisoner for whom Redmond was prepared to canvass, as shown by a letter written to him on behalf of the Invincibles confined in Maryborough prison in Ireland. The writer pressed strongly for intervention, while admitting that 'it was a terrible conspiracy', on the grounds that they were 'political prisoners' and 'did it to free Ireland to a certain extent of her oppressors'. He complained, 'I wrote to Mr. Harrington and you Mr. Redmond on one former occasion and I am surprised that my letter was not even acknowledged.' Henry Moroney to Redmond, 22 Nov. 1892, NLI Ms. 15,238 (3).
9 Hansard (4th series), 1, 502–12, 15 Feb. 1892. About 25,000 tenants had applied to purchase their farms after the 1885 Ashbourne Act, and another 35,000 did so during the 1890s following the Acts of 1891 and 1896. But these numbers were small compared with the 300,000 who were enabled to purchase by the Wyndham Act of 1903. See M. J. Winstanley, *Ireland and the Land Question 1800*–1922 (London and New York, 1984).
10 Hansard (4th series), 1, 502–12, 15 Feb. 1892.
11 ibid.
12 ibid.
13 *F.J.*, 17, 18 Feb. 1892.
14 For the outstanding account of Parnell's 'appeal to the hillsides' in his last year, see Callanan, *Parnell Split*, pp. 238–59. For a comprehensive treatment of the connections between the Redmondites and extreme nationalists, see Matthew Kelly, '"Parnell's Old Brigade": The Redmondite–Fenian Nexus in the 1890s', *Irish Historical Studies*, vol. 33, no. 130 (Nov. 2002), pp. 209–32.
15 Redmond's March 1892 lecture on 'The National Demand' was given in aid of the movement to raise funds to provide a home for James Stephens on his return from Paris. On 12 May 1892 he attended with William, Leamy and other Parnellites at the presentation to Stephens of a small house at Sutton, County Dublin.
16 Kelly, 'Parnell's Old Brigade', pp. 221–2.
17 *F.J.*, 18 Mar. 1892. Redmond, *Historical and Political Addresses*.
18 Mather to Redmond, Copy of notes of conversation, 30 Mar. 1892, NLI Ms. 15,206 (P8434).
19 Redmond to Mather, 13 Apr. 1892, NLI Ms. 15,206 (P8434); original emphases.
20 Mather to Redmond, 23 Apr. 1892, NLI Ms. 15,206 (P8434).
21 Redmond to Mather, 28 Apr. 1892, NLI Ms. 15,206 (P8434).
22 Mather to Redmond, 1 May 1892, NLI Ms. 15,206 (P8434).
23 Mather to Redmond, 11, 18, 20 May 1892, NLI Ms. 15,206 (P8434).
24 The article appeared under the title 'The Readjustment of the Union' in *Nineteenth Century* (Oct. 1892), p. 2290.
25 *F.J.*, 29 Jan. 1892.
26 ibid., 26, 28 Mar. 1892.
27 After Parnell's death, Healy maintained the personally offensive tone in his rhetoric, referring to Katharine Parnell in a Longford speech on 1 Nov. as 'a proved British prostitute'. Less amenable than ever to control by his colleagues, he moderated his

language only in response to an oblique intervention by Gladstone. See Callanan, *Parnell Split*, pp. 187–91.
28 *F.J.*, 17–21 May 1892.
29 ibid., 25 May 1892.
30 ibid., 6 May 1892.
31 Gill to Redmond, 8 Jan. 1892, Redmond Papers, NLI Ms. 15,190 (1).
32 Gill to Dillon, 17 Jan. 1892, Gill to Redmond, 4 Feb. 1892, Gill Papers, NLI Ms. 13,507 (19).
33 *F.J.*, 4 Apr. 1892.
34 ibid., 7 Apr. 1892.
35 Redmond to Gill, 8 Apr. 1892, Gill Papers, NLI Ms. 13,507 (19).
36 *F.J.*, 13 Apr. 1892.
37 ibid., 25 Apr. 1892.
38 ibid., 27 Apr. 1892.
39 ibid.
40 ibid., 5 May 1892.
41 ibid.
42 J. J. Clancy to Redmond, 24 May 1892, Dillon Papers, TCD Ms. 6747 (2).
43 ibid., 4 Jun. 1892.
44 ibid., 6 Jun. 1892.
45 News cuttings of Redmond's visit to New York 12–17 June, 1892, NLI Ms. 7418.
46 ibid.
47 ibid.
48 *F.J.*, 6, 27 Jun. 1892.
49 News cuttings, NLI Ms. 7418.
50 *F.J.*, 24 Jun. 1892.
51 *I.D.I.*, 27 Jun. 1892.
52 ibid., 30 Jun. 1892.
53 ibid., 1 Jul. 1892. Twelve years later, Redmond and other members of the reunited Irish parliamentary party would criticize the slow and inadequate operation of these early Labourers Acts, which by then had yielded on average less than 1,000 cottages per year for a labourer population of more than 200,000.
54 ibid.
55 The Parnellite candidate in East Wicklow complained in a letter to Archbishop Walsh that the parish priest of Roundwood in a sermon had told his parishioners: 'Parnellism is simply love of adultery, and all those who profess Parnellism, they profess to love and admire adultery. They are an adulterous set, their leaders are open and avowed adulterers, and therefore I say to you, as parish priest, beware of those Parnellites when they enter your houses, you that have wives and daughters, for they will do all they can to commit those adulteries.' *I. D. I.*, 1 Jul. 1892.
56 His vote was 1,676 to Sheehy's 1,293. The *Freeman* blamed Sheehy's defeat on the fact that he was prevented from carrying out a personal canvass by the 'murderous attack' made on him, although his vote improved on Davitt's of December 1891; Redmond attributed the drop in his own vote to the disenfranchisement of 'whole streets' and to 'foul libels' on him and his friends which he would take to court. See *F.J.*, 8 Jul. 1892; *I.D.I.* 8 Jul. 1892.
57 *F.J.*, 18, 26 Jul. 1892.
58 The thirteen Labour and nine Parnellite M.P.s could, if they voted together against the Government, defeat it by two votes. *I.D.I.*, 25 Jul. 1892.
59 Hansard, 6, 163–79, 8 Aug. 1892.
60 *I.D.I.*, 14, 15 Sept. 1892. However, despite persistent pressure by both factions of nationalists, and to the embarrassment of their anti-Parnellite allies, the Liberals had still not actually repealed the coercion legislation by the date of the 1895 general election.
61 ibid., 28 Sept., 15 Oct. 1892.
62 Morley to Redmond, with reply, 15 Sept. 1892, NLI Ms. 15,207 (1).
63 The memorandum is in NLI Ms. 15,207 (1).

64 *I.D.I.*, 16 Jul. 1892.
65 ibid., 1, 2 Dec. 1892. The bishop said that he held better hopes for the soul of a heretic than for that of a Parnellite. Father Tynan would 'fire the heels and toes' of those who voted Parnellite.
66 ibid., 2 Dec. 1892.
67 ibid., 24 Dec. 1892. A third, anti-Parnellite, petition was heard between the two Meath petitions to have the election of William Redmond in East Clare overturned on grounds of intimidation, but was unsuccessful.
68 'The Lesson of South Meath', *Fortnightly Review*, vol. 59 (27 Dec. 1892), pp. 1–6; reprinted in *I.D.I.*, 30 Dec. 1892.
69 Pierce Mahony was defeated by 258 votes in North Meath, while J. J. Dalton, Redmond's brother-in-law, lost in South Meath by 69 votes on a greatly increased poll. *I.D.I.*, 20, 23 Feb. 1893.
70 The federation was labelled the 'Whig Federation'.
71 *F.J.*, 5 Sep. 1892.
72 *I.D.I.*, 8 Sep. 1892.
73 ibid., 22 Aug. 1892.
74 ibid., 25 Aug. 1892.
75 ibid., 2 Sep. 1892.
76 ibid., 11 Oct. 1892.
77 ibid.
78 ibid., 27 Oct. 1892.
79 ibid., 31 Oct. 1892.
80 *F.J.*, 4 Nov. 1892.
81 ibid., 5 Jul. 1894. For the full controversy, which occupied as much column space as the Boulogne controversy of the previous year, see *I.D.I.*, 22, 25 Aug., 2, 26 Sept., 11, 12, 13, 14, 17, 18, 22, 27, 31 Oct., 2, 5 Nov. 1892.
82 *Summary of Information Contained in District Commissioners' Annual Reports for 1891*, NAI C.B.S. 3/716, Box 4, 5006/S. The National Federation increased in the same period from 199 to 640 branches, the majority of them under clerical control.
83 *I.D.I.*, 16 Nov. 1892. He was proud to say that he still had his certificate of enrolment on Butt's National roll while he was 'but a lad in college here in Dublin'.
84 NAI 3/716, Box 4, 5921/S.
85 Kelly, '"Parnell's Old Brigade"', p. 213.
86 Comparable membership figures outside Dublin at the end of 1893 were 6,514 for the National League, 8,120 for the IRB (Fenians), 1,813 for the GAA, and 47,080 for the National Federation. Estimated strengths of various Nationalist associations, 1 Jan. 1894, NAI C.B.S. 3/716, Box 8, 7828/S.
87 *I.D.I.*, 26 Dec. 1892; Hansard (3rd series), 356, 1141–51, 3 Aug. 1891.
88 Hansard (4th series), 8, 916–37, 9 Feb. 1893.
89 Quoted in *I.D.I.*, 9 Feb. 1893.
90 For Redmond's definition of political prisoner, see his amnesty speech of 11 Feb. 1892, note 7.
91 Hansard (4th series), 8, 943–55, 9 Feb. 1893.
92 *I.D.I.*, 10, 11 Feb. 1893.
93 *F.J.*, 10 Feb. 1893.
94 Hansard (4th series), 8, 1463–80, 14 Feb. 1893.
95 *I.D.I.*, 14 Feb., 7 Mar. 1893.
96 ibid., 10 Mar. 1893.
97 ibid., 18 Jan. 1893.
98 See chapter 2, note 27.
99 Hansard (4th series), 11, 234–52, 13 April 1893.
100 Quoted in *I.D.I.*, 15 Apr. 1893.
101 Sir Henry Lucy, *Diary of the Home Rule Parliament 1892–1895* (London, 1896), p. 105. Lucy also described Davitt's maiden speech, which, in spite of its 'undue length and amateurism', 'impressed the House with the conviction of its honesty, earnestness and

singleness of purpose', as one of the four great speeches he had heard that week (the others were those of Chamberlain and Asquith).

102 *The Times*, 4 May 1893.

103 Hansard, (3rd series), 304, 1053–1054, 8 Apr. 1886.

104 *I.D.I.*, 5 May 1893.

105 Hansard (4th series), 12, 79–81, 4 May 1893. The public reactions of neither Ulster Unionist nor nationalist leaders in 1886 provided grounds for Gladstone's 1893 assertions. In his winding-up speech just before the defeat of the 1886 Bill, Gladstone merely stated that while he did not recede from his earlier statement on Ulster, the Unionist leader Colonel Edward Saunderson 'emphatically disclaims the severance of Ulster from the rest of Ireland, and the hon. Member for Cork [Parnell] has laid before us a reasoned and elaborate argument on that subject today, which, as it appears to me, requires the careful attention of those who propose such a plan for our acceptance'. Hansard, 306, 1220, 7 Jun. 1886.

106 *I.D.I.*, 5 May 1893.

107 *F.J.*, 6 May 1893.

108 Hansard (4th series), 8, 1461–2, 14 Feb. 1893.

109 *F.J.*, 6 May 1893.

110 *I.D.I.*, 10, 12, 24 May 1893.

111 *F.J.*, 10 May 1893.

112 Hansard (4th series), 12, 1121–3, 16 May 1893.

113 ibid., 12, 1125–7, 16 May 1893.

114 *I.D.I.*, 21 Jun. 1893.

115 ibid., 7 Mar. 1893.

116 Redmond to Morley, 13 Jun. 1893, NLI Ms. 15,207 (1).

117 Redmond to Morley, 15 Jun. 1893, NLI Ms. 15,207 (1).

118 Redmond to Morley, 20 Jun. 1893, NLI Ms. 15,207 (1).

119 *I.D.I.*, 29, 30 Jun. 1893.

120 ibid., 11, 12, 18 Jul. 1893; *F.J.*, 11 Jul. 1893.

121 Quoted in *I.D.I.*, 26 Jul. 1893.

122 Quoted in *I.D.I.*, 1 Aug. 1893.

123 ibid., 14, 28 Jul. 1893.

124 ibid., 28 Jul. 1893. At the end of the sitting T. P. O'Connor shouted 'Judas!' repeatedly at Chamberlain, while during the division blows were exchanged between Colonel Saunderson and some of the Nationalist M.P.s.

125 The quote is from Shakespeare's *As You Like It*.

126 *I.D.I.*, 10 Aug. 1893.

127 Hansard (4th series), 16, 1503–08, 30 Aug. 1893.

128 *F.J.*, 1 Sep. 1893.

129 *I.D.I.*, 2, 9 Sep. 1893. The vote was 419 to 41.

9. The Vacuum

1 *I.D.I.*, 9 Oct. 1894.

2 *F.J.*, 18 Mar. 1895.

3 *I.D.I.*, 12 Jan. 1894.

4 *F.J.*, 10 Oct., 2 Nov. 1893.

5 *I.D.I.*, 28 Sept., 18 Oct. 1893.

6 *F.J.*, 14 Apr., 10, 31 Aug. 1893; Redmond speech in Strokestown, *I.D.I.*, 22 Jan. 1894.

7 NAI CBS 3/716, Box 4, 5757/S. Mallon wrote on 25 October 1895 that Allan, who was the 'head of the strong section of the Fenian party' had had a private office constructed within the office of the *Daily Independent* to which callers had to be announced; all the leading Dublin IRB men came there to see him. He was also engaged with others in buying up old military rifles in Britain (15 to 20 per box, three or four times a year) and shipping them to a central location in Ireland. NAI CBS 3/716, Box 10, 10712/S.

8 F. J. Allan to Redmond, 1 Sept. 1893, NLI Ms. 15,164 (2).

9 NAI CBS 3/716, Box 4, 5757/S.
10 F. J. Allan's disapproval was decidedly tolerant: in 1894 he wrote, 'these men and others have just as much right to think that the time has come for the use of these methods as others of us have to consider that the time has not yet arrived for them; or as the most modern constitutionalist has to believe that such methods should not be used at all . . . we should throw no shadow of blame upon them so long as the link between England and Ireland remains unbroken'. Serial 'Behind Prison Bars', Part 1, *Weekly Independent*, 28 Apr. 1894.
11 *F.J.*, 8 May, 3 Jun. 1893.
12 NAI CBS 3/716, Box 8, 8008/S, 8727/S.
13 *I.D.I.*, 13 Jan. 1894.
14 ibid., 10 Feb. 1894. The compositor, Walter Sheridan, was reported in April 1895 to have been dismissed from the paper 'without cause assigned'. The police's impression was that 'some of the Directors would not have him there'. NAI CBS 3/716, Box 10, 9814/S.
15 *I.D.I.*, 10 Oct. 1893.
16 ibid., 11 Oct. 1893.
17 T. P. Gill to Redmond, 13 Oct. 1893, NLI Ms. 15,190 (1); Gill's emphases.
18 T.P. Gill to Redmond, 24 Oct. 1893, NLI Ms. 15,190 (1).
19 *I.D.I.*, 30 Oct. 1893.
20 ibid., 3 Nov. 1893; *F.J.*, 4 Nov. 1893.
21 *I.D.I.*, 11 Nov. 1893, 17 Jan. 1894.
22 *I.D.I.*, 23 Oct. 1893.
23 ibid., 27 Nov. 1893.
24 ibid., 17 Sep. 1892, 28 Oct., 8, 9, 11, 13, 15 Nov. 1893. The *Independent* of 16 November, lapsing into invective more typical of the Healyite press, used religion against the agnostic Morley: 'Not being a Christian,' it observed sanctimoniously, he would not know that the acts he was prosecuting, such as the building of shelters, were enjoined by 'a law . . . that is older and more venerable . . . than Acts of Parliament'.
25 ibid., 18, 19 Dec. 1893.
26 ibid., 25 Jan. 1894.
27 ibid., 29 Jan. 1894.
28 ibid., 15 Feb. 1894.
29 ibid., 16, 20, 21, 22 Feb. 1894.
30 ibid., 5, 6 Mar. 1894.
31 *F.J.*, 13 Mar. 1894.
32 Hansard (4th series), 22, 180–9, 13 Mar. 1894.
33 *F.J.*, 19 Mar. 1894.
34 *I.D.I.*, 19 Mar. 1894.
35 ibid., 24 Mar. 1894.
36 ibid., 28–31 Mar. 1894.
37 ibid., 3 Apr. 1894.
38 ibid., 10 May 1894.
39 ibid., 5 May 1894.
40 ibid., 11, 26 May 1894.
41 ibid., 3 May 1894.
42 ibid., 24 Oct. 1892. For McKenna's briefings of Redmond in 1893 and 1894 on the financial relations between Great Britain and Ireland under the Union, see NLI Ms. 15,203 (7).
43 *I.D.I.*, 30 May, 22 Jun. 1894.
44 ibid., 20, 21 Apr. 1894.
45 ibid., 28 May 1894.
46 ibid., 20 Apr. 1894.
47 ibid., 22 May 1894.
48 *F.J.*, 8 Aug. 1894.
49 *I.D.I.*, 15, 16 Aug. 1894.

50 ibid., 24 Apr., 6, 26, 30 Jun., 6 Jul., 22 Aug. 1894.
51 William Redmond, M.P. for East Clare, was absent from Rossa's meeting at Ennis, sending a letter of apology which avoided praising him personally: 'I am glad, however, to notice that all sections are united to welcome Rossa back from exile. If we cannot agree as to the best party or methods to free Ireland, we can at least unite to show respect to men who have suffered for the sake of Ireland.' Both sections of nationalists supported a resolution condemning the Town Commissioners for refusing Rossa the use of the town hall. The hotel reception afterwards was chaired by Patrick O'Brien, a past and future Parnellite M.P., *I.D.I.*, 5, 18, 20 Jun. 1894.
52 ibid., 27 Jun. 1894.
53 ibid., 13, 23 Jul., 20 Aug. 1894. The *Freeman* commented that Rossa had repaid 'in rather curious fashion' the courtesy and kindness of those who had received him, in insulting Davitt and sneering at the peasants of Ireland. *F.J.*, 20 Aug. 1894.
54 *I.D.I.*, 5, 16, 17, 19 Jul., 20 Aug. 1894.
55 Rossa lives on in the republican pantheon as the subject of Patrick Pearse's impassioned graveside oration of 1915 on the occasion of the return of Rossa's remains to Ireland, learned by generations of Irish schoolchildren: 'The fools, the fools, they have left us our Fenian dead . . . While Ireland holds these graves, Ireland unfree shall never be at peace.' A Liffey bridge was renamed after him by Dublin Corporation, making him the second such figure, marginal even within republicanism, to be so honoured in the city (the 1930s IRA bomber of Britain and Nazi protégé Sean Russell, commemorated by a statue in Fairview Park, is the other).
56 *I.D.I.*, 3, 4, 6 Sept. 1894.
57 *I.D.I.*, 1, 3 Nov. 1894.
58 ibid., 19 Oct., 6, 9, 12, 13 Nov. 1894.
59 ibid., 5 Sept. 1894.
60 ibid.
61 ibid., 9 Oct. 1894.
62 *F.J.*, 9 Oct. 1894.
63 *I.D.I.*, 30 Oct. 1894.
64 ibid., 29 Oct. 1894.
65 ibid., 5 Dec.; *F.J.*, 5 Dec. 1894.
66 *I.D.I.*, 13 Nov. 1894.
67 Morley to Redmond, 23 Nov. 1894, NLI Ms. 15,207 (1).
68 F. J. Allan to Redmond, 30 Jul. 1894, NLI Ms. 15,164 (2); NAI CBS 3/716, Box 12, 14349/S, 7 Oct. 1897.
69 *Weekly Independent,* 2 Mar. 1895. John Twiss was hanged on 9 February 1895 for the murder of the bailiff James Donovan the previous year. A petition with 40,000 signatures protesting his innocence failed to have him reprieved.
70 M. A. Manning to Redmond, 6 Mar. 1895, NLI Ms. 15,205 (7).
71 *Weekly Independent,* 2 Mar. 1895.
72 *United Irishman*, 10, 17 Feb. 1900. On 24 October 1901, the day of Redmond's departure on a visit to the US, the *Daily Independent*, then still pro-Redmond, felt obliged to publish an exculpatory 'statement' on the Cambridge Union speech. The writer pointed out that the meeting was the first in the history of the union to which pressmen were invited, that no accommodation was provided for them and that under the circumstances the summary published was 'a necessarily imperfect one'. It urged that the speech 'should be considered as a whole before passing adverse judgment on it. It was... the straight-from-the-shoulder speech of an independent Irish Nationalist . . . The independence of the Irish Parliament, when established, was emphasised in the most emphatic manner . . .' The speech as a whole was, it claimed, 'perfectly in accord with Mr. Parnell's famous speech at Cork Opera House' 'the 'march of a nation' speech of January 1885.
73 *I.D.I.*, 21 Jan. 1895.
74 NAI CBS 3/716, Box 10, 9502/S, 21 Jan. 1895.
75 *F.J.*, 21 Jan. 1895.

76 *I.D.I.*, 24 Jan. 1895.
77 Hansard (4th series), 30, 465–80, 11 Feb. 1895.
78 ibid., 30, 480–9, 11 Feb. 1895; *F.J.*, 12 Feb. 1895.
79 *I.D.I.*, 1 Mar. 1895.
80 *F.J.*, 27 Feb., 18 Mar. 1895.
81 *I.D.I.*, 18 Mar. 1895.
82 ibid., 20 Mar. 1895. That he was on dangerous ground in quoting Lord Salisbury in the House of Lords was shown in May when the latter defined 'the people' in terms very close to Rosebery's 'predominant partner'. *F.J.*, 23 May 1895.
83 *I.D.I.*, 29 Apr. 1895.
84 Memorandum by Redmond of meeting with Archbishop Walsh, Sunday 24 Feb. 1895, NLI Ms. 18,290.
85 *I.D.I.*, 18 Mar. 1895.
86 Easter letter of Archbishop Walsh, ibid., 16 Apr. 1895.
87 *F.J.*, 25 Apr. 1895.
88 John O'Mulloy DD, PP Aughrim to Redmond, 9 Apr.1895, NLI Ms. 15,238 (6).
89 *I.D.I.*, 1 May 1895. Redmond had received from a Denis Treacy, a sympathizer in Manchester, a letter sent to him by his father, Michael Treacy of Arklow, which showed the influence of the anti-Parnellite clergy on uneducated voters: 'I say the man that gowes and gives his vote against his Bishop and priests is doing wrong. Remember when Sickness and death comes how fond you or me will be to see our good priest that we voted against in our Healthy days and at that last moment how sorry we will be for gowen against our priest our Bishop and priests ought to no right from wrong in them matters and we should be advised by them . . .' Denis Treacy professed himself 'ashamed' of his father. Denis Treacy to Redmond, 28 Apr. 1895, NLI Ms. 15,238 (6).
90 *F.J.*, 20 Mar. 1895; *I.D.I.*, 10 Jun. 1895.
91 *I.D.I.*, 10 Jun. 1895.
92 ibid., May *passim*, 6, 8, 10, 13 Jun. 1894.
93 ibid., 29 Jun. 1895. The Parnellite candidate received about 1,000 votes more than William Redmond in the same constituency in 1892, and 2,000 more than John Redmond in November 1891. The *Freeman* improbably ascribed the entire increase to the Tory vote.
94 ibid., 22 Jun. 1895.
95 ibid., 28 Jun. 1895.
96 ibid., 9 Jul. 1895.
97 ibid., 12 Jul. 1895. For a full treatment of the 'seats-for-cash' scandal, see F. S. L. Lyons, 'The Machinery of the Irish Parliamentary party in the General Election of 1895', *Irish Historical Studies*, vol. 8 (1952) pp. 115–39.
98 ibid., 19 Jul. 1895.
99 ibid., 6 Jul. 1895.
100 Douglas Hyde's famous 1893 lecture 'The Necessity for De-Anglicising Ireland', intended as a strictly non-political proposition, was in circulation in pamphlet form.
101 Walker (ed.), *Parliamentary Election Results.*
102 *I.D.I.*, 17 Jan. 1896.
103 ibid., 27 Jan. 1896.

10. New Directions, Old Quarrels

1 *I.D.I.*, 8 Jan. 1896.
2 ibid., 3 Feb. 1896.
3 *I.D.I.*, 16, 21 Aug.; *F.J.*, 1 Aug. 1895.
4 Hansard (4th series), 36, 102–11, 15 Aug. 1895.
5 He had farmed in Wyoming and on his return to Ireland had helped to set up thirty co-operative creameries by 1893.
6 Hansard (4th series), 36, 114–19, 15 Aug. 1895.
7 ibid., 36, 126–36, 15 Aug. 1895.
8 *I.D.I.*, 15 Apr., 20 Aug., 6 Sept., 19 Nov. 1895.

9 ibid., 17 Aug. 1895.
10 ibid., 5, 6, 13 Sept., 4 Dec. 1895.
11 ibid., 28 Sept. 1895.
12 NAI CBS 3/716, Box 11, 11921/S; *I.D.I.*, 26 Sep., 4 Oct. 1895.
13 ibid., Box 11, 11921/S, 12053/S, 2 Jul. 1896.
14 ibid., Box 11, 12115/S, 17 Jul. 1896.
15 ibid., Box 11, 11518/S, 23 Mar. 1896; Box 10, 10574/S, Sep. 1895.
16 ibid., Box 10, 10712/S, 25 Oct. 1895. A month later Egan and Allan were reported to have fallen out, with the former now a trusted agent of the INA leadership (one of whom was John MacBride) who were opposed to Allan, while the latter no longer took part in the amnesty movement. ibid., Box 10, 10819/S, 20 Nov. 1895.
17 See Callanan, *Parnell Split*, pp. 240–5.
18 *I.D.I.*, 27 Feb. 1895. See Chapter 9.
19 *Irish Republic* (New York), 8 Mar. 1896, in NAI 3/716, Box 11, 11518/S.
20 *F.J.*, 8, 10 Aug., 2–7 Sept. 95.
21 Quoted in *I.D.I.*, 6 Sept. 1895.
22 *I.D.I.*, 8, 14, 15 Nov. 1895; Callanan, *T. M. Healy*, p. 435.
23 *I.D.I.*, 8 Oct. 1895.
24 ibid.; *F.J.*, 8 Oct. 1895.
25 *I.D.I.*, 11 Oct. 1895.
26 ibid., 7 Dec. 1895.
27 ibid., 28 Aug., 19, 22 Oct. 1895. For an account of the establishment and deliberations of the Recess Committee, see Sir Horace Plunkett, *Ireland in the New Century* (London, 1904), pp. 213–26.
28 ibid., 24 Oct., 14, 21 Dec. 1895.
29 ibid., 7 Jan. 1896.
30 The doctrine, proclaimed by US President James Monroe in 1823, that intervention by European powers in any part of the Americas would be regarded by the US as hostile action.
31 ibid., 24 Dec. 1895.
32 Hawksley to Redmond, 25 Dec. 1895, NLI Ms. 15,193 (2).
33 Angus Maguire to Redmond, 27 Dec. 1895, NLI Ms. 15,238 (6).
34 Redmond to Maguire, 1 Jan. 1896, NLI Ms. 15,238 (7). Redmond ended by saying that he did not intend to allude to the matter again unless forced to, in which case he would ask Maguire's advice beforehand. In any case, his view was that there was no real danger of war at all.
35 *I.D.I.*, 1–7 Jan. 1896.
36 ibid., 7, 10 Jan. 1896.
37 *Cork Examiner*, 30 Dec. 1895.
38 ibid., 13 Jan. 1896.
39 ibid., 12 Oct. 1896.
40 O'Donnell, *History* vol. 2, p. 344.
41 *Irish People*, 10 Feb. 1900.
42 *I.D.I.*, 6 Jun. 1894. In January 1896 he was more generous towards Sexton when he praised 'the extraordinary industry and the brilliant ability which he displayed' at the meetings of the Financial Relations Commission in the previous months; these were 'of enormous value to Ireland' even though, as he reminded his audience, Sexton had been the spokesman of his party in opposing the appointment of the commission during the Home Rule debates of 1893. *I.D.I.*, 7 Jan. 1896.
43 *I.D.I.*, 22 Jul. 1895. The animus behind these remarks may have been a reflection of Redmond's anger at comments made by Dillon earlier in the year. Pointing to the contradiction between Redmond's calling Gladstone a fraud and a humbug when he retired and his current claim to know that his reason for retiring was his colleagues' refusal to dissolve Parliament on the defeat of the 1893 Home Rule Bill, Dillon had declared 'there is no sincerity or honesty in this man'. *F.J.*, 28 Jan. 1895.
44 *I.D.I.*, 17 Jan. 1896.

45 Memo in Redmond's hand of meeting with Henry Labouchere, 9 Apr. 1894, NLI Ms. 15,201 (3).
46 *I.D.I.*, 3 Feb. 1896.
47 ibid., 21 May 1896.
48 ibid., 15, 31 Aug., 1–4, 9 Sept. 1896.
49 ibid., 28 Sept. 1896.
50 *F.J.*, 28 Sept. 1896.
51 *I.D.I.*, 30 Sept. 1896; *F.J.*, 1 Oct. 1896.
52 Quoted in *I.D.I.*, 26 Feb. 1896.
53 Quoted in ibid., 7 Sept. 1896.
54 ibid., 16 Apr. 1896.
55 ibid., 13, 23 May 1896.
56 ibid., 29 May 1896.
57 ibid., 21 Jul. 1896. On this occasion Davitt left the House rather than vote in favour of the twelve o'clock suspension.
58 ibid., 30 Jul., 8, 14 Aug. 1896.
59 ibid., 4 Aug. 1896.
60 ibid., 10 Aug. 1896.
61 ibid., 19 Aug. 1896.
62 White-Ridley to Redmond, 3 Aug. 1896, NLI Ms. 15,222. On 9 September Redmond told the League central branch that he had come to have 'the greatest possible confidence in [White-Ridley's] kindly feeling, humanity and sense of justice'. The August releases left five Irish prisoners in British jails. One of these was Henry Wilson, alias Thomas Clarke, who on his release in September 1898 would resume his IRB activities and live to become the most senior of the strategists of the 1916 insurrection and of the signatories of the Proclamation of the Irish Republic. In a eulogy of Clarke, ironic in view of all that would happen twenty years later, Redmond told the Tipperary amnesty meeting on 27 September as Dillon stood by his side: 'Wilson is a man of whom no words in praise could be too high. I have learned in my many visits to Portland for five years to love, honour and respect Henry Wilson. I have seen day after day how his brave spirit was keeping him alive . . . I have seen year after year the fading away of his physical strength.' *I.D.I.*, 28 Sept. 1896.
63 *I.D.I.*, 9 Sept. 1896.
64 ibid., 12 Oct. 1896.
65 Newscuttings of Redmond's visit to US, Nov. 1896 to Feb. 1897, NLI Ms. 7423.
66 ibid. This lecture seems to have been a personal favourite: Redmond had it reprinted for inclusion in both *Historical and Political Addresses* (1898) and *Home Rule: Speeches* (1910).
67 *I.D.I.*, 4 Feb. 1896. 'Foreign senate' was another of his rhetorical names for the Westminster Parliament.
68 The *Independent*'s London correspondent wrote on 30 June of A. J. Balfour being one of the two most talked-of cyclists in the House of Commons: he had come to grief twice, but in spite of 'his cool, dogged daring in threading the perils of the streets . . . it must not be assumed that Mr. Balfour rides recklessly. He goes at a fair speed, and the only danger he incurs is from wheeling in and out of the busy street traffic.'
69 The first electrified tramway in Dublin had opened the previous 16 May, running from Haddington Road to Dalkey; 75,000 people had travelled on it in its first weekend. The first accident involving a cyclist and the tram took place on 1 July, when a cyclist was struck and badly injured at Booterstown. *I.D.I.*, 18 May, 2 Jul. 1896.
70 See his Commons speech on the Prisons Bill in March 1898, in which he contrasted the 'vindictive retribution' that seemed to him to characterize the British system with the humanity of the American prison systems he had seen. Hansard, 55, 1193–201, 28 Mar. 1898.
71 *I.D.I.*, 17 Feb. 1897.
72 ibid., 15 Feb. 1897.

73 Amnesty address in New York by Redmond, in Devoy Papers, NLI Ms. 18,060.
74 Quoted in *I.D.I.*, 21 Oct. 1896.
75 *I.D.I.*, 13 Nov., 14 Dec. 1896.
76 ibid., 29, 30 Dec. 1896.
77 'True' revenue inflow to the British Exchequer from Ireland increased from £7.67 million in 1894–95 to £8.15 million in 1896–97, a 6 per cent increase; of these sums £503,475 in 1894–95 and £718,000 in 1896–97 came from estate duties, a 43 per cent increase. *I.D.I.*, 3 Sep. 1897.
78 ibid., 19 Dec. 1896.
79 ibid., 22, 29 Jan., 10, 13 Feb. 1897.
80 ibid., 15, 16, 17 Feb. 1897.
81 ibid., 23 Feb. 1897.
82 ibid., 10, 13, 17 Mar. 1897.
83 ibid., 30 Mar. 1897.
84 ibid., 31 Mar., 1 Apr. 1897.
85 ibid., 8, 28 May 1897. The vote was for maintenance of harbours and lighthouses by the Board of Trade. William Redmond's suspension took place amidst laughter after he jousted with the Chairman: 'Do I understand you to say that I am grossly disorderly in simply referring to the relative taxation of Great Britain and Ireland? That would be like the ruling in one of Gilbert and Sullivan's operas.' Chairman: 'The honourable member is grossly disorderly in that last remark (*cheers*).'
86 ibid., 8 Dec. 1897.
87 ibid., 13, 22 Apr., 3 Jun. 1897.
88 ibid., 5 Jun. 1897.
89 ibid., 9 Dec. 1897.

11. Commemoration and Conciliation

1 *I.D.I.*, 30 May, 1898.
2 ibid., 1 Jun. 1898.
3 NAI CBS 3/716, Box 11, 11316/S. There had been differences of emphasis between the speeches of Redmond and Harrington on the unity question as far back as January 1896: see *F.J.*, 13, 14, 15 Jan. 1896; *I.D.I.*, 15 Jan. 1896. In June 1896 Mallon had it from a Dublin informant that Harrington had no longer anything to do with the *Independent*, and that he and Redmond 'do not agree on vital points of policy. Mr. Harrington is in favour of constitutional agitation under the policy of Parnellism, and does not regard Fenianism in any form as necessary to promote that policy. Mr. Redmond considers it more necessary now than ever to keep close to the Fenians, and in order to keep some of them, who are well known to him, from starving he actually has money paid to them.' NAI CBS 3/716, Box 11, 12013/S.
4 *I.D.I.*, 3 Dec. 1896.
5 For a full account of the tensions within the Parnellite movement in the 1890s, see Kelly, '"Parnell's Old Brigade"'.
6 *I.D.I.*, 16 Jan. 1897; *United Ireland*, 23 Jan. 1897.
7 *I.D.I.*, 23 Jan. 1897.
8 *United Ireland*, 30 Jan. 1897.
9 *I.D.I.*, 15 Feb. 1897.
10 ibid.
11 ibid., 24 Feb. 1897.
12 ibid., 21 Apr. 1897.
13 The National League had shrunk, according to a police report in late 1897, from 8,076 members in good standing in 1892 to 3,338 members in 111 branches by April 1897, and was regarded as 'practically defunct'. NAI CBS 3/716, Box 12, 14826/S.
14 *I.D.I.*, 21 Apr. 1897.
15 *Daily Nation*, 1 May 1897.
16 NAI CBS 3/716, Box 12, 13478/S.
17 NAI CBS 3/716, Box 12, 13652/S, 13748/S, 14826/S.

18 Redmond wrote to Harrington on 26 April: 'We are all (Clancy, Kenny, Carew, Pat O'Brien etc.) very unhappy at the turn things have taken and at the apparent estrangement which has arisen between us. We are all anxious to have a chat with you . . . ' Harrington replied the following day that he would be very glad to meet Redmond personally, but as to the others, 'they showed an extraordinary zeal to get rid of me and I never care to keep up appearances of comradeship where there is no genuine cordiality.' NLI Ms. 15, 194.
19 Allan to Redmond, undated (most likely Feb. 1897) NLI Ms. 15,164 (2). Two copies of Redmond's amnesty address are in Devoy's papers, NLI Ms. 18,060.
20 Allan to Devoy, 29 Dec. 1897, *Devoy's Post Bag*, vol. 2: 1880–1928. Allan wrote: 'As Mr. John Redmond is leaving for New York in the morning I think it only right to let you know for the information of our friends that the articles in the *Irish Republic* about the lecture on '98 which Redmond delivered in Dublin are disgraceful lies. There was not a single word in Redmond's whole lecture that could offend the most extreme man. As a matter of fact, the lecture was delivered to clear off the debt on a monument which was erected over one of our fellows here, Michael Seery, and our boys feel greatly riled over the *Irish Republic* articles, as they looked upon it as a gracious act on Redmond's part to lecture for us.'
21 NAI CBS 3/716, Box 11, 12013/S.
22 For an account of the contacts between Parnell and Rhodes, see Lyons, *Parnell*, pp. 442–4, 587–9.
23 *I.D.I.*, 9, 11 May 1896.
24 ibid., 12 May 1897, 25 Jan. 1899.
25 ibid., 18 May 1897.
26 ibid., 7 Sep. 1897.
27 ibid., 10, 24 Nov. 1897.
28 ibid., 8 Dec. 1897.
29 Quoted in *I.D.I.*, 7 Apr. 1893.
30 R. F. Foster, *W. B. Yeats: A Life*, 2 vols. (Oxford 1998), vol. 1, pp. 119–24. Conor Cruise O'Brien, *Ancestral Voices* (Dublin, 1994), pp. 30, 37.
31 *I.D.I.*, 17 Apr. 1893.
32 Janet Eagleson Dunleavy and Gareth W. Dunleavy, *Douglas Hyde: A Maker of Modern Ireland* (Berkeley, 1991), p. 186; *I.D.I.*, 17 Jan. 1894.
33 *I.D.I.*, 23 Jun. 1896.
34 ibid., 1 Jan. 1895.
35 ibid., 7 Jun. 1899.
36 See Chapter 12.
37 *I.D.I.*, 7, 20 Sept. 1899.
38 NAI CBS 3/716, Box 11, 12730/S.
39 *I.D.I.*, 16 Jun. 1897.
40 ibid.
41 ibid., 22 Jun. 1897.
42 ibid., 22, 25 Jun. 1897.
43 ibid., 19 Jun. 1897. One story told of a Dillonite M.P. telegraphing to London to reserve eight seats on Speaker's Green.
44 ibid., 22, 24 Jun. 1897.
45 ibid., 5 Mar. 1897. Among those who attended meetings of the committee were W. B. Yeats and Maud Gonne.
46 Allan to Redmond, 2 Mar. 1897, NLI Ms. 15,164 (2).
47 Allan to Redmond, 1 Mar. 1897, NLI Ms. 15,164 (2).
48 *I.D.I.*, 12 Apr., 10 Sept. 1897.
49 ibid., 17 Jun. 1897.
50 ibid., 23 Nov., 9 Dec. 1897.
51 NAI CBS 3/716, Box 12, 14781/S.
52 *I.D.I.*, 1, 10, 19, 25 Jan., 1, 3 Feb. 1898.
53 ibid., 7 Jun. 1895.
54 Baker to Redmond, 23 Aug. 1895, NLI Ms. 15,167 (1).

55 *I.D.I.*, 30 May 1896.
56 Police figures showed the circulation of the *Daily Independent* as having risen from 15,000 in January 1895 to 17,000 in January 1896. The *Freeman* also improved its circulation over the same period, from 23,000 to 30,000. The latter paper had been in serious decline since the split, before which its daily circulation had been 50,000. NAI 3/716, Box 13, 9468/S, Jan. 1895; 15447/S, 13 Apr. 1897.
57 Baker to Redmond, 11 May 1896, NLI Ms. 15,167 (1).
58 Baker to Redmond, 4 Jun. 1896, NLI Ms. 15,167 (1).
59 Baker to Redmond, 15 Jun. 1896, NLI Ms. 15,167 (1).
60 Baker to Redmond, 25 Jun. 1896, NLI Ms. 15,167 (1). Baker's alarm was not fully justified by the actual trend in circulation, which, according to police figures, fell only from 17,000 in January 1896 to 16,000 in April 1897 for the *Daily Independent*, a fall more than offset by the rise in circulation of the *Evening Herald* from 16,000 to 20,000 in the same period (an improvement ascribed by the police to the superiority of its sporting correspondents). The *Freeman*, meanwhile, fell back again to 26,000 by April 1897. NAI 3/716, Box 13, 15447/S, 13 Apr. 1897.
61 *I.D.I.*, 19 Jun. 1897. Mallon, who was convinced that the *Daily Independent* was 'for all practical purposes, the daily organ of the secret societies', commented that Chandler, a lawyer from Philadelphia, 'seems to have control of lots of cash', and was in Dublin 'in the interest of secret societies'. NAI 3/716, Box 12, 13974/S, 27 Jul. 1897.
62 Baker to Redmond, 10 May 1897, NLI Ms. 15,167 (1).
63 Circulation figures remained steady, at 16,000 for the *Daily Independent* and 20,000 for the *Evening Herald*, between April 1897 and April 1898. NAI 3/716, Box 13, 15945/S, 13 Apr. 1898.
64 Baker to Redmond, 22 Jul. 1897, NLI Ms. 15,167 (1).
65 Baker to Carew, 30 Jul. 1897, NLI Ms. 15,167 (1).
66 Byrne, who was already in failing health, died two years later in October 1899. In the newspaper that he had held behind Parnell almost until the end of the latter's life, now under Sexton's managing directorship, his death was recorded in a tiny paragraph that failed to mention that he had ever been editor of either the *Freeman* or the *Independent*. *F.J.*, and *I.D.I.*, 14 Oct. 1899. See also Frank Callanan's introduction to Edward Byrne, *Parnell: A Memoir*, ed. Frank Callanan (Dublin, 1991), pp. 1–10.
67 *I.D.I.*, 13 Dec. 1897.
68 ibid.
69 Allan to Redmond, 14 Feb., 18 Feb. 1898, NLI Ms. 15,164 (2).
70 Baker to Redmond, 9 Mar. 1898, NLI Ms. 15,167 (1).
71 Baker to Redmond, 16 Mar. 1898, NLI Ms. 15,167 (1).
72 Baker to Redmond, 26 Mar. 1898, NLI Ms. 15,167 (1).
73 *I.D.I.*, 24 Aug.; Aug. and Sept. 1898 *passim*. The *Independent* boasted on 24 August of being 'the first paper this side of the Atlantic . . . to secure the most perfect Printing Press ever produced'.
74 Quoted in Baker to Redmond, 20 Oct. 1898, NLI Ms. 15,167 (1).
75 Baker to Redmond, 25 Oct. 1898, NLI Ms. 15,167 (1).
76 NAI CBS 3/716, Box 15, 18281/S; *Daily Nation*, 24 Feb. 1899.
77 NAI CBS 3/716, Box 15, 18500/S, 18699/S, 18742/S.
78 *Daily Nation*, 27 Feb., 1 Mar. 1899.
79 NAI CBS 3/716, Box 15, 18778/S.
80 Allan was discharged with three months salary, and was hard up for a time while he attempted to open a book agency. In January 1900 he was appointed secretary to Lord Mayor Sir Thomas Pile, a post which placed him in embarrassing positions before his IRB comrades. In the St Patrick's Day procession that year he was sitting in the back of the lord mayor's carriage when he was strewn with broken glass and struck with a stone thrown from a crowd of nationalists incensed by the passing of Pile's resolution that Dublin Corporation present an address of welcome to Queen Victoria on her forthcoming visit. During the visit he had to organize a reception of schoolchildren for the queen in the Phoenix Park. *F.J.*, 19 Mar. 1900. Interestingly,

Allan and Pile, from opposite ends of the spectrum of Dublin Parnellism, were both English Methodists by birth. For an account of Allan's long career in republican politics, see Owen McGee, 'Frederick James Allan (1861–1937), Fenian and Civil Servant', *History Ireland* (Spring 2002), pp. 29–33.

81 Baker to Redmond, 24 Apr., 17 Jul. 1899, NLI Ms. 15,167 (1); Patterson to Redmond, 7 Jun., 14, 16 Jul. 1899, NLI Ms. 15,238.
82 *I.D.I.*, 5 Sept. 1899.
83 *F.J.*, 22 Mar. 1900.
84 *I.D.I.*, 15 Jan. 1898.
85 Hansard, 53, 371–82, 11 Feb. 1898.
86 *I.D.I.*, 15 Feb. 1898.
87 Harrington denounced Redmond's action as 'unpardonable stupidity' and 'treason', and Dillon's vote as revealing 'hopeless weakness and indecision'. *I.D.I.*, 18 Feb. 1898.
88 Quoted in ibid., 21 Feb. 1898.
89 ibid., 9 Mar. 1898.
90 Quoted in ibid., 16 Mar. 1898.
91 Hansard, 55, 446–55, 21 Mar. 1898.
92 *I.D.I.*, 16 Apr. 1898.
93 ibid.
94 ibid., 14 Mar. 1898; NAI CBS 3/716, Box 13, 15647/S.
95 NAI 3/716, Box 13, 15200/S, 16235/S.
96 *I.D.I.*, 25 Apr. 1898.
97 ibid., 3 May 1898.
98 ibid., 15 Mar. 1898.
99 O'Callaghan to Redmond, 22 Apr. 1898, NLI Ms. 15,213 (1).
100 O'Callaghan to Redmond, 13 May 1898, NLI Ms. 15,213 (1).
101 *I.D.I.*, 30 May 1898.
102 ibid., 1 Jun. 1898.
103 Quoted in *I.D.I.*, 3 Jun. 1898.
104 *F.J.*, 4 Jun. 1898.
105 *I.D.I.*, 14 Jul. 1898.
106 ibid., 9 Jul. 1898. The *Independent*, however, criticized as a tactical blunder the decision, at a meeting of the National Club convened by Harrington, to expel from the club those nationalists on the Corporation who had voted for Sexton; ibid., 12 Jul. 1898.
107 ibid., 14 Jul. 1898.
108 ibid., 14 Sept. 1898.
109 ibid., 17, 21 Jun. 1898.
110 ibid., 16 Aug. 1898.
111 ibid.
112 ibid., 6 Sept. 1898.
113 ibid., 14 Sept. 1898.
114 ibid., 7 Oct., 22 Nov. 1898.
115 ibid., 11 Oct. 1898.
116 ibid., 18 Nov. 1898.
117 Kelly, '"Parnell's Old Brigade"', p. 211.
118 Michael Laffan, 'John Redmond and Home Rule', in Ciaran Brady (ed.), *Worsted in the Game – Losers in Irish History* (Dublin, 1989), p. 137.
119 ibid.

12. Stumbling towards Unity

1 William O'Brien, *An Olive Branch in Ireland* (London, 1910).
2 *I.D.I.*, 20 Oct. 1900.
3 See Philip Bull, 'The United Irish League and the Reunion of the Irish Parliamentary Party, 1898–1900', *Irish Historical Studies*, vol. 26, no. 101 (May 1988), pp. 51–78; Philip Bull, 'The Formation of the United Irish League, 1898–1900: The Dynamics of Irish Agrarian Agitation', *Irish Historical Studies*, vol. 33,

no. 132 (Nov. 2003), pp. 404–23; Sally Warwick-Haller, *William O'Brien and the Irish Land War* (Dublin, 1990), pp. 171–93.

4 William O'Brien to Dillon, 26 Dec. 1898, O'Brien Papers, NLI Ms. 8555 (12).
5 ibid.
6 Bull, 'Formation of the United Irish League', p. 416.
7 *I.D.I.*, 3 Feb. 1898.
8 Dillon to William O'Brien, 8 Jul. 1898, O'Brien Papers, NLI Ms. 8555 (13).
9 Dillon to William O'Brien, 4 Apr. 1898, O'Brien Papers, NLI Ms. 8555 (15).
10 William O'Brien to Dillon, 26 Dec. 1898, O'Brien Papers, NLI Ms. 8555 (12).
11 Warwick-Haller, *William O'Brien and the Irish Land War*, pp. 187–8.
12 *I.D.I.*, 1 Oct. 1898.
13 ibid., 14 Oct. 1898.
14 Quoted in Bull, 'Formation of the United Irish League', p. 418.
15 *I.D.I.*, 31 Oct. 1898. The two brothers met only two days later at a rally in Wexford to lay the foundation stone for a 1798 monument there, a fact which suggests that Redmond was kept abreast of developments in the West.
16 *I.D.I.*, 14 Nov. 1898.
17 ibid., 28 Dec. 1898.
18 ibid., 3 Dec. 1898.
19 ibid., 28 Nov. 1898.
20 NAI 3/716, Box 15, 18281/S (20 Jan. 1899). O'Kelly stood to lose an annual salary of £250 (18860/S).
21 *I.D.I.*, 24, 30 Jan. 1899.
22 ibid., 7 Jan. 1899.
23 Quoted in *I.D.I.*, 23 Mar. 1899; ibid., 27 Mar. 1899.
24 *F.J.*, 31 Jan. 1899.
25 *I.D.I.*, 5 Apr. 1899.
26 Nevertheless, Unionist representation on Dublin Corporation fell in the elections of January 1899. The new City Council had 53 nationalists (including 9 Labour) and 7 Unionists, compared with 48 nationalists and 12 Unionists previously. *Daily Express*, 19 Jan. 1899.
27 *I.D.I.*, 10 Apr. 1899.
28 Quoted in *I.D.I.*, 11 Apr. 1899.
29 ibid., 24 Apr. 1899.
30 ibid., 23 May, 5 Jul. 1899. Devoy claimed in the *Boston Globe* that the Parnellite section of the electorate were 'by far the most intelligent voters in Ireland'.
31 NAI 3/716, Box 15, 18971/S; Box 16, 20299/S; *I.D.I.*, 17 Jun. 1899.
32 *I.D.I.*, 7, 8 Jun. 1899.
33 ibid., 14 Jul. 1899.
34 ibid., 14 Feb. 1899.
35 *F.J.*, 1 Apr. 1899.
36 *I.D.I.*, 4 Apr. 1899.
37 F. S. L. Lyons, *The Irish Parliamentary Party 1890–1910* (London, 1951), pp. 81–2.
38 *F.J.*, 5 Apr. 1899.
39 ibid., 8 Apr. 1899.
40 *I.D.I.*, 1 May 1899.
41 ibid., 13 May, 8 Jul. 1899.
42 Redmond to Dillon, 24 Jul. 1899, NLI Ms.15,182 (2).
43 Healy to Redmond, 24 Jul. 1899, NLI Ms. 15,196.
44 Dillon to Redmond, 26 Jul. 1899, NLI Ms. 15,182 (2).
45 *I.D.I.*, 29 Jul. 1899.
46 Dillon to Davitt, 29 Aug. 1899, NLI Ms. 15,741.
47 *I.D.I.*, 4 Aug. 1899.
48 Dillon to Davitt, 29 Aug. 1899, NLI Ms. 15,741.
49 The second Bill, opposed by the Irish Unionists led by Edward Carson and Colonel Saunderson, passed the House of Commons by a majority of 162 but was rejected by the Lords by a majority of 5, a move that caused anger and a

revival of anti-House of Lords sentiment in Ireland. *I.D.I.*, 25 Jul. 1899.
50 *I.D.I.,* 17, 18 Feb. 1899.
51 ibid., 3, 4 Feb. 1899.
52 ibid., 14 Mar. 1899.
53 ibid., 22 May 1899.
54 ibid., 6 Jul. 1899.
55 ibid., 24 Jul. 1899.
56 *F.J.*, 20 May 1899; Bull, 'United Irish League and the Reunion of the Irish Parliamentary Party', pp. 64–5.
57 Lyons, *Irish Parliamentary Party 1890-1910*, pp. 206–07, 214. The income figures increased dramatically after the reunion of 1900: between the June and December conventions of that year almost £11,000 was raised.
58 *I.DI.,* 9 Oct. 1899. Many of those active in the '98 commemoration movement, including O'Leary, Yeats, Gonne, and Arthur Griffith, together with Davitt and several Redmondite M.P.s were involved in the Irish Transvaal Committee, which staged a demonstration of 20,000 in Dublin on 1 October. The committee also distributed 1,500 posters and handbills entitled 'Enlisting in the English Army is Treason to Ireland'. NAI CBS 3/716, Box 16, 20143/S, 20142/S.
59 *I.D.I.*, 18, 21 Oct. 1899.
60 ibid., 19 Oct. 1899. The *Independent* used a primitive signalling system to indicate the progress of the war: three red lights on its building meant heavy fighting; one red light meant a British success; while a green light meant a Boer success. *I.D.I.*, 25 Oct. 1899.
61 *I.D.I.*, 16 Nov. 1899.
62 ibid., 12 Dec. 1899.
63 ibid., 13 Nov. 1899.
64 Healy, *Letters and Leaders*, vol. 2, pp. 434, 443.
65 Healy to Moreton Frewen, 10 May 1899, NLI Ms. 15,188 (9).
66 Healy, *Letters and Leaders*, vol. 2, p. 435.
67 Healy to Redmond, 4 Aug. 1899, NLI Ms. 15,196.
68 Redmond to Healy, 12 Aug. 1899, NLI Ms. 15,196; *I.D.I.*, 24 Nov. 1899.
69 *I.D.I.*, 7 Aug. 1899.
70 ibid., 21 Sept. 1899.
71 ibid., 10 Oct. 1899.
72 ibid., 9, 11 Dec. 1899. Half of the amount of £6,000 was sent by the legendary Richard 'Boss' Croker on behalf of Tammany Hall, 'for the purpose of clearing the entire encumbrance now resting upon the Parnell homestead, thus securing the retention of the home in the family'. Redmond had informed Croker that if they were unable to carry out their plan of buying the Parnell house and demesne for the nation, 'with the understanding that any members of the Parnell family who chose to occupy it should be at liberty to do so', they could at least proceed with the monument, and proposed to place a contract immediately with the eminent Irish-American sculptor Augustus Saint Gaudens. Redmond to Croker, 3 Nov. 1899; Croker to Redmond and Tallon, 21 Nov. 1899, NLI Ms. 15,236 (2).
73 Miscellaneous correspondence, NLI Ms. 15,238 (10).
74 Lyons, *Irish Parliamentary Party 1890–1910*, pp. 84–5.
75 Quoted in *I.D.I.*, 2 Dec. 1899.
76 *F.J.*, 18 Dec. 1899.
77 S. Gwynn, *John Redmond's Last Years*, p. 22.
78 *I.D.I.,* 4 Jan. 1900.
79 ibid., 18 Jan. 1900.
80 ibid., 22 Jan. 1900.
81 O'Brien to J. F. X. O'Brien, 28 Jan. 1900, J. F. X O'Brien Papers, NLI Ms. 13,427.
82 Bull, 'United Irish League and the Reunion of the Irish Parliamentary Party', p. 68.
83 *F.J.*, 16 Jan. 1900.
84 Lyons, *Irish Parliamentary Party 1890–1910*, p. 86.
85 Bull, 'United Irish League and the Reunion of the Irish Parliamentary Party', pp. 68–9.

86 *I.D.I.*, 26 Jan. 1900.
87 ibid., 31 Jan. 1900.
88 Lyons, *Irish Parliamentary Party 1890–1910*, p. 88. Davitt himself had done his utmost to convert O'Brien to this view of Harrington, writing to the latter on 23 January: 'I am informed that Harrington is now the most active enemy of the League in Dublin. His head is swollen enormously over the Conferences and it appears he is Healy's candidate for the Chair of the reunited Party!!! . . . All this is Healy's plan. He thinks Harrington will be the best tool with which to fight the League . . .' Davitt to O'Brien, 23 Jan. 1900, O'Brien Papers, NLI Ms. 914 (785).
89 According to Healy, O'Brien had received new information which led him to the mistaken belief that Harrington was after all in league with Healy, and wired the meeting: 'Vote for Redmond, and smash the Healy-Harrington conspiracy!' Redmond's election was thus 'a fluke'. Healy, *Letters and Leaders*, vol. 2, p. 446.
90 Redmond to T. P. Gill, 6 Feb. 1900, NLI Ms. 15,190 (5).
91 O'Brien, *An Olive Branch in Ireland*, p. 123.
92 *I.D.I.*, 10 Feb. 1900.
93 ibid., 12 Feb. 1900.
94 Hansard (4th series), 78, 830–41, 7 Feb. 1900.
95 ibid., 80, 402–03, 8 Mar. 1900.
96 *I.D.I.*, 14, 17, 26 Mar. 1900.
97 Dillon to O'Brien, 14 Mar. 1900, O'Brien Papers, NLI Ms. 8555 (10).
98 Healy, *Letters and Leaders*, vol 2, p. 448. Healy's astonished reaction was 'O'Brien never sent such a message,' to which Redmond replied 'savagely': 'He did, the dog!'. The 'Smash Redmond' message was used by Healy in his campaign against O'Brien later in 1900. See *I.D.I.*, 11 Jun., 28 Sep. 1900. The letter is quoted in J. V. O'Brien, *William O'Brien*, pp. 120–1.
99 Harrington to Redmond, 3 Mar. 1900, NLI Ms. 15,194.
100 *F.J.* 12 Mar. 1900.
101 Redmond to O'Brien, postscript 12 Mar. to letter 11 Mar., NLI Ms. 10,496 (2).
102 O'Brien to Dillon, 26 Mar. 1900, O'Brien Papers, NLI Ms. 8555 (10).
103 O'Brien to Redmond, 27 Mar. 1900, NLI Ms. 15,212 (5).
104 Harrington to Redmond, 30 Mar. 1900, NLI Ms. 15,194.
105 J. J. McCartan to Redmond, 29 Mar. 1900, NLI Ms. 15,239 (1).
106 Redmond to O'Brien, 29 Mar. 1900, NLI Ms. 10,496 (2).
107 Dillon to O'Brien, 5 Apr. 1900, O'Brien Papers, NLI Ms. 8555 (10).
108 O'Brien to Dillon, 6 Apr. 1900, O'Brien Papers, NLI Ms. 8555 (11).
109 *I.D.I.*, 23 Apr. 1900.
110 *F.J.*, 27 Apr. 1900.
111 *I.D.I.*, 4 May 1900.
112 Dillon to O'Brien, 16 Jun. 1900, O'Brien Papers, NLI Ms. 8555 (10).
113 *I.D.I.*, 30 May 1900.
114 ibid., 1 Jun. 1900.
115 ibid., 9 Jun. 1900.
116 ibid., 11, 12 Jun. 1900.
117 ibid., 20, 21 Jun. 1900.
118 Bull, 'United Irish League and the Reunion of the Irish Parliamentary Party', p. 76.
119 Redmond to Harrington, undated (probably Apr./May 1900), Harrington Papers, NLI Ms. 8576 (45).
120 *I.D.I.*, 11 Jun. 1900.
121 Hansard (4th series), 86, 684, 20 Jul. 1900.
122 For the full speech, see ibid., 86, 682–91, 20 Jul. 1900.
123 *I.D.I.*, 3 Sept. 1900. W. B. Yeats echoed these opinions at the central branch of the Gaelic League on 17 October when he contrasted the 'modern vulgarities' that were music-hall songs to the 'higher civilisation' to be found in Gaelic culture.
124 *I.D.I.*, 12 Oct. 1900.
125 ibid., 3 Sept. 1900.
126 ibid., 24 Sept. 1900.

127 ibid., 15 Sept. 1900.
128 *F.J.*, 20 Aug. 1900.
129 Quoted in *F.J.*, 19 Jul. 1900.
130 *I.D.I.*, 7 Aug. 1900.
131 F. S. L. Lyons, *John Dillon – A Biography* (London, 1968), p. 213.
132 *I.D.I.*, 8 Aug. 1900.
133 *F.J.*, 23 Aug. 1900.
134 Healy to Redmond, 13 May, 16 Aug. 1900, NLI Ms. 15,196; Healy, *Letters and Leaders*, vol. 2, pp. 448–9.
135 *I.D.I.*, 1 Sept. 1900.
136 *Evening Telegraph*, 23 Aug. 1900.
137 *I.D.I.*, 25 Sept. 1900.
138 ibid., 8 Aug. 1900.
139 ibid., 24 Aug. 1900.
140 ibid., 3 Sept. 1900.
141 ibid., 8 Sept. 1900.
142 ibid., 10 Sept. 1900.
143 ibid., 15 Sept. 1900.
144 ibid., 28 Sept. 1900.
145 ibid., 24 Sept. 1900.
146 Redmond to T. P. O'Connor, 27 Sept. 1900, NLI Ms. 15,215 (1).
147 Bull, 'United Irish League and the Reunion of the Irish Parliamentary Party', pp. 76–77.
148 Redmond to Blake, 3 Nov. 1900, NLI Ms. 15,170 (2).
149 *I.D.I.*, 9 Nov. 1900.
150 O'Brien to Redmond, 9 Nov. 1900, NLI Ms. 10,496 (12).
141 Redmond to O'Brien, 10 Nov. 1900, NLI Ms. 10,496 (3).
152 Healy, *Letters and Leaders*, vol. 2, p. 452.
153 *I.D.I.*, and *F.J.*, 12, 13 Dec. 1900.
154 *I.D.I.*, 13 Dec. 1900.
155 Hansard (4th series), 89, 964, 22 Feb. 1901.

13. Epilogue

1 David Lloyd George, *War Memoirs: Vol. 1* (London, 1938), p. 420.
2 John Devoy, *Recollections of an Irish Rebel* (New York, 1929), p. 480.
3 See Redmond's speech at Liverpool, *F.J.*, 16 Mar. 1903.
4 Paul Bew, *Conflict and Conciliation in Ireland 1890–1910* (Oxford, 1987), p. 113.
5 O'Brien, *An Olive Branch in Ireland*, p. 288.
6 *F.J.*, 15 Sept. 1905.

Bibliography

I Unpublished Sources

(i) Politicians' Papers

Isaac Butt Papers, National Library of Ireland
John Devoy Papers, National Library of Ireland
John Dillon Papers, Trinity College Dublin Library
T. P. Gill Papers, National Library of Ireland
T. C. Harrington Papers, National Library of Ireland
J. F. X. O'Brien Papers, National Library of Ireland
William O'Brien Papers, National Library of Ireland
John Redmond Papers, National Library of Ireland

(ii) Police Reports

Royal Irish Constabulary reports of Land League and National League proceedings, 1882–1889, INL 3/714, National Archives of Ireland
Royal Irish Constabulary Crime Branch Special reports, 1891–1900, CBS 3/716, National Archives of Ireland

(iii) Miscellaneous Papers

Redmond family tree and commentary, in possession of the Ryan family of Ballytrent House
Private verse journal of John Redmond, in possession of Fr Matt Glynn, Tagoat, Co. Wexford
Two unpublished lectures by John Redmond (NLI Ms. 15,274)
(a) 'The ballad poetry of Ireland'
(b) 'Irish Popular Leaders from Swift to Parnell'
Memoir by Sophie (Mrs William) O'Brien of John and Willie Redmond, National Library of Ireland
Transcripts 1850–1904, Registry of Deeds, King's Inns, Dublin

II Official and other Published Papers

Hansard's Parliamentary Debates, 2nd, 3rd and 4th series.
Proceedings of the Home Rule Conference, 18–21 November 1873 (Dublin, 1874).
Report of the Royal Commission on the Housing of the Working Classes (Ireland), 3rd Report, H.C. 1884–5, C.4547–I, vol. xxxi.
Report of the Special Commission, 1888, appointed to inquire into charges and allegations made against certain members of Parliament in O'Donnell v. Walter, H.C. 1890, C.5891.
Report of the Royal Commission on the Financial Relations between Great Britain and Ireland ['The Childers Commission'], H.C. 1896, C.8262, vol. xxxiii.

Report of the Recess Committee on the Establishment of a Department of Agriculture and Industries for Ireland (London & Dublin, 1896).

III Newspapers and Periodicals

(i) Irish Newspapers

Arklow Reporter
Cork Examiner
Cork Herald
Daily Express
Dublin Evening Mail
Evening Herald
Evening Telegraph
Freeman's Journal
Insuppressible
Irish Catholic
Irish Daily Independent
Irish People
Irish Times
Irish Weekly Independent
Nation
National Press
'Suppressed' United Ireland
United Ireland
United Irishman
Weekly Freeman's Journal
Wexford Herald
Wexford Independent
Wexford People
Wicklow News–Letter

(ii) Other newspapers and periodicals

(a) Newspapers

Daily News
Daily Chronicle
Daily Telegraph
Freeman's Journal (Sydney)
Gaelic American
Labour World
Manchester Guardian
Pall Mall Gazette
Saturday Review
Standard
Sydney Morning Herald
The Times

(b) Periodicals

Black and White
Contemporary Review

Fortnightly Review
New Review
Nineteenth Century
Pall Mall Magazine

(iii) Irish Annual Directories

Watson's or the Gentleman's and Citizen's Almanack, years 1830 to 1838 (Dublin)
Dublin Almanac and General Register of Ireland, years 1835 to 1837 (Dublin)
Thom's Almanac and Official Directory of the United Kingdom of Great Britain and Ireland, years 1845 to 1869 (Dublin)
Dublin University Calendar, years 1874 to 1876, Trinity College, Dublin

(iv) Miscellaneous Reference Works

Dictionary of National Biography
Who Was Who
The Catholic Encyclopaedia, Vol. XIV (New York 1912)

IV Published writings and speeches of John Redmond

Redmond, John, *Historical and Political Addresses 1883–97* (Dublin & London, 1898)

Redmond, John, *Home Rule: Speeches of John Redmond, M.P.*, ed. with intro. by R. Barry O'Brien (London, 1910)

'The Irish Local Government Bill', *Fortnightly Review,* vol. 51 (May 1892), pp. 621–33

'Readjustment of the Union: a nationalist plan', *Nineteenth Century*, vol. 32 (Oct. 1892), pp. 509–23

'A Plea for Amnesty', *Fortnightly Review*, vol. 52 (Dec. 1892), pp. 722–32

'The Lesson of South Meath', *Fortnightly Review*, vol. 53 (Jan. 1893), pp. 1–6

'Notes on the Home Rule Bill (No. II): the mutual safeguards', *Contemporary Review*, vol. 63 (Mar. 1893), pp. 311–15

'Ireland's Reply', *New Review* vol. 8 (Jan. 1893), pp. 12–17

'Obstruction (No. VII)', *New Review*, vol. 8 (Apr. 1893), pp. 392–4

'Second Thoughts on the Home Rule Bill', *Nineteenth Century*, vol. 33 (Apr. 1893), pp. 559–570

'The "gag" and the Commons (No. II)', *New Review*, vol. 9 (Aug. 1893), pp. 122–8

'What next [after rejection of Home Rule]?', *Nineteenth Century*, vol. 34 (Nov. 1893), pp. 688–97

'What has become of Home Rule?' *Nineteenth Century*, vol. 36 (Nov. 1894), pp. 655–77

'The Policy of "Killing Home Rule by Kindness"', *Nineteenth Century*, vol. 38 (Dec. 1895), pp. 905–14

'Ireland and the Next Session', *Nineteenth Century*, vol. 41 (Jan. 1897), pp. 104–112

'The Promised Irish Local Government Bill', *Nineteenth Century*, vol. 41 (Oct. 1897), pp. 640–52

'The Centenary of '98 [the Irish Insurrection]', *Nineteenth Century*, vol. 42 (Apr. 1898), pp. 612–24

V Articles, Works and Memoirs by Contemporaries

Anon., 'The Redmond Memorial, Wexford', in *The Irish Builder*, Vol. IX, 1 Apr. 1867, p. 87

Wilfred Scawen Blunt, *The Land War in Ireland – being a personal narrative of events* (London, 1912)

Byrne, Edward, *Parnell: A Memoir*, ed. Frank Callanan (Dublin, 1991)

Davitt, Michael, *The fall of feudalism in Ireland* (London, 1904)

Devoy, John, *Devoy's Post Bag*, 1871–1928, ed. William O'Brien and Desmond Ryan (2 vols., Dublin, 1948, repr. 1979)

Devoy, *Recollections of an Irish Rebel*, ed. Sean O Luing (Shannon, 1969)

Gannon, John, 'John Redmond: his schooldays', *The Clongownian*, Vol. VIII, No. 2 (June 1918), pp. 137–8

Gwynn, Denis, *The Life of John Redmond* (London, 1932)

Gwynn, Stephen, *John Redmond's Last Years* (London, 1919)

Healy, Timothy Michael, *Letters and Leaders of My Day* (2 vols., London, 1927)

Healy, Timothy Michael, 'Ulster and Ireland', *Contemporary Review*, 48 (Nov. 1885), pp. 723–31

Horgan, John J., *Parnell to Pearse – some recollections and reflections* (Dublin, 1948)

Hyde, Douglas, 'The Necessity for De-Anglicising Ireland' in Charles Gavan Duffy et al. (eds.), *The revival of Irish literature, plays, poems and prose* (London, 1894)

Kane, Fr Robert Kane, S.J., 'John Redmond as a Clongownian', *The Clongownian*, Vol. VIII, No. 2 (June 1918), pp. 138–43

Kavanagh, Patrick F., *A Popular History of the Insurrection of 1798* (Dublin, 1870)

Kettle, Andrew J., *Material for Victory*, ed. L.J. Kettle (Dublin, 1958)

Leamy, Margaret, *Parnell's Faithful Few* (New York, 1936)

Lecky, W. E. H., *The Leaders of Public Opinion in Ireland* (London, 1871)

Lucy, Sir Henry W., *A Diary of Two Parliaments* (2 vols., London, 1886), Vol. II: The Gladstone Parliament 1880–85

Lucy, Sir Henry W., *A Diary of the Salisbury Parliament 1886–92* (London, 1892)

Lucy, Sir Henry W., *A Diary of the Home Rule Parliament 1892–5* (London, 1896)

Lucy, Sir Henry W., *A Diary of the Unionist Parliament 1895–1900* (London, 1901)

Morley, John, *The Life of William Ewart Gladstone*, (2 vols., London 1908)

O'Brien, R. Barry, *The Life of Charles Stewart Parnell, 1846–91* (2 vols., London, 1898)

O'Brien, William, 'Was Fenianism ever formidable?', *Contemporary Review*, lxxi (1897), pp. 680–93

O'Brien, William, *Recollections* (London, 1905)

O'Brien, William, *An Olive Branch in Ireland* (London, 1910)

O'Brien, William, *Evening Memories* (Dublin and London, 1920)

O'Donnell, Frank Hugh, *A History of the Irish Parliamentary Party*, (2 vols., London, 1910)

Plunkett, Sir Horace, *Ireland in the New Century* (London, 1904).

Redmond, William H. K., 'Aughavanagh in Parnell's Time', *Irish Weekly Independent*, 6 Oct. 1894.

Redmond-Howard, L. G., *John Redmond – The man and the demand* (London, 1910)
Swift MacNeill, J. G., *What I have seen and heard* (Boston, 1925)
Temple, Rt. Hon. Sir Richard, *Letters and Character Sketches from the House of Commons,* ed. Sir Richard Carnac Temple, Bart. (London, 1912)
Tynan, Katherine, *Twenty-Five Years: Reminiscences* (London, 1913)
Tynan, Katherine, *Memories* (London, 1924)
Wells, Warre B., *John Redmond – A Biography* (London, 1919)

VI Historical Articles and Works

Bew, Paul, *Conflict and Conciliation in Ireland 1890–1910* (Oxford, 1987)
Bew, *John Redmond* (Dundalk, 1996)
Bolger, Patrick, *The Irish Co-operative Movement – its History and Development* (Dublin, Institute of Public Administration, 1977)
Boyce, D. George, *Nationalism in Ireland* (London, 1982)
Boyce, D. George, *The Irish Question and British Politics 1868–1986* (London 1988)
Bull, Philip, 'The United Irish League and the reunion of the Irish parliamentary party, 1898–1900', *Irish Historical Studies,* xxvi, no. 101 (May 1988), pp. 51–78
Bull, Philip, 'The formation of the United Irish League, 1898–1900: the dynamics of Irish agrarian agitation', *Irish Historical Studies,* xxxiii, no. 132 (Nov. 2003), pp. 404–23
Bull, Philip, *Land, Politics and Nationalism* (Dublin, 1996)
Callanan, Frank, *The Parnell Split* (Cork, 1992)
Callanan, Frank, *Timothy Michael Healy* (Cork, 1996)
Campbell, Fergus, *Land and Revolution: Nationalist Politics in the West of Ireland 1891–1921* (Oxford, 2005)
Campbell, Malcolm, 'John Redmond and the Irish National League in Australia and New Zealand, 1883', *History,* Vol. 86, No. 283 (July 2001), pp. 348–62
Cleary, Brian, 'The Battle of Oulart Hill: Context and Strategy', in Dáire Keogh and Nicholas Furlong (eds.), *The Mighty Wave: The 1798 Rebellion in Wexford* (Dublin, 1996), pp. 79–96
Corish, Patrick J., 'Two Centuries of Catholicism in County Wexford' in Kevin Whelan and William Nolan (eds.) *Wexford: history and society– interdisciplinary essays on the history of an Irish county* (Dublin, 1987)
Cruise O'Brien, Conor, *Parnell and his Party* (Oxford, 1957)
Cruise O'Brien, Conor, *Ancestral Voices* (Dublin, 1994)
Curtis, L. P., *Coercion and Conciliation in Ireland, 1880–92: a Study in Conservative Unionism* (Princeton, 1963).
Daly, Mary E., *Dublin – the deposed capital: a social and economic history 1860–1914* (Cork, 1985)
Davis, Richard P., *Arthur Griffith and Non-Violent Sinn Fein* (Dublin, 1974)
Denman, Terence, '"The red livery of shame": the campaign against army recruitment in Ireland, 1889–1914', *Irish Historical Studies*, xxix, no. 114 (Nov. 1994), pp. 208–33
Denman, Terence, *A lonely grave – the life and death of William Redmond* (Dublin, 1995)
Dunleavy, Janet Egleson, and Dunleavy, Gareth W., *Douglas Hyde: A Maker of Modern Ireland* (Berkeley, 1991)
Dunne, Tom, *Rebellions: Memoir, Memory and 1798* (Dublin, 2004).

Foster, R. F., *Charles Stewart Parnell: The Man and His Family* (Brighton, 1976)

Foster, R. F., *Paddy and Mr. Punch: Connections in Irish and English History* (London, 1993)

Foster, R. F., *W. B. Yeats: A Life*, 2 vols., Vol I: The Apprentice Mage 1865–1914 (Oxford, 1998)

Gailey, Andrew, 'Unionist rhetoric and Irish local government reform, 1895–9', *Irish Historical Studies,* xxiv, no. 93 (May 1984), pp. 52–68

Garvin, Tom, 'Priests and Patriots: Irish separatism and fear of the modern, 1890–1914', *Irish Historical Studies,* xxv, no. 97 (May 1986), pp. 67–81.

Garvin, Tom, *Nationalist Revolutionaries in Ireland 1858–1928* (Oxford, 1988)

Glynn, Jarlath, 'The Catholic Church in Wexford Town 1800 – 1858', *The Past (Organ of the Ui Cinsealaigh Historical Society)*, No. 15, 1984, pp. 5–39

Goodall, David, 'The Freemen of Wexford in 1776', *The Irish Genealogist,* Vol. 5, No. 4, Nov. 1977

Gutzke, David W., 'Rosebery and Ireland, 1898–1903: A Reappraisal' in Alan O'Day (ed.) *Reactions to Irish Nationalism, 1865–1914* (London, 1987), pp. 285–95

Jackson, Alvin, *Home Rule: an Irish History 1800–2000* (London, 2003)

Jordan, Donald, 'Merchants, "Strong Farmers" and Fenians: the Post-Famine Political Elite and the Irish Land War' in Charles H. Philpin (ed.), *Nationalism and Popular Protest in Ireland* (Cambridge, 1987), pp. 320–48

Kee, Robert, *The Laurel and the Ivy: the story of Charles Stewart Parnell and Irish Nationalism* (London, 1993)

Kelly, John, 'Parnell in Irish Literature', in Boyce and O'Day (eds.), *Parnell in Perspective* (London, 1991), pp. 256–7.

Kelly, Matthew, '"Parnell's Old Brigade": the Redmondite–Fenian nexus in the 1890s', *Irish Historical Studies*, xxxiii, no. 130 (Nov. 2002), pp. 209–32

Kinsella, Anna, '1798 Claimed for Catholics: Father Kavanagh, Fenians and the Centenary Celebrations' in Keogh and Furlong (eds.), *The Mighty Wave: the 1798 Rebellion in Wexford* (Dublin, 1996), pp. 139–55

Laffan, Michael, 'John Redmond and Home Rule' in Ciaran Brady (ed.) *Worsted in the Game – Losers in Irish History* (Dublin, 1989)

Larkin, Emmet, *The Roman Catholic Church in Ireland and the Fall of Parnell 1888–1891* (Liverpool, 1979)

Lee, Joseph, *The Modernisation of Irish Society 1848–1918* (Dublin, 1973)

Lyons, F. S. L., 'The machinery of the Irish parliamentary party in the general election of 1895', *Irish Historical Studies*, viii (1952), pp. 115–39

Lyons, F. S. L., *The Irish Parliamentary Party 1890–1910* (London, 1951)

Lyons, F. S. L., *The Fall of Parnell* (London, 1960)

Lyons, F. S. L., *John Dillon – a biography* (London, 1968)

Lyons, F. S. L., 'The Political Ideas of Parnell', *Historical Journal*, xvi, 4 (1973), pp. 749–75

Lyons, F. S. L., *Charles Stewart Parnell* (London, 1977)

MacDonagh, *O'Connell: The Life of Daniel O'Connell 1775–1847* (London, 1991)

Malcolm, Elizabeth, *'Ireland Sober, Ireland Free': Drink and Temperance in 19th Century Ireland* (Dublin, 1986)

Maume, Patrick, 'John Redmond – visionary, fool or traitor?', *Irish Times*, 4 Mar. 1993

Maume, Patrick, *The Long Gestation: Irish Nationalist Life, 1891–1918* (Dublin, 1999)

McCartney, Donal, *W. E. H. Lecky, Historian and Politician, 1838–1903* (Dublin, 1994)

McGee, Owen, 'Frederick James Allan (1861–1937), Fenian and civil servant', *History Ireland* (Spring 2002), pp. 29–33

Miller, David W., *Queen's Rebels: Ulster Loyalism in Historical Perspective* (Dublin, 1978)

Miller, David W., 'The Roman Catholic Church in Ireland, 1898–1918' in Alan O'Day (ed.) *Reactions to Irish Nationalism, 1865–1914* (London, 1987), pp. 187–203

Morton, Grenfell, *Home Rule and the Irish Question* (London, 1980)

Murphy, Hilary, *Families of County Wexford* (Dublin,1986)

Myers, Kevin, 'A Great Reconciler is Traduced Again', *Irish Times*, 23 Apr. 1996

O'Brien, Joseph V., *William O'Brien and the Course of Irish Politics 1881–1918* (Berkeley 1976)

O'Broin, Leon, *The prime informer – a suppressed scandal* (London, 1971)

Palmer, Norman D., *The Irish Land League Crisis* (New Haven, 1940)

Prunty, Jacinta, *Dublin Slums 1800 – 1925: a study in urban geography* (Dublin, 1998)

Shannon, Catherine B., 'The Ulster liberal unionists and local government reform, 1885–98', *Irish Historical Studies*, xviii (Mar. 1973), pp. 407–23

Thornley, David, *Isaac Butt and Home Rule* (London, 1964)

Walker, Brian M. (ed.), *New History of Ireland – Vol. VIII: Parliamentary Election Results in Ireland 1801–1922* (Dublin, 1978)

Walsh, Dan, *100 Wexford Country Houses: an illustrated history* (Wexford, 1996)

Warwick-Haller, Sally, *William O'Brien and the Irish Land War* (Dublin, 1990)

Wheatley, Michael, 'John Redmond and federalism in 1910', *Irish Historical Studies*, xxxii, no. 127 (May 2001), pp. 343–64

Whelan, Kevin, 'The Catholic community in 18th century Wexford', in T. P. Power, K. Whelan (eds.): *Endurance and Emergence: Catholics in Ireland in the 18th century* (Dublin, 1990), pp. 129–70

Whelan, Kevin, *The Tree of Liberty: Radicalism, Catholicism and the Construction of Irish Identity 1760–1830* (Cork, 1996)

White, Terence deVere, 'The Tragedy of John Redmond', *Irish Times*, 1 Mar. 1973

Winstanley, Michael J., *Ireland and the Land Question 1800–1922* (London, 1984)

Index

Page numbers in bold indicate Figures